Emily W. Leider is the author of Rapid Eye Movement and Other Poems, California's Daughter: Gertrude Atherton and Her Times, and Becoming Mae West. She also edited Yesterday: The Memoir of a Russian-Jewish Family. She lives in San Francisco.

DARK LOVER

THE LIFE AND DEATH OF
Rudolph Valentino

EMILY W. LEIDER

First published in the United States in 2003
by Farrar, Strauss and Giroux
19 Union Square West, New York 10003

First published in the United Kingdom in 2003
by Faber and Faber Limited
3 Queen Square London WC1N 3AU

This paperback edition first published in 2004

Printed in England by Mackays of Chatham, plc

Designed by Jonathan D. Lippincott

Grateful acknowledgement is made to the following individuals and institutions for permission to quote
textual material: Anthony and Margery Baragona for permission to quote from the letters of Valeria
Belletti; Columbia University for Oral History Popular Arts Project Interviews with Mae Murray (1959)
and Nita Naldi (1958); Anthony Slide for permission to quote from interviews he conducted between 1976
and 1979 with friends and associates of Rudolph Valentino.

A CIP record for this book
is available from the British Library

ISBN 0–571–21819–9

2 4 6 8 10 9 7 5 3 1

Again, always, for Bill

CONTENTS

ACKNOWLEDGMENTS

In my pursuit of Rudolph Valentino I began by relying on the kindness of strangers and ended up eager to voice gratitude. It's my pleasure to thank:

Sylvia Valentino Huber, with whom I traveled from Taranto to Castellaneta's Museo Valentino, and who has helped educate me about the Guglielmi family.

Kathy Compagno, for expert assistance in tracking Italian genealogy.

Kevin Brownlow, whose generosity to researchers is almost as celebrated as his mastery of the history and technology of silent pictures. He opened his files, answered endless queries, read the manuscript, and provided essential feedback.

Anthony Slide, who handed over transcripts of his many interviews with people connected to Valentino, tapped his vast store of knowledge to respond to my questions, and helped me get in touch with others who had information.

Betty Lasky, for her amazing memory and painstaking help.

Fellow biographer and demon researcher David Stenn, who made copies for me from his files and shared both trade secrets and insights.

In Castellaneta, Italy: Sandro Esposito of the Museo Valentino; Dominico Orlando and especially Agostino De Bellis.

At the New York City Municipal Archives: Joe Van Nostrand and especially Kenneth Cobb, who helped me track court records.

At the Margaret Herrick Library, Academy of Motion Picture Arts and Sciences, Beverly Hills: Lucia Schultz, Ed Carter, Barbara Hall, and particularly the all-knowing, ever-helpful Kristine Krueger.

At the Bibliothèque de l'Arsenal, Départment des Arts du Spectacle, Paris: Noëlle Giret.

At the Amsterdam Filmmuseum: Jasper Koedam.

At the Harry Ransom Humanities Research Center, Austin, Texas: Rachel Howarth.

At the Lilly Library, Indiana University, Bloomington: Sue Presnell.

At the Film Study Center, Museum of Modern Art, New York: Charles Silver, Terry Geesken, Mary Corliss, and especially the thoughtful, generous, and exacting Ron Magliozzi.

At the Library of Congress, Washington, D.C.: Wonderful Madeline Matz.

At the American Museum of the Moving Image, Astoria: Dana Nemeth and Mary Henderson.

The staffs of the Billy Rose Theater Collection of the New York Public Library; La Bibliothèque du Film, Paris; and the British Film Institute in London.

At the Palm Springs Historical Society: Sally McManus.

At the Pacific Film Archive, Berkeley: Nancy Goldman.

At the University of Southern California Cinema-Television Library: Ned Comstock.

At the Wisconsin Center for Film and Theater Research, Madison: Maxine Ducey.

My agents at the Wylie Agency: Jin Auh and Sarah Chalfant.

My previous and current editors at Farrar, Straus and Giroux: Elisabeth Dyssegaard and Denise Oswald.

Editorial assistant Chandra Wohleber.

Cover designer Susan Mitchell; page designer Jonathan Lippincott; copy editor Kate Scott; production editor JoAnna Kremer.

For offering information, and/or miscellaneous acts of generosity: Lutz Bacher, Anthony and Margery Baragona, Cari Beauchamp, Dr. Arthur Bogart, Celia Browne and Lisette Rice and the members of the Valentino e-group, Massimo Burlando, Diana Serra Cary, Sergio Castilla, Nan Hudnut Clarkson, Frank Cullen, Jim Curtis, Louise Di

Modica, Judy Einzig, Allan Ellenberger, Leatrice Gilbert Fountain, Bob Giroux, Thomas Gladysz, Howard Gutner, T. Gene Hatcher, Charles Higham, Donna Hill, Meri Jaye, Althea John of the Motion Picture Home, Richard Koszarski, Miles Kreuger, Gavin Lambert, Richard Lamparski, Arthur Lennig, Alfred Allan Lewis, Arel Lucas, Diane MacIntyre of Silents Majority, Mike McKelvy, Christina McKillip, Diane Mathis Madsen, Michael Morris, Patricia Neal, Stuart Oderman, Barry Paris, Mary Jane Parkinson, Barbara Ullman Phillips, David Pierce, Dorothy Ralphaelson, the San Francisco Public Library Inter-Library Loan Service, Peter Scarlet, George Schönbrunn, Bill Self, Elena Sheehan, David Shepard, Sylvia Shorris, Elyse Singer, Thomas T. Slater, André Soares, Frances Starn, the late Lura Swig, Tracy Terhune, David Thomson, Tom Turinia, Billie Tyrrell, Amanda Vaill, Connie Van Wyck, Alexander Walker, Marc Wanamaker of Bison Archives, David P. Warren, Jan Willis, Brother Robert Wood, Shela Xorges, Michael Peter Yakaitis of the Library of Moving Images.

Finally, to my family: Richard, Katherine, and Jean, for support both technical and non-. And to Bill, my tentmate of choice, for sharing every inch of the remarkable journey from the Ionian Sea to Hollywood Forever.

DARK LOVER

PROLOGUE

Rudolph Valentino probably never saw a moving picture until he was well into his teens, but he could have seen one earlier. Silent movies were born the same year he was, 1895, when the perfectly named Lumière brothers dazzled and terrified audiences in Paris by projecting down a beam of light images showing workers leaving a factory. Moving pictures of a baby eating breakfast and a train zooming toward the camera would soon follow. The first known Italian cinema display before a paying audience took place in Rome one year later, and there the famous Cines studio came into being around 1906. Valentino's family, the Giovanni Guglielmis, of Castellaneta, lived far from Rome at the time, but they had some experience with cameras, having posed regularly for unsmiling formal portraits attired in their Sunday best. And powerful lenses entered into the everyday working life of Valentino's father, a veterinarian and scientist who used a microscope for his research.

Light is what movies have always been about. The light that the camera lens captures in the same way the human eye does, by refraction. The light that at the turn of the twentieth century was magically linked with motion and projection to create a new kind of spectacle Americans nicknamed "the flickers." It was backlighting that turned Mary Pickford's crown of blonde ringlets into something supernal, like an angel's halo, and arc lamps that made her skin glow whiter than white. To the early movie directors and cameramen who filmed in black and white printed on tinted stock, contrast became a powerful dramatic tool. What quicker way to convey a villain's perfidy than to close in on his black mustache and shiny black top hat? What shot conveyed terror better than one that panned in on a shadowed alley?

Rudolph Valentino was the screen's first dark-skinned romantic hero. Before he became a star, his olive complexion and ethnic look usually limited him to villain roles. Romantic leads and hard-bitten heroes tended to be played by actors who looked all-American— square-shouldered, square-jawed, tall-in-the-saddle types like Douglas Fairbanks, William S. Hart, and Wallace Reid. When Valentino auditioned for D. W. Griffith in 1918, Griffith rejected him as "too foreign looking." He felt sure "The girls would never like him." Only after the powerful screenwriter June Mathis recognized a smoldering quality in Valentino's performance as a brutish "cabaret parasite" in *Eyes of Youth* did romantic lead roles start coming his way. Mathis persuaded the director Rex Ingram to cast him as the tango-dancing Julio in *The Four Horsemen of the Apocalypse*. In 1921, in his twenty-sixth year, Valentino became a star, although star billing would be withheld for another year. He would play leading men in fourteen feature films.

As a screen star in the 1920s—a peak of racial polarization in the United States—he specialized in portraying "exotics": Arab sheiks, Indian rajahs, South American gauchos. He helped to redefine and broaden American masculine ideals. Only after Valentino could a blonde leading lady accept and return the ardent kisses of a screen lover with dark coloring. Valentino had much to do with waking American women up to just how exciting, sensual, and romantic love and sex could be. He was alluring precisely because he didn't look or behave like a midwestern American woman's brother, boyfriend, or husband. "He is not like the nice boy who takes you to all the high-school dances," Agnes Smith would tellingly write in 1922.

Valentino, who died only five years after his leap into stardom and within weeks of the first sound movie, was well matched to his art. Light, motion, and projection intrigued this young man in love with cameras, who was a dancer before he became an actor, and who from childhood on was besotted by any means of getting somewhere fast:

steaming trains, galloping horses, and, as soon as they became available, cars. "Born in a land of sunlight, achieving fame in a sunlight land," his last spoken words supposedly were a request to keep the curtains open to "let the sunlight in." On-screen, lit by Klieg arc lamps, mercury vapor tubes, or incandescents, he gave off heat.

The silent diva Mae Murray, a friend of Valentino's who costarred with him in two movies and adored dancing with him, once defined stardom in terms of electrical wattage. "I think of glamour as a 'watt,' as a 250-watt globe," she said, "and some of us, through God, are very bulby. We get this accentuated power. . . . It's light." If 250 watts were standard for stardom, Valentino gave off gamma rays. More than seventy-five years after his death, goose bumps still rise when he strides across the screen costumed as a gaucho, guiding and sliding his partner in a deft and menacing tango. His capacity to stir in women and men the most intimate erotic and spiritual fantasies, and to pique the possessive feelings that are usually reserved for living lovers, hasn't dimmed. At the mausoleum in Hollywood Memorial Cemetery, where his young body has lain since it was placed there in 1926, the caretaker reported more than a year after his death that an occasional pregnant woman would turn up claiming that Valentino had fathered her unborn child. In the wake of his sudden death due to complications from a perforated ulcer when he was just thirty-one, thousands of New York mourners rioted; suicides spurred by grief were reported in London and Paris. Hollywood studios briefly shut down. Three grief-struck women, Jean Acker, Natacha Rambova, and Pola Negri, the first two of them former Valentino wives and the last-named claiming to be his fiancée, wrangled in public over their competing claims to be Valentino's legitimate widow and to have been his one true soul mate—and there were legions of others, less well known, who privately grieved for him as if they had lost a secret, cherished lover.

At the dawn of the twenty-first century, as I write these words, there are many fewer claimants to exclusive possession of Valentino's heart, soul, or body than there were immediately after his death, and some young and middle-aged moviegoers have never seen him on-screen, though they've probably seen his silhouette on packs of Sheik condoms. In London in 1998 throngs flocked to Britain's National Film Theatre to see Valentino on screen in *The Four Horsemen of the Apocalypse*, restored in 1990 by Kevin Brownlow and David Gill, and a host of other Valentino films. Valentino retrospectives at Bologna, Pordenone, the Library of Congress, and the American Museum of the Moving Image have also been well attended. Every year more Valentino films become available for home viewing on video or DVD, though video prints are rarely of first quality.

Fans all over who are drawn to the occult still seek psychic communion with Valentino. While writing this book, I spoke with someone, a channeler by profession, who told me he and Rudy remain in constant contact. Others cling to pieces of him the way worshippers in Italy enshrined as relics the bones or hairs of a favorite saint, by amassing pictures of him or talismanic objects he once owned: rings, hats, cigarette cases, books, swords. Falcon Lair, the Benedict Canyon house he was fixing up when he died, still draws unwelcome curiosity seekers, and can be visited on one of several Web sites devoted to Valentino.

Valentino himself believed in life after death. He spoke openly about his psychic teacher and spirit guide, an American Indian named Black Feather, and posed for photographs costumed, like him, as an Indian brave. With his second wife, Natacha Rambova, he engaged in automatic writing and attended séances that they believed broke through boundaries of space, time, and mortality to put them in direct touch with the dead of ancient Egypt or the more recent past. So it's not surprising that psychics and clairvoyants continue to buzz around the Valentino honey pot. In London I met a man born well after Valentino's demise who described the long-dead actor's speaking voice and accent to me. He expressed amazement that, in the course of a conversation with Valentino he had conducted during the 1970s with the assistance of Leslie Flint, a medium who was president of the Valentino Memorial Guild, Valentino had never once inquired about the state of cinema today or currently performing male heartthrobs.

I don't pretend to understand everything about Valentino's uncanny ability to move, arouse, and commune with his audience, men as well as women, both straight and gay, but there can be no question that he had (and still has) that ability in spades, and that such power at times entails risk. While he lived, Valentino provoked detractors' malice and envy as much as an overheated sense of loving intimacy among his fans. American men, especially male newspaper and magazine writers, regularly attempted to skin him alive. A *Chicago Tribune* editorial attacking his masculinity and labeling him a "Pink Powder Puff" wounded him so deeply he actually challenged the perpetrator to a boxing match in order to prove his superior masculine mettle.

Valentino's acting style sometimes provided ammunition to his detractors. Directed for exaggerated effects by George Melford in *The Sheik*, his eyes bulge when he wants to express lust, and a menacing stride too easily conveys threat. His billowing robes and Arab burnoose also made mainstream American coat-and-tie types uneasy. Valentino raised disturbing questions about just how decorative and beautiful a man should properly be.

Loved or reviled, Valentino stirred the passions. We're talking about something more than standard-issue Hollywood-style charisma, more than the way screen close-ups of superbeautiful, superdesirable young faces can seep into the audience's dreams and infiltrate their psyches. Rudolph Valentino's hold on his public sets him apart, pushes him into a supernova realm shared only with incandescents like Garbo.

His particular appeal has everything to do with his southern Italian warmth, the tender way he caressed a screen lover's hand or sniffed a rose she held, the affection with which, as Juan Gallardo in *Blood and Sand*, he chucked his plump mother under the chin and nuzzled her cheek. His large vocabulary of expressions and gestures was joined to a vulnerable, wounded quality that elicited compassion. Both in his well-publicized private life and on-screen, Valentino suffered greatly, and he could and did openly show his pain. His two failed marriages, bigamy trial, and fight with the Famous Players–Lasky Corporation studio bosses all made headlines, and in each instance highlighted a personal precariousness. In his first screen sensation, *The Four Horsemen of the Apocalypse*, he goes off to die at the front in the Great War. In his last movie, *The Son of the Sheik*, he is hung by his wrists and tormented;

Christlike, he suffers for us all. His anguish draws us in, making us feel close to him.

But he also has an opposite power, similar to Garbo's, derived from his sphinxlike mysteriousness. Just who was this man? Ciphers hold more fascination than things that are transparent. The obsession to define Valentino's sexuality, to label him gay, straight, or bisexual, is just the most visible mark of a generalized desire to crack his code, know the unknowable. The suddenness of his death contributes to his myth; especially in Italy, rumors that Valentino actually was murdered persist.

But if he could be precisely defined, his appeal would diminish. People are drawn to his androgynous quality, and to his mysticism, finding him a fellow seeker after truth, someone overwhelmed by the strangeness, pain, and perplexity at the heart of things.

His early death, like that of John Lennon, James Dean, Marilyn Monroe, or Princess Diana, only heightened his myth. Romanticism worships nothing more than a beautiful lover who dies young, and Valentino, whose roles included characters from Dumas and Pushkin, brought the romantic ideal to its screen apex. He became, like Keats's still unravished bride of quietness, a figure on a Greek urn always stopped in midmotion, always young. He combined mystery and openness of heart, packaged alluringly in a lithe, elegant, and sensual wrapper, his dancer's well-toned body. Rudolph Valentino promised on-screen to embody the one most of us long for: a bombshell lover who wants to, knows how to, adore. And before the camera, he most often delivered his messages of love via his eloquently yearning eyes. Love enters the soul through the eyes, the ancients believed. They were onto something.

"Everything in film depends upon eyes," Lillian Gish once said. "They tell the story better than words." June Mathis, the scenarist responsible for casting Valentino as Julio in the film that made him a star, *The Four Horsemen of the Apocalypse*, echoed this opinion, saying that eyes were the first thing she noticed about an actor, because they didn't lie. "The soul that looks out of the eyes is the real you."

Valentino's famous stare locates his power. Deep, yearning, mesmerizing, a tantalizing puzzle—the eyes had it.

1

MERCURIO

Before he can reach or grasp, turn or crawl, an infant must first learn something even more basic: how to focus his eyes and stare into another human face. This particular infant, the dark-haired, olive-skinned second son of Giovanni and Gabriella Guglielmi, born on the sixth of May, 1895, in a thick-walled, tile-roofed, stone farmhouse on Castellaneta's Via Commercio (later Via Roma), is ten days old today. He is about to be baptized Rodulphus Petrus Philibertus Raphael: Rodolfo Pietro Filiberto Raffaele. His first name means "well-known wolf," but the newborn Rodolfo's looks are not lupine; he will be nicknamed *il pipistrello*, "the bat," by his schoolmates, and as a young man of sleek grace he will be photographed as a faun and likened to a panther. His hypnotic stare, destined to be trained on screen vamps as well as angelic blondes, will conjure up images of the fabled basilisk, a mythic reptile said to be capable of killing with its eyes. Today, the intense newborn fixes his dark gaze on his petite, black-haired, French-born mother, Maria Berta Gabriella Barbin, known in Castellaneta as Donna Gabriella. As she stares back, enveloping him, his tense muscles relax. A gong from the church campanile summons the town to his christening.

On the steep, narrow streets of Castellaneta, in the Apulian province of Taranto at the instep of the Italian boot, the May sun blazes, bleaching the shuttered houses to an almost blinding whiteness. Holy Week, with its somber processions of hooded penitents, has just passed; bitter greens sprout in the rocky soil of family farm plots. Set on a hill, with a view joining coastal plain and sea, Castellaneta looks like many other Mediterranean towns; its whitewashed facades and casbahlike thresholds could be in Greece. In fact, eight hundred years before Christ the area was part of Magna Graecia, a group of Greek cities along the coast of southern Italy; Castellaneta was close to Taras, the booming port on the Ionian Sea, and there are still remnants of Greek pots to be found here, and a few weathered temple fragments near the Marina, the waterfront about twenty-five miles to the southeast, at Taranto, on the Mare Grande, a lagoon of the Gulf of Taranto. Aphrodite and her son, Eros, armed with a quiver that shoots darts of desire, once presided over lovers here. Actors in leering comic masks performed Attic plays. Centuries later, Greek words linger in the local dialect everybody speaks.

Today the sunstruck almond blossoms on the garland affixed to the door of the *casa* Guglielmi to announce the birth of their new son begin to scatter on the threshold. As the neighbors heading to church emerge from curtained doorways, their heels clicking on the white stone steps, they pass an enormous, gaping ravine, the *gravina*. They shield their faces from the sun as they skirt the cavernous gorge into which, every decade, a few poor souls fall or leap to their deaths.

Rodolfo's wet nurse, Giuseppina Ranaldi, has reported to Donna Gabriella that the ten-day-old baby suckles hungrily; she predicts the infant will thrive and asks permission to tie a horn-shaped red coral charm around his neck, to ward off *mal'occhio,* the evil eye. He is a comely baby, with a well-knit torso and strong limbs, but he must not be praised too loudly, lest he provoke the envious squint of the jealous. At present all life seems perilous, a new baby's especially so. A cholera epidemic has ravaged the south of Italy, and malarial water continues to blight river, stream, and coastline. Church bells toll often for the dead here in Puglia; in chapels votive candles burn day and night. Breath hangs in the balance, both human breath and the breath of the beasts everyone depends on—the donkeys, horses, oxen, and mules that plow the tawny wheat fields, pull high carts of water to the parched gray-green olive orchards, and haul jugs of red wine; the lambs that, if well enough nourished, give wool and meat and milk for pecorino cheese; the scrawny goats whose hides might be fashioned into vests; the cows needed for milk and boot leather.

The firstborn of Giovanni and Gabriella, a girl named Bice, lived through only two summers. Born in June 1890, a year after the wedding of her parents, she was buried soon after her first birthday, in August. Donna Gabriella regularly visits the cemetery in Castellaneta, crowded with fresh-dug graves, to pray and place flowers on little Bice's tombstone, which the stonemason marked at her request with a large black cross and engraved with the lines, in both French and Italian, that Gabriella chose from the poet Malherbe: "She lived as roses live, no longer than a morning."

It is the sixteenth of May, 1895, and Rodolfo is ten days old. Babies here die so frequently in the first week of life that christenings never take place right away; they generally occur after at least ten days have passed, enough time to show that both infant and mother have the strength to greet the world. The townspeople of Castellaneta join family members in the baptistery under the church's carved ceiling to add their blessings, some of them genuflecting to cross themselves before the altar, which is fragrant with lilies. Giovanni Guglielmi, dressed in black, his white collar stiff, stands at attention, his expression proud behind a black mustache, his tall back held ramrod straight, as befits a former Royal Army grenadier and second lieutenant of artillery trained in Rome at the State Military Academy (Regia Accademia Militare). Perhaps the family of Marchese Raffaele Giovinazzi is present at this christening; at least the name "Raffaele" on Rodolfo's birth certificate seems to honor the marchese. As Gabriella's lacy sleeves brush Rodolfo's cheek, her older son, Alberto, hovers close to his mother's long skirt and studies his new baby brother with a seriousness unusual in a child not yet three years old. Alberto was born in Rome during his father's military service there, and his bearing seems to partake of Roman dignity. But it's his mother, Gabriella, whose black brow, bright eyes, shining mouth, and sharply drawn features beckon to Rodolfo. Before sleep, after tears, the baby at the baptismal font seems alert as she tenderly cradles him, bundled in embroidered cloth of the finest white linen. Taking the infant for a moment, the priest in a long black cassock sprinkles the water that absolves Rodulphus Petrus Philibertus Raphael from the taint of original sin.

Gabriella waited long for her children. She is almost forty at Rodolfo's christening, and when she married Giovanni Guglielmi in 1889 at the age of thirty-three she was considered to be already well launched into spinsterhood. Her mother-in-law, Donna Grazia Ancona, who passed away long before Gabriella ever set foot on Italian soil, had delivered the boy who would become Gabriella's husband at the more usual age of twenty. At thirty-six, Giovanni was no youngster either when he wed Gabriella Barbin in Taranto, but it was more common for a man to marry in his thirties than for a woman. Even more unusual was the fact that Gabriella had not lived with her parents or any relative just prior to her wedding. Because both of her parents had died, she had had to make her own way in the world, and not rely on the support and protection of her family.

When she met her future husband, Gabriella was serving as the companion of a noble lady, Marchesa Giovinazzi, who lived on a large parcel of farmland that extended from the suburbs of Castellaneta to the Marina and included, in addition to a grand palazzo, smaller and poorer dwellings for the peasants and farm animals who worked the land. It was the kind of vast acreage, joining the wealthy landowner with the poor who cultivate the soil, that had existed since feudal times. Giovanni Guglielmi and Donna Gabriella Barbin met when he stopped at the Giovinazzi estate to tend their horses, pigs, or cattle. The lady of the house, Marchesa Giovinazzi, Principessa Ruffo di Calabria, was the wife of Marchese Raffaele Giovanizzi, whose father had been mayor of Taranto and who would become mayor himself. The aristocratic and powerful Giovinazzis lived grandly amidst marble floors and gilded picture frames, and they took care of their own. Over time, they adopted a protective attitude toward the gentle and cultivated Donna Gabriella, treating her with the sort of affection and generosity that is most often reserved for a daughter or sister. Only a trusted lady of great refinement would be invited to serve as live-in companion to a marchesa, a role comparable to lady-in-waiting to a queen; and only one who faithfully performed such duties as reading aloud, conversing, helping to dress the marchesa, and perhaps accompanying her when she traveled to Taranto or Naples would win the kind of favor Gabriella enjoyed. But Donna Gabriella left her noble companions on the great Giovinazzi estate to marry.

Soft-spoken, virtuous, and accomplished both in languages and with her needle, Gabriella first won the veterinarian's admiration and then his love, which she returned, prizing studious, intelligent, hard-working Giovanni Guglielmi for his ambition and his dignified devotion. Though theirs was a love match sanctified by the Church, marriage at the turn of the twentieth century remained a business contract; a bride was expected to contribute materially to her new household. Marchesa Giovinazzi held Gabriella in such esteem that she contributed handsomely—perhaps money, perhaps land, perhaps farm animals, perhaps linen—to Gabriella's dowry. Very likely Gabriella, who grew up in the Vosges, a part of France renowned for its textile arts, finished and embroidered her own linens for her trousseau and was adept at lace making. She and Giovanni chose June for their wedding, considered an auspicious month since Roman times.

Giovanni's family and the neighbors in Castellaneta treated Donna Gabriella with respect and admiration, bowing gently in her direction when they met, but they withheld their warmest kisses. Although a devout Catholic, she was not one of them, since she had been born far from Castellaneta in a tiny Vosges mountain town called Lure, in Lorraine, the region of France made famous by Joan of Arc. Much of Lorraine was annexed by Germany after the Franco-Prussian War (1870–1871), and Gabriella had moved with her family to Paris in time to live through its brutal siege by the Prussian army in 1870. The *francese* Donna Gabriella had been christened Marie Berta Gabrielle Barbin in 1856, right after the end of the Crimean War. Like her second son, Rodolfo, she had a birthday in early May, but unlike his childhood, hers was scarred by the jolting dislocations and brutal deprivations of war. Following the Siege of Paris, during a winter of extreme cold and dwindling food, fourteen-year-old Gabriella ate rats to keep from starving.

By the time she married, Gabriella had learned fluent Italian, as well as the local dialect, but she much preferred to speak French in her gentle voice, and she wrote letters to her distant family in handwriting so fine it could have been copied from an illuminated medieval manuscript. Bookish (a surviving photograph shows her posed with a small volume in hand), fastidious about her attire and her household, and well-bred, she is described on Rodolfo's birth certificate as a *gentildonna*, a gentlewoman. Gabriella liked to read the works of Alexandre Dumas Fils, to attend Mass, to recite French poetry, and to do handiwork, creating exquisite lace and embroidery. She loved beautiful things, as would her second son. She also liked the theater enough to journey to Naples to attend performances by renowned actors like the Sicilian Giovanni Grasso and the Shakespearean character actor Ermete Novelli, though she considered the private lives of theatrical types not quite respectable.

Marie Berta Gabriella Barbin and her sister Léonie had come to Taranto with their father, Pierre Filibert Barbin, a construction engineer and graduate of L'École de Chemin de Fer de Chaumont who settled in Apulia as head of a company hired to oversee work on the railroad connecting Taranto to Bari, on the Adriatic. Brigands, roving bands of plunderers, terrorized rural Apulia in the late nineteenth century, and Pierre Filibert Barbin survived his capture by a group of them while he was working in the isolated countryside. But he didn't survive by much. Rodolfo, who was given the middle names Pietro Filiberto to honor his maternal grandfather, would get to know him only through the stories he heard about him, but he became well acquainted with the railroad Pierre Filibert helped to build. Only one member of his family lived near there by 1923, when at the height of his American fame, Rodolfo, transformed into the screen star Rudolph Valentino, revisited his hometown, but he puffed up with pride at the sight of the ravine-spanning railroad bridge built by his grandfather, who had died not long after the bridge was completed.

After her father's death Gabriella decided to remain near Taranto. Though she still had family back in Lorraine, she shuddered at the memory of what Bismarck's soldiers had done to her homeland. Her sister Léonie had also married an Italian, Francesco Galeone, and lived nearby. Neither she nor Léonie wished to return to France. Gabriella wanted to stay close to her, and she had accustomed herself to Apulia, learned to love its fishing boats painted blue; the subdued lapping waves of the sky-colored Ionian Sea; the Romanesque, Norman, and Bourbon churches where she prayed; the festive dinner tables piled high on days of celebration with bowls of mussels, sea urchins, olives, and pasta. Her connection with the Giovinazzis allowed her to stay on, earning her own way. When she met Giovanni Guglielmi, laureate of the University of Naples, he had recently established his practice as Castellaneta's veterinarian. Every day he made his rounds on horseback, accepting payment from the peasant farmers most often not in money but in cheese, olive oil, sacks of grain, or wine. He had powerful clients, too, like the Giovinazzis and the Castellaneta City Hall. Evenings he toiled at the microscope in his study, researching the transmission of malaria from cattle and horses to humans.

Giovanni was not wealthy. He had wanted to study medicine in Naples, but for financial reasons switched to veterinary science, which required less training. But his learning and dedication to an essential profession elevated him to a place of honor in this hard-pressed agricultural village of about seven thousand residents, where machines had not yet displaced the wooden plow and the scythe. Neither was Gabriella wealthy, but it's likely that her engineer father left her something, in addition to what the marchesa contributed to her dowry. Compared to most of their neighbors, the industrious Guglielmis of Via Commercio lived comfortably. Neither luxuriating at the top nor scrounging near the bottom of the economic ladder, they enjoyed bourgeois amenities like fine linen, a tiled roof over a sturdy house with casement windows, a stable for horses, a nurse to help with the children, separate servant quarters on their grounds. But these were disciplined, dignified people, well acquainted with funeral Masses, toil, and hard times. Unspoiled, they lived frugally, counting each *soldo*, wasting nothing. They decorated their walls with Madonnas and crucifixes and disdained pleasure for its own sake.

Giovanni's father, Pasquale, unlike Gabriella's father, had little schooling. At the time Giovanni was born, Pasquale Guglielmi worked as an artisan, a carpenter. Pasquale's family had lived for centuries in the gleaming and stately Baroque town of Martina Franca, high on the Murge Plateau in the province of Lecce, where ancient beehive-shaped stone dwellings called *trulli* still abound and the heels of well-shod passersby still click on the alabaster stone streets. The family fled Martina Franca to nearby Castellaneta to escape attacking brigands, who posed as defenders of the peasants against the gentry and the state. Giovanni did more than flee; as an army officer, he had been enlisted by the state to fight the brigands and restore order.

"Guglielmi" translates as "Williams" in English; the name, of German origin, is common in both northern and southern Italy, and came into Italy in the ninth century as the Latin Guilihelmus. By coincidence, a Flemish or Dutch-sounding version of the same name, Willien, had belonged to Gabriella's mother before her marriage. The family of Giovanni Guglielmi, he told his sons, originated in Rome, but migrated to Puglia in the fifteen hundreds.

The less remote Guglielmi ancestors, so far as we know, were not highborn, but as he grew up Rodolfo wanted them to be. He read and was told adventure stories, and imagined himself a sword-rattling crusader, a daredevil medieval prince, or a knight in armor riding bareback to pursue brigands or dueling to protect his family's honor. The chivalric code and the medieval idea that a knight must fight to defend his good name were very much alive to him. After all, Italy, unified for only thirty-five years when Rodolfo was born, had a king: at the time of Rodolfo's birth it was King Umberto, and then, after Umberto's assassination in 1900, Victor Emanuel III. Italy and France both had histories brimming with dramatic incidents involving counts, dukes, and barons, to say nothing of queens and marchese, daggers and poison rings. Royals were the stuff of the legends Gabriella recounted to her children in the language she spoke with them, French. Donna Gabriella took Rodolfo and Alberto on outings in a horse-drawn carriage, to visit castles built by emperors, princes, kings, and dukes. Rodolfo's imagination churned. He could see himself leaping from a turret or hiding behind a tapestry. He developed a love of Renaissance carving, jewel-encrusted swords, and antique armor that he kept as long as he lived. (One of the items he owned at the time of his death was a mailed glove that had belonged to Philip II of Spain.) The most exciting things he could imagine, glory and honor and adventure, involved highborn people and the magnificence they commanded.

As a young man Rodolfo would reinvent himself as the descendant of aristocrats, endowing himself with impressive additional names that aren't present on any birth or baptismal record: "di Valentina d'Antonguolla" precedes "Guglielmi" in his account. He claimed his parents so named him, explaining that "the di Valentina is a papal title"—romantic because the word *valentino* in Italian means "sweetheart," and historic for its association with the Borgias—"and the d'Antonguolla indicates an obscure right to certain royal property which is entirely forgotten now." Rodolfo insisted that his mother told him that in a love duel his illustrious Roman forebear had killed a member of the powerful Colonna family and had been forced to flee to Martina Franca.

Perhaps Gabriella, a born storyteller who was proud of her own lineage (which may have included aristocrats), did tell Rodolfo such tales. But she apparently never impressed them on her older son, Alberto, who made no claim to lofty ancestry, or on Alberto and Rodolfo's younger sister, Maria, who was born when Rodolfo was two and always lived and dressed simply. Having a noble pedigree didn't matter much to Alberto and Maria, though they were proud indeed of their parents' accomplishments and respected position in town society; but it mattered greatly to Rodolfo. Alberto said that his brother, Rudy, wanting to justify his claim to noble ancestry, wrote from America to someone in Rome dedicated to heraldry, and that "they sent him a coat of arms" and a family history that included the name Valentino, but that Alberto knew nothing about that.

Aristocratic or not, Rodolfo was a beautiful boy, though not perfectly made. He had one slightly cauliflowered ear, the left one, and in future years cameramen would learn to shoot his "good" side. The ears also inclined to little points, like a baby faun's. His underdeveloped chest would prevent him from being admitted to the naval academy he hoped to attend. He had less than perfect vision. Rodolfo's left eye was "lazy," tending to wander, and he turned out to be quite myopic. People who knew him well in Hollywood swore that the famously arousing, sometimes menacing, often hypnotic squint signified near-sightedness more than anything else. "Rudy couldn't *see*, and he refused to wear glasses. *Myopia*—not passion."

Almond-shaped eyes under heavy brows lent Rodolfo a Middle Eastern cast; maybe there were Saracen, Byzantine, Gypsy, or Moorish ancestors way back when. As he grew up, Rodolfo welcomed this possibility. He liked his terra-cotta–colored skin, which matched the ancient dancing figures from Magna Graecia that a teacher might have taken him to see on display in Taranto. The future portrayer of sheiks and rajahs recognized a non-Western strain in himself, often casting himself as a Saracen when he played with his friends. His favorite book was *The Adventurers of India*, and he would always dream of one day being able to visit there.

Before he reached the age of six Rodolfo's right cheek was marked with a scar, the result of an unhappy early experiment with his father's razor. This was no isolated incident. Rodolfo had a reckless streak, and despite hands adept at tinkering and legs that moved with panther-like nimbleness, he got into scrapes and injured himself regularly. "Accident-prone" we'd call him now, and perhaps also "hyperkinetic." The impetuous boy lacked any trace of caution, and he could not sit still. In his twenties he could sometimes be passive, more acted upon than acting; but the child Rodolfo was all action. He would aggressively hurl objects at others, vault up cliffs, and straddle fences, often getting his clothes torn and sometimes breaking things, more out of inattention than malice. His restless energy "kept him impatient for something different all the time." One of his several nicknames was Mercury, after the lightning-swift messenger of the gods shod in winged sandals.

Motion ruled Rodolfo from the start. He hated school because there he had to stay in his seat and pay attention. His kindergarten teachers, two maiden sisters, spoiled him, but later instructors predicted he would never amount to anything. Although bright enough, "he refused to submit to the routine of schooling." Rodolfo had to run, jump, climb trees, and throw lemons, with less than knightly gallantry, at girls below. Attempting an acrobatic feat, he fell off the porch backward and cut the back of his head, leaving another scar. With his chums Alfonso Tamburrino and Giacomo De Bellis he would explore the caves along the Castellaneta gorge, some of them inhabited by hermits or decorated with frescoes, imagining an escape from marauding Saracens hurling poison darts, or pretending he led a band of brigands.

He had a special rapport with animals, especially the kinds he could ride. He rode bareback on a wild donkey nobody else dared mount— and managed to stay on it. At his uncle's property, a Moorish-looking spread outside Taranto, where the Guglielmi children spent their summers, "I used to go to the stables and fool with the mules. My mother lived in constant fear that I might be brought home with a hoof print on my stomach. My favorite occupation was to put on the harnesses, take the mules to water, hitch them up, drive the carts." His father taught him to ride the way a cavalry officer would, so that a coin placed between his knee and the horse's side would not fall.

Rodolfo shouted with excitement the day a band of Gypsies came to town. He and his friend Memeo cut school to befriend the raggle-taggle children who played clay whistles, and they gaped in wonder at the wagon caravans driven by men who wore glittering earrings and red neckerchiefs. In the fields near the caravan, Rodolfo and Memeo spent hours "picking flowers, hunting bird's eggs and spearing little snakes on wire noose hooks." They never allowed the snakes to die.

The proprietors of gardens feared a visit from Rodolfo, because he had a habit of stealing green figs. In fact, he was so fond of this fruit that people called him "green fig eater," which meant a person with impractical ideas. This proved a telling nickname, for Rodolfo was known as a dreamer who lived someplace other than the here and now. He constantly playacted, and was his own best audience. "I became to myself an imaginary figure of great excellence, daring and glamor." Children whose fantasies hold them captive can be endearing, and Rodolfo held that appeal, especially for his mother, sister, and nurse, Rosa. But his tendency to see himself as a swashbuckling hero most often landed him in the woodshed, or some version of jail. "When he was bad, which was frequent," he would take refuge with his neighbors, the Maldarizzis, who remembered, "Sometimes [he] would throw stones at his own home to get them to open the door and feed him biscuits and bread."

Rodolfo regularly had to be punished, and in the early days the punisher invariably was his father. Giovanni had been molded by a militaristic discipline that he in turn enforced at home, or tried to. "The father punished with severity. He would lock him without supper in a dark closet and listen unmoved to his passionate beating on the door." When he felt the offense merited it, Giovanni didn't hesitate to use his whip or cane. Giovanni's study, the place where he conducted his research, was off limits for the three children. "My mother held my father's study to be a sacred place where none should intrude." Of course children find forbidden places enticing, and Rodolfo, intrigued by his father's microscope and the other curious instruments around, couldn't resist sneaking into the study with his younger sister, Maria, one day when their father was out. There, borrowing his father's long-stemmed pipe, he initiated his sister into the mysteries of smoking corn silk and promptly turned green. "Father's cane seemed to shout its intentions from the corner."

Somehow Rodolfo got possession of a gun that shot wax bullets, which he aimed at Maria, a "by no means helpless young woman," who fought back with sticks and stones. "She gave valiant battle, and when my supply of ammunition gave out I took flight to the neighbor's property. There I hastily climbed a lime tree and commenced utilizing the unripe fruit against the enemy." He had fired a couple of rounds when an errant lime struck and broke his father's study window. Giovanni, at home this time, emerged with cavalry whip in hand. "He administered a brilliant beating," of the this-hurts-me-more-than-it-hurts-you variety. "I saw the tears in his eyes," Valentino later recalled.

The southern Italians have a folk saying, "Relatives are like shoes; the tighter they are, the more they pinch." In Rodolfo's experience, the family alliances broke down according to sex; the relatives who did most of the pinching were male, those who salved, applauded, and caressed, female. When he broke the rules, both parents tried to shame him, harping on the idea that the Guglielmis were a respected family with high standards of proper conduct; but only his father enforced discipline with severity.

Alberto, a practical sort, pleased his parents by studying hard and excelling at school. He tended to take his father's side; his brother's extravagant unruliness made him uncomfortable. While Rudy was "very close" to his mother and sister, Alberto instead followed his father. Sometimes, his mother or Rodolfo's nurse, Rosa, would try to intervene by hiding him or sending him out of the house where his father couldn't get at him—to a neighbor's, perhaps. The gulf between Rodolfo and his brother became even wider when they were separated by schooling. Alberto was sent to stay with his uncle's family in another town and attend school there, while his younger brother and sister stayed behind in Castellaneta.

Maria served as Rodolfo's ally, sometimes joining as his partner in mischief, very often providing the immediate responses he wanted. "She never would tag [after] Alberto, but was always waiting for me to show off." Maria enjoyed providing the attention Rodolfo sought. "Maria was the audience I strove to invoke," he would remember. Rodolfo's earliest displays of chivalry were directed toward this beloved younger sister. An early photo of them shows a pudgy-faced Rodolfo dolled up in a suit with a white lace collar, his arm draped protectively around winsome little Maria, dressed all in white.

Pleasing his mother mattered even more. Rodólfo adored her. They had an easy and tender intimacy, exchanging hugs and kisses. Gabriella made him feel loved even when he misbehaved. Although she adored all three of her children, the personalities of Alberto and Maria were more reserved and self-contained, less needy than this middle child's. She and Rodolfo had a special bond, sharing not only the French language Gabriella spoke at home but the language of beauty and emotion. Her realm—decorative handiwork, aristocratic connections, fluency in several languages, reading French poetry aloud, dramatic storytelling, soulful prayer—felt more comfortable to him than did his father's reserve, strict standards, and scientific pursuits.

Although he and his father shared a love of military uniforms and horses, Rodolfo hated science, or anything to do with doctors. "My father happened to be a doctor and though I loved and idealized him privately, professionally I never had any use for him or anyone connected with that science." Rodolfo also disliked being hemmed in or told what to do, especially by a man. And his father's tendency to reach for his cane or his cavalry whip could make the boy quake in his riding boots.

Rodolfo's strokes of approval tended to come from feminine hands, and that was the way he liked it. "A man's most coveted audience is a woman. Her approbation, the ultimate laurel wreath." The most beautiful woman he could imagine was of the Italian Madonna type, a Mona Lisa with a serene face and calm, soft eyes. Women who had children held particular appeal, because Rodolfo could never get enough mothering. A series of maternal women, ending with Teresa Werner, the aunt of his second wife, would exert a strong pull on his emotional reins throughout his short life. "What sort of little boy were you?" a reporter asked him in 1924. A troublesome one, he answered, one who caused his mother much sorrow because of his bad behavior, and one who had a habit of falling in love with grown-up ladies as old as his mamma.

According to Robert Florey, one of Rodolfo's close friends in Hollywood, who was French, Gabriella set a feminine standard that was difficult for him to match in his adult life. Rodolfo idolized her as a perfect Madonna, bestower of love, light, and sustenance, exemplary for her combination of culture, spirit, and marvelous domestic accomplishment and practicality. Florey doubted that any young woman, especially an American woman, could ever measure up. He wondered at his friend's impossible idealism; where would Rodolfo ever find the angelic virgin, ethereally beautiful, delicate, and in disposition extremely sweet, of his dreams? What Rodolfo wanted was a more beautiful version of his exalted mother.

Rodolfo's first wife, Jean Acker, who does not seem to have possessed very many of the qualities of his feminine ideal, complained after their divorce that Rodolfo expected his wife to excel at domestic skills she never aspired to: "[His] heroine is a thrifty housewife—one who can remake dresses and millinery and utilize everything to the utmost." Natacha Rambova, his second wife, at the time of his second divorce raised similar objections, claiming that not just her husband but European men in general expected their wives to defer to them and to be willing to devote themselves to husband, hearth, and children. All his life, Rodolfo would seek out other people's mothers. In Hollywood, watching one day from the sidelines on the set of *Peter Pan* (1924), he went out of his way to be kind to the Italian mother of Virginia Brown Faire, the teenager who played Tinker Bell. He would offer Mrs. Brown a chair and chat with her in Italian. When a wire broke, leaving the airborne Virginia/Tinker Bell suspended, Mrs. Brown began screaming. Her embarrassed daughter, unharmed, reprimanded her mother, accusing her of being too emotional, too Italian. Rodolfo scolded Virginia, telling her not to speak that way to her mother, and he tried to calm Mrs. Brown.

The Guglielmi family moved from Castellaneta to Taranto when Rodolfo was nine years old, because Giovanni wanted to advance his career by devoting more time to his research on malaria. Rodolfo was never a good student, and his grades plummeted to a new low after the move. He played hookey so much that he even failed French, the language he spoke fluently at home with his mother. His highest grade, the equivalent of a C+, was in calligraphy, and he received grades lower than that in conduct, Italian, French, mathematics, and art. "Flunked" (*respinte*), says his report card, preserved for all to see in Castellaneta's Museo Valentino. Shame was an emotion Rodolfo learned early and too well.

There were new joys as well as humiliations in the larger city of Taranto. The Guglielmi family home in the new quarter of Taranto was only a few blocks from the serene Ionian Sea. Sailors in dark uniforms with white caps and brass buttons made arresting appearances all over town, and Rodolfo could visit their headquarters in the fifteenth-century castle near the hanging bridge, which separated the new Taranto from the ancient one. Watching the boats on the Mare

Grande offered a new diversion for Rodolfo and his recently acquired circle of chums, and every so often they could beg or borrow a blue fishing boat and go out on their own; however, fear of contracting malaria kept them from swimming. There was a theater in town for operetta, if one could scrape up enough money for a ticket, and the circus, which Rodolfo eagerly awaited, stopped more often here than it had in Castellaneta.

But such joys abruptly halted during Rodolfo's tenth year, when, in the course of one of his experiments, Giovanni contracted malaria and succumbed to the disease he had hoped to help eradicate.

2

EARLY SORROW

Giovanni's death at the age of fifty-three in March of 1906 was the end result of his marathon exertions on behalf of his biomedical research on malaria. Throughout his final vigil he toiled incessantly with slides, microscope, and test tubes, growing haggard and closing himself off from friends, his children, everyone except Gabriella. "There had been many deaths among the cattle [and horses] of our district, and my father . . . was studying constantly for a method of checking the epidemic. He finally diagnosed the disease as malaria . . . [which] until then . . . had been considered as a disease peculiar to human beings." According to Rodolfo, his father achieved a scientific breakthrough, discovering that mosquito bites could infect cattle and horses as well as people. "My father spent months testing his theory, and then many months more working out a formula for a vaccine." Giovanni's last push to eradicate disease through tireless experiment and study seemed heroic to his family and to the wider world, too. Again according to Rodolfo, Guglielmi's findings became well known in the European biomedical community of the day, and were discussed "by many scientists, among them Professor Nocard of the Pasteur Institute" in Paris. The research affirmed Giovanni's patriotic and military allegiances as well as his scientific goals, since it was partly motivated by a desire to help Italian soldiers remain healthy both within Italy and during colonizing missions in Africa.

All three of Giovanni's children exalted their father's accomplishments and his willingness to put his own life at risk to benefit others. Giovanni "died for his work, as he had lived for it." For the remainder of his own life, Rodolfo would recoil at the premises and practices of medical science, but in his work as an actor in Hollywood he mimicked his father's tunnel vision and missionary zeal, throwing himself wholly into whatever he pursued. Like many a son, while rebelling against his father he at the same time reprised some of his father's habits. And his family pride never left him.

As Giovanni lay dying, his malarial fever and chills having given way to a gaunt, jaundiced exhaustion, he drew his sons around him. Gabriella had stepped away from her post at the foot of his bed, undoubtedly to fetch something for her enervated husband. Maria was not included in this masculine rite of passage, a heart-stopping, melodramatic deathbed scene that could have been lifted whole from a Verdi opera finale. Although weak, Giovanni on his bed of pain exerted great effort to reach for and remove a crucifix from the wall, handing it to Rodolfo. His black eyes glowed with unaccustomed gentleness as he summoned the strength to speak words that recalled his status as a former military officer as well as head of the Guglielmi family: "My boys," he told them, "love your mother and above all love your country." The words would forever resonate for Rodolfo: *Madre e Italia. Curtain.*

Later, Rodolfo claimed, he, Alberto, and Maria stood near their mother to watch the funeral coach drawn by six black horses, "the horseman in his Charon-like uniform of silver and black." Four men who had been Giovanni's closest friends each held a huge tassel attached to the hearse. This recollection may have been embellished for the benefit of movie fans who were reading Valentino's ghost-written life story in *Photoplay*, but even if the actual scene wasn't quite so picturesque, Giovanni was an important enough citizen to merit considerable pomp and ceremony.

Each member of the Guglielmi family expressed grief differently. Maria wept softly, trying not to call attention to herself. Alberto, always self-controlled, compressed his lips. Rodolfo grieved openly, sobbing wildly at times, at other moments aware that he must try to hold himself in check; people were watching him, and his mother would need him. "I [was] trying to restrain myself." When he didn't succeed, waves of emotion engulfed him.

Guilt surfaced. He had not only lost his father; he had failed him by not living up to Giovanni's standards and refusing to follow his upright, hardworking example. Giovanni used to hit him with a leather riding crop; now Rodolfo became his own emotional whipping boy. Even if he made good later on in life, Giovanni would never know, could never praise him. He had no way of hiding from this unexpressed but searing realization. In particular, Rodolfo's dismal performance in school gnawed at him, for it disgraced more than him alone, according to his father's way of thinking. Giovanni and Gabriella were ranking members of the respectable Taranto professional class, as they had been previously esteemed in Castellaneta. A son's performance in school brought honor or shame to his entire family. More tears choked him as Rodolfo wrestled with himself and his anguish.

When Rodolfo simply broke down, his mother shamed him further by her unexpected, exemplary restraint. After the funeral he saw Gabriella kneeling before the altar candles of the cathedral, "not so much praying as holding commune with him who had but preceded her." He did not see her weep behind her widow's veil, even during the funeral, although she was obviously stricken. "I couldn't understand why she did not cry . . . as I did. I wondered that she could comfort us—a pale, quiet little woman, so peacefully serene." Gabriella's faith carried her. She clearly felt that not even death could sever her marriage bond, and that in heaven she and Giovanni would one day meet again. In the eyes of her children, her fidelity even in widowhood pushed her ever closer to a kind of secular sainthood. Rodolfo grew up convinced that such unearthly goodness and soul sharing could happen; they weren't mere dreams. For the rest of his life he idealized the communion between his parents as "something beautiful and sublime. I saw, for the first time, a great, real love."

The move from Castellaneta to Taranto two years before Giovanni's passing had unhinged Rodolfo; it had required adjusting to city life, new friends, and a demanding new middle school, Dante

Alighieri, at which he did so poorly he was forced to repeat an entire year. In Taranto he no longer had access to the ready escape hatches of roaming the fields, ravines, and caves or sneaking off to the homes of accommodating neighbors he'd always known. He'd been branded a troublesome child before Giovanni died; now his unruliness accelerated and careened. He was fatherless at the age of ten, and his disobedience, untruthfulness, contempt for authority and chronic hookey playing caused his mother endless worry, bafflement, and dismay, although he smothered her with affection. "All of us loved our little mother to distraction," he would remember. "We vied jealously to serve her. And I would try to kiss and embrace her exactly as I used to see my father do." This too caused concern. His uncles and his father's friends felt Rodolfo needed strong masculine guidance; he should be separated from his mother, who tended to too readily forgive his trespasses and was easily manipulated by him. This necessity seemed all the more imperative since Alberto had been sent to another town to stay with an uncle while attending school and now Rodolfo was the only male in the house. Home had become Gabriella's place, a feminine domain.

While he lived, prudent Giovanni had paid into a fund that would qualify Rodolfo, about whom he felt understandable concern, for special schooling in the event of Giovanni's death. North of Rome, in the medieval Umbrian hill town Perugia, famous for chocolates, paintings by Fra Angelico, and feuding noble factions, had been founded the Boarding School for Orphans of Italian Health Professionals (Collegio Convitto per gli Orfani dei Santari Italiani); Rodolfo was packed off to this center of learning at age twelve to study, experience life away from his family, and, it was fondly hoped, finally accept the yoke of discipline.

Very often Rodolfo and later his biographers described his school in Perugia as a military academy; it wasn't. It was a technical school that prepared young men to work as mechanics, engineers, or accountants while also providing a foundation in the liberal arts. Rodolfo's skill at fixing motors and other machines was nurtured here; he also learned a little Spanish and improved his already quite good French. Though the Perugia boarding school wasn't a stepping stone to a guaranteed military career, it borrowed some of its structure, dress code, and pedagogy from the military model. Rodolfo and other students had to wear visored caps and brass-buttoned uniforms and clip their hair close to the scalp, and they were put through military-style paces every day. "We marched squad form to and from our meals." Rodolfo found that he enjoyed the marching and standing tall at attention, the precision turns to face right or left. He dreamed of following in his father's and a cousin's footsteps into the military and becoming a cavalry officer one day.

Along with the military one, the boarding school retained a monastic atmosphere, for the buildings had once housed monks. "A great tolling bell controlled our movements." The architecture and furnishings of the place, built around two courtyards in the fourteenth century, conveyed reverence for the past combined with solemn austerity bordering on the grimly Gothic. "The great refectory with its massive tables was adorned with pictures, mostly of ecclesiastical subjects or dignitaries of the church." In one courtyard there was a deep, ancient well where, the students whispered, "recalcitrant friars" had been "imprisoned and allowed to expiate their sins by slowly decaying in the hideous dampness."

The atmosphere at the school was designed to be forbidding; homey it wasn't. During the winter months the students had to rise at 5 a.m. and march down to the showers; after dressing and cleaning their rooms, they breakfasted on bread and hot chocolate if they had been well behaved, bread and water if they hadn't. Rodolfo often had to settle for water. His well-established pattern of disrespecting authority and studying as little as possible did not suddenly reform with the new surroundings, teachers, and schoolmates. He particularly hated math, and would attend that class armed with a book of adventure stories that he would conceal inside his text. "All would go well until the teacher would call upon me to recite." Attempts to teach Rodolfo to calculate, reason logically, and master figures proved hopeless.

The trick of counting money, especially, eluded him, and always would. He paid scant attention. Money remained a concern to his mother, who, though not poor, was now supporting herself and three children on a meager widow's pension plus the modest nest egg she and Giovanni had managed to squirrel away.

In Perugia Rodolfo first experimented with cigarettes; later he would chain-smoke. "We wore long cloaks when out of doors in the colder weather and used to steal a smoke . . . beneath their folds. But often the odor or nicotine stains on our fingers were the cause of dire punishment, so we used to scrub our hands with lemons."

The boarding-school punishments Rodolfo often endured resembled the ones he already knew so well from his earlier childhood: imprisonment of one sort or another, and deprivation. "So many times I would break the rules and be put in a jail and [be] given only bread and water." Occasionally during these times of imprisonment, his cell overlooked the courtyard with the dreadful well. Confined to a barrel with a window, he could stare at the well and "dream gruesome dreams."

Rodolfo's acting out signals that in those days he was frequently depressed as well as angry, at the world and himself. Under his cloak, the now adolescent Rodolfo took to wearing black, as if he were a grieving Prince Hamlet or a morose Count Dracula. He adopted a scowling expression that lent him a sinister or mournful air, and this, along with his skinny build and slightly pointy ears, prompted his classmates to tease him. Even in his early teens, Rodolfo reminded others of a vampire.

Sports provided one outlet for Rodolfo's energy, a haven where his athletic prowess won him admiration from his mates and he could submerge in sweat some of the dark thoughts that troubled him. A local style of soccer was his favorite, but he also ran, climbed, rowed, and wrestled. Another pleasure, enjoyed less often, came via visits to the theater. "I saw classic plays, including Shakespeare, but didn't act."

His student days in Perugia ended disastrously. "I became too active for the discipline and was finally taken out." The field he was being trained in, engineering, failed to excite his interest, and his chronic class cutting caught up with him. Rodolfo faced expulsion from school. In order to avoid having his record blemished for all time with the black mark of expulsion, Gabriella, when warned by the headmaster that disgrace was imminent, withdrew him from boarding school. In a letter to the headmaster, she begged for a show of compassion for her son, a boy she admitted had a difficult character and unruly habits, which had provoked the school's complaints about him. Rodolfo was not brilliant, she conceded, but she thought him "*abbastanza intelligente*," intelligent enough.

Writers about the Italian national character make much of the Italian preoccupation with display, putting on a good show, *bella figura*. Fine tailoring, careful grooming, and elegance all hold a place of eminence in Italy's social pantheon. Rodolfo certainly shared this love of finery. When he fantasized about his future, he tended to fix on the smart uniform and glorious blue cape, irresistible to women, that he would wear as an officer for the dragoons of Savoy. It's telling that he imagined himself playing not just any part in his future life, but a costume role. However, it was his French mother who fastened on Rodolfo's apparel and careful grooming as the indicator of propriety, status, and taste and the gauge by which others would judge his character. Gabriella had decided that fifteen-year-old Rodolfo would never qualify to train for the job he most wanted, cavalry officer. That was a position more suitable to brilliant students, or the sons of wealthier families. Rather, since he loved boats and machines, she thought he should take the examination for admission to a naval technical school in Venice. "I wanted to get into the navy. I expect the presence of so much shipping in Taranto harbor excited my imagination. I was . . . always impatient, headstrong, and inclined for a life of excitement."

But how, Gabriella reasoned in a letter to the headmaster in Perugia, could he be expected to pass muster in Venice if he showed up for his preliminary entrance examination in the threadbare, too-small military-style school uniform he had been wearing? Where to find thirty lire for a respectable new "*borghese*" (bourgeois) outfit? She suggested in her carefully ornamental handwritten letter that the headmaster in Perugia should lend Rodolfo a new uniform, promising him that it would be returned in mint condition ready for another student's use.

Gabriella's pleading letter produced the result she'd sought.

Rodolfo spent a brief preparatory period in Venice, where for the first time in his life he applied himself to study, cramming for his test, and then turned up for his exam in a handsome borrowed uniform plus a new winter coat. But despite his smart appearance and his exertions to get himself into good physical as well as intellectual trim before presenting himself to the examiners in Venice, Rodolfo once again failed to measure up. He passed the written exam, but not the physical. The Venetian naval doctors ruled that his chest measurement fell short by two centimeters. Because of this physical deficiency, he was not even allowed to continue the physical.

For Rodolfo, this was a devastating, life-shattering blow. "Here I was, fifteen, and a complete failure." The possibility that he somehow lacked the requisite masculine physique troubled him. He had nightmares that his father was reproaching and punishing him. "I returned home heart-sick and ambitionless and stayed a year. I did little except cause my dear mother worry."

Once again, Gabriella came to the rescue, proclaiming that she had never been completely convinced that a naval career best suited Rodolfo; besides, Italy already had more than enough men in uniform. She coddled and comforted him, and in short order came up with an alternate suggestion for his future. Hadn't he always enjoyed the out-of-doors, riding, spending time among the horses and cattle he'd learned to handle and care for in Castellaneta? She thought a career in landscaping, animal husbandry, or "scientific agriculture" might be just his ticket. He applied to and was accepted by the Agricultural Institute of Saint Ilario of Liguria (Istituto di Agraria di Sant'Ilario Ligure) at Nervi, a tiny village in the mountains above the Mediterranean in the province of Genoa, in the Liguria region. Gabriella, still dressed in black widow's weeds four years after Giovanni's death, accompanied him to the new school. She had written in advance to school officials that her son might not be easy to educate. "I am a bit worried because he is somewhat capricious."

In Liguria Rodolfo fell in love with the dramatic landscape, with its rocky cliffs, tall cypresses, and evergreens overlooking the calm blue Mediterranean. The Agricultural Institute stood on top of a hill in

Nervi, surrounded by terraced gardens, with rows of fruit trees and vegetable gardens, which the students helped to tend. For once Rodolfo found parts of the curriculum that were to his liking, since so much of his schooling now took place outdoors. He had matured enough to realize he would not be granted an infinite number of second chances, and he applied himself more than he ever had at school, in a far gentler climate than the one in Perugia. Here in Liguria, as in Perugia, the students wore cadet's uniforms and were drilled like soldiers. (It's hard to imagine that they performed their farming chores in cadet's uniforms, but perhaps they did.) But unlike in Perugia, in the Nervi school thoroughbred horses and prime cattle were kept, and Rodolfo became a master rider and trainer. He learned to handle a horse that bolted and reared, and to break a bull. A bucking bull or kicking horse never frightened him. When a calf escaped from the stable, Rodolfo chased and corralled it. "I always have been and still am crazy about cattle," he would write. He was taught the rudiments of fencing, continued wrestling, and as he attained his adult height, worked on improving his muscle power and expanding the scrawny chest that had disqualified him from the naval academy. He would remain a fitness fanatic for the rest of his life.

Exactly how tall he was is in question; he claimed to be five feet ten or eleven inches, but was probably closer to five feet eight. A California rancher who kept the Arabian horses Rodolfo would come to love as an adult described him as "a little squirt. Not very big. About five feet six inches." Douglas Fairbanks supposedly stood about five feet seven; an undoctored photograph of Fairbanks standing next to Valentino on the set of *The Eagle* in 1925 shows the two stars as being very close to the same stature.

In agricultural school Rodolfo was taught a great deal about how to grow maize, stake grapevines, plant orange and olive trees, and thin flowerbeds. He learned how to irrigate and cultivate terraces, how to build dry-walls, how to combine different kinds of plants in a way pleasing to the eye, and how to prune and shape hedges and trees. (The techniques were all adapted to the realities of farming in Italy circa 1911, a time when many farmers still used mules and oxen to pull wagons; eventually these would be replaced with tractors.) This was work he enjoyed.

But there were distractions. He enjoyed the companionship of his male schoolmates and wished for more opportunities to carouse with them after hours or explore the region beyond Nervi. He took piano lessons and escaped to the keyboard whenever he could. And he day-dreamed about girls. While in Nervi he had his first romance, with the daughter of the school cook. Her name was Felicita, and she was a tall, dark-haired, and graceful young woman with a serene glance. "Rodolfo would wait hours in a nearby square for Felicita, who would pass by with her two sisters." This was look-but-don't-touch puppy love, all about yearning. Evenings he would call to Felicita to come to the window, and he'd serenade her with a Neapolitan air. (Rodolfo had a pleasant baritone voice, and he could play the mandolin a bit.) Once, Felicita would recall, "when he tried to stop me on the street, a teacher gave him some smacks." Before leaving Sant'Ilario he returned to Felicita's window to call his farewell. "He sent me a kiss on his fingers. He was crying, and I was moved by emotion also."

The interview with Felicita, who later married an employee of the Italian state railroad and moved to Rome, was conducted by a reporter more than forty years after Rodolfo left Nervi and had become world-famous. Many such retrospective interviews contain self-aggrandizing distortions and should be taken with more than one grain of salt. But the story of this crush on the pretty daughter of the school cook is confirmed by Rodolfo himself in his published diary. And the picture of him as a budding Romeo, as much in love with love as with any particular object of his affections, squares with other accounts. Days after Rodolfo died, his sister, Maria, recalled him at the age seventeen, bro-kenhearted when one of his sweethearts succumbed to typhus. He didn't have the money to buy flowers, and since it was winter, there were none to pick. So "he took the flowers from the church altar and put them on her grave." That he cared more for "profane" love, worldly love, than for the sacred love sanctified in church is suggested in this innocently sacrilegious gesture; or maybe it would be closer to the truth to say that, like the troubadors of old, Rodolfo exalted the love for a woman to something close to sacred.

Rodolfo would tell *Photoplay*, "I was always in love. Young Italians always are. . . . I used to spend hours copying passages from Tasso and Ariosto . . . In this period of poetical hysteria I compared the fair one to sunsets that flame out of heaven, . . . the clouds kissed silver by a loving moon." He spoke of being in love as if it were a set of lines he could declaim, a performance that involved gestures of devotion, wallowing in sadness and molding his facial expression to communicate deep passion. "An American may speak love with his lips, the Italian must say it with his eyes."

He could testify that Italian middle-class notions of respectability, combined with the Catholic Church's insistence on sexual purity in young women, created symphonies of frustration in young men. "If the Italian is the most passionate lover in the world it may be because he is the most restrained. Rigid convention denies him all contact with the lovelier girls, who never are free from chaperons." Trying to sneak around with a girl from a respectable family just wouldn't work at school, where he was always being watched, nor would it when he went home to a city as small as Taranto. "The whole town promenaded at night on a certain piazza, . . . and the next day all of the people would know everything that had happened."

When he returned to Taranto from Nervi, Rodolfo earned new rebukes from neighbors and relatives because of his shiftlessness and the company he kept. Although, in two years, he had earned his certificate at the agriculture school and qualified for employment, he had no job. He certainly expended no energy seeking gainful employment, perhaps because he wanted to spend some time near his mother in Taranto, and the southern Italian farm economy was depressed. As a certified scientific farmer or landscape gardener he might have found a position elsewhere in Italy, had he sought one. Instead, he slept late, lazed around the public squares or the waterfront in Taranto all afternoon, and looked for good times at night. Since nice girls from "gently bred" families were off limits except in tightly supervised situations, Rodolfo sought out the companionship of dancers, singers, and actresses, most of them older than he, who performed operetta locally. These show people liked him, accepted him, and evidently found him diverting and attractive company. "I don't do anything except go to the music hall and have fun with the girl singers there," he wrote to his friend Bruno Pozzan. And perhaps he had a taste for sleazier company from the rough district in the old city, where the fishermen hung out. "My family predicted darksome fates for me." They viewed with alarm his late hours, easy pleasure seeking, and unconcern about who paid for his fun. "Good-for-nothing" is not too strong an expression for the way they thought of him. A former Castellaneta neighbor claimed he was frequently arrested for vagabonding in Taranto. Probably not true, but it shows that in polite circles he was much discussed and was the occasion of much moralistic clucking and dire prophecy.

Like many a youth brought up to become a gentleman in a puritan climate, Rodolfo struggled to reconcile his ideals with his desires. Within him contended love and lust, romance and sex. On one side amorous, poetic yearnings smoldered; on the other roared his over-heated hormones.

Cars and dancing supplied distraction. Automobiles were still a novelty in the early 1900s, but were becoming less so by the minute. In Turin, Giovanni Agnelli had joined with a group of industrialists to create Fiat; by 1903 there were four Fiat factories, turning out 1,300 cars a year, and each year until the outbreak of the Great War they increased the number. Exactly when Rodolfo first sat behind the wheel and learned to drive isn't certain, but once he did he was smitten. He dreamed of cars, haunted garages. In tune with the new century, he adored speed. He would claim in a Hollywood job application around 1919 that as a teenager he had driven a Fiat one hundred and twenty miles per hour in a race between Rome and Naples, and had come in second. Somehow he came up with the money to own a Fiat, which he sold before leaving for the United States. Because he had poor vision and maybe impaired depth perception, driving fast wasn't his best-chosen pastime, as later mishaps would amply demonstrate. But no one ever convinced him of that.

Dancing suited him better. Naturally gregarious, musical, agile as a cat, he moved across the dance floor with an elegant and effortless rhythmic grace. Rodolfo was born to dance. He never took a lesson in Italy, but gravitated to places where he could practice with a partner

the steps he found so easy to learn. He executed them with aplomb—
and he loved showing off. When he danced with a pretty, well-dressed,
and nimble partner, people took notice. Rodolfo had acquired a
tuxedo as well as a Fiat. As he smoothed back his hair and fastened his
stiff white collar, staring at himself in the mirror before stepping out
at night, he knew he cut a dashing figure. He had sprouted a hint of a
short black mustache, which he kept in perfect trim. He hoped it
made him look older than seventeen.

Taranto has a lively dance tradition. The delirious tarantella supposedly originated there; people believed that the way to cure a taran-
tula bite was to dance oneself into a trance. And much earlier, when
Taranto was part of Magna Graecia, acolytes of Dionysus with vines in
their hair and wearing leather phalluses or ornamental animal tails
spun in ecstatic, mystic initiation rites. In tamer times at the dawn of
the twentieth century, ballroom dances such as the waltz, the polka,
and *galop de bal* became part of the dancing repertoire of most young
people from "good" families. Already, at seventeen, Rodolfo found
that his dancing skills made it easy for him to meet, and impress,
good-looking women. It helped that he had concentrated on polishing
his manners. He could bow low, kiss a hand, hold open a door with
panache, deftly encircle a slender waist, as if these gestures, too, were
steps to a dance he had mastered. Among the qualities he would later
list as "most admirable in a man" was courtliness, which he himself
possessed to a fare-thee-well.

But in Taranto, he began more and more to sense that such finesse
would never find full play. Several of his former classmates had visited
Paris and had enticed him with stories about the pleasures it offered.
He spoke serviceable French and had been hearing stories about his
mother's native country all his life. After drawing on money left by his
father, he and a friend set out by train in 1912 for the City of Light.

Paris, he felt at once, belonged to him. Strolling along the grand
boulevards, losing himself in the crowds streaming through brightly lit
arcades whose polished windows beckoned, he sniffed the heady air as

if it contained helium. He was like a zoo animal released from a cage into the wild, but his wild was the cosmopolitan metropolis. In Paris he could revel in anonymity. He could go where he pleased, with whom he pleased. No one was going to check on or reproach him for staying up until morning's wee hours, or for promenading, dressed to the nines, with a showgirl. On the contrary, here in Paris the actions that in Taranto would have been tagged indiscretions won him admiring glances, and everywhere he found companions who had no more pressing occupation than to chase delight and feast on diversion.

Although Rodolfo lacked the budget for anything but the most rudimentary hotel room, and probably brought with him only one suit for daytime use and his white waistcoat and black tails for festive nights at the restaurants, cabarets, and music halls he frequented with new companions, he worked on blending in. He had no wish to advertise that he was new to Paris, solidly middle class, from a small city in southern Italy, and not a seasoned *boulevardier*. He began to practice an art he would devote himself to, the gentle art of moving into, appearing to have been born amid, fashionable and elite circles. High life beckoned to him, with its popping champagne corks, jeweled cigarette cases, nonchalant spending, and exquisite ladies in feathery décolletage flirting under crystal chandeliers.

Emerging from a café on the Rue Royale, he might have been struck by the sight of the elegant marquis de Castellane, sporting a gardenia in his buttonhole, or the Venetian magnifico comte de Beaumont flourishing a waxed mustache and gold-tipped cane. The English dandy had long been admired and much imitated in Paris. Rodolfo, too, would audition as "a Poet of Cloth . . . a Clothes-wearing man," a man who makes elegance a way of life. He knew how important good grooming and the right apparel can be in furthering social acceptance. As Balzac put it, clothes matter to "those who wish to appear to have what they do not have, because that is often the best way of getting it later on."

Chic people interested Rodolfo, and so did artistic types. Nursing an espresso at Le Café Weber, he could have noticed Claude Debussy dragging on a cigarette or a clothes-conscious Marcel Proust adjusting his woolen muffler around his neck. He might even have observed the young Russian dancer who was the talk of Paris, the sensational Ballets Russes star Vaslav Nijinsky, "half cat, half snake," pursuing down some side street one of the tarts his lover, Serge Diaghilev, wished Nijinsky could resist.

Nijinsky's performances for the Ballets Russes had electrified Paris, which wasn't accustomed to dynamic, erotically charged male ballet dancers, unpretty choreography that aped things barbaric and primitive, or Stravinsky's percussive, tradition-shattering scores. Even if he missed attending a performance of Michael Fokine's *Schéhérezade* or Nijinsky's erotic ballet *L'Après-midi d'un Faune* at the Théâtre du Châtelet, Rodolfo would have picked up on Léon Bakst's influence on Paris fashion. Bakst's Ballets Russes costumes, along with creations of Fauve painters and fashion designers like Fortuny and Paul Poiret, brought about a revolution in color trends. Instead of shy pastels or somber black, stylish women and a few theatrical men were dressing in vivid reds, electric blues, and sumptuous jewel-patterns redolent of the Orient. Schéhérezade outfits, featuring tunics slit over harem skirts, were all the rage. Rodolfo took note. One day he would luxuriate in red silk Chinese pajamas and dressing gowns of fur-lined paisley silk. And within the next few years, Rodolfo would project during his own performances something akin to Nijinsky's androgynous allure.

If on this first visit to Paris he went out dancing, or saw others dance in cafés like La Feria and the Jardin de Paris, Rodolfo would have been exposed to a wild hoodlum's dance he would later perform, in a watered-down version, on film: the Apache. In it, the male dancer, wearing a cap pulled down on one side, a knotted neckerchief, loose-fitting pants, and a buttoned suit jacket, grabs his partner's buttocks and flings and then drags her across the floor. Music-hall stars Mistinguett and Max Dearly adapted this brutal dance of the underworld, also called the "valse chaloupée," and turned it into a show-stopping performance piece. The Apache, much censored when it crossed the sea to invade New York dance halls and vaudeville stages, captured a sadistic eroticism; the male partner dominates and excites by inflicting pain, just like the sexily menacing Sheik, Ahmed Ben Hassan, in the eponymous E. M. Hull novel that would become the rage a decade later.

Another domination dance with undercurrents of violence, also with underworld and bordello roots, had caught on in fashionable prewar Paris: the Argentine tango. If he didn't see tango dancing in Taranto, demonstrated by young people who had visited Argentina, Rodolfo, destined to become the silent screen's "Mr. Tango," undoubtedly saw it, and maybe attempted it, here in Paris. It must have been a case of love at first slide. The tango's combination of style and exotic expressiveness, repression and sex, its blending of Andalusian and African rhythms, Spanish words, and Italian melodies, spoke to his very essence. The somber and passionate mood of tango movements precisely captured his own, "The tango," wrote the Argentine poet Enrique Santo Discepolo, "is a sad thought that can be danced."

We don't know for sure that Rodolfo attended movies in Paris, but movies were available there, and were beginning to be à la mode. New cinemas were opening at a rapid clip, even luxury cinemas such as the Gaumont-Palace and the Electric-Palace. Sarah Bernhardt could be seen on Paris screens as Camille, in a filmed version of the popular Dumas Fils melodrama, La Dame aux camélias, in which Rodolfo would one day play Armand Duval. The highest-paid film star in the world, in 1912, was Rodolfo's—and Charlie Chaplin's—future friend in Hollywood, the comic Max Linder, who made numerous short, extremely popular comedies for Pathé. His signature character, also named Max, always wore a dapper Parisian's elegant top hat, a frock coat, black or striped trousers, a tie, vest, and spats. In one film he would be a waiter, in another a tango professor, but most often he was a man about town. "Max rarely ever worked; instead, he either courted young women, . . . frequented restaurants and nightclubs, or indulged in various sports." He pursued "a life of 'decadence.'"

During his weeks in Paris, Rodolfo experienced at least two setbacks, folded into the glitter and excitement. The first, predictably enough, was that he ran short of funds and had to wire home for money. The second, more mysterious, involved some kind of unpleasantness with a young music-hall dancer. The Paris-born writer and director Robert Florey, who became Rodolfo's confidant in Hollywood in the early 1920s, reports that the friend he called Rudy was never completely forthcoming about exactly what transpired. He said Rudy told him that in 1912 he took up in Paris with a music-hall dancer but that for some reason she refused to go to bed with him. Subsequently, Rudy pronounced the nearly naked dancers of the Folies-Bergère uniformly ugly and much too fleshy; he insisted that they couldn't compare with Ziegfeld's New York beauties.

Rodolfo's defensive reticence on the matter suggests that the problem may have been his own. Perhaps, like many another sensitive youth, in his first sexual encounter with a woman he found to his profound embarrassment that he couldn't perform. The fact that he praised Ziegfeld lovelies to the skies hints that in New York he would find greater sexual success.

But before he boarded the boat for New York, Rodolfo had to face a few more humiliations in his own eyes and those of his family. With the money his mother sent to bail him out of Paris, he went to Monte Carlo, hoping to return home flush from his winnings at the gaming tables. "If I was a poor amateur at the boulevards, I was less than a poor amateur at the gaming tables." He lost nearly every sou he had, and returned to Taranto with empty pockets and many debts. He resumed his old ways, sleeping late, hanging out in the town square and at the cafés, perhaps going to movies at either of two Taranto cinemas, and keeping company with singers, layabouts, and dancers. He bought gifts for his girlfriends and sent the bill to his mother. As far as his uncles were concerned, he was headed straight for the gutter. They felt that he would only continue to disgrace the family and should be encouraged to move as far from Taranto as possible. "Thrown on his own resources, he'll either turn out a criminal or a man."

This decision to make a fresh start suited Rodolfo, although he hated the idea of putting an ocean between himself and his mother. Demoralized and tired of being harshly judged and living aimlessly, he agreed that he needed a jolt. "I don't want to continue the kind of idle and useless life that I've led up till now," he wrote to a friend, disclosing an introspective, not at all complacent, turn of mind.

He knew many people in Italy who had relatives in South America or the United States. The father of one of his classmates at the agricultural college had lived in the States for several years. Because of the region's chronic poverty and high unemployment, southern Italians had for the past several decades been swarming to more promising shores, mainly Buenos Aires and New York. Between 1890 and 1914 the United States had open immigration laws, and its cities were filling rapidly with people from the poorest and most oppressed sections of Europe and Eastern Europe. Rodolfo, unlike most of his emigrating countrymen, was not escaping chronic family poverty but rather his own track record and the sense of defeat it had helped to create. That, combined with a growing conviction that Italy was confining and that opportunities to make good abounded in America, decided the matter. Gabriella bought a ticket for him to sail at the tail-end of the year 1913 on the S. S. *Cleveland*, from Naples to Genoa and on to New York. Tearfully embracing his mother and then Maria, an eager Rodolfo, valise in hand, took a last lingering look at the December-gray Ionian Sea before bidding a silent farewell to Taranto and his disgraced boyhood.

3

NEW YORK TANGO

"He was shipped off to America like a lot of other unmanageable young Italians. . . . he wanted to make good in the brightlights; money burned in his pockets."
—John Dos Passos, "Adagio Dancer," *The Big Money*

When he sighted New York City from the deck of the steamship S.S. *Cleveland*, the eighteen-year-old Rodolfo, with his quickened pulse and his few well-rehearsed words of English, resembled a lot of other young Italians with sea legs crowding into New York Harbor from southern Italy. Like them, he was drenched in hope. But unlike most of the new immigrants, who were arriving from Naples and who were peasants fleeing poverty, Rodolfo crossed the ocean in a first-class cabin with a tux in his trunk and a draft from the Credito Italiano for the equivalent of four thousand dollars in his pocket. His mother, Gabriella, had purchased a second-class ticket for him, but once on board he instantly found that this arrangement didn't suit him; he preferred the services and the amenities in first class, where he could mingle with the right sort of people (the kind who might help him get ahead in America), enjoy champagne with dinner, and dance at full-dress balls. He sold the draft at a loss and paid enough extra to trade up to a first-class cabin.

Aboard the S.S. *Cleveland* Rodolfo wrote to his mother, smoked the cigarettes he couldn't do without, worked on learning English; and he pursued an attractive young American lady, a good dancer named Marion Hennion, who used the time between deck tennis and shuffleboard to teach him the one-step. Playing no favorites, he also chatted up the wealthy Miss Eleanor Post—later Mrs. Russell E. Dill—who remembered him as young, attractive, and enthusiastic. "Very few people were traveling and we had the run of the boat. Every afternoon . . . while one of us played the piano, the other danced with Rudolph." She recalled that he already knew the tango.

Unlike most of his fellow southern Italians, who came to the United States with the idea that they would return to Italy as soon as they had earned and saved some money, Rodolfo intended to make a success of himself in America and remain there, far away from his disapproving Taranto relatives; perhaps he would send for Gabriella when he could afford to look after her. He had vague ideas about going to Argentina if things didn't work out well for him in the States. But first he must try to advance himself, and get to know wealthy or socially prominent people who might offer opportunities essential to his future. He carried with him, and handed out to those he wanted to know, large calling cards, printed on parchment, bearing his name and what looked like a heraldic family crest. But the distinguished genealogy he advertised didn't stand in the way of his having a good time. A photo taken on the deck of the *Cleveland* shows him cavorting with Miss Post and another smiling young man named Vincent Vitelli; Rodolfo and the Italian gent both wear dark suits and white shirts, with a white handkerchief neatly folded in overlapped triangles to peek neatly out of each young man's dark breast-pocket. Alexander Walker, who was lent the photo by the former Miss Post, labels this nautical Rodolfo "a smart young masher" in a "jaunty cap." The high-spirited masher seems companionable, socially confident, meticulous about his appearance, and bent on pleasure.

The S.S. *Cleveland*, of the Hamburg-Amerika Line, had departed Naples on December 9, 1913, and picked up passengers in Genoa. It set anchor in Brooklyn fourteen days later, two days before Christmas, on a cheerless wintery day: "Increasing cloudiness, probably rain by tonight," the December 23 *New York Times* forecasted. Rodolfo Guglielmi informed the American immigration authorities that he was an "agriculturalist" by trade and that his middle name was "dei Marchesi," so that everyone would take him for the descendant of a marquis. Interestingly, a fellow southern Italian passenger on the list of aliens on the *Cleveland* bore the name Valentini.

After making his way to Wall Street to exchange money at Brown Brothers, he set out to find lodgings. He left his trunk behind on the *Cleveland*, planning to come back for it once he had scouted out a place to keep it. As he surveyed lower Manhattan's fabled skyline for the first time, the high buildings reminded him of Italian hill towns built in white stone, with their tall campaniles jutting into the sky.

An Italian he'd met on board the ship had given him the name of a place called Giolito's, on West Forty-ninth Street in Manhattan, where Italian was spoken and rooms were available. Meals could be taken there as well: "The Best Italian Dinner In The City, Lunch 55¢, Dinner 85¢, 108–110 W. 49th St." ran an advertisement. Unconcerned about costs, Rodolfo sprang for a suite consisting of bedroom, parlor, and bath, in the front of the house. "Nothing was too elegant for me then, as the four thousand my mother had given me seemed an inexhaustible fortune." Eager for a taste of New York excitement, he passed up the pleasures of Giolito's Italian fare and headed straight for fashionable Rector's, a palatial, newly relocated Broadway lobster palace where pretty actresses were treated to bird-and-bottle suppers by stage-door Johnnies, and elegant men-about-town gathered to dine, drink, ogle, and flirt. Rodolfo loved rubbing shoulders with stylish pleasure seekers like himself, and he soon learned that a dance floor had recently been installed at Rector's and likewise at other nearby upscale restaurants. New York was in the midst of a dance craze, he couldn't help but notice. After devouring "everything on the [lunch] menu" at Rector's he returned to the S.S. *Cleveland* to pick up his trunk, managing to get lost on the subway several times before finding his way back to Giolito's.

His choice of Midtown's theater district as the place to hang his hat, rather than one of the densely settled Italian neighborhoods in Brooklyn or lower Manhattan, is a tip-off that Rodolfo may already have begun dreaming of work connected to show business—if he thought of work at all. He certainly wanted to be at the hub of New York's amusement quarter, and if he yearned for a touch of home, there were other Italians at hand, not only in his rooming house but also a few blocks to the west in the rough neighborhood known as Hell's Kitchen. On many a New York corner he might pass an Italian hurdy-gurdy man grinding a tune for a nickel, or raising a passerby's smile by showing off his trained monkey. But it wasn't the hurdy-gurdy men or the Italians who worked all over New York digging subways and laying pipe whose company he sought. Rodolfo aspired to the *haut monde*.

Bone weary, excited by his impressions of teeming New York, and thinking of his family, before going to sleep that night he wrote to his mother some observations about his new country: "These Americans are strange people. . . . They chew all the time, and yet never put anything into their mouths. They must belong to the family of ruminants, like sheep and cows." Ford automobiles could be spotted on the streets, their horns contributing to the general hullabaloo, but only a select few could afford them; horse cars still ruled the thoroughfares of Manhattan. Fifth Avenue traffic came to a halt when heavy trucks drawn by four or six horses blocked the way, or women out shopping left their empty carriages or hansom cabs lined up at the curb.

Gloom soon overtook Rodolfo; he had never been so completely alone. He wondered whether he'd made a terrible mistake in coming to New York. With Christmas imminent, he was seized with longing for familiar faces and a warm hearth. "The loneliest ebb of my life came on that Christmas eve, only one day after my arrival in New York. The abyss of loneliness. I ate a solitary dinner in a small café, and the very food tasted bitter with my unshed tears. One doesn't dare to cry in America. It is unmanly here." Unmanly or not, he confessed (to Herbert Howe, who ghostwrote Valentino's life story for *Photoplay*) that he actually threw himself on his bed "and cried like an infant, thinking of mother and blaming myself for having been so mean toward all my family." What he meant by "mean" we can only guess at: Did he refer to his failure to shape up in Taranto as his uncles had prescribed? His bullying of his sister? His abandonment of his mother? Probably all of the above, but he didn't need to be precise. The tear ducts simply opened.

Rodolfo's ability to summon tears would eventually help him become a screen actor at ease with emotion and one with special appeal to women; it would prompt sneers from American he-men who'd grown up hearing their parents admonish "Be a man" at the sight of an incipient sob of pain or self-pity.

Social to the tips of his pointed shoes, Rodolfo needed friends. But where to begin? He wandered around Manhattan, peering into restaurants where he could see other young people laughing and having fun. Perhaps around New Year's Eve, he entered a popular café on Fortieth Street called Bustanoby's, where he found he could converse in French with several waiters. He soon was invited to join a group of continental-looking youths in evening dress who also spoke French; one of them he recognized from his time in Paris. These fashionable young swells became his cronies, the "three noble musketeers," and they jointly took Rodolfo under their wing, introducing him to women, showing him New York, and helping him learn or improve his skill with currently popular dance steps like the Castle Walk, named for the renowned husband-and-wife dance team, Irene and Vernon Castle, or the tango. Evenings, he'd go out dancing with the trio, at times picking up women dance partners along the way; perhaps they found partners for more than dancing, too, as they crowded into smoky cabarets or mingled with after-theater crowds streaming out of the Winter Garden or the Hippodrome. Locating a spot for dancing was no trick at all. All kinds of venues offered dance floors and music; not just restaurants and cabarets but hotels, theater lobbies, and even skating rinks. They'd stay up, these gadabouts in immaculate white shirts and perfectly creased trousers, partying until the wee hours: "I was a pretty wild boy."

One of the musketeers, George Ragni, was the wealthy son of an insurance agent in France. The other two were aristocratic playboys from Austria, Count Otto Salm von Hoogstraesten and his brother, Count Alex. The athletic Salm brothers, who would compete for tennis's Davis Cup in 1924, offered conviviality and good looks, Alex in particular. Alex later had a film acting career in Germany and after that was briefly married to an American heiress, whose father denounced him as a fortune-hunting vagrant. Both Salms excelled at ballroom dancing, setting an example their new friend Rodolfo eagerly followed. Right now, in New York in early 1914, the Counts Salm, with George Ragni, provided welcome camaraderie and entrée into New York café society. In their company Rodolfo spent money with abandon, behaving as if he, too, belonged to the free-spending aristocracy. "Rudy [in his early days in New York] often masqueraded as a Count or Marquis," his publicist, Beulah Livingstone, reported in 1926.

With his debonair new friends Rodolfo spoke French; at Giolito's he conversed in Italian. Since he had a gift for languages and was impatient to acquire English, he realized after a few months that if he wanted to make progress he should situate himself among people who spoke American English. He moved uptown to another boarding house, where the house language was New Yorkese, then briefly to an Italian neighborhood in Brooklyn, where rent was cheaper than in Manhattan.

He had a letter of introduction—either through a former schoolmate or perhaps someone he'd met on board the S.S. *Cleveland*—from an Italian architect to a young New York social lion named Schuyler Livingston Parsons, who lived in an apartment on Fifth Avenue (the posh restaurant Sherry's was in the same building), where Rodolfo presented himself. Parsons, an outgoing and gracious man who loved to entertain, was planning a small dinner that night, to be followed by dancing at various cabarets. Rodolfo was invited to join the dinner party, and "when the ladies saw [him] they insisted that he come along with us, and . . . he proved to be a beautiful dancer." At last, he'd been launched.

Then panic set in as he confronted that old demon, empty pockets. The money he had counted on to sustain him comfortably for an indefinite but prolonged period had almost disappeared, vanished into the mists of New York high living as it had similarly evaporated on his Paris jaunt two years earlier. He needed a job, pronto. His dependable brother, Alberto, who worked in local government in southern Italy, had provided Rodolfo with a letter of introduction to the New York commissioner of immigration. Rodolfo went to see him, describing his education at the agricultural school in Nervi. No doubt impressed by Rodolfo's courteous bearing as well as his education, the commissioner arranged for him a highly privileged interview with the millionaire Cornelius Bliss, Jr., a socially prominent philanthropist and financier whose father had been secretary of the interior under President McKinley and who happened to be looking for a landscape gardener. Bliss had recently purchased an estate in Jericho, Long Island. After interviewing Rodolfo, he hired him to plan and supervise the laying out of an Italian garden and installed him in quarters above the garage.

The new gardener didn't last long in Jericho, for several reasons. One was that when Mrs. Bliss returned from Europe she decided she would prefer a golf course to Italian gardens. Another had to do with an unfortunate accident: Rodolfo crashed a carpenter's motorcycle he'd borrowed into a telephone pole and damaged the motorcycle. He had neglected to ask the carpenter's permission before borrowing the motorcycle. Even this compound infraction might have been overlooked by Mr. Bliss, who seemed to like Rodolfo and want to help him, if the young Italian had shown a greater inclination for hard work. Supervising, rather than laboring with his hands, was what Rodolfo believed he had been hired to do. "My pride . . . would not permit me to stoop to the labor of picking bugs from the leaves of bushes, . . . nor would it permit me to eat with the other 'help,' when I had imagined myself a sort of guest of the family." Besides, he'd decided he really preferred to live in the city, not hidden away amid lawns, shrubs, and trees, where there wasn't much action once the sun set.

Bliss felt he had no choice but to let Rodolfo go, but he was kind enough to provide both a small weekly allowance to tide him over for a short term, and a letter to the parks commissioner in New York City, in which he recommended Guglielmi as an apprentice landscape gardener in Central Park. This proved, unfortunately, to be a civil service position requiring a preliminary exam that only American citizens were allowed to take.

Whether he liked it or not, Rodolfo found himself, in this and many future instances, grouped with other new immigrants who were often collectively disdained as greenhorns. Italians in particular found themselves disparaged as "swarthy" criminal types, supposedly devious, prone to explosions of violence, and ruled by the Mafia or the Black Hand. A 1913 film, *The Criminals*, showed Black Handers kidnapping a child, and a D. W. Griffith film, *Italian Blood*, focused on an Italian husband's insane jealousy. American slang contained ugly, dehumanizing epithets for Italians, who were smeared as "wops" or "dagos" and ostracized for having complexions not quite white. One American-born employer was asked by an Italian job seeker, "You don't call an Italian a white man?" The answer came back, "No sir, an Italian is a dago." When distinctions were made among Italians, those from the south got the short end of the stick. Many Americans as well as northern Italians automatically assumed that if you were southern Italian, you had to be poor, uneducated, and inclined to settle arguments with a stiletto.

Although the Federal Bureau of Immigration's open-door policy had been allowing thousands of Italians—nearly 300,000 the year Valentino arrived—to settle in the United States since the 1880s, there was pressure from "old stock" Americans, whose forebears had arrived during Colonial times, to slam the open door shut. The privileged wanted assurances that only the "right sort" of immigrants would hereafter be allowed in; they agitated against "racial aliens" and defended a narrow, nativist definition of American tradition, based on a belief in the superiority of Anglo-Saxon attitudes and ancestry. Biased against the uneducated and the nonwhite, they pushed for a literacy test as a ticket of admission. Some laborers, too, resented the southern and eastern European newcomers, blaming them for taking all the unskilled jobs and being willing to work for less than a living wage.

The agitation for immigration restriction came to an end, temporarily, with the outbreak of the European War in August of 1914, which brought a sudden and dramatic plunge in the number of foreign-born newcomers emigrating to America, and a new chilliness toward those whose native countries were engaged in war. But New York

City, where most immigrants from Europe landed and many settled, remained a polyglot city crowded with settlers from Italy, Russia, Poland, and Austria-Hungary who didn't always get along with one another, let alone with those whose antecedents had come over on the *Mayflower*. Rodolfo had plenty of "alien" company—New York had more Italian residents than any city in Italy—but that doesn't mean he felt he had allies.

Now came a time of unimagined hardship, isolation, and privation. He could no longer afford to keep up with his high-living companions. Initially too haughty to accept menial jobs, Rodolfo faced the reality after leaving the Bliss estate that if he wanted to eat and to have a roof over his head he could ill afford to pick and choose. He took anything he could get: polishing brass, sweeping up stores or sidewalks, picking up debris, washing cars. Such jobs paid very little, perhaps on a good day a few dollars. Rodolfo pawned whatever he owned that was pawnable and moved into a cubbyhole in the scruffy Mills Hotel, where rooms went for twelve cents a night. "My last landlady held my trunk, so that I didn't even have a change of such clothing as I had left."—a particular indignity to one who set so much store by his fine feathers. Even the cubbyhole had to be vacated after a single night. "I slept on park benches" in Central Park. Hungry day followed hungry day. For a few weeks he lived the life of a vagrant, never knowing where or whether he'd find a meal, or a pillow for his head.

He became adept at tracking down saloons that offered free lunches: "There was one place where they gave you a red ticket that entitled you to a dish of Irish stew with a glass of beer. I managed to show that ticket and then slip it back in my pocket" to use again. But he couldn't do that all the time. "Many a time I went hungry; many a time I washed under a hydrant."

To keep his mother from worrying, he would write to her on stationery filched from a fine hotel like the Waldorf or the Astor, assuring her in his neat, decorative handwriting that he was flourishing. On his birthday, in May, he scraped together enough to have himself photographed in top hat and tails, so he could send the picture home as proof of his success. He wouldn't want to pose in his only suit, Taranto made, which had pockets so huge he could have pulled rabbits out of them. Telling his family the truth about his struggles and hard times seemed out of the question; that would only have confirmed his uncles' dire predictions about his prodigal habits and weak character.

To add to his troubles, the European War prompted worries about his draft and immigration status. Initially neutral, like the United States, Italy joined the Allied effort in May of 1915. After that, Italy no longer allowed its young male citizens to emigrate, and those who were under forty could be called to arms, even if they lived abroad. Many Italians returned from the United States to do their military service. Those men who were called and failed to return for duty could be jailed, even put to death, as deserters. Aware of these frightening possibilities, Rodolfo tried to enlist at the Italian Recruitment Bureau but was turned down because of poor vision. When he started earning a little money he signed up for flying lessons in Mineola, Long Island, with the thought that he might serve the United States as a pilot. He wanted to do his part, to proudly don a military uniform as his father had, and to escape the dreaded tags "slacker" and "mollycoddle." By 1915 Americans more and more frequently branded those unwilling or unable to join battle as softies, cowards, and weaklings.

The war also imposed hardships on his family in Italy. Letters from home told him money was tight, and Rodolfo had to adjust to the news that from here on, even in a desperate emergency, he could no longer turn to his mother for bail-out funds. For the first time in his life he had no safety net. Worse, Rodolfo learned with alarm that his mother was not well and had left the home they had shared near the Ionian Sea. With her daughter, Maria, Gabriella had departed Taranto and returned to the Doubs region of France, southwest of the area where she grew up and close to the frontier between France and Germany. She went back to France not to be looked after herself but to help La Comité d'Assistance aux Soldats care for the war-wounded. Her blood-soaked native land was again reeling in the face of German aggression. The French army had lost a million men in the first five months of the war. There were hideous stories about atrocities: mutilated prisoners, maimed children, bayonets stuck through limbs, soldiers overcome by poison gas. To Rodolfo, Europe now felt more than an ocean away; it seemed almost another planet, but a planet scarred and under siege.

His sense of isolation increased as he worried about the war, because at first the United States under President Woodrow Wilson hardly seemed to share his concern. Unless they had relatives in Europe, in the early months of fighting, Americans tended to "flip past the war news, preferring to read about Congress passing the bill to create Mother's Day" or about a five-month coal strike. But the indifference to war news and the support for a neutral policy would both prove to be short-lived.

While living the life of a rich pleasure hound whose companions were French-speaking counts, Rodolfo had become an accomplished social dancer. He simply had the knack. His lithe body could slide into the Brazilian maxixe dance as deftly as his tongue could into a French or Spanish phrase. His talent for dancing, combined with the polished good looks that made him a sought-after partner, helped him pry open a door to employment. "One rainy evening a man hailed me on the street," he recalled in an interview, "and dragged me under an awning. He had a room nearby and we slept that night with our feet in each other's face." Rodolfo must have either told the man about, or demonstrated, his dancing adroitness, because "next morning . . . my host said, 'I noticed you picked up dancing quickly. Why don't you go around [to Maxim's] and ask for a job? You'll get your meals also.' My friend gave me money [presumably to get his trunk out of hock and make himself presentable] and I got the job." We don't know whether this open-handed new contact remained in the picture; for certain, this was not the only time the debonair, improvident Rodolfo benefited from an eager-to-please friend's financial bounty.

Maxim's Restaurant-Cabaret, on Thirty-eighth Street, right next door to Irving Berlin's music publishing company, was one of several Manhattan nightspots offering European cuisine, elegant decor, live music, and dancing in an atmosphere of luxury and Parisian sensuality.

Its Swiss-born proprietor, Julius Keller, had been a waiter at posh Del-monico's, where he'd worked his way up, learning the culinary arts, cultivating helpful social connections, and observing that a successful Manhattan restaurant must offer spectacle along with good food and drink. "The public eats with its eyes as well as its mouth, and the restaurant which displays the best showmanship catches the crowd," Keller believed. With theatrical panache he outfitted his Maxim's waiters like footmen to Louis XIV, in silk stockings, ruffled shirts, powdered wigs, satin knee breeches, and pumps with silver buckles—the kind of frippery Rodolfo himself would don in his 1924 film *Monsieur Beaucaire*. The members of Maxim's resident string orchestra wore red tuxedo coats that glowed under rosy lights. Those who dined in this frothy setting would feel transported into a fairy-tale kingdom from a romantic past that could have been invented for a staged op-eretta. At the same time the more energetic Maxim's patrons had a chance to cut loose in daring, popular new dances that broke free of convention, marking the dancers as up-to-date and fashionable New Yorkers. This yoking of old Europe with the very latest American trend made for a surefire hit.

Right before the war, Keller recalled in his memoir, *Inns and Outs*, New York "had gone slightly insane on the subject of dancing." Women with time on their hands wanted to spend their afternoons at fashion-able *thés dansants*, or "tea dances," their evenings at exciting cabarets. They wanted to shine on the dance floor and were eager to learn the latest steps: turkey trots and bunny hugs, hesitation waltzes and Ar-gentine tangos. When he installed a dance floor at Maxim's, Keller realized that in addition to offering music and space, he should also provide a covey of male dance partners for women without escorts, or with nondancing dates. "Women of all ages began thronging the places where the music was hot and the right dancing partners available. The men were slower than they in falling victims to the craze," and often a wife or sweetheart yearning to dance could not do so, because the man she was with had not mastered the steps. Also, particularly in the af-ternoon, some women ventured out unescorted. "At Maxim's we attempted to correct this unhappy condition by having a few dancing men on hand."

Rodolfo Guglielmi became one such dancer-for-hire, or "taxi dancer." Keller found him "an exceptionally good-looking chap, tall and well-built, dark and romantic in appearance." That meant the women who came to Maxim's in search of a male dance partner or dancing teacher would jump at the chance to get close to him. At the time Keller hired him, Rodolfo "had been making his living as a car washer in a nearby garage." Keller dressed him and his cohorts in smart evening suits and allowed them to eat their dinners free at the restaurant in exchange for dancing with the ladies, who, sure enough, kept coming back for more. "Signor Rodolfo," as he now fashioned himself, made no protest when a wealthy woman from the Crocker family of California made him her particular protégé.

In addition to dancing at the restaurant, he gave private lessons in an upstairs room (like the one in the 1919 Valentino film *Eyes of Youth*), which had a Victrola for playing recorded dance tunes like "Songe d'Automne." Whether sex sometimes followed one of Signor Rodolfo's dancing sessions is anybody's guess. But without knowing the particulars, naysayers in the press often damned every man in this line of work, and assumed that male dancers who were paid by women indulged in some sort of deceit or hanky-panky. A columnist for *Variety*, reporting that a dancing teacher had been arrested for taking money in advance and not giving pupils proper dancing lessons, smirked, "Who can prove what a proper dancing lesson really is?"

The fact that the hired dancing men were usually good looking, well groomed, and well dressed immediately posed a threat to mainstreamers concerned with protecting feminine virtue. Males were not supposed to be too pretty, and since the time of the American Revolution, men's finery had been yoked in Yankee puritan minds with the absurd, "effete" fussiness and affectation of European aristocrats branded as "macaronis."

The women who attended the afternoon teas and nighttime dances at places such as Maxim's tended to be from the white middle class or upper crust; it wasn't poor or "alien" women whose virtue the guardians of propriety wanted to defend, though there was a popular song called "Rosie Rosenblatt, Stop the Turkey Trot." The opportunity for mingling social classes set off alarms, as did the potential mixing of skin tones and ethnic groups. That the dancers tended to have dark hair and dark complexions, that they usually had Italian or Jewish names and were very often foreign born, invited suspicion among those inclined to distrust immigrants in the first place. "The new dancing has done much to bridge social distinctions," an article in *The New York Times* reported. "Since the tango became popular an extraordinary number of dark-skinned young men have appeared in New York as teachers of the Argentinean dance."

The body contact permitted between partners dancing the new dances elicited particular purity brigade concern at the time of the dance craze. Midshipmen being trained at Annapolis were ordered to keep their "left arms straight during all dances" and at least three inches between dancing partners. Bluenoses assumed that in the New York cabarets and tearooms a woman might find herself in the arms of a strange but alluring foreigner who was up to no good. Under the headline "TANGO PIRATES INFEST BROADWAY," *The New York Times* characterized the male "taxi dancer" as a new breed of villain who "must not be confused with the old-fashioned white slaver" who in the pre-Wilson years had set innocent young girls on the path to ruin. This new menace preyed upon wealthy women, but slyly worked within the law, avoiding the blackmail or outright robbery that could put him safely behind bars. The tango pirate tripped alarms because his glossy veneer made him so seductive. "During the Fall, Winter, and Spring these young fellows invariably wear a silk hat, usually tilted at an angle of forty-five degrees. In the summer they wear . . . the most fashionable straws. And cutaway coats. And spats—always spats." Not usually from the "lowest underworld," they were as a rule "ignorant, ill-born" flatterers who "have acquired a mere veneer of good manners" and usually have designs on a girl's or woman's money.

The whole idea of allowing women to go unescorted (often during the afternoon, when husbands or sweethearts would be at work) to places where, for a price, they could drink alcohol and be held in the arms of attractive strangers, made moral watchdogs gag. Cabarets themselves, according to an article in *Harper's Weekly*, smacked as much of evil influence as the afternoon tango palaces. "The very air of these places is heavy with unleashed passions."

The tango—one of the dances women were most eager to learn, partly because of the way it mixed skillful stepping with erotic steam—became a focus for more general anxieties about woman's changing role in society. The women who went to these dances to tango tested boundaries, experimented with new social liberties. They were putting on lip-rouge and discarding their corsets and billowing Edwardian skirts that touched the ground in favor of shorter, clinging hobble skirts and peekaboo shirtwaists. To them, the tango offered excitement: men's and women's chests, hips, and thighs came in contact as they danced, and the male partner's bending over the woman mimicked sex—*Quelle scandale*! The Roman Catholic Church in cities throughout America banned the tango as indecent and "indicative of moral decadence." A 1914 letter to the Vatican newspaper characterized the dance as an "offense against God." Well-chaperoned debutante parties banished it. When sixteen-year-old Gloria Swanson went to a fancy tea dance on Staten Island in 1914 she was warned to stand clear of the dangerous Argentinean import. Don't worry, a friend there reassured her, "They never play tangos on Staten Island."

In just a few months in Manhattan, Rodolfo seemed to have readily adopted a bold New York attitude about the interactions between the sexes, apparently leaving the constraints of his southern Italian culture far behind. In Italy's southern provinces, the Mezzogiorno, unchaperoned contact between women and males who weren't family members was strictly prohibited, as Rodolfo had been reminded every time he tried to seek out a young woman from a respectable family. His own family would have been shocked to learn how Rodolfo was now earning his living, and he himself would later admit that he felt American women went too far in their quest for independence.

Even in cutting-edge New York, tango pirates caught plenty of heat from the standard-bearers of morality. The tags used in the 1910s to describe and deride men who danced for a fee reveal the sneering contempt they commonly aroused. They were "lounge lizards," a term suggesting that they didn't really work but instead hung around all day (and all night) looking ornamental. A male dancer's sweat apparently didn't qualify as a mark of legitimate labor; instead, critics were troubled by the scent of his cologne. The term "tango pirates" implied they were predators preying on innocent, or at least gullible, females who were temporarily released from the guardianship of fathers, husbands, or fiancés. The "taxi dancers" were paid for their services for a brief ride, like cab drivers; and women did the paying, which raised both eyebrows and hackles. "Gigolo," a word that became common in the 1920s, derived from a French word, *gigolette*, for a female prostitute who would sometimes solicit at public dances.

It was customary for a man to pay the costs of a date, or even an assignation. But when the roles were reversed, old guard moralists began to sputter. A lot of American men—and many American women, too—considered the wallet an extension of the phallus. When the man paid, he asserted, and by some measures proved, his potency. When on the other hand a man took money from a woman, the feeling was that he immediately jeopardized his manhood. In taking on, even for an afternoon or a single whirl around the dance floor, the financial dependence customary for women, not men, he became a figure of ridicule or scorn, like a sponging husband with a working or rich wife and no job of his own. He became passive, not active as a manly man should be. Just as in marriage, where the man was expected to win the bread, on dates or even during brief couplings the man asserted his power via the cash he could earn and bestow. Americans saw any rented or dependent man as deplorably womanish, but Europeans took a different view. As the silent film scenarist Anita Loos pointed out, European marriages were based on the dowry system, which subsidized husbands. "No European male is ever humiliated by having to go to his wife holding his hat. Only in the crude culture of the New World was the kept man considered decadent."

In this New World, even for a man to dance well challenged popular assumptions about manliness. Real men rode horses, swung bats, wielded hammers, threw punches, drove tanks, shot howitzers. They might walk softly, as ex-president Theodore Roosevelt had famously admonished, but as they did so they had to carry that big stick. Roosevelt, ever-popular although no longer in the White House, had advocated and exemplified a masculine ideal of Bull Moose adventurousness and rough-riding athletic prowess. He thought a man should lead what he dubbed "the strenuous life, seeking out hardship, toil, and danger." American opinion found nothing strenuous in dancing done by men, whether in ballets or ballrooms. Nijinsky, who appeared in New York in 1916 with the Ballets Russes, was slammed in the press for being effete. To move with graceful insinuation, wear citified evening clothes, show off, and make a woman sigh as you swept her across the floor—sorry, it just wouldn't do, especially if the woman was picking up the tab. The gigolo's slicked-back hair became a symbol of what made him suspect. Instead of being rugged and leathery like a 100 percent American, his oiled hair and manner made him "smooth" and slithery, like the fabled snake in the grass.

As Rudolph Valentino, Rodolfo became quite defensive in later years about the time he spent as a youthful taxi dancer, protesting that he did not regard dancing as a suitable profession for a man, unless he happened to be Nijinsky, to whom he claimed (in an application for a job at Universal Studios) to have given a tango lesson. "For a man to do ballroom dancing for any other reason than absolute necessity—that I cannot understand. To be a Nijinsky—yes, that demands the highest artistry. That is beautiful, but the other—pouf." At the time he went to work at Maxim's, however, he was grateful for the chance to do something that paid decently, provided meals in a posh setting, and put his talents to use. He worked hard at dancing, even going so far as to take a few lessons himself from a tango master, Don Leno, and he effortlessly became proficient at charming his "ever-changing clientele" of women. Partnering so many women schooled him in how to quickly attune himself to feminine signals and nuanced rhythms, a skill that would later prove invaluable. As Alexander Walker says, "There is a parallel here with Greta Garbo's early experience as a lather-girl in a back-street barber's in Stockholm. She, too, would cash in later on early training in the arts of servicing and beguiling the opposite sex."

Rodolfo won such plaudits on the dance floor that he soon got a chance to step up to a more visible and respectable position as an exhibition dancer. Along the way, he began to meet people in the theater and made a first timid foray into the world of motion pictures.

4

SIGNOR RODOLFO

Working as a taxi dancer and private social dance instructor didn't satisfy Rodolfo. He wanted something more respectable that still offered variety and excitement, perhaps performing on the legitimate stage. Although he spoke with a pronounced Italian accent, his English was fluent by now, he had a pleasant baritone voice, and he certainly knew how to move. If only someone would give him a chance. He befriended the actor Harrison Ford (Harrison Ford the first, no relation to the present one, who appeared on the stage before he switched to movies), meeting theater people through him and briefly rooming with him. He began haunting Broadway studios and casting agencies, impressing Cosmo Hamilton, a playwright, as "a quiet fur-coated young man who wanted to sing but had no voice, wanted to act but was without experience, and finally wanted to dance, which he did extremely well."

Rodolfo talked an agent with a Broadway office directly over the Harris Theatre into granting him an interview; a secretary had dismissed the wistful applicant as a youth with a bad complexion who had never done anything in the theater. Said youth returned every day for the next two weeks, until the agent at last relented, not agreeing to send Rodolfo to auditions but instead to let him stick around and learn the theatrical ropes while working as an office boy. "I recall introducing him to Jack Pickford, Richard Barthelmess, Douglas Fairbanks [a Broadway actor before his 1915 film debut] and others who paid no attention to him. He was a very quiet person . . . but full of hopes." The agent, whose name was John W. Higgins, agreed to coach Rodolfo to be an actor in the theater: "I loaned him a copy of Justin Hunley McCarthy's *If I Were King*. He actually lived the role of François Villon and learned it from cover to cover. . . . One afternoon to an invited audience he . . . read his first lines, which were 'All Frenchmen who so ere ye be.' Those who heard him did not think much of him and the owner of the building told me I was wasting my time."

Higgins nonetheless had taken a shine to his eager apprentice, who accompanied him to an Al Jolson show at the Winter Garden (Rodolfo applauded enthusiastically) and took him to his first New York opera, *Thais*. Backstage after the curtain "he met the gorgeous prima donna" Lois Elwell, who sang the title role, and when she gave him a signed picture of herself as Thais she instantly converted Rodolfo into an opera fan. According to Higgins, Rodolfo easily assumed a worshipful stance toward women of talent, respecting and admiring them "for their art." The vaudeville diva Eva Tanguay, known as "the Cyclonic One" because she never stopped moving, provided inspiration because, said Rodolfo, "there was not a lazy bone in her body." Rodolfo, who'd been branded a lounge lizard but would live out his days in perpetual motion, tried to catch her every whirl.

Although he received not a whit of encouragement from Broadway theater producers, Rodolfo found it easy enough to land a few day jobs as a movie "dress" extra. He had to supply his own wardrobe, apply his own grease paint, and be willing to travel by subway or ferry to Brooklyn or New Jersey, but as an extra he got a chance to see how pictures were made, meet some screen actors and directors, and earn five dollars for each day of shooting.

Though Los Angeles was luring more and more film people because it promised sunshine and space, New York City and its environs were still a center for picture making. With the coming of feature films requiring more than four reels and the recent opening of luxury picture houses with marble entrances, plush seats, and in-house orchestras, movies were enjoying a new, high-gloss respectability. The public flocked to see gripping narratives, Keystone comedies, and favorite stars—Mary Pickford, Theda Bara, Lillian Gish, Charlie Chaplin, the cowboy William S. Hart—whose faces everybody knew by heart. "The motion picture is something more than popular. It is intimate," a trade paper of the day observed. "To an extraordinary extent it is entering into the daily thoughts of the masses." The unquenchable appetite for "photoplays" translated into a financial bonanza for a few producers, exhibitors, and stars. By 1915, what had begun as humble storefront entertainment had mushroomed into a multimillion-dollar megabusiness attractive to big investors. Chaplin was making ten thousand dollars a week, and the controversial, groundbreaking twelve-reel Civil War epic *Birth of a Nation* earned four million dollars in its forty-five-week first run.

There's no doubt that Rodolfo wanted to break into pictures. In the days when he lacked both job and room, he'd passed more than one night in a movie house that stayed open twenty-four hours. When he wasn't literally dreaming, he dreamed of seeing his own face up there on the screen. Mary Pickford recalled being interrupted by a handsome foreigner while lunching with her mother at a Manhattan restaurant. Too shy to address America's Sweetheart directly, he instead bowed correctly to her mother, gave his name, begged forgiveness for speaking without having been introduced, and said to Mrs. Pickford, "I am very eager to have your advice as to how I may get into motion pictures." Mrs. Pickford replied that he should get himself photographed by a skilled professional "in profile, full face, bust and full figure"; he should write his age, height, complexion, and experience on the back of each photo, and send copies to every single studio. It was good advice, but he waited to take it until he got to Hollywood.

Exactly when Rodolfo made his screen debut is much debated. Some claim he appeared in a movie within weeks of his arrival in the United States, as a dance extra for a *thé dansant* scene in a D. W. Griffith production called *Battle of the Sexes*—one of thousands of lost silent films and the first of two Griffith features with the same title. That Rodolfo actually appeared in this film seems unlikely, since in his first weeks in New York he spoke little English, knew few people, and hadn't yet begun to dance professionally. "I stayed in New York three months before working," he reported, "spending time with my friends when I should have saved my money for a rainy day." According to two different Griffith scholars, *Battle of the Sexes* was a "quickie" made in just four or five days in December 1913 in a Union Square loft on a shoestring; an elaborate dance hall set would have been out of the question. Rodolfo in any case gave scant thought to practicalities such as employment as he busily went through all his money. If he had met the powerful Mr. Griffith at such an early date, he surely would have mentioned the fact in one of his interviews or autobiographical pieces.

More likely his first extra role came a few months later, when he played a Cossack in Vitagraph's expensive feature *My Official Wife*— about a plot to assassinate the Russian czar—filmed in the spring of 1914 in Brooklyn. Albert E. Smith, a Vitagraph founder, claims that Rodolfo came to the Flatbush studio to assist a set decorator and stayed on to go before the camera in the film, which starred Clara Kimball Young. Her then husband, James Young, was the director and Earle Williams costarred. Since Smith also lists Leon Trotsky as a cast member, he may not be the most reliable reporter.

Clara Kimball Young, who looked like a Madonna, proved to be an important connection. After she left Vitagraph, where she'd been a top star, the dark-haired and impassioned leading lady became the focus around which a former jewelry salesman, Lewis Selznick, organized World Pictures. At World Pictures' Fort Lee, New Jersey, studio, Rodolfo worked with her again in 1916 as a bit player in Selznick's *The Foolish Virgin*, a forgotten melodrama about a drunken husband. But everyone who saw *Eyes of Youth* a few years later remembered Rodolfo's character roughing up Miss Young and delivering a mesmerizing performance as a "cabaret parasite" that set him on the path to stardom. In Hollywood, James Young, now divorced from Clara, would resurface as the director who cast Rodolfo as an Apache dancer in *A Rogue's Romance* and became a friend. Both Clara and James, when they reconnected with Rodolfo on the West Coast, drew on their knowledge of his experience as a tango pirate when assigning him screen roles.

As a New York screen extra Rodolfo definitely turns up in two movies in a tuxedo, his precisely parted hair slicked back in the authentic patent-leather style. The first bit was in the "midnight frolic" sequence of a patriotic, prowar serial called *Patria*. It starred Irene Castle as an heiress who inherits a munitions factory, and it was made in 1916 by a flag-waving, jingoistic William Randolph Hearst. In the second, *Seventeen*, based on a novel by Booth Tarkington, he's "very much in evidence grinning broadly over [Jack] Pickford's shoulder in the wedding sequence." Footage from *Patria* has survived, and there, in episode 3, Rodolfo unmistakably stands, totally at ease in white tie among the champagne-quaffing New York revelers, his younger face fleshier than the one we know from a thousand later star close-ups. At age twenty-one, pasta-loving Rodolfo weighed about twenty pounds more than the sleek twenty-five-year-old movie-star heartthrob Valentino, and to make himself look slimmer and sleeker in the new form-fitting dress suits he sometimes wore a man's corset.

His dancing prowess at Maxim's still paid his rent and caused jaws to drop. "He flowed along. He looked as though if he took a jump, he'd never land," said one Maxim's patron. He'd continue dancing after hours, for the sheer joy of it, making the rounds from Murray's, which had a revolving dance floor, to Reisenweber's, Bustanoby's, Churchill's, the Moulin Rouge, or the curfew-bending 400 Club. At the Knickerbocker Hotel, where Maxfield Parrish's celebrated mural of Old King Cole smiled down, he made the acquaintance of the acclaimed Metropolitan Opera tenor Enrico Caruso, a compatriot from Naples who lived at the Knickerbocker and would soon be making his own motion picture debut.

Rodolfo tangoed at the Knickerbocker with dainty Mae Murray, who became a soul mate. They bonded as two stagestruck seekers, fatherless transplants who'd arrived in New York as teenagers, both of whom spoke eloquently with their feet. "We were very close . . . There's a funny camaraderie that's between dancers—we clicked immediately," Mae Murray recalled. "Something happens. It's almost indestructible. It has no sex to it." Mae, a divorcée six years his senior, cherished him as an openhearted friend with a mystical quality, someone who had "that other dimension."

Later known as "the gardenia of the screen" and filmdom's "girl with the bee-stung lips," Mae Murray (née Marie Koenig) had begun to hit her stride in New York when she became a featured dancer at the Jardin de Danse, a chic roof-garden cabaret. A last-minute replacement for Irene Castle in Irving Berlin's first musical, *Watch Your Step,* she went on to appear with W. C. Fields, Ed Wynn, and Bert Williams in *Ziegfeld Follies of 1915.* Ziegfeld, taken with her tousled coif, sleepy eyes, shapely legs, and alluring white shoulders, cast her as a Persian princess who dances beside a pool and as "Merry Pickum" a takeoff on Mary Pickford, whose smiling face, surrounded by golden curls, flashed on a proscenium screen. The movies were beginning to invade the Broadway stage, as they already had invaded vaudeville. After *Follies* rehearsals, Rodolfo often picked up Mae at the New Amsterdam Theatre and they'd find a restaurant with good music for dancing, then share secrets as they walked deserted paths in Central Park.

His own star was rising since his introduction to Bonnie Glass, a well-established exhibition ballroom dancer whose partner, Clifton Webb, had given notice. A friend of Glass's, Norman Kerry, who met Rodolfo when they both signed up for flying lessons in Mineola, claimed that he was the one who arranged the introduction to Bonnie Glass, but some say the go-between was a black dancer named Bessie Dudley, the partner of Ken "Snake Hips" Johnson. In either case, Rodolfo and Glass hit it off. After a test run, Miss Glass hired Rodolfo as Webb's replacement; he looked to her "like a South American millionaire" and she agreed to pay him fifty dollars a week. Although he'd been earning more at Maxim's, Rodolfo recognized a good career move. For prestige, exhibition dancing in cabarets or vaudeville fell short of the Broadway stage, but outstripped taxi dancing by a mile. Popular "class teams" such as Irene and Vernon Castle earned as much as five hundred dollars a week for cabaret engagements, taught the latest steps to debutantes, and set standards for elegance and social cachet. If "lounge lizards" were consigned to society's bottom rung, successful exhibition dancers mingled easily with the Fifth Avenue swells who flocked to see them.

One winning dance-team formula paired an American woman with a continental-looking male partner such as Maurice Mouvet, who was "debonair and cocksure in his beautifully fitting evening dress" and, though Brooklyn-born, was a longtime Parisian. According to Robert Florey, Valentino worked as an extra in a film called *The Quest of Life*, which starred Maurice and his dance partner, Florence Walton, but Rodolfo was consigned to an obscure corner in a dance-hall scene.

Exploiting the American-woman-with-European-man trend, Bonnie Glass, a wealthy, Massachusetts-born divorcée described as "quite Irene Castle-ish from bangs and headband to smile," billed her new partner as "Signor Rodolfo." Featuring specialties like the flirtation waltz, the aeroplane waltz, "a semi-Spanish dance of many whirls," a polkalike gallop, and an African-American-style cakewalk that brought down the house, they appeared at charity benefits at Delmonico's and Rector's, on the roof of the Winter Garden, and at various Keith's vaudeville houses, Keith's being the major "big-time" circuit. At the Colonial, where "her orchestra's eccentric ebony drummer really put the [cakewalk] turn over," they were hailed for their "class" and for "bringing ever so many of the smart set to the theater." At the Palace, showpiece of the Keith vaudeville houses, they shared the bill with the powerhouse singer Sophie Tucker, the headliner who twanged "Araby" and belted out "Ballin' the Jack." Grace La Rue, a singer also on the Palace roster, recalled one Palace date that took place on a steamy August night. Suffering from both the heat and nervousness, Rodolfo "was constantly mopping his brow, and his collars wilted instantly." Horrors! "He brought to the stage a supply of fresh collars . . . to change while the special orchestra played between dances." There was no mirror in his dressing room and La Rue invited him to use hers. He thanked her, admitting to his case of nerves. "I am too soft," he told her. "I haven't danced enough. And besides, I must lose a little weight." The self-confidence that Rudolph Valentino would later project was nowhere in evidence here.

After months of touring, Miss Glass decided to open her own club, first the Café Montmartre in the basement of the old Boulevard Café, then Chez Fysher on Forty-fifth Street. "The queen of her world," she drew a posh crowd, which provided entrée for Rodolfo into the glittering circles he aspired to. At Chez Fysher, readers of *Vanity Fair* learned, New Yorkers danced and paid war prices for champagne.

"Every evening at Fysher the corks fly, the drums rattle, the brunette and banged-haired Bordoni sings her outrageous little songs, the extravagant toasts are proffered." Rodolfo continued at Chez Fysher as the partner of Bonnie Glass until she married Ben Ali Haggin (a society painter who created tableaux vivants for Ziegfeld), retired from dancing, and closed her club.

Bonnie Glass and Signor Rodolfo attracted notice in the trade press, most of it favorable. One reviewer complained that they "haven't learned to make proper exits," but Miss Glass won plaudits for her beautiful gowns and sylphlike grace. As a dancer, though, she was outshone by nimble Rodolfo, whom the *Clipper* singled out for special praise: "Miss Glass shapes up as a fair ballroom dancer, but her dancing partner, Signor Rodolfo, a Latin-appearing youth, is grace personified." So suave was he, opined another, that Miss Glass might have trouble keeping him in tow: "all the other dancing girls are trying to steal [him] away."

And stolen away he soon was, after Bonnie Glass retired, by one of the queens of exhibition dancing. Joan Sawyer had danced in Broadway musicals, managed the Persian Garden's roof cabaret, and was regularly featured, with a variety of male partners, as the leading member of a ballroom team. Admired for her flowing, legato continuity of movement, she also possessed more financial savvy and clout than most dancers, having won the right to be paid a percentage of a cabaret's total box-office take. The elegant and expensive Miss Sawyer had a taste for Latin partners; before hiring Signor Rodolfo she'd danced with Carlos Sebastian. Like Irene Castle and Bonnie Glass, she traded on her "lady" image and tried to tame and sanitize the new dances to broaden their appeal to the elite: "She even dances the much abused tango as quietly and with as much classic grace as the minuet was danced." She and Signor Rodolfo toured the major eastern cities on the Keith circuit and danced at the Woodmansten Inn, a New York roadhouse. They scored an appearance before President Wilson in Washington, as Rodolfo would proudly recollect. He was earning $240 a week, something worth writing home about.

Things finally seemed to be going his way. Rodolfo was making good money and becoming known as one of New York's outstanding ballroom dancers, a nuanced performer of exceptional suavity and élan. Though he still worried about his immigration status, he no longer felt like a total outcast. He was living on Central Park West, where he rented a hall room from a former actress named Miriam Merton, who remembered him sleeping until noon and protesting loudly the vocal exercises of a fellow boarder, a singer who liked to practice in the morning. He had acquired many friends in show business and had dined with real-estate tycoons, bankers, brokers, heiresses, and society hostesses. At Chez Fysher he'd many times held in his arms and whirled around the dance floor one of the wealthiest and most beautiful socialites in New York, a young married woman from Chile named Blanca de Saulles.

Blanca, also called Blanquita, quite took his breath away. Pale-skinned and slender, with the wide dark eyes and black hair of a Goya portrait, she awakened his capacity for worship. "For years I had cherished a picture in my mind of how the perfect woman would look, a picture composed of the things I had read and some of the great paintings I had seen. When Mrs. de Saulles stood before me it was as though the picture had come to life. I adored her. She seemed so far above me that I never dreamed she would look at a mere tango dancer." It didn't hurt that she was related by marriage to his titled friends, the Salms. Count Otto Salm had married, and his wife, a cousin of Blanca's husband, had befriended Blanca. The fact that Blanca had a young son to whom she was devoted only made her more perfect to Rodolfo, who exalted the Madonna type.

Blanca often turned up at the cabarets without her husband, eager to mingle and move. Rodolfo readily obliged. He considered her one of the most divine dancers he'd ever known, and their mutual delight in stepping to a beat first drew them together. She soon learned he could speak Spanish, and that he knew what it felt like to live far from homeland and family. As she began to confide in him, her profound unhappiness opened floodgates of compassion.

When she had married brawny Jack de Saulles, an American businessman, in the English Catholic Church in Paris in 1911, the match had been hailed as a brilliant one. The exquisite sixteen-year-old bride, a niece of the former president of Chile, belonged to a prominent silver-mining family and had inherited a fortune. Her mother, a famous beauty, had been called "the star of Santiago," and her aunt, Eugenia Erazzuriz, a trendsetter in interior design and an art patron in Europe, had been painted by Sargent and Boldini. (Eugenia Erazzuriz later befriended Cocteau, Stravinsky, and Picasso.) Señorita Blanca Erazzuriz-Vergara and John Longer de Saulles, once captain of the Yale football team, had met in Chile when he came there to promote the building of the trans-Andean railroad. He followed her to Paris and they married there a few months after their first introduction.

From the start they had their differences. They were fourteen years apart in age, came from dissimilar countries and cultures, and had disparate incomes—hers was far greater. "Jack was never over-burdened with riches," a society gossip sheet tattled, but he boasted an impeccable pedigree and impressive connections. A friend of President Wilson's, for whom he'd campaigned vigorously in New York and who once nominated him to be ambassador to Uruguay, he was a cousin of a former New York mayor, George McClellan. His father had served in the Confederate Army as a major on the staff of General Polk. His mother was a Heckscher, his aunt a Van Rensselaer—names out of New York's Blue Book of the social elite. "He became a partner with his cousin, Maurice Heckscher, son of August Heckscher, in the real estate business, the latter having given them a start."

Popular with his cronies, the clubby, hale-fellow-well-met Jack never developed much of a taste for family life. Although he loved his son, he rarely saw him, and after a few years with Blanquita, she no longer interested him sexually. He maintained a separate apartment, where he often entertained other women. He favored dancers and showgirls, and had made an unsuccessful play for Mae Murray. Joan Sawyer, on the other hand, gave him more than one tumble. He made scant attempt to conceal his philandering from his wife or their social circle. Everybody knew about Jack and his fondness for Broadway's young lovelies. Everybody felt sorry for the foreign heiress, the exquisite and neglected Mrs. de Saulles.

She consoled herself by lavishing affection on their son, John Jr., and spending her evenings at restaurants and cabarets, surrounded by music and festive throngs. "I'm feeling quite an advanced feminist trotting around alone and coming home alone at late hours with my own key," she wrote to Jack when he traveled to another city. But it wasn't the life she wanted. "I'd rather be an old-fashioned little wife and have hubby always trotting along beside me."

Still only twenty-three, Blanca decided she couldn't continue in this sham of a marriage, and, although she was a Roman Catholic, she sued for divorce in the summer of 1916. When the district attorney asked her how a woman suffering the heart pangs of neglect and marital infidelity could express delight in dancing, she countered neatly, "We do not dance with our hearts."

In order to win both a New York divorce and custody of her son, Blanca needed proof that her husband had committed adultery. She enlisted the support of her friend the dancing man. Seizing an opportunity to make himself indispensable, Rodolfo volunteered to provide evidence that would support her case in court. In exposing details about Jack de Saulles's infidelity, Rodolfo saw himself as a knight in armor leaping to rescue a noble damsel in distress.

Had he and Blanca become lovers? Nobody knows the answer. My guess is that they had not, but that Rodolfo hoped a real affair might flare up once she had her freedom. He excelled at yearning, and she for her part could ill afford to risk being found out as somebody's mistress. Blanca displayed a fervor in court, a moral righteousness that would be hard (though not impossible) to fake. She painted herself as the virtuous and long-suffering wife of a crass philanderer, and won the sympathy of every reporter present in the packed courtroom, as well as the judge. She had "faithfully lived up to her duties as a wife, having followed her husband to a strange land." Her own fidelity to her marriage vows was never publicly called into question, although *Variety* did report that she had often been seen with a professional dancer.

In his divorce-hearing testimony, which survives in court documents sealed since 1917 that I was able to examine after successfully filing a motion to temporarily unseal them for research, Rodolfo Guglielmi named Joan Sawyer as one of two co-respondents. After identifying himself as a dancer who lived at 264 West Fifty-seventh

Street, he was asked whether he had worked in any other capacity since arriving in New York. "I intended to do agriculture," he answered. "That is what I studied for, but I never had an opportunity." He falsely stated (risking perjury charges and possible deportation) that he had done no other work but dancing, "excepting the moving pictures, lately."

He then testified that he met John de Saulles for the first time in January 1916, had been several times in his apartment at 2 West Fifty-seventh Street, and had seen him in restaurants. He described de Saulles as "a medium-sized man, very muscular, clean shaved; dark hair, combed very slick, flat." He once had attended a dinner at Joan Sawyer's apartment. "There was a lady in my company, myself, Miss Sawyer and Mr. de Saulles. He called her Joan and she called him Jack and dear. He called her sweetheart."

He said that he and Joan Sawyer first worked together at Keith's Theatre in Washington. "After our theatre performance we danced for a party given to President Wilson." Instead of spending the night in Washington, the performers returned to New York together by train after the party. At Pennsylvania Station, Rodolfo put Miss Sawyer in a cab, telling the driver to take her to Mr. de Saulles's apartment, where he would pick her up the following morning at 8:45. Joan Sawyer waited for him early the next day, as planned. When she got into the cab, de Saulles, in pajamas, waved good-bye from his apartment window.

Another time, Guglielmi testified, he and Joan Sawyer remained a week together in Providence, Rhode Island, dancing at the Albee Theatre there. "I saw Mr. de Saulles Saturday in Providence at the Hotel Narragansett, closing night," he reported. "After a party in her honor, [Joan Sawyer] and Mr. de Saulles retired to her room upstairs. Her room had one large bed." The next day they all returned on the same train to New York. "Mr. de Saulles and Miss Sawyer shared a drawing room on the train. I had an upper berth in the same car, opposite their drawing room." From his berth he spotted a douche bag in Joan Sawyer's traveling bag. "How did you come to be looking through her dressing case on the train?" asked de Saulles's attorney. Answer: "She just opened it in front of me."

Rodolfo Guglielmi's testimony wasn't unique. Others testified to the same effect: de Saulles's former valet, Julius Hadamek, said he had seen Joan Sawyer at his employer's apartment many times "and that she remained there over night, sleeping in defendant's bed room, which contained but one bed" and in which he later found hair pins. Miss Sawyer's former cook reported catching de Saulles kissing Miss Sawyer. And Blanca de Saulles herself stated later that once, in London, when she called at her husband's hotel, announcing herself as Mrs. de Saulles, the clerk had asked her, "Which one?" But Rodolfo's account was the most extensive and damning. Blanca de Saulles won her divorce, although the court decided that the child should spend part of the time with his father.

John de Saulles had powerful political connections in New York. The incriminating words of Rodolfo Guglielmi, a mere tango dancer and an Italian immigrant to boot, galled him, and in retaliation he set Rodolfo up for a cruel retribution. At least that seems to be the best interpretation of the extraordinary event that followed the divorce hearing by five weeks.

At 909 Seventh Avenue, just around the corner from Rodolfo Guglielmi's own rooms on Fifty-seventh Street, lived a gray-haired woman known as Mrs. Georgia Thym who was alleged to keep a brothel in an apartment decorated with heavy draperies and suggestive oil paintings. Rodolfo Guglielmi was there on the night of September 5, 1916. Tipped off by "a well-to-do businessman who said that he had been victimized," and another witness who had been at Narragansett Pier in Rhode Island, the New York City assistant district attorney and two detectives on the vice squad raided Mrs. Thym's apartment and arrested her and Guglielmi. Assistant district attorney James E. Smith told the press, "'For many years Mrs. Thym's place has been the scene of . . . vicious parties.' Many persons of means, he said, principally 'social climbers,' had been blackmailed after indiscreet visits to this house."

The next day's *New York Times* identified Rodolfo Guglielmi as a social climber and "a cabaret dancer who said that he was a recent dancing partner of a woman well known on Broadway," obviously a reference to Joan Sawyer. The *Tribune* quoted a description of him as a "bogus count or marquis," a "handsome fellow, about twenty years old, [who] wears corsets and a wristwatch. He was often seen dancing in well-known hotels and tango parlors." The reference to the corset and the wristwatch was a slur on Guglielmi's masculinity. Americans considered corsets for men absurd. The man's wristwatch, replacing the pocket version, had been introduced recently, and though it was becoming more acceptable by 1916, it wasn't yet the norm. People sometimes still called it a "bracelet watch." Before the war began to alter the fashion, the Dallas *Times* said of a man wearing a wristwatch, "In winter we think he looks better carrying a muff."

Many questions remain about the arrest, and since the police file on the case is missing, they aren't all going to be answered. What was Rodolfo Guglielmi doing at Mrs. Thym's apartment? Had he gone there to procure the services of a prostitute? If so, none seem to have been present on the night of the raid, and we wonder how John de Saulles, presumably the businessman who tipped off the detectives, could have known in advance that Guglielmi would be on the premises. Had he been followed? The vice squad assumed that Rodolfo Guglielmi functioned not as a customer but as a proprietor at Mrs. Thym's establishment. On what grounds, if any, did they base their assumption? We simply do not know.

According to court records, Mrs. Thym and Guglielmi were not directly accused of trafficking in white slavery or indeed of any crime, although the indictment names both as operators of a bawdy house that paid protection money to a policeman. Rather, they were sent to jail for their failure to post bail of $10,000 each. They were held as witnesses against a police officer, William J. Enright, who was charged with extortion and accused of accepting protection money from the keepers of disorderly houses. The indictment states: "Rudolph Guglielmi is a material and necessary witness on behalf of the People . . . against the above named defendant [William J. Enright] who is a police officer. . . . Your deponent is informed and verily believes that said witness operates a disorderly house at premises No. 909 Seventh Ave. and has paid protection money to the said defendant for the privilege of running a disorderly house. . . . It is the intention of the People to use said witness upon the trial, and . . . unless he is committed to the House of Detention for Witnesses said witness will not be within the jurisdiction when wanted." Mrs. Thym was detained on an identical charge.

The evidence must have been flimsy, because two days after the raid their bail was reduced from $10,000 to $1,500 by Judge Otto Rosalsky. Mrs. Thym and Rudolph Guglielmi each could and did raise this smaller sum. (Rodolfo surely had to borrow it from someone.) They were released from their respective houses of detention, in his case the notorious Tombs prison.

For Rodolfo, the immediate result of these traumatic events was the loss of his livelihood and reputation. He had been arrested at a bawdy house and gone to jail, and now he had a police record. Everybody knew about it. His good name, a man's most precious possession, had been forever tarnished. Again he revisited the place called shame. The fact that he had been jailed only as a material witness was never reported in the papers; his arrest in a vice raid, and the embarrassing circumstances, made for more titillating journalism, and those associations stuck. He felt he had become infamous, joined the ranks of the untouchable. Until the end of his life, he continued to try to expunge the whole sordid episode from all records. Although he or some bigwig from a studio apparently succeeded in having the police file removed, court records survived and the story in *The New York Times* and its Index could be dug up by anyone who remembered how to spell "Guglielmi."

Blanca de Saulles never spoke up to offer thanks, solace, or her company. She withdrew with her son and a maid to a house on Long Island. When she applied for permission from the court to take her child out of the country to visit family members abroad, she argued that she had "no friends and very few acquaintances in New York."

Joan Sawyer also wanted nothing further to do with her former dance partner; he had dragged her name through the mud. When he testified at the divorce hearing, Rodolfo had appeared unconcerned about the possible consequences either to Miss Sawyer or to their professional partnership. He and Joan Sawyer remained on friendly terms, he had stated. Asked why he had decided to come forward in this way, he'd answered, "I have a special reason, which if you don't mind I won't go over." When the attorney pressed him, "Doesn't it strike you that you are doing her rather a bad turn to come here and give this testimony in this way?" he inexplicably replied, "No, I don't think so."

After this, no other woman from the world of exhibition dancing came forward with a job offer. Although Joan Sawyer soon resumed her performing career with one of her previous partners, and appeared in a 1917 movie, *Love's Law*, the dance craze in general had lost steam, and the cabarets were suffering. Afternoon tea dances "have about gone, forever," *Variety* reported in a summary of events in the entertainment world for the year 1916. "Few places of any repute permit it and when these do they are very rigid over whom they admit. . . . The recent 'white slave' blackmailing case arose from the dansant [tea dance] more than anything else." This seems to be a veiled reference to the vice squad raid at Mrs. Thym's apartment, involving a cabaret dancer, Rodolfo. Although Rodolfo had never actually been charged with blackmailing, the newspapers and local gossip associated him with that practice, with white slavery, and with the now discredited tea dance.

As Rodolfo began to look for work that would take him away from New York City, he hoped that talk about the de Saulles divorce would be displaced by some other scandal, and it would be easier to forget. But in the summer of 1917 a new de Saulles sensation rocked New York.

Blanca de Saulles, infuriated at her former husband for failing to deliver their son back to her at the time stipulated by the court, on an August afternoon took a taxi to his country home near Westbury, Long Island, pressed a revolver to his head as he stood on the porch, and demanded that he give up their son. She then pulled the trigger five times. "I killed him and I am glad I did it," she cried out at the bloody scene. "He refused to give me my child." In the aftermath of this sensational murder, the name Rodolfo Guglielmi, and the details of his testimony in the de Saulles divorce hearing, resurfaced in the papers.

Blanca stood trial, pleading that a thyroid condition had affected her brain, that she had blanked out before the shooting and only remembered Jack saying she could never have their son. She was acquitted in Nassau County Court on the grounds that her crime had been unpremeditated. The judge echoed community sentiment when he expressed understanding of a mother's overwhelming devotion to her only child; to rob the child of his mother, when he had already lost his father, would be to doubly penalize an innocent victim.

The de Saulles murder became fodder for a quickie "sensation movie," released only months after the trial. *Woman and the Law*, directed by Raoul Walsh, featured Miriam Cooper as "Blanquetta La Salle" and Peggy Hopkins (later Peggy Hopkins Joyce, best known for her six husbands) as Joan Sawyer, renamed Josie Sabel and typed as an adventuress of loose morals. The publicity frankly exploited the movie's topicality; its subtitle was "Based on the Sensational De Saulles Case." Ads posed the question, "Are there provocations which justify a woman to kill?"

By the time *Woman and the Law* hit the theaters Blanca de Saulles had moved back to Chile with John Jr. And Rodolfo Guglielmi had embarked on a new life in California.

5

"A NEW STYLE HEAVY"

When he accepted a part in the road company of *The Masked Model*, a theatrical musical headed for California, Rodolfo accomplished several goals at once: he escaped New York and its relentless rumor mill; he pulled in seventy-five dollars a week, a big drop from his salary with Joan Sawyer but better than the nothing that he earned following the de Saulles divorce hearing and his subsequent arrest; and he got free rail-passage to the Eden called California, where his hopes for a future in either farming or moving pictures might flower amid the jasmine, poppies, and palms. He remembered, "I wanted to try my hand at agriculture. California I had been told was somewhat like my own country," with a temperate climate similar to southern Italy's and a Mediterranean blend of sun, sea, and sky.

At his audition for *The Masked Model*, the theatrical agent Chamberlain Brown wrote on the back of a photo of Rodolfo, "personality and presence, fine dancer, sings a little." But since the personable dancer lacked theatrical experience he started at the bottom, as a chorus man billed as "Monsieur Rodolph" who did dance specialties and also served as understudy to the leading man, Joseph Lertora. The *Masked Model* plot hinged on a young soubrette, played by Edna Pendleton, who bets she can become engaged to a foreign nobleman. Lertora portrayed her victim, an Italian count with flashing eyes and teeth who in one scene masquerades as a rajah; a perfect role for Rodolfo—but not his role this time. John Cort directed, and the ho-hum songs by Harold Orlob and Carl Woess included "The Road to the Girl You Love" and "Meet Me in Havana."

"A Wealth of Whirling Gaiety," the ads for *The Masked Model* promised. "Company of 70 and Snappiest Chorus Ever. A Lively, Lilting, Laughing, Luxurious Musical Confection. Haunting Melodies. Dreamy Waltzes. Syncopated Dances. Rapid Action. Price $1.00. First Six Rows $1.50."

The tour began in April 1917, just as the United States entered the European War, when producers hoped audiences would be in the mood for frothy, escapist entertainment. At the same time they kept things topical by including a fox-trot from another show, *Johnny Get Your Gun*.

In the official autobiography of Valentino (ghostwritten by Herbert Howe) that was first published in 1923 in *Photoplay* and has been quoted by biographers ever since, Rodolfo says that *The Masked Model* folded in Ogden, Utah, and that he continued alone to San Francisco on the train ticket he'd been issued as part of his pay. But in May of 1917, *The Masked Model* did open for a two-week run at San Francisco's Cort Theatre, on Ellis Street, near Stockton, and from there went on to Los Angeles and back to New York by way of Canada. For unknown reasons, Rodolfo was no longer a member of the cast. There may have been a dispute about salary; Alberto Valentino told Kevin Brownlow that the producer had disappeared with the money. But if that's so, why did the others in the show stay with it? According to an Oakland theater owner who claimed he remembered, Rodolfo left the company because he'd been fired.

Once again Rodolfo found himself a stranger looking for work in a place completely new to him, but less overwhelming than New York. Despite agitation after a recent bombing and strife over labor unions, San Francisco nightlife flourished in an atmosphere of relaxed bonhomie, and there were many inexpensive restaurants serving tomatoes as red as the ones in Italy and excellent local pasta from the Italian enclave in North Beach. He took rooms in the downtown area, newly rebuilt after the devastating earthquake and fire of 1906, and began making the rounds of the dance halls and cabarets, offering his credentials as both instructor and performer. Professional male dancers were much in demand now, since so many had left the country to answer the call to arms. He saw no alternative but to revert to his gigolo past, eking out a living by giving lessons and dancing for hire at Tait's Café on O'Farrell Street and at the Cliff House, overlooking the beach on the edge of the Pacific. He also briefly appeared in vaudeville at the Orpheum, across the Bay in Oakland. He didn't like this life, and tried desperately to find an alternative.

Rodolfo managed to get an interview with A. P. Giannini, the founder and president of the Bank of Italy, and confided to him his ambition to get a job related to his training in agriculture, perhaps in the Napa Valley wine vineyards. Giannini, who started out as a produce merchant, discouraged him from such pursuits, urging him instead to "stick to your profession" as a performer, and to "save your money and invest in land of your own."

Rodolfo attended school for two weeks to train as a salesman of gilt-edge security bonds, and scored two sales (one to the head waiter at Cliff House) and two fifty-dollar commissions in his first two days. But on his third day, June 5, 1917, the United States' military draft was declared, the Liberty Bond drive began, and his business career was swiftly aborted—nobody had any interest in buying anything unrelated to the war effort.

As an alien without U.S. citizenship papers, Rodolfo was exempt from the American draft, but he still risked deportation and arrest in Italy for failing to enlist there. He reported to the Italian embassy and again failed the physical because of poor vision in his left eye. Since he had taken flying lessons in New York, he thought he might succeed with the Royal Canadian Flying Corps, but they, too, rejected him as physically unqualified. The humiliation recalled too vividly the indignity of his teens, when naval doctors in Venice had disqualified him for admission to the naval technical school because his chest measurement fell short. At a time when military valor was taken to be a key measure of virility, a single young man without a uniform raised doubts about his manliness as well as his patriotism. "Civilian apparel was a dress of shame," recalled Charlie Chaplin, who faced his own struggle to clear himself of the slacker charge.

These were paranoid times in America. Tens of thousands of draft-age men were apprehended and disciplined as draft-dodging molly-coddles. Recent immigrants were viewed with suspicion and tagged as disloyal; they might form fifth columns and take orders from foreign powers. German spies supposedly lurked behind every door. In the frenzy of patriotism that exploded, citizens felt called upon to prove they were "hundred percent Americans" and immigrants were branded "hyphenated Americans." The new laws against sedition and espionage penalized people for criticizing the U.S. government, the flag, or any-one in military uniform. You could be jailed for speaking up for any country at war with the United States or doing something to restrict the sale of Liberty Bonds.

In San Francisco, and in cities and towns across the nation, recruit-ment stations were set up at movie theaters that showed war newsreels or patriotic films exposing the bestiality of the Hun. Screenings were preceded by flag-waving speeches delivered by "Four-Minute Men," so called because the talks lasted only four minutes and the speakers re-called the heroes of the American Revolution. Mary Pickford led a marine band down Market Street and with the fellow stars Douglas Fairbanks and Charlie Chaplin raised millions for Liberty Bonds. A Liberty Bond poster showed Fairbanks delivering a one-two punch to the kaiser.

One of Mary Pickford's propaganda pictures, Cecil B. DeMille's *The Little American*, was partially shot in San Francisco. Rodolfo's friend from Mineola flying school, Norman Kerry, happened to be in town to play one of the dastardly German soldiers who menace Little Mary in the picture, and the friends reconnected during Rodolfo's stint as a bond salesman. Ramon Novarro (still called Ramon Samaniego) also had an uncredited small role in *The Little American*, but we don't know whether he, too, came north as part of the San Francisco shoot.

When they first met in New York, Norman Kerry had been Nor-man Kaiser, who worked as a salesman for his father's leather-goods business, sometimes traveling to South America to acquire hides. Nor-man disliked the leather trade, and set up shop as a theatrical agent.

But he was restless. Since Kerry possessed dapper good looks, a meticulously waxed black mustache, and a broad-shouldered, muscular, six-foot-two physique, Rodolfo had encouraged him to try his luck in the movies. He'd done just that, coming west in 1916 with a rodeo star, Art Acord, and finding ready work in pictures as a heavy or leading man. His surname had to go, though. "Kaiser" pressed all the wrong buttons among gung-ho Americans who thought of Kaiser Wilhelm as another Attila the Hun.

By all accounts Norman Kerry was something of a wild man, an adventurer, horseman, prankster, art collector, and heavy drinker who often turned up drunk on the set and once at a party bit a dog on the leg. He married four times, caroused at bars and brothels, enlisted in the Royal Canadian Flying Corps toward the end of the Great War and transferred to the American Tank Corps. Never a top silent star, he nonetheless worked regularly and prominently in the second tier, often opposite big-name talents like Lon Chaney, Marion Davies, Lillian Gish, or Pickford. He and Erich von Stroheim got along famously; von Stroheim was fired as director of *Merry-Go-Round*, the story goes, after shooting a scene featuring Kerry nude.

Rumors of a homosexual relationship between Kerry and Rodolfo persist, but remain just that: rumors. At this remove, they can't be either conclusively verified or finally put to rest. The two did form a close bond, and did share an apartment for a time in Los Angeles, but while they were together both went out with women. Kerry lent or gave money to many friends, including Rodolfo; he was so open-handed his manager in later years insisted on countersigning all his checks. Rodolfo called him "my brother" and readily accepted his mentor's career advice and financial support. Modeling himself on Kerry, he even grew a mustache and tried to copy Kerry's jokey manner. Close to the same age, the dark-haired boon buddies looked enough alike to pass as noble Italian brothers in a film called *Passion's Playground*, although Kerry was taller, had sharper features, a chunkier build, and a more macho stance. Most of Rodolfo's close male friends in California were foreign-born, but Kerry, a native of Rochester, New York, was an exception (though his mother was Hungarian).

Kerry encouraged Rodolfo to follow him from San Francisco to

Hollywood, promising to introduce him to movie people and assuring him he had a future in pictures. The war had severely reduced the number of European-made films on the marketplace, and American filmmaking burgeoned as a result. "Pictures were the new Klondike and people warmed to it like grifters to a mardigras," said publicist Harry Reichenbach. Between 1910 and 1920 the population of Hollywood would jump from five thousand to thirty-six thousand.

Before departing San Francisco, though, Rodolfo accepted a speaking part in another theatrical production, *Nobody Home*, a "rapid-fire" musical with a Jerome Kern score that had pleased audiences at New York's Princess Theatre a few years back. Richard Carle starred as an eccentric Englishman pursuing a Winter Garden actress, and "Monsieur Rodolphe" took a place among forty "funmakers, singers and dancers" in the farce booked for two weeks at the Alcazar. Though he didn't care much for his low-profile part, he had to be pleased that the show garnered good reviews, and the opening was packed. But at a time when coal was being rationed and electricity curtailed, the production faltered; it was hard to make a go of a live musical with a large cast. Dollar-a-head theater tickets became too pricey for a public bent on saving every penny for Liberty Bonds or bandages. Meanwhile, a movie at a neighborhood theater cost no more than a dime. Seat prices at the Alcazar were lowered, but *Nobody Home* took a loss; this was not a good moment for the theater business. "Theatrical conditions all over the Pacific Coast have so discouraged theatrical managers," *Variety* reported, "that they are predicting that within a few months, if improvement does not arrive, the legitimate playhouses will have to close."

Rodolfo recorded that he first traveled to Los Angeles as the guest of a troupe of players in an Al Jolson show on a train headed south from San Francisco. Frank Carter, an actor in the cast of the Jolson musical, *Robinson Crusoe Jr.*, supposedly extended the invitation, saying "there is always an extra berth on our train." If this is what really happened, Rodolfo must have left San Francisco in late July, when the Jolson show opened at the Los Angeles Opera House, and must have returned to San Francisco in the fall to work in *Nobody Home*, which opened in October. There's evidence he did land in Los Angeles before appearing in *Nobody Home*: he sent his mother a photo portrait of himself with the inscription "A ma bien aimée Maman de son petit Rodolph," and dated it Los Angeles, September 1, 1917.

A dancer by the name of Ivy Crane Wilson, who claimed she'd been responsible for hiring Rodolfo to dance at San Francisco's Cliff House, told another tale about how he got his way paid to Los Angeles, one that indicates that well before he became a movie star Rodolfo had the capacity to trigger men's sexual jealousy. She was managing the Cliff House at the time, she said, and engaged Rodolfo as dancer-in-residence after he told her he'd been stranded on the coast, with no job in sight. "So he came out [to Cliff House], and I danced with him and all the other women danced with him. Then a very important San Francisco man just didn't care too much about having this handsome, young Italian dancing around with all the women, so he paid his fare. . . . He said, 'If you'll send him down to Los Angeles, perhaps somebody down there will be interested in him.' . . . So [Rodolfo] said he'd be delighted to go." And off he went.

Both of these accounts could be true if in fact he really traveled south to Los Angeles two separate times, once in July and again in the late fall.

Rudy, as he now liked to be called, moved into the Alexandria Hotel, in downtown Los Angeles at Fifth and Spring Street, where he shared a room with Norman Kerry, who picked up the tab. "Norman Kerry not only provided me with funds which I needed so badly but he introduced me to everyone of importance in the studios." The Alexandria's grand lobby, with its marble columns, crystal chandeliers, and "million dollar" Turkish carpet, served as a social hub for the movie colony. Stars, producers, directors, and hopeful newcomers gathered there to drink, snack on free sandwiches, and dance—to see and be seen. A top earner such as Douglas Fairbanks might be spotted at the bar, and the great Griffith himself sometimes turned up on the dance floor. Theda Bara, the celebrated screen vamp, had put up there before settling in town. Chaplin twirled his cane in the foyer. Ramon Samaniego was working as a busboy. There's no certainty that he and Rudy knew each other at this time, though they might have and, despite rumors to the contrary, there's no proof that these two were ever close.

Samuel Goldwyn spotted Rudy in the crowd and was struck by the young Italian's somber eyes and graceful gestures: "Even when he leaned up against a cigar case . . . you felt that the column of some ruined temple overlooking the Mediterranean would have been more appropriate." Goldwyn reported that Rudy would walk up to a director or producer and ask, " 'Anything doing today?' 'Have you finished casting so-and-so?' 'When do you start shooting?' These questions . . . were made more touching by a very naive manner, by a slightly foreign accent. He always looked so eager when he put the question and so disappointed when he got the answer." More than anything, he wanted to act in the movies.

In order to attract notice, Rudy dressed flamboyantly, strolling down the boulevard in green golf stockings, ornate vest, and vivid tie or decked out in a Basque beret and white flannel trousers. Sometimes arriving in a borrowed Rolls-Royce, he'd show up early in the morning outside a studio wearing cowboy attire: riding breeches and boots, a shirt open at the collar, riding whip in hand. This wasn't all posing; he did go riding in the sparsely populated hills whenever he could rent or borrow a horse. At the beach on Sundays he promenaded in a white bathing suit, leading two white Russian wolfhounds on leashes. Drab he wasn't. Everybody would say, "Here comes Rudy."

Los Angeles in late 1917 still felt like a small town, with many unpaved roads, and bean fields that stretched to Santa Monica. Hollywood Boulevard, bordered by orange and lemon groves, drew such scant traffic that a pedestrian could cross it without having to look both ways. Movie scenes were regularly shot outdoors in full view of passersby. "On a Sunday it was no surprise to see a bank holdup in a real bank borrowed by some picture company," said Adolphe Menjou. Actors wandered around the streets and turned up in restaurants wearing full makeup and costumed as cowboys, bathing beauties, or silk-hatted heavies. Many who owned neither horse nor auto arrived on the lot by streetcar, or on foot. "Extras could be plucked like ripe tomatoes . . . right outside the studio," said Jesse Lasky, vice president of Famous Players–Lasky. Benches under the pepper trees in the middle of Vine Street became gathering places for people who wanted jobs.

The war had mobilized the movie industry. Beat-the-drum features like *To Hell with the Kaiser* displaced pro-peace efforts like *Intolerance*, which some audiences greeted with boos. Erich von Stroheim, regularly cast as a villainous Prussian officer, was so completely identified with this role that he was hissed when he went out in public. The Lasky studio formed its own training unit to guard the coast and to drill employees who might be sent to the front. Mrs. Cecil DeMille and Mrs. Fairbanks (the first Mrs. Fairbanks, not Mary Pickford) walked around Hollywood in nurses' uniforms, and on Wednesday nights stars made guest appearances at the Red Cross tea shop. Both Mary Pickford and Theda Bara adopted regiments and autographed flags to be carried into battle. During the winter months, studios had to shut down for half the day to conserve electricity.

When Norman Kerry departed for training camp in Toronto, Rudy moved out of the pricey Alexandria Hotel and into an eight-dollar-a-week apartment nearby at Fifth and Grand, which he shared with another friend he'd gotten to know in San Francisco, Bryan ("Brynie") Foy. Oldest of the "Seven Little Foys" who for years toured in vaudeville with their comedian father, Eddie, Brynie became a songwriter, a comedy writer for Fox, and later a producer for Warner Bros. In 1929 Foy would direct Valentino look-alike George Raft (playing a dancing gigolo) and Texas Guinan in Raft's first picture, a talkie called *Queen of the Night Clubs*. Foy never commented publicly on Rudy's gigolo background. Instead he spoke of his ex-roommate's aristocratic bearing, fine manners, and meticulous attention to what he wore. According to him, "Rudy would starve in order to buy suitable clothes."

Rudy was beginning to be recognized, but not always for the right reasons. Whispers about his scandalous New York past proved hard to shake, especially after a front-page story on Blanca de Saulles's acquittal at her murder trial appeared in the Los Angeles papers just after he arrived in town. For years after settling in the movie colony, he continued to be known as a professional lounge lizard, or worse. The actress Viola Dana enjoyed dancing with him in nightspots like the Vernon Country Club, but her escort, Tony Moreno, warned her not to. "Don't you know he has a bad reputation? He has the reputation of being a gigolo. He used to get paid for dancing with women."

He still did, as a matter of fact, but no longer as a taxi dancer. Since screen roles were slow to materialize, Rudy once again turned to exhibition dancing as his meal ticket. When Fanchon, of the exhibition dancing team Fanchon and Marco (their real names were Fanny and Mike Wolff), lost her partner to the military, Rudy replaced him, performing glides, whirlwinds, and tangos at Tait's Café in Los Angeles. He was hired at a rowdy roadhouse on the outskirts of town, Baron Long's Watts Tavern, to dance with Marjorie Tain for thirty-five dollars a week. That led to a booking in staid Pasadena at the upscale Hotel Maryland, where his partner was Kitty Phelps, whose costumes—billowing sleeves laced with ribbons—he designed. Part of his pay at the Hotel Maryland consisted of free lodging at that hostelry, which was home to many elderly women. "On one occasion, when the proprietor decided that I was not worth the weekly stipend, these old ladies rose in a body and declared that if they let me go they would leave too." His older women friends, some of them wealthy, would sometimes allow him to borrow their beautifully maintained touring cars.

He soon moved back into town on his own steam—a 1918 studio directory gives his address as 7369 Sunset Boulevard—hopeful that parts in pictures would begin to come his way. His first break came when a young Colorado-born director named Emmett Flynn, "the first director to see anything in me," hired him as a dress extra in a feature written by Hayden Talbot called *Alimony*, at five dollars a day. Another extra in the same feature was a delicate beauty called Alice Taaffe, with whom Rudy sometimes went dancing. Alice Taaffe would change her name to Alice Terry and become one of the silent screen's most accomplished leading ladies. She was twice paired with Valentino in features directed by the man she would marry, Rex Ingram.

Rudy, a born performer, still lacked confidence before the Klieg lights, and felt that the established actors looked down on him. "At first I was terrified that the other actors, the director, the crew, would see how lousy I was." He had never studied pantomime, had little acting experience, and so far had only demonstrated that he photographed well, knew how to dance, and looked good in evening dress. His instincts told him to let his sense of rhythm guide him as an actor: "There are accents in my movements much as there are accents in music." What he liked best about film was the fact that it focused on movement, and could be shot outdoors.

He didn't set his sights on romantic or heroic roles. Physical traits determined casting choices and he knew he looked foreign, which meant he would be typed as a villain. Ethnic and racial stereotypes were still rigidly fixed, and moral qualities attached to skin tone and hair color, as well as nationality. Blonde women tended to be cast as virgins, brunettes as vamps. To American directors and producers, and much of the audience, dark skin implied contamination. The most popular leading men of the moment were all clean-cut, square-jawed, all-Americans, potential Arrow-collar-ad models like Douglas Fairbanks, Harold Lockwood, and Wallace Reid, with whom Rudy couldn't hope to compete.

Rudy disagreed with the practice of pigeonholing characters as either demons or unspotted heroes because he believed "no one is entirely evil and a good man may be motivated by a spirit that is not all good." But typing according to strict moral categories prevailed in the melodramatic scenarios of the day. When he paid to put his name and picture in the 1918 *Motion Picture Studio Directory* he categorized himself as "a New Style Heavy."

As a heavy he performed dastardly deeds like shooting an opera singer from a box, then tumbling out of the box after putting the revolver to his own head (*Once to Every Woman*); leading a gang of rough crooks to kidnap a nobleman and rob a mansion (*The Wonderful Chance*); or ripping the dress from the shoulder of a respectable wife while stifling her cries (*Eyes of Youth*). Sometimes his suave good looks masked his character's wickedness. At other times, when he portrayed a scoundrel of the deepest dye, he was made up to look quite repellent; in *A Rogue's Romance*, as a Montmartre tough guy called The Ferret, his hair is plastered across his scowling forehead, his brows are thickened, his jacket is rumpled and ill-fitting as he savages his partner in a violent Apache dance; he's supercilious-looking in a monocle, top hat, and curled black mustache as a scheming Frenchman in *An Adventuress*. But even when he's allowed to look handsome, his glossy exterior usually disguises moral deviousness.

A few times his Latin looks were ignored and he was cast against type as an appealing Irishman or an eligible American bachelor, which prompted comment. Reviewing *A Society Sensation*, *Variety*, referring to him with a name from a screen credit, said "Rodolpho De Valentino makes a very American Dick Bradley despite the fact he is a fairly recent arrival from Italy."

D. W. Griffith—never known for his broadmindedness—helped perpetuate the ethnic stereotype. One night, while savoring a tasty spaghetti dinner Rudy had cooked, Griffith told him he might find a future in pictures if he could lose weight and tone down his overcharged acting style (according to Griffith, Rudy "could not be kept from sawing the air with wild gesticulations in the Latin manner"), but passed on casting him as the Mexican bandit in *Scarlet Days* because he felt his exotic appearance would not appeal to women in the audience. "He's too foreign looking. The girls would never like him." A few years later he would also pass on a chance to cast Rudy as the seducing scoundrel, Sanderson, in *Way Down East*; Rudy told an interviewer he tried for that part, which went to Lowell Sherman. A heavily made-up Richard Barthelmess got the part in *Scarlet Days*, and Griffith hired Rudy to dance for several weeks with Carol Dempster (Griffith's current off-camera favorite, who was once a Denishawn dancer) and Clarine Seymour on the stage of Clune's Auditorium in the prologue to *The Greatest Thing in Life*. The more Rudy danced professionally, the less he wanted to continue doing so. In 1919 Rudy applied for an acting job at Universal Studios; the application form contained the question, "Why did you take up a motion picture career?" to which Rudy replied, "Tired of ballroom dancing."

When a lead acting role did materialize for Rudy, again thanks to

Emmett Flynn, it was true to the stereotype of the oily Latin cad. In *The Married Virgin*, another script by Hayden Talbot, this time directed by the New Yorker Joe Maxwell, he played a devious, shifty-eyed, fortune-hunting Italian count who carries on an affair with a married woman while wed—though in name only—to her wealthy stepdaughter. The role allowed him to don spats, a derby, and a pinky ring, to sneer into the camera, to kiss a lady's hand and smoke menacingly— all gestures that became essential to his persona—and to seize the wheel of a speeding roadster and, after the car tumbles down a cliff and his illicit lover is killed, to flee on foot. During filming in San Diego, wanting to stay in character, he insisted on speaking Italian on the set, even though no one around could understand him.

For the first time he received billing as Rodolfo di Valentini, a name supposedly evocative of a papal title in the family tree, as well as of the patron saint of lovers. "Di Valentini" would be spelled many ways— De Valentino, di Valentino, and Valentine are all variations that were used—before the name Valentino was finally established. The reasons for shedding "Guglielmi" are transparent. It was too hard for Americans to pronounce, spell, or remember.

The Married Virgin gave him ample opportunity to strut his stuff and to look strikingly handsome in many close-ups, but unfortunately a dispute over the salaries of the cameramen put the picture on the shelf for more than a year after it was made. As he awaited its release and tried for new parts, devastating news arrived from Europe.

His mother and Maria waited out the war in Besançon, France, assisting wounded soldiers in the Doubs region. Maria had notified him soon after he arrived in Los Angeles that Gabriella's health was failing. On January 18, 1918, she died.

Rudy had anticipated the catastrophe. He recalled: "Every day when I returned to my little room on Sunset Boulevard I would run the last block, so anxious was I to see if a letter awaited me. One day I found a small black-bordered envelope with my sister's writing under my door. Tremblingly, I tore it open to read that my mother had been gone four weeks. There was also a farewell note she had written to me on her death bed. . . . I dropped on the bed in a spasm of grief.

"That very day I had an appointment with [the director] George Fitzmaurice to talk over a part and I had to meet him with a face swollen and a broken heart. [He didn't get the part.] The chief reason I had wanted success was for my mother's sake; she had believed in me, encouraged me and urge[d] me on. . . . My greatest comfort came in rereading my mother's letters written during our four years' separation in which she wrote so confidently of my future. I was probably the most troublesome of her three children, . . . but I was also her favorite and we were very, very close."

Many who met Rudy in the wake of his mother's death recall his desolation. Alone in his tiny apartment, he wept without stint. In the company of others, he seemed withdrawn and unhappy. "I think he was lonely, terribly lonely," the screenwriter and journalist Adela Rogers St. Johns wrote. "Men did not like him. He wasn't a mixer." Charlie Chaplin used to see him sitting forlornly in the lounge of the Los Angeles Athletic Club, "a young man, a bit player, . . . a lonely fellow named Valentino who had come to Hollywood to try his luck and was not doing very well." Another bit player, Jack Gilbert, introduced them. "Valentino had an air of sadness," Chaplin remembered.

The November armistice occasioned only momentary rejoicing in Hollywood, because it coincided with the devastating flu epidemic that closed down studios, resulting in the layoff of many actors and technicians, and claiming many more lives. Harold Lockwood, a romantic leading man, died at age thirty-one. "Film land is full of gloom and germs," reported *Motion Picture World*. Rudy thought he might escape infection by visiting friends in San Francisco, but when he returned to Los Angeles he fell ill. Dreading hospitals and suspicious of medical science, he refused to see a doctor, instead nursing himself with bed rest and a diet of boiled fruits and broth. He was living on Morgan Place now, across the street from Wallace Reid, whose saxophone playing disturbed his sleep.

The armistice closed down the market for war pictures, catching the movie industry off guard "with millions of dollars' worth of war films that the public didn't want to see." The very day the war ended, the director Fred Balshofer had finished cutting a picture in which Rudy played a supporting role, an "all-out anti-Kaiser picture" that had been advertised as "a vivid and startling story of Hun frightfulness, based on the hitherto unexposed machinations of the infamous Iron Circle of Berlin." Originally called *Over the Rhine*, it starred a female impersonator, Julian Eltinge, in the double role of Jack Perry, a patriotic young American, and Elsa Von Bohn, an employee of the United States Secret Service. Virginia Rappe, the actress who died in 1921 at the notorious San Francisco party that led to Fatty Arbuckle's arrest and trial for her murder, also played a supporting role. Balshofer pulled the picture from release, because "nobody wanted to show a war picture now that the conflict was over." He retitled it *An Adventuress* and released it two years later, but it was generally ignored. He would later recoup some of the eighty thousand dollars he lost by rereleasing it with yet another title, *Isle of Love*, after Valentino became a star.

The delay in exhibiting the Balshofer film probably had little impact on Rudy, who was already depressed and in debt. A Mercer car he'd bought for more money than he could afford had been repossessed after he failed to keep up his monthly payments and because of this he had to walk everywhere, ride the streetcar, or cadge lifts when he couldn't borrow a car. More than a year after his mother's death, he continued to see himself as a grieving loner, a bewildered, restless seeker who could find no peace. He inscribed a photograph of himself "To my only star," describing himself as a wanderer in the dark who seeks rest and solace in vain, though his guiding star brightens the way.

Who was this only star brightening his darkest hours? We haven't a clue, but Rudy seems to have found someone to love for a while. The romance didn't last, and he sought other companions. He went horseback riding on Sundays with the Gish sisters, whose riding habits he designed, and returned with them to the home they shared with their mother. "He loved to come and visit, and there was usually cooking going on," recalled Dorothy Gish. "Mother was a good cook and they got together and cooked things up." Carmel Myers, a teenaged star who picked him to play her boyfriend in two romantic comedies, says he tried to date her but was stymied by her overprotective mother, a rabbi's wife. When informed by her mother that Carmel was too young to go out with men, "he said, 'Madame Myers, when I want something I never let anyone stand in my way.' And Mama asked him, 'Even if the person standing in your way weighs two hundred and fifty pounds?' I never did have dinner with him."

Another young woman who attracted him was a script girl named Florence Mack, who met him at a party in a Wilshire district apartment. A young, dark man with a foreign accent kept following her, she recalled with a blush sixty years after the encounter. It was a warm night and she went to the fire escape for a breath of cooling air. The young man pursued her, and spoke boldly, telling her she was his ideal girl and that "I could kiss you from your head to your toes." He said he was an actor in pictures and had just appeared opposite Mae Murray in *The Delicious Little Devil*. When she saw the film, Florence Mack recognized the fire escape masher as Rudolph Valentino. Since she hadn't stayed with him long enough to even learn his name, it's clear his verbal advances left her cold.

On-screen he got the girl more often. Actresses, rather than male directors or producers, were the first to see his romantic or romantic-comic potential. Dorothy Gish prevailed upon one of D. W. Griffith's assistants, the director Elmer Clifton, to give Rudy a part opposite her in a light satire about superstition called *Out of Luck* (now lost); he's the dark man a fortune-teller predicted would enter the heroine's life. *Out of Luck,* praised as a "highly amusing farce-comedy built around the social activities of the younger set in high class metropolitan circles," boosted Rudy's stock because it paired him with a highly visible Griffith star. In his application to the Universal Pictures Studio, Rudy listed this picture as the one in which he appears to best advantage. Dorothy Gish, fresh from her triumph as "the little disturber" in Griffith's *Hearts of the World*, seems to have been less pleased with Rudy than he was with her. Although she considered him a wonderful man, she complained to her sister, Lillian, that "he was so fastidious that it took him too long to dress and he held up their shooting schedule."

Carmel Myers, whom Rudy managed to pry away from her mother long enough to take her for a turn around the dance floor at a party, persuaded director Paul Powell, a once and future journalist who'd also worked under Griffith, to give Rudy a chance to play opposite her in two comedies that have survived. In *A Society Sensation* he's Dick Bradley, the yacht-owning son of a socialite mother. (When he gets out of his villain's straitjacket in these early pictures, he's pegged as an aristocrat.) Carmel Myers plays the girl he loves, a fisherman's daughter who turns out to be a duchess after Dick proves he'd want her even if she were a poor nobody. Buried in the story about social climbing is a sequence that skews gender roles. When Dick appears to be drowning in the surf, Carmel, fully clothed, jumps in to rescue him. ("He's very nice—but awfully heavy," the title reads.) She's the one who takes physical risks and plays the swashbuckling hero. Only after that does Dick show off his brawn by decking a bunch of toughs who come aboard his yacht. "Rudolph De Valentino was a good-looking hero whom the girls will think 'just grand,'" one critic had the foresight to write in 1918. "He's a clean-cut chap and registers very well."

In *All Night*, the second comedy starring Carmel Myers and directed by Paul Powell, Rudy demonstrates a comic flair that should have been tapped more often. Flourishing an easy elegance tempered with winning ingenuousness, he's Richard Thayer, a shy and well-bred suitor too tongue-tied to propose to Carmel's character, Elizabeth. His married friends, the Harcourts, arrange a dinner party where Richard will finally get a chance to speak to Elizabeth alone, but all hell breaks loose when the party is invaded by a rich Montana boor who wants to size up the Harcourts before lending them a million dollars. The Harcourts have lost all their money, and really need the boor to bail them out. Having fired their servants, they pose as butler and maid, and ask guests Richard and Elizabeth to pretend to be them, the already married hosts. In one scene, extremely proper Elizabeth is sent to bed with pajama-clad Rudy/Richard, who hides under a blanket. By the end, his friends rescued, he's back in his tux and engaged to marry Elizabeth. Advertised as "daringly French," *All Night* won plaudits as "one of the funniest farces ever presented on the screen."

Both of these Carmel Myers comedies were made at Universal Studios, where Rudy ultimately became a regular. Presided over by the studio's founder Carl Laemmle, Universal City occupied a huge plant north of Hollywood in the San Fernando Valley. Instead of producing elaborate features with expensive, big-name stars, the studio mass-produced westerns, serials, and short features on the cheap, without bells and whistles. "Universal was the Woolworth's of the motion picture business." At Universal, a young actress named Lina Basquette recalled, Rudy "had a dressing room across from mine where he cooked spaghetti on a Sterno burner. . . . He was a mild-mannered man, was rather shy and generally ignored."

During this time at Universal Rudy forged an important friendship with Douglas ("Gerry") Gerrard, an Irish-born former Shakespearean actor who both acted in and directed movies. (He was Anna Pavlova's leading man in her only feature.) Gerrard soon displaced Norman Kerry as Rudy's closest friend. Like Kerry, he was athletic, dark-haired, high-spirited, and convivial, a big talker who enjoyed clowning and allowed himself to be the butt of other people's jokes. He had many friends and liked to entertain. "Douglas was the only one who invited me to go out with him, and whenever he gave a party he made it a point to have me."

For some reason—maybe because Gerrard wasn't doing much directing after 1920—Rudy never appeared in a picture directed by him. But at Universal he reconnected with his onetime confidante and after-hours New York dance partner, Mae Murray, now married to the director Bob Leonard and doing very well in pictures. At Mae Murray's behest, Leonard cast Rudy in the titillating *Delicious Little Devil*. Like the Carmel Myers comedies, this one addressed class snobbery and social mobility. It promised to show (said an ad) how "the daughter of a royal bricklayer makes a monkey out of royalty." Billed as "Rudolpho De Valentine," Rudy plays Jimmy Calhoun, son of a millionaire contractor who's lost touch with his bricklayer past. Mae Murray's Mary McGuire is supporting her poor family, since her father and uncle are too lazy and drunk to do much besides guzzle and play checkers while the women wait on them. Fired from her job as a hatcheck girl, she decides to try for a lucrative position as a cabaret dancer, stacking the deck in her favor by pretending to be Gloria De Moin, a scandalous Parisienne dancing artiste who's the mistress of a notorious duke. She's hired, and performs in alluring Cleopatra garb, baring her midriff (and, in a backstage bathing scene, her breasts). In love with Mary, Jimmy/Rudy sits ringside at the cabaret, brooding about her sinful past and her cavorting in skimpy, Ziegfeld-inspired getups. His father tries to expose her as damaged goods, staging an elaborate banquet at which he's sure she'll disgrace herself. Instead, Jimmy, the duke (who's really a crook), and everyone else at the table get roaring drunk. The only one to remain sober, Mary tries to get away from the no longer slumbering and now aroused duke, whose advances get more and more violent. There's an exciting car chase after Jimmy comes to his senses and realizes Mary's in danger. Rudy, always fascinated by the nuts and bolts of production, spent much time studying the director's plans for the chase. "He pored over the map Bob [Leonard] had drawn, plotting the action for the final sequence," recalled Mae Murray.

Although *Moving Picture World* found the humor "delightfully fresh and pleasing and the character work good," a critic named Henry Carlette slammed *The Delicious Little Devil* as a cheap melodrama with a lurid and artificial story. "A great big 'Why?' is the dominant thought after seeing this." It's true that Mae Murray expresses emotion here mainly by making faces: scowling, arching her brows, or forming the famous bee-stung lips into a moue. But the cabaret scenes have tremendous vitality.

According to the not always credible Miss Murray, friction on the set arose between her director-husband, Bob Leonard, and Rudy because of Leonard's jealousy. On the lot, Rudy and Mae often danced between setups. Musicians were routinely employed to provide mood music that helped actors get into character; when Mae asked them to play a tango, she and Rudy took off while Leonard seethed. He would cast Rudy opposite Mae Murray only once more, this time as the two-timing and unsympathetic fiancé of a deaf teacher, played by Mae, in *The Big Little Person*. Panned by the few reviewers who noticed it, it remained in Rudy's own memory bank only because of the pains he took to rent one of his costumes, a suit of armor.

Although still light-years from stardom, Rudy in his first Hollywood years earned his stripes as a capable professional regularly cast as either a blackguard or the romantic partner of a female star he complemented but didn't outshine. The role that lifted him out of his apprenticeship and into the foreground was a small one that on the surface resembled other "heavy" parts he'd played many times, but never before in such a costly production or one with as many big-name players: *Eyes of Youth*, with Milton Sills, Pauline Starke, and Edmund Lowe, supporting Clara Kimball Young.

The plot of *Eyes of Youth* sounds silly enough to have been invented by Monty Python. Clara Kimball Young plays Gina Ashling, a young woman at an impasse as she faces difficult choices. Her father's business is failing and as the oldest of three siblings she feels responsible for holding things together. Several men seek her hand, and she can't decide whether to accept one of their proposals, stay home and get a job, or go off to Europe to pursue an operatic singing career. A yogi from India knocks on her door and she takes him in, confiding her dilemma to the blind seer. He takes out his crystal ball and allows her to look into the future. The Path of Duty, the Path of Ambition, and the Path of Wealth unfold in turn, each dramatizing the consequences of a different choice.

Valentino appears only in the third episode, in which Gina has married a rich playboy banker she doesn't love but serves faithfully. Her philandering husband, who wants to get rid of her, hires a "cabaret parasite" named Clarence Morgan to trap the virtuous Gina in a compromising situation. As Clarence, Valentino leaps off the screen in the few minutes allotted to him. We first see him in a street scene, getting out of a cab in front of a roadhouse and pocketing the money the bad guys are paying him to entrap Gina. He's dressed for evening in a derby and fur-collared black overcoat. Now indoors in an upstairs room, Clarence strips down to his tux and crisp white shirt. Then, pretending to be a doctor, he telephones Gina and tells her that her husband has been injured in an accident and that she must come to the roadhouse at once to be with him. By the time Gina arrives, Clarence has shed jacket, tie, and collar. His helmet of black hair gleaming, his collarless white shirt a magnet for light, he's poised for seduction. Nimbly he locks the doors, eases Gina into a chair, removes her shawl with an intimate, insinuating touch, and pours her a drink. With astounding economy of movement he struggles with her, tearing her dress, and places his hand over her mouth to stifle her cries. The insidious husband and his coconspirators arrive as Clarence is saying, "Darling, I know you love me, but what of your husband?" Gina has been effectively snared.

Eyes of Youth was hailed as "a knockout" and became a box-office hit after opening to the trade in the grand ballroom of New York's Hotel Astor, where thirteen hundred viewers sat for the screening, another several hundred stood, and afterward all danced to Irving Berlin's "Eyes of Youth Waltz." Valentino's combination of stealth and steam in his cameo as the cabaret parasite convinced the screenwriter June Mathis that he could handle a major part in her script for a go-for-broke production at Metro Pictures Corporation.

On the eve of his career breakthrough, Rudy met a young Metro actress who struck him as someone he could talk to in a new way, someone who understood. Her name was Jean Acker.

6

MISALLIANCE

When Rudy first met Jean Acker, she occupied an enviable place close to the center of a social and professional circle that had gathered around the exotic and talented Russian-born actress Alla Nazimova, and he was a shunned outsider anxious for entrée.

Nazimova was a student of Stanislavsky who hypnotized American theater audiences with her interpretations of Ibsen's and Chekhov's characters and presided over a three-and-a-half-acre Sunset Boulevard spread, complete with a swimming pool shaped like the Black Sea, that was known as the Garden of Alla. There in the perfumed air, amid purple divans and buffets heaped with caviar, an international coterie gathered for costume balls, movie screenings, or Madame's demonstrations of Oriental dances. Lithe and angular, with an unruly mop of dark curls on her head and a long cigarette holder in her hand, Nazimova projected exotic sophistication, ambiguous sexuality ("My friends call me Peter and sometimes Mimi"), and absolute authority. The Metro studio, having wooed her from the stage, was paying her lavishly and agreeing to pretty much everything she requested. "All she had to do was raise an eyebrow and everyone shook."

In September 1919, a group of Metro bigwigs and stars were celebrating the completion of a Nazimova film called *Stronger Than Death*. They gathered as the guests of the studio manager, Maxwell Karger, at Venice's Ship Café, a popular nightspot housed on the pier in what looked like an old stranded galleon. Among those present were Nazi-mova's ostensible husband, Charles Bryant, the actresses Dagmar Godowsky, May Allison, and Viola Dana, and actors Bert Lytell and Milton Sills. Rounding out the party was Nazimova's current favorite, Jean Acker, a recent import from the East Coast who had just been signed to a Metro contract. "Nazimova, in a recent trip to New York, brought back to Los Angeles with her . . . a new brand of perfumed cigarettes, together with a protégé [sic] who used to be known . . . as Jeanne Acker," *Photoplay* had just reported, slyly hinting at Nazimova's fondness for partners of her own sex.

When Valentino happened to come dancing by the celebrants' table, he spotted Dagmar Godowsky, a musician's daughter and friend from New York who now sometimes gave him rides to Universal Studio. As Godowsky recounts it, he approached the group "beaming with pleasure and I started to introduce him, but Nazimova lowered her head and froze. Her little frame was rigid, and she looked as if she were having a divine fit." When Nazimova orchestrated her snub, all the others followed her lead, "lowering their heads in this shocking form of grace." Then, as Valentino withdrew in haste and humiliation, she thundered, "How dare you bring that gigolo to my table? How dare you introduce that pimp to Nazimova?" Referring to the notori-ous de Saulles scandal, she reminded everyone present that the danc-ing man had fled to California to avoid being mentioned in a ghastly society murder. She wrongly supposed that Blanca de Saulles had killed her husband out of love for Valentino.

A few days later Acker and Valentino met again at a party he at-tended with Douglas Gerrard at the newly built Sunset Boulevard mansion of the actress Pauline Frederick. Jean had been mortified by Nazimova's high-handed rebuff and was eager to make amends. Her sympathetic ear, lithe figure, and petite gamine's demeanor drew him in. "The first question he asked me was, 'Do you care to dance?' I de-cided to sit it out with him under a California moon." We can only guess at the ensuing conversation, but chords of mutual affection had been struck.

He must have told her of his desolation at his mother's death, his career ambitions and frustrations, and his feelings of isolation. She undoubtedly withheld from him the truth about her own untidy tangle of emotional and sexual involvements. Although she had come to California as Nazimova's lover, and had copped a two-hundred-dollar-a-week contract with Metro on the strength of that connection, she had within a few months begun an affair with another, less established, actress named Grace Darmond, who resented Nazimova's hold on Acker and wanted Acker to break with the older and more powerful woman and come to live with her. Unable to take this step, Acker had quarreled with Grace Darmond. She felt miserable. In Valentino she saw a possible escape hatch, a way to extricate herself from both affairs and still have someone to lean on. Wearing emotional blinders, he responded to her neediness without having a clue about its causes. He didn't even realize that Jean was primarily a lesbian, or so he would insist to his friends; people often see only what they want to see. Acker seems to have indulged in occasional relationships with men. At least in 1923 she was said to be engaged to a marquis from Madrid. Her early relationship with Rudy surely included at least some spooning.

They arranged to go horseback riding by moonlight. This was a winning formula, one they invoked a second time, and a third. Within a matter of weeks they decided to get married.

Jean Acker was a doer rather than a thinker. Born on a New Jersey farm and named Harriet by parents who separated when she was young (her mother was Irish, her father part Cherokee), she loved to drive, had owned a motorcycle, and was an expert horsewoman who once portrayed a jockey on-screen. Like Valentino she tended to leap before she looked.

"On Sundays I answer to the name of Miss Jean Acker, and weekdays I'm just Billie," she told an interviewer in 1913, when she was an obscure twenty-year-old who had played in vaudeville and stock-company drama before joining Sigmund Lubin's Philadelphia motion picture operation and moving on to the IMP (Independent Motion Picture Company) studio in New York. "I attended school at St. Mary's Seminary, Springfield, New Jersey. I'd rather jump from a moving train or ride a motorcycle fifty miles an hour or take a ride in an aeroplane than eat. I am very fond of horseback riding . . . I am five feet three and weigh 121 pounds." She wore her reddish brown hair in a neat flapper bob, with bangs like the ones later associated with Louise Brooks and Colleen Moore.

Never a big earner, and prone to complaints about ill health, she had won a ten-thousand-dollar settlement after a motorist collided with her motorcycle, and she used that money in Los Angeles to buy a big touring car. This was a major asset, as far as Valentino was concerned. "I honestly believe Rodolph would have married then any woman with an automobile," Acker once remarked. He would soon acquire a Fiat of his own, then in short order a 1914 Cadillac. Her social connections within the movie colony also attracted him. She lived at the fashionable Hollywood Hotel, a three-story mission-style structure surrounded by palms, which rivaled the Alexandria Hotel as a mecca of the moving-picture colony. "He thought it would be a very good idea to marry Jean because she knew a lot of people and that could help his career." Then there was the adhesive power of mutual need. "We were the two lowliest and loneliest people in Hollywood," Rudy explained to Adela Rogers St. Johns, conveniently forgetting that at the time Jean Acker's status was far less lowly than his own. "It was like starting to climb a mountain. If you saw someone beside you look as alone and lost as you felt, you'd offer your arm, it would be easier if you held on to each other."

In 1919, American women who married aliens forfeited their own United States citizenship, so Acker's American citizenship would not have provided an additional enticement to Rudy to marry her; in fact, she lost her citizenship. Not until 1925, after the Cable Act had changed the law and she'd been divorced for three years, would Jean Acker reclaim her American nationality.

Acker herself believed she and Rudy both fell victim to dewy-eyed romantic fantasy. They shared an eagerness to act out gauzy scenarios and moon-spoon-June song lyrics. "It was simply a case of California, the glamour of the Southern moonlight and the fascinating love-making of the man," Jean later said. Rudy concurred. "It seemed spontaneous and beautiful then. But as I look back now, it seems more like a scene for a picture with me acting the leading part."

Robert Florey, who didn't know either of the principals in 1919 but became Rudy's close friend two years later, said that Rudy's never-never-land notions about what a wife should be had absolutely no grounding in reality, that the woman of his dreams didn't exist; she had to be "angelic, virginal, serene, fascinating, elegant, beautiful in form and gentle in character." Passion is notably absent from his wish list. When it came to the love of women, said Florey, Valentino was a man both self-deceived and deceiving of others.

Rudy pressed his suit aggressively with Jean, whose temperament scarcely matched his ethereal ideal. He desperately wanted to have someone he could call his own. Getting married was his idea, his ardent wish, and she capitulated. On November 6, 1919, the *Los Angeles Times* reported:

PHOTOPLAY ACTRESS MARRIES ON A DARE
Two Month Wooing Results in Hurry-Up Nuptials of Screen People

They met two months ago and last Tuesday afternoon he dared her to marry him. She accepted the challenge and now Miss Jean Acker is Mrs. Rodolph Valentino. This is the romance of two picture players as told yesterday. Mr. Valentino met Miss Acker at a party given by Pauline Frederick in the early part of September. He pressed his case for two long months and after a dare made while they were horseback riding in Beverly Hills, she consented.

He suggested Santa Ana. She demurred and they came to the city at the suggestion of friends, arranged for License Clerk Sparks to issue one of his "hurry-up-before-it-is-too-late" kind, that are often given after the office closes.

Then they drove to the home of James I. Myers of the Broadway Christian Church and took him to the scene of the wedding. A party was being given to Mr. and Mrs. Maxwell Karger of the Metro plant and the young couple furnished a feature for the evening.

Mr. Valentino is in picture work here and his bride is
with the Metro company. Both will continue their work.
They are at the Hollywood Hotel.

If the wedding sounds like a Metro company party, that's because it
was one. Jean and Rudy hitched their wedding wagon to an already in
motion going-away fête at the home of the company's treasurer,
Joseph Engel, in honor of Metro president Richard Rowland and his
wife, who were returning to New York. Metro's general manager,
Maxwell Karger, served as best man. After the midnight ceremony
and a buffet supper, the newlyweds drove in Jean's car to the Hollywood Hotel, where a weekly lobby dance was in progress. They joined
the dancers, swaying to the band until the predawn hours. Jean went
to her room, then Rudy followed her.

Rudy turned the knob to find it would not give. He tried again,
with the same result. Jean had locked him out. Inside, he could hear
her crying and calling to him to go away at once. There would be no
wedding-night lovemaking. In fury and disbelief, he pounded on the
door, rousing other hotel guests, until he realized it would be pointless
to continue. On foot, he returned alone to his own apartment.

The distraught Jean sought comfort from the Kargers, who had
helped arrange the improvised wedding. Mrs. Anna Karger would testify that at dawn Miss Acker arrived at the Karger home. "She came to
me and said she was sorry they were married. Miss Acker threw herself on a bed and wept. She told me she thought she had made a mistake." Jean then departed for Grace Darmond's apartment.

If the desire to provoke Nazimova numbered among her confused
emotions, Jean succeeded, for Nazimova wrote to her friend Edith
Luckett (the mother of Nancy Reagan) asking whether she had heard
of Jean Acker's marriage. "It was the worst thing she had done on top
of all the other worst things she has done," said Nazimova in the letter,
and her bad behavior precipitated a break with the older woman. "She
married a professional 'lounge lizard'—that's how she herself called
him only one week before her marriage."

But as Madame Nazimova and everyone else in Hollywood would

soon become aware, the marriage didn't deserve to be called one. "Mine was not a marriage," Valentino would say. "It was a ridiculous tragedy." He became tight-lipped whenever the fiasco was mentioned, eventually turning bitter about it, and his friends avoided broaching this subject in conversation. Valentino later chided himself for not seeking an immediate annulment.

Terror at the prospect of invasive, sensationalized publicity might explain his failure to do so, for the press would surely have seized upon and magnified every titillating detail, even beyond what they did during the divorce hearing. He would have had to scream from the rooftops the humiliating facts about Jean's refusal to consummate the union and about her relationship with Grace Darmond. His own background and intimate life, he must have reasoned, would also have been subjected to cruel scrutiny. He had much to fear.

According to Patricia Neal, who got to know Jean Acker when she lived for several years in a Beverly Hills building owned by Acker and her then partner Chloe Carter, Jean said that Rudy had confessed to her immediately after they exchanged vows (perhaps in the car as they drove to the Hollywood Hotel?) that he had had gonorrhea. Whether he was still infectious at the time isn't clear. But if he was, and if Jean risked contagion if they had sex, she had every reason to be outraged by the timing of his revelation. "I don't think she ever slept with him," Neal told me, adding that she had liked Jean Acker very much, that Jean was "heavenly looking" and very funny.

It's possible that Jean's revelation to Patricia Neal should be dismissed along with many other untruths Acker uttered about Valentino. What sets it apart, and lends it credibility, is the fact that it was confided in private to a friend, not broadcast to the public in an attempt to garner publicity for herself or extract money from Rudy. Before the divorce Jean told a reporter, "In time I may have to bare some unprintable details in court, but it would break my heart now."

Following their abrupt wedding-night separation, Rudy refused to accept Jean's rejection as final. In a letter introduced as evidence in his suit for divorce when Acker sought separate maintenance, he begged her to return to him:

My Dear Jean,

I am at a complete loss to understand your conduct towards me as I cannot receive any satisfactory explanation through telephoning or seeing you.

Since I cannot force my presence upon you, either at the hotel or at Grace's, where you spend most of your time, I guess I'd better give it up. I am always ready to furnish you a home and all the comfort to the best of my moderate means and ability, as well as all the love and care of a husband for his dear little wife.

Please, dear Jean, darling, come to your senses and give me an opportunity to prove my sincere love and eternal devotion to you.

Your unhappy, loving husband
Rodolfo

He made a deposit on an apartment big enough for two in the Formosa Apartment Building, but she put him off.

In early December they met by chance, and embraced warmly. Jean seemed transformed; she was affectionate and welcoming to Rudy, who felt so elated, according to Douglas Gerrard, that he invited some friends to join them at the Alexandria for a celebration of their reunion. The two spent the night of December 5 together, their one night under the same roof, but the next morning Rudy went to Gerrard's flat to tell him Jean had again left him. Gerrard telephoned Jean for an explanation, he testified in the divorce hearing. "I asked her why she and her husband could not live together. She said: 'He is impossible, he is dictatorial.'"

But her messages to Rudy were infuriatingly inconsistent. One moment she was sending him mash notes and calling him sweetheart and darling: "Dearest boy of mine, I wish you were in my arms this very minute. Oh, I need you so. You remember the song, 'I'd Rather Be There Than Any Place I Know'? Well, that is the way I feel tonight." The next she was refusing to spend Christmas with him because she had to work (he ended up having Christmas dinner at the home of

Viola Dana), and seeming to give him permission to pursue other love interests: "Try to be as good as possible. Remember, I don't expect too much of my good-looking, dark-eyed boy."

When she went on location at Lone Pine, in Inyo County, not far from Death Valley, to film *The Roundup* with Roscoe "Fatty" Arbuckle, she did everything in her power to keep Rudy from visiting, though she did receive Grace Darmond: "Advise strongly you do not come, as I am working much too hard to entertain anyone, and hotel only has room for the company." She even wired Douglas Gerrard that he should prevent Rudy from turning up, because his doing so would "injure me." She would testify in court that her hotel room had just two single beds and that an unwritten rule stipulated that a spouse should not visit a wife or husband on location. After spending more than a hundred dollars on telegrams, Rudy decided to make an appearance at Lone Pine, even if he would not be welcomed. He wired in advance to announce that he was coming but found when he got there that Jean had already departed.

He then followed her to Grace Darmond's Los Angeles apartment, which was in a building owned by Darmond's mother. She recalled, "He called at the house and asked for his wife and when I told him she was upstairs, he pushed me aside and was very angry." He rushed up the stairs and entered the apartment. Jean called out that she could not see him, that she was in the bath. In a replay of the scene at the Hollywood Hotel on their wedding night, he pounded on the door—this time the door of the bathroom. He "started hammering on the bathroom door, threatening to break it down unless I opened it," Acker would testify. She let him in and a shouting match ensued, apparently witnessed by Grace Darmond (who testified in the divorce hearing). He cursed her for giving him the slip, allowing him to travel all the way to Inyo County to see her only to find her absent, and she yelled back that she'd never received the telegram announcing his imminent arrival at Lone Pine. Rigid with rage and frustration, he snapped. Striking her on the face, which at once became red and swollen, he knocked her to the floor. When he saw what he had done "he relented and begged for forgiveness, and I dressed and went down into the lobby of the apartment house with him." She then told him she would seek a Reno divorce, to which he replied that she should think it over first. "He said I would never lose his friendship," but that he now considered having a wife an impediment to a man's success. "A wife is like a ball and chain around my ankles."

By the time Acker and Valentino faced each other in divorce court, each charging the other with desertion, two years had passed and the balance of power had shifted. Acker had been ill enough to be hospitalized for an extended period; her doctor confirmed in an affidavit that she suffered from stomach ulcers, required rest, and at present could not work. Valentino had turned into a famous movie star, the smoldering Julio of *The Four Horsemen of the Apocalypse*, the irresistibly exotic and passionate lover known as the Sheik. He'd become a close friend of Nazimova's, had played Armand to her Camille on-screen, and had appeared in four feature films made at Metro before moving on to Famous Players–Lasky. Although he was earning far less than he was worth, his weekly paycheck of seven hundred dollars from Famous Players–Lasky put his income and earning capacity far above hers. In court Acker and her attorney tried to walk both sides of the street, demanding financial support in the form of "separate maintenance" for a woman too sick to work while insisting that she lacked mercenary motives. "I did not marry him for money," she averred, "I married him simply because I love him."

Loved him, evidently, without having gotten to know him. "I never learned his birthday," she stated. "He is an enigma. Our paths have only crossed like ships that pass in the night. Perhaps we knew each other in another world."

When questioned about her wedding-night rejection, Acker claimed she had shut the door in Valentino's face after realizing he was broke. Making a curious choice of words, she said, "I wanted to make a man of him. I did not want him at my hotel, [did not want to be] supporting him until he received work. I wanted him to go to work. I gave him money, underwear, clothes. I was not going to take him into the hotel to embarrass me." The judge could not get her to substantiate her claim that she provided funds or clothing (he did ascertain that Rudy had driven her car and helped himself to some of her expensive perfume), and pointed out her inconsistency: she chided her husband for not paying at the hotel, but refused to move into the apartment he rented for them as a couple. The judge might have pointed out that within two weeks after they married, Rudy went to work on *Passion's Playground*, that he then went east to appear in two films shot in New York, and that his being employed in no way enhanced his standing in Jean's eyes.

She also tried to make it appear that Valentino's success had changed him and implied that it had ruptured an otherwise intact union. "He was nothing when I married him, and as soon as he 'arrived' he lost interest in me," she testified.

Judge Thomas O. Toland sided with Valentino in his decision, awarding Valentino the divorce he sought while denying Acker separate maintenance. He dismissed the "bathroom incident" fight during which Rudy knocked Acker down as an accident justified by provocation, not evidence of cruelty, and found that Jean Acker had deserted her husband and not the other way around. "From the beginning," Toland ruled, "it is clear . . . that the marriage, which was rather a hasty one, was for some reason distasteful to the plaintiff. . . . She was not in that frame of mind consistent with becoming truly and seriously a wife." But along with his legal victory came a costly financial settlement. Valentino agreed to pay Jean Acker's medical bills and to make monthly alimony payments of $175 until a final settlement was reached. From the moment of this ruling onward to well beyond his demise, Rudy's estate would remain debt-plagued.

Acker was an exploiter who sued for the legal right to call herself "Mrs. Rudolph Valentino" and in 1923 toured in vaudeville with a sketch called "How She Won the Sheik." Her connection to Valentino turned out to be her chief claim to fame, something she traded on until her death at age eighty-five in 1978. But in spite of this, between Jean and Rudy there had existed something more substantial than sheer opportunism, a genuine emotional link. "She is an understanding heart," Rudy said of her. They rekindled their friendship after his second divorce, were often together in New York right before he became fatally ill. Rudy's manager, George Ullman, allowed her to visit the hospital after he lapsed into unconsciousness and she wept without restraint at his bier. Ullman permitted her to spend some time alone with the deceased—something she'd avoided when Rudy's body pulsed with life—and included her as part of the official funeral cortège.

Soon after he died, after telling a reporter she had loved Rudy as a sister or mother would, Acker wrote and published a popular song about him, "We Will Meet at the End of the Trail," with syrupy lyrics like the ones she held accountable for their romantic delusions prior to marrying. The song suggests that she and Rudy were linked souls destined for reunion in heaven:

> Tho I pine for the touch of your hand in mine
> I smile through my tears, for we'll meet sometime.
> In my dreams I caress you
> While angels all bless you.

For the rest of her days she kept a part of Rudy that Polyclinic Hospital sent to her—since no family member was at hand—after Valentino's passing: his toupée.

7

ENTER JULIO

Restlessness overtook Rudy following his marital debacle. One night, after dancing for hours at the Alexandria with a married woman, he accepted her invitation to follow her to Palm Springs, which at that time was a remote desert outpost with only one hotel, a general store, a post office, and a single gas station to its name. The married woman, Princess Helen Troubetzkoy, realized when they got to Palm Springs that it would never do for Rudy to stay at her hotel. Her husband, the sculptor Paul Troubetzkoy, an exiled Russian prince, "would not like it at all." She knocked at the bungalow door of a friend, Paul Ivano, at two in the morning to ask if Rudy could be put up in his spare room. Ivano agreed, delighted to learn that his uninvited guest spoke French. They went horseback riding together in the morning and found they couldn't stop talking. "He stayed two weeks, which was all right. I bought the food and he cooked it. He was a good cook. And we became friends."

Whether anything ever came of the liaison with Princess Troubetzkoy we don't know, but Rudy did befriend her sculptor husband; he attended at least one Los Angeles party with him, posed for one of three bronze figures he created for a World War I memorial that once adorned Westlake Park, and allowed Troubetzkoy to sculpt one of his hands in white Carrara marble. And he fell in love with the stark beauty of the desert, a place he would escape to many times to "see the truth of things, regain perspective," and savor the peacefulness born of a sense that "you are alone, yet not alone."

Paul Ivano became an important presence in Valentino's life, a so-cial ally and sometime roommate whose career as a Hollywood cam-eraman Rudy would help to initiate. Born Paul Ivanichevitch in Nice to Russian and Serbian parents, he had been gassed while serving with French forces during the Great War. Transferred to the U.S. Signal Corps, he was put to work as a still photographer. When he contracted pulmonary tuberculosis, a wealthy American Red Cross nurse invited him to Palm Springs to convalesce, which is why he happened to be there when Valentino turned up.

After Palm Springs Rudy departed by train for an indefinite stay in New York, now a very different city from the pre-Prohibition Gotham he had fled in 1917. Hip-flasks had taken over as the fashion accessory of choice. Automobiles—high-end Stutzes and Pierce-Arrows among the Fords—clogged the intersections, and glittering nightspots like Bustanoby's and Shanley's had been replaced by dimly lit speakeasies and midnight supper clubs in private homes. Young women were shortening their skirts, flattening their breasts, reddening their lips, smoking cigarettes, and learning how to dance to a jazz beat. Enjoying a new permissiveness about sex, they cuddled with their sleek-haired boyfriends in rumble seats or at the movies. Women of all ages flocked to the luxurious new picture palaces; the audience for movies was overwhelmingly female. More and more vaudeville houses were con-verted into movie theaters, and corner newsstands displayed glossy magazine covers promising to give the inside scoop on Gloria Swan-son's fabulous wardrobe or Mary Pickford's home life with her new husband, Douglas Fairbanks.

According to Ivano, Rudy considered resettling permanently in the East and not coming back to Hollywood at all. While bunking with friends in Greenwich Village and Long Island he pondered whether he should start dancing professionally again and meanwhile took on roles as a mustachioed heavy in two more screen productions. One of these films, *Stolen Moments*, introduced him to Aileen Pringle (then known as Aileen Savage), carried him briefly to St. Augustine, Florida, and cast him as a blackmailing South American novelist. In the other, *The Won-derful Chance,* Rudy played a safe-cracking, cigar-chomping gangster who trolls the gritty slums of New York. Photographed on location, it featured shots of laundry strung from actual clotheslines and authentically overstuffed garbage cans.

On the five-day train trip from California to New York, Ivano reported, Rudy had read in the original Spanish a novel about the Great War that became an international best-seller, Vicente Blasco Ibáñez's *The Four Horsemen of the Apocalypse*. Although movers and shakers in the entertainment industry were being advised to indulge the public's hunger for upbeat escapist fare and steer clear of subject matter recalling the destruction, brutality, and sacrifice of war, the popularity of this book suggested otherwise. *The Four Horsemen,* an epic three-generation family saga that begins in Argentina and ends on the blood-stained battlefields of France, had gone through more than a hundred printings and had found more than ten million readers in the United States alone. Its combination of grandeur and disillusionment hit home with a postwar American public for whom, as F. Scott Fitzgerald famously put it, "all Gods [were] dead, all wars fought, all faith in man shaken."

When he read in one of the trade papers that Metro—recently bought by Marcus Loew—had purchased screen rights to *The Four Horsemen* for an advance of twenty thousand dollars against 10 percent of royalties, had assigned June Mathis to adapt the novel for the screen, and was about to begin casting, Rudy presented himself at Metro's New York office. He thought there might be a part for him somewhere in the Argentine sequence of the story, maybe a dancing role, since the tango figures prominently in the plot. At Metro's office he was surprised to hear from Maxwell Karger, the very man who had served as best man at his wedding to Jean Acker, that scenarist June Mathis had been looking for him. She had been put in charge of the entire production. "Then June came in," he remembered. "I liked her right away. She was so friendly and so human. We talked about assorted things. . . . And then she turned to me and asked if I would like to play the leading part [Julio Desnoyers]. 'Would I?' I told them that I would, oh, so very much indeed."

June Mathis had seen Valentino in Hollywood on the lot and on the dance floor of a nightspot. Struck by his good looks and grace, she had learned his name, but they had never spoken and never been introduced. His work as the sinuous cabaret parasite in *Eyes of Youth* had persuaded her that he had what it took to portray the young libertine Julio Desnoyers, but she knew that featuring a relative unknown in such an expensive and ambitious production would seem reckless. "She deliberately didn't want to be introduced to me because she knew that might mean opposition to her choice of me for Julio. She wanted to be sure that no one could hint at anything personal in her selection. And she was right. Many people said she was crazy to give me the part. I was a heavy, they said, and would never be anything else." Among the other actors who'd been mentioned as contenders for the plum role of Julio were the Spanish-born Antonio Moreno and a leading man named Carlyle Blackwell. But Mathis held out for Rudolph Valentino, and she prevailed.

He was signed for $350 a week (less than the salary of Wallace Beery, who had a relatively small part as a ruthless German officer) and was instructed to board a train to Los Angeles, for the film was to be produced in California, much of it at Metro's Hollywood studio at Cahuenga Boulevard and Romaine Street. In New York, the director of *The Wonderful Chance,* George Archainbaud, hurried up the shooting schedule so that Rudy would be free to leave. Before embarking for California he had himself measured for more than twenty-five custom-fitted suits to wear as the man-about-town Julio in his Paris heyday. Metro would provide him with only his Argentine gaucho costume and the French soldier's uniforms of the final sequence. He would spend the next year paying off his New York tailor.

"Rudolph Valentino has been summoned from New York," *Motion Picture News* reported in August of 1920, "to play the part of the hero [in *The Four Horsemen*], the [grand]son of the rich South American who develops into a tango king in Paris in the dance frenzy that preceded the opening of the war in 1914. Mr. Valentino was selected from Miss Mathis's recollection of his playing in *Eyes of Youth*; he realized her ideal of the youthful Julio—a poetic dreamy Latin type of twenty-three years."

Along with Anita Loos and Frances Marion, June Mathis ranks as one of the most accomplished, prolific, and powerful women writers in silent-era Hollywood. The American Film Institute catalogue credits 113 films to her twelve-year career, including writing credit for *Blood and Sand* and *Ben-Hur* and editing credit for the notoriously extravagant von Stroheim film *Greed*. More than simply a writer or editor, she functioned as an executive for Metro (and later Goldwyn) who had a say in deciding which pictures would be made and exercised authority over every phase of production. "Her duties are not ended when the continuity of a story is completed," *Moving Picture World* reported. "She hovers around the stages and sets and confers with the directors daily, and she follows the film into the cutting and editorial rooms and writes the titles." According to the film historian Lewis Jacobs, "June Mathis originated the writer-director combination . . . [whose task] was to plan the film's action before any shooting began." She is also credited with developing the technique for "shooting on paper," which involved planning the placement and movement of the camera while writing the scenario.

Mathis was Valentino's senior by only eight years, but she appeared to be considerably older. Her looks fit the maternal role she played as both the discoverer and the nurturer of Valentino as a leading man. Rudy actually called her "little mother" and described himself as her adopted son. "She mothered Rudy, and my dear she worshipped him and he worshipped her," reported Nita Naldi, who had ample opportunity to observe them together on the set of *Blood and Sand*. There's no certainty that Mathis had a romantic interest in him, though she did seem to favor Italian men. She eventually married Sylvano Balboni, a cameraman she met in Rome while filming *Ben-Hur*. But there's every indication that she and Rudy did truly love one another as friends.

A squat, stocky woman with flyaway brown hair and "Paris clothes that on her looked dowdy," she had a famous temper, the capacity to work like a dray horse, and an indomitable will. No other single person did as much as she did to launch Rudolph Valentino into stardom, though Norman Kerry also played an important enabling role. Before *The Four Horsemen* had even been released, Rudy inscribed a photograph to her on November 19, 1920, "To June Mathis," expressing his eternal gratitude to her for opening the gates of opportunity with "quiet hands," and guiding him along the road to success.

June Mathis started out as a stage ingenue from the West who starred on Broadway and spent four seasons touring with the female impersonator Julian Eltinge in *The Fascinating Widow*. After taking a writing course in New York, she entered a scriptwriting competition, which yielded job offers. Her first movie script, *The House of Tears*, was directed in 1915 by Edwin Carewe, and led to a contract with Metro. Within a few years she had advanced to head of Metro's scenario (scriptwriting) department, and in 1919 she moved with her mother to Hollywood, where she wrote several scripts for Nazimova. Like Nazimova, she held exalted ideals for motion pictures, valuing the medium as an art form rather than a purely commercial enterprise whose goals were profit and entertainment. These were views Valentino would espouse, too, during his later battle with Famous Players–Lasky over artistic control of his pictures.

Mathis also had a mystical bent. Her scripts typically include characters like the Christlike prophet Tchernoff, in *The Four Horsemen*, who sees the vision of the horsemen from the Book of Revelations—War, Famine, Pestilence, and Death—riding through the sky; or the philosopher Don Joselito in *Blood and Sand*, who keeps a record of human atrocities. (Both of these characters originated in Blasco Ibáñez novels, but Mathis strongly bonded with them.) A spiritualist who believed in reincarnation, she always wore an opal ring when she wrote, convinced that its magical powers brought her ideas. She had been a sickly child who had healed herself, she believed, through sheer force of will. "Ever since I have been sure that . . . everything is mental! We can overcome anything by a sincere mental determination," she stated. Convinced that thoughts created vibrations, she maintained that communication among people was a matter of picking up these unheard messages. "If you are vibrating on the right plane, you will inevitably come in contact with others who can help you. It's like tuning in on your radio. If you get the right wave-length, you have your station."

What drew her to Valentino as the right choice for the lead in *The Four Horsemen*? Blasco Ibáñez's description of Julio Desnoyers in the novel gives a partial answer: "He was of medium height, and dark complexion, with a . . . triangular face under two masses of hair, straight, black, and glossy as lacquer," a young man of "slender elegance, medium stature and muscular agility." The actor who played Julio had to be credible as the handsome, indulged Argentinean favorite of his Castilian grandfather, Madariaga, a rich cattle baron who identifies with Julio's French patrimony, while spurning the half-German, carrot-topped von Hartrott grandsons who come by way of his younger daughter. After the Desnoyers family moves to France, Julio must be convincing as a Montmartre poseur who dons a smock to paint half-naked models and lives on the indulgence of his mother. His mastery of the tango must qualify him to become the rage of the Paris tea salons, every dowager's dream tango partner and instructor. Valentino matched the novel's physical description, and he excelled as a tango master. But the actor who played Julio had to have depths; he must convincingly mature from a selfish lady-killer into a brave soldier seasoned by love, suffering, and sacrifice who redeems himself by dying in battle. June Mathis saw a soulfulness in Valentino that resided in his eyes. "Whenever I view a possible choice for a role," she once said, "I first notice the eyes. There I find what I call soul. You may alter everything except your eyes, in these days when tucks are taken in necks, chins blunted or sharpened and noses remodeled at will. Hair may be dyed, eyebrows plucked and teeth replaced, but the soul that looks out of the eyes is the real 'you.'"

Because of their special rapport, Valentino took his cues from Mathis when he went before the cameras as Julio. "Every single day June Mathis was on that set . . . When I would rehearse I could tell by June's face whether she was pleased with the way I was doing the scene, and if she was not she would call me over to her, very quietly, and say, 'I wouldn't do it quite like that, Rudy, I think it would go better like this.' I'd watch her all the time and if there was a frown between her eyes I'd change my tactics."

June Mathis also had the good sense to pick Rex Ingram to direct *The Four Horsemen*. Handsome enough to be a leading man himself and only twenty-seven when he began what turned into his breakthrough film, Ingram, born Reginald Hitchcock in Dublin, came to the United States to study drawing and sculpture at the Yale School of Fine Arts. Before completing his studies in New Haven, he moved to New York, where he both acted and wrote for the production company Vitagraph. During the war he became a flying instructor in the Royal Canadian Flying Corps. An injury in a crash kept him from active service, but the military experience left its imprint: forevermore a khaki shirt and a trench coat would be the staples of his wardrobe. When the war ended he became a director for Universal, and there he first encountered Valentino. Although impressed by Valentino's dancer's poise and air of repose, and by his memorable face, Ingram had to be talked into allowing Valentino to play Julio Desnoyers; he argued for a Julio "stronger and more French" than Valentino. June Mathis refused to budge and he capitulated to her.

Although he and Valentino never hit it off, Ingram considered his Julio "fool-proof to photograph, except that he couldn't be shot with both ears showing." And he sensed the readiness of the American public for a new kind of hero. The Arrow-collar man's appeal had passed its peak. Audiences, as Ingram's friend Erich von Stroheim put it, "had become weary of . . . doll-like heroines and their hairless, flat-chested heroes who were as lily-white as the heroines." Women were ready to respond to a leading man whose face suggested undercurrents of cruelty and whose every gesture promised a new kind of dangerous sensuality. Whereas Douglas Fairbanks would sooner jump from an airplane than play a love scene, Valentino seemed to put women first and "looked as if he knew everything about love," said Hollywood's resident expert on romance, Elinor Glyn.

In the Buenos Aires tango scene that turned Valentino into a box-office lion, his Julio is dressed as a gaucho in a flat-brimmed hat that shades his eyes, flared three-quarter-length pants, a woven serape draped over one shoulder, and boots with spurs. He carries a riding crop that sets a tone of menace matched by his steely squint. We're in a waterfront dive in the Boca quarter of Buenos Aires, a "port of last resort" where kisses come with a price tag and the "dregs of humanity" consort. Like the fire-breathing dragon of the prophet's visions,

Julio's element is smoke. He inhales a cigarillo, burning up the screen as he exhales slowly through his nostrils. The cameraman, John Seitz (later the cinematographer for *Double Indemnity* and *Sunset Boulevard*), used a moving camera mounted on a dolly, allowing for both fluidity and intimacy in shooting the dance sequence. The cheap, garishly lip-sticked woman dancer, Beatrice Dominguez, is dancing the tango with another partner when Julio approaches and cuts in. The male rival re-sists and Julio floors him with his riding crop, sweeping Dominguez into his arms. (Rex Ingram had used a version of this cutting-in scene in an earlier film of his, set on the Bowery.) Cheered on by a rowdy crowd that includes his old debauched grandfather, "the Centaur" Madariaga, Julio and Dominguez lock eyes as they step together in perfect unison, sliding, pivoting, dropping and lifting, dipping back-ward with legs intertwined and faces almost touching. Their intricate and leisurely tango ends with a vampire kiss that prior to editing en-dured for seventy-five feet of film.

The Argentine tango scene, severely cropped in videotapes avail-able in the United States, but restored in David Gill and Kevin Brown-low's edition for Turner Entertainment TV, isn't in the Blasco Ibáñez novel at all. Ingram custom-fit it to match Valentino's abilities, re-hearsing for three days to expand a visual vignette into some of the most atmospheric footage in screen history.

Julio isn't a one-size-fits-all sort of lover. One of the keys to his ap-peal is the way he picks up the pulse of the particular woman he's with. His sadistic treatment of Beatrice Dominguez in the tango scene—he ends up throwing her off his lap as if she were a sack of po-tatoes when she laughs at Madariaga's sudden illness—is contrasted with the tender interplay between him and the married woman, Mar-guerite Laurier, who captures his heart in Paris. Portrayed by the ethereal Alice Terry, soon to become Mrs. Rex Ingram, Marguerite is everything Dominguez isn't: elegant, dainty, slender, aristocratic, blonde. (Terry wore a wig over her own dark locks.) She's a lady of fashion, beautifully turned out in a dark suit and a hat with white os-trich aigrette. Always focused on his beloved, Julio handles Mar-guerite like a piece of delicate Sèvres porcelain. With her his gestures are deferential, nuanced, never rough or outsized, and there are many close-ups of him with Marguerite that illustrate how the rest of the world falls away during their times together. The lovers speak a private language. (In fact, the actors spoke French, so that lip-readers would be impressed.) At their initial meeting, he holds on to her hand a bit too long as he kisses it, incurring the jealous wrath of her older, unloved husband. When Julio inhales the scent of a rosebud she has handed him, it's as if the perfume of her skin has infused its petals. In his Montmartre studio, he removes her shoes and dries and caresses her wet feet after she arrives during a downpour. Only once before the camera does he cut loose with Marguerite, embracing her hungrily and cupping his hand over her breast when he tells her she belongs to him, not her husband, Laurier. Usually, he keeps the lid on, holding back. "He always suggested more than he gave," said Alice Terry of Valentino. "I always had the impression that I was playing with a volcano that might erupt at any minute. It never did, but that was the secret of his appeal."

Julio's shifting attitude toward the war marks his moral progress. Initially indifferent to the news that war has begun as he pursues his life of pleasure, he soon finds it impossible to remain aloof. His upstairs neighbor, the mystic Tchernoff, prophesies the coming apocalypse, invoking Albrecht Dürer's images of the fire-breathing beast and the four masked enemies of mankind, messengers of doom who ride against the sky. Marguerite's brother and her ex-husband (who has agreed to a divorce) go off to fight, and a repentant Marguerite feels called upon to do her part. She trains to become a Red Cross nurse, dons a headdress that makes her look like a nun, and, when Laurier returns from the war, ends up caring for the dignified older husband she never loved, whose heroism in battle has left him wheelchair-bound and blind. Julio's father (wonderfully played by Josef Swickard), once a pacifist, has been galvanized into ardent French patriotism. The marauding Germans have sacked his castle on the Marne and raped his steward's daughter. To win his father's approval, match Marguerite's sacrifice, and earn his own self-respect, Julio enlists as a *poilu*, a soldier in the French army, even though as an Argentinean he is not technically required to volunteer. "I have been a coward," he acknowledges. Promoted to the rank of officer, he breaks from his self-indulgent past to render gallant service in the trenches. "He is a different Julio," a title tells us. "One hears everywhere of his unselfishness and his bravery." Drenched in mud, he dies face-to-face with one of his half-German cousins and is buried in a vast field of white crosses. In our last glimpse of him, his ghost appears before Marguerite, urging her to stay with the wounded Laurier and continue to seek atonement.

The transformation of Julio allows audiences to have it both ways. They partake vicariously in his dissolute youth, share the excitement of his adulterous affair with Marguerite, sit with him near a couple of decadent-looking lesbians at a Paris tango tea dance, and then repudiate all that as they rise with him to the exaltation of repentance, martyrdom, and redemption. Julio dies in a war not just against Germany but against a hideous, surreal barbarism. The presence of Tchernoff at the graveyard (a June Mathis flourish that isn't in the novel) signifies that by dying heroically Julio has won entry into the spirit realm. An alternate, happy ending—showing Julio and Marguerite's marriage in Argentina—was filmed but never pulled from the Metro vault. It would not have sounded the appropriately solemn and majestic notes.

June Mathis used her screenplays as a means to moral and spiritual enlightenment. For Rex Ingram, who before shooting would sketch a scene from various angles, film was one of the graphic arts, a medium joining elements from sculpture, painting, and theater. He saw the close-up as a matter of "modeling obtained by judicious arrangement of light and shade." In pursuit of the soft, mellow, and even light he associated with the tones in paintings of the old masters, he avoided shooting outdoors in direct sunlight, preferring the late-afternoon hours when "we can work with the lens wide open. There are no high lights. Every crack and crevice does not stand out. The picture . . . meets the eye restfully." When shooting indoors he would repaint a set he didn't like or rearrange items on a wall to meet his exacting standards of composition.

He was also a stickler for historical accuracy, down to the smallest details. At Valentino's urging, he brought in Paul Ivano from Palm Springs and put him to work authenticating the French soldiers' uniforms and the look of the French village on the Marne, which was meticulously reconstructed behind Griffith Park, only to be just as painstakingly destroyed in the film. Jacques d'Auray, a former French officer, also vouched for the veracity of these scenes, and a former German soldier named Curt Rehfeld drilled the actors who played Germans. Real European antiques were borrowed to furnish the various French abodes, and for the South American interiors, Argentine weavings, paintings, and musical instruments were assembled. Even the signs printed on the wall of the Boca cabaret had to ring true. The old Gilmore Ranch on La Brea was used for exterior shooting of the South American scenes, because its herds of sheep and cattle could be photographed to suggest Madariaga's vast holdings and because it still contained outbuildings "of the exact type to be seen in South America during the period of the story."

The entire company sensed that they were participating in a momentous experiment. "I never saw a director or a cast so enthused with their work," said a reporter from *Moving Picture World* who visited the set. Valentino was so fired up, he even went to watch the filming of big scenes in which he played no part.

When shooting finally ended after six months, an exhausted Valentino repaired to Paul Ivano's Palm Springs bungalow for a rest. Douglas Gerrard, Emmett Flynn, and John Gilbert, at that time a contract player for Fox, came along for the ride. "I've just made a picture that will make me the biggest star in the world," Valentino announced to the group. John Gilbert, ambitious on his own behalf, challenged him, saying, "What do you mean?" According to Ivano, the two nearly came to blows.

Hyperbole and superlatives flowed easily whenever people referred to *The Four Horsemen*. It was an early prototype of the blockbuster. According to Grant Whytock, the film's skilled editor, almost a million feet of film were shot using fourteen cameras. Metro advertised its wildly inflated claim that 12,000 people had been employed to make the film, 72 of them principals in the cast, and 125,000 tons of masonry, steel, lumber, and furniture had been used in the sets. The studio shelled out $800,000 for the production. The popular joke of the day was, "through the pockets of [Metro owner] Marcus Loew rode the Four Horsemen."

Blasco Ibáñez applauded the artistry of the screen adaptation, and when it finally hit the movie houses, American reviewers hailed it as a masterpiece on par with the best of Griffith. Ingram's production, said *Variety*, "is to the picture of today what *Birth of a Nation* was." *The New York Times* praised *The Four Horsemen* for achieving "an effect of grandeur, of exaltation of the spirit, beyond anything as yet achieved by the drama." In a bold-print editorial headlined "The Great Has Come," *Motion Picture World* saluted "a fine spectacle, a supreme drama, a vitalized sermon, a marvel of creation" destined to survive as long as the human family survives. "We find ourselves in the position of a man who tries to describe Wagner's music, only to discover that the music itself has gone beyond language and interprets thoughts impossible to put in words." The critic Robert Sherwood assured *Life* readers that the film "lifts the silent drama to an artistic plane that it has never touched before."

The reviewers were right. *The Four Horseman* has lost none of its power. Yoking epic grandeur to one family's private saga, it combines innovative photography, fine acting, and an eerie sense of foreboding. There are portentous moments—Blasco Ibáñez, June Mathis, and Rex Ingram all shared an inclination to wax philosophical—but the majesty of the whole, and its success in capturing the overwhelming ghastliness of war, make it a film worth seeking out at silent film festivals.

Although Rex Ingram awarded himself top billing and relegated Valentino's name in the credits to the same small type used for every other member of the company, critics singled out Valentino for applause. Robert Sherwood predicted he was headed for stardom, and ranked him "both in ability and appearance" above "all the stock movie heroes from Richard Barthelmess down. He tangos, makes love, and fights with equal grace." To Edwin Schallert of the *Los Angeles Times* he had already achieved stardom. "In the interpretation of Julio," he wrote, "Valentino has assumed a place among the most dominant romantic actors of the screen. He has set forth an ideal portrait of selfish, extravagant youth, with the finer soul qualities [a]waiting the moment for their revealing." Rudolph Valentino had made his mark. He hadn't merely delivered a riveting performance; he had introduced a new type. Said *Photoplay*, "Rudolph Valentino played Julio . . . and immediately the film world knew it had the continental hero, the polished foreigner, the modern Don Juan in its unsuspecting midst."

For once, the enthusiasm of the ticket-buying public matched the critical reception. Two days after a premiere before an audience of notables at New York's Lyric Theatre, long lines formed at the box office and fifteen hundred would-be patrons for reserved seats had to be turned away. A full symphony orchestra played at every screening, and an actor costumed as the apostle John read from the Book of Revelations. The Lyric's previous record, set by *Way Down East* in 1920, was surpassed, and New York succumbed to *Four Horsemen* fever. The windows of Macy's, Gimbel's, and Lord and Taylor were filled with movie stills and displays of the novel. After being feted at a dance as the guest of honor of a group of 150 New York professional women, Rudy charmed those at a postdance breakfast by insisting on cooking a Spanish omelet, and then providing tango instructions to the tune of some Argentine recordings.

The actress Constance Talmadge, who happened to be in New York at the time *The Four Horsemen* had its premiere, remembered that young women there could talk of nothing but Valentino. "Everywhere I went, I seemed to hear the buzz of girls wishing to each other that they would be lucky enough to dance a tango with that hero." Talmadge was thrilled when Valentino spotted her while she was having tea with her mother at the Biltmore and asked her to dance. Julio in the flesh! As she moved to his beat, the outside world fell away. "People, music, the floor, all attained a delightful blur," she recalled. "Here indeed was perfect rhythm."

Officialdom, too, took due notice. President and Mrs. Harding attended a private screening, as did Vice-President and Mrs. Coolidge.

At the Los Angeles Mission Theater premiere, which Valentino attended, when the screening ended a hushed silence was followed by tumultuous applause. Rudy was surrounded with well-wishers. *The Four Horsemen* ended up as one of the top moneymakers of the 1920s, chalking up more than four million dollars in theatrical rentals.

The picture was aggressively marketed in Brazil, Montevideo,

Uruguay, and Chile. It had an elaborate premiere in Madrid. In France, after initial opposition, owing to what the French considered excessive credit given to the American soldiers, its Paris premiere was attended by the French president, Alexandre Millerand, by Marshal Foch, Premier Poincaré, and the American ambassador, and the film's run was a success.

Not surprisingly, the film encountered hostility from the German press, which protested the way the German army was depicted and reported attempts to have *The Four Horsemen* banned throughout Europe. When Metro redistributed the movie in 1926, after Valentino's death, the German ambassador in Washington objected.

No future Valentino picture would appeal as much to highbrow audiences. He would always be identified with the role of Julio, and he would never top this performance for the prestige it conferred on him. A fan-magazine profile called "Enter Julio!" depicted Rudy as an aesthete who was also a man of action: "Either, to correspond with his virile physique, he should not be so aesthetically attuned, or to accord with his vigorous spirituality he should not be so immaculately groomed. . . . This phenomenal youth cannot relinquish his fidelity to Arthur Symons, D'Annunzio, Dante, Wilde, Fokine and Caruso because of his . . . interest in Hart, Schaffner & Marx [men's clothiers], thoroughbreds, surf-bathing and Dardenella [eau de cologne]. He has the indolence of Endymion who would dream, . . . the vitality of Don Juan who would woo; the extravagance of Don Quixote who would exaggerate."

Not until *Blood and Sand*'s Gallardo would Valentino again portray a man with a character so similar to his own. "In *The Four Horsemen*," he would confess in a moment of introspection, "I played what I knew to be myself, and when finished he turned out to be Julio because . . . Julio is any man . . . who lets his weakness dictate his circumstances."

The only finger-pointing to greet *The Four Horsemen of the Apocalypse* was the finger Valentino pointed at himself for possessing the human frailty he shared with Julio. From the point of view of public acclaim, Rudolph Valentino had already in a single bound vaulted to his peak.

8

THE WONDER YEAR

I n the fall of 1920, while *The Four Horsemen of the Apocalypse* was being cut and prepared for release, Rudy invited Paul Ivano to move in with him. They shared a small place in the Formosa Apartments, 9139 Hollywood Boulevard, at La Brea, a popular address among movie folk—one where he'd once hoped to nest-build with Jean Acker. The director Bill Wellman lived there, as did many starlets. During this time Rudy had begun working in a low-budget, low-profile Metro film called *Uncharted Seas*.

Although his pattern of pairing off with a woman at social gatherings made some people think of Rudy as a ladies' man (his new friend Jack Dempsey described him as one, and Nazimova's "husband," Charles Bryant, dubbed him a Lothario), Ivano said that these days he, rather than Rudy, was the real lady-killer. "[Rudy] was the greatest promoter so far as promoting dames. He talked them into believing he was the greatest lover. He would take the poor things to dinner, and then to the apartment, where we'd have a drink. And he'd sit down in the armchair, and because he was tired from the day's work he'd fall sound asleep. I would say to the girl, 'Well darling, I have to get up early tomorrow, so if you want to wait for Rudy wait here, but I'm going to bed.' Ten minutes later someone would knock on my door" and the woman would end up in bed with Ivano while Rudy spent the night sleeping upright in an armchair in the living room. The following morning he'd growl at Ivano, "You son-of-a-bitch. I promoted the dame." Ivano would insist the woman had chosen him freely. He'd kid Rudy about it. "We used to have fun."

Ivano dismissed as "a lot of baloney" the latter-day gossip that Rudy was a homosexual, angrily insisting, "He was a nice, normal human being." But he confirmed that—except when Rudy was with Natacha Rambova, the woman who became his second wife—Rudy seemed content with a passive stance when it came to actual sex. Conquest held little allure. And others who were on the scene reached similar conclusions: he did not chase skirts with an eye to removing them. Stuart Holmes, the actor who played one of the von Hartrott cousins in *The Four Horsemen*, recalled of Rudy, "All he thought about was Italian food. He'd turn those big slumberous eyes on some woman and she'd just about swoon with delight, but he couldn't have cared less. He was usually thinking about the spaghetti and meatballs he was going to have for dinner that evening."

Food certainly figures in many people's recollections of Rudy at this time. He instructed Leatrice Joy in how to bake meatballs before adding them to pasta sauce and warned the young actress Patsy Ruth Miller that unless she learned to cook she would never find a husband. He was so fond of licorice candy that his teeth would turn black and he'd have to rinse his mouth madly before going before the cameras. With Ivano he would prepare six-foot-long spaghetti so unwieldy he had to stand on a ladder as he dropped it in the pot of boiling water. There are no parallel tales attesting to his prowess as a lover, beyond Patsy Ruth Miller's account of a "long, lovely" birthday kiss from him when she turned eighteen. It's possible that he opted for the sexual sidelines at the time because he felt inhibited by the fact that he was still legally married to Jean Acker. He also could have been sobered by his alleged bout with gonorrhea, and he was surely still smarting from Jean's abrupt rejection. He seemed to be conserving his energies mostly for his career.

He had many women friends, with whom he tended either to function as a surrogate son and protégé, as with June Mathis, or to fall easily into platonic pal-ship, as he did with Dagmar Godowsky. She associated him with cooking spaghetti for her, cutting her hair, and helping her fix up her bungalow. For her, the sexual heat he projected on screen failed to ignite when she met him in the flesh, and his enormous appeal to feminine movie fans remained a mystery. Most of the actresses he worked with echoed this judgment. "Other women found him to be very seductive and sexy," Patsy Ruth Miller recalled. "I found him to be just a lot of fun, more like an older brother" who teased her, swam with her, and tried to protect her from predatory males. Nita Naldi, who would play a vamp in three Valentino movies, agreed that the off-screen Valentino was just "an ordinary young man with atrocious taste in clothes. All the girls who have worked with him feel exactly as I do. They like him . . . but not one of them has ever fallen in love with him. Yet he stirs them on the screen."

Metro showed no sign of recognizing that it had created a star. Possibly because Rex Ingram had little faith in him, they refused to give Valentino a raise beyond the $350 he earned initially and shoved him into a supporting part in a standard-issue production that must have been an anticlimax after the extravagance and ambition of *The Four Horsemen*. "Nowhere in motion pictures is there a comparable instance of a player who captured so frantic a following . . . and who himself received so pitifully few rewards for his efforts."

Uncharted Seas, his next production, concerned two rivals for the affections of a character, Lucretia Eastman, played by Alice Lake. Her drunken weakling of a husband has failed her so many times she wants to ditch him. An expedition to the Arctic Circle will give him one more chance to show that he's a real man, deserving of her love. Valentino plays Frank Underwood, a onetime suitor still stuck on Lucretia who finds himself on another ship bound for the Arctic. When her lily-livered husband turns back in fear, Lucretia jumps ship, joining Frank on an icebound adventure that culminates with their rescue and Lucretia's divorce from her unworthy spouse. Some dramatic snow scenes photographed in Flagstaff, Arizona, by John Seitz, could not compensate for the contrived plot and poor production values. One reviewer pointed out how uncomfortable Valentino looked in all his layers. He "acts well, although his emotions are smothered in fur."

The first time Natacha Rambova laid eyes on Valentino was when he appeared on the Metro back lot between setups, costumed for the frozen north. On a sultry December day in Hollywood, Nazimova—who had clearly revised her opinion of Rudy since the night she snubbed him at the Ship Café—introduced them, while streams of perspiration ran down his fur-framed cheeks. "What I could see of the face was not exactly prepossessing," Natacha would recall. "Two dark slanting eyes with eyelashes and eyebrows white with mica," which served as artificial snow. He shook her hand warmly and beamed his million-dollar smile. "That flash of even white teeth had certainly something very winning about it."

Rudy may have been the one dressed for the Arctic, but Natacha displayed the icy demeanor. He had noticed her at the studio before, and had wondered about the tall, erect, dark-haired, and haughty beauty who walked like a ballerina—toes pointed out—and took no notice of his presence as she calmly went about her work as a costume designer and art director for Nazimova. "She never looked to right or left. She seemed frozen," said Rudy. She had blue eyes and a flawless complexion and wore long, flowing skirts with flat shoes. Along with her snow-queen air, Natacha projected a theatrical sensuality that seemed to contradict it. Her oval face was made up like a dancer's, with mascaraed dark lashes, black kohl surrounding her eyes, a hint of color on each high cheekbone, and sculpted, meticulously outlined red lips. In dress she followed the lead of the Paris designer Paul Poiret, favoring uncorseted and fluid lines, brilliant colors like scarlet and purple, luxuriously draped fabrics that had sheen, turbans redolent of the exotic East, and clunky jewelry encrusted with real gems. Behind her back Rudy would joke "Here comes Pavlova" when she walked by, but Natacha saw herself as more the Cleopatra type, a *femme fatale* capable of ruling continents.

Natacha's real name was Winifred Shaughnessy and her place of birth was no more exotic than Salt Lake City, Utah. Her Irish Catholic father, a colonel on the Union side in the Civil War, afterward had become a businessman with mining interests who turned into a carousing problem drinker and gambler. Natacha's restless, capable, and much-married mother, nicknamed Muzzie, came of Mormon stock (she was a descendant of a Mormon patriarch, Heber C. Kimball). When Muzzie needed a profession that would furnish an income, she taught herself to be an interior designer and moved to San Francisco to set up shop. As her mother changed cities and husbands, young Winifred changed surnames: from Shaughnessy to de Wolfe, and eventually to Hudnut. Stability was provided by her loving maternal aunt, Mrs. Teresa Werner, an oasis of calm who treated the exquisite, talented, and headstrong child like her own daughter. In young Winifred's matriarchal world, men were expendable and transient presences, but her loving Aunt Teresa was an anchor who held fast.

In San Francisco, Winifred's mother married Edgar de Wolfe, the socially prominent but passive brother of a celebrated interior designer, Elsie de Wolfe, who was the darling of the elite on both sides of the Atlantic. Elsie de Wolfe established her reputation as an innovator in home decor by stripping away Victorian bric-a-brac. Partial to Georgian architecture, Fragonard paintings, Louis XV furniture, and the color beige, she made her taste the epitome of fashion and filled the homes of American tycoons with French antiques. Even her passion for Pekingese dogs set a trend. Muzzie's prosperity was assured when Elsie de Wolfe accepted her San Francisco sister-in-law as a business partner who could handle clients in the western United States, while she herself served those in Europe and near New York.

Natacha's mother flourished in California, becoming wealthy and socially successful, but eight-year-old Winifred proved to be a handful. She ridiculed her ineffectual stepfather and was sent home from summer camp for conduct unbecoming a young lady. Muzzie retaliated by enrolling her daughter, under protest, at an upper-class British boarding school that Elsie de Wolfe had recommended, Leatherhead Court, in Surrey. Elsie owned a house in Versailles, Villa Trianon, which served as a gathering place for the rich and distinguished, and the child could spend summers and vacations there. She could learn French, go to nearby Paris to study ballet, and benefit from Elsie's gilt-edged social and cultural connections. Elsie's live-in companion was the theatrical agent Elizabeth Marbury, who had represented major writing talents such as George Bernard Shaw and Somerset Maugham, and performers such as Irene and Vernon Castle. Anne Morgan, the daughter of the banker J. P. Morgan, was also in attendance. Together, the sapphic chatelaines of Villa Trianon knew everybody who was anybody in the interlocking spheres of art, home decor for the wealthy, and theater. Sarah Bernhardt had visited. Bernard Berenson, an annual guest, called them "the nymphets."

Winifred's nearly nine years at the British boarding school and her extended exposure to life at Villa Trianon fostered in her exceptional independence and self-sufficiency. Intense, artistic, and scornful of anything she considered superficial, she shied away from her schoolmates and quarreled with Aunt Elsie, branding her a pretentious social climber. Elsie's assiduous efforts to limit Winifred's contact with men further alienated her. The teenager, who was nicknamed Wink, prized solitude, using her time alone to refine her skill in drawing and design, to read extensively in mythology, and to study languages. Whereas Elsie abhorred anything avant-garde, Wink was drawn to Art Nouveau and the daring new design and dance arts emerging in Paris and New York. She may have rejected Elsie's conservative taste, but she learned from her example and from her own interior decorator mother that "while men still shaped the world, . . . it was the women who shaped the style in which we live."

Natacha was also a gifted ballet dancer and had trained with Rosita Meuri at the Paris Opera during the summers. She traveled to London whenever she could to attend performances by Pavlova, Nijinsky, and a virile-looking Russian alumnus of Diaghilev's Ballets Russes named Theodore Kosloff.

Right before war erupted in Europe, young Wink broke decisively with her aunt at Versailles and returned to San Francisco, where she immediately collided with her mother, who was in the midst of a divorce from Edgar de Wolfe. Wink had made up her mind to pursue ballet as a career, and she had fixed on studying with Theodore Kosloff, the dancer she found so magnetic in London, at his newly opened studio in New York. Muzzie considered this notion preposterous; to her, ballet dancing was simply another social grace, like speaking French, in the "finishing" of a young debutante daughter. Aunt

Teresa intervened, offering a solution. She would move to New York for a year and provide a home for her formidable niece during her apprenticeship as a Kosloff dancer.

Aunt Teresa proved to be no match for her strong-minded charge. Within the year, the seventeen-year-old Winifred had agreed to change her name to Natacha Rambova and had begun to perform with Kosloff's Imperial Russian Ballet Company. She took to wearing her long hair parted in the middle and in two braids that encircled her ears or were pinned on top of her head. At five feet eight inches, she was considered "too tall" to be a classical ballerina, but she moved well and had a compelling stage presence. Kosloff assigned her leading parts. He was supporting a wife and invalid daughter in Europe, but this didn't stop "Natacha" from falling in love with her teacher/director and becoming his lover.

When Muzzie learned of the affair, all hell broke loose. She instigated legal action to have Kosloff deported, charging him with kidnapping and statutory rape. Instead of returning to her mother, Natacha fled underground, escaping first to Canada and then to Bournemouth, on England's Channel coast, where she hid out for several months with Kosloff's wife and child, posing as a governess. At last Muzzie relented. She dropped the charges against Kosloff and agreed to allow Natacha to resume dancing with his company. She sweetened the deal with an offer to underwrite the cost of costumes.

Natacha returned to the States and joined Kosloff's touring company as a dancer, doubling as costume designer and seamstress. Under the spell of Léon Bakst's designs for Diaghilev and Poiret's for fashionable Paris, she specialized in exotic effects: brilliant colors, baubles, bangles, shimmering draped fabrics tricked out with feathers and sparkle, partially nude bodies slathered in body paint. After the tour ended, she joined Kosloff's unusual household in Los Angeles. Kosloff had been hired by Cecil B. DeMille as both a performer and a designer for motion pictures. In joining him Natacha took her place, to her dismay, as one of several members of Kosloff's arty harem. She and the other women dancers he had mesmerized provided sexual and professional services at his bidding. They taught at the dance studio Kosloff opened (as a teenager Agnes de Mille was a pupil), performed with his company, and assisted him, uncredited, in his design work for films. "It was practically white slavery," Ivano would comment. Natacha, who had a scholarly bent, immersed herself in research for the costumes she designed. She grew increasingly restive and unhappy as her love relationship with Kosloff cooled and he continued to steal full credit for her creative work, presenting her sketches as his own.

Kosloff met the fellow Russian emigré Alla Nazimova when she turned up at his studio for instruction in ballet. (At the same time Nazimova was studying modern dance with Ruth St. Denis.) Aware that she had her own production company at Metro, he offered his services as a costume and set designer. Nazimova agreed to try him for a planned production based on Pierre Louys's "degenerate" Greco-Egyptian novel *Aphrodite*, and one day Kosloff dispatched Natacha to deliver some sketches—sketches she herself had rendered. Natacha had a great affinity with anything connected with the imagined Orient or ancient Egypt; the costumes she planned struck Nazimova as appropriately daring, sensuous, and at the same time historically plausible. But she wanted some changes made. When Nazimova asked for revisions in the designs, Natacha took out a pencil and made them instantly, revealing that she, not Kosloff, had created the visually arresting work. Taken with Natacha's talent, beguiled by her beauty, Nazimova offered Natacha a position as art and costume designer on her productions. Natacha was guaranteed "up to $5,000" per picture and accepted with alacrity. However, fear of censorship would ultimately force Metro to shelve the *Aphrodite* project.

Now that she had a way of supporting herself, Natacha could leave Kosloff. But she would have to proceed in secret, as he would do everything to detain her if he knew her plan. While Kosloff was away on a hunting trip, she packed her bag and called for a cab. But Kosloff returned unexpectedly, and when he realized Natacha's escape was in progress he shot her in the leg with bird shot. She managed to flee to the Metro studio, terrified, bleeding, and in pain. At the studio, Ivano helped to extract the bits of lead from her leg. Natacha never pressed charges against Kosloff, probably because her wish for privacy overrode all other considerations. Her leg healed, but scars—both physical and emotional—would linger. Retreating inward, she lived more and more in her own head. She armed herself with reserve, a strategy of aloofness that had served her long before she knew Kosloff, but which her experience with him reinforced. Most people interpreted it as a blend of snobbery and coldness.

Nazimova saw beyond the frosty exterior. For a time she became the most important person in Natacha's life, but nobody knows the extent of their intimacy. The two creative dynamos, both independent "New Women" who took Russian names (Nazimova, a Jew who was born in Yalta, was originally surnamed Leventon), shared a flair for sophisticated European style and stagy self-presentation and an attraction to the bizarre aestheticism of Aubrey Beardsley and the exoticism ascribed to the Orient, but was there anything more between them? Michael Morris, Natacha Rambova's biographer, insists that they were merely good friends and that Natacha, who married a second time after Rudy's death and took several male lovers, never had sex with a woman, that she in fact disliked lesbianism. Mercedes de Acosta, the celebrated lesbian head-hunter best known for her affairs with Garbo and Marlene Dietrich, claimed to have had a close link with Natacha, based on their common interest in mythology, yoga, and astrology, but that proves nothing about Natacha's sexuality. It's worth mentioning, however, that in her will, Natacha left de Acosta a small bequest, suggesting a bond of some significance. Gavin Lambert, Nazimova's biographer, thinks she and Rambova probably did become lovers, citing as evidence the photograph of them together in Chinese pajamas, and quoting the costume designer Irene Sharaff, who was a good friend of Natacha's: "*Exactly* what happened between them I don't know for certain. . . . But they were both very deeply involved with each other for a while, and they were both sexually free." Patsy Ruth Miller, the young actress who joined Nazimova's circle as its token virgin (she would play Nichette in *Camille*), said that Madame "fell for" Natacha, but said nothing about whether the feeling was mutual.

What seems beyond dispute is that within Nazimova's international circle, as in the wider Bohemian enclave in Hollywood, sexual freedom was taken for granted and gender borders fluid. As one observer described it, "The law of the colony is that everybody is entitled to do exactly as he or she sees fit in all personal matters. If you don't like it you may stay away but you must not knock." An atmosphere of experimentation prevailed, in which long-term monogamy hardly existed and bisexuality was very much an option. As an article in *Motion Picture* put it, "In these days of suffragets [*sic*] and long-haired poets, bifurcated skirts and lisping laddies, it's hard to know who's who and what's what. It's getting to be quite the rage—this exchange of identities." This is not to suggest that every person in Hollywood experimented with bisexuality or promiscuity, merely that they were popular options, along with exclusively homosexual lifestyles and even abstinence (less popular), on a very long menu of sexual choices.

Nazimova, increasingly defined as a lesbian as she got older, still enjoyed occasional relationships with men. Around the same time she met Natacha she began an affair with Paul Ivano—who at only twenty was about half her age—that lasted on and off for several years. If Nazimova and Rambova did tumble into bed, it would not have been considered a big deal.

Ivano, Rambova, and Valentino all were engaged to work in or on Nazimova's production of *Camille*, touted as a modem version of the Dumas Fils favorite about a tubercular Paris courtesan who sacrifices her happiness to protect the reputation of her lover Armand's provincial family. Although Ray Smallwood served as nominal director, Nazimova herself called all the shots, and she took credit for casting Valentino as Armand. (June Mathis, who was writing the scenario, surely put in a good word for him, and Jean Acker just as surely smarted at his selection.)

Nazimova set about altering Rudy's appearance, tweezing his thick brows into slender, neat arches that morphed into diagonals when he expressed sorrow. She commanded him to lose weight and applied blue-black shadow to his eyelids and obvious lipstick to his lips—a common practice for male screen actors of the day, but one that resulted in a more artificial, "made-up" facial appearance than he had as Julio in *The Four Horsemen*. Natacha, in charge of sets, costumes, and the "look" of the production, turned her attention to changing his hair; she thought his signature slicked-back, pomaded style did not suit a young man from the French provinces. She had him shampoo away the patent-leather gloss, and then she fluffed his locks with curling irons. In the film's later scenes, when Armand becomes a jaded Parisian, he reclaims the slicked-back style. From the start, Natacha used Valentino as her personal manikin, turning his head and body into a canvas for her art.

Although she was a dancer, Rambova's designs have a static quality; they work best as stills, rather than in motion. But her Art Deco sets and costumes for *Camille* are stunning—they steal the picture. The image of a circular, highly stylized camellia blossom recurs, providing a unifying visual leitmotif. Nazimova's Marguerite clutches a camellia; her long kimono-like gown is decked with camellias, as is her black and silver opera cloak; her fireplace resembles a bowl; her bedroom's arches and doorways are half circles, her round bed with a rounded headboard and round area rug all echo the disk shape.

In the casino sequence the glittering camellia curtain contrasts with another startling backdrop, a white on black spiderweb with an angular German Expressionist cast. Determined to emulate the art films that were transforming filmmaking, especially in Germany, Rambova deliberately set about introducing design ideas imported from avant-garde Europe. The semicircular stairway punctuated with serpentine columns in the opening scene, in a theater lobby, quotes directly from the Hans Poelzig design for Max Reinhardt's Berlin arena theater, and the repeating arches in Marguerite's smart Paris apartment copy a plan by the Parisian designer Emil-Jacques Ruhlmann.

Nazimova's acting style seems to take its cue from the decor; she strikes exaggerated poses that emphasize stark outlines and wears white, masklike, rice-powder makeup similar to a mime's. With her wraithlike thinness and frizzed bob she's like a top-heavy blossom balancing on a slender stem. Her insistence on being filmed through gauze and filters adds to the sense of unreality. "Bobbed and bizarre Dumas reigns at the Rivoli," Alan Dale commented in the *New York American*. "Futuristic, frenetic, flamboyant Dumas. . . . Camille coiffed like Shock-Headed Peter in the children's story . . . Wonderful poses—stained-glass poses. This Camille even coughed futuristically." *Moving Picture World* suggested that the movie "should be sold as a polite freak rather than a translation of the story." Most of the reviewers considered *Camille* too rarefied and avant-garde to find wide popularity, and Metro, which soon broke with Nazimova, apparently agreed after the film made a disappointing showing at the box office.

Nazimova saw to it that *Camille* would remain *her* picture and that Valentino as Armand would be given minimal opportunity to upstage her. She permitted him few close-ups, but ample opportunity to show that he excelled at looking ornamentally dreamy-eyed and plaintive in white tie and tails—shots that take on the aspect of an Art Deco study in black and white. In the countryside sequence, he models a sporty 1920s leisure-wear getup composed of plus-fours and a belted, natural-shoulder Norfolk jacket; and in a dream sequence brought to life as he reads to Marguerite from *Manon Lescaut,* he dons an eighteenth-century nobleman's costume consisting of a white wig, a satin doublet, and ruffled collar and cuffs. One thing he had a chance to demonstrate in this picture was how elegantly he wore the clothes Natacha designed or selected for him.

But his acting skills got short shrift. His big moment in the death-bed scene was simply deleted, although Rambova said he played it so convincingly that even the extras were mopping tears from their eyes. Rudy entered fully into whatever role he was playing, "living" his parts. The original uncut deathbed scene ends with him emotionally spent, his head buried in his arms. A scene showing the auction of Marguerite's effects and Armand bidding for possession of the volume *Manon Lescaut* he'd once given her also ended up on the cutting-room floor. The only way Nazimova could monopolize the emotion was by excising Armand, a move *Variety* lamented as "arrant misconception."

Nazimova did allow Valentino a few episodes of on-camera passion. He was especially adept at shows of self-abnegation, and at one point, realizing that his beloved is sick, he falls to his knees before Marguerite, embraces her legs, and cries out (the title says) "I wish I were a relative—your servant—a dog—that I might care for you—

nurse you—make you well." After Armand's father has persuaded Marguerite to give him up, and she pretends not to love Armand anymore, Armand turns cynical and depraved. Now, without love, nothing matters. When he encounters Marguerite at the Hazard d'Or casino, he grabs her roughly and forces her arms behind her back, inflicting pain as he kisses her neck in a sadistic flourish that recalls his Apache-dancing past and foreshadows his character in *The Sheik*. He raises his arms over her throat, as if he wants to choke her. With a crazed look, he mocks her in front of the crowd: "You see that woman? I loved her more than life itself—but I was poor and could not pay! I pay her now." He reaches into his pocket and pulls out a wad of bills won at the roulette table and hurls the money at Marguerite as she drops to the floor in a heap. This was the cruel Valentino, the "sex-menace" that sent shivers down feminine spines. Combined with his ability to submit, it makes a potent love cocktail.

Off the set Rudy and Natacha were falling in love, and there are idyllic photos of them picnicking outdoors during a lunch break, Rudy resting his head on her breast. (Not too many other candid photos catch the two of them being relaxed and affectionate. Generally, in the presence of a camera, they arranged themselves in carefully choreographed poses.) The company as a whole got on well together, although the director, Ray Smallwood, resented Nazimova's usurpation of his powers, and the teenager Patsy Ruth Miller privately balked at Natacha's prima ballerina airs.

Between takes Rudy kidded a lot, and initially this irritated Natacha, who remembered: "At that time I was very serious, running about in lowheeled shoes and taking squints at my sets and costumes. Rudy was forever telling jokes and forgetting the point of them, and I thought him plain dumb. Then it came over me . . . that he was trying to please, to ingratiate himself. . . . 'Oh, the poor child,' I thought. 'He just wants to be liked—he's lonely.'" Once she perceived him as needy, her irritation melted away. They danced together at a party following a costume ball at the Ambassador Hotel, she decked out as

Cleopatra and he in his gaucho costume from *The Four Horsemen*, and from that moment their closeness increased. Rudy found himself overwhelmed by Natacha's combination of beauty, mysterious allure, and command.

In her recollections, Natacha ignores the physical side of their attraction, and in rather stilted language highlights Rudy's loneliness, sweetness, and childlike naiveté. "It wasn't love at first sight," she recalled. "I think it was good comradeship more than anything else." Natacha, who (along with other bookish Americans of the day) must have been reading Freud, said repeatedly that he appealed to her "maternal instinct." She characterized him as "at heart, a little boy, a child." The soulful outsider in Rudy, not the warmhearted enthusiast of good food and good company, appealed to her. "I liked the fact that after work he didn't go in for café life, nor did he run around with girls and women, but was quiet and rather dignified and lonely and apart." In other words, Natacha saw him as a male counterpart to herself—a nonjoiner.

She also liked his willingness to sit at her feet like an acolyte, worshipful and eager to learn. "We talk about . . . books, new plays, the modern art movement, and of course our work. Our tastes are very similar." She had the edge in worldliness and cultural sophistication, and he enjoyed playing apprentice to her sorceress. "The more cultured and accomplished a woman is, the more exquisite she is to love," he once remarked. Mother figure, Egyptian queen, tutor in culture—however Natacha played it, the power was all hers.

They spent more and more time together. He attended the Los Angeles premiere of *The Four Horsemen* at the Mission Theater with Natacha—resplendent in a white-feathered cloche hat—on his arm. Earlier, John Gilbert and his wife, Leatrice Joy, had joined them at a Santa Barbara preview of the picture. According to Gilbert and Joy's daughter, Leatrice Gilbert Fountain, whose source was her mother, the tumultuous acclaim that greeted him after the screening left Valentino trembling and all keyed up. Afterward they drove with the Gilberts to the Desert Inn in Palm Springs, where Rudy calmed down in the wee hours by commandeering its kitchen to make tiny baked meatballs for his celebrated spaghetti sauce. After dinner he took a long walk by himself in the desert, trying to come to terms with a new and terrifying acquaintance: fame.

Palm Springs would continue to play a big role in their lives, providing an escape hatch that was within easy reach of Los Angeles but had none of its tumult. On weekends they might don cowboy togs and go riding and camping in the desert canyons, "cooking huge steaks over charred embers." Rudy dreamed of playing a cowboy one day in the movies. Natacha had a friend in Palm Springs, Dr. Florilla White, who sometimes joined them on horseback; Rudy also befriended the local hermit and nature boy, the German-born William Pester, and explored the Indian baths.

Or they would stay home in Hollywood and play house. In his days of living with his mother, Rudy had acquired useful domestic skills. He loved getting his hands dirty, tinkering with carpentry tools and helping Natacha fix up her pint-sized home. Natacha had rented a one-bedroom bungalow at 6612 Sunset Boulevard, where Rudy often joined her to cook up a platter of spaghetti after work. Sometimes guests such as June Mathis and her mother, Virginia, joined them. When time allowed, said Natacha, "Rudy would come out and do all sorts of handy jobs about the house for me. He'd do electric wiring and he'd make little perfume tables and smoking stands and hang all of my prints and pictures." Together they painted all her furniture with shiny black and red paint, to make it look as much as possible like Chinese lacquer. They painted her oblong bed black. Natacha's mother, now the wife of Richard Hudnut, a wealthy cosmetics magnate, paid a visit and said (probably not out loud) that the bed looked like a casket and the bedroom like a chapel in a morgue.

Eventually, Rudy moved into the bungalow. He and Natacha spent considerable time in the casketlike bed in the morguelike bedroom. When they first lived together, their relationship was intensely passionate and physical. Two dancers with beautiful, fit bodies, they did not shy from nudity but positively reveled in it. A famous double portrait of them, taken in 1922 by James Abbe, shows them apparently nude from the waist up, and Natacha once said that Rudy "looked best nude."

She compared his perfect body to a statue in the Naples Museum—
perhaps one of Eros, or a satyr.

The chief witness to their supercharged intimacy was Paul Ivano,
who was saving money by bunking on the living-room couch at the
bungalow. (At this time he was involved with Nazimova, so the two
couples sometimes made a foursome: mixed doubles.) Decades later,
asked by Anthony Slide whether Natacha was a lesbian, Ivano responded with an emphatic, "No, no, no, no." He went on to describe
the time Rudy woke him at four in the morning, in a panic. Natacha
had passed out during lovemaking, and Rudy was sure he had killed
her. Ivano asked Rudy, who still had an erection, if he and Natacha had
been making whoopee. "He said, 'Oh yes, for quite a while.'" Ivano
then awakened Natacha by dropping a sponge soaked in water on her.

One wonders about the presence of a third person, Ivano, during
an intense love affair's first flaming. Most couples would find this intrusive and inhibiting, especially in close quarters. There were probably many occasions when Ivano absented himself from the bungalow,
but the story about the time Natacha passed out suggests that the
lovers could become so absorbed in one another they became oblivi-
ous of the outside world. When they were a threesome, all seem to
have gotten along well. Ivano stands out as the only close male friend
of Rudy's who expressed affection and compassion for Natacha.

They had to exist on a tight budget, and splitting the rent three
ways made good financial sense. Although Natacha had been legally
adopted by her stepfather, Richard Hudnut, and knew she might inherit considerable wealth someday, right now she took fierce pride in
earning her own keep and was the highest-paid member of the trio.
What she collected as a designer for Nazimova she supplemented with
income garnered from private students in design. She sold some inherited jewels, and allowed Rudy to sell her Buick runabout; he traded
it for a gas-guzzling 1914 Cadillac roadster and pocketed a four-
hundred-dollar profit on the deal. Then, the three friends devised a
plan to turn Rudy's growing celebrity into cash. They bought a printing box that allowed them to reproduce one hundred Valentino photographs a night; they dried them on the floor, then affixed a signature
on each with a rubber stamp. Since sacks of Valentino fan mail arrived

each day, they decided to answer each letter with a postcard saying that for twenty-five cents the fan could receive a signed photo of the star. The coins rolled in. "I used to open up the letters and count the quarters," Ivano remembered. "Between pictures, it fed us." Within the next year the number of fan letters became so vast that they turned the task of answering them over to Natacha's maid.

Rudy and Natacha also sometimes put food on the table by becoming hunters and gatherers. They'd collect mussels at low tide, and Rudy would cook them up into a sauce for pasta at dinnertime. Or, with Natacha at the wheel, Rudy would perch on the hood of their roadster as they cruised the Robertson-Cole ranch outside Santa Monica at dawn looking for quarry. Rudy, who had probably learned to shoot as a boy in Apulia, would take aim at and bag quails, doves, and rabbits. At night, they'd feast on that day's take.

It's somewhat surprising that hunting small game seems to have raised no ripples of guilt in two people who professed to be fanatical animal lovers. On the contrary, Natacha's account, in her memoir, of their forays into the ranch in search of edible prey serves as a prelude to her rhapsodic summary of these days as "the happiest . . . I shall ever experience in this life. They were days of laughter, days of dreams and of ambitious planning." Although Rudy's fame had begun to mushroom, they still enjoyed a degree of freedom from relentless scrutiny by the press, and they still could luxuriate in occasional anonymity.

Among Rudy and Natacha's dreams for the future was a plan to create a small zoo of their own someday. In preparation, they would visit zoos in the area and spend time with Curley Stecker, a Universal Studio animal trainer who allowed them to watch a famous comedy chimp named Joe Martin go through his paces, or Brownie the Wonder Dog perform tricks. From Curley Natacha purchased a six-week-old lion cub named Zela, who came to live at the bungalow along with their two Great Danes, a large gopher snake, and a green monkey. Although Curley warned the couple that lion cubs make poor house pets, Zela and Rudy, "infinitely patient with animals," developed a special rapport. The lion cub would follow him around "like an adoring puppy," as in a scene in the 1922 film *The Young Rajah*, in which Rudy's character keeps a baby cheetah in his rooms at Harvard. But the fact

that the adorable cub could turn nasty in tooth and claw was amply
demonstrated when Zela attacked the leg of an intruder, who turned
out to be a detective hired by Jean Acker to gather evidence that
Valentino was cohabiting with a woman not his wife. Next time her
victim might be someone more innocent. The neighbors were not
amused when Zela learned to open the catches on the window screens
and go out for a stroll. Probably fed up, Ivano decided to look for his
own place. And Rudy and Natacha reluctantly agreed to take Zela to
be boarded with a trainer outside of town.

At this early stage in their togetherness, Rudy and Natacha participated in Hollywood's social life more than at any subsequent time.
They attended Nazimova's dinner parties, where they might encounter émigré musicians such as Feodor Chaliapin or Leopold
Godowsky, or the famous theatrical actress Eva Le Gallienne. Sometimes they would go with Nazimova and her partner of that evening to
Wednesday night dances at the Sunset Inn in Venice. Wednesday was
"Photoplayers Night" and there was always a dance contest. "The cinemese toddle[d] to jazzy strains." There, Alice Lake and Viola Dana
might be engaging in slangy chatter, Buster Keaton and Fatty Arbuckle
might break up the entire room with their antics on the dance floor,
and Gloria Swanson would turn heads with her stagy entrances and
glamorous gowns. There Rudy and Charles Bryant, who had previously kept their distance, got drunk together one Wednesday night,
prompting a spat between Rudy and Natacha about whether Rudy was
fit to drive her home. He lost. She drove.

Deliriously happy with Natacha at his side and a cosmopolitan circle of
friends, Rudy found his professional life less gratifying. He was again
working under Rex Ingram, this time in *The Conquering Power*, June
Mathis's adaptation of Balzac's *Eugénie Grandet*, a family saga about the
human toll of greed that contrasts the opulence of 1820s Paris with
the austerity of a household in provincial France. During shooting of
The Four Horsemen, Rudy and Ingram had managed to maintain an uneasy peace. Now they clashed head-on over the issue of Rudy's salary,
unconsciously demonstrating that Balzac's nineteenth-century axiom

that money governs human affairs had lost none of its pith by the 1920s. Rudy asked for a raise of a hundred dollars a week. Ingram refused.

The dispute over Rudy's salary represented a wider rift over star status. Metro had two categories for actors: "artists" and "stars." Rudy had become a luminary in the eyes of the public and most movie journalists; Ingram continued to see himself as the main attraction, and he thought Rudy's new celebrity had turned the young actor's head. When an actor's ego takes off, Ingram once said, "the star plays the star, not the character in the story." He would later cut Valentino down to size by calling him "just a good-looking lucky guy who copped a sensational role [in *The Four Horsemen*] and a good cameraman and had a . . . well-publicized funeral." Ingram would soon participate with apparent enthusiasm in the elevation to stardom of Ramon Novarro, an extra in *The Four Horsemen* who would get his big break playing Rupert of Hentzau in Ingram's *The Prisoner of Zenda* and go on to star in four more Ingram pictures. So it clearly wasn't stardom that bothered Ingram, it was Rudolph Valentino as star.

Ingram complained that Valentino, cast as the Paris dandy Charles Grandet in *The Conquering Power*, no longer took direction well, that he sulked when he didn't get his way, and that he especially took umbrage at being corrected in front of his colleagues on the set. Valentino, for his part, objected to having his impulses as an actor squelched. He had devoted many days to preparing to play Charles. He read the Balzac novel and studied the Mathis script. He fretted over what the elegant, impeccable Charles should wear, insisting that every detail of costuming had to be just so, "even to the monocle worn," along with a gray suit, spats and a derby, when he arrives by chauffeured sedan at his uncle's austere home. He spent days practicing with the monocle. But Ingram would rarely let him play a scene as he wished. He gave more thought to the work of his fiancée, Alice Terry, as the gentle, trusting Eugénie and Ralph Lewis's performance as her tightfisted father.

Ingram lavished most of his attention on visual effects in which he collaborated with the art director Ralph Barton, a chum of his from Yale who later became renowned as a caricaturist, and the cameraman, John Seitz. If *The Four Horsemen* provided a wide canvas for epic vistas, *The Conquering Power* offered Ingram a chance to frame cameo portraits, candlelit domestic interiors, and intimate garden landscapes. "He had shown that he could do the overpowering Michelangelo thing and now he wanted to show that he could also excel in the quiet Vermeer genre," said critic Dewitt Bodeen decades later. Both films have their phantasmagoric moments, and both conjure visions and shadows, the cameramen using experimental lenses for what was called "spirit photography." Innovative lighting effects during the climactic scene that closes in on a mad Père Grandet's ghostly visions while he is sequestered with his hoarded gold won deserved accolades. So did *The Conquering Power*'s pictorial impact as a whole. A reviewer of the day marveled: "Mr. Ingram's groups fall, dissolve and fall again into pictures so well composed that one regrets the necessity for continuous movement." The film won high marks as a work of art, but failed to pack the wallop or match the box-office heft of *The Four Horsemen*.

June Mathis wrote the scenario for *The Conquering Power* and she did her best to turn it into a star vehicle for her pet, Valentino. Where Balzac's novel places Père Grandet, a rich, miserly, Loire Valley landowner and his saintly daughter, Eugénie, at the center of the action, Mathis attempted to shift the focus in the direction of Valentino's character, Charles, Eugénie's sophisticated Parisian cousin. She also revised Charles's moral essence, turning Balzac's shallow fortune hunter into a romantic hero whose devotion to Eugénie withstands years of enforced separation. Where the novel ends with Charles's callow engagement to a titled Parisian, the movie has him return to the faithful Eugénie just in time to save her from a loveless marriage to the ugly local magistrate. We're asked to believe that it's pure love, not the fortune Eugénie has inherited, that pulls Charles back. When it comes to converting literary gold into Hollywood corn, this happy ending ranks right up there with the finale of the Greta Garbo and John Gilbert vehicle, *Love*, a restyled *Anna Karenina* that rescues Anna from the train tracks and envelops her in Vronsky's ardent arms.

In *The Conquering Power*'s opening sequence, which has no counterpart in the novel, Charles Grandet is celebrating his twenty-seventh birthday with an extravagant, decadent party at his father's Paris mansion. Once again—this marks the third time in as many major roles—

Valentino appears as a tuxedo-clad Parisian *roué* addicted to champagne, beautiful women, and late-night revelry. It's a European upper-class version of his lounge-lizard set piece. Between cigarettes and sips of bubbly from a long-stemmed glass, he kisses his mistress, Annette, slipping a diamond bracelet onto her wrist while an alluring dancer, clad in flimsy chiffon, performs a suggestive "cooch" dance in the background. He's the pampered, idle son of a banker who has suddenly fallen on hard times. Charles's partying comes to an abrupt halt when his father soberly informs him that his bank has failed and that Charles must leave Paris at once and go to stay with his rich uncle in the Loire Valley, an uncle long estranged from Charles's father. The Charles we see after the wild party is an affectionate son who sits on the arm of his father's chair and embraces him as he tries to take in the bad news. He has no idea how grave his circumstances are, no idea that his beloved father plans to kill himself after Charles departs for the provinces.

In an opening title, June Mathis tells the audience that this film is not a costume play because "commercialism tells us that you, Great Public, do not like the costume play." Instead, "we made our story of today." Some critics objected to the intrusion of modern touches into a story set a few decades after the French Revolution. In particular, they sounded off about the chauffeured four-door sedan that delivers Charles to his uncle's cold doorstep, about the contemporary fountain pen he uses to sign a legal document, and especially about Charles's up-to-date gentleman's attire. The reviewer for the *New York Review* found it jarring to see Charles "dress like a Broadway fashion plate of the present day." But Ingram defended the seeming anachronisms by pointing out that a rich Parisian would have shown off fashionable belongings, things that would seem both novel and extravagant to thrifty, backward country folk. Ingram had a point, but the viewer's confusion about where in time the action unfolds is easy to understand.

No matter how much June Mathis wanted to provide Valentino with opportunities to shine, she could not get around the fact that in Balzac's story Charles Grandet disappears for long stretches of the action. (In the novel he goes to the Indies to become a slave trader; in the picture, Martinique is his specified destination and there's no mention

of slave trading.) Rudy's feeling that as a star he deserved more camera time could not alter this circumstance. Maybe Ingram did cut out
some of his scenes. Perhaps Valentino would have been dissatisfied
even if he'd been suitably well paid, even if Rex Ingram had valued him
and allowed him star billing. We can't know that, but we do know that
he took his role's less than stellar size as a personal insult, that he and
Ingram quarreled on the set, and that one of the points of contention
between them had to do with costuming.

Rudy loved to wear his full dress clothes at gala events either on or
off the screen and he took great pains with the details of his attire for
the opening-scene festivities. Natacha would recall, "Just as they were
about to start shooting Rex [Ingram] suddenly stopped and bawled
him out before all the extras. It was something about a vest, a black
one or a white one. Whichever it was, Rex said it should be the other
one. Words flew. . . . Rudy told Rex he knew nothing about clothes, a
trench coat being the only thing he ever wore." (Ingram did not own a
tux; he had to borrow one from Rudy for a Metro dinner.) Insulted before his peers, the volatile Rudy immediately thought of challenging
Rex to a duel, as an offended nobleman in Europe might have done a
few decades back. One of the reasons Rudy developed a reputation for
being thin-skinned is that he *was* highly sensitive and easily offended.

Part of Valentino's new celebrity resided in his European brand of
elegance. This attention-grabbing masculine sartorial splendor was
something new and fascinating to American movie audiences, especially women. While in New York with Natacha and Nazimova to attend the special screening of *Camille* at the Ritz-Carlton Hotel—an
event attended by such notables as the Gish sisters, the Talmadge sisters, D. W. Griffith, Mary Pickford, the writer Booth Tarkington, and
the movie mogul Adolph Zukor—Rudy gave interviews at his hotel to
several women reporters who commented in print on how flamboyantly and fashionably he dressed. One wrote, "He received me in his
bedroom, surrounded by two other signors and one count. He had on
a dressing gown trimmed in yellow. His nails and his manner are both
highly polished." He impressed another with his "Bright Spats and/His
Slick Hair and/His Cane and/His Lemon-colored Gloves." Yellow!

Aubrey Beardsley's favorite color. Already the line between Valentino the man and the characters he played on-screen had blurred. Before the cameras or in the privacy of his hotel, he embodied the opposite type from the all-American boy or the gun-toting rider of the purple sage: the elegant, slightly outlandish European dandy, a *boulevardier*.

Rudy and Natacha both yearned for Europe and talked about their hopes for getting back there someday to live and work. They agreed that European motion-picture centers would offer an atmosphere less saturated by commercialism and more friendly to the art film than Hollywood. They would have been willing to relocate to Paris in a minute. In New York Rudy met the French director Abel Gance, who was in the States to arrange distribution of his antiwar film *J'Accuse*; Rudy asked Gance whether he could help him make contacts with French producers. Gance reported that Valentino said, "I must get away from [America]. It's so artificial. I want to get back to Europe," but Gance advised him to stay put. "I told him I could do very little for him. He was doing well in America and he should stay."

Rudy's restlessness, money problems, and discontent with Hollywood were genuine, but at this point such grumblings were submerged by more positive and powerful feelings like excitement about his success and happiness in his love life. Louella Parsons interviewed him at the Claridge Hotel in New York and wrote him up as an enthusiastic, polite, and charming gadabout who, after watching Suzanne Lenglen play tennis doubles, "headed straight for the Palais Royal to join a party. He is young and gay and happy with all the spirit of youth and the impulse to get the most out of life while he may."

The New York visit occurred soon after Rudy had made a career decision that Natacha and Ivano thought flew in the face of his ambition to continue acting in art films. He gave up on Metro and defected to Famous Players–Lasky, a studio dedicated to making commercial pictures that would draw the widest possible audience. For his first role at the new studio, he would trade in his Parisian tuxedo for an Arab sheik's flowing robes and burnoose headdress.

9

DARK LOVER

Those who claim that Natacha Rambova masterminded Valentino's film career fail to take into account his fateful decision to sign a contract with Famous Players–Lasky in July of 1921, a move Natacha and Paul Ivano only heard of after the fact. They both exploded with anger when they learned the details: two film-contract brokers, Clifford Robertson and Eugene Webb, Jr., earned a $25,000 bonus for working out an agreement with the industry giant Famous Players–Lasky (later to become Paramount) that would pay Valentino $500 a week for his first picture at his new studio, commit him to Famous Players–Lasky for a year, and give the studio an option to renew for two additional years. Natacha and Paul thought he had undersold himself—by tens, maybe hundreds, of thousands of dollars—to the rich, aggressive production company and theater chain headed by New York's Adolph Zukor and California's Jesse Lasky. They thought he was worth far more, and that the studio could well afford to pay it. Famous Players–Lasky was a company geared to producing, exhibiting, and distributing motion pictures with gonzo commercial appeal, but his friends feared it might not have Rudy's best interests at heart. And Natacha worried that Famous Players–Lasky had no stake in making artistic or cutting-edge films like the productions she so brilliantly designed for Nazimova.

Back in 1912 when Adolph Zukor, a Hungarian-born former furrier, founded Famous Players, with its slogan "Famous Players in Famous Plays," upgrading the lowly "flicker" into high-grade entertainment had been very much on his mind. He courted opera stars and serious dramatic talents from the legitimate stage to emote before the cameras, urging them to lend their prestige in exchange for high salaries and worldwide recognition. Lasky, too, the head of the Jesse L. Lasky Feature Play Company, founded in 1913; went after "quality" talent. Both executives still liked to attract respected figures such as Somerset Maugham or J. M. Barrie to their ranks. But by the early 1920s, the battle for legitimacy had been won. American movies had secured their place as the world's most popular form of entertainment. Cinema audiences had long since broadened to include the elite and respectable middle-class types along with neighborhood immigrants and working folk. All classes mingled at posh picture palaces, soaking up the glamour that stars and their opulent surroundings projected. With the postwar consumer boom, the consolidation of Zukor's company with Jesse Lasky's, the acquisition of theaters, and of Paramount's vast distribution network, the company cared less about attracting highbrow and upscale audiences than it once had. Not that the moguls had anything against the lofty organ strains conjured by masterpieces of cinema art; prestige properties were welcome, so long as they came accompanied by a steady ring from the cash register.

The Famous Players–Lasky goal was to expand its corporate empire by turning out professional, finished, appealing pictures that drew in the multitudes without rocking any boats. That meant mass production of large numbers of features designed for mainstream marketing. A bankable star helped assure box-office success. The studio chiefs, all from Eastern European Jewish backgrounds except the West Coast–born Lasky, went to great lengths trying to pick up on current American trends and popular tastes, and then to feed them with a constant stream of new pictures. If the public clamored for a particular actor or actress, that demand had to be gratified over and over again, which meant stars had to keep working at a steady clip. "The public is never wrong" was Zukor's philosophy, and it would become the title of his memoir. Production had to function with the efficiency and speed of an assembly line. "In the twenties," Lasky later wrote in his memoir, "I was turning out a continuous flow of pictures like a frozen-custard machine, Sidney Kent was selling them like hot cakes, and Adolph Zukor was collecting theatre chains like postage stamps." Stars, too, became products to be merchandised like frozen custard, hot cakes, or stamps.

Valentino's frustration and fury at Metro's indifference to his proven drawing power is easy to understand. Here he was, the red-hot romantic sensation whose performance as Julio had helped turn *The Four Horsemen of the Apocalypse* into one of the top moneymakers in film history and who had delivered good performances in three subsequent Metro pictures, and he couldn't even get his name above the title, much less on a decent contract. He had no security, no future pictures lined up. His salary of $400 a week seemed a pittance compared to what other stars and top crew earned. Nazimova at her peak made $10,000 a week. Metro in 1921 was paying its star Viola Dana $1,750 a week, second only to Bert Lytell's $2,000-a-week salary. June Mathis was making $750 weekly and Rex Ingram $1,000. Constance Talmadge in 1920 was paid $300,000 by First National for each picture. The screen cowboy William S. Hart had been offered $200,000 a picture by Famous Players–Lasky three years earlier, but had threatened to bolt from that studio and join the newly formed United Artists because he wanted a bigger say in his films, more power over the productions his name helped sell.

At Metro Valentino had no voice whatsoever in selecting his scripts and in choosing his own screenwriters and directors; Rex Ingram, June Mathis, or Nazimova took charge of all that. In 1919 Pickford, Fairbanks, and Chaplin with D. W. Griffith had founded their own studio, United Artists, because they wanted to control and directly profit from the movies they appeared in or created. Unlike most actors employed by major studios, they were trying to be captains of their fates. At Metro Valentino was treated little better than a hired hand who could easily be replaced.

Rudy thought that Rex Ingram had it in for him, that Ingram had convinced easygoing Metro president Richard Rowland that Rudy was "just a flash in the pan, that he was impossible to direct," and that after his lucky strike as Julio he would never amount to much. Other studios were dangling offers before him (at least that's what Rudy told Louella Parsons, and it was plausible), but he chose to go with Famous Players–Lasky. We can guess at his reasons. One, surely, was that Famous Players–Lasky represented the vast resources and clout of corporate power at its zenith; it was "the United States Steel Corp. of the motion picture industry," so dominant that it would soon be accused of hogging the field through unfair trade practices. Its roster of employees and associates included five-star names such as Cecil B. DeMille (who had his own production unit), and the actors Fatty Arbuckle, Wallace Reid, and Gloria Swanson. Its productions—especially those mounted by DeMille and starring Gloria Swanson—received accolades for their glossy finish, lavish sets, and sumptuous costumes. Natacha's designs might have fit in at DeMille productions, but unfortunately her *bête noire,* Theodore Kosloff, was acting in DeMille pictures, and the designer Paul Iribe was filling the slot that might have been hers. Moreover, Jesse Lasky had signed June Mathis around the same time he signed Valentino, luring her away from Metro with the understanding that she would continue to develop and write scripts for her protégé. Rudy had faith in June Mathis. She had worked her magic for him before and he had no doubt she could do it again. He felt safe with her on board.

In his autobiography, Jesse Lasky recalls being awed by Valentino's electric performance in *The Four Horsemen.* "He had more sheer animal magnetism than any actor before or since." Lasky, a former vaudeville cornet player from San Francisco who became a booker and theater owner before entering the movie business, sensed at once that the young Italian who played Julio would become "one of the greatest box-office draws of all time." He couldn't fathom his good luck when, shortly after the Los Angeles premiere of *The Four Horsemen,* Valentino appeared at his office one afternoon to ask if Famous Players–Lasky happened to have a part for him. "At first I couldn't believe he was serious," Lasky remembered. How could a comer like Valentino remain at large and unsigned? How had those numbskulls running Metro allowed such a once-in-an-era catch to slip out of their net? With the resources at their command, Lasky felt confident that he and Zukor could turn Valentino into "the biggest star we've ever had."

Valentino's visit to Lasky didn't occur entirely out of the blue. Before the opening of *The Four Horsemen*, early in 1921, he had stopped at the Vine Street offices of Famous Players–Lasky and filled out an application that remained on file. In it he stated that he had worked at Metro, Fox, and Universal Studios, that he could ride, drive, and swim, and that he stood five feet ten and a half inches tall (really?), weighed one hundred and sixty pounds, had black hair and eyes, a waist of thirty-two and a chest of thirty-six inches. Lasky more than likely checked the file, and after seeing *The Four Horsemen* he may well have written to Valentino suggesting that he drop by for a friendly chat.

In his office Lasky wooed Valentino—who didn't need a whole lot of coaxing—by telling him that gradually, over time, as a Famous Players–Lasky leading man he could expect both higher pay and a measure of control over the choice of material and personnel on his pictures. He said he would bring in June Mathis to develop scripts custom-fitted to his talents, but that was just the beginning. Lasky mentioned as an example of how the studio treated its top actors the case of Thomas Meighan, a popular, rugged-looking all-American type whose contract gave him "say as to directors, casting, editing and other matters connected with his pictures," Valentino would attest. "Mr. Lasky also stated to me that my salary would be increased from time to time as the value of my services justified it, . . . that they would make such increases voluntarily." Lasky painted a picture of the corporate giant as a family, in which "the company would treat me like a son." They would all be partners in a joint effort. Lasky promised that "if ever anything developed that I considered needed correction, I need only speak to him or [studio manager] Mr. Charles Eyton and that they would do all that they could for my success."

Lasky put his secretary on alert; she should keep an eye out for material that would suit a Latin hero. She shot back, "But Mr. Lasky—you already have the best possible story for him!" She meant the romantic novel now all the rage in England and the United States—especially among women readers—Edith M. Hull's bodice ripper, *The Sheik*.

Lasky records in his autobiography that he paid $12,500 for the screen rights, defying a budget limit of $10,000 per property. Zukor, in *his* autobiography, swears the studio paid $50,000 for said screen rights, and *Variety* gave yet another figure, stating that the novel fetched only $7,500; so it's anybody's guess whose figure was correct. Whatever they paid, both Zukor and Lasky knew that having bagged rights to *The Sheik* they had a potential blockbuster on their hands. As a book, *The Sheik* had sold well enough to put it on the best-seller lists; it went through fifty printings in the United States alone in 1921. As a movie it could reach an even vaster audience, an audience of screen fans numbering in the millions that was estimated to be 60 percent female—and the percentage of women was on the rise.

Offered the role of Sheik Ahmed Ben Hassan, Valentino signed on after consulting his agents, Robertson and Webb, and agreeing to terms they worked out. He would begin shooting within days. He was aware that for this first picture with Famous Players–Lasky he would have to manage without June Mathis, because a script for *The Sheik* had already been written by Monte Katterjohn. Neither he nor his agents insisted on any written guarantees about his star billing. "July 5 [1921] is the date set for the start of George Melford's new Paramount production, *The Sheik*," reported *Moving Picture World*. "Mr. Lasky stated that he had engaged Rudolph Valentino for the title role. The part is considered ideal for Valentino, who is a dashing and colorful actor with unusually good looks and much ability."

At the time he purchased rights to *The Sheik* Lasky had mulled over several casting choices for the lead but had rejected them all. "Wallace Reid was too much the good-natured big-brother type, Rod La Rocque too suave and sophisticated, Thomas Meighan too wholesome and casual." Lasky didn't include in this list the name of one actor with whom he had actually discussed the role, James Kirkwood. Kirkwood, once a Griffith star, was about as foreign looking as Tom Mix, but that wasn't the only thing wrong with him. He came with too high a price tag.

When Lasky, the company vice president in charge of production in California, wrote to boss Adolph Zukor in New York about his coup in landing Valentino, "the remarkable boy" who had played Julio in *The*

Four Horsemen, for the lead in *The Sheik*, he said he was sure the young Latin would make a wonderful Sheik. Then he boasted about his prize's additional asset: he was a low-ticket, bargain-basement item. Lasky said he had managed to cut the picture's production costs by 50 percent across the board from what they'd originally projected. Valentino would be paid $500 per week, whereas Kirkwood was accustomed to earning $1,750. "Kirkwood finally came down to $1,250 after I talked with him, but refused to accept $1,000. In the meantime, we found Valentino, and Kirkwood is out of a job."

After a period of unprecedented growth, Famous Players–Lasky was facing an economic crunch and had set out to eliminate or crop all expenditures they considered excessive. Lasky announced that cutting production costs "is the only thing that is going to keep the picture industry on its feet at this time." They decided to shut down the New York studio for the present and concentrate production in Hollywood. And they attacked the matter of expensive personnel. The salaries paid to leading actors had gotten way out of hand, the top brass believed. In a statement that appeared in the very issue of *Moving Picture World* that carried news of Valentino's casting as the Sheik, Lasky warned, "Abnormal and wasteful salaries, needless and wasteful extravagance . . . must come to an end."

Worries about his relatively paltry salary and about whether his contract option would be renewed troubled Valentino somewhat while he was filming *The Sheik*, according to one of his co-players, Adolphe Menjou, but not enough to spoil his expansive mood. He was having too much fun. "Loving riding and all outdoor life as he did," Natacha recalled, "Rudy was in his element," especially when the company went on location to shoot the desert exteriors at Oxnard, in Ventura County, and the Guadalupe dunes in Santa Barbara County, "where he could be in the midst of cowboys, camels, and horses, as all the company camped out in tents." Each camp covered nearly half a square mile of sand, and over two hundred people lived there. Eight-year-old Loretta Young, dressed as an Arab, was an extra in the film, along with her sisters Polly Ann Young and Sally Blane; she remembered Rudy, accompanied by his guitar, singing songs by the campfire at night and letting her and the other young extras take rides on his horse. *The Sheik* would put to use for the first time on screen Rudy's expertise as an equestrian; he proved as swift and as capable of derring-do in the saddle as the swashbuckling hero Douglas Fairbanks.

The director, George Melford, as a youth had hoped to join a Wild West show and still loved action, horses, and guns and stalked around in boots, chaps, and a cowboy hat. Rudy got along well with him, calling him Uncle George. For his part, Melford delighted in a leading man physically capable of "doing anything." For the outdoor scenes Melford shouted orders to his cast and crew from the saddle of his horse, while a bugler, stationed near the camera platforms, "blew signals for the various formations to the cavorting horsemen." The entire scene might have been mistaken for the location for a story about Teddy Roosevelt urging his Rough Riders, "Charge!" These were grown-up men fueling a testosterone high with action, speed, and playing at tribal warfare.

With his art director, Rodolph Bylek, and cameraman, William Marshall (Paul Ivano shot the stills), Melford set up striking long shots of Arab horsemen coursing over expanses of undulating pseudo-Saharan sands, their long rifles raised high in the air; and of slow-moving camel caravans outlined in silhouette. Did a cameraman ever meet a desert he didn't like? Some evocative interiors were shot through grilles or curtained entryways. For the atmospheric crowd scenes in Biskra, a town in northeastern Algiers, Melford spliced in Pathé Company stock footage of an actual Algerian town, with its mosques and minarets. For the location scenes Melford assembled "hooded Bedouin horsemen—some of them real Arabs—and every one had his horse, most of them real Arabian steeds. There were harem girls, slave girls, market women, old hags, youngsters." All wore yellow ochre makeup, the kind "that makes the movie player look sunburnt and which, being hard to remove and bad for the complexion, is detested by them."

A realistic re-creation of the North African desert wasn't what Melford set out to evoke. Having set his sights on a popular rather than a highbrow audience, he sought a certain staginess and encouraged an exaggerated acting style. An oasis, not a natural part of the California desert landscape, had to be manufactured and carried along on motor trucks. The Sahara palm trees needed for this tale of desire under the palms were constructed out of wood, canvas, and paint in the workshops of the Famous Players–Lasky studio, where battle scenes between Arab tribes "with their picturesque flowing robes" were also filmed. Even the fake palms were the wrong kind for the African desert—coconut instead of date palms; they eventually found their way to the Cocoanut Grove at the Ambassador Hotel. This was to be a fantasy film, not an attempt at naturalism.

At the back lot of the Famous Players–Lasky studio at Vine and Selma streets a mud village was constructed, "representing the fortified stronghold of the bandit sheik Omair," the villain of the story, played by Walter Long. And, reported *Moving Picture World*, on an interior set re-creating a casino in Biskra, "the African Monte Carlo, a sensational harem scene was staged with Margaret Loomis [a dancer who had trained with the Denishawn dance company] featured in Oriental dances." The casino was fitted out like a dimly lit casbah with gorgeous draperies, curtained entrances, rugs, divans, cushions, and low tables.

"Picturesque" and "Oriental," two favorite adjectives used to describe the exotic background of *The Sheik*, conjure an imaginary world much in fashion in the 1920s and earlier, a world of mystery and fascination that Natacha Rambova and Nazimova tried to evoke whenever they burned incense, assumed Cleopatra poses, painted a table with red lacquer, donned high-collared silk pajamas, applied black kohl around their eyes, or covered their hair with jeweled turbans. At her Garden of Alla, whose very name cast an exotic spell (while punning on the name Allah), Nazimova once hosted a party where the guests were asked to come costumed as Orientals, the men as sultans or sheiks, the woman as houris of the harem. For daring, dark-haired "New Women" like Natacha and Nazimova, whose next film collaboration, *Salome*, would be called "a hot house orchid of decadent passion," the lush textures of the East provided sensual and expressive license. By adapting the style they called Oriental a woman announced herself as more open to eros and beauty than her more conventional or fair-haired sisters. Blondes, in their scheme of things, had decidedly less fun. "Madame [and Natacha, too, most likely] was contemptuous of the baby-faced blondes [like Mary Pickford and Mary Miles Minter] who were flooding the screen," recalled Patsy Ruth Miller. "The quivering lip, the downcast eye, filled her with nausea, she claimed." Not for Madame "such pallid emotions, such saintly sufferings."

The novel *The Sheik* (which, by the way, Natacha disdained as trash) perpetuated an illusion of the North African world as a hotbed of decadent indulgence, but here the men, not the women, held erotic sway. The Algerian desert of *The Sheik* is a place where lecherous potentates loll in their tents on ornately patterned, overstuffed cushions, smoking who knows what while being fanned by half-naked slaves. In this fantasy domain, the Arabs (never called Muslims or Islamites) are pegged as an inferior, primitive breed. Cruel they may be, but they have the edge when it comes to passion; their blood surges in their veins— as a group they're as hot as the burning sands. Arab men supposedly knew how to gratify their senses far better than did their "civilized" French or English masters, who were held back by inhibitions dictated by Christianity's constraints on sin. Edith M. Hull, an English author from Derbyshire, observed North Africa from an imperial perch when she lived in Algeria for a year with her soldier husband. To keep many wives as Arabs did, to trade for wives as if they were pretty rugs, she considered un-Christian and quite shockingly uncouth.

The female Arab, viewed through this imperial Western and Christian lens, enjoyed no status or power but she did hold the trump card of extraordinary sexual allure. (In Katterjohn's script a note on the scene with the native dancing girl says, "This should be within the limitations of the censors, yet rhythmic and undulating.") Part of her power to entice derives from her mysteriousness. Behind the veil, beneath the scantily covered midriff and the scarves she sheds as she twirls, the harem dancer's skin takes on a high-voltage erotic charge because it is at once undulating and concealed, unknown. The Sheik, too, is covered head to toe and therefore is covert, he, too, is exotic in draped capes, tasseled turbans, ornately decorated sashes, and embroidered vests—

his character and clothing combine the womanly quality of mysterious fascination with masculine strength, authority, and fierceness. (Natacha designed Rudy's costumes.) His desert home has shaped him, endowing him with both power and cunning. "The desert is a great hiding place," an intertitle reminds us.

Ads for *The Sheik* ballyhooed the danger, mystery, adventure, and sexual titillation inherent in the story's Algerian desert setting, which the movie camera promised to bring to life:

> SEE the auction of a beautiful girl to the lords of Algerian harems
>
> SEE the barbaric gambling fete in the glittering Casino at Biskra
>
> SEE the heroine, disguised, invade the Bedouin's secret slave rites
>
> SEE Sheik Ahmed raid her caravan and carry her off to his tent
>
> SEE her captured by bandit tribesmen and enslaved by their chief
>
> SEE the Sheik's vengeance, the storm in the desert, a proud woman's heart surrendered
>
> SEE matchless scenes of gorgeous color and wild free life and love in the year's supreme screen thrill—3000 in the cast

The ads highlight the dazzling color and spine-tingling adventure connected to the desert East, but in both book and movie, Sheik Ahmed emerges as a mixture of Western European and Eastern traits. Katterjohn's script paints the interior of the Sheik's tent quarters as "a curious mixture of Oriental luxury and European comfort. It breathes the atmosphere of the barbaric East and the soft luxury of cultural tastes. A divan is covered with black silk cushions and bearskins are spread over Persian rugs. On a Moorish stool is a cigarette bowl filled with long Turkish cigarettes. There is a large Turkish pipe, carved ivory, hammered bronze." Spread about are a few magazines and books. It's a den of iniquity with a college education, a perfect setting not just for Sheik Ahmed, but also for the European but distinctly exotic-looking Rudolph Valentino.

Valentino had been linked to sexy brutality on screen before: when he danced the Apache in *A Rogue's Romance*, when he played a foreign-looking heavy in his prestardom days, when as Julio in *The Four Horsemen of the Apocalypse* he savaged his partner during a sadistic Buenos Aires tango. Once he portrayed the Sheik, his identity as an *homme fatale* took hold on a grand scale. Millions of fans identified him with his character, attributing to him the same combination of sexual menace and air of Oriental mystery along with European polish that Ahmed Ben Hassan displayed. An article for a fan magazine zeroed in on the hypnotic cast of his eyes, attributing to them "a savor of the Orient; his lids are lost beneath the smooth continuance of his brows, lending . . . a hint of mystery. His is a passionate nature over which, for the moment, repression has gained mastery." An ad in *Motion Picture Classic* posed the question "Why Do Women Adore Valentino? Do They Love Him Because He Is: Distinguished, poised, cultured, kind, dignified? . . . Or is It Because He Is: Romantic, dark, mysterious, strong, masterful . . . intriguing?" Readers were asked to choose between the European, "civilized" Valentino and his desert-lover's cruel but enticing otherness. Either way, as a European or a "savage," to mainstream Americans he was the ultimate tall, dark, and handsome stranger. Trying to figure out his appeal, an article in a fan magazine explained, "He does not look like your husband. He is not in the least like your brother. He does not resemble the man your mother thinks you ought to marry." Of course, for legions of female fans, as for Lady Diana in the story, it was the *combination*, the fusion of both aspects, that proved so hard to resist.

Valentino's dark complexion might have been highlighted as an asset, since he was playing a hot-blooded, charismatic Arab chieftain instead of a pale-skinned Frenchman such as Armand Duval or Charles Grandet. But the producers played it safe: only in the posters and lobby cards, especially those in color, does Rudy's skin look tan or even black. On-screen, his face appears white, but his hands show darker. Instead of emphasizing the slant of his eyes, Mont Westmore, the makeup man, made them appear larger than they were by arching his brows high over his heavy lids. As the Sheik, Valentino has his signature patent-leather hair completely covered by his decorated white turban and burnoose, and his tuxedo-perfect physique is concealed under flowing white sleeves and long, draped capes, but there's still plenty of dramatic black in the frame. Patterns on his headdress and on his striped tent look black and white on untinted film. The Turkish-coffee color of his eyes becomes more emphatic with makeup that subtly outlines them with black eyeliner and darkens his already dark brows. The dark pupils stand out against the whites of his eyes, especially when he widens them to signify desire, a pantomime trick that Valentino may have picked up from Natacha (who in turn had been tutored by Kosloff) and that he overindulges shamelessly, egged on by Melford. His white steed competes with the whiteness of Sahara sand; so do the perfect teeth he flashes with the frequent sneering smiles—right out of melodrama villainy—that mock his captive Lady Diana's shows of quaking fear.

When the Sheik first sets eyes on this young, headstrong British blonde, Lady Diana Mayo, the first thing that attracts him is her beauty, which rivets his attention, eliciting a Svengali stare that she returns without a flinch. Her defiance—she even pulls a gun on him—is a challenge he belittles and enjoys. It prods her desire. Next he notices and savors her whiteness. She has invaded the Biskra casino where he's entertaining a large party at which rich merchants will gamble for their choice of harem wives. Since only Arabs have been invited, Diana has disguised herself as a veiled Arab dancing girl to gain admittance to the casino. But Sheik Ahmed isn't fooled. He recognizes her as a European woman and is smitten at once by her "pale hands and golden hair of a white woman," hands he'll soon praise when serenading her with the lyric "Pale hands I loved beside the Shalimar." (Many modern prints of *The Sheik* substitute another song lyric, the words to "Beautiful Dreamer," for "Pale hands I loved," which doesn't work.) For Sheik Ahmed as for the villainous Omair, no native woman's beauty stands a chance next to that of the fair-haired virgin Diana, whose body is decidedly unvoluptuous and who makes it clear that she disdains men.

We in the audience pick up on the sharp contrast between her "white gazelle" slender fragility and his brown-skinned, muscular brawn. His tan hands are allowed to appear a shade or two darker than his face, so that when he touches Diana's skin or light-colored garment we really notice their brownness. A note in the script says, "Sheik grasps her white, trembling hands in his firm brown grip." He's all man as he struts his broad-shouldered stuff, commanding one and all to do as he bids, puffing smoke he's inhaled from a cigarette in a long holder, fondling a pistol or decisively pulling off Diana's veil in the casino to reveal her white face. He's a phallic dream come true.

His dark stare adds to his magnetism, heightens the potent and "savage" virility that makes him fascinating to Lady Diana, who was played by one of Jesse Lasky's personal favorites, the lackluster Agnes Ayres. (Alice Terry, a far lovelier and more subtle actress, said that she was considered as a possible Lady Diana, but that Rex Ingram wanted her for *Turn to the Right*.) Lady Diana is given only a few emotions to register in her face: disdain at the outset (chin in the air, arched brows), followed by wide-eyed terror, anger (furrowed brow), and, finally, rapturous love (adoring smiles).

Valentino's animal-like sleekness leaps before the camera in a new way when he stalks his female prey with the grace, stealth, and authority of a panther on the prowl, and when he gallops his horse across the wastes of sand as if he and his mount shared the same heartbeat. All in all, Lady Diana and Sheik Ahmed personify the way opposites attract. His brute maleness counters her vulnerable femaleness, and his "savagery" her highly "civilized" Englishness; his dark offsets her white.

The idea that a white woman should be attracted to a dark man is inscribed in Western culture. Think Desdemona and Othello. "On Greek vases the men are darker than the women. In Western painting (since the Middle Ages) Adonis is darker than Venus, Adam than Eve." A movie magazine, commenting in 1923 on Valentino's power over women, explained that "dark people are always more alert, intense, and energetic. They have more concentrated power and nervous force."

But in the racially polarized world of the American 1920s, where the Ku Klux Klan was again on the rise and nativist ideas about white purity were gaining new favor and fervor, care had to be taken to ensure that color boundaries would not be too openly or brazenly breached. Valentino said he had to stay away from the beach and sunbathing in his off hours because "I am very dark in complexion an' the sun it burn me too black for pictures," and "I become like a Negro." Depicting outright miscegenation was a definite no-no, especially in the southern United States and parts of the Midwest, where racists would surely issue calls to arms. The racial passions unleashed by *Birth of a Nation,* which valorized the Klan, were still fresh in memory. Censorship, not yet nationally controlled, loomed as a big worry at the state and municipal levels. (The Production Code would specifically forbid showing miscegenation on-screen when the Hays Office set up shop in 1922.) Everyone connected with making *The Sheik,* from producers to screenwriters to those in charge of makeup, had to try to second-guess the censorship boards and tone down or cut anything in the script that might alienate them or any major portion of the mass audience. Although Valentino movies appealed to immigrants in the cities, especially Italians and Latinos, the white mainstream audience was the one the studio tried hardest to please. The only truly black-skinned actors in *The Sheik* are those who play male Nubian slaves, who have little to do but obey commands and look menacing.

At the beginning of *The Sheik*, Ahmed appears to be a privileged Arab whose wealth, Paris education, and imperious mien distinguish him and equip him to be a forceful tribal leader. He clearly worships Allah, whose name he invokes many times. He shares with other Arab men the view that women exist to obey and gratify men, and that an attractive white woman holds more allure than any woman with dark skin, however beautiful, possibly could. Yet his European background sets him apart. He is different from the other Arab men because he has no harem and because he respects the idea of mutual love as a basis for marriage. In the first words he's given in the intertitles he expresses sympathy with a tribesman who wants to marry Zilah, the Arab woman he loves, and protests seeing her simply handed over to the highest bidder. Sheik Ahmed rules in his favor: "When love is more desired than riches, it is the will of Allah. Let another be chosen." By the end of the picture we find out that Ahmed's blood is European through and through, that his father was an Englishman and his mother Spanish (with Moorish blood, according to Edith Hull), that he was abandoned in the desert and raised by a chieftain to lead an Arab tribe. So, his promised marriage to blue-blooded Lady Diana will win approval even from her snobbish British twit of a brother.

Lady Diana is cut from the same racial cloth as lily-white, virginal Griffith heroines like Lillian Gish, but she has a modern, twenties feminist twist. She's a liberated New Woman, an expert horsewoman who embarks on a desert journey other Englishwomen call reckless because she'll travel accompanied by no white man, only native camel drivers and an Arab guide. "I thoroughly disapprove of this young madcap's wild scheme," an older woman clucks. Dressed boyishly in riding breeches and high boots, Diana packs a revolver along with her riding crop and throws to the winds the cautions common to sheltered, conventional European women. Fearless, athletic, adventurous, and independent, at home in the open expanse of the desert, she abhors anything that puts limits on her freedom. Initially, the Sheik repels her because he, an apparent Arab, has dared to exclude her from the casino. "Why should a savage desert bandit keep us out of any public place?" She hates the very idea of marriage, sneering to an English suitor, "Marriage is captivity—the end of independence." She abominates the way Arab men treat their women, the way rich merchants expect their wives "to obey and serve like chattel slaves."

Jesse Lasky knew very well the timeliness of feminist themes and their appeal to some women moviegoers. As early as 1917 he asked Cecil B. DeMille and the scenarist Jeanie Macpherson to "write something typically American that would portray a girl in the sort of role that the feminists in this country are now interested in . . . the kind of girl that dominates . . . who jumps in and does a man's work."

The Sheik plays with questions about just how dominant and independent a woman should aspire to be, appealing both to women's fantasies of autonomy and their desire to be swept up in love's protective embrace. On one level, it tells the story of Diana's taming. Once defiant, then a captive, Lady Diana ends up nursing Sheik Ahmed, taking care of him after he's wounded in the act of rescuing her from Omair's stronghold. No longer compelled to stay with her Sheik, she elects to stay, having become a slave to love. Broken like a wild Arabian horse that once roamed free, she accepts the harness he offers and finds her maternal, tender side. By her changed behavior she ratifies a hardly subtle credo, one the Sheik shared with Sigmund Freud and Edith Maude Hull: that only by yielding, by shedding their boyish trousers, handing over their revolvers, and becoming nurturers can females realize themselves as fulfilled women.

The night after he first sees Diana in the Biskra casino, Ahmed sneaks into her room as she sleeps; the camera closes in on her soft and dreamy face, her loose hair a tangle of wild curls. (A note in the script says Diana should be shown in a close shot "sleeping in a scrumptious position of some sort of à la dishabille, but nevertheless languorously refined.") The next morning he follows Diana's party on horseback and seizes her as she rides, plucking her with one sweeping motion from her saddle onto his mount. After riding off with her, he sequesters her in his tent. By his lights, he requires no justification for abducting her, beyond his desire to possess her. "When an Arab sees a woman he wants, he takes her." Having seized her, he commands her to change from her riding costume into a dress: "You make a very charming boy, but it was not a boy I saw two nights ago." Later he will costume her in Oriental harem pants and an embroidered vest, humiliating her before Ahmed's visiting French friend, the elegant physician and author Raoul St. Hubert (Adolphe Menjou). "Are you going to let him [St. Hubert] see me like his?" Diana asks, horror-struck that a gentleman from Europe, one of her own kind, should discover her so hideously compromised. After he meets Diana, St. Hubert tries to shame Ahmed: "Does the past mean so little to you that you now steal white women and make love to them like a savage?"

Lady Diana's abduction onto the Sheik's white steed has become one of the camp set pieces in film history, a scene (culminating with his cry, "Lie still, you little fool") that's hard to view as anything but pure hokum and self-parody. Here it was, capsulized in a few swift moments of motion-picture action, "the tale of a lawless Arab Chief who loved an English beauty—and took her!" announced the advertisements. "Stormed her caravan—carried her off to his tent!" The Famous Players ad writers had a field day using this moment to pitch the entire picture, and the popular song "The Sheik of Araby," written in response to the book, not the movie, helped stamp it in public memory. A twenty-four-sheet (billboard-size) poster was produced that was based on a Marshall Frantz oil painting of Valentino as the Sheik, "mounted on a rearing white Arabian horse, seizing Agnes Ayres and about to lift her to the back of the steed. Brilliant contrasting colors [stand out] against the bright blue background."

Audiences in the twenty-first century howl at the scene now, as many first-time viewers—especially male viewers—did in the 1920s. Mack Sennett's lampoon film *The Shriek of Araby* (1922) showed the cross-eyed comic Ben Turpin whisking a baffled Kathryn McGuire off on a white dray horse that's considerably less svelte than most Arabian stallions. But, despite the scoffers, this abduction scene in particular made the hearts of women—not all, but many—go pitter patter. The image of a young maiden being literally swept away by a dark, handsome, and muscular man wild with desire for *her*, the one woman he wants more than any other, set off female hormonal switches. Barbara Cartland, queen of later-twentieth-century romance novelists in England, edited E. M. Hull's *The Sheik* for "Barbara Cartland's Library of Love" in 1977. In her foreword Cartland wrote that in 1921, when she was twenty years old, "We all saw ourselves in the role of Diana Mayo, we all longed to be abducted into the desert and to be forced by sheer violence into obedience by an all-conquering male."

In Edith M. Hull's novel, the abduction was followed by a violent rape that was no laughing matter. "With brutal hands he forced her to obey him, until she wondered if he would leave a single bone unbroken, till further resistance was impossible." In the book, Diana falls in love with Ahmed *because* he physically overpowers her, forcing her to submit when she had refused in the past to give an inch to any man. In the book, he softens his stance and shows love only after "the close union with his warm strong body" has "robbed her of all strength." Hull said she believed man had to prove his dominant power over woman, though she stopped short of endorsing rape. "I have been criticized in America for the so-called 'caveman' methods of my hero," she stated. "I don't wish to . . . defend the callous brutality of Ahmed Ben

Hassan. . . . But I am old fashioned enough to believe that a woman's best love is given to the man . . . she recognizes as her master."

Although ads suggested otherwise, the movie equivocates on the rape. We see the abduction itself, but no subsequent shows of brutal manhandling comparable to later scenes in which Omair captures and attempts to rape Lady Diana in his stronghold; Ahmed arrives at Omair's fort in the nick of time, heroically rescuing Diana from an unspeakable fate that in fact isn't much different from the one Ahmed himself attempted earlier. Sheik Ahmed, the rescuer, acts like a knight in shining armor, but he's demonstrated that he is no saint. He's at least a kidnapper, if not a rapist. His active sadistic side showed itself when he laughed at Diana's quaking and cringing. Once he has made Diana his captive, Sheik Ahmed leers at her, his eyes fairly popping from their sockets as he asks her whether she knows how beautiful she is. He undresses her with his eyes as he indicates the tent's inner chamber with a pointing gesture. "Why have you brought me here?" she demands to know. His lip curls as he sneers, "Are you not woman enough to know?" Although he terrorizes her, forcing a fervid embrace and a hot kiss, he politely leaves her alone to change clothes for dinner, then dines as a gentleman. Nobody actually says so, but apparently her maidenhead is still intact. Or is it? A servant refers to her as "my master's bride." The ladies of Kansas City were horrified enough to have the picture banned locally.

After going out to round up escaped horses in a sandstorm, Ahmed returns to find Diana collapsed in tears, her head buried on her arms. Here a close-up highlights Ahmed's sensitive, tender qualities for the first time. Oh! (pant, sigh) the handsome brute has a conscience after all, a sense of right and wrong! He's hurt by the possibility that Diana wants to be out of his clutches: "You hate them so much, my kisses?" He cares! Otherwise why would he send in the woman servant to comfort Diana? Ahmed, like Julio in *The Four Horsemen*, shows that he's capable of transformation. He begins to see Diana as a lovely highborn lady whom he has treated harshly, not just as the object of his savage lust as she is for the villainous Omair. He puts a rose on her tray before a servant delivers her tea. (On-screen, Valentino often speaks the language of flowers.) Diana angrily throws down the rose, but eventually forgives and yields, learning to love and obey Ahmed without having had her bones crushed by him. When she writes "Ahmed, I love you" in the sand, we know he has melted this uppity iceberg.

Many of the original reviewers of *The Sheik* complained that the movie, in toning down the rape, changed what had originally been the story of a woman overpowered by a man into one about a woman having her way with a compliant male. They argued that Hull's tale had lost its spine in the process of being adapted from book to screen. *Film Daily* reported that in New York the novel's reputation brought throngs to the movie theaters, but that same reputation sent them away "very much disappointed because the daring of the novel hasn't been put into the film version." Well, the report continued, that wasn't the fault of scenario writer Monte Katterjohn, but of the censors. The story as Edith Hull wrote it "wouldn't have a ghost of a chance in escaping the vigilance of those appointed to protect the public's morals." Less forgiving, *Variety* objected that fear of the censors' shears had "bled white" the original. Where Edith Hull's novel "won out because it dealt with every caged woman's desire to be caught up in a love clasp by some he-man," the movie failed to produce equivalent palpitations. Woundingly, they used the language of castration, speaking of the movie version as "mealy, emasculated."

But the paying audience disagreed. *The Sheik* smashed all attendance records when it opened at two theaters in New York, the Rivoli and the Rialto, on October 30. Within weeks of the opening, *The New York Telegraph* estimated, 125,000 people had seen the movie. (During that same period only 90,000 paid to see a newsreel of the July Dempsey-Carpentier fight.) "People are flocking in the maddest crowds to see it," *The New York News* reported. "The country club darlings, now in fur coats, have joined the mob." Zukor and Lasky and their sales force licked their lips as they raked in the dollars. After seeing the finished picture for the first time Lasky wired Zukor: "MELFORD HAS FAR SURPASSED ANY PICTURE HE HAS EVER MADE FOR US AND WE CAN SAFELY GET BEHIND THE SHEIK FOR THE VERY BIGGEST KIND OF MONEY." They designated the last week in November "The

Sheik Week" and arranged first runs at 250 theaters around the country. There was a market overseas, too. In Sydney, Australia, the picture played six months at the Globe Theatre. It ran for forty-two weeks at one theater in France, and was the first Valentino movie to be shown in Milan, Italy. Within a year of *The Sheik*'s release grosses exceeded one million dollars on a picture that cost under two hundred thousand to make.

Dozens of copycat pictures would try to cash in on the desert sheik craze, everything from *Burning Sands* to *Tents of Allah* to *Felix the Cat Shatters the Sheik* to Rex Ingram's *The Arab*, filmed in Algiers in 1924 and starring his new find, Ramon Novarro. A Hollywood reporter noted, "There are more sheiks here than in the Sahara." A new word entered American argot: young men on the prowl became "sheiks," their feminine counterparts were "shebas." Eventually, in 1931, Sheik-brand rubber condoms hit the marketplace. The word that originally designated a Muslim cleric became in the United States and Europe a synonym for the potent young he-man.

But this phenomenal success was a double-edged sword, and being linked to the exotic East had a downside. Caricatures began to appear showing Valentino with the exaggerated slanty eyes and horseteeth of racist cartoons depicting Chinese or Japanese men. "The mysterious East" suggested occult wisdom and romance to some, sneakiness and deceit to others. An exotic-looking man in a turban might be construed as a wise seer, like the yogi in *Eyes of Youth*, but he also might be seen as kin to the sleazy, snake-charming fakir in a tent show.

Women went completely haywire over Valentino's Sheik, creating a mania comparable to the screaming teeny-bopper frenzies spurred in later decades by Frank Sinatra or Elvis Presley. But this response to Valentino as the Sheik was by no means confined to teenagers. Females of all ages seem to have fallen under the Sheik's spell. The screenwriter Frances Marion would recall, "We called it *The Shriek*, for if you tuned in one of the female voices borne by the wind . . . the sound they made carried his name in a sort of passionate paean."

While women swooned, dreaming of a smoldering, darkly romantic lover who looked like Valentino and kissed just as passionately, the men they lived with sneered. The usually evenhanded and fair-minded writer and silent film aficionado Edward Wagenknecht confesses in his *The Movies in the Age of Innocence* that he could not say much about Valentino because, back in the twenties, he'd walked out of a showing of *The Sheik*. Apparently, so did droves of other men. A theater manager in Alabama reported, "The lady trade makes up for the men that stay at home." The more the girls and women lost their heads and hearts to Valentino, the more their dates, husbands, and fathers seethed with resentment at the hypnotic actor showing them up. Assaults targeted Valentino with a merciless, personalized venom. Because he was being worshipped as a love god, and because his Sheik was less brutish than the one in the novel, threatened men questioned his manliness. "Rudolph Valentino as the Sheik looks like a college boy dressed up for a masquerade in a tale by F. Scott Fitzgerald," carped *The Los Angeles Record* in an article titled "Movie Denatures Tale." His exaggerated acting came in for a drubbing ("Valentino depicts lust by widening his eyes and showing his teeth"), as if he personally had chosen the cartoonlike style characteristic of the whole movie. And he was made responsible for the script's concessions to censors: "He is a soft, sapless sort of Sheik beside the character delineated by Edith M. Hull," said one. *Motion Picture* scoffed that Valentino's Sheik smiled too much, "and you wonder why Diana is ever afraid of him." To many men in the American and European audience, the very fact that as the Sheik Valentino wore the long, flowing garments of the desert East compromised his masculinity. In the comic *Shriek of Araby,* Ben Turpin's Sheik appeared in an embroidered dress.

The most extended rant, penned by "Dick Dorgan" (probably a made-up name), appeared in the widely read fan magazine *Photoplay*. "Giving 'The Sheik' the Once Over from the Ringside" assumed the breezy and slangy tone of a sportswriter reporting on a match between Lady Diana and Sheik Ahmed:

> He tore after her like a prairie wolf and tackled her at the five yard line, picked her out of the saddle and yelled, "Home, James . . ." The Sheik was no small time guy. He was one of the real hot dogs of the desert, and the bell cow of this herd. The scene in the tent is where he vamps

Diana. He struts around like a prize turkey, every once in
a while stopping to give her a Svengali glare.

Dorgan went on to charge the Sheik/Valentino with "stealing Theda
Bara's stuff," adding as his own one-two punch, "He certainly was some
La La."

What really made Dorgan's blood boil was Valentino's beauty and
allure. It was okay for Theda Bara, the raven-haired, raccoon-eyed
screen vamp whose name was supposed to be an anagram for "Arab
death" and whose cannibalistic kiss in *A Fool There Was* drained the life
essence from her male victim, to assume exaggerated serpentine poses
and be vaunted as the incarnation of libido run amuck. It was *not* okay
if the vamp happened to be a gorgeous, erotically devastating foreign-
born male. Within a few months of his mean-spirited spoof of *The
Sheik*, Dorgan would use the columns of *Photoplay*—with a circulation
of more than two million—to raise the volume of his rant on Valentino
with "A Song of Hate," which began with this credo: "I hate Valentino!
All men hate Valentino. I hate his oriental optics, I hate his classic nose;
I hate his Roman face; I hate his smile; I hate his patent leather hair; I
hate his Svengali glare; I hate him because he dances too well; I hate
him because he is a slicker; I hate him because he is the great lover of
the screen; I hate him because he's an embezzler of hearts; I hate him
because he's too apt in the art of osculation . . . because he's too good
looking." Granted, there's a compliment imbedded in the ribbing;
Dorgan hates Valentino because he's so irresistible and omnipresent.
But there's plenty of genuine hostility mixed in.

For better or worse, Valentino the man became permanently melded
to his desert Sheik persona. In the only surviving recording of his
voice he is singing about Lady Diana's pale hands in a popular ballad,
based on a poem written in England around 1903, titled "Kashmiri
Love Song." Those, mainly women, who thought that Ahmed Ben Hassan as portrayed by Valentino was a dream of a lover tended to credit
Valentino the man with similarly awesome bedroom prowess. They
thought of him as someone who could whisk them away from hum-
drum lives to a romance-drenched fantasyland where no one has to pay

bills, tend children, chop onions, or do the laundry. Rudolph Valentino would be stamped forevermore as a handsome, exotic Romeo who pursues and escapes with one particular woman, the object of his desire—not just any skirt who happens by. When some of his pre-*Sheik* films were circulated after Valentino became known as the Sheik, exhibitors found that female patrons left the theater disappointed if the revived picture scanted on love scenes. A theater manager in Wisconsin complained that after seeing *The Conquering Power* his lady patrons gave him "a terrible razz . . . as they expected to see Valentino float through five or six reels of lovemaking."

The debate about the morality of men who use force to win a woman's love, the "caveman" issue, surfaced over and over again in the press, but often degenerated into a debate about Valentino's virility. An unsigned letter to *Movie Weekly* said that a man in love should use a little force now and then. "Girls will love a fellow all the more if he shows a little life but not too much. Book me down for Rudolph Valentino any time, and I'll bet anyone he is some caveman. If in real life his eyes are like on the screen, well that's enough for anyone to fear." Another letter writer wrote in the same issue, "I don't like the nicey, nice man who says 'please, dear.' . . . I like a real man who won't be ordered around." When the newspapers, as part of their coverage of the Jean Acker divorce hearings, reported on the time when Valentino, furious at her refusal to see him, pounded on Acker's bathroom door and then struck her, the headline in one paper ran: " 'SHEIK' IN REAL AND REEL LIFE, CHARGES WIFE."

Immediately following the release of *The Sheik* Valentino issued statements that seemed to endorse E. M. Hull's belief that a man must be dominant. Women, he said, "whether they are feminists, suffragettes, or so-called new women, . . . like to have a masterful man make them do things." He warned that unless man asserted himself as the dominant sex "we shall witness a cataclysmic upheaval where man becomes the domestic beast, woman the wage-earner." But as debate became more shrill, and he was being held accountable both for savagery toward women and for being a wimp, his tone changed and he tried to put some distance between himself and the Sheik who carried off a woman against her will. "The caveman method I abhor," he would state. "Who could desire a woman taken by force? Who could gain any pleasure from loving or caressing a woman who did not give in return?" He argued for a subtle, responsive brand of lovemaking: "Woman is piqued by flattery, enthralled by innuendo, snared by subtlety." He didn't increase his popularity with men by adding, "You Americans have employed none of these."

At the same time, he complained that the censor-wary script and director Melford had imposed restrictions that prevented him from endowing the role of Ahmed with sufficient virility. "I was forced . . . to play this wild Arabian charmer as though he were an associate professor of the history of English literature at Oxford." It wasn't his fault if his Sheik seemed like a patsy. "I neither acted like an Englishman nor like an Oriental," he defensively explained. "I was obliged to play like an emotional Italian. The Oriental is stolid, the Englishman prides himself on his self-control. Then why the eye rolling?"

Trying to separate his own identity from the Sheik's, Valentino also made a point of distancing himself from the film's racist portrayal of Arabs. Asked whether Lady Diana would have fallen for a "savage" in real life, he answered: "People are not savages because they have dark skins. The Arabian civilization is one of the oldest in the world. I was born in Southern Italy, where the Moorish influence is yet to be seen. The Moors are closely akin to the Arabs. I know them. The Arabians are dignified and keen-brained." He attributed his own desire to keep moving to a possible Bedouin ancestor and said he hoped one day to visit Egypt, Arabia, and particularly India.

The controversies provoked by *The Sheik* pursued Valentino for the rest of his life, and in some quarters they are still raging. One thing that has changed is the matter of Valentino's star ranking. The whole world associates Valentino with the role of Sheik Ahmed; everyone who thinks about the film at all thinks of it as his picture. But in 1921, the first viewers of this blockbuster looked in vain for the name Valentino in the title credits as they were first printed (on film, not the theater marquees) by Famous Players–Lasky. They originally read: "*The Sheik*, Starring Agnes Ayres."

10

FAUN MAN

Privacy and quiet became prized rarities for Valentino once he became known as the Sheik. For the rest of his days he would have to scramble to find time alone and would need to balance the perks of fame with its exorbitant costs. Sought after, swooned over as a love god, adulated and imitated, he was constantly reminded how special he was, how extraordinarily good looking. His hair and clothing set fashion trends. Millions saw his larger-than-life image on the screen, in lobbies, on the pages of magazines and newspapers, and he was recognized everywhere. His words, or those attributed to him, were endlessly quoted. At the same time, he had to adjust to his new fate as a hunted man, an object of both desire and derision, a moving target for besotted fans and the celebrity stalkers of the press. His every move would be scrutinized with a magnifying glass and commented upon in bold-faced type. We tend to think of the modern obsession with the activities of the beautiful and famous as a byproduct of the age of television, *People* magazine, and Princess Diana, but in fact it dates at least from that time, early in the twentieth century, when mass-circulation newspapers began publishing photo engravings of stage performers instead of drawings and sketches, and from the pre–World War I popularity of the first movie stars. Advances in halftone printing spawned the first tabloid newspaper, *The New York Illustrated Daily News*. By 1921 the prying lenses deployed by press reporters, newsreel makers, news photographers, and fan magazine columnists had a new favorite target. Rudolph Valentino was big news, and that made him fair game.

In search of more privacy, more space, and a tonier address than Natacha's Sunset Boulevard bungalow afforded, in the spring of 1921 Rudy and Natacha had moved to Whitley Heights, a secluded, fashionable hilltop residential section overlooking Hollywood's Cahuenga Pass and the surrounding hills. An earlier version of Beverly Hills, Whitley Heights was the neighborhood of choice for the screen actors Richard Barthelmess, Eugene O'Brien, and Barbara La Marr, and directors Sidney Franklin and Robert Vignola. Its stucco houses, red-clay rooftops, iron balconies, tiled fountains; its arched doorways and pots overflowing with vibrant bougainvillea recalled both the Mexican-Californian past and the Mediterranean hillsides dear to Valentino since his days at agriculture school in Liguria. Initially, Natacha alone rented the adobe-style house on 6770 Wedgewood Place that she and Rudy would soon purchase, though it needed a lot of work. The exterior had cracks, and as yet the house lacked both hot water and gas. Paul Ivano rented a place nearby, at 6820 Whitley Terrace, next door to actor Warren Kerrigan, and, officially, Rudy shared it with him. Rudy and Natacha had to maintain the fiction that they lived completely apart, though Rudy took most of his meals at Natacha's and undoubtedly sometimes slept over, too. To avoid scandal, he needed his own address, especially since his divorce from Jean Acker was still not final. Unfortunately, the divorce hearing would take place in November 1921, in the full glare of publicity following release of *The Sheik*.

Before that hearing, just as *The Sheik* was taking the United States by storm, Rudy and Paul left the Los Angeles area to go on location in San Francisco, where shooting of the screen version of Frank Norris's novel *Moran of the Lady Letty*, about the seafaring life on board a Pacific ocean schooner, would soon begin. Paul Ivano served as second cameraman on the film and Rudy was the leading man. (Ivano was promoted to take Bert Glennon's place after the first cameraman, William Marshall, got seasick and Glennon was promoted.) Green-eyed, dimpled, bobbed-haired brunette Dorothy Dalton would get the star billing. She and Rudy had worked together before: she played the

lead in *The Homebreaker* back in 1919 when Valentino was just an uncredited dance extra. Those two years seemed like a century ago.

Nobody at Famous Players–Lasky had sat down with a navigating chart
to plot the course of Valentino's career. But even as they continued to
economize by withholding star billing until his fourth picture for
them, Lasky and Zukor tried to build on the runaway success of *The
Sheik*. They kept the Valentino name before the public and his face before the cameras in four more pictures within the fifteen months following the release of *The Sheik*. And they tried to answer critics who
considered his work as Sheik Ahmed too gentle by throwing him into
a Douglas Fairbanks–type he-man role right away: Ramon Laredo in
the ripping yarn *Moran of the Lady Letty*. Rudy went along with this
casting decision in order to oblige his employers, even though he'd expressed a preference for playing bandits, Moors, East Indians, or romantic foreign and historical characters.

Perhaps because the company was at that time spending lavishly on
legal fees to defend itself against an antitrust suit, Famous Players–Lasky
slashed its production budget to a fraction of what it had been the previous year. The studio squeezed out $700 to pay Valentino for each
week of shooting—$200 more than he made on *The Sheik*—and kept
the budget for the whole picture below $200,000. Filming in San
Francisco began during the last week of September 1921.

The name Ramon Laredo did not appear in the novel; it was made
up specifically for the character Valentino plays. In Frank Norris's
novel, *Moran of the Lady Letty*, the hero, a wealthy young Yale man who
is shanghaied from the San Francisco wharves and forced to serve as
second mate to the evil Captain Kitchell, is named Ross Wilbur, not
Ramon Laredo. Before he portrayed Julio or the Sheik, Valentino
could and did occasionally play pale-faced Anglo characters with
names like Dick Bradley (in *A Society Sensation*) or Richard Thayer (in
All Night). But now that he had carved out a niche as either a Latin or
an exotic, his ethnic looks had to be acknowledged and exploited. So
Monte Katterjohn, the same screenwriter who wrote the scenario for

The Sheik, changed the name of Norris's leading male character and informed the audience in an intertitle at the beginning of the movie that "the rich man's son," Ramon Laredo, "spends the dash and fire inherited from his Spanish ancestors in leading cotillions."

Moran is yet another Valentino vehicle about a young man's transformation. In *The Four Horsemen*, Julio grows in insight, honor, and maturity through his ultimately fatal service in the Great War on behalf of France. In *The Sheik*, Ahmed Ben Hassan evolves from a cruel seducer to a loving and devoted fiancé. This time, as Ramon Laredo in *Moran of the Lady Letty*, Valentino's character is transformed from a coddled drawing-room socialite with a debutante girlfriend, a shiny top hat, and patent-leather shoes into a muscular, wind-burned sailor raring to go in jeans and a black turtleneck sweater. As *Photoplay* put it, "The parlor pet of San Francisco had become a slaying demon of the high seas. . . . The blood of the primeval tiger man leaped through him."

As the transformed Ramon Laredo, Valentino got to flaunt his biceps, fight the pirate villain—played by Walter Long, the same actor who glowered so menacingly as Omair in *The Sheik*—lift a comatose woman, and climb the rigging of a 350-foot, four-masted schooner. George Melford, the gung-ho director who presided over *The Sheik*, again called the shots, and he made it his business to broadcast what an athletic, virile guy Valentino was in his new role in *Moran*: "Wait till you see Valentino in it," he said in an interview before the picture's release. "You'll find out what a husky, red-blooded chap he is. Valentino and Walter Long fight a fist battle way up in the rigging of a schooner. . . . After the fight Valentino climbed to the very tip of the mast—just for exercise. The hard-boiled crew of the ship gasped!" This kind of talk was pitched to male moviegoers, who so far hadn't hurried to join the fold of Valentino fans. A theater manager who showed *Moran of the Lady Letty* in Alabama recommended it as a sort of corrective to *The Sheik*: "Valentino plays one of the parts that men as well as ladies like to see, . . . a fighting part."

The notion that battle hardens a fellow, turning a boy into a man, was intrinsic to the World War I propaganda climate that surrounded

The Four Horsemen. A related idea, that man-to-man fisticuffs separates the men from the boys, underlies *Moran of the Lady Letty* and macho culture in general. A guy "proved he was a man" and not a sissified namby-pamby by packing a powerful punch and flooring his opponent. Around the time he started filming *Moran*, Valentino, convinced that "an actor's stock in trade is his physical appearance" and that "there is nothing so brutally truthful as the movie camera," began sparring regularly with boxing gloves on. This wasn't completely new to him: as a kid he'd wrestled at school, and sometimes with his brother, Alberto, at home. Physical fitness was his main goal, but he didn't mind improving his chest expansion, muscle power, and general attractiveness at the same time. There are photos of him from 1921 or 1922, at the beach, tossing a heavy leather medicine ball to his buddy Jack Dempsey, the current world heavyweight champ, who was launching a sidebar career in pictures. Another photo shows Valentino, biceps bulging, his dukes up, in boxing gloves, sleeveless jersey, and shorts, alongside his new friend from France, Robert Florey, a journalist for a French cinema magazine. Florey would serve briefly as publicity director for Pickford and Fairbanks in Europe, work as a publicist for Valentino in 1923, and eventually become a well-known Hollywood film director and writer.

Florey himself was not beefcake material. Still in his early twenties when he arrived in Hollywood, he was slope-shouldered, boyish, tall, and slender, and looked more like the "97-pound weakling" shown in popular magazine ads than like the other image in those ads: the hulking, muscular champ Charles Atlas, who in a 1922 contest in Madison Square Garden was declared "The World's Most Perfectly Developed Man." In one photo of Florey with Valentino, Florey has on a sporty white sweater, as if he'd happened by after tennis while Rudy was sparring at home. Probably Ivano, who introduced Robert Florey to Rudy, snapped the picture.

At the beginning of *Moran*, Ramon Laredo is a bored, rich idler without much grit, muscle power, or purpose. We see him first at a society tea in a posh section of San Francisco, nattily turned out in coat and collar, with a dainty teacup in hand and an entourage of flighty debutantes. Like the lounge lizards and tango pirates Valentino had often portrayed in the past, Ramon serves no practical social function; a cake eater rather than a meat eater, he "spends his time dancing—and similar useful pursuits." Invited to a young deb's yachting party later in the day of the debutante tea, he wanders down in his "dude's" white ducks and blazer to the tough waterfront section of town, where at a wharf watering hole an unscrupulous old salt slips him a Mickey Finn. When he wakes from his drugged stupor, Ramon finds himself staggering on the deck of a smuggler's ship. (Valentino's pantomime of being drugged, passing out, and coming to are impressive; he shows he really can act.) Ramon has been shanghaied and will be forced to serve on Captain Kitchell's opium-smuggling, gun-running ship. When he sets eyes on Ramon, Kitchell sneers, "What d'you bring me this for? I wanted a second mate—not a dancin' master. . . . We ain't exactly doin' a quadrille on my quarterdeck." After knocking Ramon out with a single punch to the jaw, Kitchell outfits "Lillee of the Vallee" Ramon in sailor's gear, promising, "I'll make a seaman out o' him yet—seaman or shark bait!"

Kitchell succeeds in growing some figurative hair on Ramon's formerly puny chest. (In a few later movies, audiences got a peek at Valentino's actual bare chest, and a short, "The Sheik's Physique," shows him stripped down for a swim, but for now, arms with rippling biceps had to suffice.) Back in San Francisco, after reeling in buckets of bilge water, menacing Kitchell with a rifle, rescuing the heroine from near rape, climbing the rigging to the top of the mast, and toppling Kitchell to his doom, leathery Ramon no longer fits in among his manicured, too-utterly-utter former companions in his pampered city social set. At the ritzy cotillion he attends near the end of the picture, though his old blue-blooded friends warmly welcome him back to the fold, he realizes he's become a rank outsider. His pea coat and bell-bottoms mark him as different, and he walks with a rolling swagger, but it's his attitude, not his clothes or gait, that really sets him apart. Salt-cured by his experience at sea, he no longer wants to twirl around the dance floor in patent-leather shoes and stylish black tie and tails. His hands have calluses now and he prefers the risky, unprotected life of a seaman. His debutante girlfriend of bygone days has lost her allure, since he's fallen for the lady mariner Letty Sternersen, otherwise known as Moran.

Moran's no ordinary gal. Motherless, unfamiliar with womanly ways, and raised at sea by her captain father, she's as hale and hearty as any man and is a better sailor than most. Christened Letty, she's addressed by the neuter name Moran, which was her mother's surname before she married Captain Sternersen. Although Hollywood had to make her pretty, in Norris's novel Moran is supposed to be handsome rather than pretty, and at the start of the tale is downright mannish in dress and manner. Frank Norris describes her as a seafaring Brunhilde, a fearless, whiskey-swilling Norse powerhouse under whose coarse oilskin coat "one could infer that the biceps and deltoids were large and powerful." As Moran, whose father dies when his boat is suffused in fumes from burning coal, Dorothy Dalton looks commanding behind the schooner's wheel and heaves ho with the best of them, even though the squalls and winds of the Pacific never seem to smear her mascara. A stowaway on Kitchell's smuggling vessel after her father's ship is destroyed, she's protected by chivalrous Ramon and the sympathetic Chinese cook, Charlie. Of course Kitchell finds her and tries to seduce her; of course Ramon rescues and falls in love with her, although at first she baffles him. "I never knew a girl could be like you," he tells Moran. "You swear like a man and dress like a man and you're strong."

Even though she at one point (during a mutinous melee) mistakes him for a bad guy and tries to beat him up with her fists, while admitting with awe that she's as strong as he is (here he flatters himself), Ramon tells her he loves her more than he thought he ever could love anyone. Moran's first response to this is "I don't like that kind of talk. . . . I'm not made for men . . . nor other women either. I ought to have been a boy."

Moran's romantic ending, a hot embrace and an unspoken promise of future wedded bliss, is a compromise. After Kitchell's death, Moran accepts Ramon's love, puts on a skirt, and returns his fervent kiss; like Lady Diana in *The Sheik* she evolves from a she-man into a more feminine, definitely heterosexual woman at peace with her estrogen. She gives up her independence and her sexual ambiguity for love of her man. But Ramon makes sacrifices, too, forsaking the city's "soft" privileges and comforts for the sailor's "hard" and challenging life on the rolling main. He and Moran will live together aboard some schooner, facing down as a team the inevitable squalls, but it's not clear which one will be captain and which, first mate.

Moran of the Lady Letty is a fascinating, extremely well acted, directed, and photographed (mostly in natural light) movie that should be better known than it is. Aimed at a smaller audience than *The Sheik*, it elicited from Valentino a performance that is more understated and subtle, though to this viewer he's more persuasive in tails and surrounded by women than as a bruiser sailor spoiling for a fight. Opinion was divided on that point when the picture first played. One reviewer complained that Valentino "does not fit properly into the picture. As a rough and tumble hero, the glistening haired Rodolph does not register convincingly." *The New York Times* also found Valentino too slick to be believably salty, and judged the Ramon character unlikely as "the kind of youth who would be attracted to Moran, except momentarily, or attractive to her." While the critic for the *Times* deemed some of his scenes of sailor's derring-do successful, he thought that "in others it seems a pity that he ever left the ballroom." *Variety*'s Rush praised the whole as "an interesting melodrama of the sea with a wealth of action," and quarreled with the studio's decision to give Dorothy Dalton star billing. "The real star," *Variety* correctly insisted, "[is] Valentino as a rich young idler who is shanghaied and finds himself in the battle with a piratical skipper." The same *Variety* reviewer, after reporting that the large crowd at the Rivoli Theater in New York had turned out mainly to see Valentino, went on to give him a backhanded compliment: "As a rough-and-tumble fighting hero," Rush wrote, "Valentino is a revelation. Physically he looks the part, but it comes as something of a shock, probably because he has so long been identified with roles of a daintier kind."

A sneering note crept into Rush's *Variety* review. Valentino's personal taste and appearance, his way of dressing and combing his hair

Valentino's father, Giovanni Guglielmi, in Naples, ca. 1890 (British Film Institute)

Valentino's mother, Maria Berta Gabriella Barbin Guglielmi, in Castellaneta, ca.1900 (British Film Institute)

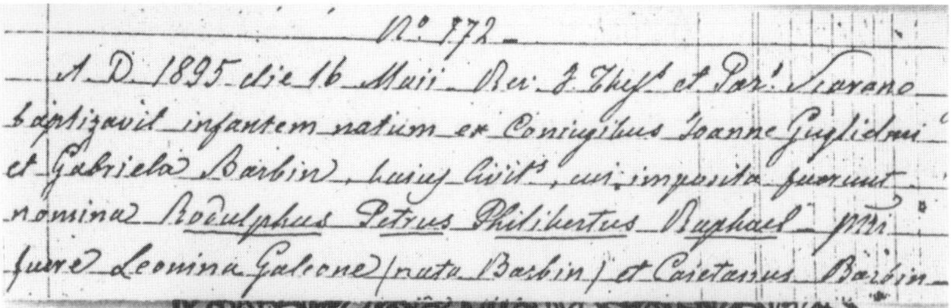

No 872

A.D. 1895 die 16 Maii. Rev. D. Theyl et Par. Searano baptizavit infantem natum ex Conjugibus Ioanne Guglielmi et Gabriela Barbin, huius civit., cui imposita fuerunt nomina Rodulphus Petrus Philibertus Raphael. Pri fuere Leonina Galeone (nata Barbin) et Caietanus Barbin.

THE ONLY BABY PICTURE OF
RUDOLPH VALENTINO
IN EXISTENCE

Rodolfo Pietro Filibert Raphael Guglielmi, photo and birth extract, Castellaneta, May 6, 1895 (Museo Valentino)

Rodolfo in cadet's uniform, ca. 1907, about age twelve (Private collection)

Older brother Alberto and Rodolfo Guglielmi, ca. 1897 (Private collection)

Rodolfo at eighteen
(Museum of Modern Art)

Joan Sawyer, exhibition dancer, with partner Carlos Sebastian, ca. 1914, before she became the dance partner of "Signor Rodolfo" (San Francisco Performing Arts Library and Museum)

(*below*) "Signor Rodolfo" with the company of the touring stage musical *The Masked Model*, 1917 (Private collection)

Rodolfo as an uncredited screen extra behind Louise Huff, Jack Pickford, and others in *Seventeen*, Famous Players, 1916 (Courtesy of the Academy of Motion Picture Arts and Sciences)

Rodolfo as a savage Apache dancer, the Ferret, in *A Rogue's Romance*, with Earle Williams and Katherine Adams, Vitagraph, 1919 (Private collection)

Virginia Rappe and "Rodolpho De Valentina" in *An Adventuress*, filmed as *Over the Rhine* in 1918, first released by Republic, 1920 (Courtesy of the Academy of Motion Picture Arts and Sciences)

"Rodolph Valentine" and Dorothy Gish in the comedy *Out of Luck* (*Nobody Home*), New Art Film Co., 1919 (Private collection)

Nell Craig, "Rudolph Valentine" as Prince Angelo Della Robbia, and Norman Kerry in *Passion's Playground*, First National, 1920 (Courtesy of the Academy of Motion Picture Arts and Sciences)

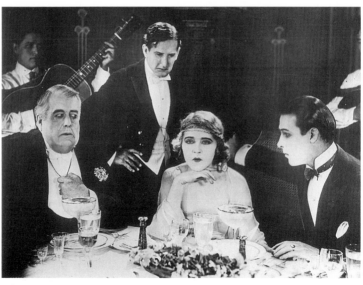

Edward Jobson, Mae Murray, and "Rudolpho De Valintine" as Jimmie Calhoun in *The Delicious Little Devil*, Universal, 1919 (Courtesy of the Academy of Motion Picture Arts and Sciences)

Jean Acker, Valentino's first wife—for just a few hours (Private collection)

(*above*) Valentino as Clarence Morgan, "a cabaret parasite," with Clara Kimball Young as Gina Ashling in *Eyes of Youth*, Equity Pictures, 1919 (Courtesy of the Academy of Motion Picture Arts and Sciences)

Demonstrating the tango with Alice Terry in a publicity photo for *The Four Horsemen of the Apocalypse*, 1921 (Museum of Modern Art)

Valentino as the gaucho Julio Desnoyers in *The Four Horsemen of the Apocalypse*, dancing the Argentine tango with Beatrice Dominguez, Metro, 1921 (Museum of Modern Art)

In a Paris tea room, the married Marguerite Laurier (Alice Terry) dances with the art student Julio Desnoyers (Valentino) as their illicit love affair catches fire, in *The Four Horsemen of the Apocalypse*, Metro, 1921. (Private collection)

Soldier Julio bidding farewell to his father (Josef Swickard) before going off to fight and die for France in the Great War, in *The Four Horsemen of the Apocalypse*, Metro, 1921 (Private collection)

Valentino, the screenwriter June Mathis, and director Rex Ingram pose with actor Pom-eroy Cannon, playing dead, on location for *The Four Horsemen of the Apocalypse*. (Courtesy of the Academy of Motion Picture Arts and Sciences)

A trade-journal ad for *All Night* (1918), revived in 1922 to cash in on Valentino's new celebrity (Private collection)

Rudy cooking his favorite extra long spaghetti, ca. 1921 (Museum of Modern Art)

Nazimova as Marguerite Gautier and Valentino as Armand in *Camille* (set and costumes designed by Natacha Rambova), Metro, 1921 (Museum of Modern Art)

Shaded by spring blossoms, Armand Duval (Valentino) reads to Marguerite Gautier (Nazimova), a tubercular demimondaine he loves. The book he reads from is *Manon Lescaut*. *Camille*, Metro, 1921 (Private collection)

In *Camille*'s casino sequence, Armand hurls his winnings from the roulette table at Marguerite, believing that she betrayed him for money. Set and costume design by Natacha Rambova. Metro (Private collection)

In *The Conquering Power* (Metro, 1921), the maid (Mary Hearn) holds the valise of the Parisian dandy Charles Grandet (Valentino) as he arrives at the provincial home of his miserly uncle (Ralph Lewis, holding lamp). Charles greets his cousin Eugénie (Alice Terry) as his aunt (Edna Demaurey) looks on. (Private collection)

Clad in an elegant silk robe, Charles caresses and kisses the hand of his cousin Eugénie (Alice Terry) in *The Conquering Power*, Metro, 1921. This kind of subtle love-making on screen made women in the audience swoon. (Private collection)

Valentino as a Chinese, à la Richard Barthelmess in D. W. Griffith's *Broken Blossoms*, ca. 1922 (Private collection)

off camera, were routinely scrutinized as part of public discussion of his work in motion pictures. Blurring distinctions between the man Valentino and the screen actor who had been hired to play a particular role, reviewers felt called upon to castigate his glossy patent-leather hair even when Valentino didn't wear that style in the role under review. Often these outbursts sprang from racial or anti-immigrant prejudice, implying that a man's slicked-back hair told of his unsavory Latin, Italian, or Asian origins. *Photoplay*'s Willard Wright published a satiric "Motion Picture Dictionary" in which he defined "antimacassar" as "a doily placed on the back of chairs to protect the upholstery from the oiled and pomaded heads of motion picture actors. Macassar oil . . . has been discarded because of its low visibility, and has been supplanted by brilliantine, patent-leather polish, Jap-a-lac, ebony veneer, bear grease, and liquid vaseline—all of which produce a superior gloss."

The attitude of the press toward screen stars in general had soured after the notorious Fatty Arbuckle scandal hit the front pages in 1921. On Labor Day weekend, only about six weeks before Valentino arrived in San Francisco with the rest of the cast and crew to begin filming *Moran*, and at the very same posh San Francisco hotel, the St. Francis, where Valentino and Ivano stayed during the shoot, the screen comic Roscoe "Fatty" Arbuckle had hosted an alcohol-drenched party that ended in catastrophe. This was the era of Prohibition and movie stars' drinking parties in themselves invited condemnation from American morality squads. But the drinking hardly registered compared to a more dire calamity. Actress Virginia Rappe (with whom Rudy had appeared in a 1919 film, *An Adventuress*), became violently ill at the St. Francis Hotel bash and died in one of its bedrooms. Arbuckle was indicted on a charge of manslaughter, and his film career was effectively destroyed—although ultimately he was exonerated in a third trial after two prior trials resulted in hung juries. A *Variety* headline says it all: "SCANDAL HITS INDUSTRY; Arbuckle Affair Furnishes Capital to Screen's Enemies—Hundreds of Exhibitors Cancel 'Fatty Comedies'—Actor Indicted for Manslaughter—Murder Charge Stands."

Arbuckle, the *Variety* story went on to reveal, "is under contract to Famous Players for three years at a salary of $3,500 a week and 25 per cent of profits on his pictures."

This was not good news for the Hollywood film industry. Guardians of public virtue rushed to condemn not just Arbuckle but his entire profession and place of residence. For censors and bluenoses, Hollywood became the new Sodom, the capital of depravity both on the screen and off. Defenders of the movie business, many of them highly regarded film professionals, rushed to oppose the blanket condemnation and fought calls for stricter censorship or new morality legislation. "The moving picture is about fifteen years old," the screenwriter Rupert Hughes argued in defense of the reviled film colony. "Sin is somewhat older than that, yet the censors would have us believe that it was not Satan but Thomas A. Edison who invented the fall of man." Since Arbuckle happened to be under contract with Famous Players—Lasky, actors connected with that studio had reason to view the whole mess with particular alarm. Just how vulnerable Valentino's situation was he would discover soon enough.

The scandal did not betray its sweeping destructive force right away. Rudy's weeks in San Francisco passed happily. Natacha had not joined him initially in northern California, because she was busily preparing her designs for the Nazimova film spectacle *Salome*, based on Aubrey Beardsley's illustrations for Oscar Wilde's play. Actress Aileen Pringle, a member of a wealthy San Francisco family and a friend of Rudy's from the time they both worked in Florida on *Stolen Moments* (1920), made her touring car available to Rudy and Paul Ivano. She'd pick them up at the St. Francis after work and they'd do the town. Dorothy Dalton, who according to Paul Ivano was the good friend of Goldwyn boss Joe Godsol, also had a chauffeured car at her disposal. She'd say, "Oh please use my car because my chauffeur is going crazy waiting for me all day." After shooting outdoors from seven in the morning until seven at night, they'd bathe, put on bathrobes, and order dinner in. Then they'd sleep a few hours, setting the alarm for midnight. After they got up and dressed, Dorothy Dalton's car, sans Dorothy, would meet them, and they'd cruise the joints on the Barbary Coast. "San Francisco was a very lively town in those days."

Maybe because she feared Rudy was having too much fun without her, Natacha turned up suddenly in San Francisco, giving no prior notice that she would be arriving in town. She telephoned one October day when Rudy was in the shower. Ivano answered, explaining that Rudy would have to call her right back. When Ivano asked, "Where are you, darling?" she snapped, "Don't call me darling" and explained that she was not calling from home but from her mother's place in San Francisco. She gave an address on California Street near the elite and sumptuous Fairmont Hotel, on Nob Hill, and said Rudy should get dressed and come at once with Ivano to see her in the Hudnuts' home.

According to Paul Ivano, Rudy had not realized how wealthy Natacha's mother and stepfather were until he visited their extravagant San Francisco abode, with its spectacular view, Louis XV antiques, and gilt-framed mirrors. Natacha had been reticent about her mother's high-society connections. She found that world suffocating and she insisted on living on what she herself earned. Ivano suspected that a figurative lightbulb went off in Rudy's head and his resolve to marry Natacha clicked on the moment he walked in and saw her resplendent beauty set against the Hudnuts' lavish, Elsie de Wolfe–style European period decor. This seems to me a harsh view. Though there might be a grain of truth in Ivano's judgment, there's every indication that Rudy's love for Natacha, and his desire to permanently join his life to hers, had emotional rather than economic wellsprings. It's true that Rudy, whose first friends in America were counts, had always been drawn to people with wealth and high social standing, and in the past had either falsified or exaggerated his kinship with the aristocracy. But by this time, because of his celebrity he had acquired his own social credentials. Glamour, fame, and money provided an American equivalent to a blue-blood pedigree. In the 1920s as in later decades, Hollywood stars hobnobbed regularly with millionaires, duchesses, and princes, each group acquiring some reflected glory from the other. Gloria Swanson would soon be marrying her marquis, and Pickfair would be hosting the duke of Alba and Lord and Lady Mountbatten, to name but a few of Doug and Mary's titled guests. Valentino's friends of this era included two actors who bore European titles and

military honorifics, too, having served their respective countries as
cavalry officers: Mario Carillo, of the noble Neapolitan Caracciolo
family, and Jean de Limur, a French count. He was proud of his close
connection to such illustrious men, even though at this point neither
actor played anything more than bit parts in the movies. All his life,
Valentino pursued luxury and identified with the nobility, but he
didn't need the Hudnuts' plush magic carpet in order to fly high.

By the time they returned to Hollywood, Rudy and Natacha had decided that they wanted to get married, which meant Rudy would have
to follow through on his divorce. Jean Acker, on the scent of money
and the kind of free publicity money can't buy, had decided to sue for
separate maintenance; Rudy, balking at having to pay her alimony and
impatient for his freedom, countersued for divorce. He realized he
would have to submit to the intrusiveness of a very public divorce
hearing in order to win his coveted prize: Natacha as his wife. Not
even the additional shrillness in the air and the hype generated by the
Arbuckle scandal would cool his ardor for Natacha or dim his determination to become her husband.

Acker and her attorney, Neil McCarthy, had no interest in playing
fair. They played to win as handsome a financial settlement as they
could get, and if that meant providing fodder for the scavenger press
by slandering Valentino, so much the worse for him. Jean had evidence
that Rudy and Natacha had been living together; she claimed that as his
lawful wife she, Jean Acker, and no other should benefit from his success, especially since, her physician maintained, poor Jean had been a
patient in October 1921 at Methodist Hospital (for an ulcer) and
could not work until January 1922 at the earliest, and maybe not even
then; "plaintiff is of an excitable nature and any undue excitement
might bring about a relapse" of her illness. Her husband, Valentino,
McCarthy claimed, had "willfully failed to provide [her] with the common necessaries of life."

Valentino and his attorney, W. I. Gilbert, insisted that he, not
Acker, was the wronged party, that he, not Acker, had been the one

deserted by a spouse, but Acker cited Valentino's carryings-on with Natacha as additional evidence of his wanton irresponsibility. Somehow Acker's attorney got his hands on a photograph of Rudy that revealed him posed in full body makeup as a half-naked horned satyr, or faun-man, curled up at Natacha's feet as he toots on silvery Pan pipes. This picture was one in a series of faun studies staged by Natacha (who borrowed the costume design from Léon Bakst) and taken in San Francisco by Helen MacGregor. One of these was eventually published in a magazine called *Shadowland* that featured arty photographs of dancers and other performers in various states of draped undress. Valentino prized the MacGregor photos depicting him as a faun with putty points tipping his ears, black and white body paint simulating goatskin on his legs, and a tail that was held in place by a barely visible leather jockstrap that also covered his privates with a fig leaf. He told Helen MacGregor in a letter he wrote to her from London in August of 1923 that her faun photos were the best pictures that had been taken of him to date.

Natacha had staged the faun studies partly as a celebration of Rudy's beautiful Greek god's body, and partly as an homage to Nijinsky, whose erotic performance in the ballet he choreographed to Debussy's tone poem "Prélude à l'Après-midi d'un faune" (inspired by a Mallarmé poem) had mesmerized her when she saw it at Covent Garden in 1913. But Jean Acker and her attorney were not depending on the public's recognition of the Nijinsky connection when they introduced the faun photo as evidence in court. It was Rudy's obvious eroticism, not Nijinsky's, that they hoped would draw gasps in the courtroom and in the sensation-hungry press. The *Los Angeles Examiner* came through for them, describing the picture brought to court as "somewhat startling to say the least." The *Los Angeles Times* ran the headline: "FAUN PICTURE CAUSES STIR; Not Questionable but Art, Declares Cinema Star."

On the stand Valentino testified that yes, he and Miss Rambova had been friends of long standing, that she and her maid helped him answer his fan mail and that Miss Rambova advised him "regarding his scenarios and artwork in his pictures." As for the faun studies, he said they were done in preparation for a movie that had been planned but canceled, *The Faun Through the Ages*. This last was probably an embellishment of the truth; it's unlikely that a faun movie ever made it to the drawing boards, though Natacha would have loved working on such a project. Rather than a film, Natacha may have been thinking that the Helen MacGregor faun photos might qualify as works of art in the same way that Adolf de Meyer's famous photographs of Nijinsky as the Faun did in 1914 when the designer Paul Iribe published them in a limited edition. In those often reproduced de Meyer images, "faint yet clear, and reminiscent of bas-reliefs," Nijinksy seems the personification of "youth itself." Without classical training in ballet or any other dance discipline, without modernist sensibility, Valentino couldn't begin to match Nijinsky as a dancer or innovator in choreography, but Natacha seems to be telling the world that her lover should be remembered as a more perfectly made and beautiful model of masculine youth than his fascinating and erratic former tango pupil.

Valentino's attorney presented to the court another, larger faun photograph that showed a scene from the picture he claimed they were planning, and a text he labeled the scenario for *The Faun*. Acker's attorney had subpoenaed Natacha Rambova and she was present in court, but since the judge hadn't determined whether the faun photos were relevant evidence she wasn't called to testify.

As the Los Angeles Superior Court slowly worked its way to a decision in Valentino's favor, granting him an interlocutory decree in January 1922 that would become final in March, 1923, Acker eventually managed to extract from Valentino a monetary settlement that was smaller than the full support she sought but larger than what Valentino thought just, or, considering his indebtedness to a long list of creditors, could easily afford. In court on November 30, 1921, he revealed that he owned three automobiles and had a total of $1,500 in cash and no life insurance. By the time Judge Toland made his ruling on alimony, it was clear that Acker could work again, in fact was working on a picture. She was awarded $175 a month from Valentino until further order of the court. She also scored some points in the court of public opinion.

The divorce hearings had informed the gossip-hungry newspaper-reading public that Valentino and Acker never lived together as man and wife, that their brief union had not included sexual intimacy. This well-publicized conclusion of the court, combined with the titillating descriptions of the faun photograph, gave ammunition to those determined to wound Valentino by questioning his virility. To many Americans, the photographs of him that highlighted his dance background disclosed effeminacy rather than primitive power and passion. Those who wanted to reduce him to a negative label couldn't be bothered with complexities. The idea that we all contain qualities that can be read as masculine or feminine, dominant or submissive, didn't enjoy wide currency. Neither did the notion that different cultures might define masculinity in different ways.

A few who wrote about Valentino could see in him both a masculine and a feminine side, and could appreciate his androgynous quality as something that increased his allure rather than diminished it: "Rudy likes music, the ballet, perfume, dance," wrote one perceptive journalist. "Counterwise, he likes to labor with his hands. He likes the sun. Rudy would rather cultivate crops than dine in . . . the Ritz Carlton. Rudy likes horses."

A rival star such as Douglas Fairbanks, who was forever vaulting fences or leaping between balconies but avoided playing love scenes, enjoyed more broad-based popularity with men in the moviegoing public and provoked far less controversy than his Italian-born future colleague at United Artists. Fairbanks looked and acted the part of Mr. Clean-cut, an all-American hero with a nimble acrobat's love of feats of valor, a boundless patriotism that had shone during the Liberty Bond campaign, and a good-natured Boy Scout's perpetual optimism and high spirits. Unlike the sometimes saturnine and mysterious Valentino, he displayed no dark side and excited few erotic fantasies. Booth Tarkington once characterized Fairbanks as "a faun who had been to Sunday school."

Fairbanks had a strong competitive streak, and he resented Valentino, even though his own stellar position as a popular hero and box-office winner was assured for as long as people continued to look at American movies. Perhaps he sensed that Valentino traded on qualities that he could not touch, for all his good looks, genuine accomplishment and appealing get-up-and-go. When Valentino called on the Fairbankses at Pickfair, Mary Pickford was mortified by Doug's coldness to Valentino. "I never saw Douglas act so fast, and with such painful rudeness, as he did in showing Valentino that he wasn't welcome," Pickford recalled. Eventually Doug and Rudy found a way to accept one another warily and become congenial associates, if not close friends. But the disparity in the way the two screen idols were treated by the press remained glaring. Doug and Mary had both been married to others when they met and became involved; they both went through messy, much publicized divorces. But you'd never know it. They somehow managed to escape blame, and in most people's minds personified squeaky-clean virtue and verve.

In November of 1921 Valentino signed a new contract with Famous Players—Lasky, at the same time borrowing $7,000 from the studio to help him pay his lawyers and Jean Acker. The new agreement, once more brokered by Clifford Robertson and Eugene Webb and signed on November 28, stipulated that Valentino would receive $1,000 a week to appear opposite star Gloria Swanson (once again he would be denied star billing) in a film to be called *Beyond the Rocks*, based on a novel by Elinor Glyn. The contract included three options of one year each. After one year Valentino's weekly pay would increase to $1,200 per week; after two years, to $2,000. By 1924, the third year, he would be making $3,000 a week for each picture. According to the naive Valentino, Jesse Lasky had assured him verbally that the numbers in the contract were not etched in stone. Lasky told him, Valentino averred in an affidavit in 1922, that the salaries specified in the contract "would be considered a minimum arrangement, since the policy of Famous Players—Lasky has always been to voluntarily pay their stars increases of salary from time to time as the value of their services warranted." It's perfectly possible that Lasky made such a vague promise. What's hard to grasp is how innocently Valentino believed him, what a babe in the woods he was about the difficulty of holding anybody to a business agreement that's not written down on paper in black and white.

Shooting of *Beyond the Rocks*, much of it on Catalina Island, off the California coast, got under way as the momentous year of 1921 drew to a close. In a way it was a compliment to Valentino that he was chosen to make love on-screen to the wildly popular and lovely Gloria Swanson; it shows that even if she got the top billing and the stellar salary to match, the studio felt he was in her league as a looker, a lover, an actor, and a box-office draw. Miss Swanson had the kind of clout with the studio that Valentino was being denied. She had the right to approve—or reject—Valentino's casting, and gave her nod to Jesse Lasky and Adolph Zukor after they agreed to pay for her trip to Europe in return for her consent. She told Zukor that her agreement to have Valentino featured would win Famous Players–Lasky more money from *Beyond the Rocks* than her trip to Europe would cost them.

Swanson and Valentino already knew one another from the days before *Four Horsemen* and got on very well. They'd gone horseback riding together in the Hollywood hills on Sunday mornings, afterward talking intimately about their bad marriages and difficult divorces as they sat on the cliffs resting their steeds. They were friendly enough for him to have presented her with a riding crop embossed with her initials as a birthday gift.

High spirits prevailed during filming, particularly on days when Madame Glyn absented herself and consequently could not annoy down-to-earth director Sam Wood with her demands, which he considered bizarre. Swanson and Valentino danced the tango together at a ball in a Catalina hotel (also in one scene in the movie), and had pillow fights after dinner in the upstairs corridors. "I never saw Rudolph Valentino so relaxed and happy," Swanson recalled. Once she played a practical joke on him while they were shooting a scene set in an inn in the Alps. In the scene, Valentino's character picks up a perfumed lace handkerchief, lifts it to his nose and smiles dreamily, the delicate scent of the hankie evoking memories of the woman he loves. Miss Swanson conspired with the prop man in preparing a duplicate handkerchief in which she concealed several pieces of garlic.

Beyond the Rocks has been listed in archives as a completely lost film, but a short fragment of it is being restored in Amsterdam by the Nederland Filmmuseum. A very complete record of the way the film was publicized and received in the press exists in Gloria Swanson's voluminous scrapbooks, meticulously preserved by her before they became part of the collection of the Harry Ransom Humanities Research Center in Austin, Texas. Gloria Swanson saved every scrap of paper, every newspaper article, interview, photograph, or press release that appeared about her in newspapers and magazines, worldwide.

The press coverage of *Beyond the Rocks* focused much attention on the stars' extravagant wardrobes. "Gloria Swanson can wear clothes," ran the opening sentence of a review in *The New York Times*. "So can Rudolph Valentino." As Theodora Fitzgerald, an impoverished but aristocratic young Englishwoman who has been forced by her straitened circumstances to marry an elderly millionaire, but falls in love during her honeymoon with the handsome, young, half-Spanish Lord Bracondale (Valentino) when he rescues her after she plunges into the sea from an overturned rowboat, Swanson dons more embroidered lace, silk, velvet, sable, and chinchilla than the usual impoverished young bride who falls out of a rowboat in a Swiss lake on her honeymoon can manage. Famous Players–Lasky took pride in its reputation for mounting lavish productions, or, as one reporter put it, excellence "in matters of gorgeousness, beauty, and good taste." An ad boasted that Miss Swanson's fifty-two new gowns had cost more than a million dollars. "Everything about [the film] is expensive—gowns, jewels, houses, restaurants, all designed to make people gasp." Glamour and ostentation were part of the Hollywood package, part of the go-for-broke mind-set of the 1920s, and the studios sold them hard. Gloria Swanson's contract stated that she should always appear in public dressed to the nines. Her lavish clothes budget was part of what made her a star. The fan magazines ran frequent features on Hollywood fashion, and often department stores and specialty shops advertised attire or decor connected with a particular star in a particular movie role. This applied to men's as well as women's fashions. To promote *Beau Brummell*, a 1924 picture starring John Barrymore, Manhattan's Harlem Opera House held a "Best Dressed Man" contest for which the prize was a suit donated by a local merchant. In 1924 the Ohio Retail Clothiers Association proclaimed Ramon Novarro the best-dressed man on the screen.

In *Beyond the Rocks* Valentino, too, wore gorgeous costumes, which according to Natacha's biographer were most likely designed by her, though she got no mention in the credits. Since the plot of *Beyond the Rocks* involved flashbacks to Versailles in the eighteenth century, Valentino had the chance to appear in some scenes decked out in eighteenth-century finery of the sort he would later show off in *Monsieur Beaucaire*—complete with powdered wig and lace cuffs. There were also sorties to make-believe Switzerland, to a fabricated baronial estate in England, and the ersatz ruins of the pharaohs.

But the studio, having splurged on the costumes, got chintzy when it came to some of the sets. A fan wrote to *Photoplay* to complain, "I walked out of this picture when the actors fell over papier-mâché rocks and grovelled in snow that poured over the cliffs like sugar."

Unlike *Moran*, which made a bid to attract male picture goers, *Beyond the Rocks* aimed for and drew a mainly female audience. The women who packed the Rivoli in New York freely expressed their preferences in the fashion department: "Miss Swanson's close fitting gowns were harshly judged and an audible preference for a soft coiffure was expressed, while they didn't seem to think Valentino photographed so well in this one." The male reviewer for *The New York Times* confessed that the picture reduced him to "a state of somniferous weariness" from which he was roused back to life by the second feature, a Buster Keaton comedy. A theater manager in upstate New York reported: "My patrons were divided on this one; the flappers said Great! because of Valentino no doubt." He added, "It's the authoress [Elinor Glyn] and cast that will pull in at the box office."

The studio banked on Elinor Glyn's name as a powerful draw for the feminine audience. A dramatic-looking English redhead with powdered white skin, vermillion lips, and a queenly bearing, Elinor Glyn was a best-selling author of spicy romantic fiction who enjoyed, even cultivated, her notoriety. Adultery—usually involving highborn Brits and/or alluring Balkan royalty—was her stock in trade. Her sensational 1907 novel, *Three Weeks*, eventually a Hollywood movie starring Aileen Pringle, featured as heroine a seductive and mysterious Lady, a Balkan queen, who receives her lover while reclining on a tiger skin. Even those who hadn't read it might be able to recite the popular ditty: "Would you like to sin / On a tiger skin / With Elinor Glyn? / Or would you prefer / To err with her / On some other fur?"

Because she had lived in Paris, was the sister of couture designer Lady Duff Gordon (known as Lucile), and had been the rather openly acknowledged mistress of Lord Curzon, Americans looked to the haughty redhead who wrote novels as the ultimate authority on continental manners, home decor, and above all, *amour*. Madame Glyn's ideas about sexual magnetism became Americanized for the benefit of Hollywood stars, but when Glyn first arrived in Hollywood in the early 1920s her European background was what qualified her as an expert on lovemaking at its most exciting, illicit best. Asked by *Photoplay* to pronounce on the question of whether artists should marry, she replied, "In my beloved Paris . . . artists do not think highly of matrimony. But I suppose here in America it is easier because of the facility of divorce and so the possibility of fairly frequent change of partners."

This oracular and exceedingly daring utterance was made before the Arbuckle scandal set off puritanical shrieks of horror, along with attendant calls for a complete Hollywood moral cleansing. Imported by Famous Players–Lasky to write titillating scenarios, Elinor Glyn needed to cool things down some by the time she wrote the scenario for and consulted during filming on *Beyond the Rocks*. Gloria Swanson reports that the picture had to be less sensual than the studio and the public had hoped, because watchdogs from the newly formed Hays Office were on hand, ready to bark at the scent of anything they judged too risky.

Hays was Will Hays, a former Presbyterian church elder and Indiana politician who in December of 1921 took the helm of a brand-new organization, the Motion Picture Producers and Distributors of

America (MPPDA), whose task was "to establish and maintain the highest possible moral and artistic standards." One of the Hays Office's new rules stipulated that kisses should run no longer than three seconds. "So we shot each kiss twice," said Swanson, once for the American market, once for the European and South American. "Poor Rudy could hardly get his nostrils flaring before the American version was over."

Though kisses had to be abbreviated, there was no impediment to showing Valentino's provocative kiss on the palm rather than the back of his lady's hand, a little trick Madame Glyn had taught him. But there was no way of getting around the fact that the plot turned on the impassioned affair between a married woman and a man who didn't happen to be her husband. The novel *Beyond the Rocks* has Lord Bracondale seizing Theodora and pulling her close to him in a torrid embrace while panting in a deep, hoarse baritone, "My darling! God, I love you so—beyond all words or sense—Oh, let us be happy for this one night—we must part afterwards I know—but just for tonight there can be no sin and no harm in being a little happy—when we are going to pay for it with all the rest of our lives. Let us have the memory of one hour of bliss—the angels themselves could not grudge us that!" This dialogue could not be transferred to screen intertitles in the Hays era, but the hot embraces could and did play out before the camera. And for their no-holds-barred love scene on the couch, Valentino and Swanson needed to warm up. Live music would be used to put actors in the right mood. In addition, for this love scene, Madame Glyn got their juices flowing by reading aloud to them from *Beyond the Rocks*. Valentino had turned to Elinor Glyn, she recalled, imploring her to "say the same words to us as are in the book." She did so, allowing herself to become very emotional, "and lovely Gloria almost wept, and Valentino was deeply moved, and it became a wonderful scene. He was so sensitive to sound and the poetic aspect of things."

In a newspaper interview that had clearly eluded studio monitors, Valentino vented his personal feelings about love between a man and woman who were practicing matrimony without a license. In his ro-

mantic view, lovemaking between unmarried lovers wasn't to be written off as sinful. The heart mattered far more than any piece of paper.
"What man-made contract is justly sufficient to hold two people apart
that love one another?" he asked, using words charged with private
meaning. "If they have been unfortunate in selection and later in life
really love one another—there is no power that should be strong
enough to keep them apart. It seems to me a greater sin to mock love,
to live with a person you have no regard for, than it is to throw down
man-made laws and go to the person you love." By his lights, conventional thinking about marriage and divorce needed revision. He had
traveled quite a distance from the values espoused by his devoutly
Catholic mother back in Italy, having adopted forgiving Frenchified
views similar to Natacha's and Madame Glyn's. "Some of our conven-
tions of civilizations today are echoes of the barbaric past."

Hollywood, and in fact postwar America in general, had been
widely exposed to the forgiving sexual morality that was freely practiced by European bohemians and sophisticates. The trend that had
started with the arrival in the American film colony of people like
Nazimova, and would continue with the importation of talents like
Pola Negri, Ernst Lubitsch, and Garbo, had picked up steam since
Erich von Stroheim had started making feature films. In his first feature, the box-office hit *Blind Husbands* (1919), he directed himself as a
philandering Austrian officer who while on leave in the Tyrol takes advantage of a frustrated and neglected American wife by seducing her.
Stroheim, like Valentino, played a sophisticated European impeccably
turned out in an officer's uniform and with a well-honed ability to kiss
a lady's hand while hinting of more intimate kisses to come. But while
Valentino had put his villainous screen cad phase behind him to
become a screen lover in earnest, Stroheim continued to revel in his
on-camera iniquity. Producers protested his costly, lengthy, much-
censored productions, but Stroheim's many fans couldn't get enough
of his delicious villainy; he was the Man You Loved to Hate.

Valentino no longer played scoundrels, but his looks continued to
suggest danger. When, after he died, one of the fan magazines asked
Elinor Glyn to comment on Rudolph Valentino and explain his appeal,

she hit on his provocative air of menace. "He looked dangerous and not to be teased with impunity. He looked as if he knew everything about love. Valentino represented the polished, sophisticated lover." His knowing ways appealed to American women but threatened their husbands. The very qualities that spelled seductiveness to Elinor Glyn and her American sisters were read with suspicion by American men.

The Vienna-born actor Joseph Schildkraut doesn't seem to have caused much of a stir when he diagnosed outbursts of moral rigidity in America as symptoms of the country's youth and provincialism. He said, "America is very young. Europe is very old. In America you are having a sex awakening. . . . The country is in a state of puberty so far as sex is concerned. . . . American women . . . are romance starved because the men here do not know the art of lovemaking. They laugh . . . to see a man kiss a woman's hand. They do not understand this gesture of gallantry. American men do not like foreigners because they are too adept at romance. American men . . . possess no fantasy. The American man dies sixteen deaths inside him before he says, 'I love you.' Yet he resents and fears the . . . innate subtlety of the foreigner." Unfortunately, when Valentino, seven years earlier, said what amounted to the very same thing—that "the American man is impossible as a lover" and resents the European male trained to make his lovemaking "exquisite and entertaining and delicate"—his attack on the amatory skills of American men became part of an ongoing public-relations disaster for him.

By the time *Beyond the Rocks* opened in New York in May of 1922, Valentino and Natacha had purchased and started fixing up the house on Wedgewood Place, settling in for what they hoped would be a time of domestic happiness, prosperity, stability, and professional productivity. But it was not to be. Less than six months after they began work on their new nest, Valentino's name screamed from headlines in every sensational newspaper in the land. Too ardent to wait, he had married Natacha before a year had elapsed after his interlocutory decree and was thus technically still wed to Jean Acker. The murder of director William Desmond Taylor in February 1922 had added fuel to the already raging furor about Hollywood morals, and a publicity-hungry

Los Angeles district attorney decided to ride the wave of public out-
rage by charging Valentino with bigamy. The front-page stories—
"VALENTINO MARRIAGE; POSSIBLE BIGAMY ANGLE DISCLOSED BY
WEDDING TO PERFUMER'S HEIRESS"—didn't hurt box office for the
Swanson-Valentino romance. "GLYN STORY WITH VALENTINO PULLS
RECORD FOR RIVOLI," another headline ran. "VALENTINO'S UNDESIR-
ABLE PUBLICITY HELPED RIVOLI."

11

THE BIGAMIST

For a wife, a man should pick out a woman who is pretty, has a good disposition, and is domestically inclined," Valentino stated (via his ghostwriter) in an article called "Woman and Love," which was published in *Photoplay* two months before he and Natacha Rambova first tied the knot, on May 13, 1922, in Mexicali, Mexico. Pretty, domestically inclined women who have good dispositions are rare these days, he went on to observe sadly, but then again, he insisted, puffing out his chest like a prize rooster, "we Europeans do not expect too much of one woman."

"We Europeans" did prefer a wife who wanted someday in the not too distant future to become a mother. "Should I try again to find me a wife," Valentino confided to his public, "let me find one who wishes to have children and who when she has them wishes to take care of them. That is the proper test for the good woman who is to share the side of your life."

His written ideas about wives have little relation to his actual choices. Neither of the two women Valentino married qualified as domestic angel or mother hen, though both scored high in the looks department. His mother, Gabriella, did fit the mold of gentle and genteel wifely devotion to husband, home, and family, but young, available versions of Gabriella, if they existed at all in postwar Hollywood, don't seem to have held much allure for Valentino. He gravitated toward women who Did Things within his world of motion pictures.

Although he was consistently attracted to advanced New Women who were accomplished, independent, and sophisticated; although he owed much of his own career success to influential, talented, and childless Hollywood Amazons such as Alla Nazimova and June Mathis, he liked to think of himself as the traditional dominant male who condescended to a deferential mate. As he put it, "A woman can never have a happy love affair with a man unless he is her superior."

It's hard to know how much of this *Photoplay* chest thumping represents Valentino's true thinking and how much was public relations drivel, designed to deliver to fans the opinions movie magazine editors and writers thought they wanted to hear. But there are other, less-processed sources verifying Valentino's Old World opinions about a woman's proper role. When he and Natacha eventually parted company in 1925, those views would come spilling into full view. He would reiterate that he'd always wanted a wife who would stay home, tend to children, put her husband's needs first. Natacha would respond in public that a career and independence had always mattered a great deal to her, and insist that Valentino should have realized this from the start.

Conservative in his views about wives, Valentino remained permissive, continental, and modern in his thinking about private pleasures; he opposed the uplifters' attempts to legislate morality, indicating his solidarity with the much-maligned Roscoe "Fatty" Arbuckle by appearing with Arbuckle in a comic short film, *Character Studies*, which was released between Arbuckle's first two trials for manslaughter. In an interview with writer Willis Goldbeck he blamed Prohibition on old biddies who have nothing better to do than to interfere with and try to correct the misbehaving, easily swayed multitude. This same group of dried-up Mrs. Grundys were also behind the current Hollywood push for a morality cleanup, he alleged, allying himself with libertarians opposed to repressive measures. American women, Valentino argued, referring to their recently won suffrage rights, "have done nothing with the vote." The frivolous young ones "concentrate on marcel waves. The power falls, then, to the disappointed woman, the old woman, the sex-starved woman. . . . She is inevitably a reactionary, a censor, and interferer." If Valentino wasn't reading Freud, his use of terms like "sex-starved" hints that he'd picked up Freudian notions about repression and sublimation that floated at large in Hollywood's orange blossom–scented air.

Natacha never sought the role of the submissive and domestic little woman. Far from it. Strong-willed and exacting, with a sense of entitlement that her privileged upbringing and beauty ratified, she possessed many talents, and in any endeavor she undertook she preferred to sit at the helm. In response to Rudy's remark to her that she would never find a husband if she couldn't cook, Patsy Ruth Miller commented that she doubted that Natacha ever learned even to make "burnt fudge." In fact, Natacha apparently could and did bake a little, enjoyed nesting when it summoned her abilities in home decoration, and was a fine seamstress. But she wanted to make her mark in the wider world of the arts and had no interest in staying in the background darning socks for her man. She loved dogs, but children did not rank high on her list of priorities. In their first days together at Natacha's Sunset Boulevard bungalow she and Rudy had enjoyed playing house. Now, on Wedgewood Place in Whitley Heights, they relegated tasks they considered menial to servants. They lived like lord and lady of the manor, as if Valentino actually received the stratospheric salary other major stars commanded. Under his new contract, while he was working he now fetched $1,250 a week, but since he had many debts, he was always in arrears. Robert Florey commented, "He earned little but spent much." The "little" is relative, of course. A star like Thomas Meighan was paid $5,000 weekly by Famous Players–Lasky, whether or not he was filming.

Natacha, now completing work with Nazimova on *Salome*, continued to contribute her salary to the household, though, having left Metro in favor of Nazimova's self-financed and *outré* productions, she now earned less than Rudy did. She supervised the remodeling and decorating of their Whitley Heights house, installing black marble floors, black velvet couches, and flame-colored curtains; but as their professional talents were much in demand, they both went off to work in the morning; at present that arrangement suited them just fine. Natacha's current project engaged all her considerable creative power. Her daring designs for *Salome*, based on Aubrey Beardsley's notorious black-and-white illustrations for the Oscar Wilde version of the biblical story, allowed her to dress a Syrian captain in mesh jersey with painted nipples and to costume Nazimova as Salome in a tunic with side slits and crown her with a headpiece made up of vibrating glass bubbles dangling from strings. Natacha was content in her work and apparently happy with Rudy. Although the seeds of later conflict between them were present from the start, just waiting to sprout, as yet they lay dormant.

Right now Rudy and Natacha made a compatible team: lovers, soul mates, companions, style setters, cosmopolites, and housemates who often collaborated in their work and who supported each other's career endeavors. In particular, she aided him, although her fame and cachet surely increased because of her intimacy with Valentino. "She is the finest woman I know," he told a reporter a few days before their Mexican wedding, "and has already had a great influence on my career." In 1922, the outside world, not internal strife about the way partners in a marriage should function, presented the chief obstacle to wedded bliss.

Since March, Rudy had been working to complete *Blood and Sand*, his first picture for Famous Players–Lasky for which he at last was granted star billing, and the first for which the studio made good on its promise to employ June Mathis as scenarist and adapter. Once again Mathis would be developing a script for Valentino based on a popular Blasco Ibáñez novel, originally published in Spanish, with Hispanic characters. It takes place in Seville, and once again (as in *The Four Horsemen*) Valentino on-screen would straighten his spine and click the heels of his boots in dramatic Latin dance tempo (flamenco this time), rough up his partner on the floor of a smoky dance café, dote on his mother back home, and romance a woman who was not his wife. Mathis again would have a chance to indulge her propensity (shared with Blasco Ibáñez) for heavy-handed sermonizing, portentous maxims ("The crowd is a beast with ten thousand heads"), and foreboding mysticism. This time the gloomy ruminations issue mostly from the mouth of the philosopher Don Joselito (Charles Belcher), whose study is filled with death's heads and torture devices from the Inquisition, and who takes a dark view of Spain's passion for bullfighting. His murky utterances are all that remains of the fierce denunciation of the cruelties of the bullring implicit in the Blasco Ibáñez novel.

Valentino plays Juan Gallardo, a doomed and impetuous matador contaminated by the sadism built into the rituals of the bullring, where "cruelty is disguised as sport." Although he rises from peasant roots to the pinnacles of wealth and popular adulation, his glory flames only briefly. Distracted by his fickle mistress and drained by dissipation, he dies in the arena, gored by a bull. No surprise. The gory death of a childhood friend has foreshadowed his own premature demise. "Happiness built on cruelty cannot survive," we've been advised.

Valentino's character, Gallardo, grows up in Seville as the curly-headed rapscallion son of a stout widow (played by Rosa Rosanova) who chases him with a broom when he misbehaves, then melts when he takes her hand and sweet-talks her. He's a charmer, an affectionate daredevil. His dead father was a shoemaker, but Juan shows no interest in working in a leather shop; instead he dreams of becoming a hero, an acclaimed bullfighter, promising his mother, "Someday I will build you a fine house."

His fond, forgiving mother is one of three women with powerful claims on Gallardo's heart as he grows older. The other two are his saintly wife, Carmen, played by Lila Lee, a petite, cameo-like beauty in a white mantilla, and the larger-than-life temptress Doña Sol, acted with over-the-top gusto by the sinuous, flashing-eyed brunette Nita Naldi. Carmen, the wife, has modesty, home, family, and tradition in her favor. She lives with Gallardo and their extended family in Seville. A devout woman who wears a cross around her neck and is given to fervent prayer, she's Gallardo's bride before God and appeals to the part of him that's tradition-loving, honorable, and faithful. But Gallardo has a shadow side, which takes over. He grapples with moral weakness, lacking the strength to resist temptations of the flesh. When vampish Doña Sol, a rich and glamorous widow, all feathers, furs, décolletage, and flounce, sets out to entrap and seduce him, she proves overpowering. Surrounded by incense burners and a turbaned black servant, she's sin incarnate. Naldi said that she was made up to resemble Dracula, and that Blasco Ibáñez himself decided to cast her as Doña Sol after meeting her at a New York dinner party. The Spanish novelist and Naldi got into a heated argument about the wealth of the Catholic Church (which he thought should be donated to the poor), and at dinner he became so angry at her (she thought his views Communistic) that his false teeth dropped into the front of her low-cut gown. Her response must have been vivid, for he instantly decided she'd be perfect to play a sadistic demon, even though his original Doña Sol, in the novel, was a blonde.

Watching Gallardo triumph as a matador, Doña Sol tosses him a ring in the shape of a serpent that had belonged to Cleopatra, then lures him to her home so they can be alone when she writhes like a boa constrictor. Just as success and the crowd's worship deceived him about what really has value, so now does a conniving vixen. He succumbs to Doña Sol, devouring her with a long, cannibalistic, and very hot kiss. Hovering close to Doña Sol's bare shoulders as she strums a harp, we see him struggling to quell desire, then yielding to it, becoming as powerless to restrain himself as a provoked bull in the ring. He's all animal, deliciously savage. As Jeanine Basinger writes in *Silent Stars*, Valentino here conveys "a passion that is slightly kinky, with a touch of rape and sadism." Turn on the air conditioning.

Valentino had enough self-confidence and generosity to allow Nita Naldi to loom large on the screen. He knew he didn't have to dominate each frame. Naldi would give him credit for playing "the big scenes with me in the foreground," adding that she thought "his willingness to cooperate with other members of the cast" played no small part in his success. But even as Naldi slinks and vamps with abandon, it's Valentino's skill in evoking Gallardo's emotional turmoil that most compels the viewer.

Gallardo's struggle, between devotion to the self-sacrificing wife he cherishes and lust for an aristocratic *femme fatale*, mirrors similar

tension in his portrayer's psyche. Valentino's private, off-screen conflicts can't be split into neat polarities—good and bad, virtuous and
sinful—like Gallardo's opposing lady loves in *Blood and Sand*. But Valentino, with one foot in nineteenth-century Italy and the other in
1920s Hollywood, did grapple with contradictory impulses and values, did seek a mate who managed to unite the Madonna and the vamp
in one body. In real life he sought both an old-fashioned stay-at-home
wife like Carmen and an aggressive, exotic siren like Doña Sol. Natacha, who looked a little like Nita Naldi, also like Naldi had Irish ancestry (Naldi was born Donna Dooley), favored the same kind of
Arabian Nights attire, and actually befriended Naldi. (The only other
Valentino leading lady Natacha cozied up to was Nazimova, but that
relationship was established before Valentino entered the picture.) As
a type, Natacha tilted more in the direction of the voluptuous, sexually liberated woman of the world than the Madonna, but Rudy had to
turn her into the embodiment of everything good, selfless, and noble,
too. He wanted her to behave like both Naldi's Doña Sol and Lila Lee's
nurturing Carmen. Natacha always spoke of her maternal feelings
toward Rudy, "the eternal boy," and in a letter to her he dubbed himself "your baby."

Natacha said that Rudy lived the role of Gallardo when he was
filming *Blood and Sand*, sometimes "leering at me the way he looked at
Doña Sol or else gazing at me with the great beseeching eyes he used
in the film toward his little wife. . . . He never dropped the part for a
moment." He was a Method actor before that term came into popular
use. (Remember, one of his on-the-job acting teachers had been Nazimova, who'd worked with Stanislavsky at the Moscow Art Theatre.)
Natacha especially admired Rudy's acting in the love scenes, many of
which were eventually cut. "They took out most of the love scenes,"
she complained. "It seemed cruel, for they were delightful, so full of
old Spain. With American men lovemaking is merely an annoying preliminary. With a Latin it is like an obligato of a delicate music motif."
And Rudy knew that score by heart.

When her busy work schedule permitted, Natacha visited the set
of *Blood and Sand*. Jesse Lasky made her welcome at the Lasky ranch in

the San Fernando Valley, where most of the film was shot. (Now it's Forest Lawn Cemetery.) She claimed she made herself useful, negotiating squabbles between Valentino and director Fred Niblo. Niblo, a veteran director of Thomas Ince productions who'd recently presided over the Douglas Fairbanks hits *The Mark of Zorro* and *The Three Musketeers*, was not Valentino's preferred choice for director. He'd favored (and would later insist he'd been promised) George Fitzmaurice but was told by Jesse Lasky that Mr. Fitzmaurice had turned down the job.

Valentino himself said he enjoyed playing Juan more than any character he'd created to date, "for there was the opportunity to show in him a complete life from early youth to death." He also said that, as he had with Julio Desnoyers, he identified closely with his character and invested heavily in his portrayal. "I felt little in common with the Sheik, but there was much in the character and experience of . . . El Gallardo that I understood intimately and sympathetically." Gallardo, however, manipulated by the crowd in the arena and by Doña Sol, "was more the puppet than Julio," Valentino pointed out. The parallels between Valentino and Gallardo would come to seem even more striking after Rudy's sudden, youthful death. The rapid rise and fall of a troubled idol, the fickleness and sadism of the crowd, a dark beauty's need to dominate, these common motifs chime eerily in both the fictional story of Gallardo and the real-life story of Rudolph Valentino.

Although the movie's melodramatic acting style and titles like "Snake! One minute I love you—the next I hate you!" sometimes prompted scoffing titters from the overflow first-run crowd at the Rivoli in New York, Valentino delivered an intense, deeply affecting performance that was admired for its "fine repression [and] sudden tenderness" by the likes of Chaplin and French director René Clair. The latter, who saw only a version of *Blood and Sand* that had been edited and apparently mauled to suit "French taste," credited Valentino for creating in Gallardo a character "at once noble, vulgar, sensual and full of pride. . . . His ennui, desire and rage . . . are the expressions of a great actor."

Valentino and Natacha had both hoped that Lasky would make good on his promise to shoot the film on location in Spain and help them to fulfill their dream of working in Europe. But to keep costs down the studio decided to buy some of the props and costumes in Spain but confine production to backlots in the Los Angeles area, relying on reflectors to simulate the blazing Spanish sunlight. Rudy would insist on shooting two versions of the scenes showing him in close-up, one in which he speaks in English and the other in which he speaks his lines in Spanish, for the benefit of the lip-readers in Spanish-speaking audiences.

Robert Florey said one excuse given for the studio's decision to film in Los Angeles was that the Hays Office (which sought to limit screen brutality) made photographing anything like a real bullfight with live actors and live bulls out of the question. Instead, film editor Dorothy Arzner spliced in existing stock footage of real bullfights and matched close-ups of Valentino to the stock long shots, sparing both Valentino's hide and the Famous Players–Lasky checkbook. Although he never faced a flesh-and-blood, charging, bleeding, fire-breathing bull, Valentino did train to use the *muleta* (a piece of crimson serge draped over a matador's stick) and cape (pink silk with red lining) to make passes like a real matador, and learned how to prod a charging bull the authentic way. In the bullfight scenes his face, made up to have thickened brows that meet in the middle, persuasively registers solemnity, defiance, and pride, and he moves with characteristic poise. His trainer, once a matador in Spain and Mexico, happened to be the father of actor Gilbert Roland, who played a bit part in the picture and helped Valentino into one of his gorgeous thirty-five-pound silver-and-gold brocade "suits of lights." But, despite the artistry of Arzner's editing and Valentino's impassioned acting, anyone viewing the bullfight scenes can't help noticing that they're watching a hokey simulation. *Movie Weekly* was on target when it called these episodes "circusy."

To compensate for his disappointment at the decision not to film in Spain, the studio promised that the next major Valentino film scheduled, *Don Cesar de Bazan*, really would be filmed in Europe.

In mid-May 1922, after completing shooting for *Blood and Sand*, Rudy found he had some unscheduled time at his disposal, and he and Natacha, with Douglas Gerrard, Paul Ivano, and Nazimova, piled into several cars and headed south toward the Palm Springs home of their friend Dr. Florilla White, a physician from the East Coast who no longer practiced medicine. On May 1 Valentino had paid Jean Acker a lump sum of twelve thousand dollars, having borrowed five thousand from the studio to do so, and now that he no longer needed to make additional support payments he believed himself to be, finally, free of any further obligation to her. He and Natacha were looking forward to living as Mr. and Mrs. Rudolph Valentino in the Whitley Heights home they'd been fixing up, and this seemed the right moment to take the plunge.

A year and a half after the Arbuckle scandal and only a few months since the headline-grabbing revelation of Wallace Reid's addiction to morphine and the subsequent (but unrelated) bizarre murder of director William Desmond Taylor, Valentino no doubt harbored well-justified anxieties about being caught living in sin with Natacha. The mucky-mucks at Famous Players–Lasky and the sensation-greedy press would point the finger of blame in their direction and deny them the tranquillity they so craved. "ZUKOR BELIEVES IT'S CLEANUP TIME AT FAMOUS-PLAYERS-LASKY LOT," a *Variety* headline warned soon after Taylor's funeral (which Valentino attended), the biggest so far for a private citizen. "[Zukor] Left This Week for Los Angeles—Film Scandals Have Uniformly Involved Famous Players–Lasky People." Now Will Hays held sway in the motion picture kingdom, keeping a lid on screen sin, and the studios would soon be requiring performers to sign contracts containing morality clauses that threatened immediate termination if an actor committed an offense that would "tend to degrade him in society or bring him into public hatred, scorn, or ridicule." Rudy and Natacha couldn't wait to make their union legal, public, and beyond reproach.

Although aware that according to California law a full year had to elapse after an interlocutory decree before either divorcing party could rewed, Rudy and Natacha both thought that by marrying in Mexico, even if it was only two months since the decree, they could bypass that loophole and legitimately tie the knot. Waiting until the final decree in March of 1923 didn't appeal to them, and they knew personally many

Hollywood people who had married out of the state, before the year expired, with no dire consequences. Friends Dagmar Godowsky and Frank Mayo, for example, got hitched in Tia Juana right after Mayo's first decree. Since others seemed to have married in Mexico with impunity, why shouldn't they? they reasoned. Dagmar Godowsky claimed in an interview with John Kobal that she was the one who had told Rudy about the option of getting married in Mexico; she'd been informed by no less an authority than a lawyer for Paramount's Cecil B. DeMille that going across the border made it okay.

On the morning of Saturday, May 13, the Valentino wedding party motored from El Centro, in the Imperial Valley, where they had spent a night at the Barbara Worth Hotel, over the California-Mexico border and on to the home of Mexicali's mayor, Otto Moller. Everything for the festive celebration and ceremony had been prepared in advance. The whole Mexican town turned out as a military brass band of forty strong blared a wedding march, and a string orchestra serenaded the celebrants from a porch. Douglas Gerrard, who served as best man, would report that Rudy and Natacha got cold feet, just briefly. They shared a moment of hesitation about whether to proceed with the wedding, and "were urged by all present to contract the marriage." American officials who were present also gave the green light.

The bride wore a knit ensemble with a white checked pattern against a dark blue or black background; the tieless groom wore an open-collared shirt, a tan sports jacket, sporty trousers, and a big grin. After a short ceremony performed by Judge Sandoval, a Mexican breakfast was served, after which corks popped and champagne flowed. The party lasted until seven in the evening, when the (probably less robust) band struck up another march as the mayor and the chief of police accompanied the newlyweds and their friends to the border.

Back in Palm Springs, the couple retired to a bungalow on Dr. White's property. Best man Douglas Gerrard slept on the outside porch, Rudy and Natacha inside. All seemed calm and joyous under the desert sky. The newlyweds intended to remain in Palm Springs, far from the Hollywood crush, for several weeks.

The following Monday morning a phone call to Rudy from the studio instantly turned the sky black. A Los Angeles superior court judge, one John W. Summerfield, had made a statement to the press calling into question the legality of the Mexicali marriage. According to the *Los Angeles Times*, the judge "stated that the entry of an interlocutory decree of divorce was nothing more than an order of the court that, nothing interfering, the parties would be entitled to a divorce after a year had elapsed, and that, if they attempted marriage within a year, the result would be bigamy." A headline ran: "VALENTINO MARRIAGE; POSSIBLE BIGAMY ANGLE DISCLOSED IN WEDDING TO PERFUMER'S HEIRESS." As Natacha would point out, "If Rudy hadn't been Rudy they wouldn't have jumped on us." She compared fame to an X-ray machine that exposes one's very heartbeats "to a gaping world." But Rudy *was* Rudy, and hundreds of thousands of newspapers could be hawked by magnifying the possible misstep of the Mexicali wedding and turning it into a major scandal. Distraught and frightened, Rudy and Natacha returned at once to Hollywood. There, at the home they wouldn't share again for years, they wept in each other's arms.

Their worst fears were realized, then surpassed, as studio lawyers advised the couple to separate. Natacha decided to leave at once for New York. She hated to go, especially since in the East she would be depending on the hospitality of her parents, who, though they liked and admired Rudy, had been less than overjoyed at the prospect of an actor son-in-law and by all the publicity following the wedding. But go she did, in extreme haste, taking with her on the train only the Pekingese puppy Rudy had given her the previous Christmas and a lone hatbox. Rudy drove her to the Union Pacific station at Pomona, bestowing a hurried farewell kiss as the train began to move. He telegraphed the Hudnuts at the Biltmore Hotel in New York, advising them that Natacha was on her way to New York. Once Richard Hudnut heard that his adopted daughter was en route, he issued the following statement: "My daughter has left California to come here for a talk with us. We requested her to do so. She may remain some time. Our confidence in Mr. Valentino is unimpaired. He is a splendid man, with plenty of character."

His father in-law's support warmed Rudy's heart, but didn't begin to calm his nerves. Rudy found himself overwrought. The eagerly sought union with Natacha had been within his grasp, had actually been sipped like a perfect glass of wine brought to his lips, only to be snatched away and abruptly shattered. Accepting the advice of his own attorney, W. I. Gilbert, he grimly turned himself in and was promptly arraigned and jailed on two counts of bigamy, one for marrying before his divorce was final and another for consummating the marriage to Natacha ("unlawful and felonious co-habiting") in Palm Springs. His nightmare of six years past—the indignity of his arrest and imprisonment in New York's Tombs on a trumped-up vice charge—was being reprised in all its shame. A more recent trauma—humiliating public scrutiny in the courtroom about the nature of his physical relationship to Jean Acker—must also have replayed in his mind. He pined for Natacha and fumed at the studio for treating her as if she were a piece of unwanted furniture that had to be shipped back to the store.

Instead of providing her a private compartment on the train, which out of respect for her as a film professional and a star's wife Rudy felt she surely deserved, "the company provided Mrs. Valentino with a ticket and a lower berth, which they charged to me, and she was compelled to make the four-day trip without any . . . privacy where she could hide her sorrow." Reporters hounded her on the train, but she refused to speak with them. Informed in Chicago that Valentino had been placed behind bars, she broke down in tears. Many who observed Natacha at other moments in her life described her as remote and hard to reach. In this situation, her guard down, she was extremely emotional, clearly heartbroken. Although she quite understandably didn't want to share her most private feelings with pushy strangers from the press, deep pain was written all over her, and she came closer to matching Rudy in her expressiveness and vulnerability than at any other point during his lifetime.

Rudy's own emotional metal turned molten. His friend the writer Adela Rogers St. Johns visited him in jail and found him "shaking the bars of his cell—his face wet with tears," shouting, "I rot here before I deny our sacred marriage. She is my wife, my wife." Bail was set at ten thousand dollars in cash.

The prosecuting Los Angeles district attorney, Thomas L. Wool-

wine, was availing himself of a choice opportunity to polish an image
that had been tarnished by recent publicity regarding his dalliance with
a female employee at certain hotels in the San Diego area. Running for
reelection, he had incurred the wrath of the Methodists, not only because of his sexual peccadillos but also because he had come out for
nullification of the Volstead Act, which enforced Prohibition. An ambitious man who ran for governor of California in 1918 and was de-
feated by Hiram Johnson, Woolwine had been keeping his name in the
papers, and scoring points as a commander in the war against sin, by
seeming to be aggressively seeking to solve the mystery of the murder
of William Desmond Taylor. Friendly with many Hollywood movers
and shakers, he often spoke at studio banquets. He personally had
journeyed to Mexicali, questioning the mayor there and obtaining the
names of witnesses to the wedding.

The executives at Famous Players—Lasky worried far more about
profits and preserving the studio's reputation than they did about
Rudolph Valentino's personal happiness or legal tribulations. Cecil B.
DeMille, currently a studio executive, sent an urgent and confidential
telegram to Zukor in New York about the mess Valentino had gotten
himself into: "DISTRICT ATTORNEY IS PREPARING TO PROSECUTE VAL-
ENTINO FOR BIGAMY ACCOUNT OF HIS MARRIAGE TO RAMBOVA AT MEXI-
CALIA [sic] AM USING EVERY MEANS AT MY DISPOSAL TO STRAIGHTEN
MATTERS AND HOPE TO BE SUCCESSFUL BUT BELIEVE YOU SHOULD KNOW
HOW MATTERS STAND AND BE PREPARED IN CASE STORM BREAKS."

Simply put, the studio's strategy was to distance itself from
Valentino, who from its point of view had acted rashly and foolishly,
contributing needlessly to an already extensive list of headaches, legal
difficulties, and public-relations problems. Valentino's jailing occurred
on a Sunday, a day when banks were closed and ten thousand dollars in
cash was not easy to raise. The studio brass made no effort to immediately come forward with the bail money and rescue the star from the
indignity of jail; they didn't want anyone to think they were in a hurry
to condone bigamy, and they very likely believed the tidal wave of publicity would only increase Valentino's box-office appeal. As a group
of producers scheduled a meeting to plan "precautionary measures
against further scandals," word went out that by refusing to immedi-

ately furnish bail to Valentino, Famous Players–Lasky hoped to make
an example of him. Their attitude resembled that of a fed-up father
who refuses to come to the aid of a teenage son who has smashed up
the family car. Let him stew in his own juices for a while; that'll teach
him.

Douglas Gerrard rushed to his friend's defense, assuring the press
that the Mexican wedding was valid. "Mr. Valentino went to Mexicali
with a letter from the Mexican consul here [Valentino's friend Manuel
Reachi], directed to the mayor of the city," he stated. "Innumerable
documents had to be signed, and there were nearly a dozen witnesses
to the marriage."

Gerrard, a native of Dublin, contacted his friend and fellow Irishman Dan O'Brien, chief of police in San Francisco, who happened to
be visiting Los Angeles, and whose son George had served as Valentino's double in *Moran of the Lady Letty*. When Gerrard called Dan
O'Brien, the popular and prosperous Famous Players–Lasky actor
Thomas Meighan happened to be with O'Brien. Meighan hardly knew
Valentino, but he came forward and put up a large chunk of the bail
money. June Mathis and director George Melford also contributed
some of the cash. So did Famous Players–Lasky attorney Frank James,
but only after Valentino had already spent two days steaming and sobbing in the slammer.

Once Valentino was freed on bail, Gerrard moved into the house at
6770 Wedgewood Place in Whitley Heights, so that in Natacha's absence his unhinged friend wouldn't be left entirely alone as he tried to
subdue symphonies of frustration and faced the ordeal of another
highly publicized and sensationalized trial. On the night he was sprung
from jail, Valentino was guest of honor at a dinner party Gerrard hosted
at the Los Angeles Athletic Club. Present, according to the *Los Angeles
Times*, were director James Young (a friend from New York days who'd
directed Rudy in two films); Fred Thompson, who was secretary of
the Motion Picture Directors' Association; and police chief Daniel J.
O'Brien of San Francisco. It didn't hurt to have a friend in court, even
if the court happened to be in another city.

Like other trials during the sensation-hungry 1920s, Valentino's
bigamy hearing became a living-theater event, a tabloid melodrama

ten times juicier than *The Perils of Pauline*. A court reporter, Reginald Taviner, described the scene in the courtroom as a bang-up affair "like a gangster's funeral, with armed guards . . . to keep the flappers from literally crushing Rudy to death. Femininity, in all shapes and ages, jammed the courtroom." Before he went down to the courtroom, Rudy won the affection of the reporters on hand in an upstairs room by sharing with them his three fingers of booze topped with a spritz of mineral water. After that, "We knew that he wasn't such a bad guy."

Valentino's public defense of his decision to marry Natacha before he had obtained his final decree in his divorce from Jean Acker only bolstered his image as a romantic hero, a twentieth-century Romeo so ardent and impetuous he couldn't wait to become husband to his lady love. He expressed profound regret for doing anything "that would lower me in the estimation of the American people who have . . . accepted me at every turn for more than I conceive to be my real worth." Love, he explained, had driven him to act hastily, but he'd been prompted "by the noblest intentions that a man could have. I loved deeply, but in loving I may have erred." In other words, he'd loved not wisely but too well.

His friends, with his lawyer, mounted an elaborate legal defense that (unfortunately for Valentino's reputation as a lover) hinged on "proving" that he and Natacha had not slept together following the wedding and the marriage hadn't been consummated. They all knew this was poppycock—the newlyweds *had* slept together—but they wanted to get Rudy off the hook. Douglas Gerrard was the one who had spent the night on the sleeping porch of the Palm Springs bungalow at Dr. White's spread and had been observed in the morning's wee hours by a passerby on horseback, an American Indian who used to ride by daily to check on his cattle. Paul Ivano perjured himself by testifying that because she had fallen ill following the wedding, Natacha had retired to bed by herself and Rudy slept on the porch; he had a witness to prove it, Ivano said. The Indian passerby was called. He actually knew nothing about the identity of the sleeper on the porch, only that he'd seen a dormant male figure, but he swore that the man he saw was Valentino, even that they'd spoken in Spanish.

During several days of court testimony, reported upon in minute detail by the press, Dr. White confirmed that the bride had become ill and stayed in a part of the house separate from Valentino. A woman employed by Dr. White as a maid, Ramalda Lugo, stated that she'd seen Nazimova at Dr. White's, clad in purple silk pajamas, and a Palm Springs deputy sheriff reported that he'd seen Valentino and "Mrs. Shaughnessy-Valentino" having breakfast on the porch of the bridal cottage, also attired in purple pajamas. "PURPLE PAJAMAS FIGURE IN TRIAL," a titillating headline ran. Valentino set the record straight: his so-called pajamas were in fact Chinese robes, and his were white, not purple. The various purple and white silk lounging garments were even displayed in court. Valentino's attorney shook his head in dismay. "It seems apparent," he said, "that the prosecution in this case is not entirely free from a desire for publicity." The entire case, he alleged, "was born in sensationalism."

Jean Acker had been extensively interviewed by the district attorney's staff, but she refused to press any bigamy charge on her own behalf. She told a reporter afterward that Valentino had called to thank her for this demur. She repaid his gratitude by announcing that she would soon be making six pictures, starring as "Mrs. Valentino." She had the legal right to that name, she declared, for several more months, and she intended to make every possible use of it. The Los Angeles papers ran photos of the two wives, Jean Acker and Natacha Rambova, adjacent to one another, while in Washington Senator Henry L. Meyers, pushing for censorship, named "one Valentino, now figuring as the star character in rape and divorce sensations" as part of the depraved Hollywood colony "where debauchery, riotous living, drunkenness, ribaldry, dissipation, free love seem to be conspicuous."

On the fifth of June, Justice J. Walter Hanby dismissed the bigamy charge on grounds of insufficient evidence of cohabitation, and argued further that the law requiring a full year's wait after an interlocutory decree should be changed. This was cause for celebration, except that Rudy was in no mood to celebrate. He grieved that he and Natacha had to live a continent apart at a time when they desperately wanted to be together. He told the press, "There is a tear of regret because of the enforced absence of the woman who has been my inspiration and counselor in my art." The tear of regret was no mere figure of speech. Sometimes, out of nowhere, because of pining for Natacha or "obscure presentiments," his eyes would flood with tears.

The Hudnuts, who had planned to embark for Europe for the summer, decided to cancel their trip and stay in New York with "wretchedly unhappy" Natacha. She hadn't wanted to join them in France, feeling that she might be able to help Rudy in New York and that commiserating with him, advising him, and being able at least to talk to him by phone came first. The Hudnuts wanted to lend every possible support to Natacha and Rudy. They left their New York hotel and opened their mountain home in the Adirondacks, Foxlair, moving into it with Natacha. From there Natacha wrote and telegraphed Rudy frequently, sometimes more than once a day. She would be driven by a chauffeur some seventeen miles of winding mountain roads to the closest town, North Creek, where she could make a long-distance call to him in Hollywood. The phone and telegraph office Natacha used was in the North Creek railroad station, the very spot where, two decades earlier, Teddy Roosevelt had come down from the mountain to learn he'd be succeeding the mortally wounded McKinley as president.

At Foxlair, between trips to North Creek, Natacha grieved and pined. Richard Hudnut's nephew Herbert would remember her as an icy beauty dressed in long skirts to hide her heavy legs, and a matching turban, "all in exotic, glorious patterns of silk." He recalled that Natacha's "gloom was impenetrable, that the atmosphere around her was funereal." But the local townsfolk, who listened in on the North Creek telephone conversations if they happened to be waiting at the railroad station, hung on every word she uttered into the receiver, and had a very different impression of Natacha, who spoke baby talk to Rudy, as he evidently did to her. They found her colorful and slightly ditzy. The star-crossed Hollywood lovers called one another Babykins, which the locals delighted to mimic, scoffing. Her names for her parents, which Rudy, too, adopted, were also babyish: her mother was Muzzie and the dignified, very proper millionaire Hudnut, who spoke with a British accent after spending much of his youth in England, was Uncle Dickie.

In her memoir, Natacha printed one of Rudy's letters to her, addressed to "My very own and only babykins." In it, he says he finds some solace in their enforced separation, because it allows Natacha to emotionally let her hair down, to show him her "adorably feminine" tenderness and vulnerability, qualities she had previously, through "false pride and a wrong idea of reserve," felt the need to hide from him (and perhaps from herself). Genuine sentiment, he said, should never be mistaken for weakness; it was the stuff of life. He goes on to say that as he rereads her letters he more and more admires in her the feminine qualities he so prized in his dear mother, whose love he believes transcends death. He knows his mother loves Natacha like one of her own children, and her love offers them protection from harm. Some people might consider him old-fashioned, he says, but he really is not; he merely admires and respects "a womanly woman, a thing which nowadays seems to be a thing of the past." Opening his own heart, he tells her she embodies for him an ideal of loveliness that is sacred. "You are to me the most precious jewel God ever gifted me with." He says he will happily put up with suffering and privation for her sake and the sake of their happiness, because "it is through suffering that the best of our nature comes forth and is molded." He assures her that she should never think that he wants to receive only happy letters from her. She should not believe she has to keep tears to herself. "If you did that I should feel that you had stopped loving me. I want to share your tears as well as your joy."

After taking a break from letter writing to have a fencing lesson, he resumes the letter, closing with the happy thought that he will be in her arms at Foxlair within six weeks. Soon after that, he hopes, they may be able to be together in France, at the Hudnut villa near Nice. In intimate Italian, the language of his childhood, he signs off "*Sempre, sempre, sempre il tuo Bambino che ti adora e viva per te sola* [always, always, always your baby, who adores you and lives for you alone]."

During their separation, Natacha remained involved in Rudy's work by designing his costumes for *The Young Rajah*, a picture that followed close on the heels of *Blood and Sand* but that has not survived except in tattered fragments. Natacha's gorgeously glittering East Indian costume designs, perhaps sketched before she fled Hollywood, may have been the only good thing about this dud, the story (based on a popular novel, *Amos Judd*, and adapted by June Mathis) of an Indian-born Hindu prince, raised in New England and educated at Harvard, who has the gift of second sight. The young rajah, who returns to India to claim the throne from a usurper, can see into the future. When he does this, a white light shines from "right in the middle of his forehead, like the little girl who had a little curl." The surviving pallid love scenes between Rudy's character, Amos Judd, and his New England sweetheart, Molly Cabot (played by Wanda Hawley), have the blandness of some of Valentino's pre-Julio love scenes, minus their spark of comedy.

Preoccupied and upset, Valentino failed to deliver a dynamic performance in *The Young Rajah*, although he looked superb posing languorously in Natacha's extravagantly sensual costumes, which echoed Léon Bakst's designs for Nijinsky as the Golden Slave in *Schéhérazade*. As the young rajah, who during his years in New England had adopted Western dress, he reverted to the splendor of the Orient. Reclining in a swan-shaped boat, or meditating with crossed legs like a temple sculpture of a turbaned young Buddha, he dons jangling bracelets on his wrists and forearms and a ring for every finger. Bare-chested, he's covered with brown body paint and draped with ropes of twined pearls. He also displayed his mostly naked body in the New England portion of the story, when he's shown as part of a college rowing crew wearing only a skimpy, revealing bathing suit. Famous Players–Lasky had learned that beefcake could make for good box office, and Valentino, proud of his fine body and not at all averse to showing it off, played along. *Blood and Sand* also offered a provocatively revealing dressing scene that unfortunately has been cut in many modern prints.

Despite the athletic rowing sequence, the critics found the mystical, androgynous, sumptuously bejeweled Valentino of *The Young Rajah* "less virile" and less intensely physical than the dynamic Valentino of *Blood and Sand*. His best roles, said *Variety*, come spiked with "a dash of paprika." Instead, this one resembled a milk shake. Or, to switch metaphors with *Movie Weekly*, a sleeping potion. It wasn't Valentino's fault, most agreed: "Rodolfo [*sic*] really does his very best with a perfectly idiotic role."

He would later fret that "my appearance altered as a result of the messages that I had from Mrs. Valentino in New York [her stories about how she was mistreated on the train, and how miserable she felt] so that some scenes had to be cut because of my bad appearance on the screen." He complained to Natacha that during filming (some of which took place on San Francisco Bay) he sometimes had to work all night and had to contend with "cheap sets, cheap casts, cheap everything." Rudy began to turn against the studio, coming to feel increasingly since his imprisonment on the bigamy charge that it behaved toward him less like a supportive friend or parent than an exploitative, dishonest, and venal enemy.

Robert Florey corroborates that during the filming of *The Young Rajah* Rudy remained constantly lonely and downcast, grumbling about the bad role, the poor directing by Philip Rosen (an experienced cameraman but an undistinguished director Rudy never would have picked), the second-rate production, and the studio's ingratitude for all he had achieved for them. He threatened to chuck it all and flee to Natacha in New York. According to Florey, Rudy now suffered his first ulcer symptoms: stomach aches plagued him and he started to medicate himself with quantities of bicarbonate of soda in powder form.

June Mathis, who had chosen the novel *Amos Judd*, adapted it, and written the script that became *The Young Rajah*, was exempted from any responsibility for the flop, as far as Rudy was concerned. He faulted Famous Players–Lasky for all the picture's failings. Valentino answered a letter from a fan who wondered whether the film's disconnectedness should be blamed on censors who made too many cuts by insisting that the picture's flaws were the studio's responsibility, not the censors'.

Before embarking for New York and Natacha, Rudy had to make a public appearance in Los Angeles at the Rialto Theatre premiere of *Blood and Sand*, where fans eager to get in waited from eleven in the morning until ten at night. As giant spotlights were turned on the stars, Valentino gratified the crowd by appearing "in person," elegantly turned out, as did Lila Lee. (Nita Naldi was in New York.) The premiere, "one of the most brilliant in film history," brought out "nearly everybody of importance in the Hollywood colony," and pleased critics as well as fans. Edwin Schallert in Los Angeles hailed the picture as "the first great tragedy we have had in cinema," classing it with Griffith's *Broken Blossoms* and *The Four Horsemen*. "It is the great art that we have been calling for," he concluded. And this time, cinema art didn't win out at the expense of commerce. *Blood and Sand* became one of Hollywood's top four moneymakers of 1922, and would outperform *The Sheik* that year.

New York critics found much to praise, but were on the whole less generous. As *Blood and Sand* set new attendance records and grossed $37,400 in its first week at the Rivoli, *Variety* carped about a lack of focus in the directing and script, which resulted in a film that "seems to have no pattern" and had trouble settling on a theme. First the theme seemed to be fame, "the humble shoemaker raised to eminence as a national hero." Then it shifted to the question "What will be the fate of a man who lives by blood and cruelty?" Then a third conflict seemed central: "the moral struggle between the wife and the other woman." The directional signals kept changing, and a viewer couldn't help but get confused.

Variety's critic had picked up on a legitimate flaw. The film does have trouble making up its mind about what it's about, but it's hard to know how much of the fault lies with Mathis's script or Niblo's directing, and how much with the wholesale cutting the studio insisted upon after shooting had been completed. Rudy, who cared very much about *Blood and Sand* and considered his work in it his best yet, argued vehemently for retention of one particular sequence, in which Gallardo, after straying from his wife and subsequently losing concentration in the arena, has been injured; although mostly healed physically, he's morally damaged. When his wife fails to give him her blessing before he returns to face down the bulls, he defiantly throws away his crutch—willfully betraying good judgment and putting his life in peril. Valentino insisted that the crutch scene was necessary to win the sympathy of the audience for Gallardo. Lasky said the picture was simply too long and the scene had to go. Bitter words were exchanged. Lasky called him an ingrate; Famous Players–Lasky had made him a star. Valentino said nonsense, the work he did at Metro was responsible for his acclaim and success.

Not only was he fighting with his employer, he was struggling with his image; his personality and style continued to excite public controversy. In addition to the fallout from his recent imprisonment on bigamy charges, he stirred anger and resentment in some quarters just for being who he was. *The San Francisco Chronicle* conducted an informal poll in which a random sample of people were asked their take on Valentino while he was spending a few days in the Bay Area. First the male and then the female point of view was sought. Women found him "triumphantly seductive," but that same seductiveness "put the lovemaking of the average husband or sweetheart into discard as tame, flat and unimpassioned." Where women saw "a modishly dressed young man of undeniable good looks," men found a fop, "stagy and temperamental. Never did a professional beauty dress with more care to display his charms than does Rudolph Valentino." One male summed it up: "Many men desire to be another Douglas Fairbanks—but Valentino? I wonder."

The New York Times was not above the fray, using a film review as an occasion for an *ad hominem* assault. Finding much about *Blood and Sand* that was colorful and gripping, its reviewer nevertheless objected to its didactic tone and got in a few digs at Valentino: "Mr. Valentino has not been doing much acting of late. He's been slicking his hair and posing for the most part. But here," it conceded, "he's an actor again." Valentino's peacocklike self-display, his wild popularity with women, combined with his ability to cut loose in his performances and give vent to fiery passion and genuine torment, worked for some males as a bait that just could not be resisted. They had to chide and jeer, knocking the love god off his pedestal.

But other males, especially young ones seeking a model to imitate, copied his style. They may have wanted to behave like Fairbanks, with cheerful, nonchalant derring-do, but they wanted to look like Valentino. Those old enough to grow sideburns like Gallardo's did so, and had flares sewn into their trousers to make them resemble Julio Desnoyers's gaucho pants. Jesse Lasky, Jr., twelve years old in 1922 and living in Hollywood, remembers swaggering about with his buddies, all with hair greased down. "Someone even made a quick fortune by inventing a hair trap that insured no possible ripple in our slick flat-tops. We were called 'Vaselinos.'"

A Latin craze that had started in the wake of *The Four Horsemen of the Apocalypse* took off like a five-alarm fire once *Blood and Sand* hit the theaters. "America is learning to fox-trot all night to the strains of 'The Venetian Love Boat' and the jazzed version of 'La Golandrina.' Our men are learning to kiss a lady's hand without shuddering. Our women are demanding them dark, daring and delightful." The flapper is fading away, reported Grace Wilcox, a columnist for the *Los Angeles Times*—prematurely, as it turned out—and in her place came "the new, illusive, mysterious woman with her long skirts and long hair." Although legislators in Washington had in 1921 passed the first Quota Act, restricting the immigration to the United States of real Italians and Spaniards, moviegoers were exalting olive skin, shiny black hair, and velvet-brown eyes. Everybody young and beautiful, it seems, wanted to be like Valentino and Rambova, and many who were not young or beautiful wanted to dream about them, worship their images, bask in their starlight.

To a young immigrant of twenty-seven, a megastar who only five years earlier had been scrounging for jobs and wondering where his next meal would come from, the contradictions must have triggered profound perplexity. How to make sense of the combination of frenzied adulation and jeering contempt? Valentino surely nodded in agreement with this *Blood and Sand* truism: "How fickle the world, how insincere its plaudits! The same voice that shouts success will croak as loudly—failure!"

To keep his balance Rudy needed and depended heavily on his male friends during the three-month interval of enforced separation from Natacha. With them he could sometimes forget his troubles, indulge his party-loving side, and simply have a good time. The inner circle, all Europeans, consisted of Paul Ivano, Douglas Gerrard, Robert Florey (now working as a gag writer for Sunshine Comedies and soon to become head of foreign publicity for Fairbanks and Pickford), Mario Caracciolo (the handsome former cavalry officer from Naples who now played character roles as Mario Carillo), and Jean de Limur from Paris, a great friend of French comic Max Linder. Linder had moved from Paris to Hollywood and sometimes participated in the group's get-togethers, although he privately complained to Florey that he found Valentino too self-centered. The cronies would gather two or three times a week at chez Rudy to enjoy a meal usually prepared by either Rudy or Carillo. Sometimes neighbors would stop by: director Robert Vignola, or actors Jack Warren Kerrigan and Eugene O'Brien. The servant Frederick (Rudy's maître d') and his wife, Louise, the cook, rarely made an appearance, but dog tender Carl Widerman, entrusted with the care of Rudy's police dogs Marquis and Sheik, sometimes partook of a glass of red wine. These events were strictly stag. "Since Natacha was in the East, we never invited ladies."

Rudy loved food, but he preferred simple fare to haute cuisine. In addition to pasta, he liked good sausages, crusty bread soaked in olive oil or rubbed with garlic, and fresh fruit. Florey or Ivano would accompany him on trips to downtown Italian groceries on Main Street to buy ingredients for antipasto, Greek olives, and chestnuts from Lombardy—all favorites. Sometimes they went out to restaurants such as François (now Musso-Frank's) or Culver City speakeasies such as The Plantation. Back home at Rudy's, late at night after an evening out, Ivano might play records on the phonograph, and Rudy, dressed in his pajamas and a top hat, would pick up his ebony baton with its silver-knob handle and dance solo, inventing all kinds of new steps, until he collapsed in exhaustion. His favorite record, according to Florey, was the ragtime keyboard standard from the 1910s, "Canadian Capers."

He and his buddies enjoyed taking daytime drives to the beach near Crystal Pier, tossing the medicine ball with Jack Dempsey on the Santa Monica sand, riding horseback, taking in the American Legion prizefights, or seeing a movie at the Iris, Apollo, or Egyptian theaters.

Sometimes they would indulge in a game of shooting craps at a friend's home. At one such session, chez Florey's friend Georges Jaumier, Rudy lost fifteen dollars to Fatty Arbuckle, which put him in a foul temper; it wasn't forking over the money that bothered him, it was rather that he didn't like to lose.

When he'd completed filming *The Young Rajah* and could begin making ready for the trip to New York and reunion with Natacha, the male cronies gathered for an endless round of going-away parties for Rudy. At the tenth and last such farewell celebration, organized by Max Linder at his home, Linder went all out, hiring almost-nude dancing cuties from Havana and a jazz band. As they empty a bottle of Armagnac, the party starts getting silly. The band plays "Caravan" and de Limur stars himself in an improvised jazz ballet. Douglas Gerrard and Florey (all six feet four of him) impersonate chorus girls. Rudy, a cigar dangling from his mouth and a cane tucked under his arm, improvises a sort of cakewalk to "The Wabash Blues," "Crybaby Blues," and "Second Hand Rose." Then, for old time's sake, he reprises "La Chaloupée" from his cabaret days and does a campy turn to "The Sheik of Araby."

Afterward, back at his own place in the wee hours, Rudy can't sleep. Florey, Gerrard, and Ivano stop by to discover him looking like a fin-de-siècle decadent, stretched out on his black velvet couch, smoking a cigarette and reading D'Annunzio. At 5 a.m. they share a breakfast that includes avocados, which they called alligator pears. Then, after a bunch of photographers dispatched to "shoot" Rudy at 10:30 have done their work and departed, it's off to Santa Monica for a swim in the surf. Rudy will be leaving Hollywood soon, not to return for several years. Farewell, chums. Farewell, bachelor life.

12

COURTROOMS AND

CLAIRVOYANTS

Early in August 1922, Rudy and his friend Douglas Gerrard made their way by train, first to New York City and then via Albany to Foxlair, the Hudnuts' magnificent twelve-hundred-acre rustic retreat in the wilderness of the Adirondack Mountains. In an attempt to preserve anonymity, Rudy wore dark glasses and had grown a beard and mustache. When Natacha caught sight of this mysterious figure at the station—he was carrying golf clubs and sporting a tweed golf suit and had pulled a soft gray cap over his shaded eyes— she had "the first good laugh she had had for weeks."

Despite the disguise, a reporter had spotted him en route in Chicago, and asked him whether he lived up to his reputation as the Great Lover. Laughing, Valentino said, "It's all tommyrot about my kissing on the screen being so sublime"; real life, he said, is never depicted on screen because real life is too sordid. But love didn't have to be sordid. "Real love is not only beautiful, it is idyllic. It is a combination of sentiment and passion. My one desire is to be before the law the husband of Miss Hudnut. [When speaking to reporters, he always referred to Natacha formally, as either 'Miss Hudnut' or 'Mrs. Valentino.'] If necessary I will marry her in every state in the Union." It's clear the prospect of being close to his would-be bride again, even if it had to be with others present much of the time, put him in a buoyant frame of mind.

He'd hoped the disguise would protect him from such intrusions by the press and would keep the studio off his scent. That too proved a vain wish. Famous Players–Lasky wanted to prevent Rudy and Natacha from cohabiting, since they weren't legally married. They didn't care a whit about the morality issue; it was all about damage control and public relations. They hoped to avoid adding to the mountain of negative publicity that had already accumulated concerning actors at Paramount, which distributed Famous Players–Lasky. Scandals involving Arbuckle, Wallace Reid, Olive Thomas (Jack Pickford's wife), and the murder victim William Desmond Taylor had exposed each one's links to the studio, and now a top moneymaker, Valentino, had joined their dubious ranks. In particular the studio sought to protect the image of one of their top stars just as a Valentino blockbuster, *Blood and Sand*, was going into mass distribution.

The studio went so far as to hire detectives from the Flynn Detective Agency to spy on the couple's movements. One detective followed Rudy to the Waldorf-Astoria on a visit he made to New York and by some misstep revealed his identity to a hotel employee. In those days, before telescopic lenses and electronic bugging devices, the detectives had a hard time penetrating the privacy of Foxlair, which was enormous and had the natural protection of the mountain wilderness. Foxlair estate encompassed the formally furnished Big House, the Tea House, a guest cottage, the Casino (where dances were held), barns, service buildings, a lake, a fishing pond, private golf links, and acres of undeveloped woodland alive with deer, chipmunks, porcupines, and foxes.

The hired gumshoes lurked in the environs and shadowed Rudy on the train when he briefly left Foxlair to confer with his lawyer in New York. The local people didn't seem to be caught up in judgmental or intrusive snooping; they respected Valentino's obvious wish for privacy. Not daring to show her face, the daughter of the farmer who brought eggs to Foxlair watched for his car from behind the curtains of her bedroom window, experiencing a thrilling *frisson* when she saw it pass.

Someone—maybe one of the Flynn detectives—invaded the Foxlair premises during a Valentino-Gerrard-Rambova poker game one night, only to be pursued by a revolver-wielding Gerrard, who was pitched by the would-be spy or robber over a veranda rail to the ground twelve feet below. Gerry miraculously escaped injury and then fired three shots, wounding the man slightly in the leg. When Rudy, fearing for his friend, tried to join the battle, he went after a shotgun the Hudnuts kept in the Big House. Natacha interceded and tried, physically, to stop him. She had enough sheer power to take Rudy on, even though he kept himself in top shape. Since Foxlair lacked electricity, only oil lamps and candles lit the house, and they scuffled in the dim light, Natacha crying out to Rudy, "Don't do it! You may be killed or disfigured for life! Remember you belong to the screen—the public!" Rudy fled and went outside to come to Gerry's aid. Natacha followed, but Gerry had already found his way back inside the Big House. The injured intruder was never identified.

If a detective had managed to get inside the Big House at Foxlair, he would have found that Rudy and Natacha had separate, but adjacent, bedrooms. Hers was done in pale blue, with a patterned rug on the floor and a white lace coverlet on the single bed. Rudy's light-filled room, looking out on stately evergreens through tall windows, had a formal feeling, with a brocade spread covering the single bed and elegant matching French armchairs surrounding it. At least in photographs, it looks as if no discarded sock had ever disfigured its picture-perfect order and symmetry.

According to the servants or their survivors, Natacha always came downstairs for meals dressed as if for a photo session, her long hair braided and coiled under a turban or a picture hat, her makeup and jewelry perfect, and trailing a lovely long linen or silk skirt or dress. No doubt she wore perfume, for she and Rudy shared a love of it and her adopted father had made his fortune in the perfume-manufacture business; he must have kept her well supplied with his widely sold Richard Hudnut scents, which had names like Cardinal Lily and Violet Sec. Or maybe she preferred pricier and more rarefied French imports.

Rudy, on the other hand, enjoying a rare opportunity to relax completely, slouched around, "uncouth looking, often in riding breeches that looked as if he had slept in them." And according to the servants, the often haughty and intimidating Richard Hudnut did not always appreciate Valentino's company at mealtime. He thought Rudy ate with too much gusto, and must have conveyed his displeasure with steely glances or grim silence. "Each meal was a tense affair."

"Uncle Dickie" Hudnut's vexation at meals was a minor ripple in an essentially calm domestic sea. The weeks at Foxlair served both Rudy and Natacha as a period of much-needed respite and recovery after months of emotional turmoil, hard work, and stress. Rudy's in-laws-to-be truly liked him. Except at meals, they found him charming, and considered him, as Hudnut had said, "a man of character." Although their manners were as formal as their furniture, and they could never be called relaxed in their approach to others, the Hudnuts were hospitable people who at various times opened their doors to Rudy's friends (such as Gerrard) and later, in France, to members of his family. Muzzie was warmer and more spontaneous than her husband (or daughter) and she and Rudy grew to be close friends over time. She didn't at all mind his celebrity, or that he looked like "an Adonis." Since his own parents were dead and kinship mattered so much to him, he appreciated belonging to an extended family with apparently bottomless resources, beautiful homes, and welcoming hearths.

Another member of Natacha's family, her mother's sister, Teresa Werner, became a fixture of their lives when summer ended and Rudy and Natacha moved to Manhattan. Since they couldn't set up house as a couple, they lived at two separate city abodes. Natacha's roommate in a hotel apartment on Sixty-seventh Street near Central Park West was her affectionate Aunt Teresa. Motherly, even-keeled, and warm-hearted, Aunt Teresa excelled at providing emotional support when it was needed and getting out of the way when it wasn't. Rudy's flat nearby on the same street was at the Hotel des Artistes, a stylish apartment building that offered residents meals sent up by dumbwaiter from its restaurant, and he, too, had a roommate, an old friend from his New York dancing days, Frank Menillo. Mae Murray also kept an apartment at Hotel des Artistes, as did ZaSu Pitts and Isadora Duncan.

In New York City Rudy and Natacha had to walk a narrow path. They could and often did appear together in public, usually in the presence of Aunt Teresa, but they had to make it clear to one and all that they respected the California law that had decreed that they could not behave like a married couple so long as Rudy was still the legal husband of Jean Acker. Crazy as it may sound today, he could actually have been prosecuted again if it could be proven that they were cohabiting without a license.

"I'll confess it is rather fun being courted by your own husband," Natacha said in an interview, making the best of a rotten deal. "We go out often for dinner and the theater . . . nearly every evening and then he brings me back to my hotel and down in the lobby he bows formally over my hand." Because she was speaking to a writer from *Photoplay*, and knew her every word would be widely and minutely scrutinized, Natacha made it appear that she and Rudy were observing strict celibacy. "Rudy and I stay in a continual state of neuter gender," she claimed. "We call it our penance for that foolish spring night. We would never have dashed to Mexico that wild way if we hadn't both been having the first vacation we had [had] . . . in two years." Whether this is true or whether instead they managed surreptitious interludes of private intimacy now and then isn't known; if they did stray from the path of righteousness, they had to do so with cloak-and-dagger stealth, so as not to be caught out. The last thing they needed was further tabloid scandal or an even crueler separation than the one they'd just endured.

The necessity to appear privately upright gained new immediacy as Valentino contemplated a daring act of rebellion against Famous Players–Lasky. Egged on by Natacha, who shared his sense of outrage, and counseled by his attorney, Arthur Butler Graham, he decided to act on his anger and stage a one-man strike. Although Famous Players–Lasky already had a script for his next scheduled picture and had begun paying director Allan Dwan weekly installments on a $15,000 salary, Valentino announced that he would refuse to return to Hollywood to begin shooting the picture, *The Spanish Cavalier*, which was based on the play *Don Cesar de Bazan*. (Eventually the script was rewritten as a vehicle for Pola Negri and Antonio Moreno and titled *The Spanish Dancer*.) The studio's insistence that he go before the cameras in California had merely fueled his rage; earlier in the year, when he'd fumed at Jesse Lasky over the decision not to film *Blood and Sand* in Spain, he'd been assured that his next Spanish-themed movie *would* be shot in Europe and that he'd at last be able to revisit his family after a separation of nearly ten years. If Europe proved out of the question as a location, Jesse Lasky had told him, shooting would "at least" take place in New York, which both Rudy and Natacha preferred because in Manhattan they could easily see a lot of each other, living as close neighbors.

He announced he had decided to accept no further paychecks from Famous Players–Lasky until the dispute was resolved, even though he owed them money. He was still paying off the debt he had incurred when he borrowed a lump sum from the studio to pay off Jean Acker. Just how risky this decision was soon became apparent.

From the days when his father had punished him for breaking a window by beating him with a cavalry whip, Rudy had a history of bristling under male authority. He would not kowtow. Though he'd dreamed of training for military service when young, he no doubt would have found taking orders from a superior officer difficult, if not impossible. In his prestardom days in motion pictures, he had gotten along fine with most of the producers and directors he worked with because they behaved like friends. But Rex Ingram changed all that. Now the stakes were higher and his bosses no longer chums. Rather, they resembled commanders who deployed dollars, casts, and crews instead of troops. Valentino was no ordinary enlisted man, he was Somebody. Famous Players–Lasky executives who failed to respect or properly acknowledge his stardom raised his hackles. Rudy was not vain about his acting and would readily admit that he still had much to learn. He felt uncomfortable posing as "the Great Lover," and always made a point of separating his hyped screen image from his real self. But he knew his worth. He had enormous pride, a good-sized ego that had not decreased with mass adulation, and he was quick to take offense.

Rudy made all business relationships personal, refusing to distinguish between a boardroom and a living room. At Metro, Rex Ingram had first aroused his wrath by ignoring his triumph in *The Four Horse-*

men. Now, ever the rebellious son, he sought to break free of servitude to Famous Players–Lasky by going absent without leave. He'd answer their collective insults with defiance. He'd retaliate against his bosses by denying them the thing they most counted on, his presence on the set.

He soon proved that he could throw the world of motion pictures into a quaking, litigious frenzy. All hell broke loose as headlines blared, moguls bit their nails, and attorneys scurried about. "TOREADOR RODOLPHO WAILS OVER NEW TROUBLE; HERO OF FLAPPERS PLANS SUIT AGAINST LASKY." For the moment he assumed command, and that must have felt delicious. But in burning his bridges Valentino left his career and financial interests totally unprotected. This is not to suggest that he didn't have legitimate, substantial grievances, nor to detract from his courage in taking on the most powerful corporation in moviedom. But his personal rancor, his haste, his refusal to educate himself about money management or legal realities, and his unbending stance would end up costing him dearly.

His fury at the studio executives had been mounting for a long time, and their decision to put snooping detectives on his tail pushed it beyond the boiling point. The us-versus-them thinking began taking shape right after the Mexicali wedding, when Valentino blamed his well-heeled (or at least so he thought) employers for failing to rescue him from prison on the bigamy charge. Budget constraints dogging the studio and the wider world of motion pictures in 1922 did not impress him. If he knew it, the fact that Famous Players–Lasky's profits were down to the tune of half a million dollars that year didn't register. He claimed in his deposition that at the end of 1921 the studio's total assets amounted to about $48,000,000, and that as the world's largest motion picture producing and distributing company they could well afford to pay him what he was worth. All civility departed when his bosses plucked Natacha from his side and sent her packing. Rudy was convinced that there had been a conspiracy to destroy his happiness and separate him from his wife. The feeling that he was being dishonored and held in contempt by his employers when he deserved to be prized as one of its most exalted and successful luminaries overrode all other concerns.

But outrage wasn't enough to make a legal case that would hold up in court, and court was where he once again found himself when Famous Players–Lasky responded to his action by suing him. A lawsuit isn't the same as a duel, even if Valentino's emotions resembled those of an old-fashioned European noble whose honor can best be restored by crossing swords with his foe at dawn. His New York lawyer, Arthur Butler Graham, sat Valentino down and insisted that he take hold of himself and list the events and issues that compelled his decision to stop working. Between the leading man and his studio there loomed major points of contention concerning film budgets, star billing and compensation, story and personnel choices for his movies, broken promises, publicity efforts, and the way he was treated on and off the set.

Valentino asserted in his affidavit that, considering his proven ability to draw large crowds into theaters and generate huge profits, his services were worth several thousand dollars a week more than his current pay level of $1,250 a week, soon to increase to $2,000 if Famous Players–Lasky exercised its option. Mary Pickford had earned $10,000 a week at the studio long before 1921, he averred. William Farnum, Norma Talmadge, and Alla Nazimova had also been paid that lofty sum. His name meant big money, and it was high time for them to begin acknowledging that. Digging up an old bone, he argued that he should have been given star billing for *The Sheik*. In fact, when *The Sheik* played in Los Angeles, Grauman's Theater, in which Famous Players–Lasky owned an interest, put only *his* name up in lights on the marquee (though on paper and in the credits Agnes Ayres was billed as star). That picture "is the most successful picture commercially ever made by Famous Players–Lasky," and his latest release, *Blood and Sand*, promised to do even better. "*Blood and Sand* is today the outstanding success of the year, even more profitable than *The Sheik*," he stated. "[It is estimated] that the gross income of the picture will exceed $2 million, that the net profit to Famous Players–Lasky Corporation will exceed One Million."

Aware that trouble was brewing, and terrified at the prospect of losing Valentino just months after they'd made the costly decision to

shelve all Fatty Arbuckle pictures, Famous Players–Lasky tried to placate him at the last minute by agreeing to increase his pay from $1,250
to $7,000 a week. *Variety* reported on the proposal right before news
of the lawsuit broke, saying that the studio had offered Valentino a new
two-year contract to replace his existing one, signed ten months back.
In a decisive moment he would live to regret, Valentino threw this
handsome and unprecedented gesture back in their faces. He'd had it.
He no longer wanted to work for Famous Players–Lasky. He felt they
had broken faith with him too many times, insulted his wife, disre-
spected his talents, and flagrantly violated the contract already in
place. Where were they when he objected to the mangling of *Blood and
Sand* and protested over the embarrassingly shoddy successor to it, *The
Young Rajah*? The studio had gone back on its verbal promise to film
the bullfight movie in Spain, and had lied to him when it claimed that
his choice for director, George Fitzmaurice, had turned down an offer
to direct the picture. "Mr. Fitzmaurice has since told me that he never
refused to direct the picture and that he would have been delighted
to direct it."

Artistic control, he insisted, lay at the heart of the conflict. "I was
willing to go on at the same salary if they would permit me to make
real photoplays instead of . . . cut-and-dried program features that
can be hacked and torn and compressed into a given number of feet of
film to fit so many cans, like so many boxes of sardines," Valentino
would explain in an "Open Letter to the American Public," published
in *Photoplay*. He charged in court that he'd been assured of the opportunity to help select his scripts and directors, and to have a voice in the
editing process, but his objections to mutilating cuts had fallen on
deaf ears. The six-minute crutch scene had been removed from *Blood
and Sand*, despite its crucial importance. Writer and director Rupert
Hughes had seen the movie before cuts and had written to Jesse Lasky
urging retention of that scene, to no avail. Jesse Lasky had told
Valentino that trimming the film to a suitable, showable length was a
business decision, pure and simple, and that the executives understood
business matters far better than he, only an actor and a relative novice,
possibly could. Period.

He'd been assured by the studio that every effort would be made to acquire the "best possible stories, produced under the best possible conditions," but in the rush to keep his name before the public in a steady stream of easily distributed new "program" films (B pictures) of no more than seven reels each, he'd been forced into mediocrity, into mass-produced pictures made on the cheap and distributed in bulk through block booking. (Block booking compelled theaters to rent all the Famous Players–Lasky films, even if they only wanted a few.) The studio had hurried him into second-rate quickies like *Beyond the Rocks* and *The Young Rajah*. None of their vows concerning creative quality had been honored, because Famous Players–Lasky, more concerned with quick bucks, quantity, and speed than with excellence, simply didn't understand or respect artists or artistic standards. Talents such as D. W. Griffith and Mary Pickford, once associated with Famous Players–Lasky, had decided to leave the fold in order to continue to grow and prosper. Speedups in the production schedule might work in a manufacturing plant, but they don't work for actors who draw on their emotions when they perform. "One might as well have a stable of race horses," states the affidavit, "and then place a limit of speed upon each horse and expect him to win, as to hold a motion picture star to the program type of picture of from five to seven and a half reels."

Valentino's charge of studio indifference to high artistic standards, his outrage at the systematic refusal to grant stars a voice in the shaping of their vehicles, had real heft and merit. He weakened his case when he shifted to more petty complaints, fussing in his affidavit about being denied a proper dressing room during the shooting of *Blood and Sand* at the Lasky Ranch and grousing that his friend Florey had been barred from the set and that Douglas Gerrard had been denied a chance to see the first cut. During shooting, his affidavit maintains, he'd been forced by manager Charles Eyton to change into his toreador costume in his open touring car while others watched, or in an exposed dressing room with no roof. "As my costumes were such that I could not wear underwear and was naked each time that I changed my costume, this condition was almost impossible." He pointed to violations of customary star treatment in these matters rather than violations of his contract.

In their "answering affidavit," Famous Players–Lacky added insult to injury by implying that Valentino was whining like a sissy. Zukor (or his attorneys) sneered: "Defendant boasts of his physical prowess, and then complains about alleged inconveniences and discomforts which no red-blooded man would notice." All traces of goodwill and good faith between plaintiff and defendant had long since evaporated. The whole dispute resembled a very public, highly acrimonious divorce.

Valentino was waging a public-relations battle as well as a fight through the courts. He didn't want to alienate his legions of devoted fans, since his bargaining power hinged on his popularity. Although issues like the size and comfort of dressing rooms have sometimes assumed huge importance in conflicts about the perks Hollywood luminaries merit, they have never played well from the public-relations point of view. Jack and Jill Public tend to withhold sympathy from aggrieved stars whom they see as already overpampered. At a time when the average American's annual income was less than $2,000, fans were inclined to withhold pity from a Valentino who insisted he was being mistreated and underpaid. Compared to most Americans, he led the life of a king. Newspapers mocked Valentino's discontent with a weekly salary of a mere $1,250—more than many Americans saw in a year.

Valentino had to try to convince the public that he didn't have a swelled head or a greedy nature. A friendly writer, Gladys Hall, described him in *Movie Weekly* as a regular fellow, without airs, who lived in a modest three-room apartment that he shared with a roommate. "No high and mightiness. He opened the door for us himself." In his "Open Letter to the American Public" he insisted, "I was not temperamental. I was not grasping. I do not consider myself a great actor yet." In asking for only what other stars got, he demanded simple fairness. "I am not a good business man," he admitted, and neither was he a selfish man, but "I am selfish to make good pictures." In real life, he said, he didn't at all resemble the Rudolph Valentino people who saw him on-screen thought they knew. "I feel quite unreal."

Among newspapers, only the *Los Angeles Times* could see the justice of his complaint that compared to most top stars "of equal importance" he'd been grossly underpaid. And no one said in print that Famous Players–Lasky Corp. should change from a for-profit behemoth turning out more than eighty pictures a year into a maker of quality art films that puts profits second but can still pay stars huge salaries.

Of course the Valentinos weren't the only ones connected with movies who were asking Hollywood to raise artistic standards and take films seriously. Erich von Stroheim consistently made the groundbreaking, unconventional movies he wanted to make, not the ones the studios could afford or easily market. Movie critic Robert E. Sherwood, who reviewed for *Life* and initiated a new annual anthology called *The Best Motion Pictures of the Year*, repeatedly tried to make the case that mass entertainment didn't have to be incompatible with intelligence and artistry. Talents like Nazimova had always insisted on high artistic standards, but when her films bombed at the box office, American producers and most critics for the popular and trade press concluded that they failed because arty stuff could not make money. Nazimova's *Salome*, with Natacha Rambova's superlative black-and-white and silver-and-gold Beardsleyesque costumes, had trouble finding a distributer, and when it was previewed in the spring of 1922 it was labeled "bizarre." An imported expressionist film from Germany, *The Cabinet of Dr. Caligari*, now regarded as a classic, initially prompted boos from American audiences and demands for refunds. In 1921 it lost money in the United States and contributed to a disastrous season for its American distributer, Samuel Goldwyn. In 1922, Famous Players–Lasky saw "quality" more as a moral than an aesthetic issue. They wanted to project the company's devotion to Hays-style standards of "decency," while keeping their eyes riveted on that all-important bottom line.

Needless to say, during the lawsuit that pitted Famous Players–Lasky against Rudolph Valentino, the studio spokesmen did not corroborate Valentino's interpretation of motives or events. They considered him improvident and were amused by his claim to be a man with "simple habits," and an "economical mode of living." They'd been eager to hire him in 1921, but now, fifteen months, one divorce, one bigamy trial, and five pictures later, had come to see him as a troublemaker completely devoid of business savvy and a sulky, demanding prima donna "obsessed with the idea that he was amenable to no rules [and that] he was entitled to special privileges." They claimed they tried to answer his demands. "We raised his salary far above the terms of his contract. That seemingly only whetted [his] appetite," Zukor wrote of the dispute. "Valentino could be charming if he wished. . . . On the other hand, he could be extremely temperamental."

In the New York State Supreme Court, Famous Players–Lasky filed a "replying affidavit" pointing out Valentino's inconsistency in arguing for both higher pay from the studio and less commercialism. If war was what he wanted, war he would get.

"Rudolph Valentino is kicking over the traces," reported *Moving Picture World*. "The star, indisputably one of the greatest drawing cards of the present day, has informed Famous Players that he will not return to its studio to begin work on 'The Spanish Cavalier,' alleging that the company has breached its contract so far as publicity and advertising [are] concerned." The trade journal was correct when it said that the rift came at a moment when Valentino's box-office value had peaked. His name carried so much clout that in June, right after the bigamy mess, a survey conducted by the fan magazine *Motion Picture Classic* found him the readers' top choice as a male cover subject, acing out the second-place contender, Thomas Meighan. That same month, some of the smaller studios in whose films Valentino had appeared in the days before he became a star scrambled to reissue and redistribute them, changing the billing, adding some new titles, and highlighting Valentino's name in the ads even if he had played only a small supporting role. *The Delicious Little Devil* (1919) was one of the pictures being brought back with new advertising and new billing—until Mae Murray stamped her dainty foot and had her name restored as star.

Precisely because he was worth so much money to them, Famous Players–Lasky decided to muster all its strength to fight Valentino, hold him to his contract, and pin him to the mat. Elek John Ludvigh, head counsel for the studio, stated that "for once Famous Players intends establishing in court whether a contract means anything."

Valentino had argued in his affidavit that he'd signed contracts that included patently unfair provisions simply because he, a relative newcomer, hadn't known any better: "I am not familiar with business affairs, and particularly was I at the time [of negotiating my contracts] unfamiliar with motion picture matters." Well, too bad for you, was the gist of the studio's response to that ingenuous plea: you signed, you consulted your own attorney and your own agent before you signed, and unless we agree otherwise, we own the exclusive rights to your performing services.

When he decided to take on Famous Players–Lasky in the courts Valentino expressed hopes that he might have his own company "as soon as litigation ends." Failing that, he indicated that he felt confident that another film company would be only too glad to employ him. Other studios had previously sought him out, his affidavit states. Goldwyn Pictures had tried to sign him while he was still at Metro. A producer named J. Parker Read had tried to hire him for a picture called *Pawned*, but he'd been unable to accept any offer without the consent of Famous Players–Lasky. Now, during his rebellion, rival studios once again were putting out feelers, making friendly gestures to show that if he became a free agent, they were interested in signing him. But it was a big if. Unless he severed his legal ties to Famous Players–Lasky, he could not be signed by another studio.

Producer Joseph Schenck had indicated that he'd be interested in casting Valentino opposite Norma Talmadge (Schenck's wife) in a new screen version of *Romeo and Juliet*. Both United Artists and Goldwyn Pictures had separately indicated that it would welcome him if he could be acquired without the risk of litigation. Valentino had left California in August so furious at Famous Players–Lasky that he no longer wanted or expected to continue working for them. In Hollywood, right before his departure he'd visited his rival, Douglas Fairbanks, one of the partners at United Artists, and told him that he planned to make contact with the United Artists office in New York. We don't know if he did go to the United Artists office in New York (since he was being tailed,

probably not), but he did make a very public appearance sitting with
Natacha in a box at the New York premiere of the new Fairbanks movie,
Robin Hood, at the Lyric Theatre—a show of support he wouldn't have
been likely to make if the old antagonism between him and Fairbanks
still held.

Goldwyn Pictures, recently separated from its founder, Samuel
Goldwyn, had under its new president, Frank Joseph Godsol, acquired
the screen rights to the play based on the immensely popular Lew
Wallace novel *Ben-Hur*. Godsol had succeeded in luring June Mathis
away from Famous Players–Lasky to take over the story department at
Goldwyn, making her the holder of "the most responsible motion picture executive position ever held by a woman," according to *Moving
Picture World*. It's likely that after learning that Valentino was breaking
free of Famous Players–Lasky, she no longer wanted to remain there
herself; he was the reason she'd switched from Metro to Famous Players in the first place. One of her first assignments at Goldwyn was to
work on adapting and writing continuity for *Ben-Hur*. The new head of
Goldwyn Pictures, Joe Godsol, also had led the charge to acquire the
pricey, hotly pursued screen rights for *Ben-Hur*, which had already
been turned into a short Kalem Company film in 1907. Now Mathis,
busily adapting the million-dollar *Ben-Hur* for a planned Goldwyn
megaproduction in Rome, decided that her first choice to play the lead
was none other than Rudolph Valentino. However, according to the
New York attorney for Fairbanks, the inside word was that "negotiations for Valentino's appearing in *Ben-Hur* were unsuccessful." The
plum role, first assigned to George Walsh, ended up going to Ramon
Novarro. (The production, beset with mishaps, dragged on for years
and ended up with a screenplay not written by June Mathis and a 1925
movie produced not by Goldwyn Pictures but by the newly formed
MGM.)

Valentino could not go to Rome to drive the chariot as Ben-Hur
because the court ruled that he had a valid and exclusive contract with
Famous Players–Lasky. In September 1922, Justice Isidor Wasservogel
of the New York State Supreme Court issued an injunction restraining
him "from appearing in any screen production other than those pro-

duced by the Famous Players–Lasky Corporation during the period he is under contract with that organization," which meant (if the company opted to exercise its option to extend his contract) not until February 7, 1924. He was also prohibited from appearing on the speaking stage. In short, he could not work as an actor at all, nor could he engage in "any other business of any kind or class whatsoever." The studio's lawyer argued that vast sums had been expended publicizing Valentino movies, "bringing him from obscurity to the limelight," and that all the charges of unjust treatment "were merely a pretense to enable him to escape from contract so he could obtain more remunerative employment elsewhere."

Meanwhile, Rudy and Natacha were falling deeper and deeper into debt. "Would you consider yourself the luckiest girl in the world if you married a man who owed $80,000?" Natacha would rhetorically ask a writer for *Screenland* after she and Rudy were finally legally wed. Although Valentino had received $43,333.33 from Famous Players–Lasky in 1922 before he stopped accepting his paychecks, his legal fees were mounting. He'd end up owing lawyer Arthur Butler Graham close to $50,000 for his services and being sued for nonpayment. He and Natacha were each paying rent in New York—not a cheap proposition even in 1922, although both shared the rent with a roommate. They still maintained their California home in Whitley Heights and were employing a skeleton crew to look after the grounds, the house, and Rudy's horses. Robert Florey was on Rudy's payroll, having been hired to manage his publicity in Europe. There were fashionable clothes to buy, expensive restaurant meals to pay for, costly wardrobes to maintain, travel expenses to cover, personal items they wanted. In New York, Rudy purchased five works at the Italian-American Art Association. A movie star has to live like a movie star even when he's not working.

Natacha wasn't worried, she revealed. She told *Photoplay*'s Ruth Waterbury: "Rudy gets horribly excited when I say this, but I do declare that if they keep him from working for two years more, then I will work and support us both. There are many things I can do. I can go back to my designing, but I don't care what it is if it only brings in

enough money for him to be able to go on fighting for decent treatment and good material." She said she'd also been courted to go before
the cameras herself as a screen actress, but she thought one actor in
the family was enough. "The ideal thing would be for me to be an art
director for Rudy when he starts to work again. I shall do what he
wants me to do."

But until one of her various schemes for top-dollar employment
panned out, or Rudy found other work, they needed a quick cash in-
fusion. They borrowed from none other than Joe Godsol, the man
who had aced out Samuel Goldwyn as president of Goldwyn Pictures,
a good-looking wheeler-dealer from Cleveland who'd made millions
in France during the Great War, had been a business partner of theater
magnate Lee Shubert, and walked around Manhattan with thousands
of dollars stuffed into his suit and coat pockets. Being a shrewd businessman, Godsol may have calculated that the loan would be more
than repaid in the future if it paved the way to a Valentino–Goldwyn
Pictures deal. However, Natacha wrote in her memoir that she saw the
loan, which she said was given without any security and which they
quickly repaid, as an "unselfish proof of friendship" that would never
be forgotten.

It must have been painful to Valentino to see Famous Players–Lasky
scrambling to sign other dark-haired and handsome European actors
who could try to substitute for him on-screen. Antonio Moreno, not
by any means a newcomer but now newly perceived (to his chagrin) as
a Valentino look-alike, was signed, as was the new discovery from the
French Basque country, Charles de Roche. When British leading man
Ivor Novello arrived in the United States and accepted an offer from
Griffith, the trade press dubbed him a "Valentino rival" who might
supplant Rudy in Spanish roles.

Three months after the court ruled that the Valentino–Famous
Players–Lasky contract could not be broken, Valentino filed a counterclaim asking $350,000 damages for alleged conspiracy and request-
ing an injunction to restrain Famous Players–Lasky "from circulating
the report he is under contract to them." The conspiracy charge involved his agent, Clifford Robertson, "who is alleged to have con-

spired with A. Zukor and J. L. Lasky to conceal the fact that larger offers have been made." (Robertson, too, would end up suing Valentino.) Valentino claimed that his agent had concealed from him the
information that he was being courted by other studios, and that
Famous Players—Lasky paid off Robertson to stay mum. This counterclaim went nowhere in court, but added to Valentino's already considerable debt to his lawyer.

What to do? Rudy and Natacha had to find lucrative employment
somehow. Valentino appealed to the court, asking to have the court injunction modified to allow him to work, if not for a rival movie company or in the speaking theater, at least somewhere. In January of 1923
he was thrown a morsel: the phrase in the injunction that forbade him
to work for himself or to work at "any other business of any kind or
class whatever," was removed. The Appellate Division of the Superior
Court of New York found that the earlier ruling had been "too stringent in that it deprived him of [the ability] to earn a livelihood in any
manner." A relieved Valentino told the press that he'd been offered
$6,000 a week to dance in restaurants and $5,000 to sing or speak into
a phonograph. He'd also been asked to write for publication.

While trying to figure out his next professional step he turned up
at the New York premiere of *The Young Rajah* and appeared on a series
of radio broadcasts, addressing the subject "What's the Matter with
the Movies?" On one broadcast, after panning "the motion picture
trust" for restricting the production of genuinely "artistic pictures," he
took on Adolph Zukor, denouncing him in such strong language that
the station abruptly cut him off. He missed no opportunity to argue
his case to an audience. At an Actors Equity meeting in New York,
sharing the podium with critic Heywood Broun, he lent his support to
the union of players, calling it "the first step toward the rescue of the
stage from factory production methods."

In private Rudy and Natacha were seeking guidance from spiritualistic
sources. This wasn't entirely a new development. Natacha, fascinated
since her teen years with ancient religions and their icons, had a certi-

tude about reincarnation and psychic forces that would eventually turn her into a dedicated and accomplished scholar of ancient Egyptian myth patterns, a writer on astrology, and a follower of the theosophist Madame Blavatsky. Rudy, too, believed that humans have had past lives, and they both were convinced that the soul survives the body in eternal life. Rudy told an interviewer in 1921 that he'd attended séances in Italy and had used the Ouija board but didn't believe in it "except as a conductor of thought without volition," but did believe in spiritualism. Organized religion never attracted him much, he confessed. His mother had been troubled by his lack of devotion to the Church. "I have never been religious," he admitted. "And I'm not now, in an orthodox sense." But he did believe in God, and longed to know "the secret of things."

In California, Rudy convinced Natacha that he'd received occasional messages from each of his deceased parents, and according to Robert Florey, he regularly visited a palm reader named "Professor Winton" or "Winston" who operated out of a storefront near Santa Monica's Crystal Pier, between a shooting gallery and a souvenir shop. One day shortly before he left for New York the palm reader told him that he would soon be making a long trip, and that he would experience more days of glory, but that he was not destined to live a long life. This upset Rudy, who didn't want to believe any such thing. He told the palm reader that he knew his life line was short but that he trusted in his lucky star, which protected him and kept him from harm. The professor said he wished that to be so. After the disturbing Crystal Pier encounter, a shaken Rudy vowed while devouring a bowl of shellfish stew with Robert Florey and lighting an endless number of Abdullah cigarettes that he would not go back to this palm reader again.

In New York, he and Natacha began experimenting with automatic and mirror writing. Costume designer Cora McGeachy served as their guide and conducted weekly séances in the apartment Natacha shared with Aunt Teresa. "Rudy was really psychic," Natacha would recall after his death. "We used to do mechanical writing a great deal." A spirit would take command of hand and pen, and move the entranced medium to write down on paper what was being dictated. If the message from the other side arrived with the letters reversed, they could decipher the writing by holding it up to a mirror. One of their frequent spirit contacts was Meselope, a member of an old Egyptian Hermetic brotherhood who provided psychic instructions and prayers. Another contact was a departed friend named Jenny, whom they believed to be the spirit of Virginia Mathis, the recently deceased mother of June. A third was Rudy's personal spirit guide, an American Indian named Black Feather. Rudy, always drawn to Indians and to the myths and artifacts of the American West, posed as Black Feather for a number of photographs at this time, dressed in a loincloth and feathered headdress.

During the automatic-writing sessions, the Valentino poems that would make up his 1923 volume, *Day Dreams*, all came into being. The poems aren't—and Rudy knew this—the polished verses of an accomplished wordsmith devoted to his craft. Instead, they're dreamy and romantic musings, thoughts on various subjects—love, self-doubt, nature, the brevity of life—expressed in sweet and wistful language that can often be touching, but sometimes veers into amorphous mush. The love poem to Natacha, "You," falls into the former category: "You are the History of Love . . . The Incentive of Chivalry/ . . . Sanctuary of my Soul." Another, celebrating the beauty of "A Baby's Skin" ("Texture of a butterfly's wing"), has real sensuous immediacy. This one, and the lines he addressed to Caruso, extolling Italy as the homeland for sun lovers, is full of yearning for something desired but out of reach: a baby, a glimpse of his native land.

"I am not a poet nor a scholar, therefore you shall find neither poems nor prose," he modestly disclaims in his preface. Rather, he offers "Just dreams—*Day Dreams*—a bit of romance, a bit of sentimentalism, a bit of philosophy, not studied but acquired by constant observation of that greatest of masters! . . . *Nature*." A drawing of a black feather, evoking Rudy's spirit guide, Black Feather, adorns the title page, and the epigraph comes by way of the Egyptian Meselope. Natacha explained in her memoir that the poems were all "psychically received" and that the initials in their dedications "stood for the names of the souls [most of them nineteenth-century writers] who had inspired them." G.S. was George Sand, B. was Byron, and W.W. stood for Walt Whitman, who according to Natacha was Rudy's favorite poet.

The poems in *Day Dreams* may derive from occult sources, but they had practical applications. Gathered in a book and published during Valentino's enforced leave from film acting, they became a best-seller that brought in royalties and kept the Valentino name before the public.

The séances had at least one other practical outcome: they forecast that Rudy would get himself a new manager. This prediction would materialize in the form of a bespectacled attorney, accountant, and businessman, S. George Ullman, who would assume a determining role in shaping the destinies of both Natacha Rambova and Rudolph Valentino.

13

THE MINERALAVA DANCE TOUR

George Ullman's character isn't easy to assess. Valentino liked his take-charge manner and became quite dependent on him, eventually turning over to him control of his career and making him executor of his estate. Natacha, too, entrusted much to him, and then became his rival; two managers for Rudolph Valentino proved to be one too many, and she lost out. Natacha, and Rudy's brother and sister as well, came to distrust Ullman after Rudy's death and to question his integrity. But Rudy himself apparently never did. The Ullmans and the Valentinos often dined together, visited one another's homes, spent holidays together. Rudy would agree to become godfather to one of Ullman's sons.

Ullman's first impression of Valentino, as Ullman tells it in the book he published soon after Valentino's death, had the emotional impact of a tsunami. "I had no idea of his magnetism," Ullman would write, "nor of the fine quality of his manhood. To say that I was enveloped by his personality with the first clasp of his sinewy hand and my first glance into his inscrutable eyes, is to state it mildly. I was literally engulfed, swept off my feet, which is unusual between two men. Had he been a beautiful woman, and I a bachelor [Ullman had a wife and two children], it would not have been so surprising. I am not an emotional man . . . but, in this instance, meeting a real he-man, I found myself moved by the most powerful personality I have ever encountered in man or woman."

Two things about this description jump off the page. First, there's Ullman's immediate, visceral response to a physical presence he found overwhelming. He instantly joined ranks with the multitudes in whom Valentino's looks, way of moving, and aura provoked both warm desire (not necessarily sexual, but certainly an ache for close connection of some sort) and possessiveness. Ullman and Valentino would remain linked, in both their working and private lives, from here on out. Within six months of this charged first encounter, infused in the telling with the heightened emotion of mourning, Ullman became Valentino's manager and career consultant.

A second thing to note in Ullman's description is his defensiveness about the depths of his feelings, which resulted in denial ("I am not an emotional man") and an exaggerated emphasis on Valentino's he-man status. This had much to do with events that occurred in the summer of 1926, right before Valentino died, to which we'll be returning later.

Ullman doesn't say where he and Valentino first met, only that it was in New York in the winter of 1922, after the flurry of publicity about Valentino's break with Famous Players—Lasky and the New York court's injunction prohibiting him from acting on stage or screen. Everyone who read the papers knew that Valentino was looking for a job, that he could dance, and that he had been offered many thousands a week to dance professionally once again. At the time, Ullman headed the advertising campaign for Mineralava, a cosmetics company that made expensive face powder and "beauty clay" complexion treatment for women, and he guessed that Valentino, with his scores of ardent feminine fans, would make the perfect hired spokesman for Mineralava products. Advertising was still a relatively young industry, but famous personalities had been earning extra money by endorsing commercial products at least since the days when Lily Langtry allowed her celebrated face and form to be used to sell Pear's soap. Women would surely heed "the Great Lover's" advice about beauty matters, Ullman thought. Why not put him to work dancing on behalf of Mineralava and (since beauty contests were all the rage these days) turn him into a professional judge of feminine charm? Beauty contests among the young women in the audience could become a regular feature of the dance tour. When Ullman realized that Natacha Rambova, "a very beautiful girl, with a marvelous complexion," also had danced professionally and would be willing and able to join Valentino as the female half of a new kind of exhibition dance team, the Mineralava dance tour began to take shape.

What was fresh and unique about this dance tour was that its success hinged on the fame of its movie star lead dancer and drew on the audience's familiarity with his screen appearances. Further, the public had new and ample opportunity to see Rudy's films, since Famous Players—Lasky, denied the possibility of issuing new Valentino movies, decided to revive previous Valentino hits, which they knew would reap profits. Early films from other companies, such as Republic's *An Adventuress*, retitled *Isle of Love,* were also making the rounds. Fans already felt they knew Valentino through the blitz of publicity his personal life had generated; they'd read all about Jean Acker, the divorce, the bigamy trial. They would soon be learning about the star's early life in Italy and struggles in New York as described in the ghostwritten Valentino autobiography, *My Life Story*, which would be serialized in *Photoplay* during the months of the tour.

When the dancer Valentino, as Signor Rodolfo, first toured the circuit around New York with Bonnie Glass and Joan Sawyer back in 1915 and 1916, exhibition dance teams had been much in fashion. By 1923 they no longer were. The war had taken a heavy toll on such teams, and Prohibition had put a major crimp in the cabaret life of the 1920s. Now dancing "cheek to cheek," with bodies close together, receded in popularity as uninhibited Jazz Age steps that stressed solo strutting, like the Black Bottom and the Shimmy, came into favor. On the Mineralava tour, however, Rudy and Natacha didn't perform the latest American dance crazes; instead, in a way they were a throwback, reviving intricate movements and a showy, finished style that had been popular years earlier in the United States. They also did dances imported from countries such as Argentina, Spain, and Russia. A flamenco number and a tempestuous Russian folk-style dance that they choreographed themselves were included in the program, along with several tangos. The Valentinos romantically evoked other times, other places. Their exotic glamour, their celebrity status, and their link to Hollywood made them red-hot and of the moment. They were fantasies in the flesh, legends with feet. And complexions!

Early in 1923, Rudy and Natacha (listed in the program as Winifred Hudnut) donned costumes—in his case gaucho hat, serape, billowing pants, and silver spurs; in hers, floor-length black velvet, red mantilla, and taffeta ruffles—and danced the "Tango from the Four Horsemen of the Apocalypse" to wide notice at New York's Century Theatre benefit for the Actors' Fund. On the same program were Jeanne Eagels in a scene from *Rain* and Will Rogers (who had recently parodied Valentino in a Hal Roach short) doing a turn as a Yankee philosopher. The dancing couple, accompanied by "Mr. Valentino's Own Tango Orchestra," were called back for twenty encores, and as they tried to leave the theater to make their way to the Actors' Equity Ball at Broadway's Hotel Astor, Rudy was "stampeded by two to three hundred feminine worshippers."

These stampeding female worshippers became a predictable part of the tour. "10,000 GIRLS MOB WORLD'S GREATEST KISSER," ran a Boston headline. According to Robert Florey, who joined the support team as a roving publicist, in order to keep from being trampled Rudy and Natacha had to escape over the roofs of dance halls or gyms in Louisville, Boston, Philadelphia, and Cincinnati. In Vancouver, British Columbia, when Rudy repaired to his dressing tent after dancing with Natacha before eight thousand spectators, "one lady tore a rent in the dressing tent to get a peek. Others followed until the canvas was well nigh ribbons." In Kansas and Arizona, young ladies snuck onto their train, concealing themselves in bathrooms, just for a chance to get close to the Sheik. Outside his Chicago hotel, the Blackstone, women grabbed the buttons off his coat and tried to steal his necktie. In Chicago's Trianon Ballroom, where the box office took in $16,500 the first three nights, during one dance "a plump lady of fifty summers hung perilously over the rail of a box. When [Valentino] came to take a bow, the lady tore off a diamond ring and flung it at him. They say . . . Rudy threw the ring back." A young woman fainted on their last night in Chicago. The ballroom manager carried her to the star's dressing room, where Natacha "fanned her and fluttered over her in solicitude to revive her." Then Rudy stepped into the room "in sombrero, spurs and all the colorful costume of the Argentine tango." The girl opened her eyes, saw that Rudolph Valentino himself hovered close, and at once fainted dead away again into Natacha's creamy arms.

Rudy enjoyed meeting his fans one at a time, and while on tour made an effort to visit schools, hospitals, settlement houses, and Italian neighborhoods whenever he could. But he found the screaming mobs both frightening and confusing. Frightening because they often jeopardized his and Natacha's physical safety. Confusing because Rudy felt that the person who inspired the fans' frenzy was a make-believe figure who had little to do with the real Rodolfo Guglielmi. Ten years earlier as a greenhorn in New York he'd been ignored and reviled when he slept out in the cold, working odd jobs and scrounging for meals. Now the same multitude that once overlooked or scorned him worshipped and exalted him. But he hadn't changed his essence; what had altered was the way people saw him. They had watched him on the screen costumed as an Arab, a toreador, a gaucho, a French soldier, and a Hindu prince, and those roles transformed him in their eyes, making him seem extraordinary and wildly romantic. The fans stood outside his window for hours, hoping for a glimpse of the demigod they thought they knew. How to explain the fickleness of the crowd?

Ullman accompanied the couple for most of the tour, joining a chef, an eleven-piece band, and twenty-odd additional staff in a luxuriously appointed private railroad car named "The Colonial." It boasted Turkish carpets, gilt mirrors, and two guest bedrooms. Scheduling the venues where the dance exhibitions would take place was put in the hands of a blue-eyed former prizefighting and wrestling promoter named Jack Curley, who knew a thing or two about the logistics of tours. He'd booked arenas and reserved hotel rooms for champs such as Jack Johnson, Jess Willard, and Georges Carpentier, all stellar attractions whose appeal spilled into the wider world of entertainment beyond the ring. Professional fighters and other sports figures who had big names and huge followings often turned to show business when they no longer had titles to defend.

Curley posed with Rudy and Natacha for photographers as they signed a contract guaranteeing them $7,500 a week plus half of the profits. The contract, originally for just six weeks, was extended to allow them to continue touring all over the United States and Canada for the better part of four months, from February through May of 1923. Often they traveled at night, arriving at a new destination in the morning. When they stopped in a small town, Natacha would recall, children often gathered near their railcar and tried to peer through the windows as they ate breakfast. Sometimes Rudy would go out to greet the fans, signing autographs and accepting their bouquets.

Curley took some heat from Natacha when, without consulting her beforehand, he promoted her in her hometown, Salt Lake City, as a local girl making good. Worse, he referred to her in advance publicity as "the little pigtailed Shaughnessy girl" who'd grown up to capture the heart of the love king in Hollywood. He arranged for a local paper to publish photos of a male schoolmate of hers who claimed he had been her first love. When Natacha saw the spread and erupted in anger, Curley acted mystified, saying he thought she'd weep tears of joy at all the fuss being made about her in her hometown. "I wept all right," Natacha answered, "but not for joy."

Since Rudy maintained that he had no further need to obey the edicts issued by Famous Players—Lasky, nor to worry about how the Hays Office might judge his morals, he and Natacha no longer had to live separately as they waited the few months left until they could finally get legally married. Although Natacha preferred to be called "Miss Hudnut," everyone now referred to them as "the Valentinos." Their appeal increased because they seemed to be living out a genuine romance. They were lovers who wanted to be married and who danced "with and for each other, for the joy of being in each other's company." Even though Valentino was recalling his role as Julio in *The Four Horsemen* by doing the tango, newspaper accounts invariably referred to him as "the Sheik."

They subsisted not on love alone. Weekly expenses for the tour were estimated at twenty thousand dollars; on a good week, grosses might reach one hundred thousand dollars. Ticket holders paid from one to three dollars to see a performance that lasted about an hour. The dance exhibitions could be held in gyms, ballrooms, armories, or even fairgrounds, but because of the court injunction they weren't supposed to be in theaters. (Sometimes they were, nonetheless.) Mineralava would pick up the hefty tab for the tour, and in return Valentino would allow his name and image to be used in magazine ads for Mineralava products; he would also talk up the beauty clay whenever he had a chance after dancing before a paying audience, and would participate in promoting beauty contests to be staged after he and Natacha danced. The contest winners were decided by audience applause, since "if Valentino made the selection, he would make more enemies than friends." When a beauty queen was selected, Valentino would promenade with her around the room, and there were whispers that she might be considered for a future screen role. Valentino presented each winner with a doll miniature of himself and Natacha, or an engraved trophy cup. The prettiest girl in each town would be invited to participate in a national contest at the end of the tour. This culminating event, which would be filmed, took place that November.

Although Rudy and Natacha had taken time out to attend the New York opening of *The Young Rajah* with June Mathis, in general Rudy now took pains to distance himself from his Famous Players–Lasky roles, especially the Sheik. In Chicago Rudy explained to a reporter that he hadn't really earned his reputation as an authority on women; people considered him one "because I was unfortunate enough to be compelled to carry off a lady and hide her in my tent—in pictures. And it isn't that I know anything about women," he said, laughing. "A man who says he understands them is either a liar or an imbecile. Why consider man the aggressor in love, anyway?" he continued. "I hold with Bernard Shaw that it is the woman who is the pursuer." He told the crowd in St. Louis, "If I ever make another Sheik picture it will be an honest-to-God last one. Why, I didn't even look like a sheik in the other one. I was a drawing-room hero."

But he wasn't consistent. One minute he argued that, contrary to popular belief, in a man-woman twosome it's the woman who usually pursues the man, not the other way around, and that was fine with him; the next minute he objected to being portrayed as a languid sensualist, as if being supine and amorous detracted from his male potency. Playing the Sheik had deprived him, he complained, "of my privileges as a man." In the public's eyes, "I am nothing but a love maker. Sometimes I have a wild inclination to hit a man squarely on the jaw and don't dare because it would be another movie scandal." By the logic at large in the land, a logic he at times seemed to adopt, loving was construed as less active and manly than fighting. Rudy blamed Famous Players–Lasky for manufacturing an image of him that was less than red-blooded: "I feel deeply distressed that I must shatter the illusions from the publicity department of my former employers depicting me as a wan and interestingly pale, beardless youth, leisurely reclining on down sofas, supported by silken pillows, smoking sheikishly perfumed cigarettes." Clearly, some of the ambivalence on this issue resided within Rudy.

The Mineralava tour itself sent the world some mixed cues. Often, during the interlude following the dancing, Valentino took the microphone and, addressing the crowd, availed himself of the opportunity to roast the "movie trust" after singing the praises of Mineralava Beauty Clay. The two topics didn't mix. Here he was, blasting the studios, and in particular Famous Players–Lasky, for turning him into a commodity, and in the next sentence he was shilling for a cosmetics firm that made no claim to be anything but a business. For top dollar, he'd sold his talents as a dancer to a company that coddled him in return for what it hoped would be handsome financial rewards. Where was the moral high road, the devotion to art and beauty untarnished by focus on the bottom line?

Not everyone who attended a performance during the Mineralava tour left it feeling satisfied. Some felt cheated, especially if they had been kept waiting, had been denied a full-length show, or if another dancer had substituted for Natacha, as happened at least once when Natacha had to make a quick solo trip to New York. A reviewer in Buffalo complained that "the program was less than half of one percent dancing. The other 99½ was bull devoted to a review of Rudy's quarrel with the motion picture trusts. And how that boy can hate! The only thing that smacked of the Arabian was the manager's visit to the box office, where he counted the shekels." In other words, this reporter concluded, "he came, he saw, he got away with murder." Chicago, a city whose press would again turn venomous on the subject of Rudolph Valentino, tweaked him for being vain, and cast aspersions on his acting ability. The *Chicago Tribune* editorialized, "The conceited rarely inherit the earth" and hinted that the Italian-born screen idol was little more than a manikin with moving parts. "As long as [Valentino] is content to remain a high class dancing man or animated statue upon whom leading ladies can drape their arms and imaginative tailors drape their costumes, he probably will survive," the paper jeered.

One reason the issue of Valentino's masculinity again surfaced was that he was endorsing cosmetics. The mainstream considered using beauty products fine for women, but questionable for a man, especially a man who was much imitated: Valentino's patent-leather hair, his Gallardo-style sideburns and gaucho pants were still setting fashion trends among the young men. George Ullman insists in his memoir that Valentino's contract with Mineralava specified that the beauty clay "should be exploited always as an adjunct to a woman's toilet." But either he misremembered, or the contract was ignored on this point, because Mineralava published ads in which Valentino did advise, many times, that Mineralava products worked for men as well as women. One ad read, "Before deciding on the present tour, Rudolph Valentino made a thorough test, practical and scientific, of Mineralava Beauty Clay, which, he declares, is just as valuable to men as it is to women." Another ad, which ran in *Photoplay*, showed a photo of Valentino in a gaucho hat and white shirt over the caption, "Every man and woman should use Mineralava. I would not be without it." This ad went on to claim that Valentino was "one of the hundreds of men and women of the Stage and Screen who endorse Mineralava. He was induced to use it through the example of his wife, the beautiful Winifred Hudnut, who boasts a flawless complexion which she attributes to the use of Mineralava." Not just the beauty clay complexion treatment, but also face powders were recommended by him and Natacha to all who wished to have beautiful skin.

Actually, without makeup Valentino's skin didn't happen to be par-

Maurice Goldberg portrait of Valentino for *Shadowland*, 1921 (Museum of Modern Art)

Valentino and the hermit William Pester in Palm Springs, ca. 1921 (Palm Springs Historical Society)

Valentino with Dr. White, local hermit William Pester, and other friends in Palm Springs, ca. 1921 (Palm Springs Historical Society)

Valentino as Sheik Ahmed Ben Hassan, threatening the virtue of Agnes Ayres as Lady Diana Mayo in *The Sheik*, Paramount, 1921 (Courtesy of the Academy of Motion Picture Arts and Sciences)

Valentino as Sheik Ahmed Ben Hassan, being nursed by Agnes Ayres as Lady Diana Mayo in *The Sheik*, Paramount, 1921 (Courtesy of the Academy of Motion Picture Arts and Sciences)

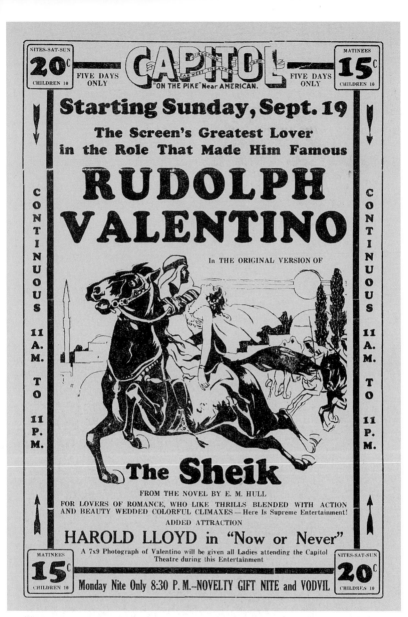

Poster ad for *The Sheik*, 1921 (Courtesy of the Academy of Motion Picture Arts and Sciences)

Ben Turpin and Kathryn McGuire clowning in *The Shriek of Araby*, Allied Productions, 1923 (Courtesy of the Academy of Motion Picture Arts and Sciences)

Dorothy Dalton as Moran, Valentino as Ramon Laredo, and Walter Long as Captain Kitch-ell in *Moran of the Lady Letty*, Paramount, 1922 (Museum of Modern Art)

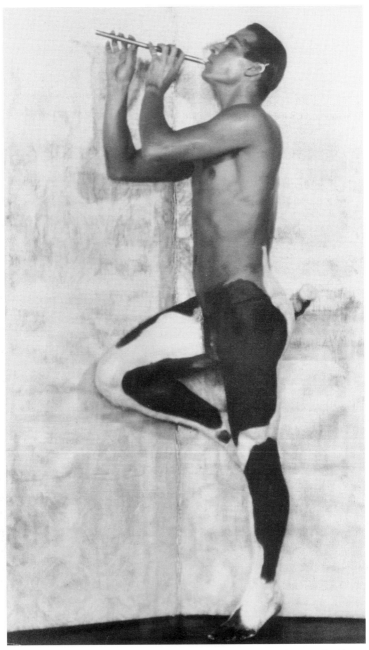

Valentino as the Faun, ca. 1921. Staged by Natacha Rambova, photographed by Helen MacGregor (Courtesy of the Academy of Motion Picture Arts and Sciences)

Valentino romancing Gloria Swanson in *Beyond the Rocks*, Paramount, 1922 (Private collection)

(*above*) Outside the court-house in Los Angeles with bondsman Thomas Meighan and attorneys after Valentino's arrest and imprisonment on a bigamy charge, May 1922 (Library of Congress)

Valentino, actor William Hart, and director Fred Niblo, 1922 (Private collection)

(*above*) Valentino as Juan Gallardo fondles Nita Naldi as the temptress Doña Sol in *Blood and Sand*, Paramount, 1922 (Museum of Modern Art)

Valentino as the torero Gallardo, with scenarist June Mathis on the set of *Blood and Sand*, 1922 (Museum of Modern Art)

Valentino, as Gallardo, demonstrates his famous hypnotic stare in a still from *Blood and Sand*, Paramount, 1922 (Private collection)

Valentino in boxing gear with friend Robert Florey, ca. 1922 (Museum of Modern Art)

Valentino costumed by Natacha Rambova as the Young Rajah, Paramount, 1922 (Museum of Modern Art)

Pals Douglas Gerrard, Valentino, Jean de Limur, and Robert Florey seem ready to dance in Whitley Heights, Hollywood, 1922 (Bison Archives)

The Valentinos' house (now destroyed) at 6770 Wedgewood Place, Whitley Heights, Hollywood (Private collection)

Double portrait of Natacha Rambova and Rudolph Valentino in profile by James Abbe, 1922 (Utah Museum of Fine Arts, University of Utah; photograph copyright Kathryn Abbe)

Natacha Rambova and Rudolph Valentino dancing the tango during the Mineralava tour, 1922 (Courtesy of the Academy of Motion Picture Arts and Sciences; photograph by James Abbe, copyright Kathryn Abbe)

(*below*) A goateed Valentino, with Natacha Rambova (second from right) and her mother and stepfather, Mr. and Mrs. Richard Hudnut, ca. 1922 (Library of Congress)

Valentino as Black Feather, ca. 1922 (Private collection)

(*below*) Three dapper men-about-town: Valentino and his Doberman, Kabar (center), with Jacques Hébertot (left) and René Clair outside the Hotel Plaza-Athénée in Paris, 1923 (Bibilothèque du Film, Paris)

Natacha Rambova in Poiret driving costume, with Valentino in "plus four" knickers, Norfolk jacket, France, 1923 (Private collection)

ticularly beautiful. A reporter who during the tour took him and
Natacha for a drive along the Cumberland River near Nashville, Ten-
nessee, remarked, "Up close, he revealed many small pockmarks in his
face. One suspected a boyhood bout with smallpox, but did not ask."

The lingering public distrust of a male screen idol who endorses
and might himself use beauty products went to the heart of an even
broader suspicion concerning the very premises of the performing
arts. Didn't actors and dancers wear makeup and dress up in costumes, and wasn't there something underhanded about all this preening and make-believe? In a masculine culture that made a fetish of
"no guff" rough-and-ready straight shooting, anything that seemed
glaringly artificial struck a nerve. For many men and a few women,
Rudolph Valentino became the embodiment of a posturing, theatrical,
look-at-me quality they found unsettling. The fact that he had taken to
complaining in public only added to his public-relations problems; real
men weren't supposed to whine. Instead of being hailed as a heroic
David, single-handedly doing battle against the greedy Goliath trusts,
to his critics he came off as a crybaby. Beneath the gleaming surface of
adulation for Valentino lurked an underlayer of ugly spite that kept
poking through.

The more thoughtful critics understood that Valentino's problem
with male put-down artists had something to do with the way his allure threatened American men. An anonymous psychologist, writing
on "The Vogue of Valentino" for *Motion Picture Magazine*, observed,
acutely, that he made mainstream husbands and boyfriends feel mun-
dane and unromantic. "American men are not lovers!" the psychologist wrote. "The American businessman has little or no imagination
for aesthetic activities and sentimental pastimes. [He] knows nothing
of the subtleties of the game of love." Crowning Valentino "the fancy
man *de luxe*," the "male Helen of Troy" (both terms that highlighted
Valentino's beauty and his androgynous quality), he dubbed him
"the Phantom Rival in every domestic establishment." And his popularity with women proved "the present great unrest among American
women," who wanted more than meat and potatoes in their lives; they
wanted champagne and roses. Valentino's gallant manner, and the
combination of indifference and fervor in his face, his beauty, and the

strength in his body made women feel he would be "susceptible to feminine wiles." Women liked that fantasy of having their way with an Adonis. Instead of ridiculing Valentino, this psychologist thought, American men would do better to "study and imitate him." Some young people apparently did this very thing, using the movies as a kind of "how-to" guide for romantic technique.

The Mineralava dance tour, which touched down at eighty-eight different locations, ended up a mixed success. It helped keep the Valentino name before the public and gave audiences in remote corners of North America, as well as big cities, a chance to see Rudy and Natacha perform live. Financially, it proved disappointing to its backers. Although toward the end of the tour they cleared $6,500 a week, Mineralava ultimately lost money, because heavy advertising budgets, along with other expenses, ran to $8,500 a week. From the public-relations point of view, the tour could be called a draw between the Valentino boosters, tens of thousands of adoring fans, and snarling detractors, some with access to print. On both sides, the emotional mercury zoomed to fever pitch. People felt they knew this star intimately; they either wanted to embrace him or punch him out. Cool heads were nowhere in evidence. The derisive tag "Vaselino" became current; that sleek pomaded hair of his just didn't look natural or ruggedly American, and it became an emblem of his differentness. Stories like this one began appearing:

VALENTINO RAZZED

Newark New Jersey, April 25. Valentino was razzed on his appearance Saturday night at the armory. About 5,000 came to see him and they greeted him with great enthusiasm. His dances with Mrs. Valentino were applauded politely, but when he began his speech, the crowd grew restless. As he denounced the "movie trust" some in the throng yelled at him and the hall became very noisy. Finally the sheik lost his temper and without

even mentioning the beauty clay he advertises, he rushed
off the stage and broke his way to his dressing room.
There he apologized to reporters for not finishing his
talk, but refused to return.

By this time, April 1923, the Valentinos had been lawfully wed at last.
On March 13 a final decree of divorce from Jean Acker was entered in
Los Angeles County Superior Court. The next day, Rudy and Natacha
tried to marry in Chicago, but since they couldn't get permission to do
so (Illinois law required still more waiting), they drove on frozen roads
from the Blackstone Hotel, Chicago, to Crown Point, Indiana, where
Justice of the Peace Howard H. Kemp pronounced them man and wife
at 6:05 p.m. Both "Winifred de Wolfe," born January 19, 1897, and
"Rodolfo Guglielmi," born May 6, 1895, had to unromantically affirm
in their applications for an Indiana marriage license that neither was
"an imbecile, feeble-minded, idiotic, or insane," nor was either party
"afflicted with epilepsy, tuberculosis, venereal, or any other conta-
gious or transmissible disease." At the Crown Point ceremony Natacha's
side of the family was represented by Mrs. R. E. de Wolfe of Salt Lake
City. No one represented Rudy's family, but an Italian friend from
Chicago, Mr. Michael Romano, served as best man. After the brief exchange of vows, "the bride and bridegroom returned to Chicago,
where they appeared Wednesday night in a dancing act at a cabaret."

Naturally, everyone wanted to learn about the new Mrs. Valentino.
Published photographs of her highlighted her "Oriental" beauty and
sophisticated fashion sense. Widely distributed double portraits taken
by the well-known theatrical photographer James Abbe showed her in
costume, dancing the tango with Valentino, or posing in profile with
him, her dark hair drawn back from her face, looking every inch the
prima ballerina assoluta, or like a Roman noblewoman whose face is
etched on a coin.

Anna Prophater, a reporter for *Screenland*, took a different tack,
praising the new Mrs. Valentino's practical know-how about career
matters. "Mrs. Valentino is one of the few wives of influence," wrote

Prophater admiringly. "She reminds you of Mary Pickford. She talks business in a sane, cool-headed way. She is engrossed in her husband's success and his ambitions. Like Mary Pickford, she is the Disraeli . . . of the household. Mary also fought her way through lawsuits and matrimonial difficulties." These sympathetic comments deserve underlining in red because they praise the very same abilities that would later be read negatively, as indications that the Mrs. "wore the pants," put her own ambition first, and behaved like a green-eyed virago. Anna Prophater found no fault with Natacha for wanting to advance her husband's career and for steering Valentino toward serious, demanding roles and away from "Sheik stuff." She quotes Mrs. Valentino as saying of her husband, "People have the wrong idea about him. Perhaps the lawsuit has brought us closer together. We both believe in the independence of the artist."

Since the Valentinos, like Mary Pickford and Douglas Fairbanks, had a much-publicized Hollywood marriage that attracted endless comment in the press, their relationship became part of the ongoing 1920s debate about woman's proper role and how power should be divided between husband and wife. Doug and Mary were depicted as a dream team, partners in life and business who used the spotlight that came with celebrity to turn themselves into role models. During the war they helped with the patriotic Liberty Bond campaign, and after the war the press made it seem as if they devoted themselves to the cause of clean living. They worked hard, kept in shape, spent their money prudently, entertained the hoi polloi at Pickfair, and stayed away from the kind of scandalous parties that had ruined Fatty Arbuckle's career and given Hollywood a black eye. The Valentinos were another story. They were "Oriental," sensuous, foreign. They weren't regarded as either 100 percent American or 100 percent morally upright, and one very vocal segment of the public couldn't forgive these trespasses. Natacha's strong-mindedness and ambition got far more negative feedback than did Mary Pickford's—even though Little Mary wasn't meek and mild by anyone's yardstick. Rudy, for all his accomplishment as an equestrian, a fitness fanatic, and a lover of surf, sun, and the great outdoors, couldn't shake his image as a hothouse orchid, a drawing-room ornament, a dancer rather than a sportsman, and an oily idler who slithered around, dabbled in poetry, and expected rich ladies to take care of him. Already there were rumors that he was henpecked. A reporter in Washington made much of an overheard bit of dialogue, in which, during their tour, Natacha scolded Rudy for flubbing a dance step three times in a row; he would have to practice alone, she told him.

Back in Italy, Rudy's family—his sister, Maria, and brother, Alberto— had never seen a Valentino movie. They had little grasp either of the extent of their brother's American fame or of the controversy he provoked, but they, too, wanted to know more about Natacha. Alberto and his wife, Ada, and Maria remained in close touch with Rudy by mail. They cheered his success (Rudy joked to a reporter that to his family, his voice test at a recording studio in New York amounted to a debut at the Metropolitan Opera) and shared his wish that their parents, especially Gabriella, had survived to witness it. Anxious for him to be happy, they wondered about the sort of wife Rudy had chosen. Would she take good care of him like a dutiful, domesticated Italian wife? Would she warm to his relatives? What sort of person was she? "Rudy says his people asked anxiously in their last letter whether Natacha Rambova is expansive like Italian women or cold and distant like English women."

Rudy, too, grew more and more impatient to return to Europe with Natacha and give Alberto and Maria a chance to meet his bride. He hadn't set foot in his native country for almost ten years, and he pined for it. He wanted Natacha to see the places that had shaped him. He was also curious to see for himself what was happening in Italy since Mussolini had assumed power, in 1922. Many in America had kept open minds about the new Italian Fascist leader, who wasn't yet perceived by most as the hated dictator and Axis ally he would later become. Some who viewed Bolshevism as a greater threat than Fascism admired Mussolini for stomping rabble-rousers and improving Italy by modernizing it and fostering both discipline and national pride. Valentino unsuccessfully tried to gain an audience with him in 1923. (Doug Fairbanks and Mary Pickford had more luck when they visited Italy in 1929.) "The most applauded men in the current world," wrote Herbert Howe in *Photoplay*, "are Valentino and Mussolini. In Rome we witnessed the Fascisti revolution and cheered for Mussolini and Vittorio Emanuele. In London we witnessed *Blood and Sand* and cheered for Valentino." Suddenly, according to Howe, all the actors wanted to be Italian.

Since Famous Players–Lasky had refused to send Valentino abroad to make pictures, now that he had free time he could go there on his own steam, perhaps somehow even arrange to act in a film over there. The Italian production company Cines, based in Rome, was trying to obtain his services to star in a planned production of *Quo Vadis*. Valentino promised Florey that if the project materialized, Florey could be its associate director. Even if he couldn't legally go to work in Europe, while there he could drum up European interest in the Hollywood films he'd already made.

Valentino had reason to be concerned about the way his films were being overlooked on the European market. Compared with Chaplin, Fairbanks, and Pickford, much-traveled international stars whose screen images crossed oceans and national borders, he faced a more limited recognition, in large part because his films had not been well distributed in Europe and he hadn't yet toured there in person. In England, to be sure, he had an enthusiastic following, and he was somewhat known in France. But Rudy thought that in both countries, as well as his native Italy, his ratings and earnings could be vastly improved, with the right publicity combined with better distribution.

Publicity was one aspect of the business world that actively interested Valentino. In a letter to James Quirk, the editor of *Photoplay*, he offered Quirk either a commission or a percentage if he would agree to handle publicity for Valentino's book of poems, *Day Dreams*, which was to be released in May by the publisher and physical-culture zealot Bernarr Macfadden. Rudy also wrote to Robert Florey, who had left the Mineralava dance tour and gone ahead to New York, to tell him that he'd posed for new publicity photos and had chosen twenty-eight different images and two hundred glossy reproductions of them, to be sent on by Florey to magazines in London and Paris. Florey was to plan the Valentino visits to those two cities, as well as Italy, and would serve as advance man in Europe. He would generate further publicity by arranging to serialize in movie magazines Rudy's planned diary account of his travels, and perhaps he'd arrange to shoot documentary footage of the trip, which might be turned into an extended newsreel. Valentino's "My Own Story of My Trip Abroad" would end up serialized over many weeks in *Movie Weekly*, but the home movies have never been shown in theaters. Film footage of the trip, some of it apparently shot by Valentino himself, turned up in "The Legend of Valentino," a Wolper-Sterling television documentary made in 1961 and recently released on DVD.

Rudy depended on Florey so much that when he heard a rumor that Florey was going to abandon him to get married and remain in the States instead of serving as European advance man, he saw red, not realizing the rumor was false. In a burst of what sounds like self-interested jealousy he warned Florey by letter that if he really did plan to bail out in order to marry, Florey would be jeopardizing his own promising future, and that opportunities to marry were a dime a dozen: "to lose one woman is to find a thousand," Rudy wrote. This is a truly extraordinary outburst, coming from a man who usually treated women with the utmost deference and respect. Florey assured Rudy that he had no present marital plans (he would eventually marry twice) and went ahead to London. Florey and Valentino would remain good friends, but their business relationship didn't survive the European tour. No one knows exactly what went wrong. In his considerable writing about Valentino, Florey remained tight-lipped about Natacha. He only comments in a general way about Rudy's unrealistic ideals regarding what a wife should be, and his bad luck in sustaining relationships with women. It seems likely that Florey and Natacha didn't especially take to one another. There would continue to be a lot of jockeying for power and emotional supremacy within Rudy's inner circle.

———

Their Mineralava tour behind them, the Valentinos returned to Rudy's rooms at the Hotel des Artistes in New York to prepare for their European journey, which would serve as a delayed honeymoon. Before they embarked, some important business matters had to be settled, and career decisions made. In preparation for what he hoped might lead to a recording contract, Rudy took some voice lessons in New York with a vocal coach by the name of Mazziotti. For Brunswick Records he made a test recording of two songs: Woodforde and Finden's "Kashmiri Love Song," from *The Sheik*, and José Padilla's "El Relicario," a Spanish song (sung in Spanish) that scores castanets in the orchestral background. It is the only known recording of his voice. Since he had a pleasing but not completely professional-sounding baritone voice, and sound recording had become a big business, it's not clear why the disc stayed in the vault for so long, but it did. Valentino's English pronunciation may have been the problem. His (to my ears delightful) Italian accent is evident, and the English lyrics of the "Kashmiri Love Song," immortalizing those "pale hands I love beside the Shalimar," sometimes come off indistinct. The recording was not commercially released until after Valentino's death.

Under Ullman's direction, he had hired a new lawyer, Max Steuer, and sent his old one packing. Steuer, a slight, bald man who earned a million a year and was so effective in court he was called "the magician," could only take charge of Valentino's complicated legal portfolio after a settlement was reached with his predecessor, Arthur Butler Graham. Graham had been kept on a retainer and was asking to be paid $65,000 for his legal services to Valentino. Max Steuer arranged a settlement with Graham of $20,000, which Valentino paid. Valentino also paid back a personal loan (probably from Joe Godsol, but it could have been from Joseph Schenck, who'd also lent him money), all in cash. "He enjoyed the feel of the crisp new bank-notes between his fingers," said Ullman. "A check would not have meant nearly so much to him." Ullman was right to insist that Valentino try to dig himself out of his financial hole in order to move forward. In return for his advice and help, Ullman asked for and got total control of the Valentinos' finances.

Now the door opened for negotiations with Famous Players–Lasky; if successful they would clear the way for Valentino to return to film acting, which he yearned to do. Dancing for a living didn't satisfy his soul the way screen acting did. A rumor circulated in the trade papers that banker A. P. Giannini, from whom the then unknown Rodolfo Guglielmi had once sought career advice in San Francisco, had convinced Adolph Zukor to strike a deal with the insurgent star, arguing that "any continuance of the differences between Famous Players and the star would only work a hardship on exhibitors, and the industry would practically be cutting their nose to spite their face if they continued the policy to keep him off the screen." The names of two producers, Joseph M. Schenck and J. D. Williams, crept into reports of a deal in the works. Russian-born Schenck, once a partner of Marcus Loew, now produced the films of his wife, Norma Talmadge, her sister, Constance Talmadge, and his brother-in-law, Buster Keaton. *Variety* reported that Schenck and Valentino had held several meetings, and that Schenck was going to join the backers of a new company, to be headed by J. D. Williams.

J. D. Williams was no stranger to Valentino or the movie business. An Australian who'd helped found First National Pictures, under that company's banner he had distributed two early Valentino films, *Alimony* (1917) and *Passion's Playground* (1920). Now he was forming a new firm, to be called Ritz-Carlton Pictures; he hoped to negotiate a deal with Famous Players–Lasky that would allow Valentino to fulfill his existing contract with them and free him to sign a new agreement with Ritz-Carlton. Exercising its option to employ Valentino for an additional year, Famous Players–Lasky would make two more pictures starring him. His pay would be $7,500 a week, starting immediately, and in 1924 the two films would be made in New York, not Hollywood. Valentino would have a say in the choice of director and cast, and Natacha would stand at his side as designer and consultant. A July dinner at the Ritz-Carlton Hotel in Manhattan celebrated the agreement whereby Valentino "would make a series of productions for Ritz-Carlton Pictures over a number of years." Valentino's rebellion against Famous Players–Lasky had in effect been quashed. Although the stu-

dio had capitulated in the matters of salary, star participation in production decisions, and venue, Valentino had lost more than a year out
of his on-screen working life and now was being forced to break his
vow never again to work for Famous Players–Lasky. His *bête noire*,
Adolph Zukor, the man responsible for putting detectives on his tail,
again loomed large. At the Ritz-Carlton dinner "every speaker could
not let pass the opportunity to express a word of appreciation for
Adolph Zukor, the individual."

Despite the Zukor factor, Rudy felt jubilant at the prospect of going before the cameras again when he returned to New York after the
European sojourn. He liked J. D. Williams, assumed Williams had the
necessary financial backing for the new endeavor, and looked forward
to dealing with a small company, where he thought the films he made
would be custom-fit to his specifications. The offer from Cines in
Rome to star in *Quo Vadis* had to be turned down, which he regretted
but didn't cry over. Onward!

While in New York, Rudy and Natacha were enjoying nightlife, going dancing at clubs and dining in restaurants in the spring and early-
summer weeks before they left for Europe. At a place called Victor
Hugo's they initiated *Photoplay*'s Herbert Howe into the joyous mysteries of a rich Italian dessert called zabaglione. Friends gave them a
farewell dinner at an East Side Italian trattoria, Villa Penza, which had
a fake garden draped with artificial wisteria. Rudy always gravitated to
friendly eateries, where he could talk Italian to the owners, wait staff,
and other customers. He loved the high life, but when it came to food,
he had an instinct for the homey and unpretentious.

At the King Cole Club, where wise-cracking, sharpshooting Texas
Guinan presided as hostess, Rudy and Natacha had an unpleasant encounter with the first Mrs. Rudolph Valentino, Jean Acker. Jean just
would not go away. While stopping in Minnesota on the last lap of the
Mineralava tour, they'd been dismayed to find the town plastered with
signs advertising "Mrs. Rudolph Valentino," otherwise known as Jean
Acker, who was appearing locally in a Keith circuit vaudeville show as
"A Regular Girl." Valentino, who had just married Natacha, went to
court to try to stop Jean from using the Valentino name, which had

never been legally hers in the first place; she'd married a guy named Guglielmi.

Tex Guinan, who'd done Hollywood time starring in westerns and was now famous for working the crowd at the clubs she hosted, and in some cases co-owned, kidded the inevitable "butter and egg man" from out of town, a hayseed who'd pay top dollar for a watered-down glass of Prohibition booze. "Hello, suckers" was her famous greeting, and she'd introduce members of her chorus line by saying "Give this little girl a great big hand." She kept moving from nightclub to nightclub to keep federal anti-alcohol agents off her scent. She'd had her clubs padlocked so many times, she'd taken to wearing a fake padlock around her neck. This month she'd decided to boost business at her latest club by staging a series of "movie nights." Tonight the guest of honor was Rudolph Valentino. The Barrymores, Anita Stewart, and former Ziegfeld beauty Peggy Hopkins Joyce sat ringside in the crowded, smoky room, along with actors Ivor Novello and Lowell Sherman and socialite Mrs. W. K. Vanderbilt, Jr. "Stage, screen, opera, bolshevism, and capitalism sat side by side," wrote one observer. Peggy Hopkins Joyce had shelled out one hundred dollars to reserve a table near the Valentinos. Miss Joyce's guest, a mysterious lady with a spiked hairdo and ropes of pearls, was introduced as "the Countess of Itch." The countess noisily rattled her dishes as Rudy and Natacha danced. Then the Valentinos and Texas Guinan realized simultaneously that the alleged Countess of Itch was none other than Jean Acker. Said Guinan, "when I realized it was Jean Acker in disguise . . . I didn't know whether to commit suicide or sing 'Baby Shoes.'" She did neither. She roared with laughter. So did Rudy. What else could he do? Natacha's response was not recorded, but we can imagine.

Well, Jean's tiresome self-promoting antics wouldn't be able to pursue them to the other side of the Atlantic. On July 23, 1923, Mr. and Mrs. Rudolph Valentino pushed through a throng of well-wishers to board the *Aquitania*, bound for Cherbourg.

EUROPE, 1923

The moment they boarded the four-funnel Cunard ocean liner *Aquitania*, a feeling of freedom, a buoyant exhilaration, lifted their spirits, and they remained aloft for the whole crossing. At last they'd escaped to a place where they could be alone when they chose, one with no lawyers to plague them, no pushy journalists, and only a handful of polite gawkers on hand. Their traveling companion, Aunt Teresa Werner, presented no problems. She was a great respecter of privacy, and in any case would be leaving them at Cherbourg to go on to the Hudnuts' villa at Juan-les-Pins in the South of France, while the newlyweds continued on to Southampton and then made their way to London. London-born actor George Arliss and his wife were fellow passengers, and the two couples became friendly, getting to know each other over elaborate shipboard dinners set with many crystal goblets. Arliss provided a kind of social bridge to London, where the two couples intended to meet again for dinner.

Another British passenger in their midst, grande dame Elinor Glyn, recorded that she thought Valentino had changed for the worse since their days with Gloria Swanson on the set of *Beyond the Rocks*. In a classic instance of the pot calling the kettle black, she tacitly accused him of turning into an arrogant snob. "He was being fearfully civil to people whom he imagined were of importance in Europe," Glyn would write in 1927, when Rudy no longer was around to defend himself. Madame Glyn probably felt jealous. She hadn't yet scored her sensational success with the concept of "It," and her name and presence no longer guaranteed the flutters of excited attention that they had prompted in Hollywood a few years back. The Valentinos, now far more celebrated than she, weren't going out of their way to dine with her on the *Aquitania*. Unlike them, *she* wouldn't be greeted at Southampton by thirty reporters eager for a story, nor was she going to be cheered by about a thousand tireless autograph seekers when she arrived at her London destination late on a rainy July night.

Valentino did try to curry favor with the rich and titled, but this was nothing new in the man who, ten years back, had fashioned himself "dei Marchesi" when he first landed in America at age eighteen.

Valentino drew up a list of notable names he could rattle off in his account of the British visit. He'd lunched with millionaire Benjamin Guinness at his Ascot estate and at the Savoy in London had been presented to Lord Glencomer, politician T. P. O'Connor, and conservative Lord Birkenhead, now secretary of state for India after a long career in Parliament. Lord Birkenhead had only the dimmest notion of who Valentino was. But his twelve-year-old daughter, Lady Pamela Smith, knew exactly. She charmed Valentino—who had a special way with young people—more than any other.

Rudy took pride in his invitation to stop in at the Wyndham's Theatre dressing room of leading man Sir Gerald du Maurier after watching him act opposite Tallulah Bankhead in *The Dancers*, a play about dance mania that du Maurier coauthored. He also would boast that he'd shaken the magical hand of pianist Arthur Rubinstein, and had been introduced to actress Gladys Cooper, whose performance in a play called *Kiki* he found inferior to one by Lenore Ulric he'd recently seen in New York. He confided this to his diary, not Miss Cooper.

Receiving Fleet Street reporters and photographers on his first morning in London at his and Natacha's royal suite at the Carlton Hotel, on Haymarket, Valentino wore a "magnificent dressing-gown over purple pajamas and sported rings on his fingers and red Russian leather slippers on his toes." Described by one writer as quiet, shy, and patient, he revealed to the assembled company that one of the things he counted on doing in London was refurbishing his wardrobe. "I have not had a decent suit in ten years," he announced. He also said that he and Natacha, who joined him at the interview, would not be accepting

any of the invitations to dance in public in England that had been pour-
ing in. They'd had their fill of exhibition dancing, thank you. "To dance
when one has to dance is not the same thing as dancing when one
wants to dance." This trip was intended to be primarily a vacation.
"What is your motto?" a reporter inquired. "Live and let live," he
replied. It was a philosophy Valentino often wished American journalists would adopt toward him.

Off to the shops of Jermyn Street they went, visiting and placing
Rudy's orders with tailors, hatters, and shirtmakers before motoring
to Natacha's old school, Leatherhead Court, in Epsom, Surrey. En
route they stopped at a kennel where Natacha purchased three pint-
sized Pekingese dogs to join the one she already had and had brought
along. Traveling light would never be their style. The Valentinos had
departed New York hauling fifteen pieces of luggage. By the time they
returned home in the fall, after his shopping spree in London and hers
in Paris, they would have twice as many trunks, a new custom-made
car (to be picked up later), and rare paintings and old books acquired
in Italy.

Because she had attended school nearby, Natacha knew the London
area well. But England was all new and exciting territory to Rudy, who
acted the wide-eyed tourist on visits to Westminster Abbey, Windsor
Castle, Hampton Court, and the Tower of London.

The proprietors of the Carlton Hotel balked at the mess the four
Pekes created in the pricey suite, which had been previously occupied
by Marshal Foch, Count Sforza, Paderewski, and the king and queen of
Belgium. They also would complain vociferously about—and ask to
be paid extra for—the stains left by black hair paste on Rudy's lace pil-
lowcases. He had taken to using the oily paste, which resembled shoe
polish, to cover an incipient bald spot. This foreshadowing of the cruel
effects of aging wounded his vanity, and it worried him, since his box-
office appeal depended partly on his youthful and photogenic good
looks.

After a fortnight in London they set off by plane from Croydon for Le
Bourget, the airport outside Paris. Rudy, who gravitated to all things

speedy, had taken flying lessons in Mineola, New York, when the Great
War erupted, in hopes of being able to serve as a pilot, but he'd never
before flown as a commercial passenger. He loved the idea of flight and
also couldn't wait to return to France, though his feelings for the
country of his mother's birth were now colored by its sorrowful associations with the war, and his mother's death in France five years earlier. "I said to Natacha before we reached France," he wrote in his
diary, "that I felt I did not care to see the battlefields of France . . . and
few of the ruins. To me the wounds of the earth, the despoliation of
ancestral beauty would be like gashes in fair flesh." Paris, he would
write after seeing it again, "still wears flowers in her hair," but now
they were "flowers plucked from graves." Even though he hadn't
served in the war, his intense identification with the role of Julio in *The
Four Horsemen* and the personal loss he had suffered made him feel
more like a participant than an observer.

Aunt Teresa had left them at Cherbourg, but Robert Florey, who'd
preceded them to London, accompanied them on the flight to France.
That made them a party of three, a common number during Rudy and
Natacha's marriage. Florey went on to set things up in Rome soon after arriving in Paris. During their years as a couple there often was a
male friend of Rudy's tagging along: Paul Ivano, Douglas Gerrard,
Florey, and eventually the Spanish painter Federico Beltrán-Masses.
Rudy leaned on his friends. Natacha, a less dependent person than he,
didn't want full-time companionship. Other than Auntie, the only
woman friend who ever joined them on a trip during the marriage was
Nita Naldi, a friend of both of theirs. At the time they met, Natacha's
involvement with Nazimova occupied much of her time, but Nazimova's influence had gone into eclipse once Rudy superseded her as a
star. In general, Natacha prized her privacy. Rudy, on the other hand,
disliked solitude, except when he felt troubled. He'd been raised with
family around, siblings, cousins, aunts, and uncles. Later he'd always
lived among schoolmates, and after that, in New York, he'd found
fellow young blades to go on the town with. Rudy preferred to do
things—ride, swim, dine, travel, carouse—in a duo or a pack. Natacha
didn't satisfy all his needs for support and conviviality, and she was
happy to give him room.

Their plane was greeted at Le Bourget by three to four hundred enthusiastic fans, and a new friend: the impresario and editor Jacques Hébertot, one of the movers and shakers on the Paris theater scene. Hébertot, an elegant man from an old Normandy family, had appointed himself unofficial Paris host to the Valentinos. A man of dynamic energy, Hébertot edited several periodicals, including *Comoedia* and *Théâtre et Comédie Illustrée*. As administrative director of the Théâtre des Champs-Elysées, he'd showcased a variety of richly talented, avant-garde performing groups, including Rolf de Maré's Swedish Ballet (Ballets Suédois) and Erik Satie's Les Six. In future years he would produce the first plays of Jean Cocteau, André Malraux, and Albert Camus, and assign to Gerard Phillippe his first acting role.

Hébertot squired the Valentinos to their Paris hotel, the Plaza Athénée, on Avenue Montaigne, quite close to his own office. He explained some of the arrangements he'd made for the distinguished visitors from Hollywood. On their second night in town, they were to be feted at a "dinner among friends" he'd gone to great lengths to plan. This dinner in Valentino's honor would introduce him and Natacha to people of note from the Paris newspaper, theater, and cinema worlds. Before he even met Valentino, Hébertot had sent dozens of personal letters of invitation to editors, actors from the Comédie Française, directors, and journalists from French, English, and American publications. About thirty guests were able to attend, but an equal number declined with regret. This was August, it was hot, and many Parisians had escaped the city. "No one is in Paris in late summer," Rudy would write.

The Paris press people who remained in town took due note of the presence in their midst of "the handsomest man in the world." A reporter for one of the dailies, indulging in a bit of imaginative hyperbole, told readers that Valentino earned $125,000 for each of his movies, and that he received seven thousand fan letters every week (this part came closer to the truth). Valentino met with reporters at his hotel, as he'd done with the London press corps. "He doesn't appear wearied by the trip from London to Paris," one resulting story read. "He seems young, extremely young, in his pajamas of grey pearl and red slippers. He has a small, slim, and dark appearance, and narrow eyes, like a Japanese."

Rudy planned to do a lot of driving in Europe, and for that he needed a car. Not just any car. "I looked at seventeen different makes of cars and finally went to see the Voisin people and ordered two cars from them. . . . I ordered an open car for my own use and a closed car for Natacha. The Voisin people put a car at my disposal to go through Italy in, and another one to use while I remained in Paris." The car he ordered to be custom built for later American delivery, a sporting model, had a two-tone gray body, maroon trim, maroon leather interior, and wire wheels. Ordering a custom-made car was distinctly à la mode. Rex Ingram, now living in the South of France, drove a Rolls Royce with no body, just two basket chairs.

Natacha shopped for gowns and day wear at the couture house of Paul Poiret, which basked in the publicity she generated. She was photographed by James Abbe and featured in magazine and newspaper spreads, magnificently turned out in a Poiret walking suit of "black velvet with trimmings of red suede and horizontal bands of crushed gold braid on the sleeves and bodice." With this she wore a tricorne hat with a crown of red suede and a black velvet brim. She also modeled a regal gown that was cut to bare one shoulder. It had a bodice of pearl-embroidered satin and an ivory velvet skirt. With it she carried a vermillion feather fan. Valentino gloried in his wife's fashion sense. Not for her the staid creations of more conventional designers, who turned out "wishy-washy things of pastel shades with oddments of flowers here and there." No, as a strong-minded woman with liberated taste she opted for "vivid colors . . . that are violent and definite. Scarlets, vermillions, strong blues, blazoning purples."

Jacques Hébertot arranged to lead them on a trip to his family's home turf on the Normandy coast. They'd looked forward to a sun-soaked holiday at Deauville, the fashionable seashore resort, and had packed bathing suits, sunshades, and cameras so that Rudy could take pictures. Rudy, who'd once raced a Fiat, had also hoped to watch the Grand Prix auto race. Of course the Valentinos knew they would be photographed along the way and they dressed for the occasion, she in a nunlike black Poiret creation with a draped tunic and a hooded, chadorlike cowl covering her neck and hair, he in knickers, Norfolk jacket, and cap. They traveled in state in several cars. Hébertot led in his chauffeur-driven open sportscar; Rudy drove the borrowed open Voisin, accompanied by Natacha; and a driver transported the massive pile of Valentino luggage in a closed car. As they approached Deauville it started to pour: not a mere shower, but a pounding rain that would not cease. "Natacha finally . . . refused to drive with me any longer in the open car," wrote Rudy; she complained that her Poiret outfit would be ruined. She got into the closed car with the chauffeur and the luggage, Rudy boarded Hébertot's tourer, and they headed for a Deauville villa (pre-engaged by Hébertot), which, however, offered small comfort to the weary, drenched party. The house fires were out, there were no telephones or hot water, and the housekeeper on the premises showed little desire to make the guests comfortable. Humor saved the day. "We burst into simultaneous and irrepressible shrieks of laughter," over the situation and the housekeeper merrily participated.

The next morning, they were disappointed to learn that the Grand Prix had been rained out. When the weather finally cleared they went motoring to an old farmhouse in the countryside. Hébertot, who'd grown up here, showed them the very bedroom in which (at least according to legend) William the Conqueror had slept before he set out for England. They feasted, country style, at a table set with wonderfully fresh butter and sweet-smelling bread.

They much preferred the Normandy farm country to the atmosphere at the Casino in Deauville, where during a compulsory visit they observed men and women staying up all night, losing fortunes at the gaming tables, and trying to look more fashionable than they were. Rudy and Natacha stuck their noses in the air. "There were no smart women. There were no smart men." These were mere provincial tourists trying to appear fashionable by showing up at the year's favorite resort, the Valentinos decided.

Although the villa Hébertot had rented left much to be desired, his solicitous shepherding and introductions made all the difference. The attentiveness he showed has prompted speculation about his motives. Was he making a play for Rudy? Hébertot made no effort to conceal the fact that he happened to be a homosexual, because he didn't have to. In the wide-open sensual playground that was Paris in 1923, being gay didn't raise eyebrows; artists, theater folk, and bohemians did as they pleased. The head of the Swedish Ballet, the wealthy aristocrat Rolf de Maré, a friend and associate of Hébertot's who in fact had installed Hébertot as administrator of the Théâtre des Champs-Elysées, had moved to Paris from Stockholm in part to escape antihomosexual prejudice in his native Sweden. At the moment, de Maré was the lover of his ballet company's lead dancer, Jean Börlin, a brilliant performer and choreographer who'd been vilified in the Swedish press for his "feminine affectation and his vaseline-plastique" body makeup. People said Börlin was to Rolf de Maré what Nijinsky had been to Diaghilev at the Ballets Russes, except that de Maré had more money.

David Bret insists in his book *Valentino: A Dream of Desire* that Hébertot's interest in Valentino was primarily sexual and that the two became a hot item. He gives as his source an unpublished manuscript by one of Hébertot's male lovers in the 1940s, actor-singer Roger Normand, who claimed to be repeating tales Hébertot told him about Valentino. The premise of Bret's book is that Valentino was a closeted gay man whose close friendships with men involved sex, but his argument is weakened by scant documentation and carelessness about his facts; in the caption to a photo of Rudy with his brother and Natacha, for instance, he identifies Alberto as André Daven, one of Rudy's lovers. Bret also maintains that Natacha was exclusively a lesbian who enjoyed setting up her husband with other men. I beg to differ. As I see it, Natacha grew to resent Rudy's attachments to friends such as Douglas Gerrard, Florey, and later Beltrán-Masses. At the same time, she held relaxed views about homosexuality. Though primarily heterosexual herself, she may very well have experimented with bisexuality and didn't judge it harshly in others. It doesn't seem to have occurred to Bret that not every tale of sexual conquest (especially if relayed at second hand) has a basis in reality, or that men can have close friendships that don't involve sex. He fails to allow for the fantasy factor:

Valentino exerted and continues to exert enormous power as an object of desire for both sexes. Lusting after him, imagining him as your lover, telling somebody that he was, isn't the same as bedding him.

Hébertot's surviving letters to Valentino have an intimate, warm, and friendly but not sexy tone. It's worth noting that until 1925 they are usually addressed to both Rudy and Natacha, and that many of his letters inviting people to the welcoming dinner in Paris explain that Madame Valentino, too, is being honored and that she is in her own right a distinguished film costume designer and a dancer. In one of the journals he edited Hébertot published a photograph of Natacha Rambova that he had taken. And Natacha was very much a part of the journey to Normandy. One of Valentino's several telegrams to Hébertot from Juan-les-Pins is signed with one word: RUDYNATACHA.

The Valentinos met René Clair through Hébertot, and he and Rolf de Maré came to join them in Normandy on their day in the country. Clair, who was writing regularly for one of Hébertot's magazines (he'd publish a rave review of *Blood and Sand*, in which he'd call Valentino a great actor), had done some acting himself and was just starting his career as an innovative film director. Clair, Hébertot, and Rolf de Maré's Swedish Ballet were collaborating in the antic Francis Picabia–designed ballet *Relâche,* which would include the avant-garde film masterpiece Clair directed, *Entr'acte,* featuring choreography by Jean Börlin and a score by Erik Satie. Collaboration among artists was the order of the day in Paris, and artists tended to pick up cues from other artists. Rolf de Maré's Swedish Ballet brought together the likes of Fernand Léger, Darius Milhaud, and even Cole Porter. Both Rudy and Natacha found the cross-fertilization that went on enviable. It wasn't just Paris, the beautiful and sophisticated city, that captivated them; it was the climate for creativity they marveled at, less commercial, more interactive, and more open to experimentation than anything they'd known in Hollywood or New York. Several of Rudy's letters to Hébertot stress how happy they were in Paris, how they hated to leave, and how ardently, when absent, they yearned to return.

However, when they returned to Paris from Normandy for a few days before embarking for the Hudnut château in the South of France,

Paris nightlife let them down. Ciro's was dead, and the Folies-Bergère disappointing. Rudy found the scantily clad Folies beauties flabby. The fabled streets of Montmartre bulged with grossly drunken American tourists. Paris by day, however, continued to divert. The Voisin car firm allowed Rudy to hang around the garage as men worked on assembling engines, an activity he'd enjoyed versions of since his teenage years. And Rudy had made one new friend he wanted to get to know better: André Daven.

Valentino's writing about André Daven in his book *My Private Diary*, which first ran as a series of articles in *Movie Weekly*, is curious, because he goes to great lengths to imply that Natacha's interest in Daven matched his own. A friend of both Robert Florey's and Hébertot's, the young, talented, and handsome Daven, later an actor, film producer, and the codirector of the Théâtre des Champs-Elysées, was working in 1923 as a reporter for *Bonsoir*. He joined the gaggle of journalists who interviewed Valentino at his hotel when he had just arrived in Paris. Valentino doesn't refer to Daven in the sequence written in Paris. Rather, he writes about him retrospectively from Juan-les-Pins, saying that Natacha has read his diary and reminded him not to overlook André. And he does write about André, at some length. "The minute he came into the room I spotted him as a 'type,'" he begins. "Young Daven is an extraordinarily good-looking chap . . . with amazing eyes, fine physique and of a compelling attraction." Valentino says he immediately thought of the current vogue in American movies for foreign types like Ramon Novarro and decided that he'd made a discovery. Daven should try for a career before the movie cameras. Valentino adds in an aside that he believes he would have made a good casting director; he has an eye for spotting talent and beauty in men as well as women. "Almost any man can 'spot' a beautiful woman. But very few men, so Natacha tells me, can recognize the unusual or attractive in another man." He says he recognized Daven's possibilities the moment he set eyes on him. "And I was not wrong, I had confirmation of that by the fact that Natacha's eyes met mine . . . and we nodded as if to say, 'Ah, you recognize him too.'"

But André Daven was primarily Rudy's friend, and a spark of mutual attraction had ignited between them. Before leaving Paris, Rudy convinced André that he must quickly learn English, come to America, and work as an actor in films. Rudy said he would help him, give him his first role in a movie. Daven's decision to accept the invitation must have come after a period of wrestling with the possibilities. He spoke no English, and he hadn't especially wanted to leave Paris. Before he decided to accept the offer and journey to New York, he and Rudy spent some time together at the end of December, after Rudy had returned to the States with Natacha and then come back to Europe alone. After a few weeks in New York Rudy sailed by himself on the *Aquitania* back to Cherbourg (Natacha followed ten days later) to spend Christmas of 1923 with the Hudnuts. A radiogram was sent to the vessel by Hébertot, announcing that André would meet his boat, and the fact that Hébertot sent the message, rather than Daven himself, suggests that the two were close friends.

Part of Daven's appeal for Valentino—and he did have a special appeal—had a narcissistic basis: he resembled Rudy. Looking at André was a bit like looking in the mirror and liking what you saw. A reporter who wrote about Daven after he'd come to the States to appear in *Monsieur Beaucaire* noted on the set that Rudy had picked Daven "thinking he would make a good screen brother. And really the resemblance is remarkably pronounced, especially in makeup." Norman Kerry, who had once served as "brother," also bore a striking physical resemblance to his best friend.

But André had to be left behind in Paris when Rudy and Natacha set off in August of 1923 for the French Riviera in the borrowed Voisin touring car. The long drive didn't go smoothly. From their earliest days together, Rudy's reckless driving had made Natacha anxious and sometimes angry. The truth is, he probably shouldn't have been driving without eyeglasses, which he refused to wear. He didn't see well, and he drove too fast on dusty roads full of hairpin turns on steep escarpments. Rudy refused to surrender the wheel, and Natacha exploded at him, though Rudy tried to placate her with assurances that he enjoyed some sort of immunity. He truly believed that when he took death-defying risks his spirit guides would protect them both from harm.

Once they arrived at Juan-les-Pins, things calmed down. Natacha's parents, Muzzie and Uncle Dickie, welcomed them warmly and wanted to hear all about their adventures. Servants waited on them. The landscape was soothing. The Côte d'Azur, soon to burgeon as the summer playground of the international set of the rich and arty, was still a place for quiet retreat under a serene aquamarine sky. Rudy felt supremely contented and mentally healthy. "I think I shall never be psychoanalyzed," he wrote in his diary. "I have no inhibitions that I know of. I have neither neuroses nor complexes." By 1926, when he was reading Freud, he would not be so sure.

The only reminders of the road trip and its hazards and bickering were some lingering physical complaints of Rudy's: "I have calluses all over both hands, and my shoulder and arm muscles are horribly out of commission from the terrific pumping up and down [I did while driving] on narrow mountain passes." Natacha nursed him as an acupuncturist might (had she learned this technique while dancing with Kosloff?), by using a pinprick on his shoulder, prompting him to comment: "The mother in woman is kind, but the female in woman is of the tigress-cat variety, and delights in subtle cruelties, in testing power, in watching the opposite species [men] suffer at her hands." This was Rudy trying to be funny, but it hints that he no longer saw Natacha as feminine perfection incarnate.

The date palms, pines, lemon trees, roses, and heliotrope of the French Riviera, abutting what one writer called "that blue jewel of a sea," reminded Rudy of the landscape at Nervi, where he'd studied agriculture, but here his accommodations were far more posh. The Hudnut villa, originally of pseudo-Moorish design, and used as a hospital during the war, had been purchased the preceding year from an impecunious Russian prince. The American Hudnuts, taking a cue from Muzzie's former sister-in-law, Elsie de Wolfe, had remodeled it into something resembling a Louis XV palace, but with rooms for the young people decorated "in gay modern things," to please Natacha.

Rudy dreamed of one day owning such a place himself. Anticipating his future California home, Falcon Lair, he told readers of his diary,

"I should like to have such a place, done somewhat in the medieval style. I am not particularly keen for modernity in either house, dress, or woman. I like a touch of the Old World. A flavor of tradition . . . old golds, somber reds, dulled blues . . . grays that are like smoke, drifting. I should like to *know* my house, make a shrine of it, where all the beautiful things I am able to garner from the four corners of the globe would find abiding place." Again, there are inklings of later differences with Natacha. They shared many tastes, and a belief in the pull of the past, but Rudy felt far less affinity with modern styles than did she.

After a little more than a week of relaxing and unwinding at Juan-les-Pins, they set out for Italy. With Aunt Teresa Werner in the backseat of the roadster lent by Voisin they drove along the coast. Rudy, once more at the wheel, promised to spare their necks, "but what is a man to do when the dream of speed possesses him?" Self-control had never been Rudy's strongest suit. The borrowed Voisin did not appear to be especially suited to racing, however. On its hood were strapped six valises, two hat boxes, a box of tools for car repair, extra tires, three cameras, and a huge leather steamer trunk.

At the Italian border they ran into trouble, despite—or more likely because of—Rudy's Italian passport bearing the name Rodolfo Guglielmi, and the expensive-looking American ladies who rode with him. Italian nationals living in America were not popular in Fascist Italy; Mussolini considered them unpatriotic turncoats. The customs officers at Ventimiglia presumed that Valentino's luxurious car and costly clothes had come to him by way of an advantageous marriage to an American heiress, and the officials made no effort to conceal their contempt. They asked him to pay a huge duty on the six hundred French cigarettes he was bringing into the country.

The insulting customs officers behaved like many others encountered in Italy to whom the name Rudolph Valentino meant nothing and who met shows of imported wealth with resentment. The face that launched a million American swoons failed to impress Italians because Valentino's movies had rarely been shown outside of Milan and his fame had not spread widely. (The Valentinos did pass one theater in the town of Lido d'Albaro where *The Conquering Power* was being shown.) Because of this gap in distribution Robert Florey had a hard time trying to "sell" publicity about him to the Italian newspapers and magazines.

Like many other celebrities, Valentino was ambivalent about his fame. He'd gotten accustomed to certain perks, which he missed when they were withdrawn. But anonymity had its compensations, too. It could be both restful and humbling. After Rudy returned to New York when the European sojourn had ended, the actress Bebe Daniels asked him whether he'd been mobbed by fans during his Italian trip. He told her, "Nothing happened, because I look like every other Italian on the street."

Even so, Rudy's heartbeat quickened as they approached familiar turf and his anticipated family reunions. Natacha later remembered how emotional he became, and reported that he felt his mother's presence. Gabriella had accompanied him to Liguria when he began agricultural school there, and tender memories of her flooded his consciousness.

His first chance to show Natacha and Aunt Teresa his old stomping ground came near Genoa, when they stopped in Nervi at the Sant' Ilario Agricultural Institute, Rudy's former school. Since it was still August, school was not in session, but Luigi, the old gentleman who tended the cattle, was on hand and recognized Rudy, who noted, "He knew nothing of pictures, but remembered how well I could handle a bull." At a lace shop Rudy reencountered the cook's daughter, on whom he'd once had a serious crush. Now she was stout and the mother of many, Natacha would recall with a sniff.

Natacha did not turn out to be a good traveler on this leg of the journey. Rudy's driving (sometimes on one wheel) continued to upset and terrify her; she felt in peril, because she was. Furthermore, neither the roads nor the accommodations met her standards. (Rudy, too, complained about lax service at their hotels.) She didn't sleep well, and she soon became utterly exhausted. Natacha liked to be in control, and on the road she was anything but. One midnight at their Genoa hotel she simply went to pieces. Rudy called it a nervous breakdown.

"Between the dust, the rumbling of the motor, the sense of impending and immediate danger, she was absolutely fagged out." It shocked Rudy to see her so undone. "I have never seen her so before. She sobbed and wept like a child, and could not be quieted." Rudy began to think that perhaps she should not continue the trip. She was less hardy than he'd supposed.

Although a night's rest revived her spirits, and the party continued on toward Milan, Natacha again came unglued when Rudy crashed the car into a telephone pole in Bologna, bending a fender. That same day, he collided with a cart driven by an "ancient crone." Obviously Natacha wasn't the only one who'd become weary, distracted, and stressed. Rudy's temper flared when they stopped at a café and a group of officers ogled Natacha appreciatively, "boldly looking her up and down," Rudy wrote. "I was just about getting ready for a good fight. Then it came to me that I probably did the same thing before I left Italy." So he decided to forgive the "mental undressing," or at least not to blame the oglers.

Robert Florey joined them for this lap of the Italian expedition, and that may have made Natacha even more unhappy; she and he weren't friends. However, Florey, quite gossipy when it came to Rudy's worries about his nascent bald spot, remained mum about Natacha's breakdown.

In Milan Rudy accomplished one of his goals for this journey: reunion with his beloved sister, Maria. When the long-separated siblings met, their already highly keyed emotions pitched even higher because of a mix-up in plans. The Valentinos' arrival in Milan had been delayed because of their accidents, and Rudy had wired to tell Maria this, but the cable didn't reach her. She became so anxious when they failed to turn up at the appointed time and place that she boarded a train to Genoa in hopes of finding them. In the end things got straightened out, and they met. When Rudy at last saw his sister, "We just embraced and then embraced again. We were crying and everyone else was crying. . . . I saw not only my dear sister, Maria, but all our childish scenes together, pranks and larks, quarrels and makings-up."

Maria had suffered greatly during the war years in France, and it showed. Some of the light in her eyes had been quenched, Rudy found; she seemed older than her twenty-six years. On her own since her mother's death in 1918, she'd studied violin, perfected her lace-making skills, and learned typing and shorthand so that she could get a job. She now held a responsible position as secretary in a large cotton and silk company. Rudy wanted very much to lighten her burden, and suggested that she take an extended vacation at the Hudnut château at Juan-les-Pins. She did visit there, but did not stay long. She had her own life in Milan, and wanted to return to it. But perhaps she might have lingered if she'd felt more at ease with the Hudnuts.

Natacha and Maria regarded each other warily. Like her mother, Maria was a devout Catholic, and she must have been distressed to discover that her brother and sister-in-law had fallen away from the faith. She evinced far more interest in showing off Milan's cathedrals than Natacha did in seeing them. The two women's styles clashed, Maria's striking Natacha as woefully "old fashioned." And Natacha, in turn, seemed to Maria alarmingly modern. It troubled Maria that her brother's wife concealed her marital status by covering her wedding ring with a glove. Natacha's abundant use of powder, lipstick, and perfume shocked her proper sister-in-law, who associated heavy makeup with prostitutes. And Maria's plainness equally appalled Natacha. "Our first task was to buy her clothes, and, above all, a box of face powder," Natacha recalled. Maria accepted the makeover without altering her mind-set or warming to her new relative. The feeling was mutual. Although Natacha fell short of outright rudeness to Rudy's family, she didn't really bond with them, nor they with her. They lived on different planets.

Rudy desperately wanted Maria to comprehend a little of what he had accomplished, and he arranged for her to see *The Four Horsemen of the Apocalypse*. He'd later do the same for Alberto in Campobasso. Maria commented after seeing it that she'd had no idea he would be "as good as that." Watching her face as she looked up at the screen to see him as Julio the gaucho or Julio the French soldier made Rudy glow with pride.

A few weeks later, Maria would accompany Rudy for a September

visit to Alberto. For the moment they embraced and said good-bye as
the baggage-laden Voison set off, after five days in Milan, toward
Rome via Tuscany. The Valentinos stopped along the way to take in the
paintings, furnishings, and armor collected at Castello Vincigliata,
near Florence, and to shop for books on historic costumes, to add to
their collection. In Siena they bought what they mistakenly took to be
a genuine Holbein painting of Anne of Cleves.

Rudy had visited Rome as a boy, but his sense of kinship with the
city on seven hills went beyond that. If the stories he'd been told about
the Guglielmi origins were true, he had Roman roots, and he believed
he had stored ancestral memories. "I am of the Romans, and the atmosphere is already in my blood." As he and Natacha took a carriage ride
from the Piazza di Spagna "up and down and about such streets as the
Via Babuina, the Via Sistina, the Via Quirinale, stopping there in the
Square for the view," everything seemed familiar. It felt like coming
home.

New to him, and much admired, were the results of Mussolini's
modernizing efforts: new roads, wider streets, demolished slums, improved sanitation. They tried to arrange a meeting with Il Duce, but he
showed no interest. However, a good friend of Mussolini's, Baron
Fassini, could not do enough for them.

Here in Rome, for once, at the hands of their wealthy host, the
Valentinos received star treatment. The name Valentino registered
with Baron Fassini, a former managing director of Rome's Cines studio, as did the name Hudnut; the baron had his own place on the Riviera. He knew exactly who his guests were, and went to great lengths
to entertain them royally, taking them through the moonlit Colosseum
and inviting them to his castle to the southwest at Nettuno, where Roman emperors had once vacationed at the edge of the sea, where Caesar Borgia had hosted wild parties, and where Mussolini now came for
an occasional rest. The underground passages and secret dungeons at
Castello Nettuno so intrigued Rudy that he decided he wanted to return someday to make a film there, a costume picture exploiting the
castle's history of ancient "blood and bravery, treachery and love, dark
as wine." For the rest of his life he would speak of his plan to portray
Caesar Borgia.

Baron Fassini introduced them to the count who was secretary of the Unione Cinematografica Italiana (Italian Union of Cinema Workers), who invited them to the set of *Quo Vadis*, a German-Italian production being shot at Cines studio in Rome. Although Italy had a great tradition of epic filmmaking, since the war Italian cinema had been forced to make do on a shoestring. "They have no lighting to speak of. They have no equipment," Rudy observed. "Their laboratories are very bad indeed, and there is, in fact, none of the modern equipment we have in America." Even so, Valentino would have happily agreed to remain in Rome to work there. The role of Nero in *Quo Vadis* had been given to Emil Jannings only after Valentino had to turn it down because of his Famous Players–Lasky obligations. Rudy had been excited by the possibility of playing a historical role such as Nero against authentic settings, and working under codirector Gabriellino D'Annunzio, the son of the writer and patriot Gabriele D'Annunzio. (Rudy was an admirer of the senior D'Annunzio's novel *Triumph of Death*.) Now that a peace accord had been hammered out between him and Famous Players–Lasky, he dearly wished the studio would reconsider, but they wouldn't. The chief of Cines, Commendatore Barattolo, had been warned by Famous Players–Lasky that Valentino still had a binding contract that forbade him to work for others until after 1924. Just as he had been forced the previous year to pass up the chance to play opposite Lillian Gish in *The White Sister*, also shot in Rome, Rudy was again stymied.

Although Emil Jannings spoke only German, and communication with him depended on interpreting by his English-speaking wife, Valentino and Jannings hit it off talking shop. Over lunch with their wives at the Borghese Gardens, the two actors compared notes. Valentino didn't report on what Jannings told him, but in his published diary he repeated part of his end of the conversation. Jannings had seen *The Four Horsemen* in Paris and, much impressed, wanted to hear about the production and how Valentino had created his characterization of Julio. By living the part, Valentino told him, "entering into the very skin of the role." For the benefit of the readers of his "private diary" Valentino stressed that when acting he never played himself. "I try, have always tried, NOT to be Rudolph Valentino in the various roles I have played. To do that would be something like playing the same tune over and over on the same instrument." This somewhat contradicts his earlier remark that he and Julio shared human failings, but it confirms what Ivano and others said about the way Valentino immersed himself in whatever role he was playing.

The stay in Rome went well, but that did not prevent Natacha from parting company with Rudy and her aunt to take a solo train ride back to Nice and the comforts of Juan-les-Pins. She just wasn't up to facing the demands of the next item on Rudy's itinerary, motoring in southern Italy—with Rudy again at the wheel. Although she had expressed some small interest in exploring his childhood haunts, her desire and need for rest, safety, and creature comforts prevailed. Since she expected to do some work on Rudy's behalf from her parents' home, arranging details of their return to New York and Rudy's comeback in pictures, she could justify her decision.

"Natacha has gone," Rudy wrote the day she departed, September 11. "I knew that she should go. . . . She really is not up to further motoring." An ominous loneliness overtook him. "I am alone today for the first time in many months. It is like a mist from the sea striking chill to the bone."

Maria traveled from Milan to Rome to join Rudy and Aunt Teresa on the journey south to meet Alberto. The three living children of Giovanni and Marie Berta Gabriella Barbin Guglielmi hadn't been in the same room in more than ten years.

Maria sat in the backseat with Auntie, reported Rudy, "so that they may not know the worst that the road (and again my driving!) has to hold for them." The landscape kept shifting, even the people, their costumes and dialects. "It was one panorama of continuous change."

Alberto was working as a poorly paid but high-ranking city administrator (secretary general) in Campobasso, the regional capital of Molise, an isolated province in the Apennine Mountains, just south of the province of Abruzzo. Today, tourists who venture to the Molise, now connected to the rest of Italy by a *superstrada*, are still warned about the wolves who haunt the surrounding wild forests, and are in-

vited to see the annual June procession, the Festival of the Mysteries
of the Body of God (Sagra dei Misteri di Corpus Domini), when children impersonating angels, devils, and saints are suspended beneath a
Madonna figure. Even in 1923, though, Campobasso was a rather large
city. It had a hotel where Rudy and Aunt Teresa put up, since Alberto
and his wife, Ada, didn't have room for three guests.

They arrived on market day, when people from the neighboring
villages and countryside, dressed in local costume and carrying produce in baskets on their heads, were returning home with their cattle
and pigs and the cheese, milk, and wine they'd either bought or offered for sale in town. To Rudy the spectacle seemed "more like a page
out of some old medieval volume than an actual sight seen in this modern twentieth century." He longed for a movie camera, to make a
record of the procession, but on this leg of the journey he didn't have
one at hand. He was reminded anew of how much better it is to shoot
movies on location rather than in make-believe settings.

The reunion with Alberto and his Taranto-born wife, Ada, was not
as highly charged as the one with Maria, but was nonetheless a joyful
occasion. Rudy arranged a screening of The Four Horsemen, not just for
Alberto and Ada but for the public, as a benefit to raise money to turn
a castle into a monument for the local heroes who had died during the
war. But for Rudy the emotional high point came when he met his
nine-year-old nephew, Jean, for the first time. "He just looked at me
once, straight in the eyes, and said, 'Uncle Rudy!' I said 'Yes!' and then
he made a fast spring, and was about my neck, hugging me tight."
Rudy, who longed for a son or daughter of his own, immediately recognized the boy as a version of his earlier self. Jean, like the nine-year-
old Rodolfo, loved motion, was fascinated by machines and gadgets,
and had trouble sitting still. Slender, with neatly combed black hair
and a penetrating, pensive gaze, he even looked like Valentino. Rudy
resurrected his own long-ago nickname, calling Jean Mercurio, quick-
silver.

Jean was dazzled by his glamorous uncle, who'd arrived laden with
gifts and immediately took the boy for a ride in the amazing Voisin
roadster. Jean had never seen anything remotely like it before. He
tooted the horn and tried to grab the wheel, "an absolute, reincar-

nated Mercury," Rudy said. Later he sent Jean his first bicycle and paid
for his piano lessons.

Compared to Campobasso's intense joys, the return to Apulia
seemed a bit anticlimactic. Along the way Rudy had to repair three flat
tires, "sprawling in the dust of the sunny road in my overalls." As he
drove farther and farther south on dusty roads, other cars became
more and more infrequent. He encountered farmers returning from
the fields, driving donkey carts. Children along the way would shriek
and squeal with excitement at the sight of the Voisin, some of them
trying to climb onto a fender for a ride. Wherever he went, the car
was a bigger draw than its driver. His last flat tire occurred just as they
approached their Taranto hotel. Thank goodness it hadn't happened in
the middle of nowhere: Rudy had run out of spares.

Here on home turf the absences stung: no mother, father, aunts, or
uncles came to welcome him with kisses on each cheek and waiting
bowls of steaming pasta. And no Natacha. Natacha had written to him
at Campobasso, reporting that she felt rested and was enjoying the
sunshine and late flowers at Juan-les-Pins. "She also gave me detailed
accounts of the various dogs." Maria and Aunt Teresa provided warmth
and solace, but Rudy ached for his wife.

In Taranto that first night Rudy retired feeling excited, but strange.
He was winding back to past times, "back into my youth," he wrote.
"Tomorrow I should get straight back to my babyhood. The house
where I was born. The streets and garden where I had made the
proverbial mud pies—and where I had pitched my first ball."

Taranto had functioned as a major naval base during the war, and
it had subsequently become a more modern city than the one Rudy
left behind in 1913. Now its citizens rode in electric streetcars instead
of horse-drawn carriages, and turned on switches for light, but his hotel, the best one in town, still lacked bathtubs or showers. Guests were
advised they could go around the corner to the Turkish bath, and
Rudy's blood boiled at the backwardness of his countrymen: "Bathing,
fresh air, exercise, diet, all these requisites of the simplest physical culture regime are unknown to them," Rudy wrote. How American he
sounded, complaining about the primitive plumbing in a southern Italian hotel. As he sponged off the dust and grime in cold water, he

flashed on a recollection of the Ritz in New York "with longing and regret."

A cousin who still lived in the area met him and they went together to a café where Rodolfo the teenager had spent long hours, nursing cups of coffee and shooting the breeze with other idle youths. Rudy was shocked at the way his old acquaintances had remained stuck in time; mentally they seemed exactly as they had been ten years before. "They were the only thing about the old town that had not changed." Here were his former companions, "sitting around the same old table, in the same indolent postures . . . still exchanging the same narrow and stultifying ideas," gossiping about some young woman's pretty ankle or last night's fun. There but for the grace of God go I, Rudy thought. For him the atmosphere had been stifling. "I realized that the luckiest thing that ever happened to me was getting away and going to America. I might so easily have become one of them."

Rudy sensed a more satisfying, less painful connection with the remote past in Rome than he did with his more immediate past in Taranto. For Taranto provoked, along with nostalgia and fond memories, reminders of his family's bygone lack of faith in him, of his father's sternness and his own failures and disappointments.

With his cousin he visited the property at Caresino, outside Taranto, where his late uncle and aunt had lived and where Rudy, Maria, and Alberto had spent childhood summers. The dilapidated place had been vacant for a long while, though the cousin's family still owned it. In the musty house Rudy found a cupboard with heavy, cracked doors where his aunt had locked him up once to punish him for some misdeed. "Here seventeen or eighteen years later I found the same door and the same cracks," an unpleasant reminder of his reputation as a problem child. The cousins had lunch at Caresino, sharing a Marsala that had been bottled the year Rudy's uncle was born.

Afterward they stopped at the home of an old family friend, a onetime classmate of Rudy's father who was now quite sick. "My God, you aren't Rodolfo, are you?" the old friend asked. "And then, affectingly, this man of sixty began crying like a child." Rudy was profoundly moved.

On to Castellaneta to see the white stone house at 116 Via Roma where he was born and the nearby railroad bridge built by his engineer grandfather. Today, that house has a fresh coat of cream-colored paint and a plaque marking it as the birthplace of Rudolph Valentino. In 1923 it looked shabbier, and had no plaque. No one in town had heard of Rudolph Valentino or his fame in America. A crowd clustered around when Rudy stopped there—not to hail him but to see the car and the Graflex camera he carried. Those who remembered Rodolfo greeted him as the son of the town's former veterinarian. Rudy handed out some paper money to children who came out to greet him, but according to one informant, it wasn't appreciated, because people were accustomed to coins. Former neighbors, the Maldarizzis, who years before had provided shelter and sweets when he'd been sent away in disgrace from his own home, invited him in for coffee and biscuits called *friselle*. One of the daughters of the household would tell a reporter more than fifty years later that as a boy Rodolfo had been an idler, but *simpatico*.

Before taking leave of Castellaneta Rudy took photographs of the monument to unknown soldiers in front of City Hall and of the field near the ravine where his nurse used to take him to play. He stopped, seized with sorrow, at the cemetery where the sister he never knew, Bice, lay buried. He cleared away the vines that were making the lines of poetry on the grave's marker hard to read, got back behind the wheel, and drove off toward Pompeii and a less troubling chapter of the more distant past.

Ready to swear off driving by the time he made it back to Juan-les-Pins, Rudy regaled Natacha with stories about his trip, and kisses. He felt ecstatic to be reunited with her. "I am going home," he wrote at the Hudnut château. "I *am* home, for I am again with Natacha." They prepared their many trunks for their return sailing to America and geared up for a meeting with J. D. Williams in London and a final round with Famous Players–Lasky in New York.

15

THE COMEBACK

I n light of the disappointing outcome, Rudy's optimism as he prepared to go back to work is poignant. He had great hopes that the
contracts hammered out, first with Famous Players–Lasky and
then with J. D. Williams and Ritz-Carlton Productions, would provide
some of the artistic control he'd long sought and that the result would
be high-quality films. No more second-rate assembly-line productions
for Rudolph Valentino. He believed he'd at last have his pick of directors, designers, and scripts, and that for the first time he would be paid
as well as other top screen stars.

Rudy couldn't wait to get going. "I have not been happy away from
pictures," he said. First up before the cameras would be the two pictures he owed Famous Players–Lasky, to be made in New York City at
the Astoria Studios in Queens (the site of today's American Museum
of the Moving Image). On both projects he looked forward to working closely with Natacha, who would now get full play as his artistic
collaborator.

The film to mark the much-hyped Valentino comeback, after his
two years away from the screen, would be *Monsieur Beaucaire*. Based on
a once popular turn-of-the-century Booth Tarkington novel that was
adapted as a play and then an operetta by André Messanger, it was now
being adapted as a film scenario by Forrest Halsey. Booth Tarkington
usually wrote books about his native Indiana (Valentino was an extra in
a 1916 film based on his Hoosier puppy-love tale, *Seventeen*), but with

Monsieur Beaucaire he created a lightly satiric, pseudohistorical romance set in Georgian England. It involved a young French nobleman and gambler, the Duke of Chartres, who defies his cousin, King Louis XV of France, and refuses to marry Princess Henriette on command. He escapes from Versailles to Bath, England, where he masquerades as a barber, pursues a titled beauty, and fends off conniving villains. *Monsieur Beaucaire* gives equal time to eighteenth-century aristocratic frippery and American democratic sentiments: the point of the story is that a barber or "lackey" is just as good as a duke, and that however beautiful she may be, a woman in love with a man's title rather than the natural man deserves rejection. Lady Mary Carlisle, the "belle of Bath" courted by the disguised French duke, comes up empty-handed when she shuns the advances of a mere barber, a "monsieur" instead of a duke. The unmasked Duke of Chartres returns to Versailles and the welcoming arms of Princess Henriette, who loves him for himself. As in *The Conquering Power*, there's a romantic clinch at the end, set in a lovely French garden.

In creating the script, which expands the portion of the plot that takes place in France, Forrest Halsey consulted with Booth Tarkington and received his blessing. This was going to be a trip to Versailles via Indiana. Halsey enlarged the role of Princess Henriette (played by Bebe Daniels), eliminated the mystery about Monsieur Beaucaire's true identity, and added some fervid love scenes. In the book, Beaucaire "merely touches Lady Mary's hand; in the movie this is translated into lengthy osculation," *The New York Times*'s critic dryly observed.

Douglas Fairbanks had originally owned the screen rights but had sold them to Famous Players–Lasky. Then William de Mille, the elder brother of Cecil B., was to make the picture, but the director Sidney Olcott displaced him. According to Natacha, *Beaucaire* "was chosen by Famous Players and submitted to us for our approval. We accepted it, yes, but no one ever heard that it had been in the first place their own choice." Well, that's partly true. The Valentinos were asked to choose between two properties, *Beaucaire* or a sea adventure based on Rafael Sabatini's *Captain Blood*, and they picked the former. It's easy to see why they made the choice, considering their close ties to France and their love for historical court costumes.

Jesse Lasky held Natacha accountable for what would prove to be a poor choice for Valentino's comeback vehicle. He blamed her for "insist[ing] on [Valentino's] doing perfumed parts like *Monsieur Beaucaire* in powdered wigs and silk stockings. We had to take him on her terms to have him at all." Natacha took the heat for a misstep in Valentino's career that she participated in but by no means initiated, as if she alone had steered Valentino away from the steamy "sex menace" roles that had made his name. Studio executives, lawyers, and Rudy himself shared responsibility for the decision. It's likely that Rudy favored a lavishly mounted historical costume picture that would suit Natacha's talents and interests, but nothing was forced on him. He very much looked forward to playing a role that would allow him to make love to two beautiful women and showcase his adeptness at comedy. He could at the same time parade in gorgeous finery, strut half naked in another prolonged dressing scene, and exhibit his skill in fencing. Determined to prove that Douglas Fairbanks had nothing on him when it came to wielding a rapier, he'd been taking lessons, practicing his *en garde* and perfecting his parry and thrust at the New York Athletic Club.

Quite a few people in the film industry had decided by this time to peg Natacha as a harpy who exercised undue control over her husband. They painted her as a designing, power-hungry she-devil, a real-life Doña Sol, who had bewitched a defenseless Gallardo. Douglas Gerrard, who'd been best man at the Mexicali wedding and a guest of Natacha's parents at the Hudnut estate in the Adirondacks, wrote in confidence to Famous Players–Lasky president Adolph Zukor that he thought Valentino had been a fool to break his original contract with the studio, and that his decision to sign with J. D. Williams had been sadly misguided. Proclaiming himself an authority on Rudy after serving as his close friend for the preceding eight years, Gerrard told Zukor that Valentino was a mere tool in his wife's hands. Valentino would eventually come to realize this, Gerrard predicted; he was really a very loyal, decent, sincere fellow, who had been completely misled and badly advised. Probably because he hoped to find employment as an actor or director, Gerrard buttered Zukor up, calling him one of the squarest and most sympathetic men in the industry and advising Zukor that he, Gerrard, had told Rudy as much. He had been in con-

stant correspondence with "Rodolfo," and had recently urged him to
return to Zukor and Famous Players—Lasky, or risk ruining his career.
Gerrard hinted that there was much in Valentino's new contract with
Ritz-Carlton Pictures that he might fault in a personal conversation,
but which he would rather not write about. Battle lines for future contention were being drawn.

Rudy and Natacha had some unfinished business to attend to when
they first got back to the States. They'd decided to sell the Hollywood
house in Whitley Heights, and Natacha immediately left for California
to initiate the process. From New York's Vanderbilt Hotel, Rudy
wrote to Hébertot of their intentions, but for unknown reasons the
Valentinos did not follow through on the real estate plan. Perhaps
when she saw the improvements that had been made on the property
in their absence Natacha had second thoughts about selling, or maybe
they just needed more time to find another California home. Natacha
returned to New York without having put their Wedgewood Place
house on the market and it was still in Valentino's estate when he died.

While working in Astoria, the Valentinos lived in the Ritz-Carlton
Hotel in Manhattan, but there's no doubt they were planning a move
to a large house with space enough for hoards of antiques, which they
set about collecting. In New York they attended art sales and auctions,
acquiring sixteenth-century portraits, tapestries, and fifteenth-century
carved chests. Their days of frugal living were behind them.

Rudy still had an outstanding obligation to the Mineralava company
to judge a beauty contest. All the young ladies who had won the local
contests during the Mineralava dance tour earlier that year were to be
invited to compete for the ultimate title of "Queen of Beauty" at New
York's Madison Square Garden. A date in late November was chosen,
and the publicity wheels were set in motion. Paul Whiteman and his
celebrated band were hired to play background music during the contest. One hundred "celebrity judges" were appointed to help Valentino
pick the winners. The contestants, eighty-eight young ladies from
eighty-eight locations in Canada and the United States, were first

whisked to Washington, D.C., where they were photographed at the Capitol with a hale-looking senator. Then, corralled in Manhattan, they received a crash course in how to smile prettily, turn their bobbed heads slowly to one side for cinematic head shots, and promenade like graceful Little Bo Peeps, with a shepherdess's crook in one hand. Girl-ish charm rather than womanly beauty ruled the day. The winner of the contest, Miss Toronto, received a jeweled crown "patterned after the famous crown of Catherine, Empress of Russia," and her court of top-placing also-rans received engraved trophy cups. In the surviving short film of the event, Valentino, in white tie and tails, looks dandy without makeup and is totally at ease as he talks nonstop into the cam-era when the judging is over. Surrounded by worshipful throngs of young women, he seems to be in his element.

David O. Selznick, at the time a twenty-one-year-old Columbia University dropout who had worked for his father, Lewis J. Selznick, in his film company, had the bright idea of recording the contest on camera and distributing it as a news short. (The senior Selznick's com-pany in 1920 had produced *The Wonderful Chance*, in which "Rudolph De Valentino" played a thug.) When Selznick Pictures went bankrupt, young David struck out on his own, making independent newsreels. He'd already completed one that focused on boxer Luis Firpo. His second independent newsreel, financed in part by George Ullman and by Valentino's recent director, Philip Rosen, became the two-reeler *Rudolph Valentino and His 88 American Beauties*. Young Selznick, the fu-ture Hollywood legend who would later produce *Gone with the Wind*, was savvy enough in 1922 to realize that the filmgoing public, after two years with no new Valentino picture in theaters, would be clam-oring to see him on-screen again. Selznick's only expenses were film and lights in Madison Square Garden, and he would clear $15,000.

All kinds of behind-the-scenes maneuvers were going on within the film industry concerning Rudolph Valentino's future. He had signed with J. D. Williams's new company, Ritz-Carlton Pictures, but the ambitious Williams was trying to bolster his new firm's standing by working out a marketing or distribution affiliation with United Artists. Williams attempted to use Valentino's cachet to attract other stars and push himself into the top producing ranks. He hinted to an associate of Douglas Fairbanks's that the wildly popular Harold Lloyd might be signing with Ritz-Carlton. Seeking publicity, he called the newspaper gossip columnist Louella Parsons to tell her that Mary Pickford and Douglas Fairbanks, both of them with United Artists, were also signing with Ritz-Carlton. Parsons in turn called United Artists president Hiram Abrams for confirmation of the scoop, and was told to kill it; it wasn't so, and she should not publish false information in her column. Parsons said she was going to print the story anyway.

Williams then floated the rumor that Famous Players–Lasky had agreed to waive its option on extending Valentino's contract—which was again a complete fabrication, a mere wish. Charlie Chaplin, also one of the principals of United Artists, had spoken to Valentino about a possible distribution hookup between him and United Artists, but Chaplin's lawyer warned him not to continue these conversations until Valentino procured "a cancellation or release from his present contract." Douglas Fairbanks, too, had spoken privately to Valentino in California almost two years back about the possibility of his joining United Artists, but Fairbanks's lawyer warned him that he would land in legal hot water if he followed up. "I quite agree," the lawyer wrote, "that Mr. Valentino would be a desirable acquisition, and we should make efforts to procure him provided we can do so without becoming involved in any serious litigation. . . . No matter how much of a drawing card he was when he quit pictures, his comeback has to be handled very carefully and he must have an unusual picture. Of course, that is his problem, not ours. Apparently Mr. Valentino will insist on taking full charge of the making of his next picture." This lawyer, Cap O'Brien, expressed doubts about the soundness of Valentino's business judgment. In a letter he wondered, "Has he had sufficient experience in pictures, and has he sufficient intelligence, to do this successfully?"

The people around Douglas Fairbanks seemed united in a belief that acquiring Valentino without J. D. Williams would make a much better bargain than Valentino *with* J. D. Williams. And they agreed that

Valentino's career choices did not inspire confidence. Fairbanks's right-hand man, H. D. Buckley, said as much: "It seems that Valentino has not reached the point where he can personally conduct his business affairs."

It's quite true that Valentino demonstrated no flair for business. This shortcoming can be partly explained by the fact that he'd been a resident of the United States for only ten years, and didn't feel completely competent in English. But he'd never been good at figures, or sitting still and reading the fine print, and was content to rely on others to act on his behalf in contract matters. Various lawyers and agents had taken advantage of his innocence and passivity, and it had cost him dearly. Now he looked to J. D. Williams, George Ullman, and, above all, Natacha. Boyish and fancy-free, he refused to hunker down and learn to be smart about finance, contracts, and the market. Rudy demanded to be treated and paid well, and he gave his all to acting and preparing his roles, but off the set he didn't really want to behave like a grown-up. Natacha became his prime business adviser and spokesperson, not because she was highly qualified or experienced but because she liked to take charge and Rudy trusted her judgment. She knew English better than he did and was willing to play the adult. Somebody had to run the show, and since Rudy couldn't or wouldn't, the job fell to her.

The wheeling and dealing between Williams and various people at United Artists remained private, but the details of the final agreement worked out with Famous Players—Lasky became public in December of 1923, just as the Valentinos were preparing to return (separately) to France for Christmas. "3-CORNERED VALENTINO TANGLE ENDS WITH CONTRACT SIGNING," a headline in *Variety* read. "Zukor and J. D. Williams Fix Up Agreement This Week—Sheik's Wife Revealed as His Real Business Manager." Zukor and Williams had once been partners at First National (back in 1917) and it must have pleased Williams to see his name linked with that of the mighty Zukor in the trade papers again.

Given power of attorney, Natacha negotiated an agreement whereby Valentino was to appear in six productions by the end of 1924, two of

them for Famous Players—Lasky and four for Ritz-Carlton. He would
be paid $7,500 a week. When Natacha signed the contract, Rudy was
already on board the *Aquitania* yet again. While he was spending ten
days in Paris, enjoying the company of Jacques Hébertot and André
Daven and "studying the Pompadour period," she was conducting business on his behalf. "It is gratifying," she stated to the press after signing
the contract, "to reach a satisfactory conclusion and see Rudolph again
in a position to pursue his career under satisfactory conditions." She
added that she thought that since his last appearance before the cameras Valentino had advanced in his "character development and
artistry." He was now ready, she rather pretentiously added, "to carry
on the interrupted march he began toward the highest goal of dramatic achievement." Zukor, who had caved in to many of Valentino's
original demands because losing him had proved so costly, said, "I
think the signing of this contract is an excellent Christmas present to
the motion picture public."

Natacha followed Rudy to Europe and the reunited Valentinos enjoyed a brief vacation at the Hudnuts' château in Juan-les-Pins before
resuming work. Natacha had packed and carried to France many
ornaments—yards of silver and gold tinsel, stars, colored balls, and
candy-filled cornucopias—for a Christmas tree, and at the château she
and Rudy insisted on decorating the tree themselves, strewing the
enormous pine's branches with cotton snow and lighting it with real
candles. The tree promptly caught fire and was doused with buckets of
water, which quashed the flames but left a residue of black smoke and
ruffled nerves. The Hudnuts' Gobelin tapestry and Saint Cire needlepoint chairs were spared damage, and even the Christmas gifts were
rescued by gallant, quick-witted, but ever calm Aunt Teresa. It turned
out to be a happy if smoky Christmas, after all.

The year 1924 was ushered in with a party under Baccarat chandeliers at the opulent seafront Negresco Hotel in Nice at which Rudy
and Natacha, the guests of honor, both drank too much of the excellent, free-flowing champagne. In the middle of the dance floor, an
ebullient, inebriated Rudy replayed a solo scene from *Blood and Sand*,
prodding with his cane an imaginary bull. His mother-in-law later dis-

covered him with his arms around a dancer, Jane Day. Rudy was telling her she would make a wonderful movie actress, but Miss Day was almost asleep and didn't respond. Natacha, also in her cups, was discovered being embraced simultaneously "by at least eight men." Ushered to safety by her mother, Natacha then kept delivering various pretty girls to Rudy for him to dance with, "making herself very popular." We know about all of these alcohol-induced high jinks because Mrs. Hudnut chose to write about them in Natacha's memoir—a tip-off on her relaxed views concerning drinking and extramarital flirtations. After all, she lived in the South of France now, not Mormon Salt Lake City. Both Valentinos had hangovers on New Year's Day when they boarded the New York–bound liner *Belgenland*.

Rudy entered the Astoria Studios to begin shooting *Monsieur Beaucaire* with many eyes trained on him in eager expectation. He was under great pressure to redeem himself at the box office and win back some of the fans and goodwill he had lost during his struggle with Famous Players–Lasky. *Photoplay*'s James R. Quirk moralized in print that Valentino had been toppled from his throne as king of screen heartthrobs because of his pigheadedness. "That so-called beauty contest for the cosmetic concern didn't augment his popularity any. . . . Nor did his eternal ranting about the demon producers. . . . Over a year ago Famous Players–Lasky offered him everything he professed to be fighting for and seven thousand dollars a week thrown in. He should have done it then. He has since learned that publicity cannot replace photography and that fans want to see their favorites on the screen, not hear them on the corner soapbox."

Publicists milked the comeback for all it was worth, and at the outset both Valentinos knocked themselves out to be as welcoming to the press, as good-natured and cooperative, as they could possibly be. They desperately wanted, and needed, a success. A gaggle of New York City–based film reporters and reviewers were invited to the set to report on the first day's shooting. "Everyone connected with the studio was . . . prepared for the worst," *Variety* reported, "but Rudy fooled 'em all. Instead of an imperious entry, as was expected, Valentino showed [up] on the scene amiable and ingratiating."

The cast and crew were treated by the Valentinos to a catered lunch and then the glittering set was shown off to the reporters, who watched as cameras rolled on the opening scene at the lavish Versailles court of Louis XV. "The floor shone like a mirror and every time a scene was shot a stagehand would run forward and polish it furiously with a mop." In the background, musicians with stringed instruments played soft "love motifs" and "candles flared above the crystal chandeliers." The gorgeously arrayed actors sparkled in their "brilliant satins and pale silks threaded with gold and silver, diamond garters and extravagantly embroidered stockings, fragile lace flounces and cuffs, embroidered slippers with jeweled buckles, powdered ringleted wigs." Valentino wore a powdered wig and a green satin coat "emblazoned with silver brocade, a lustrous pair of green satin breeches, with gray silken hose ornamented by jewelled garters and pumps that were resplendent under buckles sparkling with precious stones." Even the prop men got into the courtly spirit, draping bits of jewelry or lace around their hammers and monkey wrenches.

The mood on the set suggested bountiful times, but in fact the movie industry was going through a rough patch. It faced a major slump, one of the worst since American movies began. "Production has practically stopped," *Photoplay* revealed a few months before *Beaucaire* shooting began. "Thousands have been thrown suddenly out of work. Famous Players–Lasky has announced a shut-down [in Hollywood] of ten weeks." The reasons for the crisis included widespread investment in the new panchromatic film, which would allow for more naturalistic cinematic tones; mounting legal expenses in the fight between the Federal Trade Commission and Famous Players–Lasky, which was charged with monopolistic block booking practices; and overspending by several studios on extravagant productions like Stroheim's *Greed* at MGM (originally forty-two reels long and not released in edited ten-reel form until 1925) and Cecil B. DeMille's spectacular *The Ten Commandments* at Famous Players–Lasky.

Famous Players–Lasky had decided to make *Monsieur Beaucaire* another go-for-broke ten-reel extravaganza, a sumptuous feast for the eyes. Convinced that a returning Valentino was a surefire winner at the box office, and banking on the American fondness for European splendor mingled with lacy Valentine-card romance and Fairbanks-style adventure, they invested hundreds of thousands, confident that their outlay would be returned many times over in profits. *Movie Weekly*'s Dorothea Herzog reported that 350 wigs, costing $40,000, were being used in the production, and that $85,000 worth of antique jewelry was being worn. Apart from the jewelry, the bill for costumes ran to $90,000.

The payroll had to allow for a cast that included fifteen principals and about one hundred players of smaller parts, and an enormous crew that included a specialist in painting simulated tapestries. Among the leading players were several popular (and expensive) stars: Bebe Daniels as Princess Henriette, and as the Queen of France Lois Wilson, who had just made a splash in *The Covered Wagon*, a huge moneymaker. New York–bred Doris Kenyon, cast as the haughty English beauty Lady Mary, joined the company as a last-minute replacement for the more English-looking Helene Chadwick. The veteran director Sidney Olcott didn't come cheap. Long associated with costume pictures featuring big casts and lots of local color, and fresh from directing Marion Davies in *Little Old New York*, Olcott's salary in 1926 was $30,000 per picture and was probably close to that in 1924.

Olcott proved his mettle—as a hero, if not as a director—very early in the shooting schedule when Bebe Daniels's skirt caught on fire during a scene involving lighted alcohol torches. "Mr. Olcott, standing nearby, saw the danger and made a flying tackle, football fashion, upon her skirt, beating the flames out and incidentally knocking Bebe over. Miss Daniels was not hurt but was quite unnerved." Olcott, too, escaped serious injury, but did not prove to be a dynamic director. Doris Kenyon called him "useless."

Cameraman Harry Fischbeck had been encouraged to develop a new lighting system, which used bright spotlights to make the actors stand out boldly against a shadowy background. Fischbeck used this innovative highlighting technique to shoot the first part of the movie, which takes place in Versailles. The second half, which simulated aristocratic Bath, England, he shot entirely in more sensual soft focus. Unfortunately, the surviving prints don't retain much of the original nuance, but those who saw *Beaucaire* when it first played remarked on its gorgeous sheen and fine detail in the Versailles sequence and the lushness of the love scenes in the latter half. "A good cameraman is a magician," Valentino once said.

Valentino's dispute with Famous Players–Lasky had started out as a fight to defend Natacha from the studio's insulting disrespect after the Mexicali wedding. In his mind and in hers, *Beaucaire* was going to provide the chance to showcase her talents and make up for past slights. Natacha was an artist and this was to be an "art" picture. Although she got no official credit as Sidney Olcott's assistant director, she did function as such, in addition to being one of two presiding art directors (with Wilfred Buckland, who supervised set building) and costume designers. She threw herself into the work, sitting at Olcott's side during shooting and insisting on historical accuracy for both sets and costumes. She brought in period etchings and eighteenth-century French prints to show the craftsmen who did the building. For Natacha, work on this picture signaled not just a journey into France's storied past, but a summoning of her own youthful summers with Elsie de Wolfe at the Villa Trianon. Fragonard, frills, and furbelows hadn't at all appealed to her way back when, but now her conversance with rococo style served her well.

Some of the costumes were made in New York, but about forty were created in France, designed by illustrator-designer Georges Barbier and sewn at Max Weldy's Paris costume house. Weldy and Barbier were a celebrated team who for many years created the eye-popping feathers-and-sequins outfits worn by Folies-Bergère dancers. The Folies beauties wore little, but the actors in *Monsieur Beaucaire* were weighted down with colorful finery the black-and-white film only partially captures. One of Barbier's costumes for Valentino was a walking ensemble of pale gray velvet with chenille braid. Lined with purple and red taffeta, it had a waistcoat of pink velvet embroidered with silver, and breeches and boots of gray suede.

Natacha and Rudy had seen Barbier's costume designs on Broadway when they attended a performance of Maurice Rostand's play *Casanova* at the Empire Theatre, soon after they returned from Europe. They loved what they saw, and were also much taken with the starring stage turn of Lowell Sherman, the debonair actor who'd been chosen, years back, instead of Rudy to play the cad, Sanderson, in Griffith's *Way Down East*. Sherman, who in the early 1930s would direct Mae West in *She Done Him Wrong*, ended up being cast as foppish King Louis XV in *Monsieur Beaucaire*.

Eager to be liked, the Valentinos made generous gestures to the *Beaucaire* company, such as taking them all out one night to see a Broadway play and going on to dinner and dancing with them after the show. According to one cast member, Lois Wilson, a spirit of fun and camaraderie prevailed during shooting. "The genuine feeling of good fellowship that pervaded the set made working in the production a delight," she reported. In the opening scene Lowell Sherman (in powdered wig and lipstick, a beauty mark on his cheek, a gilded scepter in his hand) is shown sitting next to the Queen, Lois Wilson, at a court performance. As the King watches the dancers, musicians, and players, he's simultaneously working on his needlepoint, a tip-off that he's as swish as most of the snuff-sniffing, lace-collared courtiers around him. Lois Wilson had trouble preserving decorum—she was supposed to be sitting still, ramrod stiff, and unsmiling in her billowing panniered gown—when Sherman, a notorious cutup, muttered under his breath, "Oh, don't worry, Queenie, I'm knitting a little bra for you." Wilson cracked up, and the scene had to be retaken.

The two Valentinos had contrasting ways of relating to others on the set. Not surprisingly, Rudy was warmer and more outgoing. He asked the prop man to call him Rudy, while Natacha preferred to be addressed by cast and crew as Madam. Once, during shooting of a scene in which he didn't appear, Rudy took his guitar in hand and serenaded the players for an hour and a half as the cameras rolled. Lois Wilson described him as a hard worker who got to the studio at 5 a.m. each morning to train and exercise for two hours before shooting began, but who also could be a bundle of deviltry, "as expert in flourishing a bon mot as he is in handling a rapier." He was a kidder whose jokes "were not at my expense—oh, no!—he is too entirely a gentleman to be rude—but they have that continental flavor that is fascinating and sometimes so risqué." He reminded Wilson (as he did Natacha) of "an overgrown little boy. One of those kiddies with huge brown eyes and a guileless expression [caught] in the act of robbing the family jam closet. You would wipe the incriminating evidence from his countenance and kiss away the hurt look in his eyes."

A close friend's presence contributed to Rudy's good mood on the set. André Daven had come over from Paris to play his brother, the Duke of Nemours. Though Daven had only a small part, he appeared in scenes at both ends of the shooting schedule, which necessitated his presence throughout. In the dressing scene, as Valentino's character, the Duke of Chartres, stands shirtless, flexing his muscles for a good five minutes while his shirt is being warmed for him, it's Daven's Duke of Nemours who finally helps him into the silk garment, concluding the elaborate morning toilette ritual. Daven wrote to a friend in Paris that in addition to acting in *Beaucaire* for sixty dollars a week he was earning another fifty dollars a week assisting in publicity. He said that Rudy wanted to give him a bigger role in his next picture, and that he insisted that Daven take meals with him and ride in his car. After shooting was completed, Rudy and André would spend a week fishing in Florida together, traveling without Natacha. "The two of us are living in a little bungalow, away from everything," Daven wrote in a letter home. "It's restful." Exactly what they did and felt we don't know, but this seems to have been a genuine love affair. Daven ended up returning to France suddenly after the Florida trip, not staying on to make a second film with Rudy. He explained in a letter that the reasons for his early return were too delicate to explain in writing, but that "nothing has been broken—on the contrary." Perhaps Daven feared they were becoming too attached to one another.

If Natacha considered Daven a threat, no one seems to have picked up on it. "His sun rises and sets in Natacha," Lois Wilson said of Rudy. A photo exists showing the three of them, Rudy, Natacha, and André, taking lunch together at the Astoria Studios commissary; they're off by themselves, not mingling with the rest of the company. Rudy sits next to Natacha and across from André. Each occupies an island of space.

There were differences of opinion as to whether or not Madam acted too bossy. Lois Wilson thought not. She saw Natacha as a charming woman who stuck to the job of designing and did not interfere elsewhere. According to Wilson, "She has beauty, charm, grace, and ability. It is miraculous what she can do with a piece of cloth, a pincushion, and an ornament." But Dutch-born actress Jetta Goudal, originally scheduled to appear in *Beaucaire*, bowed out because she clashed with Natacha, whom she considered a know-it-all. According to Goudal, the studio recognized her difficulties with Madam Rambova, and therefore excused her, which Goudal thought was very kind of them. Doris Kenyon, who played Lady Mary Carlisle, "the belle of Bath," remembered Natacha sitting on the side of the set, gesturing to Valentino as he acted a scene to indicate how he should play it. Kenyon found Valentino "a little flirty," but Rambova, she said, kept him under close watch.

Studio publicist Harry Reichenbach complained in print that Madam intervened when an interviewer from a magazine arrived to speak to Valentino. The would-be interviewer was told he should speak instead to Mrs. Valentino. Reichenbach, furious that an interview he'd gone to pains to arrange was being sabotaged, stormed away, barking, "If Mrs. Valentino has anything to say, tell her to phone Mrs. Reichenbach between seven and eight some evening."

Gavin Lambert, Alla Nazimova's biographer, thinks that by calling herself "Madam," Natacha engaged in conscious or unconscious competition with her former best friend, Nazimova. He also believes the same competitive motive prompted her to invite Nazimova's former mentor, the pathbreaking Russian director Konstantin Stanislavsky, to the *Beaucaire* set, but surely there were nobler impulses at work, too. Of course the entire cast would be excited at the chance to meet the great Stanislavsky. His acclaimed Moscow Art Theater was performing in New York that spring, and Natacha arranged for the Russian director and a few of his players to join the *Beaucaire* cast at lunch in

Astoria and then watch some of the shooting. That day they were filming a scene in which the Queen cries. Each time the cameras rolled for
another take, Lois Wilson had to summon tears. Stanislavsky was
amazed. He said he would never expect an actress in his company to
play an emotional scene involving tears over and over many times in
rapid succession—it was too demanding, too draining. Although he
expressed admiration for studio discipline and the precision of Olcott's directing, the whole process of making movies left him under-
whelmed. Stanislavsky reportedly told his interpreter that Valentino
had no concept of the right way to wear period costumes, but he failed
to say exactly what he found wanting.

Valentino had been tutored in acting by Nazimova, and he was
quite capable of summoning powerful emotions—for instance in his
spurned-lover scene with Nazimova in *Camille*. But the kind of in-
depth character work that Stanislavsky pioneered had no place in a
confection like *Monsieur Beaucaire*, which ended up more like a gorgeous satin-and-gauze ballet than an affecting comedy or drama. The
whole point being made about court life in the eighteenth century was
that it was a place and time where trifles were inflated, where much
ado was made about nothing. The movie suffers from the same imbal-
ance. The settings and costumes overwhelm the slender premise, and
there are so many characters in wigs and lace that it's often hard to tell
one from another.

The script tried to create a contrast between the preening effeminacy of the King and the energetic heterosexual exploits of Valentino's
character, the Duke of Chartres, but this difference didn't emerge
very clearly. Because of the film's bland, tableaulike stasis—its emphasis on fey, arched-eyebrow joking and bespangled prettiness—the
whole production feels precious. Not a whole lot happens. Yes,
Valentino's Duke of Chartres shaves himself (to the consternation of
his attendants), flirts with Madame de Pompadour, fends off a band of
British scoundrels wielding rapiers, vaults over a balcony, shows kindness when he comforts a distraught child servant, switches his affections from Lady Mary back to Princess Henriette, and kisses many a
dainty hand, but it's hard to care. You can't take your eyes off the

skintight satin knickers he wears, the powdered curls, beauty marks, and jeweled garters and the elaborately choreographed minuets. They set the preening, mincing tone that many American viewers found hard to stomach. In fact, Valentino's performance in *Beaucaire*, like his later one in *The Eagle*, allowed him to gently spoof his lover-boy image, but most people didn't pick up on the distance between him and his character and didn't get the joke. Beaucaire's relief at not being looked at, for once, not being pursued by women when he assumes his disguise, plays with Valentino's real-life situation, but the parody disappeared in a cloud of wig powder.

The New York Times made a disparaging comparison between Valentino as Chartres/Beaucaire and John Barrymore's recent screen appearance as Beau Brummell, another male clotheshorse from the eighteenth century. "In Brummell, Barrymore ends up a withered dandy with matted gray hair and threadbare attire," the *Times* critic wrote. "Would Valentino, we wonder, have cared to obliterate his own looks with such a makeup for the sake of artistic success?" The true answer—not the one the reviewer implied—is yes. In *The Four Horsemen*'s battle scenes Valentino appeared looking rumpled, weary, mudsplattered, and anything but glamorous. But the anonymous critic for the *Times* chose not to remember that, hinting that Valentino's personal vanity stood in the way of his acting. The charge was unfair. Valentino played his role in *Beaucaire* as it was written, directed, and designed. But he got blamed, once again, for too closely resembling the character he played.

The resentment nascent in the *Times* review echoed elsewhere. Although the picture's visual splendors inspired many rhapsodic reviews and the film did excellent box office in London, Paris, New York City, and Chicago, it flopped elsewhere in the United States, and prompted some venomous outbursts directed at its star. *Photoplay* published a photo of Valentino in profile, nude from the waist up, chin resting on fist, with the following jeering caption: "Rudolph Valentino is suggestive of [Rodin's] 'The Thinker' in this pose. Perhaps he is wondering how it will seem to wear a wig and satin knee panties in . . . his next picture." Men, warned one critic, are not going to take to the "dolled up" Rudolph "in his white wig, silks, lace and satin knickers." *Beaucaire* was typed as a "women's film." At the packed Strand Theater opening week in New York, "girls made up three quarters of a sweltering house." But some women found Valentino's Beaucaire off-putting. A female fan upbraided him: "You are trying to be too artistic. In fact, the whole picture seemed to me to be artificial. I don't want to see Rudy turned into a hothouse flower." Another fan had complained earlier, "I would like to know just who it was that started the pretty young man vogue in films? Whom shall we blame—Rex Ingram? Then lead him on for the slaughter. Continue to give us rugged types such as Thomas Meighan, Milton Sills."

A particular flashpoint in *Beaucaire* was the dressing scene at Versailles, which allowed Valentino to display his naked upper body. The scene had been created as a conscious piece of beefcake titillation, calculated to provide spice. *Variety*'s critic liked the picture, and praised Valentino's performance, but took issue with the amount of footage given over to "his being nude above the waist, thereby giving the populace an informed view of his muscular development." A woman reviewer named Mildred Spain had no problem at all with the scene, issuing an invitation to "Ladies! Ladies!" to take a good look, and pronouncing Valentino "nude but not naughty. A picture for the health magazines. A plaster statue of a young athlete he might be."

Dressed or undressed, Valentino in *Beaucaire* tripped emotional switches. People felt called upon to take a stand as if he were running for public office. Once again *Photoplay*'s James R. Quirk delivered a lecture: "Something has happened to the Valentino of *The Sheik* and *Blood and Sand*," he began. "I am afraid the dyed-in-the-wool Valentino fans will be a little disappointed in their idol in *Monsieur Beaucaire*. Rudy is trying to be an actor at the expense of the personality that made him a sensation." The fans, Quirk explained, "like their Rudy a little wicked," and that Rudy was nowhere to be found here. Despite some "rattling good sword fights," in this film "he doesn't look a bit dangerous to women."

One could argue that the controversy over Valentino in *Beaucaire* proved how important he remained; people only quarrel or poke fun when they care. Ben Turpin got busy again with a two-reel Mack Sennett spoof, *Monsieur Don't Care*—alas, a lost film.

The old debate about how ordinary people should view ostentatious European aristocrats, a debate that lay at the heart of both the French and American revolutions, was rehashed in the arguments over this film. The American puritan strain trusts rough-hewn plainness and rejects what seems elaborately fussy; the Duke of Chartres didn't stand a chance. Royalty, on the other hand, loved the movie. In England, *Beaucaire* was screened at the ballroom of Sandringham House at a command performance celebrating Queen Alexandra's birthday. But in a small town in New Mexico, a movie exhibitor complained, "Advertised it like a house afire but it flopped. It might be that it will not take in small towns and is only a picture for big cities. [People are] tired of costume productions. Valentino in a production that happened in 1924 would have pulled them in."

Despite the criticism, Valentino remained a major star, and a trendsetter. Famous Players–Lasky, anticipating his defection, hired Ricardo Cortez (né Jacob Krantz) to play "Valentino roles." Rudy continued to receive as much fan mail as any other star, and two employees were necessary to handle it. A *Film Daily* poll ranked him fourth in popularity among male talents, after Harold Lloyd, Tom Mix, and Thomas Meighan, but another trade paper placed him at the top of the list. At the Theatre Owners' Ball at New York's Hotel Astor in March 1924, Valentino and Marion Davies were crowned "King and Queen of the Movies." Eddie Cantor, Fannie Brice, Richard Barthelmess, Hope Hampton, Anita Stewart, and Governor Al Smith were among the luminaries who looked on at the coronation.

To the studio, no amount of press and fan attention could compensate for a disappointing financial return. If Famous Players–Lasky had spent less mounting *Monsieur Beaucaire* it would have considered its box office quite respectable. Although *Film Daily* ranked it ninth among top-grossing 1923 movies, the lavish production budget became a club to use against the Valentinos, especially Natacha. For the studio's next—and last—Valentino movie, *A Sainted Devil*, the executives would see to it that the same mistakes would not be repeated.

Rudy would return to a red-blooded he-man role. A tried and true South American setting would replace Europe. And the budget would be more modest.

The Valentinos eagerly awaited being cut free of Famous Players–Lasky. After this one last picture, they looked forward to a golden age of independence and productivity at Ritz-Carlton Pictures under the baton of J. D. Williams. Williams confidently announced that he had great plans, plans that would take Valentino to shooting locations in Egypt, India, Morocco, and Corsica. At last they would be working abroad. Like a tree laden with spring blossoms, their world seemed to burst with promise.

16

SLIPPAGE

J esse Lasky believed that Valentino achieved his stardom by "playing earthy tigers. Physical lovers smelling of the bullring. And desert chieftains dragging women into his tent." For his last picture under Lasky and Zukor's banner, *The Sainted Devil*, the earthy tiger once again would be uncaged and allowed to go on the prowl, and Famous Players–Lasky hoped to cash in.

Joseph Henabery, who had a long association with Famous Players–Lasky, was brought in to direct *The Sainted Devil* after Natacha had already started work on the production. A former railroad man from Nebraska, the well-liked Henabery had been drawn to the world of motion pictures during Hollywood's infancy. As an actor he played Lincoln in *The Birth of a Nation,* later becoming an assistant to D. W. Griffith and then a busy director who worked with such actors as Douglas Fairbanks and Mary Miles Minter. In the early summer of 1924, when Henabery arrived in Astoria from Hollywood, he found that some of the sets for *The Sainted Devil* had already been erected, and that the shooting script—not one he especially admired—had been completed by Forrest Halsey and approved. Since Natacha took charge of the casting, and the costumes were in the works, Henabery can hardly be called the auteur of this lost picture; he was more like a chauffeur hired by a boss who prefers to do the driving. "Mrs. Valentino assumed responsibility for most all matters concerning production," Henabery recalled, "but after my arrival at the studio she usually consulted with me in these matters."

Henabery apparently had no problem with Natacha's assumption of authority. She had won his respect. "She knew the degree of exaggeration necessary for stage or picture work. I learned a lot from her," he said. *The Sainted Devil*, a story of love, betrayal, and mistaken identity, included scenes requiring Valentino to run through a gamut of emotions, writ large: romantic bliss, grief, anger, cynicism, ennui, despair, and dissipation, the latter state helped along by Henabery's insistence that Rudy endure a siege of sleeplessness that lasted thirty-seven hours. If Natacha served as Rudy's acting coach, she knew how to get him to pull out all the stops. Surely her understanding of the "exaggeration" Henabery mentions had something to do with her training, via Kosloff, as a Diaghilev-tutored dancer and pantomimist; facial expressions became part of the language of gesture, part of the attempt to make the whole body speak eloquently in a way clearly visible to those sitting in the back rows of a theater. Rudy's emotional pyrotechnics also owed much to Nazimova's acting style, which ran to highly stylized poses and grand, theatrical gestures.

Either at Natacha's bidding or on his own, Henabery instructed the *Sainted Devil* cameraman, Harry Fischbeck (the same gifted cameraman who'd used innovative lighting on *Monsieur Beaucaire*) to shoot many soft-focus close-ups, which gave "full face, profile, ear, eye, nose and throat views of Rudy." This may have been a sop for the fans. All those close-ups, *Variety*'s Sisk commented, "may be what women want." The excessive number of close-ups and the sometimes sleep-inducing pace made for a picture that couldn't hold its audience. One reviewer complained, "The action drags, frequently it hesitates and occasionally it actually stops." Like other films imprinted with Natacha's stamp, it showed what can happen when the quest for cinematic visual perfection is divorced from any drive toward propulsive action. "The poor man has become suddenly paralyzed," the *Graphic*'s critic concluded as she watched one of Valentino's stalled moments after he concludes that his bride has been untrue. A firm editorial hand would have helped. Since we don't know who exerted final authority, we can't say whether the primary fault lay with Natacha, the studio, Halsey, or Henabery. No doubt they each contributed to a mix that in the end pleased few.

Natacha definitely made her creative presence felt. Henabery admired her intelligence and energy, and was convinced that Valentino owed his stardom to his wife. "But for her influence, he would probably have suffered poor stories, low budgets—and ended up discarded and forgotten," he averred. Henabery thought Natacha's foresight and determination had "made" Valentino, that her demand for control forced the studio to spend more and meet higher production standards than it otherwise would have; and that in a later era she would have been frankly called the producer and given credit as such. He agreed with others that Natacha could be stubborn, and he knew that where money was involved she often proved to be improvident, investing a great deal on set furniture or props that because of lighting and camera angles would hardly show up when a scene was actually shot. She tended to be weak on collaboration and communication.

Henabery respected Natacha's mind and eye more than he did Rudy's, but he liked both Valentinos, and the feeling was mutual. They took to calling him Uncle Joe and would elect to work with him again. Things went smoothly on the set as long as Rudy and Natacha agreed with each other, but not when they got into a tug-of-war over some issue on which they had opposing views. On many a night Henabery ended up leaving the Astoria Studio with them and repairing to their apartment at the Ritz. Over dinner they would wrangle for hours. "Often I thought they were both wrong." Sometimes he lingered until two or three in the morning, but he wouldn't leave until the conflict was resolved. Unfortunately, Henabery doesn't specify what the points in dispute were. He does say that no matter how tired they were, the Valentinos insisted on getting up early to resume shooting the next morning, not wanting to lose a minute's time. "Delays were upsetting to the Valentinos. They wanted to get away from Paramount as quickly as they could." Their legal battles had "left them bitter."

Using a "top hits" mentality, the studio tried to combine in *The Sainted Devil* elements from two past Valentino winners, *The Four Horsemen* and *Blood and Sand*. It wanted to dim impressions of the prettified, lace-collared, beauty-marked Valentino of *Monsieur Beaucaire*, even though the sumptuousness of that production had been widely hailed. Once again the public would get to watch a virile Valentino doing the tango in a crowded South American cabaret, fighting bandits, arrayed like a magnificent toreador, or riding over the pampas in a slouched sombrero and billowing trousers. One more time there would be romantically framed soft-focus love scenes shot in picturesque courtyards, yet again a lovely wife (newcomer Helen D'Algy) wearing a lace mantilla, a saintly type contrasted with not one but two scheming vamps, Nita Naldi and Dagmar Godowsky. The Valentino character, Don Alonso Castro, just like Gallardo in *Blood and Sand*, becomes dissipated and cynical, in this instance because he believes his bride has betrayed him with the villain, El Tigre (George Siegmann). The studio ballyhooed the idea that it had resurrected the popular, smoldering Valentino of the past. "Rudy is himself again, the good bad man," ran the publicity paragraphs in both *Photoplay*, read by fans, and the trade paper *Moving Picture World*, aimed at exhibitors. "With all the lure of romance of Julio and the wickedness of Juan Gallardo, . . . he comes back as Don Alonso in a story of wild loves and adventures in the Argentine. Slouched hat, high boots, striped shirt, gay neckerchief, draped serape, wide trousers, knife and loaded riding whip. And he makes love to all the girls." Here the familiar Valentino returned, one critic said, "entirely surrounded by women and wardrobe."

Nobody at Paramount figured out that unless some new ingredient is added, a too-familiar formula stales and that old hats, even when they're slouched sombreros, wear thin pretty fast. Nor did they recognize that as Julio Desnoyers and Juan Gallardo, Valentino had scorched the screen playing soulful characters who feel deeply and grow internally; high-voltage emotional intensity and conviction powered the earlier hits. Latin locales, castanets, and decorative costumes, although they contributed color, didn't in themselves create cinema magic. Don Alonso Castro, the Valentino character in Forrest Halsey's *Sainted Devil* script, unlike his predecessors, has little substance and less motivation, changing from good to bad, romantic to cynic, trusting soul to firebreathing devil in a single instant. He's been a love-struck grandee, serenading his pure and lovely Julietta beneath her balcony and kneeling before a saint after his wedding, but when he believes Julietta, now his wife, is letting El Tigre, the bandit who's captured her, make love to her, he instantly turns into a snarling brute, spurning her and all womankind. He fends off advances from the two scheming, man-hungry vamps and ends up back in the wedding chapel with his beloved Julietta, who proves to be untainted by sin after all.

According to Natacha, the script she and Rudy originally approved, based on a Rex Beach story, had a war background that lent it urgency and suspense. Because of worries about losing the market in Europe, the studio cut out the war plot. As Natacha put it, "The spinal column of the beast was amputated." All that remained was a melodramatic, contrived, and far-fetched Latin love story involving mistaken identity, just an excuse for some fight scenes, dancing, histrionics, and striking visual effects. Natacha had been enthusiastic about the project before beginning work on it, but she completely lost interest along the way.

Considerable energy and money went into the costumes, which, because no print of *The Sainted Devil* has surfaced, can now be admired only in surviving stills. Jetta Goudal, a former stage actress originally designated to play one of the vamps, had her own scheme for dressing flamboyantly that clashed with Natacha's (probably equally outré) costume designs for Goudal's character, Doña Florencia. After Natacha showed Goudal her sketches, the two had words, and Goudal found herself hastily replaced by Rudy's old friend Dagmar Godowsky. The gossip columns tried to turn Goudal's fiery exit from the film into a fight for Valentino's affections, but this gambit was apparently the creation of studio publicists. Goudal recalled that they tried to portray her as another Pola Negri, another temperamental European actress. She went to the publicity department to ask why they circulated such baseless stories. They said, because that's what the public likes. Unfortunately, the groundless but titillating gossip had already circulated and done its work.

Though her people skills were imperfect, Natacha did have an uncanny ability to spot talent. She tapped two designers slated for future major careers in fashion to create costumes for *The Sainted Devil*: Norman Norell and Adrian Gilbert, at that time both in their early twenties, fresh out of design school, and until recently known as Norman Levinson and Adolph Adrian Greenburg; Greenburg ultimately became famous as, simply, Adrian. We don't know exactly who did what; it may be that Natacha asked Adrian to take over designing Valentino's costumes after she rejected the "crabbed sketches" of Norell. Apparently Norell did design at least one vamp costume for Dagmar Godowsky and Natacha herself designed several more. It's clear that Adrian emerged the favorite, for he was invited to follow the Valentinos to Hollywood to work on their next picture. He would travel with them when they took the train back to California.

When it was too late to do anything about it, Natacha realized that gorgeous sets and costumes can't rescue an otherwise misguided picture. She conceded afterward that she'd "lost sight of the fact that if beauty is only used as a shallow satisfaction for the eye and not combined with food for the soul as well . . . it is but an empty gilded shell."

When *The Sainted Devil* had its premiere in the fall of 1924, the Strand Theater in New York initially did excellent business, attracting "everybody from flappers to grandmothers," but the crowds quickly dwindled. A planned three-week run was cut to two weeks. *Variety* dismissed it as another women's picture, designed to please Valentino's fans, who were mostly female. The reports from movie theaters in the hinterlands made it sound as if Valentino's heyday had passed. A theater manager in Guthrie, Oklahoma, groused, "This should have been called 'Scented Devil,' because people could smell it out in the street. Terrible. I can't put this star over. It cannot be done. . . . Lost me money? Sure it did." Another, in Illinois, offered this grim prognosis: "I blamed my flop [with] Beaucaire on costume, but now after playing Rudy in his own type of picture, I am convinced that he is a dead one. Draw very poor and only satisfied a scant few." At least in some quarters, Valentino was being written off as a has-been before he'd even turned thirty.

Rudy and Natacha didn't pay much attention to the grumblings about *The Sainted Devil*. They were too busy preparing for their first Ritz-Carlton picture, which would have a story written by Natacha herself, under the pen name "Justus Layne." (Was this name choice a hint that at last the Valentinos would be done justice?) The new movie, a costume epic, was to be the culmination of their dreams, their masterpiece. Tentatively titled *The Scarlet Power* (*The Flame of Destiny* was another title they considered before they ultimately settled on *The Hooded Falcon*) and loosely based on the legend of El Cid, it was set in the fourteenth-century Spanish court and involved Spaniards, Moors, and Jews. Originally, Valentino was to play a young noble who falls in love with a beautiful Moorish princess. The script went through several revisions, in the course of which Valentino's character became himself a dark-skinned Moor.

Louella Parsons reported that Mrs. Valentino was working on the script as the shooting of *The Sainted Devil* came to an end. Eight weeks later, in August, she revealed that the Valentinos had met with June Mathis and that Mr. Valentino had emerged from the conference with a smile on his face. "I am willing to bet a dollar to a doughnut," Parsons wrote, "that before the snow flies we shall see Miss Mathis and Valentino working together."

June Mathis was still under contract as editorial supervisor with Goldwyn, but things were not working out well for her at what was now MGM; her script for *Ben-Hur* had been rejected and now, back from Rome, she was being blamed for everything that had gone wrong on that protracted and apparently star-crossed production. At present she was freelancing, while in the process of negotiating a move to First National to develop scripts for Colleen Moore. Moore played jazz-baby flapper roles quite out of step with Mathis's mystical and somber bent, but Mathis took what work came her way. Keeping herself "as busy as the proverbial one-armed paperhanger," she was being pulled in many disparate professional directions. Her mother had recently died, and her suddenly tumultuous private life provided little respite. She had left for Rome while rumored to be engaged to actor George Walsh, but returned with a fiancé she'd met in Italy and would soon marry, cameraman Sylvano Balboni. Rudy now pressured her to agree to take on writing the continuity for his Spanish Moor picture. Natacha had outlined the story, but the script needed fine-tuning by a professional scenario writer. It needed the Mathis touch. June Mathis had never been able to say no to Valentino before, and she didn't this time. "Miss Mathis declares herself fascinated by the acting possibilities of the role to be played by Mr. Valentino."

The Valentinos soon experienced the first of several disappointments with the man who now controlled their professional destinies, J. D. Williams. They had hoped to shoot the Spanish picture in Spain, but Williams told them that would be too expensive; the pockets of Ritz-Carlton Pictures were not that deep. They'd looked forward to selecting their own stories for development into Valentino movies, but would discover that, without consulting them first, Williams had gone ahead and bought screen rights for a current Broadway success, a modern play by Martin Brown, called *Cobra,* that on-stage starred Louis Calhern and Judith Anderson. Worse still, they would learn that Williams had worked out a distribution deal between Ritz-Carlton and Famous Players–Lasky, the very company Valentino had spent the last two years battling in court and attempting to flee.

Henabery considered the Valentinos "babes in the woods in business" because they'd signed a contract with Williams "without any knowledge as to how and where he was going to get the required finances." Henabery found out about the bargain struck between Williams and Famous Players–Lasky when he told Adolph Zukor that he, Henabery, would be leaving that studio to make a costume picture with Valentino's new producer. He'd telegrammed the studio's West Coast office to say he was eager to accept the offer because this would be a big picture and provide a great opportunity. Zukor stunned Henabery by revealing that Famous Players–Lasky had put up the money and would release the upcoming Valentino pictures. Henabery recalled, "You could have knocked me over with a feather. I knew the Valentinos would be furious when they discovered they were still tied up with Paramount."

The conversation between Zukor and Henabery took place while the Valentinos were off on another jaunt to Europe. They had departed on the S.S. *Leviathan* in late August, seen off at the New York pier by Harold Lloyd and his brother, Gaylord. Nita Naldi, who would soon join them in France, and hundreds of fans also turned up to wave good-bye.

Rudy took along his trainer, Chris Schnurrer, and he told a reporter that while abroad he expected to wrestle and fence every day to stay in top shape. By this time Rudy had become a full-fledged fitness guru. His exercise regime, based on army training workouts, had been published in a book called *How You Can Keep Fit*, which was serialized in a newspaper under the title "Valentino's Beauty Secrets" and also would appear in an upcoming magazine article. Readers were advised to do their exercises wearing as little clothing as possible and were told they could transform themselves as Rudy had "with no other equipment than a bench, a stout wooden pole, and a bar on which to chin." Beefcake images of him flexing his muscles in a pair of skimpy shorts had adorned the cover of *Movie Weekly*, whose publisher, Bernarr Macfadden—also the founder of *Physical Culture* magazine— gave interviews standing on his head.

The Valentinos stopped in Paris to pick up the custom-made open Avion-Voisin touring car, gray with a red leather interior, that Rudy had ordered the previous year, and to accept Jacques Hébertot's gift of a Doberman pinscher Rudy had admired and named Kabar. André Daven's name must have come up in conversation, but he seems to have departed from Hébertot's inner circle. He was currently involved with Rolf de Maré, who would put Daven in charge of the Théâtre des Champs-Elysées (replacing Hébertot), as it was being converted from a showcase for avant-garde groups like the Swedish Ballet into a music hall. There Daven would in 1925 produce the all-black *Révue Nègre*, starring Josephine Baker, which took Paris by storm.

After driving south, Rudy and Natacha arrived at Juan-les-Pins looking like prototypes of the glamorous fantasy figures they were: Rudy sat behind the wheel of the Voisin wearing a fur-collared leather coat and racing goggles, the enormous Doberman, Kabar, at his side. Sweltering in the back, Natacha showed off a new fur coat, even though it was August, and was joined by the five yelping pedigreed Pekingese dogs she had just acquired, one of them for a mere fifteen hundred dollars.

Cap d'Antibes had yet to take off as one of the world's most fashionable summer resorts, but it was about to. This was the summer, as F. Scott Fitzgerald reported in a letter, when "there was no one at Antibes except me, Zelda, the Valentinos, the Murphys, Mistinguet [*sic*], Rex Ingram, Dos Passos, Alice Terry, the MacLeishes." As far as we know, Valentino never met any of the writers mentioned, but he did know Gerald and Sara Murphy, the wealthy and stylish American couple on whom the Divers in Fitzgerald's *Tender Is the Night* were based.

They lingered at the Hudnut château long enough for Rudy to cause a power outage in the attempt to screen *Monsieur Beaucaire*, and to create further havoc by dismantling an electric piano he couldn't put back together. Fortunately, Mrs. Hudnut had a soft spot for Rudy and a forgiving nature. She simply wrote to the manufacturer in England to send a repairman. Rudy gave tango lessons to his sister, Maria, who was visiting for a few days, and took impromptu cruises all over the Riviera in a rented motorboat. "It was a beautiful sight to see him standing at the wheel, bareheaded, in his black suit, the white spray dashing up [in] his face," his indulgent mother-in-law would recall. Rudy was feeling buoyant. He lolled on the beach at Antibes, where Honoria Murphy, the young daughter of Gerald and Sara, developed an enormous crush on him. He kept coming up with grandiose schemes predicated on the "millions upon millions" he expected to make. He talked about building a boathouse on the Hudnut château grounds that would dwarf the main house and require the digging of a tunnel to the sea. He dreamed aloud about buying and restoring a castle on one of the Lérins Islands, near Cannes. Nothing seemed impossible.

Juan-les-Pins marked only their starting point. This was to be a research and prop acquisition trip in preparation for *The Hooded Falcon*. Since they couldn't make their dream picture in Spain, they would do the next best thing: travel to that country to visit historic sites and buy authentic period jewelry, armor, and costumes, to be shipped to America. Collecting had become for both a driving passion, an ongoing quest for countless Holy Grails. Neither Rudy nor Natacha can be called the more extravagant; this was a shared compulsion, a true *folie à deux.* Money seemed to have little reality. They simply spent it, the way they breathed the air. If they couldn't *do* whatever they wished, they would *have:* Renaissance doors, Gothic chairs and chests, painted screens, tapestries, old ivories, silver, jeweled swords with curved blades, cuirasses, spears, helmets, pearl-inlay muscats, the mailed glove of Philip II, a great shield traced in gold, even a crimson throne. Natacha spent ten thousand dollars on exquisite antique shawls, saying she planned to resell them, with a high markup, to Fifth Avenue shops, but she never got around to doing so. J. D. Williams had advanced them forty thousand dollars to pay for Spanish props and costumes, but by the time they left they had gone through close to a hundred thousand.

Everything had to be packed for shipping to Ritz-Carlton Pictures in New York. Because the Spanish roads were poor, Rudy had agreed to leave behind his precious Voisin. They traveled by train, taking Natacha's mother along, and always occupying three first-class compartments: a double for Rudy and Natacha, a single for Mrs. Hudnut, and a third for hand luggage and Rudy's several cameras, including a movie camera. Rudy intended to photograph all that he saw.

Madrid was their first stop, but their hearts and imaginations were more stirred by Seville, where Blasco Ibáñez had set *Blood and Sand.* There Rudy visited the humble house where the torero who inspired the character Juan Gallardo had lived. From a dealer in costumes worn by deceased heroes of the bullring, he purchased several toreador ensembles, including one treasure embroidered in gold, with a purple silk velvet cape. They attended a bullfight, horrified but transfixed by the bloody spectacle, and thrilled to discover that King Alfonso XIII and his family were seated in a box near them. Rudy got so carried away that he stood on the balcony rail, cheering until he became hoarse, and came close to jumping into the arena. With tears in his eyes, he forswore acting in movies and shouted his intention to move to Spain and become a toreador. Mrs. Hudnut conjectured that this ability to meld identities with characters he found fascinating explained his success as an actor.

They spent several entranced days in Granada, absorbing the atmosphere of the palace and gardens of the Alhambra, the last Moorish stronghold. "In wandering through the shadowy marbled halls, through arches of fantastical design and delicacy, Rudy seemed above all haunted by the utter sadness of the place." Natacha, whose words these are, ascribed this ghostly sensation to his psychic ability to sense the despair felt by the last Moorish sultan and his "vanquished court." He took hundreds of photographs, indoors and out, in every kind of light, fascinated by the small arched notches in the thick walls that once had held bronze lamps and incense burners, and by other architectural details he and Natacha intended to duplicate on-screen.

After studying paintings of medieval Spanish princes, Rudy decided he must grow a beard for his forthcoming role. "We noted from the old portraits that all the men, as they grow older, wore beards. Only the youths were smooth-shaven." With his new goatee and his excellent Spanish, he was mistaken for a Spaniard wherever he went, even at the bank where he presented his letter of credit and Italian passport to an incredulous clerk. He sent jokey postcards to several friends, showing a picture of himself posed beside a billy goat and the message, "The one with the whiskers is the goat."

Nita Naldi was to play a major role in *The Hooded Falcon*. The costumes Natacha designed for her were to be fitted and sewn in Paris, where Naldi and the Valentinos met before setting out together for a tour of the Loire Valley châteaux. Mrs. Hudnut and her young niece, Margaret Dinwoodey, joined the party, and at times the slangy, uninhibited Naldi, a born New Yorker whose real name was Donna Dooley, brought blushes to their ladylike cheeks. "Usually in hotel dining rooms her shrill voice could be heard above all others as she recounted her backstage Winter Garden reminiscences" of her days as a Broadway showgirl. "Her shins must have been raw, as we were continually kicking her under the table, as most of her stories were a bit risqué for the public," Mrs. Hudnut recalled. At the château Chaumont, when Naldi noticed that the bedrooms of Catherine de Medici and of her astrologer were connected by a short passageway, she commented, "These old guys had nothing on Hollywood morals."

Château de Chambord, with its four hundred rooms, double spiral staircases, and extensive grounds, immediately inspired in Rudy a vision of himself as its munificent lord, hosting yearly hunting trips and banquets for all his friends. If Francois I had done it, why not Rudolph Valentino? At Châteaudun he carried the real estate fantasy to another level, arranging a tour with a sales agent. He and Natacha vanished into the off-limits tower, whose floor had collapsed. They emerged unscathed, but less eager for ownership.

After three months in Europe, it was time to return to New York. Rudy spent a few days with Alberto at Juan-les-Pins before departing for American shores. The brothers posed there, in beautifully tailored matching white suits, for the photographer James Abbe. Natacha missed most of Alberto's stay. She had to oversee the progress on Nita Naldi's costumes, which were being made in Paris, so she and Alberto intersected at Juan-les-Pins for just one day. It would be their sole encounter.

American news photographers greeting the Valentinos' arrival in New York on the *Leviathan* zoomed in on Rudy's new reddish goatee. Since he set trends in men's fashion, a change in his appearance was considered newsworthy. Prodded by publicist Harry Reichenbach, the Associated Master Barbers of America soon issued a statement threatening a boycott of Valentino pictures by its members for "as long as he remains bewhiskered." The barbers claimed they feared that the male population would be guided by the famous actor "to the extent of making beards fashionable again," which "would not only work harmful injury to barbers, but would . . . make American citizens difficult to distinguish from Russians." J. D. Williams exploited the publicity by staging a banquet in Valentino's honor at New York's Ritz-Carlton Hotel to mark Valentino's initiation as a Ritz-Carlton Pictures star. Every male guest was presented with a fake red beard and mustache.

Although conviviality and high spirits prevailed at the banquet, tension surfaced at subsequent private meetings between the Valentinos and Williams. He admonished them for reckless spending in Europe, informed them of the financial involvement of Famous Players—Lasky in his new endeavor, and explained that the budget for *The Hooded Falcon* could not exceed $500,000. He went on to tell them that he had bought the screen rights to *Cobra,* unwelcome news both because he had acted without consulting them and because *Cobra's* modern setting held little allure; to provide the romance his fans wanted, Valentino felt he needed scripts about "other races and other ages. I find it hard to be romantic in a sack suit," he said. Then Williams dropped the bombshell that *The Hooded Falcon* would have to be filmed in Hollywood, which had more studio space available than New York. The Valentinos had just signed a long-term lease on an expensive apartment at 270 Park Avenue at Forty-fifth Street, and had completely furnished it with antiques purchased in Europe. Moving back to California had not figured in their plans. Even after Williams's announcement they decided to keep the Park Avenue place as a luxurious *pied à terre*, since they expected to be shuttling back and forth between coasts.

A former New York City policeman, Luther ("Lou") Mahoney, drove them to the train station in late November 1924. Mahoney had met Rudy a few months earlier, during production of *The Sainted Devil.* An extortionist group of criminals called the Black Hand had threatened Valentino in a letter, and the New York City police force, taking no chances, assigned Mahoney to serve as his short-term bodyguard. Mahoney and Valentino instantly hit it off. "Meeting him was like meeting an old friend," Mahoney remembered. "He joked about the Black Hand but said he hoped I was a good shot. The day I accompanied him to the train taking him back to Hollywood he said, 'Remember, Luther, if you ever come to Hollywood, look me up. I'll put you on my payroll.'" Within the year, Mahoney had moved to California and joined the Valentinos' staff, leaving his initial job as a studio carpenter and car mechanic to become their factotum, friend, and indispensable overseer of buildings and grounds.

The costume designer Adrian accompanied the Valentinos on the train trip west, as did Nita Naldi, J. D. Williams, Joseph Henabery, George Ullman, Ritz-Carlton publicity chief Joseph Jackson, and Natacha's pet monkey, who took a shine to Adrian and refused to be ousted from the costume designer's sleeping berth. Adrian, whose first Hollywood assignment was to be designing the costumes for *The Hooded Falcon*, said later that he found Natacha commanding, but graceful in her machinations. He described Rudy as a delightful overgrown boy.

A flotilla of motorcycle police, the president of the Los Angeles City Council, and thousands of fans jammed the platform to hail the returning Valentinos. "Probably no film star ever received the ovation accorded Rudy when he stepped from the train at Santa Fe station," *Movie Weekly* reported.

Although he was hit at once with a lawsuit filed by his former agents, Robertson and Webb, who asked to be paid the percentage they would have earned if Rudy had stayed with Famous Players–Lasky, Rudy was delighted to be back in California. "One can live a simple life in Hollywood, despite reports to the contrary," he said. "You can be out in the open. You can ride horseback and even go swimming in the winter. New York has its decided advantages—plays, operas, art exhibits, auctions—and I would not want to stay away from it too long. But frankly, I would rather work in Hollywood." He found that the two years and three months he'd been absent had brought changes to the landscape that he didn't altogether welcome. Hollywood, he worried, was mushrooming into a city. "Hollywood Boulevard now has tall office buildings and heavy traffic—qualities pleasing to the Chamber of Commerce and many property owners, but I like to think of Hollywood as a small town."

Natacha much preferred living in New York, but she immediately set about further improving their Whitley Heights property. The house presided over a steep hill, and its modern interior's sleek lines, gleaming surfaces, and dramatic colors reflected her taste, not Rudy's. The entry was on the upper level; to get to the dining room, furnished with Chinese red lacquer chairs upholstered in black velvet, you descended a graceful staircase with a wrought-iron railing. A scarlet-and-black Spanish shawl was thrown over the rail, but few other recent European purchases were in evidence. The living room, down another short flight of stairs, had a black marble floor, yellow walls, and low divans heaped with bright-colored cushions. Making use of Lou Mahoney's skills, Natacha soon had a six-sided swimming pool built on the side of their hill. She decided she wanted an aviary with running water, perches, and a nesting area for the birds. Mahoney drew a design for an octagon-shaped wire cage, which he showed to set designer William Cameron Menzies. Menzies redrew the design, to scale, and construction began. Water had to be brought down a hill via a concrete slab. When the aviary was completed Natacha was so pleased, she threw her arms around Mahoney and asked if he would next turn his attention to building a fish pond. The accommodating and resourceful former cop was happy to oblige, and the completed pond featured at each end a frog that spouted water.

As Natacha's rapport with Mahoney increased, her relationship with George Ullman, who in addition to being Rudy's manager was serving as production manager at Ritz-Carlton Pictures, grew more tense. Ullman resented Natacha's tight grip on the reins of Valentino's career; it impeded his own influence. He saw Natacha as a beguiling but sinister dominatrix whose beauty, talent, and magnetism allowed her to have her way. "She exercised to the fullest her uncanny ability to charm" those "whose allegiance she desired to secure . . . to serve her own ambition, or to forward any project of her own." Mahoney, clearly under Natacha's spell, did not get along with Ullman. "Every move that Ullman made was directed against me," he claimed. Ullman kept his hand on the till, curbing the Valentinos' penchant for reckless spending, but Mahoney needed money to finance the improvements he'd been hired to make, and resented having to go to Ullman to clear every expenditure. A three-cornered battle for ascendancy ensued.

If Rudy had ruled his own roost with a firmer hand, those around him would have felt less called upon to jockey behind the scenes. Content to entrust management detail to others, he responded to pressure by throwing himself into physical activities, rising at dawn to go riding in the hills for hours with his old friend Mario Carillo, or hiking with his dogs. At home, "like a boy who had a toy to play with," he loved to tinker with his cars, cameras, or other gadgets. On Christmas Eve, he stayed up all night putting together on the black marble living-room floor an elaborate network of electric trains, tracks, and tunnels, to be presented to the Ullmans' six-year-old son as an early-morning surprise.

Natacha turned her attention from the house back to *The Hooded Falcon*. The cast and crew had been put on salary before leaving New York, and continued to gobble up the budget as one delay followed another. The original crew had included June Mathis, Adrian, Joseph Henabery, and photographer Harry Fischbeck, all proven talents the Valentinos had worked with before. New to the team was William Cameron Menzies, whose fantasy set designs for the Fairbanks film *The Thief of Bagdad* had contributed much to its success, and who had been working since July on his designs for *The Hooded Falcon*. Natacha considered him the best set designer in movies, once again exhibiting her instinct for spotting giant talents. "Sets are being erected at the United Studios," *Movie Weekly* had reported weeks before the Valentinos returned to California.

J. D. Williams publicly patted himself on the back for creating the perfect environment for Valentino to work in: "With our company he is surrounded by a group whose hopes for his success are second only to his own. Of course we want to make money, but we are a unit in believing that the fine, the artistic, the intelligent picture will appeal to the greatest number. We do not believe it necessary to play down to the . . . fourteen year old intellect. Nor do we believe in paltry or blatant sex appeal." At Ritz-Carlton Pictures, the new, improved Valentino would become "the master of his own production ship—the captain of his own artistic soul."

In spite of Williams's chest-thumping, signs that *The Hooded Falcon* was in trouble surfaced even before the Valentinos unpacked their trunks at 6770 Wedgewood Place. On the train, Rudy, Natacha, and Joseph Henabery had each read the hurriedly written June Mathis scenario and had agreed that it simply would not do. Since June was now too busy at First National to make the necessary revisions, Henabery wanted to enlist the help of Anthony Coldewey as script doctor, and Rudy thought of calling in Rafael Sabatini. George Ullman was dispatched to inform Mathis that her script had not passed muster. After Ullman's meeting with her, "June refused to have anything further to do with us," Natacha wrote. In one stroke, the close and important long-term friendship with Mathis seemed irreparably damaged, to the sorrow of all parties. Natacha complained that she'd been unfairly singled out and made a scapegoat, although the rejection of the Mathis script had been a group decision: "As it was the usual procedure to credit all disagreeable things to my account, this instance was not an exception."

It's quite true that Natacha was being depicted as an ambitious martinet who led poor Rudy around by the nose: "Talk about your dutiful husbands! Show us anywhere a husband who can match the screen sheik, Rudolph Valentino, in impersonating a meek lambkin in the presence of his wifie dear. Rudy never disobeys," meowed a columnist in *Zit's Weekly*, who joined the chorus that assigned responsibility for the rift with Mathis to Natacha.

Rudy and Natacha felt called upon to defend their partnership. In a fan magazine article titled "Valentino Is Not a Henpecked Husband," Rudy argued that he would be a fool not to listen to his wife's counsel concerning the choice of actors, stories, and directors. "She is a woman of the highest culture. She has a sane, judicious mind. I know that she is loyal to my interests." Natacha later acknowledged that all the negative talk took a heavy toll: "We were both happier trying to get up the ladder than teetering on the top of it. Success is a cruel and bitter dish. We find ourselves the target for unkind and unjust criticism."

The symbol of Valentino's subservience to his dominant wife was taken to be the platinum slave bracelet she had given him for Christmas in 1924 and which he always wore. (He had given her a watch she'd admired, set with diamonds and with its face embedded in a moonstone.) Made at Tiffany's from Natacha's sketch, the much-discussed slave bracelet had heavy interlocked links. George Ullman saw Natacha "place the now famous slave bracelet on Rudy's wrist" and "witnessed his kiss of fervent gratitude for the symbolism it expressed. [Rudy] declared that he was the slave of her beauty and kindliness."

The platinum slave bracelet was his favorite, but it was not the first bracelet that Rudy had worn, nor was it his only one (he owned silver and gold versions, and sometimes wore one on each wrist), nor was

Valentino and Natacha Rambova returning to the United States on the *Aquitania*, October 1923 (Museum of Modern Art)

Valentino as the foppish Duke de Chartres in *Monsieur Beaucaire*, Paramount, 1924 (Museum of Modern Art)

Valentino with André Daven in *Monsieur Beaucaire* dressing scene (Museum of Modern Art)

At left table, Valentino, Natacha Rambova, and André Daven lunching at Astoria Studios, during shooting of *Monsieur Beaucaire*, 1924. Lowell Sherman, Bebe Daniels, Sidney Olcott, and Doris Kenyon are at right table. (Museum of Modern Art)

Valentino in felt fedora, with sideburns, custom-tailored British suit, pinky ring, and walking stick: a trend-setting man of fashion, ca. 1925 (Private collection)

Valentino, his chauffeur, and the custom-made Isotta Fraschini town car, 1925 (Museum of Modern Art)

Valentino, surrounded by crew for *The Sainted Devil*, loading film into his 35mm Debrie movie camera. Director Joseph Henabery is seated at right, in straw hat, near his Bell and Howell camera, 1924. (Private collection)

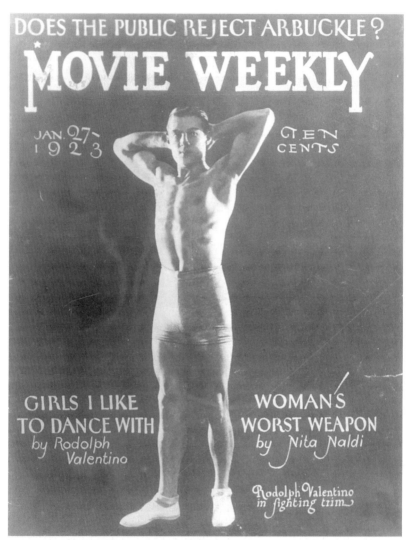

Valentino, "in fighting trim," as a buff physical-fitness cover boy, 1923 (Private collection)

Valentino, a mask of tragedy as Don Alonso Castro, in *The Sainted Devil*, Paramount, 1924 (Museum of Modern Art)

(*below*) Valentino, made up for his role as Count Rodrigo Torriani in *Cobra*, with friend and boxing coach Jack Dempsey, 1925 (Private collection)

Valentino costumed by Adrian in a publicity still for his uncompleted film *The Hooded Falcon*, 1925 (Courtesy of the Academy of Motion Picture Arts and Sciences)

(*below*) Valentino, Natacha Rambova, and Federico Beltrán-Masses in formal attire at the Ambassador Hotel, Los Angeles, 1925. Valentino's much-discussed platinum slave bracelet, a gift from Natacha, is visible at left. (Courtesy of the Academy of Motion Picture Arts and Sciences)

Federico Beltrán-Masses, Valentino costumed as Dubrovsky in *The Eagle*, and his manager, George Ullman, 1925, at Valentino's United Studios bungalow (Private collection)

Clarence Brown, Joseph Schenck, Valentino as Dubrovsky, and Douglas Fairbanks at United Studios, June 1925, during shooting of *The Eagle* (Wisconsin Center for Film and Theater Research)

Valentino with Mae Murray in Paris, January 1926 (Museum of Modern Art)

Valentino returning by ship from Europe after his second divorce, with Kabar, January 1926 (Museum of Modern Art)

Valentino with Vilma Banky, in a publicity still for *The Son of the Sheik*, 1926 (Private collection)

(*below*) Valentino with Vilma Banky as Yasmin, in *The Son of the Sheik*, United Artists, 1926 (Museum of Modern Art)

(*above*) Valentino in *The Son of the Sheik* torture scene, United Artists, 1926
(Private collection)

Valentino as the son of the Sheik, with director George Fitzmaurice, signing autographs, 1926
(Private collection)

Falcon Lair, 1926 (Bison Archives)

Best man Valentino, maid of honor Pola Negri, bride Mae Murray, and groom Prince David Mdivani, June 27, 1926 (Wisconsin Center for Film and Theater Research)

Crowd lining up outside the Million Dollar Theater, Los Angeles, for preview of *The Son of the Sheik*, July 1926 (Private collection)

Party group at the Santa Monica home of Constance Talmadge, May 1926. Top row, from left: Roscoe "Fatty" Arbuckle, Mae Murray, Ward Crane, Virginia Valli, Ronald Colman, Bessie Love, Jack Pickford, Rudolph Valentino, Pola Negri. Middle row: fourth from left, Lila Lee, between Louella Parsons and Carmel Myers; fourth from right, standing, in white cloche, Agnes Ayres; Richard Barthelmess, in white sweater, is just left of center, between Claire Windsor and Constance Talmadge, who stands next to Bea Lillie. Bottom row: left, squatting, Antonio Moreno; far right, Howard Hughes, next to Marshall Neilan and (seated) Blanche Sweet (Palm Springs Historical Society)

One of the last formal portraits of Valentino, the so-called trance portrait, by Bruno of Hollywood, 1926 (Courtesy of the Academy of Motion Picture Arts and Sciences)

Sheet-music cover, "We Will Meet At the End of the Trail," by Jean Acker, 1926 (Lilly Library, Indiana University)

Dime-store window display to commemorate the death of Valentino and advertise a recording of a song written in his memory, "There's a New Star in Heaven Tonight," 1926 (Museum of Modern Art)

Composite photo from the New York *Graphic*, August 25, 1926. Valentino is being welcomed into heaven. In the background, a film still shows an army of souls crossing the River Styx. (Private collection)

Castellaneta, Italy, 1961: local citizens celebrating the dedication of a ceramic sculpture of Valentino as the Sheik (Private collection)

Castellaneta, 1998: the birthplace of Rudolph Valentino (William Leider)

such adornment unique to him. In Paris circa 1912 a group of young male artists who worked for *La Gazette de Bon Ton* were called the Beau Brummells or Knights of the Bracelet because, in addition to wearing coats with pinched-in waists and broad-brimmed hats set at a tilt, they all sported bracelets on their wrists. A bracelet on a male in Paris signaled an artistic bent, and in Spain, South America, or southern Italy men of every stripe adorned themselves with jewelry to indicate both wealth and religious devotion. Gold chains, crosses on chains, rosary beads, and St. Christopher medals were and still are customary, and Italian male babies sometimes wore little religious medals or amulets pinned to their undershirts.

Other men in the world of Hollywood movies who favored wrist jewelry included Ramon Novarro, whose bracelet was silver, Rex Ingram, who sported a gold bracelet on his left wrist, and Rod La Rocque. "Maybe it's the fashion for men to wear jewelry," commented *Photoplay.* "If so, Rod La Rocque . . . is certainly à la mode. Rod is wearing one of these new-fangled chain bracelets, with a large clasp, a half-dozen rings and a variety of stick pins." Erich von Stroheim always wore a gold and enamel bit-chain bracelet and white gloves; he carried a walking stick, and "would as soon appear in public in his shirtsleeves as [go] without them," it was said.

But Valentino's bracelet drew the lion's share of comment, and many assumed that fad had originated with him. When a writer for a fan magazine claimed that Ramon Novarro had taken to wearing a bracelet in imitation of Valentino, a reader pointed out that both actors came from Latin cultures in which men routinely wore chain jewelry.

Valentino refused to abandon his slave bracelet, a love token he took to his grave. But the reddish beard that had caused almost as much comment had vanished, at least for the present, now that *The Hooded Falcon* had to be postponed yet again for script doctoring. While work continued in preparation for that epic, the Valentinos would divert their attention to *Cobra,* the contemporary story J. D. Williams had insisted could be filmed on the cheap, and in a hurry.

THE CRACK-UP

Cobra left most of those involved in its production dissatisfied. Natacha did some sketches for the costumes and stuck around for the first weeks of shooting, but then dropped out. "I was far too absorbed in work on the 'Falcon,'" she explained. "Besides, it was a modern story and modern stories always bored me to tears." The only part of the picture she liked was a sequence in which ancestors in a portrait gallery come to life dressed in costumes from the Renaissance. Before she lost interest, though, she squandered a wad of Ritz-Carlton money on a lavish supper-club set that required the illumination of 150 Klieg lights, spotlights, and Cooper Hewitt mercury-vapor lamps. She also clashed with Rudy's friend Mario Carillo, who played a bit part, and supposedly with other actors on the set as well.

Photographer Harry Fischbeck, who had come West on behalf of Ritz-Carlton Pictures after working behind the camera on *Monsieur Beaucaire* and *The Sainted Devil*, quit in the middle of shooting. At issue was his use of low-key lighting, which director Joseph Henabery thought he was overdoing after his success with it in the two previous films. When, after viewing rushes, Natacha backed Henabery, Fischbeck took off in a huff.

Dev Jennings, his replacement, avoided shooting Rudy's left side, to conceal his cauliflowered left ear. He remembered Valentino as a man very much in love with his wife, and very jealous of her; also as a man who lived to eat. "He had a great love of Italian cooking and loved garlic in his food," said Jennings. "He used to have Italian food in his dressing room at lunchtime. . . . Nita Naldi said she was going to chew garlic for revenge."

Joseph Henabery came down with pleurisy during shooting and directed with his chest strapped with tape. He complained about having to work on a mammoth, freezing indoor set, heated only by portable "salamander" stoves, with a cast that (with a few exceptions) had been assembled to act in *The Hooded Falcon* instead of the picture at hand. "None of the supporting players would have been my choice for the parts they played [in *Cobra*]," he admitted.

He balked at the silly plot as well. It revolved around the friendship between Rodrigo Torriani (Valentino) and Jack Dorning (Casson Ferguson), two young men who become partners in an antiques business and fall in love with the same woman, Jack's blonde goody-goody secretary Mary (Gertrude Olmstead). Both friends also fall prey to the same scheming, dark-haired vamp, Elise (Nita Naldi), who in time marries Jack for his money. She tries to seduce Rodrigo on the side and ends up punished for her sins, "burnt to a crisp in a hotel fire." In case we miss the symbolism, we're reminded that Elise represents the cobra of the title and Rodrigo her helpless victim. A close-up shows a bronze sculpture of the cobra mesmerizing a tiger, as the cobra morphs into a slinky human temptress. In the seduction scene Elise sheds her fur coat to reveal a black sheath adorned on one side with a huge dragon (hint, hint) embroidered in silver sequins. "I dare you to kiss me and then let me go," says Elise in a title. Tempted, Rodrigo goes to the hotel for an assignation, but once there he has second thoughts and leaves before anything truly compromising occurs. One of many flaws in the story is that Rod doesn't turn out to be entirely helpless before the mesmerizing cobra after all.

The two leading men are a study in contrasts. Jack Dorning is American, rich, scrawny, and shy around women. Valentino's character, Count Rodrigo Torriani, is an incorrigible skirt chaser possessing an impressive Italian pedigree; he has good looks, perfect manners, and an extensive wardrobe, but little ready cash. When we see him for the first time he's in his native Italy, seated alone at a café table, sipping wine, smoking, and flirting with a pretty woman at a nearby table. Impeccably turned out in a dark jacket, white flannel trousers, and two-tone shoes, he establishes a light, comic-opera tone, gently sending up his portrayer's image as a man who's catnip to women. Soon he's trying to elude the grasping father of one of his female conquests and is bailed out by his new pal, tourist Dorning. He follows Dorning to America after Dorning talks him into joining his antiques business and there makes a success of himself, working long hours at Dorning's showroom, and encouraging roommate Dorning to date attractive women. Dorning marries the fortune-hunting Elise, unaware until after she dies that she's been a faithless wife. At work the secretary, Mary, seems at last to be encouraging Rodrigo's tender attentions, but the blooming romance has no future. Putting loyalty to his male buddy above his own chance for romantic happiness, Rod (as he is called in America) forswears "the one pure, clean love he has ever known," so that Jack Dorning, a widower now, can wed Mary. The final shot shows Rodrigo on his way back to Italy, alone on the deck of a steamer, mournfully scattering into the sea the rose petals that symbolize his love for Mary. As a review pointed out, "Rudy escapes for perhaps the first time since he has been in pictures, without a wife. The only woman present in the final fadeout is the Statue of Liberty."

Martin Brown's play *Cobra*, based on an actual fire in a hotel frequented by illicit lovers, had starred Judith Anderson as a cobralike wife. It needed to be altered beyond recognition in order to work as a vehicle for Valentino, who here plays an Italian for the first time since his days as a supporting player of "heavies." Those who had seen the play scarcely recognized the screen adaptation. "The locale of the story has been changed so that it opens in Italy instead of the dormitory of an American college. And the leading woman is a majestic siren played by Nita Naldi instead of the lisping and grasping young flapper so strikingly portrayed on the stage by Judith Anderson." An earlier treatment of the script stuck closer to the original. Written by Rudy's old friend and early supporter James Young, it was tossed on the rubbish heap when Anthony Coldewey came on board as scenarist.

Rudy had a fight scene in this movie—his character answers with a knockout punch a rival's charge that he's an "indoor sheik"—and he went into training to improve his boxing skills. He would rise every morning at five, and after a dawn horseback ride or swim would get to the set by seven. There he would spar for two hours with a lightweight boxer, Gene Delmont, who had joined Rudy's staff. Jack Dempsey sometimes turned up to exchange gloved punches, and the two were photographed together lunching at the Brown Derby.

Although *Cobra* has some striking William Cameron Menzies sets and a few antic moments, it's a jumbled affair—part comedy, part melodrama—in which Valentino, upstaged by his wardrobe, delivers an uneven performance. Amused and amusing in the Italian sequence, touching as the lover who loses in the end, he sags in the middle, losing steam opposite Naldi's Elise. This was Naldi's third turn vamping Valentino, and it may be that the repetition had begun to tell on both of them. Instead of sizzling, they merely go through the motions of lovemaking. Nita Naldi told Dagmar Godowsky that she and Rudy "would scream with laughter through their purple scenes." They were having fun, but keeping on their emotional brakes. Gertrude Olmstead, who praised Valentino for his consideration and patience, plays her role as a total simp.

When the film was finally released after being shelved for several months, the ho-hum-ness of it all prompted critical swipes. "Valentino has many affairs but he's afraid to display his customary ardor," wrote the reviewer for *Motion Picture Magazine*. Another growled, "Valentino stalks through the action . . . quite disinterestedly, with only occasional bursts of emotion." In the scene in which Elise dares him to hold her in his arms, "one was never quite sure that he really wanted to." When the picture at last opened, patrons yawned. An exhibitor in the West reported, "This one killed Valentino for good as far as Kalispell, Montana is concerned. Absolutely terrible."

The hot male screen lover of the moment was no longer Rudolph Valentino, but John Gilbert, who had soared to major stardom in 1925 with two breakthrough roles in a row, Danilo in *The Merry Widow* and Jim, a World War I infantryman, in *The Big Parade*. "Not since Rudolph

Valentino flashed across the screen in *The Four Horsemen* has there been such a performance in a glowingly romantic role," wrote James Quirk of Gilbert's work in *The Merry Widow*. Although a survey by the British *Picturegoer* of its readers named Valentino the most popular screen star, in the States "his fame seems to be slipping from him and many of his former admirers are cheering for other favorites. He is facing an uncertain future and he knows it. His pedestal is an insecure one now, and no one knows it better than himself. Valentino appears today to be an earnest, troubled young man, frankly regretting his mistakes." At least this was the verdict of a writer for *Movie Weekly*.

Nothing seemed to be going right for the Valentinos since their return to Hollywood. June Mathis wouldn't speak to them. Joseph Henabery had pleurisy. *Cobra* sat on the shelf, not to be released for distribution by Paramount until after Valentino had made another, stronger picture. "The star realizes that his fame, at present, hangs precariously in the balance. If he comes back smashingly, in a role just suited to him, he will probably remain a reigning favorite. But another poor picture after *Sainted Devil* will be almost fatal to his future. And those who have seen *Cobra* are not enthusiastic," ran another truthful but wounding item in *Movie Weekly*.

Socially, they were keeping to themselves. Natacha disliked parties, so they rarely attended them. "We live a very simple and quiet life . . . here at home with our dogs and pictures," she told a reporter. "We rarely go out." Rudy's male friends seldom came by these days. They did not feel welcomed by Natacha, whose aloofness was read as snobbishness, and whose commanding manner was usually construed as interference. "I've been called everything from Messalina to a dope fiend," she told the nineteen-year-old Myrna Loy, who had tried out for the role of Mary in *Cobra* but failed the screen test.

Natacha, rather than J. D. Williams, George Ullman, or Rudy himself, got blamed for Valentino's recent decline in popularity. *Variety* ran a blind item touching on film colony talk about "the manner in which a cameraman [Fischbeck] resented the criticism of his work by a star's wife. . . . Reports have been current for some time that 'the Mrs.' has been running matters. It is said that when actors would appear ready for work the wife would approach them, scan their appearance and makeup carefully and then order them to make changes which she suggested." Myrna Loy recalled that Rudy, sweet, childlike, and eager to be liked, always agreed to everything, "expecting [Natacha] to get him out of it. His wife became the villain."

To counter the negative buzz, Rudy and Natacha began turning up more often at high-profile events like the premiere of the Marion Davies picture *Zander the Great*. They attended a dinner at the Cocoanut Grove held to welcome Gloria Swanson back to Hollywood from France with her new husband, the marquis de la Falaise de la Coudraye. They gave a party at the Sixty Club that was attended by Norma Shearer, Blanche Sweet, Mickey Neilan, and Allan Dwan, and another at their Whitley Heights home at which director Eddie Sutherland had to sit at a separate table all by himself, to avoid the risk of assembling an unlucky thirteen at the main table. Both Valentinos were highly superstitious.

Natacha remembered this as a time of forced sociability and artificial gaiety. "We danced, we gossiped, we giggled, we flirted, we drank," she recalled, "and succeeded in being exceedingly bored." They attended the fights at the American Legion on Friday nights and made expeditions to the Venice beach amusement pier, "where we ate hot dogs, rode on the merry-go-round and pretended we were having a hilarious time." They even invited a reporter to their home for a formal dinner. Jellied bouillon, lobster mousse with fish sauce, and broiled squab, prepared by the cook, Rose Klein, and deftly served by the very correct butler, Frederick, made up the menu on this stilted and joyless occasion. Italian cutwork doilies adorned the polished glass table. Red roses made the centerpiece, and orange candles in red-and-black holders "cast a glamorous light." Mrs. Valentino appeared "in an apple-green frock, a white satin turban wrapped around her glossy black hair." Was Rudy present? Presumably yes, since the article is called "Dinner with the Valentinos." But it devotes not one word to him, or to the conversation, if there was any.

Restless and dispirited, Rudy and Natacha decided to try changing their luck by altering their surroundings. They would move to a larger, grander house at the top of Benedict Canyon, overlooking the exclusive new neighborhood of choice for Hollywood's elite, Beverly Hills. Screenwriter Frances Marion and husband Fred Thomson, an expert horseman and actor in westerns, would be their nearest neighbors. Charlie Chaplin, Marion Davies, John Gilbert, Thomas Ince, and Douglas Fairbanks and Mary Pickford were already installed close by, and Buster Keaton and Harold Lloyd has begun building lavish spreads; Lloyd's would even have its own waterfall and golf course. The new residence, chosen by both Valentinos, was a two-level, sixteen-room Spanish-style villa at 2 Bella Drive, with stucco walls, a red-tile roof, hardwood and travertine floors, grand fireplaces, and wood-beamed ceilings. Purchased from a realtor, George F. Read, it had been built in 1923 on an eight-acre lot, which was large enough to accommodate stables for Rudy's horses, kennels for their many dogs, a multicar garage, and servants' quarters. The property adjoined some undeveloped acres that they also acquired, where they hoped one day to build tennis courts, install a swimming pool, and have a private airport. They spent $150,000 for the house and $25,000 more for the adjoining acres, having taken out a $100,000 loan to make it possible. Rudy himself would oversee the landscaping and the planting of the gardens.

They named the house Falcon Lair, in honor of *The Hooded Falcon* and six falcons that Rudy had imported from Europe. With the help of Lou Mahoney and a professional bird trainer, Rudy was teaching the dangerous predators, which had to wear man-made hoods to keep them from attacking, to settle on his arm. The falcons would be used in the film, which they still hoped to complete.

But *The Hooded Falcon,* like a desert mirage, kept receding further from sight as they approached it. Sets and costumes existed, and a cast had been assembled that included Sally Long, Dorothy Revier, Emily Fitzroy, Anthony d'Algy, Hector Sarno, and Gustav von Seyffertitz. The actors hung around, collecting their paychecks and awaiting orders to report to United Studios. Shooting was about to begin, they kept hearing, as postponement followed postponement. Now, as ongoing problems with the script resisted resolution, and the budget hemorrhaged, the choice of director became one more vexed question. Rudy and Natacha had selected Alan Hale, a large and likable

man better known as an actor (he played the German brother-in-law
Karl von Hartrott in *The Four Horsemen*) and an inventor (he patented
a theater chair that slides back) than as a director. J. D. Williams ve-
toed Hale, insisting that a costly costume epic required a far more experienced hand at the helm. When Williams suggested that the
underqualified Hale would never have been picked if not for Natacha,
Rudy took umbrage and walked out of the meeting, shouting, "Stop
right there. Don't you ever dare mention my wife again as long as you
live . . . [or] I'll give you the worst licking you ever had in your life.
You leave my wife's name out of our business disagreements, do you
understand?" Williams immediately announced that work on *The
Hooded Falcon* would again be postponed, and Rudy and Natacha took
off for Palm Springs. There they would be spared reading the *Variety*
headlines: "MRS. VALENTINO CAUSE OF BREAKUP WITH WILLIAMS;
WIFE'S INTERFERENCE RESENTED; ULTIMATUM BY PRODUCERS."

Palm Springs, with its "wind swept desert sands, great rocks and
giant palms bent into weird shapes," had often provided refuge. They
had an open invitation to stay at Dr. Florilla White's guest bungalow,
site of their interrupted post-Mexicali honeymoon, but were rarely
found indoors. They swam, camped, and went horseback riding on the
sandy trails, savoring the spectacular sunsets over the San Jacinto
Mountains and the solitude. In Palm Springs Valentino had first met
Paul Ivano; to Palm Springs he'd retreated after the opening of *The
Four Horsemen*, to reckon with his sudden fame. The desert mountains
now provided the backdrop for yet another pivotal scene. George Ullman telephoned to tell them that J. D. Williams was pulling the plug.
The Hooded Falcon, on which $150,000 had already been spent, would
be scuttled, and Valentino's contract with Ritz-Carlton was being terminated. The company, which had already begun cutting staff, would
completely disband, since without Valentino it had no further reason
to exist. Ullman says in his memoir that he wasn't sorry to see *The
Hooded Falcon* go under, and he apparently made no effort to salvage it.
He'd never had much enthusiasm for the prospect of Valentino portraying a Moor, convinced that the sight of him with a beard and dark-
ened skin would have dismayed many of his fans.

Natacha left Palm Springs immediately to consult with Ullman, who told her that a contract between Valentino and United Artists was in the works. Initially this pleased her, because she thought that finally Rudy would be given his due and that they would have the chance to work together on the kind of major productions they had always sought, projects like the Fairbanks pictures—*Robin Hood* or *The Thief of Bagdad*—which they considered exemplary for successfully combining art with commerce. She may even have believed *The Hooded Falcon* would be picked up by United Artists. She indicated her agreement and returned to Rudy in Palm Springs.

She soon learned that the deal Ullman had struck with producer Joseph Schenck of United Artists offered many of the requisites Rudy had long sought: he would be paid ten thousand dollars a week, make three pictures a year, and receive a percentage of profits. He could select his own costar. His name would receive "chief prominence" in advertising, and he would be promoted on the same basis as the other principals of United Artists, Mary Pickford, Douglas Fairbanks, Norma Talmadge, and Charlie Chaplin. There would be no block booking requiring theaters to show lesser films if they wanted the good ones, and no pressure to mass-produce Valentino films. But there was a major hitch. Mrs. Valentino was to be excluded. Natacha Rambova would no longer participate in the making of Rudolph Valentino's pictures or the shaping of his career. Instead of Natacha, Benjamin Glazer, a sometime attorney, playwright, scriptwriter, and translator on leave from MGM, would supervise Valentino's United Artists productions.

Rudy agonized over his decision, recognizing its consequences for Natacha. If he signed, she would be devastated. People like George Ullman believed that ambition on her own behalf had propelled her, but Natacha always insisted that for five years she had devoted herself wholly to advancing Rudy's career. Under the United Artists contract, her reward would be banishment.

In the end Rudy felt that he had no choice but to accept United Artists' terms. Everyone agreed that his career hung in the balance, that his next picture had to be a success, and that Natacha's unpopularity, combined with his record of quarreling with producers, had weakened his hand. He had no reason to suppose that he would ever receive a better offer. And unless he signed the contract, his loan of $100,000 for the new property would not be approved by the lender.

The press reminded Rudy of the precariousness of his position. "Valentino has been badly advised," James Quirk observed in *Photoplay* in response to the news that Valentino and J. D. Williams had parted company. "He has been swayed by absurd and silly influences. He was a screen sensation rather than an established success." An accompanying cartoon showed throngs rushing to see movies starring Ramon Novarro and Tony Moreno as Rudy and Natacha stand off by themselves, on a pedestal, with a single grizzled fan cheering them on. Rudy, in spats and tails, exclaims, "I'm for art!" The turbaned Natacha shouts, "Down with the producers!" *Movie Weekly* compared the fight with Williams to the earlier dispute with Zukor and Lasky, and rushed to judgment. "With no wish to be unkind, we remind Rudy that no one in the world has ever been so great that they are supreme."

In an attempt to mollify Natacha, Ullman threw her a bone: he would put up $30,000 to help finance a film she could write and supervise herself. The film, which received only limited, delayed distribution, ended up costing $100,000, and eventually was lost, was a satire of the beauty industry called *What Price Beauty?* It starred Nita Naldi as a vamp who competes with a country girl for the affection of a handsome beauty parlor manager. The cameraman was Dev Jennings, who'd replaced Harry Fischbeck on *Cobra*; Adrian designed the costumes. Alan Hale was announced as director, but for unknown reasons he didn't complete the job and Thomas Buckingham, usually a director of comedies, took over for him. This film's claim to fame is that, in a futuristic dream sequence, it introduced a slinky, sloe-eyed young dancer in a small but eye-catching role: Myrna Loy, clad in red velvet pajamas, representing "the intellectual type." *Motion Picture Magazine* called her "piquant, elfin, boyish, lithe, vivacious, the essence of grace." Mrs. Valentino heralded her as "the 1926 flapper model."

As Natacha began work on her own picture, she withdrew from Rudy and their marriage. "When she ceased to collaborate," Ullman reports, "she also failed to cooperate with him in more ways than one.

Valentino could not fail to detect her failing interest and to feel a profound hurt. Her fancy was straying into other paths." She told Lou Mahoney that she was having a power boat built, and planned to go off to an island somewhere "and do things that I know I am capable of doing." She hardly ever stayed home, and refused to participate in overseeing the renovations and improvements at Falcon Lair, making it clear she had no plans to move in. Her one contribution to the new residence was to design a steel pennant with a stylized "V" to adorn the center roof tower.

Although Natacha accompanied him to a United Artists dinner at the Biltmore Hotel, she took no particular notice of Rudy's thirtieth birthday a few days later. She went off to work, and he remained at home, dressed in blue overalls and soiled tennis shoes, tinkering with his cars. (He'd recently acquired a black Isotta Fraschini town car, adorned on the hood with a silver cobra, his emblem.) When Natacha got home, they dined in, joined only by George Ullman.

While he awaited finalization of his new contract, Rudy languished, uneasy that Natacha, not he, departed for the studio at dawn and returned home late and exhausted. Without a clear purpose, he busied himself overhauling his cars or poring over plans for Falcon Lair. Playing house husband at this juncture proved difficult. His sense of masculine command eroded. He felt abandoned, adrift, solitary. He missed having family around him, and he increasingly resented Natacha's immersion in her own career activities outside the home. When he and Natacha were together, they fought. "In the canyon where they lived neighbors often heard quarreling at night."

An issue in the marriage that had smoldered for a long time now flamed into prominence: he wanted children and Natacha didn't. Natacha reminded him that if he'd counted on babies he should have married someone else. She didn't believe in having children and then turning them over to nursemaids. She's always worked, and never pretended to qualify as a domestic angel. He knew that. She attacked his male egotism and his European belief that in a marriage the wife should serve the husband. "In Europe boys are taught to consider themselves much more important than girls," she would tell a reporter. "Those boys expect a wife to be subordinate. Marvelous love-making, romance, passion, poetry, and adoration may precede the marriage. But what a foreign husband must have in a wife is this: she must minister to his wants." And she must furnish an heir. Rudy especially "wanted a boy, a *son*. That was a secret annoyance to me. European men are male worshippers. They want a male child as a mirror of their own magnificent masculinity. Then, he wanted this son to be brought up abroad and sent to an Italian military school. I couldn't bear that."

Nita Naldi, so recently on the warmest terms with Natacha, turned against her, siding with Rudy. She circulated the information that she had accompanied Natacha to one abortion and that Natacha had terminated two other pregnancies during her marriage to Rudy. Natacha herself once said, in the 1950s, "I always told my mother that I would see to it that I would never have any children." We have no way of verifying the alleged abortions, but Natacha's determination not to become a mother seems authentic and ironclad. As the marriage faltered, to Rudy it came to represent all other points of contention.

In her present mood she wanted to prove more than that she could flourish independent of Rudy; she seemed to be mocking him. As Natacha put it, "Here was an inversion of domestic roles indeed! Madame Wage Earner off to business bright and early every morning and Monsieur at home all day, perhaps to arbitrate some domestic dispute below stairs. A man might as well don an apron and be done with it." Natacha knew Rudy well enough to be aware how best to injure him. According to one source, she taunted him in front of his United Artists associates at a dinner, making a comparison between Spanish lovers who are "real men," and Italian "gigolos who only know how to make love with their eyes, on film. In life their prowess extends no further than the edge of the bed." Stung, Rudy supposedly countered, "If you have a complaint about me, Natacha, don't include all Italians. They are not responsible for my unhappiness in loving you." This dialogue, reported at thirdhand long after it occurred, may be nothing more than hearsay. But Natacha's willingness to inflict pain was real. She disappeared to parts unknown for several days once her film was completed, refusing to continue the charade of togetherness. Their sex life surely must have reflected their estrangement in all other departments, offering more anguish than pleasure. Rudy may well have become impotent, in which case Natacha may have turned his failure in bed into one more sign of her superior mettle.

Natacha took a lover, a camera technician (Jennings?) who worked on *What Price Beauty?*, and she would retreat with him into the darkroom for hours at a time. "We generally rush for some anaesthetic to deaden our misery," she would explain in her memoir, and her drug of choice was sex. The affair didn't last, but at the time she justified it to herself as necessary. Her lover, she told Lou Mahoney, "was the only one that seemed to understand my problems." Suspicious, George Ullman took it upon himself to hire private detectives, who tailed her day and night for several weeks. When Rudy found out about the detectives, he turned on Ullman for having acted on his own. "I know nothing of detectives," Rudy told a reporter who got wind of this development, "and as for Mr. Ullman, what interest could he possibly have in the matter?" But the evidence of Natacha's infidelity seemed conclusive, and it sent Rudy reeling. The role of cuckold, ancient butt of crude jests, was humiliation itself. "To be labeled a cuckold was one of the strongest insults in the southern Italian vocabulary," one historian has stated—and an insult particularly stinging to a man deeply in love with his wife and celebrated all over the world as the Great Lover. He grabbed a gun and threatened to kill Natacha's lover. Ullman seized the weapon and tried to calm him down.

A double standard operated here. If Rudy truly had an affair with André Daven, he seems to have forgotten about it, or at least to be applying a set of rules that absolved the straying partner of guilt if the cheating happened with a lover of the same sex. "She had a right to expect me to have no affairs with women," Rudy would comment after they separated, "but not to alienate me from my men friends." Of course, it's also possible that they were better equipped to handle the amorous intrusions of others when their relationship was on sturdier ground. Natacha's rebellion went beyond mere infidelity, however. The issue was rejection. Rudy felt spurned, and questioned whether his wife had ever really loved him. "Women do not fall in love with

me," he would lament. "I fall in love with them. I do not think one
woman in my life has ever loved me sincerely, deeply. I think it is because I make the mistake of falling so deeply in love with them. In
every love union there is one who loves more than the other. . . . In
my romances—that one has been I. When I have heard myself referred
to as a 'great lover' I have often thought to myself, 'The great lover—
loved by all, but his loves.'"

Alone in Palm Springs Rudy was discovered by the locals wandering in the desert at night. "We dunno what's the matter with that guy,"
one observer remarked. "We thought he must have a [gold]mine
staked out, but all he does is look at the stars."

Aunt Teresa, who'd move to Los Angeles to live nearby in her own
home on Sycamore Street, tried her best to negotiate marital peace.
"Not a day passed in which she was not in the house in Whitley
Heights," said Ullman. To each of the warring contenders she offered
a sympathetic ear and a shoulder to cry on. She succeeded in winning
some temporary truces, and the loving gratitude of both parties.

Another who tried to mediate was Rudy's friend the Spanish portrait painter Federico Beltrán-Masses, who was staying with Rudy and
Natacha. "I loved them both equally," Beltrán-Masses recalled, "and
their disaccord pained me greatly. I urged them to be patient." According to him, Rudy thought with his heart and Natacha with her
head. Rudy first met the painter in 1924 in New York, where Beltrán-
Masses had an exhibit of large canvases at the Wildenstein Gallery.
Beltrán-Masses was a painter of the old school, on whom modernism
had left no mark. Known both for his sensuous nudes and as a "court
painter," he had done portraits of the king of Spain and others in his
court. Intrigued by the prospect of being immortalized like a royal,
Rudy invited Beltrán-Masses to be his guest in Hollywood specifically
because he wanted the Spaniard to paint him. Beltrán-Masses made
several canvases of each of the Valentinos, showing Rudy as a gaucho
and as a Moor in full armor, and Natacha in Spanish costume and in *La
Gitana* as a reclining, nearly naked Gypsy. The latter would hang above
Rudy's bed in Falcon Lair; he later took painting lessons from Beltrán-
Masses and copied it several times.

Rudy had assured Beltrán-Masses that once in Hollywood he would be able to get commissions from other stars, and he helped to arrange for Marion Davies to sit for him. When the Marion Davies portrait was ready to show, Davies and Rudy decided to host an exhibition and reception for Beltrán-Masses at the Ambassador Hotel. Natacha almost sabotaged the glittering event, which was attended by the elite of Hollywood, including Charlie Chaplin, Mary Pickford and Douglas Fairbanks, Bebe Daniels, the Talmadge sisters, the Tom Mixes, Colleen Moore, Richard Barthelmess, Irving Thalberg, John Gilbert, Mae Murray, Dorothy Gish, Harold Lloyd, Barbara La Marr, and Gloria Swanson. When the night of the reception arrived, Natacha refused to dress, and Rudy waited for her with mounting alarm. Finally she agreed to get ready, and they arrived, late and tense. Natacha, in a jeweled turban, a striking Poiret ensemble, and clanking bracelets, made a queenly entrance, sweeping by "with a faint, fixed smile, or a slight inclination of her head. Poor Rudy trailed behind, trying to be friendly and natural." When dinner still had not been served by ten-thirty, one influential guest, the writer Adela Rogers St. Johns, decided she'd had enough and bolted.

Rudy's embarrassment at the late entrance and dinner fiasco was all the greater because on this night, in addition to honoring the paintings of Beltrán-Masses, he was to confer a gold "Rudolph Valentino Medal" on John Barrymore, in recognition of his performance in *Beau Brummell* as the best by a film actor or actress in the preceding year. Two years before the Academy Awards were instituted, Rudy had come up with the idea of conferring an annual screen-acting award, as a way of fostering interest in the cinematic arts. Rupert Hughes and film magazine editor Rob Wagner helped him determine the winner, who was chosen by polling seventy-five critics for newspapers, fan magazines, and trade papers. Every actor except Valentino was eligible. As it turned out, the Rudolph Valentino Medal for screen acting would be conferred only this once.

As his marriage disintegrated, Valentino awaited word on when his first picture for United Artists would begin production. His new boss,

Joseph Schenck, a wily, Russian-born old-timer whose wife, Norma Talmadge, called him Daddy, initially announced that he would star Valentino as a Spanish bandit in a story of early California called *The Bronze Collar*, to be directed by Clarence Brown. Then *Variety* reported that another film had been substituted. "Clarence Brown feels *The Bronze Collar* is not a big enough story for the star."

The selection of Clarence Brown as director immediately lent prestige and promise to Valentino's first United Artists undertaking. Later known as Garbo's favorite director and still later as the director of celebrated talkies such as *Intruder in the Dust*, *National Velvet*, and *The Yearling*, Brown was a former automobile engineer who had served as assistant to the director Maurice Tourneur. An expert on lighting with an instinct for pacing and a naturalistic style, he had scored critical successes with *Smouldering Fires* (1924), starring Pauline Frederick, and *The Goose Woman* (1925), which turned Louise Dresser, a veteran of Broadway musicals, into a screen star. Mindful of the backlash against frippery in *Monsieur Beaucaire*, Brown set out to find a "virile" role for Valentino, something "that will appeal to men moviegoers as well as women."

Rudy knew how important it was to find the right director. His disappointment at being denied George Fitzmaurice to direct *Blood and Sand* had been a sticking point in his battle with Famous Players—Lasky, and Philip Rosen's unsatisfactory command of *The Young Rajah* had fueled his discontent. Asked to comment on some of the high-profile directors of the mid-twenties, Rudy extolled the skill of Erich von Stroheim, saying he'd like nothing better than to be directed by him, "given the proper story." He praised Ernst Lubitsch, but said, "I doubt if my style would appeal to him." As it happens, a writer who'd often collaborated with Lubitsch, Hans Kraly, was hired to create the witty script that Clarence Brown was about to direct. Brown sat in on the writing, claiming that was his way of getting to know his characters.

Valentino and Clarence Brown fell right into step, sharing a love of technology and compatible senses of humor. "[Brown] never wastes any time on comedy that isn't genuinely funny and to the point of the story," said Rudy, who commented when filming was done that he wished he could stay on to make future movies with Clarence Brown and that he wanted to do more comedy. He hailed Brown as a great director, one who "directs like the leader of an orchestra—not so much by words as by tone." For his part, Brown would retrospectively link Valentino with Garbo as the silent screen's great immortals. "Garbo and Valentino are the two who are going down through posterity."

The story finally chosen, based on "Dubrovsky," an unfinished novelette by Pushkin, went through several title changes. First it was to be called *The Untamed,* then *The Black Eagle*. Since that sounded too close to Fairbanks's work in progress, *The Black Pirate,* the title was changed to *The Lone Eagle,* and finally shortened to the one that stuck, *The Eagle*.

Pushkin had less impact on the picture than Douglas Fairbanks, Valentino's model in this film. Since his sensational success with *The Mark of Zorro* in 1920, Fairbanks had continued to enchant the public with shows of his athletic prowess in movies that combined swashbuckling adventure and irreverent humor with period costumes and picturesque settings. Hans Kraly's script for *The Eagle* borrows *Zorro*'s black mask, physical daring, and the theme of dual identity. Only *The Eagle* goes one better, giving the hero not just two but three personas: the Cossack lieutenant Vladimir Dubrovsky of the Imperial Guards, the masked Tartar bandit Black Eagle, and the French tutor Marcel Le Blanc in top hat and waistcoat. *Robin Hood*–like, the masked Dubrovsky steals from a rich marauder to give back to a peasant woman money that was rightfully hers. But unlike a Fairbanks hero, Dubrovsky puts love before justice or revenge, before everything.

Kraly's script and Brown's direction gave Valentino another chance to poke fun at his own screen image. He couldn't have played Dubrovsky this way early in his career because audiences were supposed to catch the references to his previous roles. Again he's an exotic in a foreign setting, but this time he plays a Slav, not a Latin, and the stylized William Cameron Menzies sets aren't allowed to steal his thunder. Again he lifts a blonde beauty onto his saddle, but this time it's a rescue, not a kidnapping. Again he dances with a lady love, but for a change, the dance is a mazurka. Once more two women vie for his affections, but the rival for once is an amorous czarina, Catherine the Great (Louise Dresser), not a vamp, and because she's older and much too aggressive she holds no allure. As usual he gives his costume designer (Adrian) plenty to do, but here he's no mere manikin, he's an action hero in perpetual motion, chasing runaway horses, fleeing through a window, or battling a menacing bear. The old formulas have acquired new ingredients and there's a fresh point of view.

As Dubrovsky, Valentino flirts with death (the spurned czarina puts a price on his head) and has his share of smoldering love scenes, but he also has a chance to kid around. His ring gets stuck on his finger when he tries to bestow it as a token of devotion that he pretends had been entrusted to him by the Black Eagle. Distracted by the young beauty sitting beside him at a banquet, he puts too much pepper in his soup and gasps when he tastes it. When Catherine the Great tries to sneak in a cuddle, he wipes off her kiss the moment her back is turned. He appears to be strangling the crude villain, Kyrilla, but really he's only administering a neck massage. But when he massages the neck of Kyrilla's lovely daughter, Mascha, his movements turn sensuous and Mascha's face registers ecstasy.

Choosing Vilma Banky to play the romantic Mascha was a stroke of casting genius. She and Valentino had real chemistry. A graceful and ethereal blonde, with high cheekbones, expressive eyes, and very little English, the Hungarian-born Banky had been appearing in Germany, in productions of the giant UFA film combine, when Samuel Goldwyn spotted her and brought her to the States in 1924 to play opposite Ronald Colman in *The Dark Angel*. Joseph Schenck saw rushes of *The Dark Angel* and decided on the spot that he simply had to borrow her from Goldwyn, with whom she'd signed a five-year contract, to play opposite Valentino in *The Eagle*. Valentino, whose contract guaranteed him veto-power, gave his ringing approval. Supposedly he'd seen her on horseback, cantering in the Hollywood hills.

Once shooting began in July it had to proceed quickly. The idea was to release *The Eagle* in late fall, so that it could preempt and overshadow *Cobra*, which Paramount planned to distribute in early December.

Considering the level of tumult in his emotional life, Valentino's ability to concentrate and give his all to the role of Dubrovsky might seem surprising. But after five months away from a set, he welcomed the release acting gave him and the structure a tight shooting schedule provided. "Charlie Chaplin once told me," he revealed, "that his best work was done while under great personal strain. With me it is the same." What a relief to be able to become someone else, and what a pleasure finally to be working under ideal conditions, with a top-rate costar and support team, good pay, and luxurious surroundings. Off camera, he could relax in his studio bungalow, a six-room house decorated with mounted swords and spears. It had its own kitchen and did double duty as dressing room and office. Beltrán-Masses sometimes joined him for lunch at the bungalow, where he gave Rudy painting lessons.

About four weeks after shooting began on *The Eagle*, Natacha announced that she and Rudy had decided to take a "marital vacation." Accompanied by her aunt and George Ullman, she had boarded a train bound for New York, via Chicago. Rudy saw her off. The farewell became another staged event, recorded by a pack of reporters and photographers and witnessed by a crowd of curious fans. As usual, both Valentinos appeared perfectly turned out, each in cool summer attire and a hat, their emotions masked with smiles. They kissed good-bye affectionately, as if they expected to be together again by the next weekend. As the train started to move, "Rudy clung to the steps of the observation car as long as he dared and then ran along the platform" as she drifted out of sight. He must have sensed the finality of their separation.

Natacha announced the split soon after her arrival in New York; it caught Rudy off guard. When she left, he said, he thought they had agreed not to make their troubles public for a while. "Mrs. Valentino and I are the best of friends," he told a reporter. "Owing to temperamental differences, we decided to separate for a while. It is impossible for me to tell what the future will bring forth. For Mrs. Valentino I have the greatest respect and admiration. We have been happy together, and we may be again. I am sorry this had to happen, but we cannot always order our lives as we would like to have them." The talk of possible reconciliation contradicted his revelation that a property settlement had already been made. Before she left, Natacha signed a quit-claim, whereby she turned over the Falcon Lair acreage to Rudolph Guglielmi. A few days later, Valentino filed articles of incorporation for his own company, Rudolph Valentino Productions, listing himself, George Ullman, and Ullman's wife, Beatrice, as the three incorporators. Economically, the Valentinos had already parted ways.

Natacha tried to emphasize that the separation had been amicable. She said that she and Rudy remained in close touch, by phone and letter. "Rudy and I have had no big quarrel," she told Louella Parsons. "We have not been getting along very well for some time, principally because he wanted me to give up my career, but I cannot say anything unkind about him. . . . He is a dear boy, charming and delightful, but I think we need a vacation from each other." An undercurrent of anger surfaced when, during a meeting with reporters at the Park Avenue apartment she and Rudy had leased together, she broached the subject of her career, and Rudy's demand that she give it up. "With butlers, maids and the rest, what work is there for a housewife? I won't be a parasite. I won't sit home and twiddle my fingers, waiting for a husband who goes on the lot at five a.m. and gets home at midnight and receives mail from girls in Oshkosh and Kalamazoo."

Rudy tried to gain the upper hand by issuing an ultimatum: "Mrs. Valentino cannot have a career and be my wife at the same time," he threatened. Later he would modify his stance, claiming he did not object to her having a career, so long as it was "her own career." But he disliked being managed by a wife whose manner alienated so many colleagues.

Within days of Natasha's departure, Hollywood buzzed with the news that Rudy's leading lady, Vilma Banky, was helping him forget his troubles. He had escorted her to the preview in Venice, California, of her debut American movie, *The Dark Angel*. A young secretary of Samuel Goldwyn, Valeria Belletti, couldn't wait to share the gossip with her best friend, Irma, back East. "Last night," she wrote in a letter, "Valentino took Vilma to the preview. Everybody was astonished at this. After the preview . . . we went home and we rode behind Valentino's car—and Vilma was with him. This morning, the whole studio was talking about it and the papers carried a big story. . . . Mr. Goldwyn asked me to get Vilma to come over to see him. I located her in Valentino's bungalow! . . . I heard Goldwyn tell her that she must not do anything that will in any way ruin her reputation. When she came out, she gave me a wicked wink."

Vilma and Rudy danced together at the Cocoanut Grove, and on consecutive Sundays he lay at her feet in the sand at the beach. This was no love affair, however. "I know their relations are not at all intimate— they are just friends," wrote the young secretary who'd seen them together. Vilma offered the heartbroken Rudy her extremely pretty shoulder to cry on. She was new in town, quite friendless, and very willing to be sought out by her handsome and famous leading man. As Valeria Belletti, the young secretary, put it, "Valentino is a very quiet sort of chap, very dignified, polite and ultra refined. He doesn't mingle with the usual Hollywood crowd and doesn't go in for wild parties at all. Vilma is the same type—therefore they enjoy each other's company a great deal."

Vilma joined him when he sought advice from a crystal-ball-gazing Santa Monica seer, Dareos, who told a reporter that Valentino had come to him in a confused state, confessing his undying love for Mrs. Valentino and begging for a glimpse into the future. Dareos foretold that the separated couple would never be reconciled, that Mrs. Valentino would refuse to give up her career in favor of home and children. "I told him he was born to have many romances and that he should never get married." Informed that Dareos had leaked all this to the press, Rudy admitted he had consulted the seer, but said the prediction was all wrong, that a reconciliation between him and Natacha was eminently possible.

When Natacha announced her plans to go to Paris to establish residence in order to seek a divorce, hopes for reconciliation vanished. Rudy said he would honor his wife's wishes, but he was clearly distraught. When driving he became ever more reckless and accident-prone than usual. First he was arrested for speeding on Santa Monica Boulevard; appearing in court costumed as the Cossack Dubrovsky, he pleaded feebly that the speedometer on his French car registered speed only in kilometers and that he didn't know how fast he had been going in miles, since he was "not much of a mathematician." Then, a few days after the speeding incident, he fell, wrenching his right wrist and getting kicked by a horse, during shooting of the opening scenes of *The Eagle* near Lankershim, in the San Fernando Valley. A publicist explained that Clarence Brown had suggested, to no avail, that a stunt double rather than Rudy himself risk the tricky maneuver, which required him to make a flying leap from his own mount to a runaway horse and bring the offending animal to a stop. "The horse was simply traveling too fast for Rudy to catch hold of his bridle securely," reported the *Los Angeles Times*.

Rudy confided to Beltrán-Masses that he would rather die young than grow old. "I would like to disappear at the height of my powers, in an accident," he said. "I find nothing more stupid than to die of a disease." On September 1, 1925, he wrote a new will, leaving only one dollar to Natacha and dividing the rest of his estate among his siblings, Alberto and Maria, and Natacha's aunt, Teresa Werner. His secretary, Margaret Neff, typed a page of additional instructions, directing George Ullman to "perpetuate my name in the picture industry by continuing Rudolph Valentino Productions until Jean Valentino shall have reached twenty-five." The day he rewrote his will, according to Beltrán-Masses, Rudy tried to kill himself. "I found him with a Browning [automatic pistol] in his hand, having written his last will, and ready to make the fatal gesture. I wrested it from his hand and threw it in a drawer, crying, 'That's idiotic.' Rudolph threw himself into my arms weeping."

Rudy recovered his equilibrium enough to be able to continue working and to make the move into Falcon Lair. He soon began going out again, seeing old friends and forming new attachments. But the break from Natacha left a wound that never fully healed. "Materialists see love as a chemical reaction," he would say, "but spiritualists, of whom I am one, see it as the irresistible attraction of two souls." In his eyes Natacha would remain bound to him as his soul mate, for eternity.

Natacha did her share of suffering, too. Reporters who tracked her in Paris found her "pale, upset and nervous when Rudolph's name was mentioned, snapping angry answers while she clenched her palms." Asked whether she still loved the man she would soon divorce, she stonewalled, saying, "that is a question I cannot answer." Her tear-stained last letter to Rudy, addressed to "Rudy darling," offered a less guarded reply. "You were my first real love and you will be my last one," she wrote. "With my arms around you, I give you my last kiss."

18

TANGO NOTTURNO

*T*he Eagle scored only moderately at the box office, winning "a decision but no knock-out," but it did succeed in pleasing critics and helped put Rudolph Valentino back in the running as a top contender. "Rudy is doing considerable of a comeback with this picture and if Joe Schenck can follow it with another as good, the chances are that he will have this star on the road to popularity," said *Variety.* "It is a dandy," reported a theater manager who had screened *The Eagle* in Proctor, Minnesota. "The best Rudolph Valentino picture I have seen since *The Four Horsemen.* It pleased the men besides the women." The part about pleasing men seems on the mark. The week following the New York premiere, of the five thousand-plus fan letters Rudy received, more than half were from men.

Rudy himself believed he had done some of his finest work in *The Eagle,* which he described as "the first film in which I have played which has really been of my own choosing." Because he wanted to help it succeed he decided to attend the New York premiere at the Strand Theater, "to study the audience reaction and also to see the film with the musical score which has been arranged by Louis Gottschalk." He planned to go on to Europe to attend the London premiere, and to connect there with Alberto and his family. Since he expected Natacha's Paris divorce action to take place during this trip, calling him to Paris, he was going to need his brother's support.

In early November of 1925 he entrained for New York.

His *Eagle* leading lady, Vilma Banky, didn't join him in Gotham for the premiere because Samuel Goldwyn, fearing scandal, wouldn't permit her to make the trip. He directed his secretary to advise Joseph Schenck "that in view of the relations between Mr. and Mrs. Valentino and the fact that Vilma is quite friendly with Valentino, it wouldn't be good policy to have Vilma in New York when Valentino is there, too."

En route to the Strand Theater premiere with United Artists publicist Beulah Livingstone, Rudy handed out through the car window brass coins minted for the occasion; they looked like rubles, with an eagle embossed on one side and on the other a likeness of Valentino as a Cossack. At the theater they found a crowd of thousands clamoring to get in, despite drenching rain. Those who made it inside saw an opening stage show featuring an orchestra performing Tchaikovsky's "1812 Overture," and folk dances executed by costumed maidens in a simulated Russian country garden, to the accompaniment of balalaika music. After the screening, Rudy stepped on stage to make a short speech, saying that he hoped quality films like *The Eagle* would win him back friends that had slipped away when he made inferior movies. He and Livingstone then headed downtown, accompanied by an escort of motorcycle police, for a spaghetti dinner in Little Italy, causing a traffic tie-up from Mulberry Street to Mott Street. In front of the Pearl Street restaurant his car was mobbed. "It was impossible for Rudy to comply with all the demands for autographs, so he solved the problem by shouting, 'Women and children first!'"

Natacha, too, returned briefly to New York, with forty trunks in tow, to act opposite Clive Brook in a movie tentatively titled *Do Clothes Make the Woman?*, an adaptation of a novel by Laura Jean Libbey in which she would star as an actress who gives up her stage career to help her inventor husband. "A powerful and heart-stirring story of a woman's supreme devotion and sacrifice for a man who paid the penalty of 'forgetting' when success came to him," or so the publicity for her sole screen performance promised; but although she looked stunning in front of the cameras, Natacha's acting was self-conscious. Her producer said, tactfully, "Natacha Rambova belongs definitely to the new school of screen artists who repress rather than express their deepest emotions." The brief surviving footage of the film, which would ultimately be released (to Natacha's horror) with the title *When Love Grows Cold*, shows her saying good-bye to her sleeping son; in light of the much-publicized conflict between Rudy and Natacha about her rejection of real-life motherhood, it's a scene full of resonance. Because of the title choice and advertising that exploited the film's echoes of her off-screen life, the film did reasonably well, but Natacha was so angry she washed her hands of moving pictures for all time.

Rudy and Natacha did not meet in New York. Their Park Avenue apartment sat vacant, as Natacha had rented another place at 9 West Eighty-first Street and Rudy was staying at the Ritz-Carlton Hotel. "If he wants to see me he can call me up," Natacha told reporters, before she began work on her film. "And you can say I am going on with my work. . . . In a day or so I shall begin work on a moving picture for which I have signed a contract to act." Rudy did see his mother-in-law, Mrs. Hudnut, and learned from her that a Paris divorce decree would be granted if Rudy came to France. According to French law, both parties had to be at hand if a divorce action was to be completed. Natacha's mother had hoped for a reconciliation between "these over-tired and temperamental children," but sadly conceded defeat: "they were both too proud, too hasty and impetuous."

Rudy told Mrs. Hudnut he would expedite his wife's wishes by going to Paris. "As I understand it, all I have to do is to establish a domicile in France, which I will do. . . . There is no plan on my part to consider marriage to anyone else. The time will come, probably, but it is far off. When that time comes, I shall choose a wife whose tastes are thoroughly domestic and who is inclined to have children." With this statement he vented his frustration with Natacha and made public the desires he *wanted* to have, not those he already did have: when it came to selecting a mate Rudy had never in his life sought out a domestic-minded woman. At other moments he swore off any future marriage altogether, pointing out that female fans prefer single actors. "A married actor is never so romantic."

Before leaving New York Rudy took one decisive step he had been putting off for years: he went to the Federal Building to apply for United

States citizenship, bringing along as his sponsor William J. Burns, former chief of the United States Secret Service and founder of the famous Burns Detective Agency. He had not acted earlier to become naturalized primarily because he feared complications and negative publicity about his failure to serve in the military during the Great War. To qualify as a citizen he needed to prove to the American authorities that he had a clean military record, but he had learned that his record bore a stain. In Taranto he had been listed as a slacker, an evader of military service. Someone in Italy intervened to correct the error, attesting that Valentino had tried to enlist when Italy entered the war but had been rejected because of defective vision in his left eye. Producing a certificate showing his honorable release from Italian military duties, Valentino also truthfully stated that during the war, after being rejected by Italy, he'd tried to enlist in the Canadian or American armed forces, but had been turned down for the same physical defect.

As he resolved one problem with Italian officials, he created another one even more thorny. The preliminary citizenship papers for the United States required the applicant to take an oath renouncing forever all allegiance and fidelity to any foreign prince, potentate, or state, including Victor Emanuel III, king of Italy. In Mussolini's ultranationalistic Italy this had dire repercussions. When word got out in Italy of Valentino's initial application, he was denounced as a turncoat. In Rome, placards went up calling him a traitor, and warning that bombs would go off if he dared enter the country. A boycott of his films was organized and in Bergamo a demonstration broke out at a theater during a screening of *Monsieur Beaucaire*. A pamphlet published in Milan charged, "If there were a war tomorrow Valentino would remain peacefully in his new country, where he would continue to play pretty boys, dandies, while our poor soldiers endure the trenches." Profoundly distressed by this turn of events, Valentino canceled his plans to visit Italy while in Europe. He wrote a letter to Mussolini explaining that economic and career considerations had motivated his decision to change citizenship, not a lack of love for his native land. He later demonstrated his goodwill by visiting the Italian embassy in Washington, D.C., and posing for a photograph with the Italian am-

bassador and other consulate dignitaries. Mussolini responded by calling up Fascist militia detachments in Rome to halt the anti-Valentino
boycott. Either because he wanted to avoid further agitation against
him in Italy, or because he simply never got around to it, Valentino did
not follow through on his application for U.S. citizenship. He never
took the final oath. He died an Italian subject.

As he disembarked from the *Leviathan* in Southampton, reporters
questioned Rudy about his breakup with Natacha. He confirmed that
a divorce was only weeks away, but said, "Up to the hour I sailed for
Europe I would have welcomed [Natacha] with open arms if she had
given up her idea of a career." He repeated that what he had wanted
from marriage was a wife, not a business partner, and went on to be-
rate Natacha for isolating him from others, especially his men friends.
"I woke up from my dream of love finally to find myself lost from my
friends," in particular those down-at-the-heels types (such as Douglas
Gerrard) who had failed to make successes of themselves. "I expect
now to lead a new life, absolutely free, but you never can tell. Love is
such a fever, it is liable to catch you at any time."

Rudy was far from being emotionally free. One of his best friends
in Hollywood, the Mexican diplomat Manuel Reachi, current husband
of the very pregnant Agnes Ayres, had sailed to Europe with him and
would later travel with him on the continent. Reachi said of Rudy,
"The boy is mad. He thinks only of Natacha. For two days on the boat
he talked of nothing but her."

The London premiere of *The Eagle* at the Marble Arch Pavilion
found Valentino once again besieged by fans, who blocked the theater
entrance and overturned advertisement boards. After the screening,
he was forced to escape via a cellar staircase under the stage. Lady
Curzon attended, but she could not keep her promise to Rudy that she
would be joined by members of the royal family. The queen mother,
Alexandra, had just died and during the mourning period the family
decided to cancel all public appearances.

Rudy lingered only a few days in London but would return to

spend Christmas there with Alberto, Ada, his nephew, Jean, and his sister, Maria. The Hudnuts had written to invite him to Juan-les-Pins for Christmas, but Rudy decided that would be too painful. "My heart is too full of sorrow to spend the holidays in the home where the happiest days of my life were spent. I will come to you in early January," he promised.

He was anxious to get to Paris and put the divorce behind him. Arriving at the Gare du Nord on a frigid December day, he was greeted by a throng of two thousand fans, mostly women, who broke through police lines and ran amuck. Rudy emerged with clothes torn, hat lost, and hair rumpled—the physical equivalent of his frayed emotional state. After installing himself at the Plaza-Athénée, he felt, if anything, worse. This was the very same suite he had shared with Natacha in 1923. The only thing to do was try to submerge his misery in a binge. His first night of partying in Montmartre ended up with breakfast at 5:30 a.m. at Mitchell's, a club in Rue Blanche featuring black entertainers, all the rage in Paris since the opening of Josephine Baker's *Révue Nègre*. After consuming quantities of champagne mixed with beer he and a divorcée named Laura Gould won a dance contest. Earlier he'd gone to the theater and on to Club Florida, where a group of South American customers greeted him with an ovation. He'd danced his new favorite dance, a hybrid of the tango and the Charleston, with Jean Nash, "the best-dressed and most extravagant woman in Europe."

Mae Murray, in Paris on the rebound after her recent divorce from Robert Z. Leonard, often kept Rudy company on his nocturnal rounds as she had a decade earlier when they were both young dancers in New York. They danced together at the Lido, Ambassadeurs, and Ciro's, prompting the usual rumors that they were engaged, or at least an item. "Just a sister to him, that's all," she assured reporters. Murray's biographer claims that Mae tried to arrange for Rudy to reconnect with Blanca de Saulles, who had remarried and was staying with her son in Paris, but that Blanca would not see him.

The Paris bacchanal provided distraction but little genuine joy. He visited the music-hall stars the Dolly Sisters and befriended an Egyptian prince, who invited him to Cairo. For three weeks Rudy slept only

two hours a night, according to Manuel Reachi. "He goes on an endless round of parties [one of them at a château near Fontainebleau]
which I'm sure he doesn't enjoy." By the time he left Europe, Rudy's
appearance had altered shockingly. He looked haggard, his face pale
and puffy; he had huge rings under his eyes and the famously sleek helmet of hair had thinned and receded. Within less than a month he
seemed to have aged ten years.

In Europe he spent money with his customary abandon, ordering a
new custom-made Isotta-Fraschini convertible roadster, acquiring antique firearms for his collection, Venetian and Bohemian glassware for
Falcon Lair, Arabian costumes for his next movie, thirty-odd new suits
and three dozen pairs of hand-turned shoes in London. He would take
a ribbing in the columns of *Photoplay* for his latest flights of sartorial
fancy: "A fur-lined bathrobe was the *pièce de résistance* of the Paris
wardrobe that Rudolph Valentino brought home with him. The
bathrobe . . . is paisley lined with white fur. Rudy also has a wasp-
waisted evening dress, and his new sable evening overcoat leaves the
coat checkers at the night-clubs simply gasping."

One much-reported escapade from this stay in Paris belongs in the
annals of publicity, not history. Strategically placed press reports
spread the news that a jealous Hungarian, Baron Imre Lukatz, in love
with Vilma Banky and claiming to be betrothed to her, had aimed a
right hook in Rudy's direction in the lobby of the Mogador Theater and
challenged his imagined rival to a duel. The story went that Beltrán-
Masses, now living in Paris, intervened to stop the fistfight, but the
following dawn Valentino took a pair of dueling swords to the park of
a private château. There, instead of dueling, the baron rescinded his
challenge and apologized, issuing an invitation to breakfast. According
to Samuel Goldwyn's biographer, A. Scott Berg, the ersatz baron was
actually an actor who'd been hired by the Goldwyn organization and
the whole story was a mere hoax designed to promote Banky in *The
Dark Angel*.

Once Natacha had filed her petition for divorce and Rudy had established residence in Paris, the final decree would follow as a matter
of course. In the meantime, Rudy had no reason to remain in Paris,

and no wish to do so. On a whim he headed for Berlin with Manuel Reachi, paying no heed to German visa restrictions. He planned to stay at the Adlon Hotel, where Mae Murray also happened to be putting up. A crowd of curiosity seekers in which "the male element predominated" greeted them. So did a band of demonstrators protesting the defamation of Germany in *The Four Horsemen of the Apocalypse*. Mae Murray told reporters that she and Rudy were not engaged, just old friends, and Rudy revealed that he was worried about the campaign against him in Italy. He was surely discomfited as well by the show of anti-Valentino sentiments in Berlin.

He and Reachi accepted an invitation to visit the Expressionist director F. W. Murnau at the UFA's Neubabelsberg studio. Murnau, who would be leaving for Hollywood in a matter of weeks to direct *Sunrise*, was completing work on *Faust*. We don't know whether Emil Jannings, who played Mephisto, was present during the visit or whether Rudy had a chance to observe Murnau's innovative "moving camera" in action. We do know that when it came time to depart Germany, Rudy's lack of a visa and his record of participation in the anti-German *Four Horsemen* caught up with him and he was denied permission to leave. Fortunately, his traveling companion, Reachi, had good diplomatic connections. Reachi contacted Ortiz Rubio, the Mexican ambassador to Germany, who intervened on Valentino's behalf.

Rudy took off at once for Christmas in London, but was back on the continent in a trice. He played baccarat at Monte Carlo and celebrated New Year's Eve there with Mae Murray and Reachi. American newspapers reported that Rex Ingram and Alice Terry expected to join the celebration, which is remarkable if true; Rudy and the Ingrams could hardly be called friends. At the stroke of midnight Rudy made a vow never to marry again, backing his pledge with a five-to-one bet of ten thousand dollars that he would still be unmarried in 1930.

He had promised the Hudnuts that he would come to Juan-les-Pins in January to say farewell to them and the château, and he drove there alone. Muzzie found him "the same sweet, loving boy" she had always known. This time, though, he was too sad to linger long. "He often went to Natacha's room to sit there awhile by himself, and when he came out he would kneel beside me and bury his head in my lap and cry like a baby."

The following week, wearing long, pointed sideburns, Rudy set off from Southampton for New York with Alberto and his family. He learned from a reporter as he boarded the *Leviathan* that the divorce had been granted, on grounds of desertion and nonsupport, by the Seine tribunal of three judges. Pronouncing the coincidence of departure and divorce an excellent omen, he declared, "I cross the ocean a free man." Pausing to reflect, he added: "That closes a chapter in my life. It only remains to turn the page and begin anew." In private he would tell a friend, "In the courts she divorces me. Can you divorce the heart?"

Alberto, Ada, and young Jean had remained an entire month in London at Rudy's behest, but the restless, distracted Rudy actually spent little more than a week with them. Well, he could tell himself, soon I will have Alberto's family with me all the time. They had agreed to come to live with him in California at Falcon Lair. In the fall Jean would resume his schooling in Italy, but would join his parents during long summer vacations. Rudy nourished hopes that Jean, on whom he doted, would find a future profession in the film industry. Alberto would be making frequent trips back to Europe, for he was going to take over foreign publicity for Valentino's pictures. Ada, to the extent permitted by her precarious health, would play the domestic role Italian wives traditionally took.

Falcon Lair was being transformed. Outdoor floodlights had been installed, and new awnings protected the windows from the sun's glare. The antiques Rudy and Natacha had acquired in Europe had been moved there from the Park Avenue apartment. Italian cypress trees had been planted and Florentine carved oak doors installed that depicted Roman horsemen in combat. For the first time, Rudy himself presided over his home and determined its style, which from the pennant on the central turret to the crusader's gauntlet engraved with the crest of St. George that was displayed in the living room to the Indo-Persian shield mounted in the reception hall suggested a medieval castle somewhere in Spain or Italy, defended by armored knights and inhabited by a ruler who sat on a throne embroidered with a crown. This was Valentino's private kingdom. "Three or four years ago," he acknowledged, "I would not have dared to do my rooms like this. But lately I am doing things more to suit my own tastes. The location was just what I wanted. The name is one I selected myself. The [living-room] furnishings are red because it is the color I prefer above all others."

Despite all of this, reminders of Natacha lingered in Rudy's lower-level bedroom, whose modern furniture came from the house in Whitley Heights. Rudy's king-sized bed had a dark blue lacquered headboard and yellow coverings; a built-in perfume lamp at its foot, once Natacha's, suffused the room with fragrance when lit.

When Lou Mahoney began supervising construction of a surrounding concrete retaining wall and wrought-iron gates and fences, Rudy tellingly asked him, "Do you think you can make it look like a fort?" Work on the retaining wall began on the heels of an emergency soon after Rudy returned from Europe. During a relentless rainstorm, Rudy had been awakened by an ominous rapping from the walls and floors. The pillars that held up the front gate were collapsing; the shale under the foundation had fractured, and the house was beginning to slip down the hill. "Probably it won't be long before [the house] comes falling down on me," an unnerved Rudy told a visitor. If Falcon Lair was a fortress, it was a fortress under siege.

The night Falcon Lair's foundation threatened to give way, Rudy and Alberto, Ada, and Jean took refuge in the white-pillared, pseudo-plantation-style Beverly Hills mansion of Pola Negri, the new woman in Valentino's life.

Valentino first saw the Polish actress Pola Negri on the screen at a private showing of *Madame Du Barry* before he had become famous or she had left Europe. He wrote her a fan letter, enclosing his photograph, and describing himself as "a worm worshipping at the feet of a great star." By the time he and Negri were introduced by Raoul Walsh, late in 1924, during the period when Walsh was directing Negri in *East of Suez*, Negri had moved to Hollywood, had become a major Famous

Players—Lasky luminary, and had developed a lively interest in getting to know her once abject fan, whose letter she claimed to remember; but Rudy preferred to talk to Walsh about a horse he wanted to buy from him.

They met again at a costume party hosted by Marion Davies shortly before Rudy left for Europe in the fall of 1925, and this time, with his divorce from Natacha under way, they clicked. The floor cleared as they danced a tango, she in the white kid boots, white fox fur, and the ball gown she had worn as Catherine the Great in *Forbidden Paradise*, he in his jeweled torero costume from *Blood and Sand*. Negri was smitten. "It was the way he moved! I was a novitiate being led by some over-powering feline." The attraction was more than physical. The unhappiness in him, she said, called out to the unhappiness in her. According not only to Negri, a notorious fabricator, but to Paul Ivano, who heard it from Rudy, they soon became lovers. In the months preceding his death, when Rudy was in California, Pola Negri was his constant companion and frequent overnight guest. According to Lou Mahoney, Pola kept a supply of her negligées at Falcon Lair.

Born in Poland to an aristocratic but impoverished mother and a revolutionary Slovak father who supposedly had Bohemian Gypsy blood and spent much of his life as a political prisoner, Apolonia Chalupiec changed her name to Pola Negri when she auditioned at the Imperial Academy of Dramatic Arts in Warsaw. Trained as a ballet dancer, she turned to the theater after a bout with tuberculosis, becoming a leading interpreter of roles by Ibsen and Gerhardt Hauptmann at Warsaw's Rozmaitosci Theater while still in her teens. After appearing in a popular two-reel Polish film into which she interpolated a Salome dance, she was tapped by Max Reinhardt to perform onstage in Berlin as an exotic mulatto harem dancer in the pantomime *Sumurun,* based on a tale in the *Arabian Nights.* At Reinhardt's theater she met Ernst Lubitsch, who began earning his directing stripes with a series of highly successful costume films in which Negri starred: *The Eyes of Mummy Ma*, *Carmen*, *Madame Du Barry* (retitled *Passion* in America), and *Sumurun* (released in the United States as *One Arabian Night*). Negri also acquired and quickly shed a husband whose main contribution was his title; he allowed her to be known as Countess Dambski. Linked with many lovers and twice divorced, Negri's most enduring emotional attachment so far was to her mother, who lived with her in Beverly Hills.

Negri won acclaim in Europe as an accomplished and electrifying dramatic actress with considerable range, but Hollywood typed her as a glamorous but earthy vamp, a bejeweled spitfire given to emotional tempests, excesses of black kohl eye makeup, and uninhibited displays of passion. *Photoplay* called her "a Goya woman. Frost white skin with blood scarlet lips. . . . She seems the eternal Carmen—the reckless, Bohemian, impulsive, loved and loving gypsy, passionate, elemental, primitive." She was just learning English, and in the United States her heavy foreign accent ("I am Slav. We Slavs loff to suffer") contributed to her mystique. To Americans she seemed the embodiment of everything exotic, fiery, and continental—qualities she shared with Valentino.

She also shared his love of luxury. Her Beverly Hills house, modeled on Mount Vernon, had damask walls, polar-bear-skin rugs, Venetian furniture inlaid with gold, a swimming pool, a sunken garden, a screening room—and a huge portrait of herself over the fireplace. She ordered her clothes from Vienna, choosing black silks or velvets to match her hair or creamy whites to highlight her pale skin. Draping herself in ermine or chinchilla and dripping with diamonds, emeralds, or rubies, she rode in state in a limousine with a liveried chauffeur. When she took Valentino to the train station they traveled in her cream-colored Rolls-Royce trimmed with ivory and upholstered in white velvet. She claims Valentino brought her from Europe a monogrammed black onyx cigarette case studded with diamonds.

Unlike Valentino, she had a penchant for relentless self-promotion, which eventually contributed to her fall from favor with the public. When Pola Negri was around, a press agent was never far behind. Theatrical to the tips of her painted red fingertips, she stole any scene she could, placing herself at center stage. In her self-vaunting memoir, other actresses are always jealous of her, never the other way around. (She does admit that the much-reported feud between her and Gloria

Swanson was drummed up by studio publicists and had no basis in fact.) Instead of telling about the famous personalities she met, she lists the celebrities who wanted to meet her. A line from a Mae West play, "So glad to have you meet me," comes to mind. According to Negri, Chaplin was half crazy with love for her, and she only reluctantly yielded to his blandishments. The romance with Chaplin, and the rumored engagement of "the king of comedy and the queen of tragedy" during her first months in the United States, in 1922, helped secure her place as the darling of fan magazines and gossip columnists.

In her memoir Negri depicts Valentino as the great love of her life, the only man she ever truly wanted, but one who awakened in her dark premonitions as well as passion. She believed herself predestined for tragedy in her love life, and their happiest times together were always shadowed by this sense of impending doom. Valentino, too, in her telling, is a haunted soul prone to wild mood swings, one moment the "carefree schoolboy taking delight in his athletic ability," the next a "brooding ascetic torturing himself with bitter memories and dire forebodings." Although both Alfred Allan Lewis, the ghostwriter of Negri's autobiography, and George Schönbrunn, the friend who supported her petition for U.S. citizenship, peg her memoir as a work of fiction, "a lie," there are asides in it that have the ring of authenticity. For instance, she quotes Rudy characterizing himself, after their first lovemaking, as a "man so locked within himself that he is paralyzed and cannot move." She describes him as a sophisticated lover, but one who harbored doubts about his manhood. She says he sometimes doubled over with abdominal pain but that he dismissed these episodes, "morbidly frightened of displaying any signs of illness, as if they made him somehow less manly." According to her he believed his symptoms were caused by the medicine he took to retard baldness.

Her representations of Rudy's feelings for her can't be trusted at all. She makes him out to be as besotted by love as she, a wild romantic strewing rose petals on their bed of bliss. She completely erases Natacha from the picture, although many who spent time with Rudy after the separation and divorce have attested to his lingering preoccupation with her. Agnes Ayres reported, for example, that during shooting of *The Son of the Sheik*, he would rave about Natacha between scenes: "He was crazy about Natacha." Negri insists that she and Rudy became engaged, despite his frequent denials or evasions. "Ask the lady," he would often answer when pressed for clarification. In San Francisco in February of 1926 he told a reporter in no uncertain terms, "I'm engaged to no one. I've been married twice and I'm very glad to have my freedom for a while. I don't intend to get married to anybody." Adela Rogers St. Johns said that Rudy likened Negri to an erupting Mount Vesuvius or cascading Niagara Falls—far too histrionic for him. "In the home, I love quiet."

However, he never denied his deep affection for Pola, and Alberto and Beltrán-Masses both said they believed he expected to marry her. A photograph in Negri's book, taken at her pool, shows his hand resting on her upper thigh, a gesture of casual intimacy, as she reclines in a lounging chair, sipping champagne. He hung her photograph in his bedroom (she had a fit when she discovered it had been taken down during the visit of a certain Lady Sheila Loughborough from England) and he inscribed one of him to her, "To my imperative yet imperially darling Polita, whom I love more than life itself." This last phrase, lifted from *Camille*, he wrote in French, which was the language they spoke together. Pola was just learning English and didn't know Italian or Spanish. Rudy lacked her German or Polish.

Pola Negri was bisexual and spent her last years living with and being supported by Margaret West, a wealthy Texan. The passive Rudy was surely attracted to her commanding, "imperially darling" personality, but he may not have known of her attraction to women; both before and immediately after the time they were together Negri's sexual relationships were consistently with men. Other male lovers included Rod La Rocque and Yucca Troubetzkoy, as well as Chaplin. The year following Valentino's death she married adventurer Serge Mdivani and would become pregnant by him.

In contrast to Natacha, Pola Negri had a warm, spontaneous, and social nature. Friendly with fun-loving Marion Davies, she enjoyed Hollywood parties and attended with Rudy a birthday celebration for Richard Barthelmess at the Santa Monica home of Constance Talmadge; a famous group photograph taken on that occasion shows them sitting on a fence laughing together, joined by other guests: Fatty Arbuckle, Mae Murray, Ronald Colman, Bessie Love, Jack Pickford, Bea Lillie, Antonio Moreno, and Buster Keaton. Again unlike Natacha, Pola was willing to spend casual time with Rudy's family, to throw a gala birthday party for him at the Ambassador Hotel, or to be photographed looking less than perfect, with tousled hair. Rudy's young nephew, Jean, who had his own little horse, sometimes joined them when they went riding in the hills. During weekend excursions to Catalina on Rudy's yacht, the *Phoenix*, she savored his pastas and sauce Milanaise, his scrambled eggs named in her honor "Pola-naise." High-spirited home movies were taken of Pola frolicking with Rudy. In one she sits astride a rubber sea horse in her pool as Rudy dives to upset her and treat her to a dunking. In another they clown a melodrama in which Pola plays a temptress whose reward for seducing a married man (Alberto) is to be spanked by Rudy.

They also both loved to dress up. Elinor Glyn and Erich von Stroheim, judges at a costume ball at the Sixty Club, awarded them the prize for "best and most beautifully costumed couple." They came as Spanish dancers, Rudy again in his cloth-of-gold torero costume and cape, Pola in flounced skirt and dangling hoop earrings, flourishing a tambourine. "When they took the floor together and did a glorified tango they were a sensation." For Mae Murray's wedding (her fourth) to Prince David Mdivani, at which Rudy served as best man and Pola as matron of honor, they donned formal attire, Rudy in cutaway coat, wing collar, foulard tie, and pin-striped trousers. Following the ceremony at the Church of the Good Shepherd in Beverly Hills, Rudy hosted a wedding breakfast at the Ambassador Hotel.

Periodically Pola's Vesuvian temperament erupted at Rudy and a shouting match ensued. "From day to day," *Photoplay* tattled, "you cannot tell whether they are in the midst of a flaming romance, or whether they are engaged in a none-too-private war." Pola often had her chauffeur wait for her when she visited Falcon Lair at night, in case she suddenly felt the need to flee. When Rudy hosted a dinner for the visiting beauty Lady Sheila Loughborough, a jealous Pola embarrassed him by making a very public scene. Supposedly she slapped him. "Darling," Norma Talmadge said to Pola later, "you must learn how to hide your emotions. You're too transparent." The lovers soon made up. "When they are on-again they really are quite entrancing. When they do the tango together they give you chills up and down your spine. They look quite mad about each other."

Pola didn't want Rudy out of her sight. She canceled plans for a European vacation with her mother, electing to stay closer to home and go instead to Lake Arrowhead, in the San Bernardino Mountains. When Rudy went on location to shoot some desert scenes for *Son of the Sheik* in the Southwest, she followed him. Valeria Belletti wrote to her friend, "The only dirt on the lot now is that Pola Negri today drove to Albuquerque to meet Valentino—she has an awful crush on him. When Joe Schenck heard about it he wanted his press agent to drive after her and prevent the meeting because Schenck is afraid there'll be some adverse criticism and scandal—but it couldn't be done so I suppose it will get out in the papers." It did, but with none of the negative spin Schenck had feared. Trying to be discreet, Negri and Valentino returned to California separately. Soon, gossips reported they had been spotted together at Coronado Beach, San Diego. When Rudy stayed late for shooting in the United Artists Studio, Pola would join him for candlelit dinners.

On a weekend without Pola in San Francisco, Rudy got into trouble. After attending a nightclub called the Tiffin Room with Douglas Gerrard and two local socialites, he showed up the next morning to take a lesson in Charleston dancing from Fontella La Pierre, a dancer at the club. He hired a new valet in San Francisco and headed home. Driving back to Los Angeles at breakneck speed, he crashed his Italian car into a pole near the railroad tracks in Santa Margarita, north of San Luis Obispo. He was thrown twenty-five feet and suffered cuts and bruises. The *Los Angeles Examiner* took this opportunity to chastise him as a reckless upstart with a swelled head and thundered: "His dangerous career should be rudely interrupted by the strong hand of the law."

While Rudy was still in Europe Joseph Schenck had decided to acquire the rights to E. M. Hull's *The Sons of the Sheik* (about twin sheiks) and to cast Valentino in another sheik role, basing his choice on market research and his own hunches about what would win popular favor. Fairbanks, who followed *The Mark of Zorro* with *Don Q, Son of Zorro*, had helped to popularize sequels. A poll of fans showed that 90 percent of them favored Valentino in one more sheik picture teeming with action, color, romance, and adventure. George Ullman relayed the message that he was to curtail his European stay and return to Los Angeles at once. Shooting would begin in February 1926.

Rudy had made no secret of his weariness of the sheik label. In an interview titled "I'm Tired of Being a Sheik," conducted late in 1925 by J. K. Winkler, he said, "Heaven knows I'm no sheik! Look at this 'sleek black hair.' Getting a bit thin about the temples, isn't it? . . . I had to pose as a sheik for five years! . . . A lot of the perfumed ballyhooing was my own fault. I wanted to make a lot of money and so I let them play me up as a lounge lizard, a soft handsome devil whose only aim in life was to sit around and be admired by women. And all that time I was a farmer at heart and still am. . . . No more posing Apollo stuff for me. If any producer comes to me with a sheik part I am going to murder him! I am going to show I am a real actor if I have to play Hamlet in a waiter's tuxedo." He saw his time running out as a persuasive romantic lead, anticipating that as he got older the public would become bored and that in the future he would devote himself to playing historical characters like Cesare Borgia or perhaps an American Indian. Being typed as a Great Lover only invited resentment from males and incredulity from women, he had concluded. "The feminine portion [of the public] begins to challenge you. 'All right—if you're so exciting—let's see you excite *me*,' they say. The whole thing is false and artificial. You can't go on and on with it." On the screen, he said, "one appears to be what others desire, not what one is in reality." He could easily foresee a time in the not too distant future when he would retire altogether from film acting and become a producer and occasional director who would devote himself mainly to ranching and farming.

Frances Marion, the expert cowriter of the *Son of the Sheik* scenario, remembered that Rudy had hoped to play in an adaptation by her of D'Annunzio's *The Flame of Love*, but was stoical about accepting this new sheik assignment. "He made no complaint; he was too tired to combat the overwhelming forces that governed his career." She described the love scenes as "tempestuous tussles in a tasseled tent," and her private name for the movie was "Son of a Bitch." The script that we know from the movie was her second attempt. Originally she wrote a satire of *The Sheik* that the director, George Fitzmaurice, found hilarious, but had to reject; it had no role for Vilma Banky, who had already been signed.

Several circumstances helped Rudy see an upside to his new undertaking. One was that he would at last be directed by George Fitzmaurice, the Paris-born director he'd sought from his earliest days in Hollywood. Known for his careful preparatory work and his interest in psychology, Fitzmaurice had just directed *The Dark Angel*, employing the same leading lady, Banky, photographer, George Barnes, and scenarist he would be using in *Son of the Sheik*. He and Rudy shared mutual respect and excellent rapport.

Second to Rudy's satisfaction with Fitzmaurice came the pleasure of working again opposite Vilma Banky, a responsive actress, a graceful dancer with a delicate, flowerlike beauty, and someone he truly liked. When he lifted her for a scene in the moonlit ruins, prop man Irving Sindler reported, he didn't want to put her down.

And then came the matter of the script, which furnished an opportunity to try a dual role even more virtuosic than the triple-switch he undertook in *Cobra*. The E. M. Hull novel *Sons of the Sheik* had twin protagonists, but the twins in the screen version were fused into one son. Instead of twin sons, the dual role in the film would involve two generations of sheiks. Valentino insisted on playing both the father, chieftain Ahmed Ben Hassan of the original *Sheik*, still married to Lady Diana Mayo (Agnes Ayres), but now made up with a lined face, mustache, and partly gray beard, and Ahmed's headstrong young adult son, attired in authentic Arab costumes Valentino had bought abroad. Through the use of the split screen, father and son could appear in the same frame, the young man moving with erotic fire, his father with imperious dignity. Rudy savored the challenge of playing an older man, something new for him. Fitzmaurice said, "He loved character work.

As the father in *Son of the Sheik* he was even happier than in the name role." But Rudy confessed afterward, "I didn't enjoy seeing myself old." Reminders of his body's mortality troubled him. "I don't want to be an old man," he told Norma Talmadge, repeating words he'd spoken to Beltrán-Masses. "If I meet death at forty I'll be quite satisfied."

The sequel allowed him to correct some of the flaws in *The Sheik*. This time the young, virile Ahmed does not equivocate. He stands up to his father, insisting on selecting his own bride and straightening a piece of iron his father has bent to demonstrate his superior strength and equal authority. And he does not shrink from forcing himself on a woman. No one would be able to call him a patsy.

Young Ahmed has fallen in love with Yasmin, a street dancer who helps support her father, a dissolute Frenchman, and his roving band of thieving Arab entertainers, with whom she travels. When Ahmed is captured by Yasmin's father's troupe, one of the thieves lies to him by telling him that Yasmin, whose love he thought he'd won, was paid to lure him into the trap that led to his capture and torture. Before he learns that Yasmin didn't really betray him and loves him after all, a furious young Ahmed abducts her, taking her to a desert camp.

We don't actually see young Sheik Ahmed's rape of Yasmin. But we know it has taken place because we do see the preamble, in which Ahmed removes his belt and lights a cigarette as he stalks his kidnapped prey, roughly tossing her onto a divan in his tent and approaching her with measured pace, staring her down (there's a close-up of her terrified eyes, all pupil, staring back), ignoring her pleas for mercy, embracing her with muscular arms, and kissing her despite her defiant cry that she hates him. "For once your kisses are free!" he exclaims during a struggle. (Banky didn't like being treated roughly. "I am grabbed this way and that," she complained. "I am all the blue and the black.") Then, after a fade-out, we see the aftermath: Yasmin swooning on the round bed, crying into her pillow, and Ahmed looking guilty when his father arrives and commands that Yasmin be released.

The fade-out shields us from rape's cruelest brutalities, and the rough stuff we do witness is made somewhat more forgivable by our awareness of Yasmin's underlying love for Ahmed, the tenderness he's already demonstrated, the suffering he's endured when tortured, and his contrition when he realizes she's innocent of any participation in his entrapment. Ahmed's sheer physical allure helps us forgive him. Valentino—free of the eye popping that marred the original *Sheik*, costumed in genuine Arabian robes, embroidered vests, and jewel-studded belts—had never looked more handsome on-screen. The grotesque Arabs—the dwarf who's there to clown and the grimacing, predatory Moor, Ghabah (Montague Love), who's there to menace—offset Ahmed's valor and attractiveness. Omnipresent, Ahmed is the steamy lover who, in an early tryst, covers Yasmin's face with kisses even before revealing his name to her: "I am he who loves you—is that not name enough?"; he's the half-naked victim you want to rescue when he's strung up by his wrists and flogged; the sex menace narrowing his gaze and crossing his bulging arms in front of his broad chest as he advances on Yasmin; the swashbuckling hero who jumps from a balcony to swing from a chandelier; the mysterious figure who lurks in the shadows as Yasmin dances, his face half hidden by his dark burnoose; the horseman vaulting onto an Arabian stallion as it rears, or, racing, a black silhouette cutting a trail of hoofprints across the limitless expanse of white sand dunes.

Rudy went to great lengths to acquire the horse he most wanted to ride in this picture. As the young sheik he would mount his own black gelding Firefly in long shots, and a dark bay in close shots, but as the father he hoped to ride a horse he'd seen and admired but did not own. Before going to the Yuma Desert in Arizona for shooting he sent a telegram to the cereal baron and horse rancher W. K. Kellogg, asking permission to borrow from the Kellogg Arabian Ranch in Pomona both the white Arabian stallion Jadaan and Jadaan's trainer, Karl Schmidt, and promising to return the horse and trainer by the first of May. "WE WILL GIVE YOU TREMENDOUS CLEAR ADVERTISING AND PUBLICITY CAMPAIGN," he wired, pressing his case by arguing that the exposure would help convince the world of the gentility and nobility of purebred Arabian horses. Kellogg agreed, provided that Valentino paid the horse's transportation and insurance costs, paid trainer Schmidt's salary, gave screen credit to the Kellogg Ranch, and honored the May 1 deadline.

Valentino reneged on more than one promise. He returned the horse late, after transporting him to Falcon Lair, and Kellogg's son suspected he had used Jadaan for breeding, not just to ride in the movie. The first prints of the film included no credit line for the Kellogg Ranch, though one was added in later versions. But in the end the Kelloggs got plenty of interest on their loan. Jadaan became a screen star in his own right, appearing in several subsequent movies, including *Under Two Flags*, and turning up at the Tournament of Roses and in photographs posed with the saddle, red velvet saddle cover, and gold breast collar Valentino had used in the film. A Kellogg employee, Spide Rathbun, even tried to bring Jadaan to Hollywood Memorial Cemetery in 1933 for the ceremony commemorating the seventh anniversary of Valentino's death, but the cemetery director testily ejected him with the words, "Get that horse out of here."

Shooting in the Yuma Desert proved to be an ordeal. The relentless heat was stifling. Because temperatures could rise to one hundred and twenty in full sun, and there was no shade available, most scenes were shot between four and nine in the morning or in the late afternoon. Cast and crew were plagued by the flies that followed the horses and also the camels that had been used for *Beau Geste*, which had just been filmed at the same site. The entire company had to bathe in citronella. "I guess that's art," said Rudy, who remained civil and friendly to all, always saying hello and inviting company members into his tent for drinks.

His horse fell twice, and despite his fine appearance Rudy wasn't feeling very well himself. Frances Marion described him as "physically worn out and at times in nagging pain," and Norma Talmadge remembered that he complained of a pain in his side, but refused to see a doctor. June Mathis, back in touch now after a reconciliation eased by Natacha's absence, visited the Hollywood set several times and begged him to take a long rest.

But he needed to keep working to pay his debts. Vilma Banky would not be available for his next projected picture, based on the life of Benvenuto Cellini, and before Estelle Taylor was chosen as leading lady there was talk that Dolores Del Rio or even Greta Garbo would take Banky's place. George Fitzmaurice would again direct. Valentino signed a new contract with John Considine, United Artists' general manager, under which he was to make three pictures in the coming year for a salary of $7,500 a week, plus a percentage of the profits. After that he would coproduce with Joseph Schenck as a full partner entitled to half the profits. Although he would be taking a pay cut, he'd be assuming greater control.

Four months before the official release of *Son of the Sheik*, Los Angeles got an advance look via a preview run at the Spanish-style Grauman's Million Dollar Theatre. Business was brisk, with weekly returns of close to $32,000. On opening night, July 8, 1926, at the close of the first screening Valentino came onstage to make a brief speech. As he prepared to exit, he noticed that a huge decorative vase on the side of the stage was about to fall and could perhaps injure patrons in the front row. He tried to steady the heavy vase by putting his shoulder against it, but its weight toppled him backward. He managed to deflect the fall of the vase so that instead of falling on members of the audience it fell into the orchestra pit, but so did he, landing flat on his back. He was knocked unconscious for several minutes. Doctors were hastily summoned and he came to. "Then he staggered to his place in the audience, amid the most terrific applause." The battered star greeted well-wishers, among them June Mathis and the costume designer who conducted séances, Cora McGeachy, outside the theater. Then he and his party—which included Pola Negri in a silver sheath and diamond tiara, Mae Murray, David Mdivani, Louella Parsons, and Chaplin—repaired to the Cocoanut Grove to toast the film's success and wish Rudy good luck on his upcoming trip.

He had agreed to go on tour to promote *Son of the Sheik*, and he wanted to be on hand in New York to see off Alberto, who with his family would be leaving for Europe at the beginning of August. Rudy's first stop would be San Francisco. Pola and a group of fans came down to the red-brick Santa Fe Station, with its one solitary palm, to wave good-bye. She kissed him quickly, and then, as he shouted farewells, the train gathered speed and he vanished from sight.

19

DEATH OF A GOD

The short stay in San Francisco had been planned as a recreational break, only indirectly connected to publicity for *Son of the Sheik*. The mayor of the city, James Rolph, Jr., greeted their train and whisked Valentino and George Ullman off to Nob Hill for a press luncheon at the Fairmont Hotel. "[Valentino] wore a silver ring on each hand, both set with chrysoprase [a green semiprecious stone], and the same stones were set on his silver cuff links," reported the *San Francisco Chronicle*. "On each wrist there was a heavy silver chain bracelet. His necktie was a gray striped butterfly bow. He was much exercised over the persecution he is enduring at the hands of the Italian Fascisti because of his taking out U.S. citizenship papers."

Mayor Rolph, whose genial personality earned him the moniker "Sunny Jim" and who later became governor of California, enjoyed socializing with movie stars and took an avuncular interest in Rudy. He invited him home to meet the Mrs. and presented as a gift a black cocker spaniel Rudy had admired. The next morning the weary Rudy and Ullman, his omnipresent manager, took off by train for the East in the midst of a horrendous heat wave. "Rudy donned a Chinese lounging suit and, after a weak attempt to read a book . . . calmly went to sleep," said Ullman.

At the Blackstone Hotel in Chicago, as Rudy awaited a connecting train to New York, Ullman handed him a newspaper. Rudy turned pale as he scanned the now notorious "Pink Powder Puffs" editorial in the

Chicago Tribune. The words he read with shock and disbelief wounded him more than any previous printed attack, casting a pall over his last days and no doubt contributing to the exacerbation of his long festering but untreated gastric ulcer. The epithet "Pink Powder Puff" stung anew each time he read or said it, and according to Ullman, "Rudy repeated the words more times than I heard him utter any other phrase in all the years that I knew him."

The writer of this inflammatory editorial held Valentino responsible for a decline in the masculinity of the American male. He charged that at a new public ballroom [the Aragon] on Chicago's north side, powder vending machines had been installed in the men's washroom.

> The glass tubes contain a fluffy pink solid, and beneath them one reads an amazing legend . . . : "Insert coin. Hold personal puff beneath the tube. Then pull lever."
>
> A powder vending machine! In a men's washroom! Homo Americanus! Why didn't someone quietly drown Rudolph Guglielmo [*sic*], alias Valentino, years ago?
>
> And was the pink powder machine pulled from the wall or ignored? It was not. It was used. We personally saw two "men" . . . step up, insert coin, hold kerchief beneath the spout, pull the lever, then take the pretty pink stuff and put it on their cheeks in front of the mirror. . . .
>
> It is time for a matriarchy if the male species allows such a thing to persist. Better a rule by masculine women than by effeminate men. Man began to slip when he discarded the straight razor for the safety pattern. We shall not be surprised when we hear that the safety razor has given way to the depilatory.
>
> Who or what is to blame is what puzzles us. Is this degeneration into effeminacy a cognate reaction with pacifism to the virilities and realities of the war? Are pink parlors and parlor pinks in any way related? How does one reconcile masculine cosmetics, sheiks, floppy pants,

and slave bracelets with a disregard for law and an apti-
tude for crime more in keeping with the frontier of half
a century ago than a twentieth century metropolis?

Do women like the type of "man" who pats pink powder on his face in a public washroom and arranges his
coiffure in a public elevator? Do women at heart belong
to the Wilsonian era of "I Didn't Raise my Boy to be a
Soldier?" What has become of the old "caveman" line?

It is a strange social phenomenon and one that is running its course not only here in America but in Europe as
well. Chicago may have its powder puffs; London has its
dancing men and Paris its gigolos. . . . Hollywood is a
national school of masculinity. Rudy, the beautiful gardener's boy, is the prototype of the American male.

Hell's bells. Oh, sugar.

Just as he had been horrified to find his 1916 arrest in New York reported in the pages of *The New York Times*, so Valentino bridled at seeing this new slur upon his good name entered into the public record.
"It is a printed utterance—and automatically becomes part of my biography, which some day I will not be here to defend," he explained.
But the hurt went deeper than that, prodding his own self-doubt and
wounding his dignity. His honor, along with his masculinity, had been
impugned. The Italian code of chivalry ranked honor as the highest
concern of a gentleman. The most serious offenses, according to this
code, could be resolved only by an open letter of abject apology, or a
duel.

Valentino issued a challenge, in the form of a letter that was published in the Chicago *Herald Examiner*. Addressed to "The Man (?) Who
Wrote the Editorial Headed 'Pink Powder Puffs' in Sunday's 'Tribune,'" it accused the editorial writer of attacking "me, my race, and
my father's name. You slur my Italian ancestry; you cast ridicule upon
my Italian name; you cast doubt upon my manhood." Then came the
summons to battle:

I call you, in return, a contemptible coward, and to prove which of us is the better man, I challenge you to a personal test. This is not a challenge to a duel in the generally accepted sense—that would be illegal. But in Illinois boxing is legal. . . . I, therefore, defy you to meet me in the boxing . . . arena to prove in typical American fashion . . . which of us is more a man. I prefer this test of honor to be private, so I may give you the beating you deserve, and because I want to make it absolutely plain that this challenge is not for purposes of publicity. I am handing copies of this to the newspapers simply because I doubt that any one so cowardly as to write about me as you have would respond . . . unless forced by the press to do so. I do not know who you are or how big you are but this challenge stands if you are as big as Jack Dempsey.

I will meet you immediately or give you a reasonable time in which to prepare, for I assume that your muscles must be flabby and weak, judging from your cowardly mentality and that you will have to replace the vitriol in your veins for red blood—if there be a place in such a body as yours for red blood and manly muscle. . . .

Hoping I will have an opportunity to demonstrate to you that the wrist under a slave bracelet may snap a real fist into your sagging jaw and that I may teach you respect of a man even though he happens to prefer to keep his face clean, I remain with

Utter Contempt

Rudolph Valentino

P.S. I will return to Chicago within ten days.

The writer of the *Chicago Tribune* editorial, later identified as a man called John Herrick, never responded. Alberto claimed that they eventually heard that he was suffering from tuberculosis and was close to death. Valentino chose to interpret his attacker's "heroic silence" as proof of the writer's cowardice, and as a "tacit retraction" that vindicated him.

When he arrived in New York's Grand Central Terminal Rudy carried a volume of Freud under his arm, an interesting choice. "He was jaunty, friendly, suave, and clad with quiet elegance." But he was spoiling for a fight. Jack Dempsey, who had recently undergone plastic surgery on his broken nose and who was in the East training for his September world championship bout with Gene Tunney, soon got a phone call from a Rudy quivering with anger. "Valentino felt that he was being attacked because he was a foreigner making a living courtesy of the American dollar," Dempsey said. "He felt the damage had been done, [and] now the public would always have its doubts regarding his masculinity." Rudy asked Dempsey to help him set up and get into shape for an exhibition bout at which Dempsey would serve as referee. Dempsey agreed to ask Frank "Buck" O'Neil, sportswriter and boxing authority for the *New York Evening Journal* to spar with Valentino on the roof garden of the Ambassador Hotel. Press photographers and newsreel cameramen were on hand to watch O'Neil, thirty pounds heavier than Rudy and several inches taller, drop to the mat once and to hear him say "That boy has a punch like a mule's kick." A headline ran, "POWDER PUFF? WHAM!"

Similar scenes were reprised when Rudy returned to Chicago for the Roosevelt Theater opening there of *Son of the Sheik*. He wanted to storm the *Chicago Tribune*, but Dempsey had advised him not to. Instead, he flexed his biceps for reporters and boxed with welterweight "Kid" Hogan before members of the press at a gym in the Loop. Again he repeated his offer to fight the editorial writer, characterizing him as either a decrepit old man or the victim of an inferiority complex: "READY FOR ALL COMERS!" a photo caption announced. "Here's brawn, girls and boys! Rudolph, the Sheik, demonstrating at a Loop gym that a man can wear a slave bracelet and still be a Goliath."

In Atlantic City for a *Son of the Sheik* opening, Rudy fought off adoring fans, made a radio broadcast from the Steel Pier, and attended a Gus Edwards revue (Edwards was a vaudeville old-timer) at which

Edwards presented him with a pair of boxing gloves. Rudy later agreed to dance the tango with a dancer in the revue. It would be his last public tango. An actor named Lorenzo Tucker, who later became known as "the Black Valentino," saw Rudy strolling on the boardwalk and discerned scratches on his cheeks and jaw. He concluded they had been inflicted by Pola Negri, but more likely they were battle scars from his recent exhibition boxing bouts.

All the "Powder Puffs" publicity helped sell movie tickets. In a single week in Chicago, Son of the Sheik took in $29,700. At New York's Strand, where on opening night a double line stretched two blocks in ninety-eight-degree heat, returns soared even higher, totaling $75,000 over two weeks. Valentino was mobbed as he tried to make his way to a car after the first screening. Fans tore off his tie and ripped the cuff links from his shirt.

But the biggest news on Broadway was Don Juan, a Warner Bros. costume picture starring John Barrymore, which opened August 6 at the "Refrigerated Warner Theater" as part of the first all-sound film program. Don Juan lacked spoken dialogue, but it had sound effects and a synchronized Vitaphone musical score. Before the feature, Will Hays appeared on screen announcing "the beginning of a new era in music and motion pictures." The Jazz Singer would follow fourteen months later. Nobody knows how successfully Rudolph Valentino would have made the transition to talkies. He had a pleasing baritone speaking voice with only a trace of an Italian accent, and had a record of eager receptiveness to new technologies. How he would have adapted to the sound era's less romantic sensibility and more naturalistic acting style remains an open question.

In New York Rudy hurled himself into a whirlwind of nonstop social activity as the weather alternated between blistering heat and tumultuous thunderstorms. He dined at the restaurant in the Ambassador Hotel with Jack Dempsey and his then wife, Estelle Taylor, who had been signed to play opposite Rudy in a planned upcoming movie on the life of Cellini. At the Colony he had lunch with his old nemesis, Adolph Zukor, and supposedly told him that he now realized his strike against Famous Players—Lasky had been a mistake. He seemed to dread solitude, even when in his rooms at the Ambassador Hotel on Park Avenue and Fifty-first Street. An interviewer from *Theatre* magazine found him there "in the blaze of midday, with [electric] fans going, bottled water flowing, servants hurrying and reporters scurrying," surrounded by an entourage that included his personal publicity man, general press agent, secretary, photographers, and his buddy Jack Dempsey. George Ullman and his wife occupied adjoining rooms.

If Pola Negri was on his mind he didn't show it, and he made no effort to appear monogamous. On the contrary, he gave every indication that he relished the chance to play while the cat was away. He attended several weekend parties at "Pleasure Island," the Long Island retreat of wealthy man-about-town Schuyler Parsons, and was photographed there with his arm around Margaret Keene's shoulders. Jean Acker was a frequent companion, joining him for late lunches or on drives out to the country. Her grasping, attention-seeking exploits in bygone days no longer mattered to Rudy; she was a link with his past, someone he could talk to who provided comfort and sympathy. Another old friend, Aileen Pringle, was his date for the premiere of *Son of the Sheik*. Alberto had left for Europe on the *France*, seen off at the dock by Rudy himself, and Rudy very much needed the moorings of continuity and connection.

Acker and Pringle, along with Ullman and *Photoplay*'s Jimmy Quirk, joined Rudy's party after the Strand Theater opening of *Son of the Sheik*. They repaired to Tommy Guinan's nightclub, the Playground, at which Tommy's sister, Texas Guinan, presided. A magician, the "fakir" Rahman Bey, attired as a sheik, asked for volunteers who would help him show that he could pierce human skin with a hatpin without drawing blood or causing pain. Someone in the crowd called out, "How about the he-man, Valentino?" Rudy, put on the spot, felt he had to come forward. He removed his coat, and the crowd tittered: he was wearing red suspenders. Ullman insisted that Rudy's arm, rather than his cheek, be offered. "Rahman started to pierce Rudy's arm with a hatpin and Rudy shouted 'Ouch!' That was laugh Number Two, and Rudy couldn't stand being laughed at, so he let the pin go all the way," reported *Variety*. Ullman says there was no blood, but that he nonetheless sent for alcohol and cleansed the arm. Even the usually hard-nosed *Variety* was moved to comment, "It must be terrible to be a celeb."

All the partying failed to reverse Rudy's fundamental unhappiness. Asked whether he considered himself a success, he answered in the negative. He was gratified by the warm response to *Son of the Sheik*, but to him success meant "a sequence of artistic achievements," which he hadn't yet delivered; he didn't expect to do so until he had achieved economic independence. "He was frightened of his future, worried about finances. . . . He felt that upon the success or failure of *Son of the Sheik* hung his whole professional future." To the writer of those words, an interviewer from *Theatre* magazine, he wailed, "I have never had anything that I *really* wanted! Never!" He told Adela Rogers St. Johns, "I have everything—and I have nothing. It's all too terribly fast for me. . . . A man should control his life. My life is controlling me."

Aileen Pringle had introduced him to the renowned editor and critic H. L. Mencken, with whom Rudy was anxious to discuss his victimization at the hands of hostile newspapermen. Mencken found himself much touched by this "curiously naive and boyish young fellow," who had "some obvious fineness in him." As they shared a meal in the sweltering heat, Rudy unburdened himself, talking not only about the Chicago attack but also about his family and early life in Italy. Mencken "advised him to let the dreadful farce roll along to exhaustion. . . . His [Rudy's] words were simple and yet somehow very eloquent. I could still see the mime before me, but now and then . . . there was a flash of something else. That something else, I concluded, was what is commonly called, for want of a better name, a gentleman."

Mencken picked up on Valentino's underlying and profound discontent. "It was not that trifling Chicago episode that was riding him; it was the whole grotesque futility of his life." His vast success felt hollow. He was nothing more than the hero of the rabble. "Valentino's agony was the agony of a man of relatively civilized feelings thrown into a situation of intolerable vulgarity, destructive alike to his peace and dignity."

The emotional malaise so many sensed surely owed a great deal to, and in turn accelerated, the physical discomfort he was suffering. Rudy felt and looked ill, but denied it, refusing to take care of himself or seek help. Dismissing his abdominal pain and pallor as "nervous indigestion," he overindulged, downing three dozen snails at a sitting and then reaching for the bicarbonate of soda. He was getting very little sleep. Asked whether he smoked, he answered, "Yes, from forty to fifty cigarettes a day." And if he drank? "Yes, frequently." As to his eating habits, "I eat everything I please." Yet Schuyler Parsons observed him being "seized with terrible pains" while motoring to a party, and heard his butler remark on the enormous quantity of bicarbonate of soda Valentino was taking.

Saturday, August 14, found Rudy squiring Marion Benda, a dancer in the *Ziegfeld Follies* who'd been introduced to him by designer Ben Ali Haggin, the man who had married Rudy's dance partner of a decade back, Bonnie Glass. Benda had a roommate, fellow dancer Dorothy Wigman (later Raphaelson), who remembers her as "highly intelligent." According to Raphaelson, a living-room conversation between Rudy and Benda touched on the theories of Professor Jung. Marion Benda, who was cast as a Venetian girl in Haggin's *Follies* tableau "Treasures of the East," described Valentino as "a perfect gentleman. I have never been treated with more courtesy and deference by any man than he has displayed in the short three weeks of our friendship," she said.

His other companion that night, Barclay Warburton, Jr., like Rudy was emerging from a recent marital breakup. Warburton's wife was granted a Paris divorce on this very date, August 14, 1926, and would soon marry W. K. Vanderbilt, Jr. A good-looking, fair-haired, natty dresser still in his twenties, Barclay Warburton, Jr., had met Rudy through Schuyler Parsons and attended the same weekend parties at Pleasure Island in Islip. He enjoyed the advantages of wealth and an impressive pedigree, being the grandson of Philadelphia merchant prince John Wanamaker and the son of the mayor of Palm Beach. A sportsman and pilot who'd served in the Signal Corps during the war, he'd dabbled in tabloid journalism and was described in the press as a broker, but he lacked a serious calling, preferring to devote himself to high living in a Park Avenue apartment "full of soft lights, low couches and luxury." Warburton loved to carouse and host rowdy parties, to the distress of his East Side neighbors. One of them sued, complaining that repeated noisy gatherings that lasted until dawn deprived him of rest and forced him to move. Strangely, both Marion Benda and Warburton would commit suicide, Benda in 1951 and Warburton on Thanksgiving Day, 1936.

On this particular August Saturday night Rudy and Warburton took in a show, George White's *Scandals* at the Apollo Theatre, near Times Square. It featured Erté costumes, a rousing rendition by Ann Pennington of the dance called the Black Bottom, and a love duet delivered by Harry Richman and Frances Williams. Richman and the chorus segued into a song called "Lucky Day," but this day wasn't. Coming backstage after the curtain, Rudy invited Richman and Williams to a party Warburton was throwing at his apartment on Park Avenue at Eightieth Street. Marion Benda must have joined them after her own *Follies* performance. "We had some drinks, music, and dancing, until about 1:30 o'clock when Rudy was taken violently ill and was rushed to his apartment at the Ambassador," Harry Richman recalled. Warburton summoned his own physician, Dr. Paul Durham, and after examining Rudy the doctor called an ambulance. Rudy was suffering excruciating pain. He had a rapid pulse and a rigid abdomen. Ullman's secretary, Estelle Dick, rode with him and George Ullman in the ambulance to Polyclinic Hospital, on Fiftieth Street near Eighth Avenue. It was close to noon.

A double operation, for acute appendicitis and perforated gastric ulcers, was undertaken by Dr. Harold Meeker at four-thirty in the afternoon. By that time Valentino had gone into "profound shock, with a pulse of 140." Why the delay of almost five hours, when all signs indicated that the patient's life was in grave danger? There are two possible answers, and we don't know which one provides the true explanation. Alberto—who was not on the scene, having just arrived in France—maintained in an interview with Kevin Brownlow that surgery was delayed because on this Sunday in August only an attending resident, a doctor still in training, was initially on hand at Polyclinic

Hospital and it took several hours to track down and bring in Dr. Meeker, an experienced senior physician. But Dr. Arthur Bogart, a physician who trained at Polyclinic in the late 1940s, maintains that one of Valentino's doctors who was still on the staff informed him that Valentino himself had postponed the operation, until his deteriorating condition left no alternative. "The doctor told me his patient refused surgical intervention which might have saved his life—because he was terrified of surgery." He had an "Italian fear" of hospitals.

There was such a thing as a southern Italian antipathy to hospitals, based on the tradition that persisted well into the early twentieth century that only sick people without homes or relatives to look after them had to rely on institutional care, from monks and nuns in monasteries. An old Neapolitan curse translates, "May you end your days in the hospital." Apparently, dying in a hospital was regarded as the worst fate imaginable. We know that Valentino avoided doctors his whole life (though he must have had to undergo physicals required for studio insurance policies), and his intense focus on his own body may have made him especially dread the prospect of cutting and scarring it. But the delay in undertaking surgery worsened his chances for survival.

When he recovered from the ether the next morning, Valentino's first words to George Ullman were, "Did I behave like a pink powder puff or like a man?" He had internalized the Chicago attack on his manhood to such an extent that he saw his bed of pain as a proving ground.

At Rudy's request, Ullman sent a cable to Natacha at Juan-les-Pins, informing her of his sudden illness and the operation. Natacha, seized with regret and concern, sent a wire: "HAVE JUST HEARD OF YOUR ILL-NESS. WE ARE PRAYING HOURLY FOR YOUR RECOVERY. MUCH LOVE." She believed a reconciliation had taken place, and that their past differences counted for nothing in light of the present catastrophe. Re-united in spirit, they exchanged telegrams almost to the death. Aiding her efforts to stay in touch was a medium, George Wehner, who'd been installed at Juan-les-Pins to conduct séances. A special room in the château, decorated with a portrait of Madame Blavatsky, had been set aside for making spirit contact. Rudy was heartened by Natacha's show of solicitude. He asked Ullman to phone Natacha's half sister,

Mrs. Nora Van Horn, to inquire when Natacha would return to New York. Clearly, he hoped to see her again.

Other women in his life vied for the inside track. Pola Negri besieged the hospital switchboard with her calls. In the midst of filming *Hotel Imperial* under Mauritz Stiller's direction in Hollywood, she wanted to rush to Rudy's side, but the studio was loath to halt production, and would not give her leave for another week. "I am stunned and shocked beyond description," she said of the emergency. "I had no inkling that he was so sick. I would like to rush to him now but . . . I am in the middle of a picture and cannot see how I can get away now, much as I would like to hasten to his bedside." Negri later said that Stiller, recently displaced by John Gilbert in the affections of his protégée Greta Garbo and nursing his wounds, bonded with her as a fellow sufferer and offered consolation.

Jean Acker announced that she had canceled her plans to depart on a trip to Europe because she wanted to remain close to Rudy in his hour of need. She was not allowed at present to visit the eighth-floor sickroom (which had once been occupied by Mary Pickford). Only doctors, nurses, and George Ullman were permitted in. An armed guard stood at the door.

At first the medical bulletins were guardedly optimistic. The patient was doing as well as could be expected, although his condition remained serious. Seventy-five percent of those who have surgery for appendicitis recover, the hospital spokesman stated. Peritonitis, an inflammation of the membrane that lines the walls of the abdominal cavity, had set in, but had not spread. Rudy himself expected to be out of the hospital soon. Ullman did not tell him about the peritonitis and did his best to shield his client from knowledge of the gravity of his illness. Rudy was not allowed to read newspapers.

Rudy thanked his nurses and expressed regret over postponement of a planned visit to Philadelphia. Asked whether he wanted to send for Alberto, Rudy answered, "By no means. Just cable him that I am a little indisposed and will soon be all right. And wire Pola the same." He talked about where he would go to rest once he left the hospital and indicated he expected to go back to work before long. From Ullman he requested a mirror. Ullman complied with reluctance; his illness had left marks on Rudy's face that Ullman did not want him to see. (Exactly what sort of marks Ullman does not reveal.) Rudy studied his ravaged visage in the mirror and said, "I just want to see how I look when I am sick, so that if I ever play the part in pictures I will know how to put on my makeup."

Crowds of well-wishers kept vigil outside the hospital, and phone messages poured in, many from ordinary citizens, others from people with famous names: Mayor Jimmy Walker, Representative Fiorello La Guardia (with whom Rudy had once appeared at a New York City Columbus Day celebration), Gloria Swanson, Marion Davies, Mae Marsh, Jack Dempsey. Vilma Banky requested hourly updates on the star's condition. Two extra switchboard operators had to be hired to handle the calls. Stacks of Bibles arrived. Douglas Fairbanks and Mary Pickford cabled a message of hope, as did Chaplin and John Gilbert. A young dancer tried to send in her pet monkey, "to amuse him." Flowers by the truckload piled up. Only a few stems were permitted in Rudy's room, and he asked that the rest be distributed to patients in the wards. He also asked, "How much longer is this damned thing going to last?"

As Valentino battled for his life, tabloid newspapers cashed in. The New York *Graphic* published on its front page the first of several of its notorious faked composite photographs, this one showing Valentino naked, in profile on the operating table, eyes wide open, a sheet draped over his lower body, surrounded by doctors and nurses. One of the nurses is unaccountably smiling and another caresses the patient's hair. "RUDY BRAVE IN THE FACE OF DEATH," the headline read. The next day's two-and-a-half-inch headline brayed "RUDY DEAD," and in smaller type in a sidebar, "Broadway Hears. Cry Startles Film World as Sheik Rallies." The premature death report prompted phone calls to the hospital at the rate of two thousand an hour. This was followed by a story suggesting that Valentino's illness was just a publicity stunt.

Valentino's vital signs appeared in daily press bulletins issued by Drs. Meeker, Durham, and a third who had been brought in, T. Randolph Manning:

August 17: temperature 103, pulse 100, respiration 26
August 18: temperature 103, pulse 108, respiration 26
August 19: temperature 101, pulse 90, respiration 22

On August 20 came an announcement that Valentino had passed the crisis point and that his physicians would issue no further daily bulletins "unless unexpected developments occur." His temperature was normal and he was allowed a meal of chicken broth and Vichy water. Gloria Swanson and the marquis de la Falaise, her husband, were turned away when they attempted a visit, but Valentino asked to keep a French book the marquis had left, *The Prisoner of Chance,* by Bernard Grasset. He ordered roses for his day nurse, Pearl Franks, and asked if he might continue his recuperation at his hotel.

Then came an alarming turn for the worse. On August 20 Valentino complained of severe pain in the left side of his chest and abdomen. In the absence of yet-to-be-discovered antibiotics, infection took hold, invading the lining of his heart and riddling his body. The peritonitis was spreading, his doctors revealed, and pleurisy, an inflammation of the membranous sacs that enclose the lungs, had developed on the left side. He had pneumonia in his left lung and his temperature soared to 103, then even higher. He passed a restless night. A fourth physician, a lung specialist, Dr. Eugene Pool of New York Hospital, was called in. The possibility of a blood transfusion was discussed but rejected. By a strange coincidence, Barclay Warburton, Jr., was admitted to another hospital for a "minor" operation whose precise nature was kept secret. Rumors flew that bad liquor or bad food had been served at Warburton's party.

Jean Acker arrived at Polyclinic Hospital carrying a huge oblong box to be left for Valentino. It contained a ruffled white linen bedspread (called a "counterpane" in some newspapers) that she had embroidered herself, and a pillow cover with "Rudy" embroidered in each corner.

Although he had been given opiates, Rudy remained awake intermittently as all hope for his recovery fell away. On Sunday evening, August 22, George Ullman decided to call in two priests, even though

Rudy had been a lapsed Catholic, twice married outside the Church and twice divorced. "Why should I go to church to pray," he once asked, "since God knows all, and He is everywhere?" Father Edward Leonard of St. Malachy's, the "actor's church" on West Forty-ninth Street, administered the Last Rites after Father Joseph Cangedo, who had been raised in Apulia and claimed to have known Valentino since childhood, heard his confession and granted absolution.

Joseph Schenck had sent a cable to Alberto in Paris with the news that his brother was dying and urged him to return to New York on the first available ship.

Schenck was allowed to visit the sickroom while his wife, Norma Talmadge, waited, weeping, in an adjoining room. "Hello, Chief," Rudy greeted him. "Can't you get me out of here? I've got to go on that fishing trip in Maine." He asked after Constance and Norma Talmadge. The Schencks left the hospital in tears.

Frank Menillo, the real estate man Rudy had roomed with at the Hotel des Artistes in 1922, later came to the bedside, speaking to Rudy in Italian. Rudy answered in English, "Thank you, Frank. I'm going to be well soon." Ullman, Menillo, two nurses, and the resident, Dr. William Bryant Rawls, kept watch all night as rain fell outside. Over radio station WEAF, Major Edward Bowes admonished listeners to concentrate on wishes for Valentino's recovery. In the early morning, a feverish, semiconscious Rudy called to Ullman, "Wasn't it an awful thing that we were lost in the woods last night?"

Ullman claims that Rudy's last coherent words were spoken in the early morning, when Ullman tried to pull down the blinds. "Don't pull down the blinds! I want the sunlight to greet me." Dr. Meeker reported another dialogue, which might have taken place after the one with Ullman. "Doctor," Rudy asked, "do you know the greatest thing I am looking forward to? I am looking forward to going fishing with you next month. I hope you have plenty of fishing rods. Mine are in California." Editorial writers for *Moving Picture World* would seize on the detail that "California" was among the last words he uttered, and press for his burial there. "California was his kingdom. There the king should lie."

Before lapsing into a coma at about 8 a.m. on August 23, Rudy cried out at intervals in Italian. No one at his bedside understood, and these words were not recorded.

Jean Acker was Rudy's last visitor. "His breathing was heavy. He didn't know she was there."

Rudolph Valentino Guglielmi died at 12:10 p.m. on Monday, August 23, 1926. He was thirty-one years old. A front-page headline in *The New York Times* announced: "VALENTINO PASSES WITH NO KIN AT SIDE . . . He died alone save for his three doctors and two nurses."

George Ullman, who had not slept for four days and nights, stood outside the sickroom. "Mr. Ullman broke down when he was informed that Valentino was dead. Doctors ordered him to bed." Dr. Durham suffered a mild heart attack.

The death certificate, hastily completed by the New York City Board of Health and signed by the chief resident physician, William B. Rawls, is awash with errors—another reminder that for all his fame, Valentino died a stranger in a strange land. The certificate gives Valentino's surname as "Guglielina" and his father's first name as "Giovandi" and misstates his mother's place of birth as Italy. It names the Ambassador Hotel as Valentino's residence. No autopsy was performed, and therefore, Dr. Rawls stated, "I am unable to state definitely the cause of death; the diagnosis during last illness was: Ruptured Gastric ulcer with general peritonitis. Contributory: septic pneumonia and septic endocarditis." News that there had been no autopsy, coupled with the admission of a degree of uncertainty about the cause of death, was fodder for those convinced that Valentino had been murdered, perhaps poisoned or shot by a jealous husband—rumors that were exploited by the tabloids and persist to this day. Dr. Meeker's statement to the press that "there was a hole in the stomach with the diameter of a dime" seemed to some especially suggestive of foul play. When he arrived in New York on the first of September, Alberto was met by a committee of Italians who urged him to order an autopsy; despite his feeling that there was something mysterious about his brother's sudden death, he never granted permission.

The public received news of Valentino's death with shock, grief, and disbelief. How could this vital young man, the very embodiment of physical perfection, an athlete who'd been photographed just weeks ago in boxing trunks that showed off his muscular legs and whose latest movie pictured him swinging from a chandelier, be so suddenly struck down? In Washington, D.C., women on F Street purchased and read the first "extra" newspaper edition ever prompted by an actor's death. Many wept openly, "and that is something that has never happened here, even upon the death of a President," reported *Variety*. In Chicago, photographs of Valentino during his recent stop in the city were flashed on movie screens, and news of the death was posted in theater lobbies.

But his passing, while shocking, had been well rehearsed. Valentino's fans had grown accustomed to images of him in the throes of death— as Julio, succumbing to shell fire on the battleground, or as mortally gored Juan Gallardo—or suffering physical agony as the sheik whose head is bandaged or who, in the last Valentino movie, is strung up by his wrists and whipped by sadistic torturers. His romantic allure always included a shadow side, an edge of menace and fatality. His velvet eyes beckoned toward unknown realms in the beyond. A fortune-teller had predicted he would have a short life, and he had told several friends he expected to die young and had no wish to grow old.

Valentino's spiritual quality, his emotional intensity, had consistently drawn in people who lived on the edge: the depressed, the mentally unstable, or the merely strange. His death opened a Pandora's box. One New York woman, Agatha Hearn, a mother, shot herself while clutching a sheaf of Valentino photographs. In London a depressed twenty-seven-year-old actress named Peggy Scott took poison while surrounded by photographs of him and left a note saying "with his death my last bit of courage has flown."

As throngs blocked traffic in front of Polyclinic Hospital, the body, in a plain wicker basket covered with a gold cloth, was removed through a side door and transported to Campbell's Funeral Church at Broadway and Sixty-sixth Street. The *Graphic* had already rushed to print a faked photograph of the late actor lying in state and would soon put together two others: one showing Valentino in white robes and conversing with an angel in the great beyond and another depicting him engaged in heavenly discourse with Enrico Caruso. Five policemen were needed to disperse the crowd that had gathered at the funeral home in hopes of getting in to see the body. Although funeral arrangements awaited a decision by Alberto, Campbell's announced that they were preparing the Gold Room—furnished with a grand piano, adorned with tapestries, and filled with treasures that had belonged to Napoleon—for a public viewing. Clothed for the last time in formal evening dress, his famous brows penciled, his blemishes powdered over, the embalmed remains of Valentino were transferred to a glass-covered casket made of silver and bronze, and worth ten thousand dollars.

Tributes poured in. George Fitzmaurice called the actor he had just directed in *Son of the Sheik* "one of the finest gentlemen as well as one of the most finished character actors whom I have ever directed." He said, "Rudy knew everybody in the company from the prop man up, and he could call each by name." Film colony movers and shakers, from Will Hays to Marcus Loew to Goldwyn and Zukor, joined a chorus of mourners in business suits, collectively acknowledging Valentino's significance to the industry he suddenly came to represent.

"We are grieved and shocked at the great loss," said Joseph Schenck. "Every one hoped for the best, especially since the boy had waged so brave a fight against the huge odds." Ever the astute businessman, Schenck arranged for massive distribution of prints of *Son of the Sheik*, parlaying the publicity generated by the star's death into worldwide grosses of $1 million within a year. His company, United Artists, cashed in on Valentino's life insurance policy, worth $250,000.

Chaplin, responding to "one of the greatest tragedies in the history of the motion picture industry," honored his deceased friend's talent: "His ability as an actor, for which he is seldom given credit," was "the great reason for his success." Chaplin added that Valentino had possessed one of the most interesting faces he'd ever seen. Gloria Swanson hailed him as a leader in his profession, adding, "May the thoughts and prayers of the millions who loved Rudy help him on his journey to the unknown."

Most poignant were the words of June Mathis, who said simply, "My heart is too full of sorrow at this moment to speak coherently. My grief is deep."

Editorials tried to sum up Valentino's contribution. The New York *Daily News* cited him as a one-man revolution who changed the meaning of the word "sheik" and created a new kind of American hero, "the type-man of the postwar period." This new type looked different from previous heroes such as Theodore Roosevelt or James J. Corbett, adopting slick hair, sideburns, and balloon trousers. He also had a different attitude toward life, the *Daily News* stated, leaving it up to the reader to figure out that that meant an attitude more sensual, more worldly, and more woman-centered than any before.

The *Los Angeles Times* addressed the vexed issue of Valentino's masculinity, arguing that Americans and Italians assess that quality in different ways, and that Valentino, although lampooned as an "exquisite," had attracted many male fans in America and had proved himself a fighter who had grit. "He passed through the depths before he attained the heights and had to fight his way up as a stranger in a new country. And in his last struggle with the grim reaper he displayed a spirit worthy of the highest admiration." In the same paper, Harry Carr gave him credit for breaking down barriers of prejudice against Latins that had existed for generations in English-speaking countries. "When I was a little boy it would have been almost unthinkable to represent an Italian in popular melodrama as anything but the arch villain. Over night, Rudolph Valentino made the Latin the lover of the world."

Some carped at the amount of space the press allotted to Valentino's life and death, seeing the all-Valentino, all-the-time coverage as evidence of America's skewed values. Why did the educator and former Harvard president Charles W. Eliot rate only a column on the obituary page, while Valentino stories filled page after page for more than a week? editorials asked. But *Variety* took the spectacle of a nation "placing itself prone before an actor" to be heartening proof of the film industry's preeminence. Along the same lines, *Moving Picture World* rhapsodized: "What a power is this fragile strip of celluloid in which he played! It remained for this boy of thirty-one to die to give such tragic proof of its all-conquering power. He died lest we forget that [celluloid's] anchors in the heart of humanity are youth and romance. The Great Arab has folded his last tent. Rudolph Guglielmi has gone to eternal youth, to eternal romance."

At dawn on Tuesday, August 24, a crowd began to assemble outside Campbell's Funeral Church, awaiting an afternoon viewing of Valentino's body that had been announced by the mortuary's publicist, Harry Klemfuss. By eleven the line wound around the block. By noon the streets surrounding the building were jammed, and by one it was impossible to approach as about thirty thousand mourners and curiosity seekers jockeyed for space. Soon after it began to rain in pelts, rioting erupted. The crowd rushed the doors. Mounted police charged, swinging clubs, trying to beat them back. With a deafening crash, a huge plate-glass window in front of the mortuary shattered into pieces. More than a hundred people were injured, including several policemen. Five women fainted. Some called the police Cossacks. "The sidewalk was strewn with glass slivers, with straw hats, with broken umbrellas, with torn pieces of clothing, with odd shoes and rubbers. There was a girl in her stocking feet, weeping hysterically, soaked to the skin, crying, 'I must see him.'" An hour after the first window shattered, a second window, this one at an auto rental agency, gave way. A Ford sedan was overturned. An impromptu emergency room was set up in the funeral parlor reception room, where several doctors and a nurse provided first aid.

During the afternoon a select few invited mourners were allowed near the bier. One was Jean Acker, who arrived with her mother and cousins; weeping without restraint, she was taken to an upstairs room to regain her composure. Others granted entry were Michael Romano, the Chicago assistant district attorney who had been best man at Rudy and Natacha's Indiana wedding, and Natacha's half sister, Mrs. Nora Van Horn.

At four the doors opened to the public, but only briefly. "One person a second passed the body of Rudolph Valentino." Later, that figure was increased a bit and seventy-four people gazed at the dead man each minute. "It was like the ceaseless tramp of an army." To the dismay of columnist Mark Hellinger, they showed little respect. "The people chatted and they laughed. On the way out they passed comments in voices none too soft." Many of those who tramped through the Gold Room left carrying a souvenir: a flower perhaps, a frond of fern, or a bit of ribbon from one of the many floral offerings. The doors were closed when George Ullman and the Campbell Funeral Church's directors decided to move the casket to a plainer room, set out with candles and a small statue of the Virgin, that had exit doors, allowing for a more orderly dispersal of foot traffic onto the streets. They reopened as an after-work crowd swelled the ranks. By closing time, midnight, an estimated fifty thousand had passed by the bier. A police captain said that in his twenty years on the force he had never seen such a crowd. In number and unruliness, they outstripped any other. Most news accounts suggested that women in the crowd far outnumbered the men, but overhead photographs taken from a high window show masses of straw boater hats worn by men. A claim by Lawrence Quirk, a nephew of James Quirk, that a wax effigy had been substituted for the actual body of Valentino has never been substantiated.

The size and frenzy of the demonstration at Campbell's owed something to what the public felt for Rudolph Valentino, and a great deal to the drama inherent in the sudden death of a young, beautiful, romantic idol. Already a legend, by dying in the prime of youth after suffering torment Valentino was lifted to the mythic stratosphere. "It was not so much a motion picture actor who lay dead," as Heywood Broun put it, "as Pan or Apollo."

Also at work were the raucous aftereffects of a solid week of sensational tabloid headlines, combined with the manipulations of publicists determined to turn the death of an idol into a colossal media event. In 1930, George Ullman would testify in court that Valentino's lying in state had been "worked up for advertising purposes" to create an increased demand for his films and help lift his estate out of debt. Campbell's had agreed to offer its mortuary services free of charge in return for the exposure they knew they would receive in newspapers, magazines, and newsreels.

On August 26, *The New York Times* reported that a group of men clad in black shirts and describing themselves as representatives of the Fascisti League of North America had stationed themselves as an honor guard beside the coffin. The *Times* printed the names and addresses of the Black Shirts, but a reporter for the *Graphic* who was present at Campbell's insists that the Fascisti were merely paid actors hired by Campbell's publicist Klemfuss. Klemfuss, according to this reporter, even went so far as to order a large wreath with a blue satin ribbon and the message "From Benito Mussolini," and display it prominently near the bier. Pietro Allegra, secretary of the Anti-Fascist Alliance of North America, mistook the Black Shirts for the real thing and issued a protest, pointing out that Valentino's films had been boycotted by the Fascists in Italy. Valentino in fact had been eager to gain Mussolini's goodwill. But the wreath bearing Mussolini's name was bogus, and the Italian government denied having sent it.

Another twenty to forty thousand viewers stood on line to get a glimpse of the body on the second day, which passed more calmly than the first. One hundred twelve police were on hand, plus a special detail of detectives. The doors of the funeral chapel were closed at midnight and George Ullman announced that henceforth, up until the day of the funeral, which was now announced for Monday, August 30, only friends and associates of Valentino's would be allowed in to view his body. "This has gone far enough," he said. "The lack of reverence shown by the crowd, the disorder and rioting since the body was first shown, have forced me to this decision."

In California, Pola Negri prepared for the four-day journey east. She had vacated her big Beverly Hills house when Rudy left town and moved into a bungalow on the grounds of the Ambassador Hotel in Los Angeles, where she thought she would feel less desolate. Here she had received the news of Rudy's death with moans, sobs, and shrieks. "Pola Negri Prostrated at News," newspapers around the country reported, usually describing her as Valentino's fiancée. Filming of *Hotel Imperial* was temporarily suspended as she succumbed to grief. "I have lost not only my dearest friend, but the one real love of my life," she said. Attended by two doctors and a nurse, and accompanied by friends Charles Eyton (a Paramount executive who had clashed with Valentino during the shooting of *Blood and Sand*) and his actress wife, Kathlyn Williams, she insisted on leaving her bed to make a pilgrimage to Falcon Lair. "Weeping as she went from room to room, the actress called to Valentino. Her friends followed her discreetly in the background." Soon after, she boarded the train for New York.

The day before the funeral, Mr. and Mrs. George Ullman met her train at Grand Central. Heavily veiled and outfitted in three thousand dollars' worth of widow's weeds, she had brought along her secretary, Florence Hein, a nurse, and a Paramount publicist. "She is on the verge of a mental collapse," Ullman told hovering reporters. In the lobby of the Ambassador Hotel, where Rudy had so recently occupied a suite, she fainted into the arms of her secretary and Mrs. Ullman. "After she spent several hours weeping in her hotel room, she was escorted to the Gold Room at Campbell's where the casket stood under its bank of flowers. She wept as they drew back the lid, exposing through the glass the face of the departed star. She knelt and prayed for fifteen minutes." When she attempted to rise, she again fainted. "POLA SWOONS AT RUDY'S BIER," the world heard. Helped to her feet, she lost control once more in her hotel when Mary Pickford handed her a note from Dr. Meeker telling her that at Polyclinic Hospital in the early morning just hours before he died Valentino had managed to say, "Pola, if she does not come in time—tell her I think of her."

Although friends like Mary Pickford and Raoul Walsh defended her emotional displays as genuine, Pola Negri's reputation in America never fully recovered from the charge that she was a histrionic scene-stealer who, in the words of Ben Lyon, one of the ushers at the New York funeral, tried to turn Valentino's funeral into "a premiere for Pola Negri." Lyon claimed he scotched her plan to adorn the casket with an arrangement of white roses spelling "Pola." In her own defense Pola said, "I cannot help that I have not the restraint of the Anglo-

Saxon. My emotions seem to them exaggerated, but I am not acting."
Her credibility took another hit when a doctor who had volunteered
to oversee her care in New York turned out to be an imposter who had
once been an inmate at a hospital for the criminally insane.

With Pola present, the funeral could be postponed no longer. New
York law required that it take place within seven days of death, which
meant that they could not wait for Alberto's return.

On the morning of Monday, August 30, under clear skies, a subdued crowd of thousands sat in windows, climbed on buildings,
jumped on boxes, or stood on tiptoes, lining both sides of Broadway
and clustering into side streets to watch the hearse proceed from
Campbell's, at Broadway and Sixty-sixth, to St. Malachy's, at 241 West
Forty-ninth Street, between Broadway and Eighth Avenue. The church
happened to be just steps away from Giolito's, the rooming house
where eighteen-year-old Rodolfo, right off the boat, had spent his
first nights in New York. Honorary pallbearers had gathered outside
Campbell's and stood by as the casket, blanketed with roses, was lifted
into the hearse. On the right were Marcus Loew, Nicholas Schenck,
Hiram Abrams, Richard Rowland, Sidney Kent, and the director Mal
St. Clair. On the left stood Adolph Zukor, James Quirk, Joseph
Schenck, Douglas Fairbanks, and Frank Menillo, "all plainly showing
their grief." A convoy of motorcycle police escorted the twelve-car
cortege as it slowly made its way down Broadway. George Ullman had
arranged the ranking within the procession. In the first car, immediately behind the hearse, rode the Ullmans and a veiled Pola Negri. Behind them came Jean Acker with her mother and cousin. The third car
held Natacha's half sister, Nora Van Horn, and the fourth carried Mary
Pickford and the sisters Norma and Constance Talmadge. As the
hearse passed, men in the crowd doffed their hats.

Inside the church, five hundred mourners each carried a printed
and numbered invitation, which served as a ticket of admission to a
solemn High Requiem Mass to be celebrated at 11 a.m. At that hour,
in Los Angeles, all work at the movie studio ceased for two minutes.
In addition to Ben Lyon, ushers at St. Malachy's included Richard Dix,

the marquis de la Falaise, and Clifton Webb, who in 1916 had dropped out as the dance partner of Bonnie Glass, to be replaced by Signor Rodolfo. The tearful throng seated in the pews included Gloria Swanson (swathed in gray fur), Lois Wilson, Marilyn Miller, Hope Hampton, Texas Guinan, Dorothy Mackaill, Ruby Keeler, Bonnie Glass, singer Gene Buck, lawyer Nathan Burkan, broadcaster Major Edward Bowes, detective William J. Burns, and magician Harry Houdini. Actress Louise Brooks, another dancer turned movie star, "cried unashamed." A first-aid station was set up in the church vestibule to administer to those in need of special assistance.

Conspicuous in their absence were all the revelers who had attended Barclay Warburton, Jr.'s party on the night Rudy took ill. Perhaps blaming them for having failed to protect Valentino from life-threatening overindulgence, Ullman simply sent no invitation cards to Harry Richman, Marion Benda, or Warburton himself.

Father Edward F. Leonard, rector of St. Malachy's, presided, assisted by the priest who had heard Valentino's confession, Reverend Father Joseph Congedo of the Church of the Sacred Heart of Jesus and Mary. As the Mass was being sung, Pola Negri leaned forward with head bowed, several times slumping forward as if overcome. Photographers were ejected for disrupting the service.

Gounod's "Ave Maria" was sung by Dimitri Onotri of the San Carlo Opera, and Guido Ciccollini of the Chicago Civic Opera sang Massenet's "Elegy." As the coffin was carried out to be transported back to Campbell's and the organist Joseph Davis played Chopin's "Funeral March," a man later identified as Nicola Abrazze of Brooklyn sank to his knees and cried out, "Good-bye, Rudolph! Good-bye, my friend. I will never see you again."

Arrangements for a second funeral in Los Angeles were taking shape well before Alberto's ship, the White Star liner *Homeric*, docked in New York. George Ullman and Pola Negri had both pressed for burial in California, and a committee of prominent Hollywood producers, directors, and stars had signed the following telegram to Alberto: "We, of the Hollywood motion picture colony, who knew, worked with and loved Rudolph Valentino, urge you to order that his mortal remains be allowed to rest forever here, where his friendships were formed and where he made his home." Charles Spencer Chaplin, the Warner Brothers (Harry, Albert, Sam, and Jack), Marion Davies, Patsy Ruth Miller, Antonio Moreno, Ramon Novarro, Mae Murray, Norma Shearer, Jack Gilbert, Clarence Brown, King Vidor, Norman Kerry, Carmel Myers, Louis B. Mayer, John W. Considine, Jr., John Barrymore, Buster Keaton, and William Cameron Menzies were among the signers. Alberto and Maria, who was living in Turin and was about to be married, agreed that California, which Valentino had loved and where his name had become a legend, should be his final resting place.

Natacha's plea for cremation and preservation of the ashes at the Hudnut vault in Woodlawn Cemetery in the Bronx was never seriously considered, but the fact that she made such a plea hints at the reserves of remorse that bled into her grief.

After being greeted at the dock by Pola Negri, George Ullman, and Frank Menillo, Alberto Guglielmi was driven to Campbell's Funeral Church. He seemed bewildered, distracted. Upstairs, he spent thirteen minutes gazing at what remained of Rudy, barely able to recognize the thin, shockingly altered face. *"Mio fratello, mio fratello,"* he was heard to utter in his Taranto dialect, *"che disgrazia."* "My brother, my brother, what a disaster."

20

AFTERMATH

A Valentino funeral train consisting of two special coaches attached to the Lake Shore Limited departed from Grand Central Station on September 2 at 6:30 p.m., headed for Chicago, where the cars would be hitched to the California-bound Golden State Limited. A baggage car carried the silver-bronze casket. In the other, a passenger coach, rode Alberto Guglielmi, Pola Negri with her nurse and secretary, the mortician Frank Campbell, and George Ullman.

Along the way, ordinary citizens gathered at train stations to bid farewell to the departed star. In Pennsylvania, Alberto was awakened just before dawn by a group of mourners from Erie, most of them Italian, who came with guitars and mandolins and asked permission to play some Italian songs "for the memory of Rudy." He was deeply touched.

Reporters who came on board asked Alberto and Ullman whether Valentino had really been engaged to Pola Negri. The two men's opinions differed, an early sign of tension in the relationship. Alberto said, "We were all one family in California when I visited my brother there. Pola and Rudy were sweethearts, happy in having found each other. They were to be married in the spring and then go to Europe on a honeymoon." Pola, he added, "is like a sister to me now," and she is "tormented by the doubts cast upon the sincerity of her grief." Ullman denied that the couple had been engaged, contending that he surely would have been aware of any such announcement. Pressed to clarify the matter of wedding plans, Pola conceded that there had been no formal engagement. "Rudy never believed in formal engagements— nor do I. Last April we frequently talked of our plans to marry. Our close friends knew of our love. We decided that our private life be- longed alone to us and we did not care to make it public." Alberto agreed: "He never told me of a formal betrothal." Grateful for Al- berto's support and very much thrown together with him, Pola con- tinued to play to the hilt the role of bereaved widow.

At Chicago's La Salle Street Station an "eddying multitude" of many thousands waited to see the funeral car at the transfer point, some of them breaking through police lines to run onto the tracks. A few women fainted under torchlights lit by newsreel cameramen and several people were trampled. Police made twenty-five arrests for dis- orderly conduct. Most of the spectators saw little, but members of the Valentino Memorial Association of Chicago were allowed to place a six-foot-high floral horseshoe beside the casket. Their leader, Judge Francis Borelli, offered a brief prayer in Italian.

As the funeral train traveled farther west, summoning memories of the funeral train of Abraham Lincoln, knots of farmers, ranchers, and laborers gathered to greet it, some of them kneeling in prayer on both sides of the tracks. In Yuma, Arizona, where Rudy and his Arabian steed had galloped over the desert sand during shooting of *Son of the Sheik*, locals paid homage. A lone horseman lifted a broad white som- brero and bowed his head. Alberto got off the train and walked along the platform, explaining that because Rudy had been fond of the area he felt close to his brother there.

Pola Negri had sent a telegram to Marion Davies, asking her to meet the train and board it near Pomona. Davies did so, along with her sister, Mr. and Mrs. Charles Eyton, and John Considine, Jr. Pola and the others in the funeral party detrained into waiting automobiles.

Everyone involved wanted to avoid another major demonstration involving huge, out-of-control crowds. For that reason, details of plans to transfer the casket from the train to the hearse had not been an- nounced in advance. Even so, a crowd of several hundred had assem- bled, along with police and photographers. In Alhambra, a suburb outside Los Angeles, at the intersection of Boulevard Park, Pasadena Boulevard, and Alhambra Avenue, a gray hearse met the train. The casket was transferred to the hearse, and the *Los Angeles Times* reported that "Miss Negri sobbed quietly and lifted a great bouquet of ivory colored rosebuds to the casket where it was placed on the golden pall as the casket was placed in the hearse." From there the coffin was transported to the Los Angeles chapel of the Cunningham & O'Connor mortuary at 1021 South Grand Avenue near Olympic Boulevard. Outside the mortuary, the crowd of spectators consisted of "adult men and women, mostly men." For a quarter a young boy sold badges bearing Valentino's picture and name, and the words "Born in 1895, At Rest 1926." Police escorted him away.

Although an elaborate California funeral was being planned, little provision for burial had been made. United Artists was about to collect $250,000 on Valentino's life insurance policies, and profits from *Son of the Sheik* were mounting, but no one seems to have considered using any of the income to pay for a cemetery plot and monument of appropriate grandeur for him. "They didn't even buy him a grave," an embittered Paul Ivano would charge. George Ullman, the executor of the estate, expressed his preference for erecting a cemetery statue depicting a horseman in a flower garden. However, worried about paying off Valentino's debts, Ullman failed to propose a plan to use funds from the estate to carry out his vision. Instead, June Mathis came forward to offer what she thought would be a temporary solution. When her mother, Virginia Ruth Mathis, had died a few years back, Mathis had purchased a family vault in Hollywood Memorial Cemetery's mausoleum that included niches for Mathis and her husband, Sylvano Balboni. Until more permanent arrangements materialized, Valentino's casket could be placed in one of the as yet unoccupied spots in the Mathis vault. So June Mathis, who had done so much to champion Rudolph Valentino in his career and who cherished him as a friend, once again came through. He would not have been surprised. To his "beloved June," Rudy had once said, "In life or death forever our souls are in tender, austere alliance."

A private memorial to Valentino had already taken place in California, just five days after he died. Valentino had joined the Los Angeles Breakfast Club, and fellow club members followed Norman Kerry as he held the bridle of a riderless horse, one that Valentino had often mounted; a pair of riding boots were placed reversed in the stirrups. Eulogies and prayers were recited and the bugler played "Taps," as in a military ceremony.

On the day of the official funeral, Tuesday, September 7, at every studio flags were lowered to half-mast, work was stopped for part of the day, and five minutes of silence was observed. Outside the Beverly Hills Church of the Good Shepherd, where only a few months earlier Valentino had stood up as best man at the wedding of Mae Murray and David Mdivani, three thousand looked on from behind police cordons. Inside, the casket rested in front of the sanctuary, and three great white candles burned on each side. High Mass was celebrated by Father Michael J. Mullins, pastor of the church and founder of the Catholic Motion-Picture Guild. Incense burned, holy water was sprinkled, prayers for the repose of the soul offered. A baritone from the Chicago Grand Opera, Richard Bonnelli, sang "Ave Maria." "The ceremony moved with a simple dignity, many in the audience . . . rising and kneeling after the manner of their faith. What tears were shed, and there were many, were shed in silence and dignity, except that at times Miss Negri was unable to restrain herself in silence. For the most part she remained kneeling with her head occasionally on the mourner's rail."

Alberto, Pola Negri, and Kathlyn Williams (Mrs. Charles Eyton) sat to the right of the bier. Immediately behind them sat Mr. and Mrs. George Ullman, Charles Eyton, and James Quirk; then Douglas Fairbanks and Mary Pickford, and behind them Harold and Mildred Lloyd. On the left sat the pallbearers: Charles Chaplin, Emmett Flynn, George Fitzmaurice, Douglas Gerrard, John Considine, Jr., and Samuel Goldwyn. Goldwyn had been summoned at the last minute to substitute for Norman Kerry, who had broken his ankle the previous day and arrived at the funeral on crutches. Rex Ingram turned down an invitation to serve as a pallbearer because he thought Valentino would not have wanted him to be there. Among the ushers, all actors, were Montague Love, Antonio Moreno, Mario Carillo, George O'Brien, John Gilbert, and Lon Chaney. Honorary pallbearers included Cecil B. De-

Mille, Mack Sennett, Louis B. Mayer, Hal Roach, Robert Vignola, Jesse Lasky, Manuel Reachi, William Hart, George Ullman, and John Barrymore. Spotted in the crowd of six hundred invited mourners were June Mathis and Sylvano Balboni, Elinor Glyn, the banker A. P. Giannini, Mayor James Rolph of San Francisco, William Randolph Hearst, Marion Davies, the writer-director Paul Bern, Sidney Olcott, Aileen Pringle, Ben Turpin, Mabel Normand, Ernst Lubitsch, Bebe Daniels, Agnes Ayres, Estelle Taylor, and Erich von Stroheim. The Italian government sent a representative, Vice-consul Gradeningro. Notably absent were two of Valentino's closest friends, Paul Ivano and Robert Florey—perhaps they felt the event had been taken over by studio executives and publicists. Also missing were two of the women Rudy had loved most deeply: his sister Maria and Natacha.

Along Santa Monica Boulevard, patient onlookers behind police barriers watched the hearse and a cortege of cars pass the studio where Valentino had so recently worked and proceed from the church to the cemetery. When the bier was being carried to its resting place an airplane dispatched by Lou Mahoney and other Valentino employees swooped low, dropping roses over the mausoleum. People in the crowd, estimated at seven thousand, "stretched their fingers skyward in order to catch some of the petals that descended 'like tears shed by the very heavens.'"

In life, Valentino had visited the Mathis crypt, which had a stained-glass window, to bestow flowers in memory of Mrs. Mathis. Now his casket was lifted and placed above hers. Alberto uttered a prayer and sobbed audibly, *"Addio, Rodolfo, addio."* Pola Negri kissed the coffin many times, then collapsed. She was helped to a divan, where she soon recovered her composure. Alberto stood before the still-open aperture, his head bowed. "He leaned toward the casket, touched its end with his forehead, kissed it, and turned away. He was the last to touch it. The crypt was closed with a marble panel."

For Alberto the death of Valentino marked a calamity from which he would never fully recover. Although he and his brother had not been especially close as children, and did not see each other at all between

1913 and 1923, after Natacha left him Rudy turned to Alberto as a drowning man reaches for a life preserver. Alberto responded, providing ballast. A sweet, dignified, and unworldly man entirely lacking his brother's volatility or dash, he was the soul of responsibility, a devoted and dependable family man who had shown himself a competent bookkeeper and administrator. He had pulled up stakes in Italy, believing that Valentino's fame and success in America offered him and his wife and son their best hope for a comfortable and secure future. When Rudy died, Alberto was in the process of establishing himself as head of European publicity and distribution for Valentino productions, but now, with no new pictures to publicize or distribute, he could not continue along that path, and would need to find another way of making a living. Alberto had spent only a few months in California, in 1926; now he planned to stay at least until the estate was settled. His English was poor and he knew nothing about American laws and next to nothing about its customs.

Neither he nor Maria had any idea what sums they might be inheriting, but they assumed the amount would be substantial. (Ullman would in time dole out cash advances from the estate, allowing Alberto $36,211 and Maria $18,188.) Describing Maria as "grief stricken" in Turin, Alberto conveyed her gratitude for the expressions of sympathy she had received from Rudy's friends and fans in America and confessed himself bewildered and weary.

One of the first things Alberto did after Rudy's death was to adopt "Valentino" first as his middle name, then as his legal last name. His next move was to hire his own lawyer in Los Angeles, Milton Cohen. When Valentino's will was made public in probate court in October, Cohen attacked it for being vague and indicated that Valentino's siblings, Alberto and Maria, both beneficiaries, might try to contest its provision entitling Natacha's aunt, Mrs. Teresa Werner, to one third of any assets. This tack entailed risks, since the will limited the claim of anyone contesting it to a legacy of one dollar. In the end, the will was not contested. Cohen wanted Alberto to be named coexecutor with S. George Ullman, and if that could not be accomplished he wanted Ullman placed under a bond (guaranty) of $100,000, as insurance, although the will named Ullman executor without bonds and empowered him to hold the estate in trust for the three heirs, Alberto, Maria, and Teresa Werner. This legal maneuver also came to naught, but in 1927 the Guglielmis filed a complaint objecting to Ullman's accounting.

Ullman, too, faced a crisis both personal and professional. "Everybody talks about what Valentino's death did to the family," he would complain privately, "but nobody talks about what it did to me." He had lost his major client, and a dear friend, his son Bobby's godfather, and someone from whom he'd rarely been separated in the past year. He'd been left in charge of settling a mound of debts and dispersing a hoard of possessions, none of them his own. He would do his best to continue his career as a manager and agent, taking on such clients as Baby Peggy and Theda Bara, who was trying to restart her career.

Valentino's estate, it turned out, owed the U.S. government more than $100,000 in back taxes. It owed $15,000 to Pola Negri for a personal loan, and $49,500 to repay George Ullman the money he had advanced to finance Natacha's movie *What Price Beauty?* United Artists had advanced Valentino $21,300 on his future salary, and there were lawyers' fees, debts to London haberdashers, funeral expenses, and outstanding mortgages on two houses to be paid. Ullman decided that the best way to raise cash in a hurry would be to conduct an estate auction.

Ullman spent $35,000 of estate funds composing, printing, distributing, and publicizing the "Catalogue for the Public Auction of the Estate of Rudolph Valentino," which sold for two dollars a copy, listed more than two thousand possessions, and contained many photographs. The auction began on December 10, 1926, at Hollywood's Hall of Art Studios on North Highland Avenue under the gavel of A. H. Weil, auctioneer, and continued for several days.

Ullman was first and foremost a businessman and was not above minor chicanery. "I resorted to some tricks," he admitted. "For instance, Rudy had lots of books, but he had only autographed a few of them, and he didn't have a book mark [a book plate]. I had [one] designed [by William Cameron Menzies], stuck it inside the covers of his books, which were worth about two bits a piece, and at the sale they fetched about three dollars a piece. And nobody knows the difference."

In his foreword to the catalogue, Ullman pretended to take the public into his confidence, acknowledging "heart-felt regret" at his capitulation to "the unfeeling course of law" that required him to sell off Valentino's belongings. But what had to be, had to be. "Although I dislike the necessity of putting up for public sale things which Mr. Valentino loved with such boyish enthusiasm, still my aversion to such a sale is lessened when I realize that it will give those who loved him the opportunity of possessing a cherished memento of one of the most honored personalities of this age." Despite Ullman's professed regrets, the catalogue shows signs of hasty production. The booklist, especially, is rife with typos and it's clear there had only been time to research the antiques superficially.

Even so, reading through the catalogue is like entering Valentino's home in his absence; touring the rooms he had occupied and furnished with such care; opening doors to his garage, kennels, and stable; scanning his bookshelves; even peering into his closets. He was a tireless collector, a man who never stopped acquiring beautiful or unusual artifacts and animals and who expressed his personality through them. His collection of antique arms and armor alone took up twelve pages of the ninety-five-page catalogue.

His books attest to an avid interest in the history of costume, the decorative arts, travel, history, French literature, heraldry, and dance. There are several titles on Nijinsky and a few, probably Natacha's, on Russian ballet and the art of Léon Bakst. There are novels in French by Stendhal, Flaubert, Zola, Balzac, Colette, and Proust and a couple in Spanish by Blasco Ibáñez.

Valentino owned seven cameras, two of them for taking motion pictures: a French Debrie and a German Ica-Kinamo. He had a vest-pocket camera, a Gaumont stereo camera for taking stereoscopic pictures, and two Graflex cameras made by Eastman—nothing but the best.

He had hung Italian and Spanish Renaissance portraits on his walls, as well the three modern portraits by Federico Beltrán-Masses. He'd possessed five Gustav Klimt watercolors and many lengths of antique embroidery, brocade, and tapestry. Natacha surely had a hand in selecting many of these rare fabrics, but Ullman made no attempt to represent her interests, and she herself failed to make any claim on the estate beyond that of her aunt.

Evidently, despite Prohibition and ulcers, Rudy had enjoyed imbibing alcohol. He kept two oak whiskey kegs, several cocktail shakers, many antique wine bottles, a silver flask, and a gold corkscrew.

He'd saved two Argentine sombreros he wore in *The Four Horsemen*; a red and gold embroidered cape from *Blood and Sand*; breeches, a white wig, jeweled stockings, and rhinestone garters from *Monsieur Beaucaire*; and Persian belts with silver buckles worn in *Son of the Sheik*. He'd kept eighty-six men's fourteenth-century costumes for *The Hooded Falcon*, and thirty-eight black hoods, never worn.

Four of his horses were offered for sale, including the Black Arabian gelding Firefly, which he rode in *Son of the Sheik* and Haroun, the gray gelding he rode in *The Eagle*. Dogs included pedigreed Great Danes, and an Irish setter from the William Randolph Hearst kennel. Kabar, Rudy's favorite, a black Doberman presented as a gift by Jacques Hébertot, stayed with Alberto, pining for his master.

The custom-made Avion Voison with red leather upholstery that he bought while in Paris was listed, as well as the eight-cylinder, five-passenger Isotta-Fraschini town car, "upholstered with taupe colored Italian broadcloth, with silver mountings and panels inlaid with two-toned walnut and silver." Rudy's personal emblem, a rearing cobra, adorned the hood of each.

Falcon Lair itself was put on the block, as was the two-level Spanish stucco house he'd shared with Natacha in Whitley Heights. Here were the French throne chair "covered solid with fine red Genovese velvet, beautifully embroidered with heavy appliqué"; the Hallet and Davis player grand piano with 136 piano rolls; Natacha's mah-jongg set; two pairs of boxing gloves; Indian moccasins and a bow and arrow; a gold-plated Gillette safety razor; sterling-silver flatware for twelve monogrammed RVG; Rudy's lacquered blue bedroom suite, and the low circular lamp table of his own design that wafted perfume through the air when lit.

The items in Valentino's "personal wardrobe" conjured up the man so eloquently that George Ullman decided he couldn't bear to part with the garments and purchased most himself. Rudy had ordered many of these suits, shirts, ties, shoes, and hats on his most recent trip to London, and they were new, having been delivered after his death. "All of his clothes," the catalogue reads, "are made of the finest materials and were tailored by the most exclusive tailors in London. His numerous pairs of shoes were all made to his special order; . . . his hats are of the finest Italian felt; his neckties are handwoven and brocaded silk." Valentino had owned 30 business suits, 7 riding coats, 7 Palm Beach suits, 60 pairs of gloves, 7 dressing robes, 10 complete dress suits, 4 lounging suits, 6 colored Japanese pajamas, 111 assorted ties, 6 high silk dress hats, 9 gray and 8 white felt hats, 26 white full-dress ties, 146 pairs of socks, 28 pairs of assorted spats, 22 white vests, 13 assorted canes, 17 white silk drawers, 59 pairs of assorted shoes, 110 silk handkerchiefs (embroidered with the initials RVG), 10 overcoats, 1 black velvet English riding habit, 1 gray corduroy hunting suit, 10 pairs of suspenders, 6 pairs of garters with tassels. And this is just a partial list.

His jewel cases contained fifteen rings set with rubies, sapphires, emeralds, cat's-eyes, or diamonds, several of them platinum; scarf pins, cuff links, and shirt studs set with rubies, sapphires, emeralds, and pearls; a wristwatch on a platinum-and-gold chain-link bracelet and an onyx pocket watch inlaid with diamonds in a cobra design; a custom-made white-gold cigarette case, matching cigarette holder and match case inlaid with cut diamonds in a cobra design; and the notorious "original Valentino slave bracelet," with two and a half ounces of pure platinum links. George Ullman said that Valentino was buried wearing the slave bracelet Natacha had designed and presented, but he may have been mistaken. What happened to the slave bracelet listed in the catalogue remains a mystery.

On the first day of the auction a crowd gathered in the doorway, blocking the sidewalk on North Highland Avenue. "Women stood with their faces pressed against the window, while others strained to hear the voice of the auctioneer." Most of the prices paid by bidders failed to match the value or original cost of the items sold. A New

York jeweler, Jules Howard, offered $145,000 for Falcon Lair, which without the elaborate carved Florentine front doors and all the other improvements he made had cost Valentino $175,000 in 1925. The power boat *Phoenix*, purchased for $9,000, went for $2,910. A $2,000 Spanish shawl was sold for $350. Shares of stock in the Hollywood Music Box, a theater, valued at $2,000, fetched only $500. The top bid for the Whitley Heights house, only $10,000, was rejected as too low. It stood unoccupied and subject to vandalism for years and was finally torn down in 1951 to make way for the Hollywood Freeway.

When a white Carrara marble sculpture Prince Paul Troubetzkoy had made of Valentino's hand was placed on the table a hush fell. The marble hand had been modeled from life, probably in Palm Springs in 1920, and the broken lifeline on the Buddha-like palm was clearly visible. The index finger pointed upward, indicating (some thought) a warning. Bidders hesitated, but a woman came forward, willing to take it home with her for $150.

All told, this first auction and a second one conducted in San Francisco a few months later netted a disappointing $96,654.

Some who bid successfully had known Valentino well. Mrs. Teresa Werner arrived in time to offer $300 for an album of Chinese costumes that had probably been Natacha's, and $400 for the Beltrán-Masses portrait of Valentino as *le faucon noir*. Adolphe Menjou came away with an antique Tuscan cabinet and a Spanish screen. Bebe Daniels purchased antique firearms. Using a proxy to bid on his behalf, Alberto acquired his brother's new Franklin coupé auto. He also arranged with Ullman to acquire most of the jewelry, before the auction began.

Alberto naively believed that if he adopted the name Valentino and altered his profile through plastic surgery he might find a future on the screen. The ever-sympathetic June Mathis promised to write a screenplay for him, and Rudy's friend Mario Carillo, who had undergone nose surgery himself, recommended a certain Dr. William Balsinger to perform the operation. Alberto endured not one but seven operations on his face, but he emerged still looking like Alberto, not Rudolph Valentino. "I try to get the Grecian nose and I get the hook," he commented mournfully. He did play small parts in a few movies (one was *Tropic Madness*, starring Leatrice Joy and directed by Robert G. Vignola), but Alberto concluded that acting was not his strongest suit. In the 1930s, after a stint as a foreign dialogue writer, he settled into a job as an auditor for Fox. Alberto lived until 1981. His son, Jean Valentino, grew up to become a successful Hollywood sound engineer for both films and television, winning an Emmy in 1971. Jean died in 1996, and is survived by two married daughters, Jeanette and Sylvia, and nine grandchildren.

In 1932, George Ullman was forced to resign as the estate's executor and to relinquish control to the Bank of America; he was ordered by the court to pay the estate a settlement of $183,754. The Guglielmis had charged him with mismanagement, fraud, and misappropriation of funds. Ullman admitted that without authority he had loaned Rudy's friend Frank Menillo $40,000, which remained unpaid; he had also paid himself $22,300 and failed to give a full accounting of Valentino's interest in his two last films. By this time, the Depression had hit hard and Ullman didn't have $183,754. He contested the amount, again through the courts. A final settlement was reached two years later, reducing Ullman's debt to the estate to about $26,000 and exonerating him of charges of mismanagement. By then, eight years after Rudy's death, the estate's value had shrunk from $772,252 to about $250,000. Falcon Lair had been sold a second time, to an architect, Juan Romero, for a mere $18,000. Unlike the first owner, Jules Howard, who never occupied the premises, Romero moved in, forcing out Alberto, who had been living with his family in the servants' quarters and earning a small salary as Falcon Lair's caretaker. Over the years, Falcon Lair has had many occupants, including renter Gloria Swanson. Tobacco heiress Doris Duke acquired it in the 1950s and died there in 1993. Supposedly she had lined the living-room ceiling with ostrich feathers. In 1997, her estate offered Falcon Lair for sale for $3.9 million. The next year a Florida architect bought it for just under $3 million.

Ullman did not cover himself with glory as executor. He took advantage of Alberto and Maria's unfamiliarity with the estate's holdings and was less than forthcoming with them about the precise value of the assets. But Ullman himself did not become rich managing Valentino's affairs, and the job of unscrambling the financial morass Valentino left would have tested even a saint. Alberto and Maria, understandably frustrated and angry, blamed Ullman for their ordeal, but it was Rudy who had spent beyond his means and failed to pay his taxes, Rudy who selected Ullman as his manager in life and as executor of his estate afterward.

June Mathis survived Valentino by less than a year. While attending a performance of *The Squall* with her grandmother in New York she suffered a fatal heart attack on July 27, 1927. She was about thirty-nine. Valentino's casket was moved to a niche next to hers. After Mathis's husband, Sylvano Balboni, returned to live in Italy, the Guglielmis bought what would have been Balboni's space from him, and it became Valentino's permanent resting place.

As a kind of substitute for a cemetery monument, a memorial sculpture dedicated to Valentino was unveiled in Hollywood's De Longpre Park in 1930. Titled *Aspiration*, the sculpture in gold-plated bronze, created by Roger Noble Burnham and subsidized by fans depicts a broad-shouldered, abstract nude male figure astride a globe. At the unveiling, Dolores Del Rio pulled the cord that let the velvet covering drop, and the sculptor spoke, describing *Aspiration* as "a torch lighting the world with the fire of romance." Much vandalized, the figure was removed in 1954 but has since been restored. A mounted bronze bust of Valentino stands beside it.

Ullman rushed his memoir *Valentino As I Knew Him* into print. Probably written with the help of a ghostwriter, it was released before the end of 1926 and served to bolster Ullman's position as the ultimate authority on Rudolph Valentino. Natacha Rambova, characterized by Ullman as Rudy's one true love but also as a selfish, power-hungry Cleopatra, answered with her own "intimate portrait" of the man she had lived with for five years. Her book, first published in Britain and then in a shorter American edition, is strangely reticent, a testament to Natacha's conflicting impulses to retain her privacy while revealing to the world her version of what happened. The result is a composite of her own words, her mother's recollections, and messages alleged to be from the departed Valentino, delivered with the help of the medium George Wehner by means of automatic writing and published in the last section of the book. Emphasizing Rudy's psychic powers, Natacha claimed an ongoing close relationship with her late, ever-loving former husband, who addresses her from the other side as *"carissima."* At first, Natacha claims, Rudy's messages revealed his unhappiness at having been taken away from his earthly pursuits before completing the work he had set out to do. But after the last rites in Hollywood, she maintained, the founder of theosophy, Madame Helena Blavatsky, had manifested herself to Rudy and his attitude changed. "He seemed more reconciled to his new surroundings and told us of his meetings with Wallace Reid and Olive Thomas," two Hollywood stars who had also died young. On the astral plane now, he encountered Caruso, heard the great tenor sing, and attended the opera with him. Joyous and content, Rudy spoke of Hollywood as a place full of undeveloped souls "being suffocated by the intense materialism of that artificial life."

When a reporter asked Natacha whether Rudy mentioned Pola Negri in any of his messages, she snapped, "He spoke only of significant things, and subjects that mean something." In Natacha's book, however, one of Rudy's dictated messages does include a reference to Pola as a person who possessed psychic powers but didn't realize it.

Natacha did not make a career out of being the ex-wife of Rudolph Valentino. She appeared on the stage, acting in both vaudeville and the Broadway theater, covered a sensational murder trial for a newspaper, and wrote a play, *All that Glitters*, based on her experience of Hollywood as a "gilded hell" (it was never produced). Toward the end of 1927 she opened an elite couture dress shop off Fifth Avenue. "I'm in business, not exactly because I need the money, but because it enables me to give vent to an artistic urge," she explained. She urged American women to express their individuality through dress and not to submit blindly to the latest fashion trends.

On a trip to Europe she met Alvaro de Urzais, the man who became her second husband, in 1934. A British-educated Spanish aristocrat, the dark and slender Alvaro could have doubled for Valentino. After closing her New York shop, Natacha lived with her new husband on the island of Mallorca, where she was engaged in the business of buying and modernizing old villas for tourists. Richard Hudnut had died in 1928, leaving capital to Natacha that financed the real estate enterprise. When the Spanish Civil War erupted, Alvaro sided with the pro-Fascist Nationalists, befriending Franco and becoming a naval commander. Initially in agreement with his monarchist, anti-Communist views, Natacha survived bombings and privation, photographing some of the carnage she witnessed. She fled in haste to Nice after an angry confrontation with a pro-Franco bishop who failed to provide sanctuary to a woman friend when leftists were being rounded up and shot. Soon after, though not yet forty, Natacha suffered a heart attack. The collapse of her marriage to Alvaro de Urzais, another childless union, soon followed. Natacha traded in her coiled braids for a bob, abandoned turbans, and began to dress more simply and to allow herself to be photographed looking relaxed. She became a disciple of George Gurdjieff, drawn to his interest in psychic connections to ancient cultures and his system of altering consciousness through music and movement.

After the Nazis invaded France, Mrs. Hudnut gave up the château in Juan-les-Pins and moved back to the States. Relocated near her mother in New York, Natacha published articles on healing and astrology while there. In the 1940s, supported by the Bollingen Foundation, she undertook a study of universal symbolism that brought her to Egypt, a place she believed had been her home in a previous life. Her participation in research on ancient scarabs and tomb inscriptions resulted in her editing a series of publications, "Egyptian Religious Texts and Representations." Back in New York, she conducted classes in her apartment on myths, symbols, and comparative religion and wrote a chapter on symbolism for the final volume of the series she edited. In 1951, the twenty-fifth anniversary of Valentino's death, she turned away would-be interviewers and threatened to sue Columbia Pictures

if a biographical film in the works, starring Anthony Dexter as
Valentino, dared to involve any impersonation of her. (It didn't.) In the
mid-1960s, stricken with scleroderma, an illness that made it difficult
for her to swallow, Natacha became emaciated, malnourished, and
delusional. A cousin brought her to Pasadena, where she died of a
heart attack in June of 1966 at the age of sixty-nine. She had donated
her collection of Egyptian antiquities to the Utah Museum of Fine
Arts and willed a major collection of Nepali and Lamaistic art to the
Philadelphia Museum of Art. Her death certificate describes her as a
"housewife."

Pola Negri claims in her memoir that she took the $15,000 repaid to
her by Valentino's estate and gave it to Alberto to help him bring his
family to America. Determined to immortalize herself as Valentino's
best-beloved, she commissioned a painting by Beltrán-Masses showing a spectral Valentino hovering over her likeness. Beltrán-Masses
painted the picture she requested, but charged his customary price for
a double portrait.

   Less than a year after Valentino died, Negri married Serge Mdivani, a self-proclaimed Georgian prince and the brother of Mae Murray's sometime husband, David Mdivani. She lived with him at her
château in Seraincourt, France; she shortly after suffered a miscar-
riage, after which they separated, in 1929. Mdivani had not wanted
her to work, but even if he had, Negri would have run into trouble
finding movie roles. Her Polish accent scared away American directors
during the transition to talkies, and her popularity in the States declined as a result of her emotional displays at Valentino's crypt. Paramount decided not to renew her contract when it expired in 1928. No
longer rich after the crash of 1929, Negri needed to resume her career. She appeared in films wherever she could: in England first, briefly
back in the States, and then in Germany, where she made five pictures
for UFA when it was controlled by Joseph Goebbels. She did not flee
the homeland of the Nazis until after Germany invaded Poland. Although rumors of an affair with Hitler were groundless, she spoke out
against him only after she had returned to the United States via France

in 1941. She became an American citizen in 1951 and was supported in her last decades by her wealthy companion, Margaret West, first in Santa Monica and then in San Antonio, Texas, West's home turf. Negri's final picture, Disney's *The Moonspinners* (1964) cast her in a cameo role as a millionairess who leads a cheetah on a leash. Negri, who died in 1987, insisted to the last that her heart belonged to Valentino. "He was the only man I ever lawved," she told A. J. Liebling, pointing to the silver-framed inscribed photograph that occupied a place of honor on her dressing table. "But I am fated always to be unhappy in lawv." The ghostwriter of her autobiography says she choked up at the mere mention of Valentino's name.

Jean Acker attempted to cash in on her link with Valentino by writing a popular song about him, "We Will Meet at the End of the Trail," the sheet music for which features pictures of both of them on the cover. Published soon after Rudy's death, the song's lyrics hint of a physical relationship between Acker and Valentino in the afterlife that tops the one they had on earth: "In my dreams I caress you/While angels all bless you." Acker's song lost out commercially to "There's a New Star in Heaven Tonight," which turned out to be much more popular. The sheet music and Rudy Vallee's recording of the song, which bids Valentino good-bye while welcoming him to heaven, were released at about the same time.

Acker played movie bit parts, usually uncredited, until the early 1950s. She had walk-on roles in *San Francisco* (1936), *Spellbound* (1945), and *It's a Wonderful Life* (1946) and was credited as Jean Acker Valentino in *Something to Live For* (1952), her last film. Continuing her tradition of trying to fatten her wallet through litigation, in 1930 she sued William Delehanty, a New York real estate broker and politician, for reneging on his contract to pay her $18,400 a year for the rest of her life. The married Delehanty denied he had signed any such contract, but admitted he had spent many thousands on Jean Acker. Acker died in 1978 at the age of eighty-five and was survived by her companion, (Lillian) Chloe Carter. They are now buried side by side in Holy Cross Cemetery, Los Angeles.

Ditra Flamé, whose connection to Valentino was far more tenuous than Jean Acker's, is another who rode on Valentino's coattails in a quest for public attention. A few years after Valentino died, and every year thereafter until the mid-1950s, a mysterious veiled "Lady in Black" would appear at the mausoleum and/or the memorial *Aspiration* and deposit a red rose. Her identity was at first kept secret, but the mourner turned out to be Ditra Helena Mefford, a former vaudeville dancer and violinist with the stage name Ditra Flamé, who claimed that Valentino, once a friend of her mother's, had visited her in the hospital when she was a child, bringing with him a single red rose. He told her that she would recover and outlive him, and that if he died first he wanted her to return the favor, remembering him with roses. This ritual she faithfully observed until she decided too much commotion accompanied her yearly appearances. She vanished, only to reappear in 1977, having by that time amassed a large collection of Valentino memorabilia and become the president of the Hollywood Valentino Memorial Guild.

There have been many other women who claimed to be the Lady in Black, including Estrellita del Regil and Marion Benda, later called Marion Wilson, the Ziegfeld Follies dancer Valentino dated in New York. Clearly delusional, Wilson insisted that she and Valentino had married and become the parents of two children. She was only one in a small army of women who insisted that Valentino had impregnated them.

A favorite with newspaper reporters and photographers, the term "Lady in Black" may in fact have been the brainchild of a reporter, producer, and publicist named Russell Birdwell, who hired an actress to mourn Valentino in a movie about Hollywood. By 1938, when *The Sheik* was rereleased, the idea of planting professional Valentino mourners had gained favor among Paramount marketers. A press book article suggests to exhibitors, "For this stunt, hire a woman dressed entirely in heavy black mourning, complete with veil, and have her visit all the local newspaper[s] . . . and ask permission to go through their files for stories and pictures of Rudolph Valentino. Instruct her to be as mysterious as possible. During the showing of *The*

Sheik, she should attend every performance and always sit in the same seat. You should be able to plant stories in local newspapers. . . . The woman can be primed to speak of how she spends her life seeking close contact with his spirit."

Mourning has become a hallmark of the cult of Valentino, much of it heartfelt, some of it tongue-in-cheek, and some of it obsessive. After Valentino's sole sound recording ("Kashmiri Love Song," with "El Relicario") was commercially released, one woman who bought it reported "she had seen Rudy 432 times on the screen. She goes to see *Blood and Sand*, when it is showing in her neighborhood, twice a day. She said she would go more often, but she is not able to stand the emotional strain."

Every year, the anniversary of Valentino's death, rather than his birth, is commemorated with a ceremony at Hollywood Memorial Cemetery, newly restored under the ownership of the Cassity family and now renamed Hollywood Forever. Year after year, on August 23, the ceremony begins promptly at 12:10 p.m., the exact hour of Valentino's passing in New York. Nobody, apparently, has yet figured out that New York time is three hours later than California's.

Recently, the cemetery administrators have initiated the practice of screening a Valentino movie, projected on the side of the mausoleum housing Valentino's remains, a few days before the anniversary. The screenings are free and are well attended. Some fans arrive in hearses, some dress in costume. People are encouraged to spread out blankets on the grass and bring picnic dinners.

Ever since 1951, when Alberto and Jean Valentino protested the carnival atmosphere, replete with black veils and sheik costumes, as "out of place at a tomb," the mausoleum program has attempted to preserve a modicum of dignity, with only partial success. The observances remain, as Lisa Mitchell put it in the *Los Angeles Times*, "part *Day of the Locust* and part 'Day of the Dead.'" Objects lent by Valentino collectors are displayed behind glass. The latest audiovisual technology is applied to project a brief narrative account of Valentino's career. Between pitches to sell cemetery plots, somber musical tributes are offered by tenors crooning "Kashmiri Love Song" or "The Sheik of

Araby." Poems by Valentino are read. Eulogies used to be delivered by actors who knew Valentino——James Kirkwood and Mary MacLaren were among them——or singer Rudy Vallee, who had recorded "There's a New Star in Heaven." Now that most of these have died, the latest actor to portray Valentino is likely to make an appearance. In 1975 it was Franco Nero, star of a 1975 ABC-TV movie based on Valentino's life; Nero arrived in a black chauffeured limousine and posed for photographers inside the mausoleum. In 2001, the seventy-fifth anniversary of Valentino's death, Charles Mandracchia, dressed as the Sheik, sang in his stalwart baritone an excerpt from a planned musical about Valentino that he has composed. In 2002 a new Lady in Black made her debut, a former film-school student named Karie Bible. Ms. Bible replaces Vicki Callahan, an attractive brunette whose junior high school drama teacher was Anthony Dexter, the first screen Valentino impersonator.

England's Valentino Memorial Guild was founded in 1927 as a charitable organization that raised money for a children's ward at the Italian Hospital in London, sent poor children on country vacations in the summer, and provided clothing to refugees. The emphasis shifted to spiritualism when the "direct voice" medium Leslie Flint took the helm. Flint, a former cinema usher and cemetery gardener, conducted séances in his London flat at which the voice of Valentino——described as similar to that of Charles Boyer——was often conjured. When Flint visited Los Angeles, Mae West and Bea Lillie were among those who participated in sessions at which Valentino's spirit voice supposedly spoke. Before his demise in 1994——his death coincided with the demise of the Valentino Memorial Guild——Flint amassed one of the largest known collections of Valentino clippings, books, posters, films, stills, publicity postcards, and other memorabilia. He owned a snippet of footage from *The Young Rajah*——so far the only known surviving remnant of that film.

In Italy, although Fascist protests in 1925 had severely limited distribution of Valentino films after he applied for American citizenship, all was forgiven when he died. "Now that Valentino is dead the theaters and newspapers are full of him," Stark Young reported from Rome in

October 1926. Screenings of *The Four Horsemen*, *The Sheik*, and *The Young Rajah* were well attended. Later in the 1920s *The Eagle* and *Son of the Sheik* were widely shown in Italian theaters "because of popular demand."

In 1966 Marcello Mastroianni starred, the only male opposite eleven actresses in a stage musical about Valentino called *Ciao Rudy* that allowed him to indulge his fondness for comedy and dancing. Before it opened in Rome Mastroianni told Israel Shenker of *The New York Times* that for any actor a reputation as the Great Lover was bound to inhibit real-life sexual performance, making him "a little impotent." He mused about Valentino's plight: "If people tell you you're a great lover, how can you make love with this heavy baggage on your back?" Mastroianni later said he resented the label "Latin lover," which he inherited, as either so vague as to be meaningless or a stereotype as confining as a pair of handcuffs.

Castellaneta was slow to honor its famous native son. The plaque on the house on Via Roma where Valentino was born, with its bas-relief of Nike, the Winged Victory, was placed there in the 1930s by American fans from Cincinnati, Ohio. Not until 1961 did the citizens of Castellaneta unveil a monument to Valentino, a garish ceramic sculpture by the Roman artist Luigi Gheno, which endows Valentino with the yellow-and-red robes of a sheik and a purple-blue face. "It doesn't serve Rudolph Valentino well," a young employee of Castellaneta's Museo Valentino opines.

The small museum, where one can see a photograph of Valentino as a schoolboy dressed as a cadet, view his unsatisfactory Taranto student record and a copy of his birth certificate, touch a manikin costumed as the Sheik, and watch the Kevin Brownlow–David Gill documentary *Swanson and Valentino* dubbed in Italian, was founded to mark the one hundredth anniversary of his birth. The centenary also prompted a Valentino film retrospective at Il Cinema Ritrovato in Bologna; release of a new silent film about an obsessed Valentino fan, *Taxi Dancer*, by the Belgian Dalemans brothers; and an exhibit in Turin, "The Gaze of Narcissus" (*"Lo Sguardo di Narciso"*), organized around the photograph collection of Valentino's sister, Maria Strada, which is now owned by poet Chicca Guglielmi Morone, a distant cousin whose mother befriended Maria's daughter Gabriella.

In Hollywood the quest for a "new Valentino" began when Rudy was still alive, during his strike against Famous Players–Lasky, and picked up speed after August 23, 1926. Ramon Novarro, Gilbert Roland, Ricardo Cortez, and Antonio Moreno were among those cast as exotic dark-haired romantic leads in the 1920s and named as Valentino's successor. Antonio Moreno, who had made his mark in Hollywood well before Valentino became a star, protested being asked to fit the Valentino mold. "I'm not imitating him. I don't want to steal a dead man's thunder," Moreno said. "Just you tell folks that if they won't have me for myself and my own acting, then I don't want them to have me because they think I'm like Rudolph."

An editorial in *Moving Picture World* in September 1926 scolded those who thought Valentino "had left a vacant position another might fill," pointing out that he rose to prominence at a particular time, when America was reshaping itself and needed new idols. That time had passed. Attempting to explain Valentino's hold on the public in the 1920s, *Moving Picture World* traced his appeal in post–World War I America to rebellious young women seeking new forms of pleasure and a new independence. "The war brought into being the flapper and her male companion became the sheik. Valentino became the King of Sheiks, idolized by women of all ages, emulated by all youths."

His enormous impact on the era's young men has been underappreciated. At the time of *The Sheik* he appealed mainly to women, but with *Blood and Sand* that changed. Among youths, the sleek Latin look became the rage. As Gilbert Roland told an audience attending a screening of *The Four Horsemen* marking the fiftieth anniversary of Valentino's death, "When he wore sideburns, we wore sideburns. We combed our hair à la Valentino. If he wore a beret, we wore a beret."

In the 1930s, George Raft—who had known Valentino in New York, had also worked as a dancer-for-hire, and had battled the gigolo tag—was considered an heir of the Sheik. Raft sported a persuasive version of the slicked-back cap of dark hair and played both a bull-fighter and a tango dancer on-screen, but he projected a very different emotional quality: tougher, harder, and less vulnerable to pain than Valentino. In the opinion of Rudy's former director Sidney Olcott, no screen actor who followed Valentino in the thirties, with the possible exception of Leslie Howard, could touch his depth of understanding for emotional drama, combined with a whimsical flair for comedy.

Cary Grant balked at attempting the part of Gallardo in a planned remake of *Blood and Sand*, saying "it would be my finish. I couldn't stand the inevitable comparison [to Valentino]." The part went to Tyrone Power. Commenting on the fruitless quest for another Valentino, Alberto Valentino suggested that "the studios must find a soul like his, not a body."

As early as 1938, producer Edward Small talked of making a film based on the life of Valentino. He first planned to cast Jack Dunn, former skating partner of Sonja Henie, in the lead, but Dunn died a few days after signing the contract. The role eventually went to a Nebraskan who called himself Anthony Dexter; he was a decent enough dancer who had a midwestern American accent. Dexter wore clothes well and looked like Valentino, but he brought nothing the least bit mysterious or European to his performance. In *Valentino*, the 1951 Columbia Pictures release directed by Lewis Allen, he's saddled with a soap-opera script (by George Bruce) that seems to have been molded by fear of lawsuits: Jean Acker, Natacha Rambova, June Mathis, Pola Negri, and Alberto Valentino do not appear as characters, though the film does include a Lady in Black. All the women in Valentino's Hollywood life are rolled into one character, an actress Valentino madly loves, played by Eleanor Parker. Despite Columbia Pictures' caution, Alice Terry ended up suing the studio, claiming that because the Eleanor Parker character was an actress married to a director, the movie slandered Terry by hinting that she and Valentino had been lovers. She won an out-of-court settlement.

Jean Valentino sued the producers of a 1975 ABC television biopic, *The Legend of Valentino,* arguing that they had no right to exploit Valentino's life without the family's consent. This production took liberties with the facts of Valentino's life—June Mathis became a glamorous dish (Suzanne Pleshette) who meets the young Valentino when he tries to burglarize her home—that inspired outrage. The suit was ultimately dismissed when the California Supreme Court ruled that Jean Valentino did not own the rights to Valentino's biography, because a person's "right of publicity" expires upon death.

In an effort to visually document the real story of Valentino's life, the family had cooperated on an earlier TV documentary, also called *The Legend of Valentino*, which used family photographs and home movies, as well as excerpts from many commercial Valentino movies. Coproduced by Paul Killiam and Saul Turell and benefiting from the input of film historian William Everson and friends Paul Ivano and Robert Florey, it's a solid, valuable source now available on DVD.

But distorted versions of the life of Valentino kept coming. Physical beauty and dancing ability, not passion or soul, governed Ken Russell's casting of Rudolf Nureyev as the star of his tawdry, sensationalized *Valentino* (1977) which treats us to a naked Rudy making love to a naked Natacha (Michelle Phillips) in Technicolor in the Sheik's tent. Although Nureyev brought to the role none of Valentino's warmth or inwardness, he delivered a magnificent tango duet with Anthony Dowell as Nijinsky and made some telling off-camera comments about the man he portrayed. Nureyev believed that Valentino was "probably not very active sexually" and that his immigrant status isolated him: "To be a foreigner always creates problems." The Russian-born ballet star saluted Valentino as an instinctive dancer who "moved with great elegance. He was remarkable for his feline suppleness, his animal way of propelling himself with a minimum of gesture and great naturalness. He would hold still and just turn his head or move his hand to indicate an emotion." Finally, said Nureyev, it was his intensity that set Valentino apart. "It wasn't his looks which counted but his acting. He had conviction."

So far, the most persuasive screen interpretation of Valentino that I've seen comes in *Good Night Valentino* (2002), a short film from Mineralava Productions starring Edoardo Ballerini, who also cowrote the script and directed. Ballerini, a young Italian-American with dual citizenship, plays Valentino just before his final illness, dining with H. L.

Mencken (John Rothman) in New York at the Ambassador Hotel. In a sensitive, compassionate performance, he suffuses his character (presented as Mencken described him) with exactly the right mix of pride, elegance, grace, and anguish. On-screen Ballerini's resemblance to Valentino is uncanny.

As a man, Valentino endured endless frustration. He hoped for a career in the cavalry or the navy, but both eluded him. He wanted a happy marriage, but was rejected by two wives. His dream of a home with children remained that, a dream. He established a reputation as a dancer of insinuating grace, but that accomplishment had to compete with the negative associations that plagued a former taxi dancer. On the screen, although he broke the mold of the foreign-looking "heavy," another stereotype, that of the exotic heartthrob, held him captive. The artistic independence he sought never came to him, although at United Artists he ended up with a bigger say in his projects, and a larger share of the profits, than he'd ever achieved before. His native Italy, which he loved, turned on him. He strove for recognition as a skilled actor, able to play comedy as well as romance, aging warriors as well as hot-blooded heroes, but the sheik mythology boxed him in. He wanted, as John Dos Passos put it in *The Big Money*, "to make good in he-man, two-fisted, bronco-busting, poker-playing, stock-juggling America." Make good he did, but without winning the approval of America's macho mainstream.

As a symbol, however, Valentino succeeded beyond anybody's reckoning. He lived the American immigrant's rags-to-riches dream. He rose to the top in silent films, the most popular form of entertainment in the 1920s and a medium for which his gifts for movement, gesture, and nonverbal emotional communication seemed made to order. Dos Passos included him—along with figures like Isadora Duncan, Frank Lloyd Wright, and Henry Ford—among the biographies in *The Big Money* because his extravagant life seemed emblematic of an era of excess. The exotic costumes he wore, his fur-lined bathrobe and jangling bracelets, his spending sprees, overpublicized divorces, custom-made cars, Arabian horses, and lordly homes—even the rioting after his shocking death—partake of that excess. He shared the decade's worship of youth, indulgence, beauty, and speed, and because he died so young he became something close to the personification of those qualities. But he went beyond representing his era, exhibiting a depth of feeling, a capacity for suffering, an artistry, and a princely bearing that belonged to him alone.

To his contemporaries he sent mixed cues. While unlocking women's fantasies of savage, forbidden passion, he was pilloried by men—and sometimes by women, too—for being too ornamental, too dependent, too much like the stereotypic female. Both earthy and artificial, he managed to pose a threat for suggesting two opposite qualities: on the one hand, sex menace, the violent but irresistible magnetism of the ardent brute; on the other, the pretty boy, the deferential gentleman, the "powder-puff" lounge lizard reviled so cruelly on the editorial page of the *Chicago Tribune*. It's impossible to separate the outcry against his polished gigolo image from pure ethnic prejudice. But his foreignness and perceived exoticism, while targeting him for attack, were also intrinsic to his seductive power.

Rudolph Valentino helped deflower postwar America, teaching it by his screen example the limits of emotional restraint and erotic innocence. And he reconfigured its ideal of the desirable man. Along with flamboyant male fashion trends, Valentino offered his adopted country a new masculine ideal: sensual, continental, and far more attuned to women than earlier models, darker in both complexion and mood, more willing than any before (or since?) to respond to beauty, show passion, and give his all—even die—for love.

His appeal in the twenty-first century hinges partly on lingering nostalgia for the 1920s, the era that saw the dawn of so much of the media-saturated, youth-worshipping, celebrity-obsessed culture of our own day, while flaunting a style, freedom, and élan we envy and would like to recapture. Today, although only residents of cities like London, Paris, New York, Washington, or Los Angeles have occasional opportunities to see Valentino movies (and other silents) as they were originally seen, on the big screen, with sharp images and live music, audiences have the best chance they have had since the 1930s to get to know his pictures, through screenings of restored prints on cable television, video, and DVD. Valentino's at times exaggerated acting style, and the hokey quality of some of his scripts, can create distance, locking him into a period straitjacket. But the mysterious and highly charged eroticism he projects seems timeless.

To acolytes, Valentino remains the ultimate romantic leading man, the dream lover whose kisses are conjured in fantasies. In a short story by Frank O'Connor, a wife who isn't attracted to her husband is told by a friend that she might try following the example of another such wife: "One night she pretended to herself that her husband was Rudolph Valentino, and everything was all right."

FILMOGRAPHY: EARLY

VALENTINO FILMS

MY OFFICIAL WIFE

11 August 1914; 5 reels.

Directed by James Young; produced by Vitagraph; distributed by General Film Co.; adapted by Marguerite Bertsch; camera, Robert A. Stuart.

Cast: Clara Kimball Young (Helene Marie), Earle Williams (Sacha Weletsky), Harry T. Morey (Arthur Bainbridge Lennox), Mary Anderson (Marguerite Lenox); RV is a bit player as Russian Cossack.

Source: *My Official Wife*, by Richard Savage.

THE QUEST OF LIFE

25 September 1916; 5 reels.

Directed by Ashley Miller; produced by Famous Players; scenario by Ashley Miller; camera, Walter Stradling.

Cast: "Maurice" Mouvet (dancer Maurice Bretton), Florence Walton (Ellen Young), Julian L'Estrange (Alec Mapleton); RV is an extra in dance scene.

Source: *Ellen Young*, by Edmund Goulding and Gabriel Enthoven.

SEVENTEEN

2 November 1916; 5 reels.

Directed by Robert G. Vignola; produced by Famous Players; distributed by Paramount; scenario by Harvey Thew.

Cast: Jack Pickford (William Sylvanus Baxter), Louise Huff (Lola Pratt). Winifred Allen (May Parcher), Madge Evans (Jane Baxter), Walter Hiers (George Cooper), Helen Lindroth (Mrs. Baxter), Anthony Merlo (Mr. Baxter); RV is an extra in wedding sequence.

Source: *Seventeen*, by Booth Tarkington.

THE FOOLISH VIRGIN
26 December 1916; 6 reels.

Directed by Albert Capellani; produced by Clara Kimball Young; distributed by Lewis J. Selznick Enterprises; scenario by Albert Capellani; camera, Jacques Monteran, Hal Young, George Peters.

Cast: Clara Kimball Young (Mary Adams), Conway Tearle (Jim Anthony), Paul Capellani (Dr. Mulford), Agnes Mapes (Ella Swanson), Catherine Proctor (Nance Anthony), Sheridan Tansey (Jim); RV is an extra.

Source: *The Foolish Virgin*, by Thomas Dixon.

PATRIA
6 January–5 May 1917; part 3 of a 15-episode serial.

Directed by Leopold and Theodore Wharton; produced by Wharton Inc. / Eastern / Hearst; distributed by International Film Service; scenario by Louis Joseph Vance; adapted by Marguerite Bertsch; camera, Levi Bacon, John Holbrook, Ray June, Lew Tree.

Cast: Irene Castle (Patria/Elaine), Milton Sills (Capt. Donald Parr) Warner Oland (Baron Huroki), Jack Holt, Wallace Beery; RV is a dancer in midnight frolic scene.

Source: "The Last of the Fighting Channings," by Louis Joseph Vance.

ALIMONY
3 December 1917; 6 reels.

Directed by Emmett J. Flynn; produced by Paralta Plays, Inc.; distributed by First National; scenario by Hayden Talbot; camera, L. Guy Wilky; art director, R. Holmes Paul; production manager, Robert Brunton.

Cast: Josephine Whittell (Bernice Bristol Flint), Lois Wilson (Marjorie Lansing), George Fisher (Howard Turner), Wallace Worsley (John Flint), Arthur Allardt (Elijah Stone), Joseph Dowling (William Jackson), Ida Lewis (Mrs. Lansing), Marguerite Livingston (Florence); RV is a dress extra.

A SOCIETY SENSATION
23 September 1918; 5 reels.

Directed by Paul Powell; produced by Universal/Bluebird Photoplays; scenario by Hope Loring and Paul Powell; Camera, E. G. Ullman.

Cast: Carmel Myers (Margaret Parmelee), Lydia Titus (Mrs. Jones), Alfred Allen (Capt. Parmelee), ZaSu Pitts (Mary), Fred Kelsey (Jim), Harold Goodwin (Tommy), Rodolpho De Valentina (Dick Bradley).

Source: "The Borrowed Duchess," by Perley Poore Sheehan.

ALL NIGHT
30 November 1918; 5 reels.

Directed by Paul Powell; produced by Universal/Bluebird Photoplays; scenario by Fred Myton; story by Edgar Franklin.

Cast: Carmel Myers (Elizabeth Lane), Rodolfo di Valentina (Richard Thayer), Charles Dorian (William Harcourt), Mary Warren (Maude Harcourt), William Dyer (Bradford), Wadsworth Harris (Colonel Lane).

Source: "One Bright Idea," by Edgar Franklin.

THE MARRIED VIRGIN

December 1918 (reissued 1920 as *Frivolous Wives*); 6 reels.

Directed by Joseph Maxwell; produced by Joseph Maxwell, Maxwell Productions; distributed by States Rights, General Film Co., and Fidelity; scenario by Hayden Talbot.

Cast: Kathleen Kirkham (Mrs. John McMillan), Vera Sisson (Mary McMillan), Frank Newberg (Douglas McKee), Edward Jobson (John McMillan), Rodolfo di Valentini (Count Roberto di San Fraccini).

THE DELICIOUS LITTLE DEVIL

20 May 1919; 6 reels.

Directed by Robert Z. Leonard; produced by Universal; scenario by Harvey Thew; camera, Allan Zeigler.

Cast: Mae Murray (Mary McGuire), Harry Rattenbury (Patrick McGuire), Richard Cummings (Uncle Barney), Ivor McFadden (Percy), Bertram Grasby (Duke de Sauterne), Edward Jobson (Michael Calhoun), Rudolpho De Valintine (Jimmie Calhoun).

Source: "Kitty, Mind Your Feet," by Harvey Thew and John Clymer.

VIRTUOUS SINNERS

25 May 1919; 5 reels.

Directed by Emmett J. Flynn; produced by Pioneer.

Cast: Norman Kerry (Hamilton Jones), Wanda Hawley (Dawn Emerson), Henry Holden (Eli Barker), David Kirby (Stool Pigeon), Bert Woodruff (Bert "Twenty Years" McGregor); RV in a bit part as a down-and-outer in the slums.

THE BIG LITTLE PERSON

May 1919; 6 reels.

Directed by Robert Z. Leonard; produced by Universal; scenario by Bess Meredyth.

Cast: Mae Murray (Arathea Manning), Clarissa Selwynne (Mrs. Manning), Rodolphe De Valentina (Arthur Endicott), Allan Sears (Gerald Staples), Mrs. Bertram Grasby (Marion Beemis).

Source: *The Big Little Person*, by Rebecca Eastman.

A ROGUE'S ROMANCE

9 June 1919 (reissued 1922); 5 reels.

Directed by James Young; produced by Vitagraph; scenario by James Young; camera, Max Dupont; story by H. H. Van Loan.

Cast: Earle Williams (Jules Marier, also known as Monsieur Picard and Armand Du Bois), Katherine Adams (Mlle. Helen Deprenay), Maude George (Jeanne Deprenay), Sid Franklin (Burgomaster), Brinsley Shaw (Henri Duval), Rudolph Valentino (The Ferret, an Apache dancer in Montmartre).

THE HOMEBREAKER
11 July 1919; 5 reels.
Directed by Victor Schertzinger; produced by Thomas Ince Productions; distributed by Paramount; camera, John S. Stumar; story by John Lynch; adapted by R. Cecil Smith.

Cast: Dorothy Dalton (Mary Marbury), Douglas MacLean (Raymond Abbot), Edwin Stevens (Jonas Abbott), Beverly Travers (Marcia), Nora Johnson (Lois Abbott), Mollie McConnell (Mrs. White), Frank Leigh (Fernando Poyntier); RV is an uncredited dance extra.

OUT OF LUCK / NOBODY HOME
24 August 1919; 5 reels.
Directed by Elmer Clifton for D. W. Griffith; assistant director, Leigh R. Smith; produced by New Art Film Co.; distributed by Famous Players–Lasky and Paramount; camera, John Leezer and Lee Garmes; scenario by Lois Zellner.

Cast: Dorothy Gish (Frances Wadsworth), Ralph Graves (Malcolm Dale), Vivian Montrose (Florence Wellington), Vera McGinnis (Mollie Rourke), George Fawcett (Rockaway Smith), Emily Chichester (Sally Smith), Norman McNeil (Rosebud Miller), Kate V. Toncray (Strong-minded Aunt), Porter Strong (Eddie the Pup), Rodolph Valentine (Maurice Rennard).

EYES OF YOUTH
26 October 1919; 7 reels.
Directed by Albert Parker; produced by Garson Productions; distributed by Equity Pictures; camera, Robert Edeson; scenario by Albert Parker; adapted by Charles Whittaker.

Cast: Clara Kimball Young (Gina Ashling), Gareth Hughes (Kenneth Ashling), Pauline Starke (Rita Ashling), Sam Sothern (Asa Ashling), Rudolfo Valentino (Clarence Morgan, a "cabaret parasite"), Vincent Serrano (the Yogi), William Courtleigh (Paolo Salvo), Edmund Lowe (Peter Judson), Ralph Lewis (Robert Goring), Milton Sills (Louis Anthony).

Source: *Eyes of Youth,* by Max Marcin and Charles Guernon.

AN ADVENTURESS
10 April 1920 (original title *Over the Rhine*; reissued 1922 as *Isle of Love*); 5 reels.
Directed by Fred J. Balshofer; produced and distributed by Republic; scenario by Charles Taylor and Tom G. Geraghty; camera, Tony Gaudio.

Cast: Julian Eltinge (Jack Perry/Mam'sell Fedora), Alma Francis (Eunice), Fred Covert (Lyn Brook/Thelma), Virginia Rappe (Zana), Stanton Beck (Grand Duke Nebo), Leo White (Prince Albert), William Clifford (Dick Sayre), Rodolpho De Valentina (Jerrold/Jacques Rudanyi).

PASSION'S PLAYGROUND
April 1920; 6 reels.
Directed by J. A. Barry; produced by Katherine MacDonald Pictures; distributed by First National; camera, Joseph Brotherton; scenario by C. N. and A. M. Williamson.

Cast: Katherine MacDonald (Mary Grant), Norman Kerry (Prince Vanno Della Robbia), Nell Craig (Marie Grant), Edwin Stevens (Lord Dauntry), Virginia Ainsworth (Lady Dauntry), Alice Wilson (Dodo Wardropp), Howard Gaye (James Hanaford), Fanny Ferrari (Idina Bland), Sylvia Jocelyn (Molly Maxwell), Walt Whitman (Curé of Roquebrune), Rudolphe Valentine (Prince Angelo Della Robbia).

Source: *The Guests of Hercules,* by C. N. and A. M. Williamson.

THE CHEATER
7 June 1920; 6 reels.
Directed by Henry Otto; produced by Screen Classics Inc.; distributed by Metro; supervised by Maxwell Karger; scenario by Lois Zellner; camera, W. M. Edmond.

Cast: May Allison (Lilly Meany/Vashti Delthic), King Baggot (Lord Asgarby), Frank Currier (Peg Meany), Harry Van Meter (Bill), Percy Challenger (Prall), Lucille Ward (Mrs. Prall); RV is an uncredited extra.

Source: *Judah,* by Henry Arthur Jones.

ONCE TO EVERY WOMAN
6 September 1920 (original title *Ambition*); 7 reels.
Directed by Allen Holubar; produced by Carl Laemmle for Universal; distributed by Universal; scenario by Allen Holubar and Olga Linek Scholl; camera, Fred Leroy Granville.

Cast: Dorothy Phillips (Aurora Meredith), William Ellingford (Matthew Meredith), Margaret Mann (Mother Meredith), Emily Chichester (Patience Meredith), Elinor Field (Virginia Meredith), Robert Anderson (Phineas Scudder), Mary Wise (Mrs. Thorndyke), Rosa Gore (Mrs. Chichester Jones), Frank Elliot (Duke of Devonshire), Dan Crimmins (Mr. Chichester Jones), Rodolfo di Valentino (Juliantimo Visconti).

THE WONDERFUL CHANCE
27 September 1920; 5 reels.
Directed by George Archainbaud; produced by Selznick Picture Corp.; distributed by Select Pictures; scenario by Mary Murillo and Melville Hammett; story by H. H. Van Loan; camera, Jules Cronjager.

Cast: Eugene O'Brien (Lord Birmingham/"Swagger" Barlow), Tom Blake ("Red" Dugan), Joe Flanagan (Haggerty), Warren Cook (Parker Winton), Martha Mansfield (Peggy Winton), Rudolph De Valentino (Joe Klingsby).

STOLEN MOMENTS

14 October 1920; 6 reels.

Directed by James Vincent; produced by American Cinema Corp.; distributed by Pioneer; scenario by Richard Hall; story by H. Thompson Rich.

Cast: Marguerite Namara (Vera Blaine), Walter Chapin (Richard Huntley), Alex K. Shannon (Campos Salles), Gene Gauthier (Alvarez Salles), Rudolph Valentine (José Dalmarez), Albert Barrett (Hugh Conway), Aileen Savage [later Aileen Pringle] (Inez Salles).

Appendix B

FILMOGRAPHY: VALENTINO

FEATURE FILMS,

1921–1926

THE FOUR HORSEMEN OF THE APOCALYPSE
6 March 1921; 11 reels.

Directed by Rex Ingram; assistant directors, Walter Mayo and Curt Rehfeld; produced and distributed by Metro; adapted by June Mathis; photography, John F. Seitz; art directors, Joseph Calder and Amos Myers; editor, Grant Whytock; music, Louis F. Gottschalk; art titles, Jack W. Robson.

Cast: Rodolph Valentino (Julio Desnoyers), Alice Terry (Marguerite Laurier), Pomeroy Cannon (Madariaga, the Centaur), Josef Swickard (Marcelo Desnoyers), Brinsley Shaw (Celendonio), Alan Hale (Karl von Hartrott), Bridgetta Clark (Doña Luisa), Mabel Van Buren (Elena), Virginia Warwick (Chichi), Nigel De Brulier (Tchernoff), John Sainpolis (Senator Laurier), Jean Hersholt (Professor von Hartrott), Stuart Holmes (Captain von Hartrott), Wallace Beery (Lieutenant-Colonel von Richthoffen), Curt Rehfeld (Major Blumhardt), Beatrice Dominguez (dancer), Bull Montana (French Butler), Edward Connelly (Lodgekeeper), Noble Johnson (Conquest); Richard Arlen and Ramon Samaniego [later, Ramon Novarro] are uncredited extras.

Source: *Los cuatro jinetes del Apocalipsis,* by Vicente Blasco Ibáñez.

UNCHARTED SEAS
25 April 1921; 6 reels.

Directed by Wesley Ruggles; assistant director, Arthur Lamb; produced and distributed by Metro; scenario by George Elwood Jenks; photography, John F. Seitz; art director, John Holden.

Cast: Alice Lake (Lucretia Eastman), Carl Gerard (Tom Eastman), Rudolph Valentino (Frank Underwood), Robert Alden (Fred Turner), Charles Mailes (Old Jim Eastman), Rhea Haines (Ruby Lawton).

Source: "The Uncharted Sea," by John Fleming Wilson.

CAMILLE

26 September 1921; 6 reels.

Directed by Ray C. Smallwood and Nazimova (uncredited); produced by Nazimova Productions; distributed by Metro; adapted by June Mathis; photography, Rudolph Bergquist; art director and costumes, Natacha Rambova.

   Cast: Nazimova (Camille, Marguerite Gautier), Rudolph Valentino (Armand Duval), Arthur Hoyt (Count de Varville), Zeffie Tilbury (Prudence,) Rex Cherryman (Gaston), Edward Connelly (Duke), Patsy Ruth Miller (Nichette), Consuelo Flowerton (Olimpe), William Orlamond (Monsieur Duval), Mrs. Oliver (Manine).

   Source: *La Dame aux Camélias*, by Alexandre Dumas Fils.

THE CONQUERING POWER

Released 8 July 1921; New York premiere, 28 November 1921; 7 reels.

Directed by Rex Ingram; produced by Metro; adapted by June Mathis; photography, John F. Seitz; art directors, Ralph Barton, Harold Grieve, Amos Myers; editor, Grant Whytock.

   Cast: Alice Terry (Eugénie Grandet), Rudolph Valentino (Charles Grandet), Eric Mayne (Victor Grandet), Ralph Lewis (Père Grandet), Edna Demaurey (Mme. Grandet), Edward Connelly (Notary Cruchot), George Atkinson (Cruchot's son), Willard Lee Hall (the Abbé), Mark Fenton (M. des Grassins), Bridgetta Clark (Mme. des Grassins), Mary Hearn (Nanon), Ward Wing (Adolph), Eugène Pouyet (Cornoiller), Andrée Tourneur (Annette).

   Source: *Eugénie Grandet*, by Honoré de Balzac.

THE SHEIK

30 October 1921; 7 reels.

Directed by George Melford; produced by Famous Players–Lasky; distributed by Paramount; scenario by Monte M. Katterjohn; photography, William Marshall and Paul Ivano; art director, Rodolph Bylek; costumes for Valentino, Natacha Rambova.

   Cast: Agnes Ayres (Diana Mayo), Rudolph Valentino (Sheik Ahmed Ben Hassan), Adolphe Menjou (Raoul de St. Hubert), Walter Long (Omair), Lucien Littlefield (Gaston), George Waggner (Youssef), Charles Brindley (Mustapha Ali), Ruth Miller (Slave Girl), F. R. Butler (Sir Aubrey Mayo), Gretchen [later Loretta] Young (uncredited extra).

   Source: *The Sheik*, by Edith Maude Hull.

MORAN OF THE LADY LETTY

12 February 1922; 7 reels.

Directed by George Melford; produced by Famous Players–Lasky; distributed by Paramount; adapted by Monte M. Katterjohn; photography, William Marshall; assistant photography, Bert Glennon and Paul Ivano.

   Cast: Dorothy Dalton (Moran/Letty Sternersen), Rudolph Valentino (Ramon

Laredo), Charles Brindley (Captain Sternersen), Walter Long (Captain Kitchell), George Kuwa ("Chopstick" Charlie), Emily Jorgenson (Nels), Maude Wayne (Josephine Herrick), Cecil Holland (Bill Trim).

Source: *Moran of the Lady Letty,* by Frank Norris.

BEYOND THE ROCKS
7 May 1922; 7 reels.
Directed by Sam Wood; produced by Famous Players–Lasky; distributed by Paramount; adapted by Jack Cunningham; photography, Alfred Gilks; art director, Max Parker; costumes for Valentino, Natacha Rambova.

Cast: Gloria Swanson (Theodora Fitzgerald), Rodolph Valentino (Lord Bracondale), Edythe Chapman (Lady Bracondale), Alec B. Francis (Captain Fitzgerald), Robert Bolder (Josiah Brown), Gertrude Astor (Morella Winmarleigh), Helen Dunbar (Lady Ada Fitzgerald), Raymond Blathwayt (Sir Patrick Fitzgerald), F. R. Butler (Lord Wensleydon), June Elvidge (Lady Anningford).

Source: *Beyond the Rocks*, by Elinor Glyn.

BLOOD AND SAND
10 September 1922; 9 reels.
Directed by Fred Niblo; assistant director, Henry Hathaway; produced by Famous Players–Lasky; distributed by Paramount; scenario by June Mathis; photography, Arthur Edeson and Alvin Wyckoff; edited by Dorothy Arzner.

Cast: Rudolph Valentino (Juan Gallardo), Lila Lee (Carmen), Nita Naldi (Doña Sol), George Field (El Nacional), Rosa Rosanova (Señora Augustias), Walter Long (Plumitas), Charles Belcher (Don Joselito), Leo White (Antonio), Jack Winn (Potaje), Marie Marstini (El Carnacione), Gilbert Clayton (Garabato), Harry La Mont (El Pontelliro), Sidney De Gray (Dr. Ruiz), Dorcas Matthews (Señora Nacional), William Lawrence (Fuentes).

Source: *Sangre y arena,* by Vicente Blasco Ibáñez.

THE YOUNG RAJAH
12 November 1922; 8 reels.
Directed by Philip Rosen; produced by Famous Players–Lasky; distributed by Paramount; adaptation and scenario by June Mathis; photography, James C. Van Trees; sets and costumes for Valentino, Natacha Rambova.

Cast: Rodolph Valentino (Amos Judd), Wanda Hawley (Molly Cabot), Pat Moore (Amos Judd as a boy), Charles Ogle (Joshua Judd), Fanny Midgley (Sarah Judd), Robert Ober (Horace Bennett), Jack Giddings (Slade), Edward Jobson (John Cabot), Josef Swickard (Narada), Bertram Grassby (Maharajah), J. Farrell MacDonald (Tehjunder Roy), George Periolat (General Gadi), George Field (Prince Musnud), Maude Wayne (Miss Van Kovert), William Boyd (Stephen Van Kovert), Joseph Harrington (Dr. Fettiplace), Spottiswoode Aitken (Caleb).

Source: *Amos Judd*, by John Ames Mitchell.

MONSIEUR BEAUCAIRE
18 August 1924; 10 reels.
Directed by Sidney Olcott; produced by Famous Players–Lasky, distributed by Paramount; screenplay, Forrest Halsey; photography, Harry Fischbeck; art directors, Natacha Rambova and Wilfred Buckland; film editor, Patricia Rooney; costumes, George Barbier and Natacha Rambova; technical adviser, André Daven.

Cast: Rudolph Valentino (Duke de Chartres/Beaucaire), Bebe Daniels (Princess Henriette), Lois Wilson (Queen Marie of France), Doris Kenyon (Lady Mary Carlisle), Lowell Sherman (King Louis XV), Paulette Duval (Madame Pompadour), John Davidson (Richelieu), Oswald York (Miropoix), André Daven (Duke de Nemours), Flora Finch (Duchesse de Montmorency), Louis Waller (François), Ian MacLaren (Duke of Winterset), Frank Shannon (Badger), Templar Powell (Molyneux), H. Cooper Cliffe (Beau Nash), Yvonne Hughes (Duchesse de Flauhault), Harry Lee (Voltaire), Florence O'Denishawn (Columbine).

Source: *Monsieur Beaucaire*, by Booth Tarkington.

A SAINTED DEVIL
17 November 1924; 9 reels.
Directed by Joseph Henabery; produced by Famous Players–Lasky; distributed by Paramount; adaptation and scenario by Forrest Halsey; photography, Harry Fischbeck; art directors, Lawrence Hitt and Natacha Rambova; costumes, Gilbert Adrian, Norman Norrell, Natacha Rambova.

Cast: Rudolph Valentino (Don Alonso Castro), Nita Naldi (Carlotta), Helen D'Algy (Julietta), Dagmar Godowsky (Doña Florencia), Jean Del Val (Casimiro), Antonio D'Algy (Don Luis), George Siegmann (El Tigre), Rogers Lytton (Don Baltasar), Isabel West (Doña Encarnación), Louise Lagrange (Carmelita), Rafael Bongini (Congo), Frank Montgomery (Indian Spy), William Betts (Priest), Edward Elkas (Notary).

Source: "Rope's End," by Rex Beach.

THE EAGLE
8 November 1925; 7 reels.
Directed by Clarence Brown; assistant director, Charles Dorian; produced by John W. Considine, Jr./Art Finance Corp.; distributed by United Artists; scenario by Hans Kraly; titles by George Marion, Jr.; photography, George Barnes and Dev Jennings; art director, William Cameron Menzies; costumes, Adrian; editor, Hal C. Kern.

Cast: Rudolph Valentino (Vladimir Dubrovsky), Vilma Banky (Mascha Troekouroff), Louise Dresser (Catherine the Great), Albert Conti (Captain Kuschka), James Marcus (Kyrilla Troekouroff), George Nichols (Judge), Carrie Clark Ward (Aunt Aurelia), Spottiswoode Aitken (Dubrovsky's Father), Mack Swain (Innkeeper), Gustav von Seyffertitz (Footman); Gary Cooper, Mario Carillo, and Otto Hoffman are uncredited extras.

Source: "Dubrovsky," by Alexander Pushkin.

COBRA

30 November 1925; 7 reels.

Directed by Joseph Henabery; assistant directors, Richard Johnson and Barton Adams; produced by J. D. Williams/Ritz-Carlton Pictures, distributed by Paramount; editor, John H. Bonn; scenario by Anthony Coldeway; photography, Harry Fischbeck and Dev Jennings; art director, William Cameron Menzies; gowns, Gilbert Adrian and Natacha Rambova; production manager, George Ullman.

Cast: Rudolph Valentino (Count Rodrigo Torriani), Nita Naldi (Elise Van Zile), Casson Ferguson (Jack Dorning), Gertrude Olmstead (Mary Drake), Hector V. Sarno (Victor Minardi), Claire De Lorez (Rose Minardi), Eileen Percy (Sophie Binner), Lillian Langdon (Mrs. Huntington Palmer), Henry Barrows (Store Manager), Rosa Rosanova (Marie).

Source: *Cobra*, by Martin Brown.

THE SON OF THE SHEIK

5 September 1926; Los Angeles premiere, 8 July 1926; 7 reels.

Directed by George Fitzmaurice; assistant director, Cullen Tate; produced by John W. Considine, Jr./Feature Productions; distributed by United Artists; adaptation and screenplay by Frances Marion and Fred de Gresac; photography, George Barnes; property master, Irving Sindler; art director, William Cameron Menzies; titles, George Marion, Jr.

Cast: Rudolph Valentino (Ahmed/The Sheik), Vilma Banky (Yasmin), Agnes Ayres (Diana), George Fawcett (André), Montague Love (Ghabah), Karl Dane (Ramadan), Bynunsky Hyman (Pincher), Bull Montana (Ali), Edward Connelly (Zouave).

Source: *The Sons of the Sheik*, by E. M. Hull.

NOTES

ABBREVIATIONS IN NOTES

AMMI: American Museum of the Moving Image, Astoria

AMPAS: Academy of Motion Picture Arts and Sciences, Margaret Herrick Library, Beverly Hills

Arsenal: Bibliothèque nationale de France, Bibliothèque de l'Arsenal, Dèpartment des arts du spectacle, Paris

AV: Alberto Valentino

BiFi: Bibliothèque du film, Paris

BFI: British Film Institute, London

JV: Jean Valentino

HRC: Harry Ransom Humanities Research Center, University of Texas, Austin

L of C: Library of Congress, Washington, D.C.

MoMA: Film Study Center, Museum of Modern Art, New York

n.p.: no page number

NR: Natacha Rambova

NYPL: New York Public Library, Billy Rose Theater Collection

RV: Rudolph Valentino

SFPALM: San Francisco Performing Arts Library and Museum

UA: United Artists

Wisconsin: Wisconsin Center for Film and Theater Research, Wisconsin Historical Society, Madison

PROLOGUE

3   *Lumière brothers:* "Where It All Began," Episode One, *Cinema Europe: The Other Hollywood,* produced by Kevin Brownlow and David Gill, Photoplay Productions, 1995.

3   *Italian cinema:* Peter Bondanella, *Italian Cinema* (New York: Continuum, 1995), p. 1.

3   *Cines*: David A. Cook, *A History of Narrative Film*, 2nd ed. (New York: W. W. Norton, 1990), p. 57.

4   *"too foreign looking"*: D. W. Griffith, quoted by Lillian Gish, *Dorothy and Lillian Gish* (New York: Scribner, 1973), p. 81.

4   *"He is not like . . ."*: Agnes Smith, "Not Quite a Hero," *Picture Play*, August 1922, p. 49.

5   *"Born in a land . . ."*: *Los Angeles Times*, August 24, 1926, n.p.

5   *"I think of glamour . . ."*: Mae Murray Interview, 1959, Columbia University Oral History Project Transcript, p. 1239.

8   *"Everything in film . . ."*: Lillian Gish in "The Trick of Light," Episode 11 of *Hollywood: The Pioneers*, produced by Kevin Brownlow and David Gill, Thames Video, 1980.

8   *"The soul that looks . . ."*: June Mathis in *Motion Picture Magazine*, April 1926, p. 43.

1: MERCURIO

9   *baptized*: Rudolph Valentino (henceforth, RV) baptismal record, Museo Valentino, Castellaneta, Italy. Birth extract no. 182, dated May 9, 1895, Castellaneta Public Records Office (Ufficio dello stato civile).

11   *Bice*: The Malherbe verses on the grave are now all but obliterated. Quoted and identified as Malherbe by Jeanne de Recqueville, *Rudolph Valentino* (Paris: France-Empire, 1978), p. 16. Author's translation. Bice's full name, as given on her June 5, 1890, birth extract, is Grazia Bice Maria Ceresa Amalia Guglielmi.

11   *Royal Army grenadier*: Roster of enrollment *(ruoli matricolari)*, 1873–1878, Taranto State Archive (Archivio di stato).

11   *Regia Accademia Militare*: Leo Pantaleo, *Il Mistero Rodolfo Valentino, Romanzo* (*The Mystery of Rodolfo Valentino: A Novel*) (Milan: Idea Books, 1995), p. 27.

11   *Alberto was born*: Alberto Valentino (henceforth, AV), taped interview by Jean Valentino (henceforth, JV), 1976, courtesy Sylvia Valentino Huber. Although Alberto said he was born in Rome, his April 21, 1892, birth extract is from Castellaneta. Since the birth extract bears a date two weeks after Alberto's birth on the seventh, the family may have transported him as a newborn infant.

12   *Donna Grazia Ancona*: Birth extract of Giovanni Antonio Giuseppe Fedele Guglielmi, born February 8, 1853, Public Records Office, Martina Franca.

12   *Giovanizzi family*: Agostino De Bellis (of Castellaneta), letter to author, May 15, 1999, based on his interview on my behalf with his ninety-six-year-old grandfather, Nicola Napoletane, also of Castellaneta.

13   *a business contract*: Trafford R. Cole, *Italian Genealogical Records* (Salt Lake City: Ancestry Incorporated, 1995), p. 94.

13   *Gabriella's dowry*: Pantaleo, *The Mystery*, p. 28.

13   *wedding*: Marriage license *(atto matrimoniale)* of Giovanni Antonio Guglielmi and Marie Berta Gabriella Barbin, June 22, 1889, Taranto State Archive (Archivio di stato).

13 *christened:* Birth certificate of Marie Berthe Gabrielle Barbin, Vesoul, France, Canton of Lure, May 8, 1856.

13 *ate rats:* Sylvia Valentino Huber, personal communication, April 17, 1999.

14 *not quite respectable:* RV, *My Private Diary* (Chicago: Occult Publishing, 1929), p. 11.

14 *L'École de Chemin de Fer:* AV, interview by Kevin Brownlow, June 3, 1977.

14 *railroad bridge:* RV, *My Private Diary,* p. 273.

15 *Francesco Galeone:* Family tree provided by Sylvia Valentino Huber.

15 *cheese, olive oil:* Pantaleo, *The Mystery,* p. 27.

15 *powerful clients:* De Bellis letter to author.

15 *researching . . . malaria:* AV, Brownlow interview.

15 *wanted to study medicine:* AV, JV interview.

15 *seven thousand residents:* de Recqueville, p. 14.

15 *amenities:* RV, "My Life Story," part 1, *Photoplay,* February 1923, p. 32.

16 *Pasquale:* Birth extract of Giovanni Antonio Giuseppe Fedele Guglielmi, born to Pasquale Guglielmi and Donna Grazia Ancona, February 9, 1853, Martina Franca.

16 *brigands:* RV, "My Life Story," p. 32; Martin Clark, *Modern Italy, 1871–1995,* 2nd ed. (London: Longman, 1996), p. 49.

16 *"Guglielmi":* Emidio De Felice, *Dizionario dei cognomi italiani (Dictionary of Italian First Names)* (Milan: Mondadori, 1978), p. 144.

16 *Willien:* Birth certificate of Marie Gabrielle Barbin, Canton of Lure, May 8, 1856.

16 *originated in Rome:* AV, JV interview.

17 *"di Valentina":* RV, "My Life Story," p. 34.

17 *"they sent him a coat of arms":* AV, Brownlow interview.

18 *"Rudy couldn't see . . .":* Adela Rogers St. Johns, *Love, Laughter, and Tears: My Hollywood Story* (Garden City, N.Y.: Doubleday, 1978), p. 164.

18 *His favorite book:* RV, "My Life Story," p. 34.

18 *a scar:* RV, *My Private Diary,* p. 174.

18 *"kept him impatient . . .":* Ethel Sands, "A Fan's Adventures in Hollywood," unsourced clip, 1922, private collection.

19 *"he refused to submit . . .":* Hiram Kelly Moderwell, "When Rudy Was a Boy," *Photoplay,* January 1928, pp. 84, 118.

19 *"I used to go to the stables . . .":* RV, *My Private Diary,* p. 270.

19 *"picking flowers . . .":* Beulah Livingstone, *Remember Valentino: Reminiscences of the World's Greatest Lover,* pamphlet, 1938, p. 18.

19 *"I became to myself . . .":* RV, *My Private Diary,* p. 228.

20 *"When he was bad . . .":* Maldarizzi family member quoted in *The New York Times,* August 26, 1926, p. 5.

20 *"The father punished . . .":* Moderwell, "When Rudy Was a Boy," p. 84.

20 *"My mother held . . .":* RV, "My Life Story," p. 253.

20 *"by no means helpless . . .":* Ibid., p. 32.

20 *"Relatives are like . . ."*: Quoted by Susan G. Berkowitz, "Familism, Kinship, and Sex Roles in Southern Italy," *Anthropological Quarterly* 57, April 1984, p. 86.

21 *Rudy was "very close"*: AV, JV interview.

21 *"She never would tag . . ."*: RV, "My Life Story," p. 32.

21 *"Maria was the audience . . ."*: RV, unsourced clip, Valentino scrapbook, NYPL.

21 *An early photo*: Reproduced in Chicca Guglielmi Morone and Antonio Miredi, *Rodolfo Valentino: Una mitologia per immagini* (*Rodolfo Valentino: A Mythology in Pictures*) (Turin: Libreria Petrini, 1995).

22 *"My father happened to be . . ."*: RV, *Movie Weekly* clip, 1923, Wisconsin.

22 *"A man's most coveted . . ."*: RV, *My Private Diary*, p. 104.

22 *"What sort of little boy . . ."*: Alma Whitaker, *Los Angeles Times*, December 21, 1924, section 3, p. 30.

22 *Florey doubted*: Robert Florey, *La lanterne magique* (*The Magic Lantern*) (Lausanne: La Cinémathèque Suisse, 1966), p. 167.

22 *"[His] heroine is . . ."*: Jean Acker, quoted in *Los Angeles Times*, September 3, 1922, n.p.

23 *European men*: Natacha Rambova (henceforth, NR), in Elizabeth Redfield, "May a Wife Deny Her Husband Children?" *Liberty*, January 2, 1926, p. 18.

23 *Mrs. Brown*: Priscilla Bonner, quoted in Tony Villecco, *Silent Stars Speak* (Jefferson, N.C.: McFarland, 2001), p. 27.

24 *Giovanni . . . succumbed*: Death certificate of Giovanni Guglielmi, March 24, 1906, Taranto State Archive.

2: EARLY SORROW

25 *"There had been many deaths . . ."*: RV, "My Life Story," part 1, *Photoplay*, February 1923, p. 34.

25 *"by many scientists . . ."*: RV, affidavit, in *Movie Weekly*, October 21, 1922, n.p.

26 *"died for his work . . . silver and black"*: RV, "My Life Story," p. 34.

27 *"I [was] trying . . . preceded her"*: RV, *My Private Diary* (Chicago: Occult Publishing, 1929), p. 121.

27–28 *"I couldn't understand . . . my father do"*: RV, "My Life Story," p. 34.

28 *school in Perugia*: Attilio Fontana, "La verità sulla giovinezza di Rodolfo Valentino" ("The Truth About the Youth of Rodolfo Valentino"), *Cinema Roma*, November 10, 1938, p. 310.

29 *"We marched squad form . . ."*: RV, "Valentino's Adventurous Life, by Himself," *Movie Weekly*, February 18, 1922, n.p.

29 *"All would go well until . . ."*: RV, unattributed clip, NYPL.

30 *widow's pension*: Fontana, "La verità," p. 309.

30 *"We wore long cloaks . . . dreams"*: RV, "Valentino's Adventurous Life," *Movie Weekly*, February 25, 1922, n.p.

30 *soccer*: *Movie Weekly*, undated clip.

30 *"I saw classic plays . . . taken out"*: RV, "Valentino's Adventurous Life," *Movie Weekly*, February 18, 1922, n.p.

31 "abbastanza intelligente": Gabriella Guglielmi, letter to Perugia headmaster, quoted in Fontana, "La verità," p. 309.

31 bella figura: See Luigi Barzini, *The Italians* (New York: Atheneum, 1986), chapter 4.

31 *the smart uniform:* RV, "My Life Story," p. 35; Robert Florey, *La lanterne magique* (*The Magic Lantern*) (Lausanne: La Cinémathèque Suisse, 1966), p. 152.

31 *"I wanted to get into . . .":* RV, "Valentino's Adventurous Life," *Movie Weekly*, February 18, 1922, n.p.

31 *Gabriella's pleading letter:* Reproduced in Fontana, "La verità," pp. 309–10, translation by Frances Starn.

32 *He passed the written:* AV, JV interview, 1976, courtesy Sylvia Valentino Huber.

32 *chest measurement:* Fontana, "La verità," p. 310.

32 *"Here I was . . .":* RV, "My Life Story," p. 35.

32 *He had nightmares:* "Hitting the Hookah with Rudy," uncredited magazine clip, Wisconsin.

32 *"I returned home . . .":* RV, "Valentino's Adventurous Life," *Movie Weekly,* February 18, 1922, n.p.

32 *Istituto di Agraria:* The school still exists as Istituto Bernardo Marsono, Agraria, and is located between Genoa and the Cinque Terre, according to Massimo Burlando (Genoa), personal communication.

32 *"I am a bit worried":* Note from Gabriella Guglielmi to headmaster, quoted in *New York Journal-American*, March 29, 1952, n.p.

32 *on top of a hill:* NR, *Rudy: An Intimate Portrait of Rudolph Valentino by His Wife* (London: Hutchison, 1926), p. 83.

33 *"I always have been . . .":* RV, *My Private Diary*, p. 129.

33 *"a little squirt":* Quoted in Mary Jane Parkinson, *The Kellogg Arabian Ranch: The First Fifty Years* (Arabian Horse Association of Southern California, 1977), p. 28.

34 *He took piano lessons:* AV, JV interview.

34 *"Rodolfo would wait":* Signora Felicita Sessarego to John Casserly, *New York Journal-American*, March 29, 1952, n.p.

34 *"he took the flowers . . .":* Maria Guglielmi, quoted in *The New York Times*, August 26, 1926, p. 5.

35 *"I was always in love . . . chaperons":* RV, "My Life Story," p. 104.

35 *"The whole town promenaded . . .":* RV, *My Private Diary*, p. 247.

35–36 *"I don't do anything . . .":* RV, letter to Bruno Pozzan, quoted by autograph dealer Charles Hamilton, *New York World Telegram-Sun,* August 23, 1962, n.p.

36 *"My family predicted . . .":* RV, *My Private Diary*, p. 243.

36 *A former Castellaneta neighbor:* The New York Times, August 26, 1926, p. 5.

36 *Fiat factories:* Denis Mack Smith, *Modern Italy* (Ann Arbor: University of Michigan Press, 1997), p. 221.

36 *Hollywood job application:* "When Rudy Applied for a Job," unsourced clip, Wisconsin.

36   *to own a Fiat:* RV, "Valentino's Adventurous Life," *Movie Weekly*, February 18,
     1922, n.p.

37   *courtliness:* "A Mental Photograph of Rudolph Valentino," *Pantomime*, April 15,
     1922, n.p.

37   *he and a friend:* RV, "Valentino's Adventurous Life," *Movie Weekly*, February 18,
     1922, n.p.

38   *marquis de Castellane:* Jules Bertaut, *Paris, 1870–1935*, trans. R. Millar (New
     York: D. Appleton, Century, 1936), p. 206.

38   *"a Poet of Cloth":* Thomas Carlyle, "Sartor Resartus," quoted in Michael Batter-
     berry and Ariane Batterberry, *Mirror Mirror: A Social History of Fashion* (New
     York: Holt, Rinehart & Winston, 1977), p. 212.

38   *"those who wish . . .":* Honoré de Balzac, "Lost Illusion," quoted in Valerie Steele,
     Paris Fashion: A Cultural History (New York: Oxford University Press, 1988),
     p. 60.

39   *Nijinsky:* Nigel Gosling, *The Adventurous World of Paris, 1900–1914* (New York:
     Morrow, 1978), p. 171; Peter Ostwald, *Vaslav Nijinsky: A Leap into Madness*
     (New York: Lyle Stuart, 1991), p. 65.

39   *a revolution in color:* Steele, *Paris Fashion*, pp. 215–29; Meredith Etherington-
     Smith and Jeremy Pilcher, *The "It" Girls: Lady Duff Gordon and Elinor Glyn* (Lon-
     don: Hamish Hamilton, 1986), p. 161.

39   *the Apache:* International Encyclopedia of Dance, ed. Selma Cohen et al., s.u.
     "Apache" (New York: Oxford University Press, 1998), vol. 1, p. 95.

40   *the Argentine tango:* Ibid., s.u. "Tango," vol. 6, p. 98.

40   *New cinemas:* Richard Abel, *The Ciné Goes to Town: French Cinema, 1896–1914*
     (Berkeley and Los Angeles: University of California Press, 1998), p. 54.

40   *Max Linder:* Ibid., p. 236.

40   *a music-hall dancer:* Florey, *Lanterne*, p. 167.

41   *"If I was a poor amateur":* RV, *My Private Diary*, p. 245.

41   *empty pockets:* RV, "My Life Story," p. 105; Florey, *Lanterne*, p. 153.

41   *sent the bill:* AV, JV interview.

41   *"Thrown on his own":* RV, quoting his relatives to Herbert Howe, "Success—and
     the Morning After," *Picture Play*, August 1921, p. 31.

41   *"I don't want to continue":* RV, letter to Bruno Pozzan, quoted by Charles Hamil-
     ton, *New York World Telegram-Sun*, August 23, 1962, n.p.

3: NEW YORK TANGO

43   *"He was shipped off . . .":* John Dos Passos, *The Big Money* (New York: New Amer-
     ican Library, 1969 [1936]), p. 206.

43   *four thousand dollars; trade up to a first-class cabin:* AV, JV interview, 1976.

44   *Marion Hennion:* Unsourced Valentino clip, Wisconsin.

44   *"Very few people . . .": calling cards:* Mrs. Russell E. Dill, letter, quoted in Norman
     A. Mackenzie, *The Magic of Rudolph Valentino* (London: Research Publishing,
     1974), p. 24.

44 *most of his fellow:* Humbert S. Nelli, "Italians," in *Harvard Encyclopedia of American Ethnic Groups* (Cambridge, Mass.: Belknap Press, 1980), pp. 549–55.

44 *Vincent Vitelli:* MacKenzie, *The Magic*, photo caption facing p. 80.

44 *"a smart young masher":* Alexander Walker, *Rudolph Valentino* (New York and London: Penguin Books, 1976), p. 11.

45 *"agriculturalist":* Unsourced Valentino clip, May 26, 1922, MoMA.

45 *list of aliens:* Manifest of alien passengers for the United States arriving from Genoa on the S.S. *Cleveland* on December 22, 1913, Passenger and Crew Lists of Vessels Arriving in New York, June 16, 1897–December 31, 1942, National Archives, Washington, D.C.

45 *"The Best Italian Dinner . . .":* Advertisement, *Variety*, January 4, 1918.

45 *"Nothing was too elegant . . .":* RV, "My Life Story," part 2, *Photoplay*, March 1923, p. 54.

46 *"These Americans . . .":* Ibid., p. 55.

46 *horse cars still ruled:* Alan Chester Valentine, *1913: America Between Two Worlds* (New York: Macmillan, 1962), p. 65.

46 *"The loneliest ebb . . .":* RV, *My Private Diary* (Chicago: Occult Publishing, 1929), p. 258.

46 *"and cried like an infant":* RV, "My Life Story," part 2, p. 55.

47 *one of them he recognized:* Chicago Tribune, January 17, 1924, n.p.

47 *"I was a pretty wild boy":* RV, in John K. Winkler, "I'm Tired of Being a Sheik," *Colliers*, January 16, 1926, p. 28.

47 *Count Alex:* Variety, November 11, 1925, p. 36.

48 *"Rudy often masqueraded":* Beulah Livingstone, *Remember Valentino: Reminiscences of the World's Greatest Lover*, pamphlet, 1938, p. 25.

48 *in Brooklyn:* AV, JV interview.

48 *"when the ladies saw [him] . . .":* Schuyler Parsons, *Untold Friendships* (Boston: Houghton Mifflin, 1955), p. 124. I owe this reference to David Stenn.

49 *Cornelius Bliss, Jr.:* Obituary, *The New York Times*, April 6, 1949, p. 29.

49 *"My pride . . .":* RV, *My Private Diary*, p. 264.

50 *Italians in American films:* Kevin Brownlow, *Behind the Mask of Innocence* (New York: Knopf, 1990), pp. 310–13.

50 *"You don't call an Italian . . .":* Quoted by Thomas J. Fleming, *The Golden Door* (New York: Grosset & Dunlap, 1970), pp. 92–94.

50 *immigration policy:* Richard D. Alba, *Italian Americans* (Englewood Cliffs, N.J.: Prentice-Hall, 1985), pp. 64–66; Francis G. Wickware, ed., *The American Year Book: 1914* (New York: Appleton, 1915), p. 385.

51 *New York had:* Mark Sullivan, *Our Times: The United States, 1900–1925*, vol. 5, *Over Here* (New York: Scribner's, 1933), p. 202.

51 *"My last landlady . . .":* RV, *My Private Diary*, p. 265.

51 *"There was one place . . .":* RV, in Josephine Shelton, "Signore Valentino Herewith Presents His New Leading Lady, Fräulein Banky," *Motion Picture Magazine*, November 1925, p. 90.

51 *photographed in top hat:* Walker, *Rudolph Valentino,* facing p. 14.

51 *his only suit:* Robert Florey, "Valentino tel qu'il est" ("Valentino as He Is"), *Ciné-Miroir* 82, September 15, 1925, p. 295.

52 *those who were under forty:* Trafford R. Cole, *Italian Genealogical Records* (Salt Lake City: Ancestry Incorporated, 1995), p. 147.

52 *tried to enlist:* The New York Times, November 11, 1925, p. 16.

52 *La Comité d'Assistance:* Jeanne de Recqueville, *Rudolph Valentino* (Paris: France-Empire, 1978), p. 30.

52 *atrocities:* Sullivan, *Our Times,* vol. 5, p. 78.

53 *"flip past the war news":* Abel Green and Joe Laurie, Jr., *Show Biz: From Vaude to Video* (New York: Henry Holt, 1951), p. 112.

53 *"One rainy evening . . .":* RV, in Winkler, "I'm Tired of Being a Sheik," p. 28.

54 *Julius Keller:* Lewis Erenberg, "Impresarios of Broadway Nightlife," in *Inventing Times Square: Commerce and Culture at the Crossroads of the World,* ed. William R. Taylor (New York: Russell Sage Foundation, 1991), p. 161.

54 *"had gone slightly insane . . .":* Julius Keller, *Inns and Outs* (New York: Putnam's, 1939), p. 124.

55 *an upstairs room:* RV, "My Life Story," part 2, p. 112.

55 *"Who can prove . . .":* Tommy Gray, *Variety,* August 27, 1915, p. 7.

55 *"macaronis":* Ellen Moers, introduction, *The Dandy: Brummell to Beerbohm* (New York: Viking Press, 1960), p. 11.

56 *the dancers tended:* Erenberg, "Impresarios of Broadway Nightlife," pp. 162–63.

56 *"The new dancing":* The New York Times, January 4, 1914, section 5, p. 8.

56 *"left arms straight":* Valentine, *1913: America Between Two Worlds,* p. 83.

56 *"TANGO PIRATES . . .":* Richard Barry, "Tango Pirates Infest Broadway," *The New York Times Magazine,* May 30, 1915, section 5, p. 16.

56 *"The very air . . .":* Quoted by Julie Malnig, *Dancing till Dawn: A Century of Exhibition Ballroom Dancing* (Westport, Conn.: Greenwood Press, 1992), p. 9.

57 *"indicative of moral decadence":* The New York Times, January 2, 1914, p. 3.

57 *A 1914 letter:* Judith L. Hanna, *Dance, Sex, and Gender: Signs of Identity, Dominance and Desire* (Chicago: University of Chicago Press, 1988), p. 164.

57 *"They never play tangos":* Gloria Swanson, *Swanson on Swanson* (New York: Random House, 1980), p. 33.

58 *"Gigolo":* Irving Lewis Allen, *The City in Slang: New York Life in Popular Speech* (New York: Oxford University Press, 1993), p. 81.

58 *"No European male":* Anita Loos, *Kiss Hollywood Good-Bye* (New York: Ballantine, 1975), p. 17.

59 *"For a man to do ballroom dancing . . .":* RV, in C. Blythe Sherwood, "Enter Julio!" *Motion Picture Classic,* June 1920, p. 75.

59 *a few lessons:* Livingstone, *Remember Valentino,* p. 34.

59 *"There is a parallel . . .":* Alexander Walker, *Stardom: The Hollywood Phenomenon* (New York: Stein & Day, 1970), p. 158.

4: SIGNOR RODOLFO

60 *Harrison Ford:* RV, in Russell Holman, *Pantomime*, February 11, 1922, p. 12.

60 *"a quiet fur-coated young man . . .":* Cosmo Hamilton, *Unwritten History* (Boston: Little, Brown, 1924), p. 322.

60 *"I recall introducing him . . .":* John W. Higgins, undated typescript, Valentino scrapbook, NYPL.

62 *"The motion picture is something more . . .":* Editorial, *Motion Picture News*, December 20, 1913, p. 28.

62 *more than one night in a movie house:* Robert Florey, *La lanterne magique* (Lausanne: La Cinémathèque Suisse, 1966), p. 163.

62 *Mary Pickford recalled:* Pickford, *Sunshine and Shadow* (Garden City, N.Y.: Doubleday, 1955), p. 133.

62 Battle of the Sexes: Listed in Diane Kaiser Koszarski, "Filmography," in *There Is a New Star in Heaven: Valentino,* ed. Eva Orbanz (Berlin: Verlag Volken Spiess, 1979), p. 32; and in Vittorio Martinelli, "Filmografia," in *Valentino: Lo Schermo della passione (Valentino: In Defense of Passion),* ed. Paola Cristalli (Ancona, Italy: Transeuropa, 1996), p. 135. These listings are based on James Card's sighting of Valentino as a dance extra in a J. Stuart Blackton compilation, *The March of the Movies.*

62–63 *"I stayed in New York . . .":* RV, in Robert Florey, "Valentino tel qu'il est" ("Valentino as He Is") *Ciné-Miroir* 83, October 1, 1925, p. 311.

63 *Griffith scholars:* Anthony Slide, personal communication, October 15, 1999; Arthur Lennig, personal communication, July 24, 2000.

63 *a Cossack:* Albert E. Smith, *Two Reels and a Crank* (Garden City, N.Y.: Doubleday, 1952), pp. 192–94.

63 The Foolish Virgin: John Cocchi, "Updating the First 18 Issues of Screen Facts," *Screen Facts* 3, no. 6 (1968), p. 63.

64 *"very much in evidence . . .":* Anthony Slide, "Rudolph Valentino: Latin Lover," in *Close-ups: Intimate Profiles of the Movie Stars by Their Co-Stars, Directors, Screenwriters, and Friends* (New York: Workman, 1978), p. 131.

64 Patria: MoMA has footage from this film. Credit for spotting RV in it goes to Dewitt Bodeen, "Rudolph Valentino," *Screen Facts* 3, no. 5 (1968), p. 8.

64 *"He flowed along . . .":* Taylor Holmes, *The New York Daily Compass,* August 23, 1949, n.p.

64 *Caruso:* Dagmar Godowsky, in John Kobal, *People Will Talk* (New York: Knopf, 1985), p. 61.

64 *"There's a funny camaraderie . . .":* Mae Murray, unpublished interview, 1959, transcript, Columbia University Oral History Research Office, p. 1233.

64 *Mae Murray:* Jane Ardmore, *The Self-Enchanted: Mae Murray, Image of an Era* (New York: McGraw Hill, 1959), pp. 31–35.

65 *Norman Kerry . . . claimed:* Norman Kerry, interview, *Los Angeles Mirror,* March 31, 1951, n.p.

65 *Bessie Dudley:* Irving Shulman, *Valentino* (New York: Trident Press, 1967), p. 105.

65 *"like a South American millionaire":* Beulah Livingstone, *Remember Valentino: Reminiscences of the World's Greatest Lover,* pamphlet, 1938, p. 36.

65 *One winning dance-team formula:* Julie Malnig, *Dancing till Dawn: A Century of Exhibition Ballroom Dancing* (Westport, Conn.: Greenwood Press, 1992), p. 41.

65 *Maurice Mouvet:* Julian Street, *Welcome to Our City* (New York: John Lane, 1913), p. 164.

66 The Quest of Life: Robert Florey, "Valentino tel qu'il est" ("Valentino as He Is") *Ciné-Miroir* 82, September 15, 1925, p. 295.

66 *"quite Irene Castle-ish . . .":* *New York Dramatic Mirror,* June 3, 1915, n.p.

66 *"ever so many":* Ibid., January 8, 1916, n.p.

66 *Sophie Tucker:* *New York Clipper,* January 15, 1916, p. 8.

66 *"was constantly mopping his brow . . .":* Grace La Rue, "My Vaudeville Years," in *Selected Vaudeville Criticism,* ed. Anthony Slide (Metuchen, N.J.: Scarecrow Press, 1988), p. 299. I owe this reference to Ron Magliozzi.

67 *"Every evening at Fysher . . .":* *Vanity Fair,* April 1916, p. 48.

67 *"haven't learned to make . . .":* *Variety,* January 14, 1916, p. 16.

67 *"Miss Glass shapes up . . .":* *New York Clipper,* January 8, 1916, p. 7.

67 *"all the other dancing girls . . .":* *New York Dramatic Mirror,* January 8, 1916, p. 7.

67 *Joan Sawyer:* Barbara Cohen-Stratyner, *Biographical Dictionary of Dance,* s.u. "Joan Sawyer" (New York: Schirmer Books, 1982), p. 795.

67 *"She even dances . . .":* Unsourced Joan Sawyer clip, Harvard Theater Collection, Cambridge, Mass.

67 *He was earning:* RV, quoted in *Movie Weekly,* February 23, 1922, n.p.

68 *living on Central Park West:* L. B. N. Gnaedinger, "Valentino as a Hall Roomer," *Movie Weekly,* February 14, 1925, p. 4.

68 *"For years I had cherished . . .":* RV, in Adela Rogers St. Johns, "Valentino: The Life Story of the Sheik," part 2, *Liberty,* September 18, 1929, p. 66.

69 *"Jack was never over-burdened . . .":* *Town Topics,* August 3, 1916, p. 6.

70 *"I'm feeling quite an advanced feminist . . .":* Blanca de Saulles, letter to her husband, quoted in *The New York Herald,* November 28, 1917, section 2, p. 6.

70 *"We do not dance . . .":* Ibid., p. 1.

70 *"faithfully lived up to her duties . . .":* Affidavit annexed to final divorce decree, *de Saulles v. de Saulles,* April 12, 1917, New York City Municipal Archives.

70 *she had often been seen:* *Variety,* August 10, 1917, p. 15.

70 *court documents sealed:* In New York, divorce testimony remains sealed for one hundred years. The de Saulles files will be unsealed in 2017.

71 *"I intended to do agriculture":* RV, testimony, Stenographer's Minutes, *de Saulles v. de Saulles,* December 1916, New York City Municipal Archives.

72 *Blanca de Saulles herself:* *The New York Herald,* November 28, 1917, section 2, p. 6.

72 *"For many years Mrs. Thym's place . . .":* *The New York Times,* September 6, 1916, p. 6.

73 *"bogus count . . .":* quoted by Shulman, p. 113.

73 *"In winter we think":* Quoted by Alan Chester Valentine, *1913: America Between Two Worlds* (New York: Macmillan, 1962), p. 198.

73 *The indictment:* Case #111396, Court of General Sessions, *People v. William J. Enright,* September 5, 1916, New York City Municipal Archives. My gratitude to Kenneth Cobb, New York City's municipal archivist, for his help in locating this document.

74 *They were released:* Records of the Court of General Sessions, September 17, 1916, New York City Municipal Archives.

74 *"no friends":* Affidavit annexed to final divorce decree, *de Saulles v. de Saulles,* April 12, 1917.

75 *"have about gone":* *Variety,* December 22, 1916, p. 125.

75 *"I killed him . . .":* Blanca de Saulles, quoted in *The New York Times,* August 4, 1917, p. 1.

76 *She was acquitted:* *The New York Herald,* December 2, 1917, p. 1.

76 *"Are there provocations . . . ?":* Advertisement, *Variety,* March 15, 1918, p. 43.

5: "A NEW STYLE HEAVY"

77 *"I wanted to try my hand . . .":* RV, quoted in *Movie Weekly,* February 23, 1922, p. 6.

77 *"personality and presence . . .":* Chamberlain Brown, quoted in Beulah Livingstone, *Remember Valentino: Reminiscences of the World's Greatest Lover,* pamphlet, 1938, p. 38.

77 *The Masked Model:* Clip, *San Francisco Call and Post,* May 21, 1917, Hartley Chronological Clipping Files, SFPALM.

78 *"A Wealth of Whirling Gaiety":* Ibid., May 14, 17, 1917, n.p.

78 *Johnny Get Your Gun:* Clip, Pittsburgh, Penn., April 10, 1917, Robinson Locke Collection, NYPL.

78 *went on to Los Angeles:* *Variety,* July 20, 1917, p. 9.

78 *the producer had disappeared:* AV, interviewed by Kevin Brownlow, June 3, 1977.

78 *an Oakland theater owner:* George Ebey, quoted in *San Francisco Chronicle,* February 11, 1951, n.p.

79 *at the Orpheum:* RV, quoted in *Movie Weekly,* February 23, 1922, p. 6.

79 *A. P. Giannini:* RV, "My Life Story," part 2, *Photoplay,* March 1923, p. 112.

79 *"Civilian apparel . . .":* Charles Chaplin, *My Autobiography* (New York: Simon & Schuster, 1964), p. 225.

80 *new laws against sedition:* Mark Sullivan, *Our Times, the U.S.: 1900–25,* vol. 5, *Over Here, 1914–1918* (New York: Scribner's, 1933), pp. 140, 472.

80 *Norman Kerry:* Paramount biography, AMPAS; Truman B. Handy, "Scotch & Seltzer," *Motion Picture Classic,* March 1920, n.p.; George Katchmer, "Norman Kerry," *Classic Images,* February 1986, pp. 15–18.

81 *von Stroheim was fired:* Richard Koszarski, *The Man You Loved to Hate: Erich von Stroheim and Hollywood* (New York: Oxford University Press, 1983), p. 300, n. 19.

81   *he was so open-handed:* Ruth Waterbury, "Hoot Mon! He's the Best Guy in Hollywood," *Photoplay*, August 1927, p. 97.

81   *Modeling himself on Kerry:* NR, *Rudolph Valentino (Recollections) Intimate Reminiscences of the Life of the Late World-Famous Star* (New York: Jacobsen-Hodgkinson, 1927), p. 11.

82   *"Pictures were the new Klondike . . .":* Harry Reichenbach with David Freedman, *Phantom Fame: The Anatomy of Ballyhoo* (London: Noel Douglas, 1932), p. 153.

82   *Between 1910 and 1920:* Bruce T. Torrence, *Hollywood: The First Hundred Years* (New York: Zoetrope, 1982), p. 87.

82   Nobody Home: *San Francisco Post and Call*, October 15, 1917, n.p.

82   *"Theatrical conditions . . .": Variety*, November 16, 1917, p. 12.

82   *as the guest of a troupe:* RV, "My Life Story," part 2, p. 113. *Robinson Crusoe Jr.* dates thanks to Miles Kreuger.

83   *with the inscription:* Chicca Guglielmi Morone and Antonio Miredi, *Rodolfo Valentino: Una mitologia per immagini* (Turin: Libraria Petrini, 1995), p. 129 (photograph).

83   *"So he came out . . .":* Ivy Crane Wilson, interview by Anthony Slide, July 20, 1976.

83   *"Norman Kerry not only . . .":* RV, "My Life Story," part 3, *Photoplay*, April 1923, p. 49.

84   *Ramon Samaniego:* Allan R. Ellenberger, *Ramon Novarro: A Biography of the Silent Film Idol, 1899–1968* (Jefferson, N.C.: McFarland, 1999), p. 14.

84   *"Even when he leaned up . . .":* Samuel Goldwyn, unsourced clip, Valentino scrapbook, NYPL.

84   *"'Anything doing today?'. . .":* RV, quoted in Samuel Goldwyn, *Behind the Screen* (New York: George H. Doran, 1923), p. 186.

84   *green golf stockings:* Livingstone, *Remember Valentino,* p. 44.

84   *At the beach:* Carmel Myers, in Anthony Slide, "Silent Stars Speak," *Films in Review*, March 1980, p. 132.

84   *"On a Sunday . . .":* Adolphe Menjou and M. M. Musselman, *It Took Nine Tailors* (New York: McGraw Hill, 1948), p. 77.

85   *"Extras could be plucked . . .":* Jesse L. Lasky with Don Weldon, *I Blow My Own Horn* (Garden City, N.Y.: Doubleday, 1957), p. 105.

85   *The war had mobilized:* Kevin Brownlow, *The War, the West, and the Wilderness* (New York: Knopf, 1979), pp. 108, 142.

85   *"Rudy would starve . . .":* Brynie Foy, quoted in S. George Ullman, *Valentino As I Knew Him* (New York: Macy-Masius, 1926), p. 40.

85–86 *Blanca de Saulles's acquittal: Los Angeles Times*, December 2, 1917, p. 1.

86   *"Don't you know? . . .":* Viola Dana, quoted in Kevin Brownlow, *Hollywood: The Pioneers* (New York: Knopf, 1979), p. 184.

86   *When Fanchon:* Barbara Cohen-Stratyner, "Fanchon: Popular Entertainment Entrepreneur," *Women and Performance* 2, no. 1 (1984), p. 63.

86 *Hotel Maryland:* Ruth Biery, "Valentino's Unknown Love," unsourced article, Wisconsin.

86 *"On one occasion . . .":* RV, quoted in *Brooklyn Eagle,* October 23, 1921, n.p.

86 *His older women friends:* Biery, "Valentino's Unknown Love," unsourced article, Wisconsin.

86 *"the first director . . .":* RV, "My Life Story," part 3, p. 50.

86 *sometimes went dancing:* George C. Pratt, "Alice Terry Reminisces," in *Image: On the Art and Evolution of the Film,* ed. Marshall Deutelbaum (New York: Dover, 1979), p. 183.

87 *"At first I was terrified . . .":* RV, in Dagmar Godowsky, "The Secret Valentino Taught Me," *Guideposts,* August 1975, p. 30.

87 *"There are accents . . .":* Quoted in James Card, "Rudolph Valentino," *Image,* May 1958, p. 112.

87 *"no one is entirely evil . . .":* RV, to Louella Parsons, *The New York Telegraph,* September 11, 1921, n.p.

88 *"Rodolpho De Valentino makes . . .":* *Variety,* October 4, 1918, p. 49.

88 *"could not be kept from sawing . . .":* D. W. Griffith, "Recollections of Rudolph Valentino," in *There Is a New Star in Heaven: Valentino,* ed. Eva Orbanz (Berlin: Verlag Volken Spiess, 1979), p. 23.

88 *"He's too foreign looking . . .":* Griffith, in Lillian Gish, *Dorothy and Lillian Gish,* ed. James E. Flasher (New York: Scribner's, 1973), p. 81.

88 *Sanderson:* Clip, *Photo Drama Magazine,* December 1921, n.p., Valentino scrapbook, NYPL.

89 The Married Virgin: Thanks to film restorer David Shepard and Ed Carter of AMPAS for arranging a screening of this film, now available on video and DVD.

89 *speaking Italian:* Robert Florey, *La lanterne magique* (Lausanne: La Cinémathèque Suisse, 1966), p. 160.

89 *in Besançon:* Jeanne de Recqueville, *Rudolph Valentino* (Paris: France-Empire, 1978), p. 30.

89 *"Every day when I . . .":* RV, "The Darkest Hours," *Motion Picture Classic,* October 1922, pp. 52, 87.

90 *"I think he was lonely . . .":* Adela Rogers St. Johns, "Valentino: The Life Story of the Sheik," part 2, *Liberty,* September 28, 1929, p. 67.

90 *"a young man, a bit player . . .":* Chaplin, *My Autobiography,* pp. 186–87.

90 *"Film land is full of gloom . . .":* Quoted in Leslie M. DeBauche, *Reel Patriotism: The Movies and World War I* (Madison: University of Wisconsin Press, 1997), p. 147.

90 *nursing himself:* Livingstone, *Remember Valentino,* p. 49.

90 *across the street from Wallace Reid:* *Ciné* clip, RV scrapbook, Arsenal.

90 *"with millions of dollars' worth . . .":* Brownlow, *Hollywood: The Pioneers,* p. 81.

91 *"a vivid and startling story . . .":* Advertisement, *Wid's Year Book, 1918* (reprint, New York: Arno Press, 1971), n.p.

91 *"nobody wanted to show . . ."*: Fred Balshofer and Arthur Miller, *One Reel a Week* (Los Angeles: University of California Press, 1967), p. 139.

91 *a Mercer car:* RV, "My Life Story," part 3, p. 52.

91 *"To my only star":* Inscription on RV portrait, dated April 1919, William Self private collection.

91 *"He loved to come and visit . . ."*: Dorothy Gish, in John Kobal, *People Will Talk* (New York: Knopf, 1985), p. 42.

92 *"he said, 'Madame Myers' . . ."*: Carmel Myers, quoted in her obituary, *Los Angeles Times*, November 16, 1980, n.p.

92 *Florence Mack:* Unpublished excerpt from an interview by Sylvia Shorris and Marion Abbott Bundy, conducted for the book *Talking Pictures* (New York: The New Press, 1994), courtesy Sylvia Shorris.

92 *"a highly amusing farce-comedy . . ."*: *Motion Picture News*, September 6, 1919, n.p. *Out of Luck* was alternately titled *Nobody Home*.

92 *"he was so fastidious . . ."*: Dorothy Gish, in L. Gish, *Dorothy and Lillian Gish*, p. 81.

93 *"Rudolph De Valentino . . ."*: *Wid's Daily*, October 8, 1918, n.p.

93 *"one of the funniest farces . . ."*: *Variety*, December 6, 1918, p. 39.

94 *"Universal was the Woolworth's . . ."*: Koszarski, *The Man You Loved to Hate*, p. 33.

94 *"had a dressing room . . ."*: Lina Basquette, in Michael G. Ankerich, *Broken Silence: Conversations with Twenty-three Silent Film Stars* (Jefferson, N.C.: McFarland, 1993), p. 33.

94 *"Douglas was the only one . . ."*: RV, "My Life Story," part 3, p. 96.

94 Delicious Little Devil: Thanks to the Nederland Filmmuseum and MoMA's Ron Magliozzi for making this film available to me.

94 *"the daughter of a royal bricklayer . . ."*: *Moving Picture World*, April 26, 1919, p. 577.

95 *"He pored over the map . . ."*: Jane Ardmore, *The Self-Enchanted: Mae Murray, Image of an Era* (New York: McGraw Hill, 1959), p. 100.

95 *"delightfully fresh . . ."*: *Moving Picture World*, April 26, 1919, p. 577.

95 *"A great big 'Why? . . ."*: Unsourced Valentino clip, MoMA.

95 *danced between setups:* Ardmore, *The Self-Enchanted:* p. 100.

97 *"a knockout":* *Variety*, November 7, 1919, p. 96.

97 Eyes of Youth *opening:* *Moving Picture World*, November 15, 1919, p. 335.

6: MISALLIANCE

98 *Garden of Alla:* Gavin Lambert, *Nazimova: A Biography* (New York: Knopf, 1997), pp. 205ff.

98 *"All she had to do . . ."*: Dagmar Godowsky, *First Person Plural: The Lives of Dagmar Godowsky* (New York: Viking Press, 1958), p. 64.

99 *"Nazimova, in a recent trip . . ."*: *Photoplay*, September 1919, p. 104.

99 *"beaming with pleasure . . ."*: Godowsky, *First Person Plural*, p. 69.

99 *She wrongly supposed:* Dagmar Godowsky, in John Kobal, *People Will Talk* (New York: Knopf, 1985), p. 62.

99 *"The first question he asked . . .":* Jean Acker, quoted in *Variety*, October 6, 1922, p. 47.

100 *so he would insist:* Robert Florey, written interview by Anthony Slide, August 20, 1976.

100 *Born on a New Jersey farm:* Obituary of Jean Acker, *Los Angeles Times*, August 19, 1978, n.p.

100 *"On Sundays I answer . . .":* Jean Acker, quoted in *Motion Picture Magazine*, August 1913, Acker clipping, n.p., NYPL.

101 *"I honestly believe . . .":* Jean Acker, quoted in "The Truth About Valentino's Divorce, *Movie Weekly*, October 28, 1922, p. 11.

101 *"He thought it would be . . .":* Paul Ivano, interview by Anthony Slide, May 12, 1976.

101 *"We were the two lowliest . . .":* RV, in Adela Rogers St. Johns, *Love, Laughter, and Tears: My Hollywood Story* (Garden City, N.Y.: Doubleday, 1978), p. 169.

101 *reclaim her American:* San Francisco Chronicle, February 4, 1925, n.p.

101 *"It was simply a case of . . .":* Jean Acker, quoted in *Movie Weekly*, October 28, 1922, p. 11.

101 *"It seemed spontaneous . . .":* RV, "My Life Story," part 3, *Photoplay*, April 1923, p. 96.

101 *Robert Florey: La lanterne magique* (Lausanne: La Cinémathèque Suisse, 1966), p. 167.

102 PHOTOPLAY ACTRESS MARRIES . . . : *Los Angeles Times*, November 6, 1919, section 2, p. 5.

103 *"She came to me and said . . .":* Mrs. Anna Karger, unsourced clip, Valentino scrapbook, NYPL.

103 *"It was the worst thing . . .":* Nazimova, letter to Edith Luckett, quoted in Lambert, *Nazimova*, p. 223.

104 *"Mine was not a marriage":* RV, in Willis Goldbeck, "The Perfect Lover," *Motion Picture Magazine*, May 1922, p. 94.

104 *turning bitter:* Robert Florey, written interview by Anthony Slide, August 20, 1976.

104 *Jean said that Rudy had confessed:* Patricia Neal, personal communication, April 22, 1998.

104 *"In time I may have to . . .":* Jean Acker, quoted in *Movie Weekly*, June 10, 1922, p. 5.

105 *My Dear Jean:* RV to Jean Acker, November 22, 1919, letter introduced as court evidence, quoted in *Movie Weekly*, June 10, 1922, p. 5.

105 *"I asked her why . . .":* Douglas Gerrard, quoted in *Los Angeles Times*, November 30, 1921, section 2, p. 11.

105 *"Dearest boy of mine . . .":* Acker to RV, December 15, 1919, letter introduced as court evidence, quoted in *Movie Weekly*, June 10, 1922, p. 5.

106 *"Try to be as good . . .":* Ibid.

106 *"Advise strongly you do not come . . .":* Acker to RV, January 16, 1920, telegram, quoted in ibid.

106 *to Grace Darmond's Los Angeles apartment:* Los Angeles Times, November 23, 1921, section 2, p. 7; November 24, 1921, section 2, p. 1.

107 *her doctor confirmed:* Dr. Josiah Cowles, affidavit, Guglielmi V. Guglielmi, October 22, 1921, Los Angeles Superior Court.

107 *"I did not marry . . . another world":* Acker testimony, quoted in *Movie Weekly,* June 10, 1922, p. 5.

107 *"I wanted to make a man . . .":* Acker, quoted in *Los Angeles Times,* November 24, 1921, section 2, p. 1.

108 *"He was nothing . . .":* Acker testimony, quoted in *Movie Weekly,* June 10, 1922, p. 5.

108 *"From the beginning":* Judge Thomas O. Toland, divorce ruling, Superior Court of Los Angeles, January 10, 1922.

108 *"How She Won the Sheik":* Toledo Blade, January 31, 1923, clip, NYPL.

108–109 *"She is an understanding heart":* RV, in Adela Rogers St. Johns, "Valentino: The Life Story of the Sheik," part 4, *Liberty,* October 12, 1929, p. 73.

109 Tho I pine . . . : "We Will Meet at the End of the Trail," words and music by Jean Acker, Shapiro, Bernstein & Co., copyright 1926, copyright not renewed.

109 *his toupée:* William Self, personal communication, August 18, 1999.

7: ENTER JULIO

110 *"would not like it at all":* Paul Ivano, interview by Anthony Slide, May 12, 1976.

110 *posed for one of three:* Ruth Biery, unsourced clip, Wisconsin.

110 *one of his hands:* "Catalogue, the Estate of Rudolph Valentino" (Hollywood: Eureka Press, 1926), pp. 42–43, AMPAS.

110 *"see the truth of things . . .":* RV, quoted in unsourced clip, Wisconsin.

111 *he had been gassed:* Robert Florey, *Hollywood d'hier et aujourd'hui* (Paris: Editions Prisma, 1979), p. 53.

111 *the audience for movies:* Miriam Hansen, "Pleasure, Ambivalence, Identification: Valentino and Female Spectatorship," *Cinema Journal* 25, no. 4, summer 1986, p. 6.

111 *Rudy considered resettling:* Ivano, Slide interview.

111 *carried him briefly to St. Augustine:* DeWitt Bodeen, letter to Anthony Slide, August 27, 1976.

112 *a hundred printings: Moving Picture World,* February 26, 1921, p. 1060.

112 *"all Gods [were] dead . . .":* F. Scott Fitzgerald, *This Side of Paradise* (New York: Scribner's, 1920), p. 282.

112 *"Then June came in":* RV, in Gladys Hall and Adele Fletcher, "We Discover Who Discovered Valentino," *Motion Picture Magazine,* June 1923, p. 93.

113 *"She deliberately didn't want . . .":* Ibid., p. 94.

113 *custom-fitted suits:* Ivano, Slide interview.

113 *"Rudolph Valentino has been summoned . . .": Motion Picture News,* August 21, 1920, p. 1525.

114 *"Her duties are not ended . . .": Moving Picture World,* June 18, 1921, p. 719.

114 *"June Mathis originated . . .":* Lewis Jacobs, *The Rise of the American Film* (New York: Harcourt, Brace, 1939), p. 328.

114 *"shooting on paper":* Vincent Tajiri, *Valentino* (New York: Bantam, 1977), p. 50.

114 *Rudy actually called her:* Quoted by Diane Mathis Madsen to author, personal communication, September 20, 2001.

114 *"She mothered Rudy . . .":* Nita Naldi, Columbia University Oral History, 1958, pp. 17–18.

114 *"Paris clothes . . .":* Adela Rogers St. Johns, *Love, Laughter, and Tears: My Hollywood Story* (Garden City, N.Y.: Doubleday, 1978), p. 167.

114 *Rudy inscribed:* Diane Mathis Madsen, personal communication.

115 *a stage ingenue:* Thomas J. Slater, "June Mathis: A Woman Who Spoke Through Silents," *Griffithiana*, spring 1995, p. 135.

115 *opal ring:* Gavin Lambert, *Nazimova: A Biography* (New York: Knopf, 1997), p. 201.

115 *"Ever since I have been sure . . .":* June Mathis, quoted in *Motion Picture Classic*, February 1927, n.p.

115 *"If you are vibrating . . .":* June Mathis, quoted in *Motion Picture Magazine*, April 1926, p. 43.

116 *"He was of medium height . . .":* Vicente Blasco Ibáñez, *The Four Horsemen of the Apocalypse* (London: Constable, 1928), pp. 15, 101.

116 *"Whenever I view . . .":* June Mathis, quoted in *Motion Picture Magazine*, April 1926, p. 43.

116 *"Every single day . . .":* Hall and Fletcher, "We Discover," p. 94.

116 *Rex Ingram:* Liam O'Leary, *Rex Ingram, Master of the Silent Cinema* (Dublin: Academy Press, 1980).

117 *"stronger and more French":* Robert Florey, *La lanterne magique* (Lausanne: La Cinémathèque Suisse, 1966), p. 161.

117 *"fool-proof to photograph . . .":* Ingram, quoted in *Oakland Tribune*, August 23, 1949, n.p.

117 *"had become weary of . . .":* Erich von Stroheim, in Kevin Brownlow, *Hollywood: The Pioneers* (New York: Knopf, 1979), p. 249.

117 *"looked as if he knew . . .":* Elinor Glyn, quoted in *Modern Screen*, May 1927, n.p.

118 *an earlier film of his:* Motion Picture Magazine, November 1924, p. 25. According to Kevin Brownlow (personal communication, March 8, 2001), the dance-hall scene may also have been inspired by a similar scene in *The Woman and the Puppet*, directed by Reginald Barker.

118 *endured for seventy-five feet:* Moving Picture World, September 25, 1920, p. 466.

119 *"He always suggested more . . .":* Alice Terry, in O'Leary, *Rex Ingram*, p. 110.

120 *An alternate, happy ending:* Kevin Brownlow, notes to *The Four Horsemen of the Apocalypse*, National Film Theatre, London.

120 *"modeling obtained by . . .":* Ingram, quoted in *Moving Picture World*, February 19, 1921, p. 923.

120 *"we can work with the lens wide open . . ."*: Ingram, quoted in *Photoplay*, August 1921, p. 43.

120 *When shooting indoors*: O'Leary, *Rex Ingram*, p. 77.

120 *historical accuracy*: Kevin Brownlow, *The War, the West, and the Wilderness* (New York: Knopf, 1979), p. 181.

121 *"of the exact type . . ."*: *Motion Picture News*, August 14, 1920, n.p.

121 *"I never saw a director . . ."*: *Moving Picture World*, August 21, 1920, p. 1005.

121 *he even went to watch*: O'Leary, *Rex Ingram*, p. 84.

121 *"I've just made a picture . . ."*: Ivano, Slide interview.

121 *almost a million feet*: George Marcher, "An Afternoon with Grant Whytock," *American Cinemeditor* 25, no. 4, winter 1975, p. 7.

122 *"is to the picture of today . . ."*: *Variety*, February 18, 1921, p. 40.

122 *"an effect of grandeur . . ."*: *The New York Times Book Review*, March 27, 1921, p. 10.

122 *"a fine spectacle . . ."*: *Moving Picture World*, March 12, 1921, p. 134.

122 *"lifts the silent drama . . ."*: *Life*, March 24, 1921, n.p.

122 *"both in ability and appearance"*: Ibid.

122 *"In the interpretation of Julio"*: Clip, *Los Angeles Times*, March 10, 1921, AMPAS.

123 *"Rudolph Valentino played Julio . . ."*: *Photoplay*, September 1921, p. 21.

123 *at New York's Lyric Theatre*: *Variety*, March 11, 1921, n.p.

123 *The Lyric's previous record*: Ibid., April 8, 1921, p. 1.

123 *The windows of Macy's*: *Moving Picture World*, April 30, 1921, p. 961.

123 *as the guest of honor*: Beulah Livingstone, *Remember Valentino: Reminiscences of the World's Greatest Lover*, pamphlet, 1938, p. 9.

123 *"Everywhere I went . . ."*: Norman R. Mackenzie, *The Magic of Rudolph Valentino* (London: Research Publishing, 1974), p. 51.

123 *President and Mrs. Harding*: *Moving Picture World*, May 21, 1921, p. 312.

123 *a hushed silence*: NR, *Rudolph Valentino (Recollections) Intimate and Interesting Reminiscences of the Life of the Late World-Famous Star* (New York: Jacobsen-Hodgkinson, 1927), p. 16.

123 *more than four million dollars*: James Card, "Rudolph Valentino," *Image*, May 1958, p. 107.

123 *in Brazil*: *Moving Picture World*, July 30, 1921, p. 531.

124 *Paris premiere*: Ibid., April 8, 1922, p. 625.

124 *German objections*: Brownlow, *The War, the West*, p. 181; O'Leary, *Rex Ingram*, p. 162.

124 *"Enter Julio!"*: C. Blythe Sherwood, *Motion Picture Classic*, June 1920, p. 19.

124 *"In The Four Horsemen"*: RV in *The Bookman*, February 1923, n.p., AMPAS.

8: THE WONDER YEAR

125 *Formosa Apartments*: Paul Ivano, interview by Anthony Slide, May 12, 1976.

125 *"[Rudy] was the greatest promoter . . ."*: Ivano, quoted in Anthony Slide, "Ivano and Valentino: A Unique Partnership," *American Cinematographer* 66, no. 8, August 1985, p. 37.

126 *"a lot of baloney"*: Ivano, Slide interview.

126 *"All he thought about . . ."*: Stuart Holmes, quoted in *Los Angeles Mirror*, February 28, 1961, n.p.

126 *He instructed Leatrice Joy:* William M. Drew, *Speaking of Silents: First Ladies of the Screen* (Vestal, New York: Vestal Press, 1989), p. 68.

126 *his teeth would turn black:* Jean Acker, in Gladys Hall, "The Two Camilles," unpublished manuscript of magazine article, Gladys Hall Collection, AMPAS.

126 *"long, lovely" birthday kiss:* Patsy Ruth Miller, *My Hollywood: When Both of Us Were Young* (West Hanover, Mass.: O'Raghailligh, 1988), p. 42.

126 *cooking spaghetti for her:* Dagmar Godowsky, *First Person Plural: The Lives of Dagmar Godowsky* (New York: Viking, 1958), p. 71.

127 *"Other women found . . ."*: In Michael G. Ankerich, *Broken Silence: Conversations with Twenty-three Silent Film Stars* (Jefferson, N.C.: McFarland, 1993), p. 200.

127 *"an ordinary young man . . ."*: Adela Rogers St. Johns, "What Kind of Men Attract Women Most?" *Photoplay*, March 1924, p. 110.

127 *"Nowhere in motion pictures . . ."*: James Card, "Rudolph Valentino," *Image*, May 1958, p. 107.

127 *"acts well, although . . ."*: Unsourced review of *Uncharted Seas*, MoMA.

128 *"What I could see of the face . . ."*: NR, *Rudolph Valentino (Recollections) Intimate and Interesting Reminiscences of the Life of the Late World-Famous Star* (New York: Jacobsen-Hodgkinson, 1927), p. 8.

128 *"She never looked to right . . ."*: RV, "My Life Story," part 3, *Photoplay*, April 1923, p. 98.

128 *"Here comes Pavlova"*: Patsy Ruth Miller, in Michael Morris, *Madam Valentino: The Many Lives of Natacha Rambova* (New York: Abbeville, 1991), p. 8.

128 *Winifred Shaughnessy:* For the facts of NR's early life I am indebted to Michael Morris, *Madam Valentino*, chapters 1 and 2.

129 *Elsie de Wolfe:* Alfred Allan Lewis, *Ladies and Not-So-Gentle-Women* (New York: Viking, 2000), pp. 218–19.

130 *"the nymphets"*: Ibid., p. 249.

130 *Elsie's assiduous efforts:* Morris, *Madam Valentino*, p. 39.

130 *"while men still shaped . . ."*: Lewis, *Ladies*, p. 283.

130 *trained with Rosita Meuri:* Mercedes de Acosta, *Here Lies the Heart* (New York: Arno Press, 1975), p. 144.

130 *Muzzie considered:* Morris, *Madam Valentino*, p. 41.

131 *Aunt Teresa proved:* Ibid., pp. 42–50; *"too tall"*: p. 43; *his lover:* p. 44; *legal action:* p. 46; *Bournemouth:* p. 47; *She dropped the charges:* p. 49; *Kosloff's unusual household:* p. 50.

132 *"It was practically white slavery"*: Ivano, Slide interview.

132 *he continued to steal full credit:* Ivano, Slide interview.

132 *Ruth St. Denis:* Godowsky, *First Person Plural*, p. 64.

132 *Aphrodite:* Morris, *Madam Valentino*, p. 69; Ivano, Slide interview.

132 *Natacha took out a pencil:* Ivano, Slide interview.

132 *"up to $5,000":* Note, dated August 23, 1920, weekly payroll, Metro Picture Corp., vol. 1, ledger book, Special Collections, AMPAS.

132 *Kosloff returned:* Morris, *Madam Valentino*, p. 63; Ivano, Slide interview.

133 *disliked lesbianism:* Morris., *Madam Valentino*, p. 246.

133 *a close link:* de Acosta, *Here Lies*, pp. 144–45.

133 *a small bequest:* NR, Last Will and Testament, July 23, 1964, New York City Surrogate Court.

133 *"Exactly what happened . . .":* Irene Sharaff, quoted in Gavin Lambert, *Nazimova: A Biography* (New York Knopf, 1997), p. 235.

133 *Madame "fell for" Natacha:* Miller, *My Hollywood*, p. 29.

134 *"The law of the colony . . .":* Mary Winship, "Oh, Hollywood," *Photoplay*, May 1921, p. 112.

134 *"In these days . . .":* Quoted in Anthony Slide, "The Silent Closet," *Film Quarterly* 52, no. 4, summer 1999, p. 30.

135 *She had him shampoo:* NR, *Rudolph Valentino*, p. 10.

135 *Poelzig; Ruhlmann:* Morris, *Madam Valentino*, p. 70.

135 *"Bobbed and bizarre . . .":* Clip, *New York American*, October 22 [1921], *Camille* file, NYPL.

136 *"should be sold as . . .":* *Moving Picture World*, September 24, 1921, p. 446.

136 *deathbed scene:* NR, *Rudolph Valentino*, p. 13.

136 *the auction:* *The Brooklyn Eagle*, October 23, 1921.

136 *"arrant misconception":* *Variety*, September 16, 1921, p. 35.

137 *the "sex-menace":* Alexander Walker, *Rudolph Valentino* (New York & London: Penguin, 1976), p. 37.

137 *"At that time I was very serious . . .":* NR, in Herbert Howe, "Her Years as Valentino's Wife," *The New Movie Magazine*, undated Valentino clip, Wisconsin.

138 *"It wasn't love at first sight":* NR, in Herbert Howe article, *Photoplay*, December 1922, p. 58.

138 *"I liked the fact . . .":* NR, "Why I Married Rudy," *Movie Weekly*, December 16, 1922, p. 7.

138 *"We talk about . . . books . . .":* RV to Herbert Howe, "Her Years as Valentino's Wife," undated Valentino clip, Wisconsin.

138 *"The more cultured . . .":* RV, "Woman and Love," *Photoplay*, March 1922, p. 42.

138 *they drove with the Gilberts:* Leatrice Gilbert Fountain, personal communication, December 8, 2000.

139 *"cooking huge steaks . . .":* Herbert Howe, "Success—and the Morning After," *Picture Play*, August 1921, p. 96.

139 *William Pester:* Identified by Sally McManus, of the Palm Springs Historical Society.

139 *"Rudy would come out . . .":* NR, "Why I Married Rudy," p. 7.

139 *bungalow dinners; painting the furniture:* NR, *Rudolph Valentino*, p. 12.

139 *the bed looked like:* Mrs. Hudnut, in NR, *Rudy: An Intimate Portrait of Rudolph Valentino by His Wife* (London: Hutchinson, 1926), p. 43.

139 *"looked best nude"*: Quoted by Morris, *Madam Valentino*, p. 127.

140 *"No, no, no, no"*: Ivano, Slide interview.

140 *allowed Rudy to sell*: NR, *Rudolph Valentino*, p. 23.

141 *"I used to open up . . ."*: Ivano, quoted in Kevin Brownlow, *Hollywood: The Pioneers* (New York: Knopf, 1979), p. 185.

141 *to Natacha's maid*: *Los Angeles Times*, December 1, 1921, section 2, p. 1.

141 *with Natacha at the wheel*: NR, *Rudolph Valentino*, p. 27.

141 *"the happiest . . ."*: Ibid., p. 29.

141 *"infinitely patient with animals"*: Ibid., p. 32.

142 *Zela attacked*: Ivano in Brownlow, *Hollywood*, p. 184.

142 *Sunset Inn*: NR, *Rudolph Valentino*, pp. 15–18.

142 *"The cinemese toddle[d] . . ."*: "Hitting the Hookah with Rudie," uncredited clip, Valentino file, Wisconsin.

143 *Rudy asked for a raise*: Ibid., p. 20.

143 *"the star plays the star . . ."*: Rex Ingram, *Los Angeles Daily News*, August 18, 1949, Valentino clip, AMPAS.

143 *"even to the monocle . . ."*: NR, *Rudolph Valentino*, p. 20.

143 *Ingram would rarely*: Robert Florey, *La lanterne magique* (Lausanne: La Cinémathèque Suisse, 1966), p. 162.

144 *"He had shown that . . ."*: Dewitt Bodeen, "Rex Ingram and Alice Terry," part 1, *Films in Review*, February 1975, pp. 82–83.

144 *"spirit photography"*: Metro press book for *The Conquering Power*, Australia, 1923, MoMA.

144 *"Mr. Ingram's groups . . ."*: Quoted in *Moving Picture World*, July 23, 1921, p. 422.

145 *"dress like a Broadway fashion plate . . ."*: *The New York Review*, July 9, 1921, n.p.

146 *"Just as they were about to . . ."*: NR, *Rudolph Valentino*, p. 21.

146 *special screening*: *The New York Telegraph*, September 11, 1921, n.p.

146 *"He received me . . ."*: Donah Benrimo, quoted in *The Brooklyn Eagle*, October 23, 1921, n.p.

146 *"Bright Spats . . ."*: Delight Evans, "A Few Impressions," *Photoplay*, December 1921, p. 49.

147 *Gance reported*: Kevin Brownlow, *The Parade's Gone By* (New York: Knopf, 1968), p. 539.

147 *"headed straight for the Palais Royal . . ."*: Louella Parsons, *The New York Telegraph*, September 11, 1921.

9: DARK LOVER

148 *contract with Famous Players–Lasky*: Paul Ivano, interview by Anthony Slide, May 12, 1976; *Variety*, July 16, 1924, p. 20.

149 *The studio chiefs*: See Neal Gabler, *An Empire of Their Own: How the Jews Invented Hollywood* (New York: Crown, 1988).

149 *"In the twenties"*: Jesse L. Lasky with Don Weldon, *I Blow My Own Horn* (Garden City, N.Y.: Doubleday, 1957), p. 130.

150 *salaries:* Metro Weekly Payroll, vol. 1, July 2, 1921, ledger book, Special Collections, AMPAS.

150 *Constance Talmadge:* Alexander Walker, *Stardom: The Hollywood Phenomenon* (New York: Stein & Day, 1970), p. 122.

150 *William S. Hart:* Tino Balio, "Stars in the Business," in *The American Film Industry*, ed. Tino Balio (Madison: University of Wisconsin Press, 1976), p. 163.

150 *"just a flash in the pan . . .":* Adolphe Menjou and M. M. Musselman, *It Took Nine Tailors* (New York: McGraw Hill, 1948), p. 94.

151 *"the United States Steel Corp. . . .":* Film Daily, quoted in Richard Koszarski, *An Evening's Entertainment: The Age of the Silent Feature Picture, 1915–1928* (New York: Macmillan, 1990), p. 69.

151 *unfair trade practices:* The New York Times, September 1, 1921, n.p.

151 *"He had more sheer animal . . .":* Lasky, *I Blow My Own Horn*, pp. 147–48.

152 *"the biggest star . . .":* Jesse Lasky, Jr., *Whatever Happened to Hollywood?* (New York: Funk & Wagnalls, 1975), p. 33.

152 *an application:* Motion Picture Magazine, February 1923, p. 29.

152 *"say as to directors . . .":* RV, affidavit, *Famous Players–Lasky v. Rudolph Valentino*, in *Movie Weekly*, October 21, 1922, n.p.

152 *"But Mr. Lasky . . .":* Lasky, *I Blow My Own Horn*, pp. 146–47.

153 *Zukor . . . swears:* Adolph Zukor with Dale Kramer, *The Public Is Never Wrong* (New York: Putnam's, 1953), p. 207.

153 *yet another figure:* Variety, December 9, 1921, p. 33.

153 *60 percent:* Koszarski, *An Evening's Entertainment*, p. 30.

153 *"July 5 . . .":* Moving Picture World, July 9, 1921, p. 226.

153 *"Wallace Reid was too much . . .":* Lasky, *I Blow My Own Horn*, p. 145.

154 *"Kirkwood finally came down . . .":* Lasky, letter to Zukor, July 2, 1921, Zukor Collection, AMPAS.

154 *"is the only thing . . .":* Moving Picture World, July 9, 1921, p. 177.

154 *Worries:* Menjou, *It Took Nine Tailors*, p. 95.

154 *"Loving riding . . .":* NR, *Rudolph Valentino (Recollections) Intimate and Interesting Reminiscences of the Life of the Late World-Famous Star* (New York: Jacobsen-Hodgkinson, 1927), p. 33.

154 *Guadalupe:* Peter Brosnan, personal communication, September 9, 2001.

154 *Each camp covered:* Moving Picture World, October 8, 1921, p. 4.

154 *Loretta Young:* Kevin Brownlow, personal communication, 1998.

155 *"doing anything":* George Melford, quoted by Louise de Modica in personal communication, February 12, 2001.

155 *"blew signals . . .":* Unsourced clip, on *The Sheik*, NYPL.

155 *Pathé Company stock footage:* Monte Katterjohn, *Sheik* script, Paramount Collections, AMPAS.

155 *"hooded Bedouin horsemen . . .":* The New York Telegraph, September 18 [1921], clip, Valentino scrapbook, AMPAS.

156 *a certain staginess:* Steven C. Caton, "The Sheik," in *Noble Dreams, Wicked Pleasures: Orientalism in America, 1870–1930,* ed. Holly Edwards (Princeton: Princeton University Press, 2000), p. 116.

156 *fake palms at the Cocoanut Grove:* Kevin Brownlow, personal communication, March 8, 2001.

156 *"the African Monte Carlo . . .":* Moving Picture World, October 1, 1921, p. 534.

156 *costumed as Orientals:* Leonard Mosley, *Zanuck* (Boston: Little, Brown, 1984), p. 44.

156 *New Women and Orientalism:* Gaylyn Studlar, "Out-Salomeing Salome," in *Visions of the East: Orientalism in Film* (London and New York: Routledge, 1997), pp. 99–129.

157 *"Madame [and Natacha, too, most likely] was contemptuous . . .":* Patsy Ruth Miller, *My Hollywood: When Both of Us Were Young* (West Hanover, Mass.: O'Raghailligh, 1988), p. 26.

157 *"This should be within . . .":* Sheik script, note to Scene 80, Paramount Collection, AMPAS.

158 *SEE the auction . . . :* Ad in *Los Angeles Examiner,* October 30, 1921.

158 *"a curious mixture . . .":* Sheik script, p. 173, Paramount Collection, AMPAS.

159 *"a savor of the Orient . . .":* Willis Goldbeck, "The Perfect Lover," *Motion Picture Magazine,* May 1922, p. 40.

159 *An ad:* Undated clip, Valentino scrapbook, NYPL.

159 *"He does not look like . . .":* Agnes Smith, "Not Quite a Hero," *Picture Play,* August 1922, n.p.

159 *arching his brows:* Frank Westmore and Muriel Davidson, *The Westmores of Hollywood* (Philadelphia: J. B. Lippincott, 1976), p. 56.

161 *"Sheik grasps her white . . .":* Sheik script, scene 94, Paramount Collection, AMPAS.

161 *a phallic dream:* Bram Dijkstra, *Evil Sisters: The Threat of Female Sexuality and the Cult of Manhood* (New York: Knopf, 1996), pp. 335ff.

161 *Alice Terry . . . was considered:* Alice Terry, in George C. Pratt, "If You Beat Me, I Wept," in *Image: On the Art and Evolution of the Film,* ed. Marshall Deutelbaum (New York: Dover, 1979), p. 183.

161 *"On Greek vases . . .":* Richard Dyer, *White* (London and New York: Routledge, 1997), p. 57.

161 *"dark people are always . . .":* Mary Towers, "Valentino's Power Over Women Explained," *Movie Weekly,* April 7, 1923, p. 25.

162 *"I am very dark . . .":* RV, quoted in Gordon Gassaway, "The Erstwhile Landscape Gardener," *Motion Picture Magazine,* July 1921, p. 92.

163 *"write something typically American . . .":* Jesse Lasky, letter, in Sumiko Higashi, *Cecil B. DeMille and American Culture: The Silent Era* (Berkeley: University of California Press, 1994), p. 143.

164 *"sleeping in a scrumptious position . . .":* Sheik script, scene 113, Paramount Collection, AMPAS.

164 *"the tale of a lawless Arab . . ."*: Advertisement, unsourced clip, Valentino scrap-book, NYPL.

165 *"mounted on a rearing . . ."*: *Moving Picture World*, September 24, 1921, p. 430.

165 *"We all saw ourselves . . ."*: Barbara Cartland, foreword to *The Sheik*, by E. M. Hull (New York: Bantam, 1977), p. 1.

165 *"With brutal hands . . ."*: E. M. Hull, *The Sheik* (Boston: Small, Maynard, 1921), p. 54.

165 *"the close union . . ."*: Ibid., p. 58.

165 *"I have been criticized . . ."*: E. M. Hull, "Why I Wrote 'The Sheik,'" unsourced clip, Valentino scrapbook, NYPL.

166 *Kansas City . . . banned locally*: *Variety*, November 11, 1921, p. 46.

167 *"very much disappointed . . ."*: *Film Daily*, November 13, 1921, p. 5.

167 *"bled white"*: *Variety*, November 11, 1921, p. 37.

167 *125,000 people*: *The New York Telegraph*, November 13, 1921, n.p.

167 *"People are flocking . . ."*: *The New York News*, November 8, 1921, n.p.

167 *"MELFORD HAS FAR SURPASSED . . ."*: Lasky to Zukor, August 31, 1921, Zukor Collection, AMPAS.

168 *In Sydney*: *Moving Picture World*, August 19, 1922, n.p.

168 *in France*: Kevin Brownlow, notes for *The Sheik*, National Film Theater, London.

168 *in Milan*: Jeanne de Recqueville, *Rudolph Valentino* (Paris: France-Empire, 1978), p. 51.

168 *grosses, production costs*: RV, affidavit, in *Movie Weekly*, September 30, 1922, p. 7; Anthony Slide, "Ivano and Valentino: A Unique Partnership," *American Cinematographer* 66, no. 8, August 1985, p. 38.

168 *"There are more sheiks here . . ."*: Herbert Howe in *Photoplay*, October 1923, p. 57.

168 *"We called it* The Shriek *. . ."*: Frances Marion, *Off with Their Heads: A Serio-Comic Tale of Hollywood* (New York: Macmillan, 1972), p. 85.

169 *he'd walked out*: Edward Wagenknecht, *The Movies in the Age of Innocence* (New York: Limelight Editions, 1997), p. 198.

169 *"The lady trade . . ."*: *Moving Picture World*, April 12, 1924, p. 560.

169 *"a college boy dressed up"*: *Los Angeles Record*, November 19, 1921, n.p.

169 *"Valentino depicts lust . . ."; "He is a soft, sapless . . ."*: James W. Dean, unsourced clip, Valentino scrapbook, NYPL.

169 *"and you wonder why . . ."*: *Motion Picture Magazine*, January 1922, n.p.

169 *"He tore after her . . ."*: Dick Dorgan, "Giving 'The Sheik' the Once Over from the Ringside," *Photoplay*, April 1922, pp. 90–92.

170 *"I hate Valentino!"*: Dorgan, "A Song of Hate," *Photoplay*, July 1922, p. 27.

170 *based on a poem*: Thanks to Helen K. Marshall of the Valentino e-group for supplying information about the source of "Kashmiri Love Song."

171 *"a terrible razz . . ."*: *Moving Picture World*, December 9, 1922, p. 568.

171 *"Girls will love a fellow . . ."; "I don't like . . ."*: Letters to *Movie Weekly*, November 17, 1921, n.p.

171 "'SHEIK' IN REAL AND REEL . . .": Clip, *Boston Advertiser*, December 17, 1921, NYPL.

171 "*whether they are feminists . . .*": RV, quoted in *Baltimore News*, October 22, 1921, NYPL.

171 "*we shall witness . . .*": RV, quoted in Goldbeck, "Perfect Lover," p. 94.

172 "*The caveman method . . .*": RV, "Woman and Love," *Photoplay*, March 1922, p. 98.

172 "*Woman is piqued by . . .*": RV, quoted in Goldbeck, "Perfect Lover," p. 94.

172 "*I was forced . . . to play . . .*": RV, in "The Motion Picture Novel," *The Bookman*, February 1923, n.p., Valentino Core Collection/Biography clip, AMPAS.

172 "*I neither acted like an Englishman . . .*": RV, quoted in unsourced Valentino clip, Wisconsin.

172 "*People are not savages because . . .*": RV, "The Psychology of the Sheik," *Movie Weekly*, October 8, 1921, p. 4.

172 *a possible Bedouin ancestor:* RV, quoted in Herbert Howe, "Success—and the Morning After," *Picture Play*, August 1921 p. 96.

10: FAUN MAN

174 *Whitley Heights:* Richard Alleman, *The Movie Lover's Guide to Hollywood* (New York: Harper & Row, 1985), pp. 30–33; NR, *Rudy: An Intimate Portrait of Rudolph Valentino, by His Wife* (London: Hutchinson, 1926), p. 46; Robert Florey, *Hollywood d'hier et d'aujourd'hui* (Paris: Editions Prisma, 1979), p. 51.

174 *Bert Glennon's place:* Anthony Slide, "Ivano and Valentino: A Unique Partnership," *American Cinematographer* 16, no. 8, August 1985, p. 38.

175 *a preference for playing bandits:* RV, quoted in Herbert Howe, "Success—and the Morning After," *Picture Play*, August 1921, p. 96.

175 *budget:* *Variety*, December 9, 1921, p. 33; contract, cited in unsourced Valentino clip, July 11, 1939, Core Collection, AMPAS.

176 "*The parlor pet . . .*": *Photoplay*, April 1922, p. 103.

176 "*Wait till you see . . .*": George Melford, quoted in *Pantomime*, February 11, 1922, p. 12.

176 "*Valentino plays . . .*": *Moving Picture World*, April 12, 1924, p. 560.

177 "*an actor's stock in trade . . .*": RV, in Seamus Dillon, "How Valentino Keeps His Figure," *Liberty*, December 27, 1924, p. 64; reprinted fall 1971.

177 *Robert Florey:* See Brian Taves, *Robert Florey, the French Expressionist* (Metuchen, N.J.: Scarecrow Press, 1987).

179 "*one could infer that the biceps . . .*": Frank Norris, *Moran of the Lady Letty* (Garden City, N.Y.: Doubleday, 1928), p. 212.

180 "*does not fit properly . . .*": *The Evening Mail*, February 7, 1922, clip, Valentino scrapbook, NYPL.

180 "*the kind of youth who would be . . .*": *The New York Times*, February 6, 1922, p. 9.

180 "*an interesting melodrama . . .*": Rush, *Variety*, February 10, 1922, p. 34.

181 "*a doily placed . . .*": Willard Wright, "A Motion Picture Dictionary," *Photoplay*, April 1922, p. 79.

181 *"SCANDAL HITS . . .":* Variety, September 16, 1921, p. 39.

182 *"The moving picture is . . .":* Rupert Hughes, quoted in *Photoplay*, October 1921, p. 119.

182 *She'd say, "Oh please . . .":* Paul Ivano, interview by Anthony Slide, May 12, 1976.

184 *"plaintiff is of an excitable nature . . .":* Guglielmi v. Guglielmi, affidavit of Frederick Speik, case D-8364, Dept. 13, Los Angeles Superior Court Documents, October 22, 1921.

185 *eventually published:* In *Shadowland*, August 1923.

185 *He told Helen MacGregor:* RV, letter to Helen MacGregor, August 14, 1923, Special Collections, BFI.

185 *Natacha had staged:* Michael Morris, *Madam Valentino: The Many Lives of Natacha Rambova* (New York: Abbeville, 1991), p. 102.

185 *"somewhat startling . . .":* Los Angeles Examiner, December 1, 1921, n.p.

185 *"FAUN PICTURE CAUSES STIR . . .":* Los Angeles Times, December 1, 1921, section 2, p. 1.

186 *"faint yet clear . . .":* Philippe Jullian, "Biographical Essay," *de Meyer*, ed. Robert Brandau (New York: Knopf, 1976), p. 34.

187 *"Rudy likes music . . .":* PhotoDrama Magazine, December 1921, n.p., clip, Valentino scrapbook, NYPL.

187 *"a faun who had been . . .":* Quoted in Richard Schickel, *His Picture in the Papers: A Speculation on Celebrity in America Based on the Life of Douglas Fairbanks, Sr.* (New York: Charterhouse, 1974), p. 221.

188 *"I never saw Douglas . . .":* Mary Pickford, quoted by Eileen Whitfield in *Pickford: The Woman Who Made Hollywood* (Lexington: University Press of Kentucky, 1997), p. 221.

188 *new contract:* Clifford Robertson affidavit in *Movie Weekly*, January 6, 1923, p. 18.

188 *"would be considered a minimum . . .":* RV, affidavit, *Famous Players–Lasky v. Rudolph Valentino*, in *Movie Weekly*, October 21, 1922, n.p.

189 *She told Zukor:* Zukor, night letter to Lasky, March 15, 1922, Zukor Collection, AMPAS.

189 *They'd gone horseback riding:* Gloria Swanson, *Swanson on Swanson* (New York: Random House, 1980), p. 171; Swanson, television interview, *Today*, NBC, August 23, 1976.

189 *"I never saw Rudolph . . .":* Swanson, *Swanson on Swanson*, p. 174.

190 *a duplicate handkerchief:* Clip, *Placerville Mountain Democrat*, September 9, 1922, Gloria Swanson Collection, HRC.

190 *"Gloria Swanson can wear clothes":* Clip, *The New York Times*, May 8, 1922, Swanson Collection, HRC.

190 *she plunges into the sea:* Clip, *Screenland*, May 6, 1922, Swanson Collection, HRC.

190 *"Everything about [the film] . . .":* Advertisement, *Moving Picture World*, May 20, 1922, n.p.

190 *Gloria Swanson's contract:* Alexander Walker, *Stardom: The Hollywood Phenomenon* (New York: Stein & Day, 1970), p. 130.

191 *"Best Dressed Man": Moving Picture World*, June 28, 1924, p. 832.

191 *Ramon Novarro:* Ibid., April 5, 1924, p. 83.

191 *costumes designed by Natacha:* Morris, *Madam Valentino*, p. 106.

191 *"I walked out . . .":* Letter to *Photoplay*, September 1922, p. 80.

191 *"Miss Swanson's close-fitting . . .":* Clip, *Film Daily*, May 14, 1922, Swanson Collection, HRC.

191 *"a state of somniferous weariness":* Clip, *The New York Times*, May 8, 1922, Swanson Collection, HRC.

191 *"My patrons were divided . . .": Moving Picture World*, December 9, 1922, p. 664.

192 *"In my beloved Paris . . .":* Elinor Glyn, "In Filmdom's Boudoir," *Photoplay*, March 1921, p. 30.

193 *"to establish and maintain . . .":* Quoted in Kevin Brownlow, *Behind the Mask of Innocence* (New York: Knopf, 1990), p. 15.

193 *"So we shot each kiss twice":* Swanson, *Swanson on Swanson*, p. 173.

193 *a little trick:* Walker, *Stardom*, p. 163.

193 *"My darling! . . .":* Quoted in "Behind the Camera with Elinor Glyn," *Screenland*, May 6, 1922, p. 27.

193 *"say the same words . . .":* RV, in Elinor Glyn, "Rudolph Valentino as I Knew Him," *Modern Screen*, May 1927, n.p.

194 *"What man-made contract . . .":* RV, quoted in undated *Capital News* clip, Swanson Collection, HRC.

195 *"He looked dangerous . . .":* Glyn, "Rudolph Valentino as I Knew Him," n.p.

195 *"America is very young . . .":* Joseph Schildkraut, quoted in "What Is IT?," *Photoplay*, June 1929, n.p.

195 *"the American man . . .":* RV, "Woman and Love," *Photoplay*, March 1922, n.p.

196 *"VALENTINO MARRIAGE . . .": Los Angeles Times*, May 16, 1922, section 2, p. 1.

196 *"GLYN STORY . . .": Variety*, May 26, 1922, p. 44.

196 *"VALENTINO'S UNDESIRABLE . . .":* Ibid., May 26, 1922, p. 36.

11: THE BIGAMIST

197 *"For a wife":* RV, "Woman and Love," *Photoplay*, March 1922, pp. 42, 98.

198 Character Studies: Thanks to David B. Pearson of the Valentino e-group and the Web site "Silent Ladies and Gents" for information about this 1922 short film, in which Buster Keaton, Douglas Fairbanks, Harold Lloyd, and Jackie Coogan also appeared.

198 *"have done nothing with the vote":* RV, quoted in Willis Goldbeck, "The Perfect Lover," *Motion Picture Magazine*, May 1922, p. 40.

199 *"burnt fudge":* Patsy Ruth Miller, *My Hollywood: When Both of Us Were Young* (West Hanover, Mass.: O'Raghailligh, 1988), p. 30.

199 *"He earned little . . ."* Robert Florey, *Hollywood d'hier et aujourd'hui* (Paris: Editions Prisma, 1979), p. 5.

199 *Thomas Meighan: Variety*, October 6, 1922, p. 46.

199 *black marble floors:* S. George Ullman, *Valentino as I Knew Him* (New York: Macy-Marsius, 1926), p. 114.

200 *"She is the finest woman I know":* RV, quoted in *Photoplay*, July 1922, p. 95.

202 *at a New York dinner party:* Nita Naldi, 1958 interview transcript, Columbia University Oral History, p. 19.

202 *"a passion that is slightly kinky . . .":* Jeanine Basinger, *Silent Stars* (New York: Knopf, 1999), p. 284.

202 *"the big scenes . . .":* Nita Naldi, quoted in *Movie Weekly*, May 3, 1924, p. 3.

203 *"leering at me . . . music motif":* NR, quoted in *Photoplay*, December 1922, p. 117.

203 *Natacha visited:* Michael Morris, *Madam Valentino: The Many Lives of Natacha Rambova* (New York: Abbeville, 1991), p. 108.

204 *"for there was the opportunity . . .":* RV, quoted in *The Bookman*, February 1923, n.p., AMPAS clip.

204 *"I felt little in common . . .":* RV, in Theodore Huff, "The Career of Rudolph Valentino," *Films in Review*, April 1952, p. 146.

204 *"was more the puppet than Julio":* RV, quoted in *The Bookman*, February 1923, n.p., AMPAS clip.

204 *scoffing titters: Variety*, August 11, 1922, p. 32.

204 *"fine repression . . .":* Chaplin, quoted in *Los Angeles Times*, August 24, 1926, p. 3.

204 *"at once noble, vulgar . . .":* René Clair in *Filius* (November 1923): n.p.; Arsenal clip.

205 *shooting two versions:* Naldi interview, Columbia University Oral History, p. 20.

205 *the Hays Office:* Robert Florey, interview by Anthony Slide, August 20, 1976.

205 *Dorothy Arzner spliced in:* Kevin Brownlow, *The Parade's Gone By* (New York: Knopf, 1968), p. 23.

205 *His trainer:* Gilbert Roland in *TV Guide*, November 22, 1975, p. 8.

205 *"circusy": Movie Weekly*, September 30, 1922, p. 24.

205 *the studio promised:* RV, affidavit, *Famous Players–Lasky v. Rudolph Valentino,* in *Movie Weekly*, November 25, 1922, p. 12.

206 *a lump sum:* Vincent Tajiri, *Valentino* (New York: Bantam, 1977), p. 71.

206 *"ZUKOR BELIEVES . . .": Variety*, February 10, 1922, p. 38.

206 *"tend to degrade . . .":* In Leatrice Gilbert Fountain, with John R. Maxim, *Dark Star* (New York: St. Martin's, 1985), p. 197.

207 *who had married out of the state:* NR, *Rudolph Valentino (Recollections) Intimate and Interesting Reminiscences of the Life of the Late World-Famous Star* (New York: Jacobsen-Hodgkinson, 1927), p. 42.

207 *Dagmar Godowsky claimed:* John Kobal, *People Will Talk* (New York: Knopf, 1985), p. 64.

207 *cold feet: Los Angeles Times*, May 17, 1922, section 2, p. 6.

207 *"were urged by all present . . .":* RV, quoted in *Los Angeles Times*, May 21, 1922, p. 1.

207 *the couple retired:* Paul Ivano, interview by Anthony Slide, May 12, 1976.

208 *"stated that the entry . . .":* Los Angeles Times, May 16, 1922, section 2, p. 1.

208 *"If Rudy hadn't been Rudy . . .":* Ruth Waterbury, "Wedded and Parted," *Photoplay*, December 1922, p. 59.

208 *returned at once:* NR, Rudolph Valentino, p. 43.

208 *less than overjoyed:* NR, in Waterbury, "Wedded and Parted," p. 59.

208 *only the Pekingese puppy:* Morris, Madam Valentino, p. 114.

208 *He telegraphed:* Los Angeles Times, May 18, 1922, section 2, p. 1.

208 *"My daughter has left . . .":* Richard Hudnut, quoted in Los Angeles Times, May 22, 1922, section 2, p. 2.

209 *"the company provided . . .":* RV, affidavit in Movie Weekly, December 23, 1922, p. 21.

209 *she broke down:* Morris, Madam Valentino, p. 115.

209 *"shaking the bars . . .":* Adela Rogers St. Johns, The Honeycomb (Garden City, N.Y.: Doubleday, 1969), p. 171.

210 *dalliance with a female:* Tajiri, Valentino, p. 72.

210 *the wrath of the Methodists:* "Methodists Flay Woolwine," Los Angeles Times, October 17, 1921, p. 2.

210 *he often spoke at:* Robert Giroux, A Deed of Death: The Story Behind the Unsolved Murder of Hollywood Director William Desmond Taylor (New York: Knopf, 1990), p. 128.

210 *"DISTRICT ATTORNEY IS PREPARING . . .":* DeMille, letter to Zukor, May 17, 1922, Zukor Collection, AMPAS.

210 *a meeting to plan:* Variety, May 26, 1922, p. 38.

211 *"Mr. Valentino went . . .":* "Valentino Chum Tells of Wedding," Los Angeles Times, May 17, 1922, section 2, p. 6.

211 *whose son George:* Kevin Brownlow, personal communication, March 8, 2001.

211 *bail money:* San Francisco Chronicle, May 21, 1922, n.p.

211 *Los Angeles Athletic Club:* Los Angeles Times, May 20, 1922, section 2, p. 1.

212 *"like a gangster's funeral . . .":* Reginald Taviner, "Why Was Valentino Tried for Bigamy?," unsourced article, author's collection.

212 *"that would lower me . . .":* "Valentino Defense Plea," Los Angeles Times, May 21, 1922, p. 2.

212 *an American Indian:* Ivano, Slide interview.

213 *"PURPLE PAJAMAS . . .":* Los Angeles Times, June 2, 1922, section 2, p. 7.

213 *she refused to press:* Movie Weekly, October 28, 1922, p. 11.

213 *She had the legal right:* San Francisco Chronicle, June 6, 1922, n.p., Chronicle clippings, California Historical Society, San Francisco.

213 *"where debauchery . . .":* Congressional Record, June 29, 1922, n.p., quoted in Brad Steiger and Chaw Mank, Valentino (New York: MacFadden-Bartell, 1966), p. 112.

213–14 *"There is a tear of regret . . .":* RV, quoted in "Bigamy Charge Dismissed," Los Angeles Times, June 6, 1922, section 2, p. 5.

214 *his eyes would flood:* Robert Florey, *La lanterne magique* (Lausanne: La Cinéma-thèque Suisse, 1966), p. 169.

214 *"all in exotic, glorious . . .":* Nan Hudnut Clarkson, *An Adirondack Archive: The Trail to Windover* (Utica: North Country Books, 1993), p. 192.

214 *the local townsfolk:* Nan Hudnut Clarkson, personal communication, September 14, 2000.

215 *"My very own and only babykins":* NR, *Rudolph Valentino*, pp. 44–46.

216 *"right in the middle . . .":* *Movie Weekly*, December 9, 1922, p. 14.

216 *"less virile":* *Moving Picture World*, November 18, 1922, p. 268.

216 *"a dash of paprika"; "Rodolfo [sic] really does . . .":* *Variety*, November 10, 1922, p. 42.

216 *a sleeping potion:* *Movie Weekly*, December 9, 1922, p. 14.

217 *"my appearance altered . . .":* RV, affidavit in *Movie Weekly*, October 21, 1922, n.p.

217 *"cheap sets, cheap casts . . .":* NR, in Waterbury, "Wedded and Parted," p. 118.

217 *his first ulcer symptoms:* Robert Florey, *Hollywood d'hier*, p. 52.

217 *faulted Famous Players–Lasky:* RV, letter to Winifred Lander, August 23, 1923, Tracy Terhune private collection.

217 *"one of the most brilliant . . .":* Edwin Schallert, quoted in *The New York Morning Telegraph*, August 6, 1922, n.p.

218 *top four moneymakers:* Richard Koszarski, *An Evening's Entertainment: The Age of the Silent Feature Picture, 1915–1928* (New York: Macmillan, 1990), p. 33.

218 *outperform* The Sheik: RV, affidavit, *Movie Weekly*, October 21, 1922, n.p.

218 *"seems to have no pattern":* *Variety*, August 11, 1922, p. 32.

218 *crutch scene:* RV, affidavit, *Movie Weekly*, December 16, 1922, p. 22.

219 *an informal poll:* *San Francisco Chronicle*, July 31, 1922, p. 3.

219 *"Mr. Valentino has not been . . .":* *The New York Times*, August 7, 1922, p. 11.

220 *"Someone even made . . .":* Jesse Lasky, Jr., *Whatever Happened to Hollywood?* (New York: Funk & Wagnalls, 1975), p. 33.

220 *"America is learning . . .":* *Los Angeles Times*, August 20, 1922, section 3, p. 13.

221 *he privately complained:* Florey, *La lanterne magique*, p. 170.

221 *The cronies would gather:* Ivano, quoted in Anthony Slide, "Ivano and Valentino: A Unique Partnership," *American Cinematographer* 66, no. 8, August 1985, p. 38.

221 *"Since Natacha . . .":* Ibid., p. 38.

221 *His favorite record:* Florey, *Hollywood*, p. 52.

222 *Rudy lost fifteen dollars:* Florey, *La lanterne magique*, p. 170.

222 *Linder went all out:* Robert Florey, "Une journée avec Rudolph Valentino," ("A Day with Rudolph Valentino"), *Cinea*, September 15, n.d., n.p., scrapbook clip, Arsenal.

12: COURTROOMS AND CLAIRVOYANTS

223 *"the first good laugh . . .":* Mrs. Winifred Hudnut, in NR, *Rudy: An Intimate Portrait of Rudolph Valentino by His Wife* (London: Hutchinson, 1926), p. 56.

223 *"It's all tommyrot . . .":* "Denies He's Great Lover," *Los Angeles Times*, August 5, 1922, p. 1.

224 *One detective followed:* RV, affidavit, *Famous Players–Lasky v. Rudolph Valentino*, in *Movie Weekly*, December 30, 1922, p. 31.

224 *Foxlair:* Elizabeth Hudnut Clarkson, *An Adirondack Archive: The Trail to Windover* (Utica: North Country Books, 1993), pp. 155ff.

224 *the daughter of the farmer:* Ibid., pp. 192–93.

225 *intruder:* NR, *Rudy*, p. 57.

225 *Hudnut scents:* Clarkson, *An Adirondack Archive*, p. 149.

225 *"uncouth looking . . .":* Ibid., p. 194.

226 *"Each meal was a tense affair":* Ibid., p. 193.

226 *Hotel des Artistes:* Kenneth T. Jackson, ed., *The Encyclopedia of New York City* (New Haven: Yale University Press, 1995), p. 563.

227 *"I'll confess it is . . .":* Ruth Waterbury, "Wedded and Parted," *Photoplay*, December 1922, p. 118.

227 *paying director Alan Dwan: Variety*, October 6, 1922, p. 46.

228 *Jesse Lasky had told him:* RV, affidavit in *Movie Weekly*, November 25, 1922, p. 12.

229 *"TOREADOR RODOLPHO . . .": Los Angeles Times*, September 1, 1922, section 2, p. 1.

229 *profits were down: Variety*, March 12, 1923, n.p.

230 *comparative salaries:* RV, affidavit in *Movie Weekly*, October 21, 1922, p. 31.

231 *"Mr. Fitzmaurice has since . . .":* Ibid., November 22, 1922, p. 12.

231 *"I was willing to go . . .":* RV, "An Open Letter to the American Public," *Photoplay*, January 1923, p. 35.

232 *"One might as well have a stable . . .":* RV, affidavit in *Movie Weekly*, January 6, 1923, p. 19.

232 *"As my costumes . . .":* Ibid., December 2, 1922, p. 19.

233 *"Defendant boasts . . .":* Zukor's answering affidavit in ibid., November 25, 1922, p. 30.

233 *average American's annual income:* Scott Derks, *The Value of a Dollar: Prices and Incomes in the U.S., 1860–1989* (Detroit: Gale Research, 1994), p. 175.

233 *"No high and mightiness . . .":* Gladys Hall, "Girls I Like to Dance With," *Movie Weekly*, January 27, 1923, n.p.

233 *"I was not temperamental . . .":* RV, "An Open Letter," pp. 34–35.

234 *"of equal importance": Los Angeles Times*, September 2, 1922, section 2, p. 11.

234 *"bizarre": Photoplay*, August 1922, p. 61.

234 *In 1921 it lost money:* Carol Easton, *The Search for Sam Goldwyn* (New York: Morrow, 1976), p. 60.

234 *"simple habits":* Zukor's answering affidavit, in *Movie Weekly*, November 25, 1922, p. 30.

235 *"obsessed with the idea . . .":* Ibid., p. 13.

235 *"We raised his salary . . .":* Adolph Zukor with Dale Kramer, *The Public Is Never Wrong* (New York: Putnam's, 1953), pp. 211–12.

235 *"Rudolph Valentino is kicking over the traces"*: *Moving Picture World*, September 9, 1922, p. 110.

235 *Mae Murray stamped*: *Variety*, June 2, 1922, p. 38.

235 *"for once Famous Players . . ."*: *Moving Picture World*, September 9, 1922, p. 110.

236 *"I am not familiar . . ."*: RV, affidavit, in *Movie Weekly*, October 21, 1922, p. 31.

236 *"as soon as litigation ends"*: *Variety*, September 29, 1922, p. 47.

236 *Other studios*: RV, affidavit, in *Movie Weekly*, January 6, 1923, p. 19.

236 Romeo and Juliet: *Film Yearbook, 1924*, p. 321.

236 *he'd visited . . . Fairbanks*: Letter from Fairbanks's attorney, Cap O'Brien, to H. D. Buckley, September 24, 1923, UA Collection, Wisconsin.

237 *the New York premiere*: *Moving Picture World*, November 11, 1922, p. 139.

237 *screen rights to . . . Ben-Hur*: Kevin Brownlow, *The Parade's Gone By* (New York: Knopf, 1968), p. 388.

237 *"the most responsible motion picture executive position . . ."*: *Moving Picture World*, December 2, 1922, p. 420.

237 *"negotiations for Valentino's appearing . . ."*: Cap O'Brien to Robert Fairbanks, September 12, 1923, UA Collection, Wisconsin.

237 *an injunction*: "Valentino Loses Out," *Moving Picture World*, October 14, 1922, p. 552; *The New York Times*, January 20, 1923, p. 13.

238 *"Would you consider . . . ?"* Anna Prophater, "Rudolph Valentino and Marriage," October 1923, *Screenland,* n.p.

238 *$43,333.33*: *Variety*, July 16, 1924, n.p.

238 *sued for nonpayment*: Ibid., February 7, 1924, p. 4.

238 *purchased five works*: *Los Angeles Times*, October 5, 1922, section 2, p. 11.

238 *"Rudy gets horribly excited . . ."*: Ruth Waterbury, "Wedded and Parted," *Photoplay*, December 1922, p. 59.

239 *"The ideal thing . . ."*: NR, "Why I Married Rudy," *Movie Weekly*, December 16, 1922, p. 7.

239 *Joe Godsol*: Kevin Lewis and Arnold Lewis, "Include Me Out: Samuel Goldwyn and Joe Godsol," *Film History* 2 (1988), p. 148; A. Scott Berg, *Goldwyn: A Biography* (New York: Knopf, 1989), p. 93.

239 *"unselfish proof of friendship"*: NR, *Rudy*, p. 63.

239 *"Valentino rival"*: *Variety*, December 22, 1922, p. 1.

239 *filed a counterclaim*: Ibid., p. 39; *The New York Times*, December 9, 1922, p. 11.

240 *"too stringent . . ."*: *The New York Times*, January 20, 1923, p. 13.

240 *radio broadcasts*: *Variety*, January 25, 1923, p. 47.

240 *the station abruptly*: "Valentino Suddenly Cut Off," *Billboard*, February 24, 1923, n.p. I owe this reference to Frank Cullen.

240 *"the first step toward . . ."*: Unsourced clip, November 5, 1922, MoMA.

241 *"except as a conductor . . ."; "I have never been . . ."*: RV to Herbert Howe, "Success—and the Morning After," *Picture Play*, August 1921, pp. 32, 96.

241 *a palm reader:* Robert Florey, *La lanterne magique* (Lausanne: La Cinémathèque Suisse, 1966), pp. 151–52.

241 *Cora McGeachy:* Ruth Biery, "Valentino's Unknown Love," unsourced clip, Wisconsin.

241 *"Rudy was really psychic":* Frederick James Smith, "Does Rudy Speak from Beyond?," *Photoplay*, February 1927, n.p.

242 *spirit contacts:* NR, *Rudy*, pp. 64–65.

242 *Jenny . . . Virginia Mathis:* George Ullman, quoted in Harry T. Brundidge, *Twinkle, Twinkle, Movie Star* (New York: E. P. Dutton, 1930), p. 73.

242 *poems:* RV, "You," "A Baby's Skin," "Italy," Preface, *Day Dreams* (New York: Macfadden, 1923).

242 *"psychically received":* NR, *Rudy*, p. 69.

13: THE MINERALAVA DANCE TOUR

244 *"I had no idea . . .":* S. George Ullman, *Valentino as I Knew Him* (New York: Macy-Masius, 1926), p. 58.

246 *"a very beautiful girl . . .":* Ibid.

246 *receded in popularity:* Julie Malnig, *Dancing till Dawn: A Century of Exhibition Ballroom Dancing* (Westport, Conn.: Greenwood Press, 1992), p. 109.

247 *benefit for the Actors' Fund:* Century Theatre program, Friday, January 19, 1923, Dance Collection, NYPL.

247 *"stampeded by two to three hundred . . .":* Unsourced Valentino clip, February 3, 1923, MoMA.

247 *"10,000 GIRLS MOB . . .":* quoted in Miriam Hansen, *Babel and Babylon: Spectatorship in American Silent Film* (Cambridge, Mass.: Harvard University Press, 1991), p. 358, n. 38.

247 *escape over the roofs:* Robert Florey, *Hollywood d'hier et aujourd'hui* (Paris: Editions Prisma, 1979), p. 54.

247 *"one lady tore a rent . . .":* *Photoplay*, August 1923, p. 68.

247 *In Kansas and Arizona:* Robert Florey, *La lanterne magique* (Lausanne: La Cinémathèque Suisse, 1966), p. 164.

247 *Chicago's Trianon:* *Variety*, February 22, 1923, p. 47; Herbert Howe, *Photoplay*, May 1923, p. 57.

248 *"fanned her and fluttered . . .":* Valentino clip, February 23, 1923, Chicago Historical Society.

248 *made an effort to visit schools:* Typescript, March 9, 1923, Photoplay Collection, MoMA.

248 *Now the same multitude:* Florey, *La lanterne magique*, p. 164.

248 *Jack Curley:* Alva Johnston, "Cauliflowers and Pachyderms," *The New Yorker*, July 14, 1934, p. 21.

249 *children often gathered:* NR, quoted in Anna Prophater, "Rudolph Valentino and Marriage," *Screenland*, October 1923, p. 96.

249 *Sometimes Rudy would:* Florey, *La lanterne magique*, p. 163.

249 *"I wept all right":* NR, quoted by Jack Curley in Alva Johnston, "Cauliflowers," p. 25.

249 *"with and for each other . . .":* Ullman, *Valentino*, p. 64.

249 *tour expenses, grosses: Variety,* March 1, 1923, n.p.

250 *"if Valentino made the selection . . .":* Ullman, *Valentino*, p. 64.

250 *Valentino presented each winner: Variety,* March 29, 1923, p. 5.

250 *"because I was unfortunate enough . . .": Los Angeles Times,* February 13, 1923, section 2, p. 10.

250 *"If I ever make another . . .": Variety,* April 12, 1923, p. 27.

251 *"I am nothing but a love maker . . .": Los Angeles Times,* February 13, 1923, section 2, p. 10.

251 *"I feel deeply distressed . . .":* RV, quoted in *Movie Weekly,* August 11, 1923, p. 3.

251 *"the program was less than . . .":* Quoted in *Motion Picture News,* April 28, 1923, n.p.

252 *"The conceited rarely . . .": Chicago Tribune,* March 7, 1923, n.p.

252 *"Before deciding on the present tour . . .":* Unsourced clip, MoMA.

252 *"Every man and woman . . .":* Ad, *Photoplay,* August 1923, p. 80.

253 *"Up close, he revealed . . .":* Ralph McGill in *Pittsburgh Post Gazette,* July 6, 1966, n.p.

253 *"American men are not lovers!":* "The Vogue of Valentino," *Motion Picture Magazine,* February 1923, pp. 27ff.

254 *Mineralava finances:* Unsourced clip, MoMA.

254 VALENTINO RAZZED: *Variety,* April 26, 1923, p. 24.

255 *"an imbecile, feeble-minded":* Application for marriage license, State of Indiana, Lake County Circuit Court, Crown Point, March 14, 1923.

255 *"the bride and bridegroom returned . . .":* Clip, Toledo *Blade,* March 15, 1923, NYPL.

255 *"Mrs. Valentino is one of the few wives of influence":* Anna Prophater, "Rudolph Valentino and Marriage," *Screenland,* October 1923, n.p.

257 *Natacha scolded Rudy:* Unsourced scrapbook clip, Tracy Terhune private collection.

257 *"Rudy says his people . . .": Motion Picture Magazine,* October 1923, p. 49.

258 *"The most applauded men . . .":* Herbert Howe, *Photoplay,* February 1923, p. 58.

258 *a planned production: Variety,* July 12, 1923, p. 20.

258 *Valentino promised Florey:* Florey, interview by Anthony Slide, August 20, 1976.

258 *he offered Quirk:* RV, letter to James Quirk, March 22, 1923, Photoplay Collection, MoMA.

258–59 *he'd posed for new publicity photos; "to lose one woman . . .":* RV, letter to Florey, May 20, 1923, quoted in Florey, *La lanterne magique,* p. 166.

260 *vocal coach:* Undated memo to Mr. Quirk, Photoplay Collection, MoMA.

260 *Max Steuer:* Colin Evans, *Super Lawyers: America's Courtroom Celebrities* (Detroit: Visible Ink Press, 1998), pp. 227–31.

260 *settlement was reached . . . Graham: Moving Picture World*, July 28, 1923, p. 283.

260 *"He enjoyed the feel . . .":* Ullman, *Valentino*, p. 73.

261 *"any continuance . . .":* Quoted in *Variety*, January 5, 1923, p. 47.

261 *"would make a series . . .": "every speaker . . .": Moving Picture World*, July 28, 1923, p. 283.

262 *New York dinners: Photoplay*, June 1923, p. 114, and October 1923, p. 86.

262 *in Minnesota: Variety*, May 30, 1923, p. 19.

263 *Jean Acker at Texas Guinan's: Photoplay*, June 1923, p. 41; Louise Berliner, *Texas Guinan: Queen of the Nightclubs* (Austin: University of Texas Press, 1993), pp. 94–95.

14: EUROPE, 1923

264 *"He was being fearfully civil . . .":* Elinor Glyn, "Rudolph Valentino as I Knew Him," *Modern Screen*, May 1927, n.p.

265 *notable names:* NR, *Rudolph Valentino (Recollections) Intimate and Interesting Reminiscences of the Life of the Late World-Famous Star* (New York: Jacobsen-Hodgkinson, 1927), p. 63; RV, "My Own Story of My Trip Abroad," *Movie Weekly*, March 8, 1924, p. 6.

265 *He also would boast:* RV, in *Movie Weekly*, February 23, 1924, p. 6.

265 *"magnificent dressing-gown . . .":* Wilton Lane, *Picturegoer*, September 1923, p. 39.

266 *"To dance when one has to . . .":* RV, in Neal Botham and Peter Donnelly, *Valentino: The Love God* (London: Everest Books, 1976), p. 142.

266 *"Live and let live":* RV, quoted in "English Fans Rush to Greet Valentino," unsourced clip, Valentino scrapbook, NYPL.

266 *visits to Westminster Abbey:* NR, *Rudolph Valentino*, p. 62.

266 *black hair paste:* Robert Florey, *Hollywood d'hier et aujourd'hui* (Paris: Editions Prisma, 1979), p. 54.

267 *"I said to Natacha . . .":* RV, "My Own Story," *Movie Weekly*, March 15, 1924, p. 10.

267 *Paris . . . "still wears . . .":* Ibid., p. 28.

268 *Théâtre des Champs-Elysées:* Jules Bertaut, *Paris, 1870–1935*, trans. R. Millar (New York: D. Appleton Century, 1936), p. 278.

268 *In future years:* Obituary of Jacques Hébertot, *Variety*, July 1, 1970, n.p.

268 *invitations:* Preserved in the Hébertot Collection, Arsenal.

268 *"No one is in Paris . . .":* RV, "My Own Story," March 22, 1924, p. 22.

268 *"the handsomest man in the world"; "He doesn't appear . . .":* Unsourced scrapbook clips, 1923, Arsenal, author's translations.

269 *"I looked at seventeen different . . .":* RV, "My Own Story," March 15, 1924, p. 28.

269 *custom-made car:* Mary Blume, *Côte d'Azur: Inventing the French Riviera* (New York: Thames & Hudson, 1992), p. 87.

269 *She was photographed:* "Natacha Valentino Inspires Paul Poiret to Create for Her This Exotic Wardrobe," *Photoplay*, January 1924, pp. 42–43.

269–70 *"wishy-washy things . . ."; "Natacha finally . . .":* RV, "My Own Story," March 15, 1924, p. 22.

270 *"There were no smart women . . .":* RV, "My Own Story," March 22, 1924, p. 22.

271 *Rolf de Maré:* Erik Naslund, "Animating a Vision: Rolf de Maré, Jean Börlin, and the Founding of the Ballets Suédois," in *Paris Modern*, ed. Nancy Baer (Seattle: University of Washington Press, 1995), p. 48; Amanda Vaill, *Everybody Was So Young* (New York: Houghton Mifflin, 1998), p. 122.

271 *Hébertot's interest:* David Bret, *Valentino: A Dream of Desire* (London: Robson Books, 1998).

273 *"The minute he came . . .":* RV, "My Own Story," April 15, 1924, p. 27.

274 *on the* Aquitania: Hébertot, undated [December 1923] Hébertot radiogram, Arsenal; travel dates in *Variety*, December 27, 1923, p. 27.

274 *"thinking he would make . . .":* Unsourced clip, Valentino scrapbook, March 11, 1924, NYPL.

274 *reckless driving:* RV, "My Own Story," March 29, 1924, pp. 14–15.

275 *"I think I shall never . . .":* Ibid., April 5, 1924, p. 28.

275 *"I have calluses . . .":* Ibid., p. 10.

275 *"in gay modern things":* NR, *Rudolph Valentino*, p. 67.

276 *"I should like to have . . .":* RV, "My Own Story," April 5, 1924, p. 11.

276 *"but what is a man to do . . .":* Ibid., p. 28.

276 *On its hood:* Ibid., May 3, 1924, p. 12.

276 *The customs officers:* NR, *Rudolph Valentino*, pp. 67–68.

277 *Robert Florey had a hard time:* Florey, Slide interview.

277 *"Nothing happened, because I look like . . .":* Bebe Daniels to Anthony Slide, in *Close-ups: Intimate Profiles of the Movie Stars*, ed. Denny Peary (New York: Workman, 1978), p. 133.

277 *Natacha later remembered:* NR, *Rudolph Valentino*, p. 70.

277 *"He knew nothing of pictures . . .":* RV, "My Own Story," April 12, 1924, p. 28.

277 *the cook's daughter:* NR, *Rudolph Valentino*, p. 70.

278 *"Between the dust . . .":* RV, "My Own Story," April 12, 1924, p. 28.

278 *car crashes:* Ibid., April 26, 1924, p. 27.

278 *"boldly looking her up and down":* Ibid., May 3, 1924, n.p.

278 *"We just embraced . . .":* RV, *My Private Diary* (Chicago: Occult Publishing, 1929), pp. 143–44.

279 *"Our first task was . . .":* NR, *Rudolph Valentino*, p. 78.

279 *"as good as that":* RV, *My Private Diary*, p. 155.

280 *"I am of the Romans . . .":* Ibid., pp. 188–89.

280 *Nettuno:* Ibid., p. 171; NR, *Rudolph Valentino*, p. 79.

281 *"They have no lighting . . .":* RV, *My Private Diary*, p. 185.

281 *The chief of Cines:* Florey, Slide interview.

281 *The White Sister:* James Abbe, *James Abbe, Photographer* (Norfolk, Va.: Chrysler Museum of Art, 2000), p. 70.

281 *"entering into the very skin of the role"*: RV, *My Private Diary*, p. 184.

282 *"Natacha has gone"*: Ibid., p. 206.

282 *"so that they may not know . . ."*: Ibid., p. 208.

283 *the annual June procession*: Carol Field, *Celebrating Italy* (New York: Morrow, 1990), p. 476.

283 *"more like a page out of . . ."*: RV, *My Private Diary*, p. 210.

283 *"He just looked at me . . ."*; *"Mercurio"*: Ibid., pp. 213–15.

284 *his first bicycle*: JV, interview by Kevin Brownlow, June 3, 1977.

284 *"sprawling in the dust . . ."*: RV, *My Private Diary*, p. 225.

284 *"She also gave me . . ."*: Ibid., p. 222.

284 *"Tomorrow I should get straight back . . ."*: RV, "My Own Story," May 31, 1924, p. 30.

284 *"Bathing, fresh air . . ."*: RV, *My Private Diary*, p. 239.

285 *"They were the only thing . . ."*: Ibid., p. 241.

285 *"Here seventeen or eighteen . . ."*: Ibid., pp. 272–73.

285 *"My God, you aren't . . ."*: RV, *My Private Diary*, p. 272.

286 *greeted him as the son*: Nicola Napoletane to Agostino de Bellis.

286 *paper money*: Unsourced Valentino clip, August 21, 1976, BFI.

286 *One of the daughters*: The New York Times, October 16, 1976, p. 2.

15: THE COMEBACK

287 *"I have not been happy . . ."*: RV, "When I Come Back," *Motion Picture Classic*, December 1923, p. 22.

288 *"merely touches Lady Mary's hand . . ."*: The New York Times, August 12, 1924, p. 12.

288 *Douglas Fairbanks; William De Mille*: Kevin Brownlow, program notes to *Monsieur Beaucaire*, National Film Theatre, London; personal communication, June 25, 2001.

288 *"was chosen by Famous Players . . ."*: NR, *Rudolph Valentino (Recollections) Intimate and Interesting Reminiscences of the Life of the Late World-Famous Star* (New York: Jacobsen-Hodgkinson, 1927), p. 117.

288 *asked to choose between*: Brownlow, *Monsieur Beaucaire* program notes.

289 *"insist[ing] on . . . perfumed parts . . ."*: Jesse Lasky, *I Blow My Own Horn* (Garden City, N.Y.: Doubleday, 1957), p. 148.

289 *fencing lessons*: Unsourced clip, NYPL.

289 *a mere tool*: Douglas Gerrard, letter to Adolph Zukor, December 19, 1923, Zukor Collection, AMPAS.

290 *Rudy wrote*: RV, letter to Jacques Hébertot, November 13, 1923, Arsenal.

290 *art sales and auctions*: Unsourced clip, April 1924, NYPL.

291 *"patterned after the famous crown . . ."*: Unsourced Valentino clip, Wisconsin.

291 *David O. Selznick*: David Thomson, *Showman: The Life of David O. Selznick* (New York: Knopf, 1992), pp. 52–53.

291 *Selznick's only expenses*: Rudy Behlmer, ed., *Memo from David O. Selznick* (New York: Viking, 1972), p. 6.

292 *He hinted:* H. D. Buckley of Douglas Fairbanks Pictures Corp., letter to Dennis "Cap" O'Brien, September 15, 1923, UA Collection, Wisconsin.

292 *Louella Parsons:* Cap O'Brien, letter to H. D. Buckley, September 25, 1923, UA Collection, Wisconsin.

292 *"a cancellation . . .":* Nathan Burkan, letter to Cap O'Brien, September 13, 1923, UA Collection, Wisconsin.

292 *"I quite agree":* Cap O'Brien to H. D. Buckley, September 24, 1923, UA Collection, Wisconsin.

293 *"It seems that Valentino . . .":* H. D. Buckley to Cap O'Brien, October 3, 1923, UA Collection, Wisconsin.

293 *"3-CORNERED VALENTINO TANGLE . . .":* Variety, December 15, 1923, p. 17.

294 *"studying the Pompadour period":* Unsourced clip, December 14, 1923, NYPL.

294 *"character development and artistry":* NR, quoted in *Los Angeles Times*, "Valentino Coming Back," December 26, 1923, section 2, p. 11.

294 *"to carry on . . .":* NR, quoted in *Movie Weekly*, January 8, 1924, p. 29.

294 *"I think the signing . . .":* Adolph Zukor, quoted in *Movie Weekly*, January 8, 1924, p. 29.

294 *Christmas tree:* Mrs. Winifred Hudnut, in NR, *Rudolph Valentino*, pp. 84–85.

295 *"by at least eight men"; "making herself very popular,":* Ibid., p. 87.

295 *"That so-called beauty contest . . .":* Photoplay, March 1924, p. 27.

295 *"Everyone connected with . . .":* Variety, February 14, 1924, n.p.

296 *"The floor shone . . .":* Motion Picture Magazine, May 1924, p. 109.

296 *"emblazoned with silver . . .":* Movie Weekly, March 15, 1924, pp. 4–5.

296 *It faced a major slump:* Photoplay, January 1924, p. 74; *Moving Picture World*, January 19, 1924, p. 174.

297 *Dorothea Herzog reported:* Movie Weekly, May 31, 1924, p. 8.

297 *New York–bred Doris Kenyon:* Doris Kenyon, quoted by Anthony Slide, personal communication.

297 *Olcott . . . salary:* Richard Koszarski, *An Evening's Entertainment: The Age of the Silent Feature Picture, 1915–1928* (New York: Macmillan, 1990), p. 213.

297 *"Mr. Olcott, standing nearby . . .":* Movie Weekly, March 15, 1924, p. 21.

297 *"useless":* Doris Kenyon, conversation with Anthony Slide, personal communication.

297 *a new lighting system:* Koszarski, *An Evening's Entertainment*, p. 151.

298 *soft focus:* Variety, March 26, 1924, p. 17.

298 *"A good cameraman . . .":* RV, "Confidences et Souvenirs," *Ciné-Miroir*, February 3, 1928, p. 83.

298 *Weldy and Barbier:* Movie Weekly, May 31, 1924, p. 8.

298 *a walking ensemble:* Motion Picture Magazine, August 1924, p. 30.

299 *"The genuine feeling . . .":* Lois Wilson, "The Rudolph Valentino I Know," *Movie Weekly*, June 27, 1925, p. 10.

299 *"Oh, don't worry, Queenie . . .":* Lowell Sherman, quoted by Lois Wilson, interview by Anthony Slide, July 13, 1979.

299–300 *"as expert in flourishing . . .":* Lois Wilson, "The Rudolph Valentino I Know," p. 9.

300 *Daven wrote to a friend:* Jeanne de Recqueville, *Rudolph Valentino* (Paris: France-Empire, 1978), pp. 88–89.

300 *"The two of us are living . . .";* *"nothing has been broken . . .":* André Daven letters, quoted by de Recqueville, p. 91.

300 *"His sun rises and sets in Natacha":* Lois Wilson, "The Rudolph Valentino I Know," p. 10.

301 *did not interfere:* Wilson, Slide interview.

301 *"She has beauty, charm . . .":* Wilson, "The Rudolph Valentino I Know," p. 10.

301 *whom she considered:* Jetta Goudal, interview by Anthony Slide, 1979, Astoria Oral History, AMMI.

301 *Doris Kenyon:* Anthony Slide, personal communication.

301 *"If Mrs. Valentino . . .":* Cal York quoting Harry Reichenbach in *Photoplay*, July 1924, p. 52.

301 *conscious or unconscious competition:* Gavin Lambert, *Nazimova: A Biography* (New York: Knopf, 1997), p. 271.

302 *He said he would never:* Wilson, Slide interview.

302 *admiration for studio discipline:* Kevin Brownlow, program notes to *Monsieur Beaucaire*, National Film Theatre, London.

302 *Stanislavsky reportedly:* Lambert, *Nazimova*, p. 271.

303 *"In Brummell . . .":* *The New York Times*, August 17, 1924, section 7, p. 2.

303 *"Rudolph Valentino is suggestive of . . .":* *Photoplay*, April 1924, p. 43.

303–4 *"dolled up":* Unsourced clip, NYPL.

304 *"girls made up three quarters . . .":* *Variety,* August 13, 1924, n.p.

304 *"You are trying to be . . .":* Margaret O'Brien, letter to *Photoplay*, December 1924, n.p.

304 *"I would like to know just who . . .":* Ruth Mathews, letter to *Photoplay*, October 1923, p. 14.

304 *"his being nude . . .":* *Variety*, August 13, 1924, n.p.

304 *"Ladies! Ladies!":* Mildred Spain, quoted in unsourced clip, NYPL.

304 *"Something has happened . . .":* *Photoplay*, September 1924, p. 27.

305 *Monsieur Don't Care:* *Moving Picture World*, May 2, 1925, p. 69.

305 *command performance:* Norman Mackenzie, *The Magic of Rudolph Valentino* (London: Research Publishing, 1974), p. 104.

305 *"Advertised it like . . .":* *Moving Picture World*, October 11, 1924, p. 490.

305 *fan mail:* *Variety*, December 31, 1924, n.p.

305 *Film Daily poll:* Koszarski, *An Evening's Entertainment*, p. 262.

305 *another trade paper:* Richard Dyer MacCann, *The Stars Appear* (Metuchen, N.J.: Scarecrow Press, 1992), p. 9.

305 *"King and Queen of the Movies":* *Movie Weekly*, March 15, 1924, p. 13.

306 *great plans:* J. D. Williams, quoted in *Los Angeles Times,* May 18, 1924, section 3, p. 22.

16: SLIPPAGE

307 "playing earthy tigers . . .": Quoted by Jesse Lasky, Jr., Whatever Happened to Hollywood? (New York: Funk & Wagnalls, 1975), p. 34.

307 Joseph Henabery, who: Kevin Brownlow, The Parade's Gone By (New York: Knopf, 1968), pp. 42ff.

307 "Mrs. Valentino assumed . . .": Joseph F. Henabery, Before, in, and After Hollywood, ed. Anthony Slide (Lanham, Md.: Scarecrow Press, 1997), p. 240.

308 "She knew the degree . . .": Ibid., p. 244.

308 a siege of sleeplessness: Ibid., p. 243.

308 close-ups: Variety, November 26, 1924, p. 24.

308 "The action drags . . .": Regina Cannon, New York Graphic, November 23, 1924, n.p.

309 "But for her influence . . .": Henabery, Before, p. 240.

309 "Often I thought . . .": Ibid., p. 245.

310 publicity paragraphs: Photoplay, October 1924, p. 44; Moving Picture World, October 25, 1924, n.p.

310 "entirely surrounded . . .": The New York Sun, November 24, 1924, n.p.

311 "The spinal column . . .": NR, Rudolph Valentino (Recollections) Intimate and Interesting Reminiscences of the Life of the Late World-Famous Star (New York: Jacobsen-Hodgkinson, 1927), p. 118.

311 Goudal recalled: Jetta Goudal, interview by Anthony Slide, 1979, Astoria Oral History, AMMI.

312 "crabbed sketches": Robert Riley, American Fashion (New York: Quadrangle, 1975), p. 20.

312 "lost sight of the fact that . . .": NR, Rudolph Valentino, p. 119.

312 another women's picture: Variety, November 26, 1924, p. 24, and December 3, 1924, n.p.

312 "This should have been called . . .": Moving Picture World, February 14, 1925, p. 687.

312 "I blamed my flop . . .": Ibid., January 24, 1925, p. 363.

313 a young noble who falls in love: Exhibitor's Trade Review, November 1, 1924, n.p.

313 Louella Parsons reported: The New York American, June 11, 1924, n.p.; August 13, 1924, n.p.

313 "as busy as the proverbial . . .": The New York Morning Telegraph, September 28, 1924, n.p.

314 "Miss Mathis declares herself . . .": Exhibitor's Trade Review, November 1, 1924, n.p.

314 "babes in the woods in business": Henabery, Before, p. 252.

314 because this would be: Henabery, telegram to Jesse Lasky, August 14, 1924, Henabery Collection, AMPAS.

314 "You could have knocked me over . . .": Henabery, Before, p. 250.

315 his trainer: Unsourced clip, NYPL.

315 training workouts: How You Can Keep Fit (New York: Macfadden, 1923).

315 "Valentino's Beauty Secrets": The New York Daily Mirror, June 24–28, 1924, n.p.

315 *"with no other equipment . . .":* Seamus Dillon, "How Valentino Keeps His Figure," *Liberty*, December 29, 1924, p. 64.

315 *involved with Rolf de Maré:* Erik Naslund, "Animating a Vision: Rolf de Maré, Jean Börlin, and the Founding of the Ballets Suédois," in *Paris Modern: The Swedish Ballet, 1920–1925*, ed. Nancy Baer (Seattle: University of Washington Press, 1995), p. 53.

315 *Rudy sat behind the wheel:* Mrs. Winifred Hudnut in NR, *Rudolph Valentino*, p. 89.

316 *"there was no one at Antibes except . . .":* F. Scott Fitzgerald, letter quoted by Amanda Vaill, *Everybody Was So Young* (New York: Houghton Mifflin, 1998), p. 163.

316 *power outage:* NR, *Rudolph Valentino*, p. 90.

316 *"It was a beautiful sight . . .":* Mrs. Hudnut, in NR, *Rudolph Valentino*, p. 89.

316 *an enormous crush:* Amanda Vaill, personal communication, May 4, 1999.

316 *spending in Spain:* Irving Shulman, *Valentino* (New York: Trident Press, 1967), p. 263.

317 *Rudy got so carried away:* Mrs. Hudnut, in NR, *Rudy: An Intimate Portrait of Rudolph Valentino, by His Wife* (London: Hutchinson, 1926), pp. 114–15.

318 *"In wandering through . . .":* NR, *Rudolph Valentino*, p. 105.

318 *"We noted from the old portraits . . .":* RV, to Gladys Hall, *Movie Weekly*, December 13, 1924, p. 12.

318 *"The one with the whiskers . . .":* S. George Ullman, foreword, *Catalogue, Estate of Rudolph Valentino* (Los Angeles: Eureka Press, 1926), p. 5.

318 *"Usually in hotel dining-rooms . . .":* Mrs. Hudnut, in *Rudolph Valentino*, p. 110.

319 *Châteaudun:* Ibid., p. 109.

319 *just one day:* AV, interview by Kevin Brownlow, June 3, 1977.

319 *"as long as he remains bewhiskered":* Beulah Livingstone, *Remember Valentino: Reminiscences of the World's Greatest Lover*, pamphlet, 1938, p. 66.

319 *a fake red beard: Moving Picture World*, November 29, 1924, p. 407.

320 *"other races . . .":* RV, to Gladys Hall, *Movie Weekly*, December 13, 1924, p. 29.

320 *"Meeting him was like . . .":* Luther Mahoney, in Raymond Lee, "The Legend of Valentino," *Movie Classics*, August 1973, p. 9.

321 *Adrian . . . said later:* Howard Gutner, personal communication, March 8, 2000.

321 *"Probably no film star . . .": Movie Weekly*, December 27, 1924, p. 23.

321 *"One can live a simple life . . .":* RV, quoted in *Movie Weekly*, January 31, 1925, p. 31.

321 *its modern interior's sleek lines:* "Dinner with the Valentinos," *The Movie Magazine*, September 1925, n.p. Thanks to Lucia Schultz and Kristine Krueger of the Margaret Herrick Library, AMPAS, for help in locating this article at the NYPL Performing Arts Collection.

322 *Mahoney drew a design:* Jack Scagnetti, *The Intimate Life of Rudolph Valentino* (Middle Village, N.Y.: Jonathan David, 1975), pp. 70–71.

322 *"She exercised to the fullest . . .":* S. George Ullman, *Valentino as I Knew Him* (New York: Macy-Masius, 1926), p. 94.

322 *"Every move that Ullman . . .":* Luther Mahoney, in Scagnetti, *Intimate Life*, p. 95.

322 *"like a boy . . .":* Ibid., p. 73.

322 *On Christmas Eve:* Ullman, *Valentino*, p. 127.

323 *"Sets are being erected . . .":* *Movie Weekly*, November 1, 1924, p. 19.

323 *"With our company . . .":* J. D. Williams, quoted in *Exhibitor's Trade Review*, November 1, 1924, n.p.

323 *Sabatini script doctor:* AV, quoted in *Motion Picture Magazine*, September 1934, p. 82.

323 *"June refused . . .":* NR, *Rudolph Valentino*, p. 115.

324 *"Talk about your . . .":* Zit's Weekly columnist, quoted in *Photoplay*, February 1925, p. 62.

324 *"She is a woman . . .";* *"We were both . . .":* Harry Carr, "Valentino Is Not a Henpecked Husband," *Motion Picture Magazine*, August 1925, n.p.

324 *"place the now famous . . .":* Ullman, *Valentino*, p. 129.

325 *Knights of the Bracelet:* Valerie Steele, *Paris Fashion: A Cultural History* (New York: Oxford University Press, 1988), p. 222.

325 *Italian male babies:* Frances M. Malpezzi and William M. Clements, *Italian-American Folklore* (Little Rock, Ark.: August House, 1992), p. 122.

325 *"Maybe it's the fashion . . .":* *Photoplay*, January 1924, p. 131.

325 *"would as soon appear . . .":* Ibid., May 1924, p. 40.

325 *a reader pointed out:* Unsourced clip, Valentino scrapbook, NYPL.

17: THE CRACK-UP

326 *"I was far too absorbed . . .":* NR, *Rudy: An Intimate Portrait of Rudolph Valentino, by His Wife* (London: Hutchinson, 1926), p. 131.

326 *she squandered:* Joseph E. Henabery, *Before, in, and After Hollywood* (Lanham, Md.: The Scarecrow Press, 1997), p. 256.

326 *She also clashed with:* Unsourced clip, Valentino scrapbook, NYPL.

327 *"He had a great love of . . .":* *Los Angeles Mirror*, September 12, 1951, n.p.

327 *"None of the supporting players . . .":* Henabery, *Before*, p. 254.

327 *"burnt to a crisp . . .":* Unsigned *Cobra* review, Robert Z. Leonard Scrapbook 9, Robert Z. Leonard Collection, AMPAS.

328 *"Rudy escapes for perhaps . . .":* *Philadelphia Public Ledger*, December 15, 1925, n.p.

328 *"The locale of the story . . .":* Helen Klumph, *Cobra* review, unsourced, in Robert Z. Leonard Scrapbook 9, Robert Z. Leonard Collection, AMPAS.

328 *An earlier treatment:* James Young, *Cobra* treatment, Joseph and Jeanne Henabery Collection, AMPAS.

329 *"would scream with laughter . . .":* Dagmar Godowsky, *First Person Plural: The Lives of Dagmar Godowsky* (New York: Viking Press, 1958), p. 71.

329 *"Valentino has many affairs . . .":* *Motion Picture Magazine*, March 1926, p. 64.

329 *"Valentino stalks through . . .":* Klumph, *Cobra* review.

329 *"This one killed . . .":* Moving Picture World, April 3, 1926, p. 357.

329–30 *"Not since Rudolph Valentino flashed . . .":* James Quirk, Photoplay, October 1925, p. 27.

330 *survey by the British:* Picturegoer, April 1925, p. 18.

330 *"his fame seems to be . . .":* Helen Carlisle, Movie Weekly, June 20, 1925, p. 43.

330 *"The star realizes . . .":* Ibid., August 15, 1925, p. 33.

330 *"We live a very simple . . .":* Quoted by Harry Carr, "Valentino Is Not a Henpecked Husband," Motion Picture Magazine, August 1925, p. 115.

330 *"I've been called . . .":* Quoted by James Kotsilibas-Davis and Myrna Loy, Myrna Loy: Being and Becoming (New York: Knopf, 1987), p. 37.

330 *"the manner in which . . .":* Variety, February 4, 1925, n.p.

331 *"expecting [Natacha] to get him . . .":* Kotsilibas-Davis and Loy, Myrna Loy, p. 38.

331 *to welcome Gloria Swanson:* Motion Picture Magazine, August 1925, p. 67.

331 *at the Sixty Club:* Photoplay, August 1925, p. 96.

331 *to avoid the risk:* Ibid., p. 101.

331 *"We danced, we gossiped . . .":* NR, Rudolph Valentino (Recollections) Intimate and Interesting Reminiscences of the Life of the Late World-Famous Star (New York: Jacobsen-Hodgkinson, 1927), pp. 119–20.

331 *"in an apple-green frock . . .":* "Dinner with the Valentinos," The Movie Magazine, August 1925, n.p., NYPL.

332 *Falcon Lair:* Catalogue, Estate of Rudolph Valentino (Los Angeles: Eureka Press, 1926), p. 9; Jack Scagnetti, The Intimate Life of Rudolph Valentino (Middle Village, N.Y.: Jonathan David, 1975), p. 72.

332 *Hooded Falcon cast:* Variety, March 11, 1925, p. 28.

333 *"MRS. VALENTINO CAUSE . . .":* Variety, March 4, 1925, p. 1.

333 *"wind swept":* Adela Rogers St. Johns, "Valentino: The Life Story of the Sheik," part 4, Liberty, October 11, 1929, p. 68.

333 *he wasn't sorry:* S. George Ullman, Valentino as I Knew Him (New York: Macy-Masius, 1926), p. 101.

334 *like the Fairbanks pictures:* NR, Rudolph Valentino, p. 118.

334 *deal with United Artists:* Memorandum, May 5, 1925, box 201, UA Collection, Wisconsin.

334 *Benjamin Glazer:* Los Angeles Times, March 10, 1925, section 2, p. 8.

335 *his loan of $100,000 . . . would not:* Jack Scagnetti, Intimate Life, p. 86.

335 *"Valentino has been badly advised":* James R. Quirk, "Presto Chango Valentino," Photoplay, May 1925, p. 36.

335 *"With no wish to be . . .":* Movie Weekly, April 4, 1925, p. 23.

335 *"piquant, elfin . . .":* Motion Picture Magazine, September 1925, p. 27.

335 *"When she ceased to collaborate":* Ullman, Valentino, p. 131.

336 *"and do things . . .":* NR, in Scagnetti, Intimate Life, p. 89.

336 *Rudy's thirtieth birthday:* Los Angeles Times, May 7, 1925, section 2, p. 2.

336 *"In the canyon . . .":* Variety, August 26, 1925, p. 1.

336 *"In Europe boys are taught . . .":* Quoted by Elizabeth Redfield, "May a Wife Deny Her Husband Children?," *Liberty*, January 2, 1926, p. 19.

337 *"I always told my mother . . .":* Louise Di Modica, personal communication, November 12, 1998.

337 *"Here was an inversion . . .":* NR, in James Whittaker, *The New York Daily Mirror*, undated clip, Valentino scrapbook, NYPL.

337 *she taunted him:* Reported by Theodore Huff, quoted by Jeanne de Recqueville, *Rudolph Valentino* (Paris: France-Empire, 1978), p. 105.

338 *"We generally rush . . .":* NR, *Rudolph Valentino*, p. 121.

338 *"was the only one . . .":* NR, in Michael Morris, *Madam Valentino: The Many Lives of Natcha Rambova* (New York: Abbeville, 1991), p. 169.

338 *"I know nothing of detectives":* RV, quoted in *Los Angeles Times*, October 3, 1925, section 2, p. 1.

338 *"To be labeled . . .":* Richard D. Alba, *Italian Americans* (Englewood Cliffs, N.J.: Prentice-Hall, 1985), p. 34.

338 *He grabbed a gun:* Morris, *Madam Valentino*, p. 168.

338 *"She had a right to expect . . .":* RV, quoted in *Los Angeles Times*, November 22, 1925, p. 13.

338–39 *"Women do not . . .":* RV, in Walter Ramsey, "The Undiscovered Valentino," *Modern Screen*, April 1927, p. 130.

339 *"We thought he must have . . .":* *Motion Picture Magazine*, July 1925, n.p.

339 *"Not a day passed . . .":* Ullman, *Valentino*, p. 153.

339 *"I loved them both . . .":* Federico Beltrán-Masses in Guillot de Saix, "Valentino, son revolver et le serpent d'argent," *Comoedia*, September 25, 1926, n.p., Arsenal clip.

339 *copied it several times:* Morris, *Madam Valentino*, p. 172.

340 *"with a faint, fixed smile . . .":* Adela Rogers St. Johns, *Love, Laughter, and Tears: My Hollywood Story* (Garden City, N.Y.: Doubleday, 1978), p. 173.

340 *"Rudolph Valentino Medal":* *Moving Picture World*, August 1, 1925, p. 508.

341 *The Bronze Collar:* Ibid., April 25, 1925, p. 805.

341 *"Clarence Brown feels . . .":* *Variety*, April 22, 1925, p. 26.

341 *a "virile" role:* Clarence Brown, unsourced Valentino clip, Wisconsin.

341 *comments on directors:* RV, to Charles Edward Hastings, *Moving Picture World*, November 21, 1925, p. 208.

341 *Brown sat in:* *Los Angeles Times*, August 23, 1925, section 3, p. 17.

342 *"directs like the leader . . .":* RV in *Motion Picture Magazine*, November 1925, p. 90.

342 *"Garbo and Valentino . . .":* Clarence Brown, in Kevin Brownlow, *The Parade's Gone By* (New York: Knopf, 1968), p. 146.

343 *Joseph Schenck saw rushes:* *Variety*, August 12, 1925, n.p.

343 *Supposedly he'd seen her:* *Movie Weekly*, August 15, 1925, p. 33.

344 *"Charlie Chaplin once . . .":* RV, in Joan Cross, "Why the Valentinos Separated," *The Movie Magazine*, October 1925, p. 97, NYPL.

344 *studio bungalow:* Ullman, *Valentino*, p. 152; *Variety*, March 4, 1925, p. 34.

344 *"Rudy clung to the steps . . .":* Ullman, *Valentino*, p. 147.

344 *"Mrs. Valentino and I . . .":* RV, quoted in *Los Angeles Times*, August 21, 1925, p. 3.

345 *quit-claim:* Recorder's office, Los Angeles County, August 17, 1925.

345 *articles of incorporation: Variety,* August 19, 1925, p. 30.

345 *"Rudy and I have had . . .":* NR to Louella Parsons, unsourced clip, Valentino scrapbook, NYPL.

345 *"With butlers, maids . . .":* NR, quoted in *Los Angeles Times*, August 21, 1925, p. 3.

345 *"Mrs. Valentino cannot . . .":* RV, quoted in *Los Angeles Times*, October 25, 1925, p. 10.

345 *"her own career":* RV, "Why Marriage Was a Failure in My Case," *The New York American*, September 5, 1926, n.p.

346 *"Last night":* Valeria Belletti, letter to Irma, August 21, 1925, Special Collections, AMPAS. Thanks to Cari Beauchamp for alerting me to these letters.

346 *Vilma and Rudy:* Adela Rogers St. Johns, "Valentino: The Life Story of the Sheik," part 4, *Liberty*, October 12, 1929, p. 70.

346 *"I know their relations . . .";* *"Valentino is a . . .":* Valeria Belletti to Irma, September 12, 1925, AMPAS.

346 *"I told him he was born to . . .":* Dareos, quoted in *Los Angeles Times*, November 14, 1925, p. 2.

347 *arrested for speeding:* August 22, 1925. Reported in *Los Angeles Times*, September 1, 1925, section 2, p. 5.

347 *appearing in court: Los Angeles Times*, September 12, 1925, section 2, p. 2.

347 *"The horse was simply . . .":* Ibid., September 10, 1925, section 2, p. 20.

347 *"I would like to disappear . . .":* RV, quoted by Beltrán-Masses, Guillot de Saix, "Valentino, son revolver," *Comoedia*, September 25, 1926, pp. 1–2.

347 *wrote a new will:* Last Will and Testament of Rudolph Guglielmi, signed September 1, 1925, filed November 10, 1926, Superior Court of Los Angeles.

347 *additional instructions:* Unsourced Valentino clip, November 7, 1930, Core Collection, AMPAS.

347 *"I found him . . .":* Beltrán-Masses to Guillot de Saix, "Valentino, son revolver," *Comoedia*, September 25, 1926, pp. 1–2.

347 *"Materialists see love . . .":* RV, "Confidences et souvenirs," *Ciné-Miroir*, February 3, 1928, p. 83.

348 *"pale, upset . . .": Los Angeles Times*, October 28, 1925, p. 13.

348 *"that is a question . . .":* Ibid., November 11, 1925, p. 1.

348 *"You were my first . . .":* NR, letter to RV, [October?] 1925, item 442, "Catalogue, Lady in Black Collection," Odyssey Auctions, Corona, California, 1993.

18: TANGO NOTTURNO

349 *"a decision, but no knock-out": Motion Picture Classic*, June 1926, p. 17.

349 *"Rudy is doing considerable . . .": Variety*, November 11, 1925, p. 38.

349 *fan letters:* John K. Winkler, "I'm Tired of Being a Sheik," *Collier's*, January 16, 1926, p. 28.

349 *"the first film in which . . ."*: RV, quoted in *Picturegoer*, January 1926, p. 62.

349 *"to study the audience . . ."*: RV, quoted in *Moving Picture World*, November 14, 1925, p. 136.

350 *"that in view of the relations . . ."*: Goldwyn, quoted by Valeria Belletti in letter to Irma, November 2, 1925, Special Collections, AMPAS.

350 *stage show*: *Moving Picture World*, November 21, 1925, p. 275.

350 *"It was impossible . . ."*: Beulah Livingstone, *Remember Valentino: Reminiscences of the World's Greatest Lover*, pamphlet, 1938, p. 71.

350 *"A powerful . . ."*: Trailer, *When Loves Grows Cold* (1926), Motion Picture Division, L of C.

350 *"Natacha Rambova belongs definitely . . ."*: J. J. Schnitzer, FBO (Film Booking Office) vice president, in *Moving Picture World*, December 26, 1925, p. 796.

351 *"If he wants to see me . . ."*: NR, quoted in *Los Angeles Times*, November 11, 1925, p. 1.

351 *"they were both too proud . . ."*: Mrs. Winifred Hudnut, in NR, *Rudolph Valentino (Recollections) Intimate and Interesting of the Life of the Late World-Famous Star* (New York: Jacobsen-Hodgkinson, 1927), p. 122.

351 *"As I understand it . . ."*: RV, quoted in *Los Angeles Times*, November 14, 1925, p. 2.

351 *"A married actor . . ."*: Ibid., November 22, 1925, p. 13.

351–52 *he applied for citizenship*: *The New York Times*, November 22, 1925, p. 16.

352 *calling him a traitor*: *San Francisco Chronicle*, July 16, 1926, n.p.

352 *A boycott*: *The New York Times*, January 9, 1926, p. 14.

352 *"If there were a war . . ."*: Quoted by Jeanne de Recqueville, *Rudolph Valentino* (Paris: France-Empire, 1978), p. 113.

352 *letter to Mussolini*: *The New Republic*, October 13, 1926, p. 218.

352–53 *posing . . . with the Italian ambassador*: L of C photo.

353 *Mussolini responded*: *Los Angeles Times*, December 7, 1925, p. 5.

353 *"Up to the hour . . ."*: RV, *Los Angeles Times*, November 22, 1925, p. 13.

353 *"The boy is mad . . ."*: Manuel Reachi, quoted in Herbert Howe, "The Last Days of Valentino," unsourced article, Wisconsin.

353 *Lady Curzon*: S. George Ullman, *Valentino as I Knew Him* (New York: Macy-Masius, 1926), p. 157.

354 *"My heart is too full . . ."*: RV, quoted by Mrs. Hudnut in NR, *Rudolph Valentino*, p. 122.

354 *breakfast . . . at Mitchell's*: *Variety*, January 6, 1926, p. 10.

354 *"the best-dressed . . ."*: *Los Angeles Times*, November 29, 1925, p. 10.

354 *"Just a sister . . ."*: Mae Murray, quoted in *Photoplay*, March 1926, p. 104.

354 *Mae tried to arrange*: Jane Ardmore, *The Self-Enchanted: Mae Murray, Image of an Era* (New York: McGraw-Hill, 1959), p. 164.

354 *Dolly Sisters; Egyptian prince*: Ullman, *Valentino*, p. 158.

355 *"He goes on an endless round . . ."*: Reachi, in Howe, "Last Days of Valentino."

355 *he spent money*: Livingstone, *Remember Valentino*, pp. 72–73.

355 "A fur-lined bathrobe . . .": Photoplay, March 1926, p. 113.

355 Baron Imre Lukatz: A. Scott Berg, Goldwyn: A Biography (New York: Knopf, 1989), p. 150; Photoplay, March 1926, p. 108.

356 "the male element predominated": The New York Times, December 22, 1925, p. 9.

356 visit . . . Murnau: Kenneth Anger, "Valentino Remembered," in There Is a New Star in Heaven: Valentino, ed. Eva Orbanz (Berlin: Verlag Volker Spiess, 1979), p. 20; photo of RV, Reachi, and Murnau at UFA studio, unsourced Valentino clip, Wisconsin.

356 he was denied permission: Howe, "Last Days of Valentino."

356 New Year's Eve: Los Angeles Times, December 29, 1925, p. 16.

356 backing his pledge: Norman A. Mackenzie, The Magic of Rudolph Valentino (London: Research Publishing, 1974), p. 119.

356 "the same sweet . . .": Mrs. Hudnut in NR, Rudolph Valentino, p. 122.

357 "I cross the ocean . . .": RV, quoted in unsourced clip, AMPAS.

357 "That closes a chapter . . .": RV, quoted in Los Angeles Times, January 20, 1926, p. 1.

357 "In the courts she . . .": RV, in Adela Rogers St. John, Love, Laughter, and Tears: My Hollywood Story (Garden City, N.Y.: Doubleday, 1978), p. 178.

358 "Three or four years ago": RV, in Walter Ramsey, "The Undiscovered Rudolph Valentino," Modern Screen, April 1927, p. 29.

358 bedroom: Los Angeles Times Home Magazine, April 26, 1953, p. 41.

358 "Do you think you can . . .": RV to Lou Mahoney, quoted by Jack Scagnetti, The Intimate Life of Rudolph Valentino (Middle Village, N.Y.: Jonathan David, 1975), p. 74.

358 an ominous rapping: Ibid., p. 73.

358 "Probably it won't be long . . .": RV, in Ramsey, "The Undiscovered Rudolph Valentino," p. 74.

358 "a worm worshipping . . .": RV, letter to Negri, in Livingstone, Remember Valentino, p. 69.

358 he and Negri were introduced: Raoul Walsh, Each Man in His Time: The Life Story of a Director (New York: Farrar, Straus & Giroux, 1974), p. 173.

359 "It was the way . . .": Pola Negri, Memoirs of a Star (Garden City, N.Y.: Doubleday, 1970), p. 260.

359 The unhappiness in him: Ibid., p. 264.

359 to Paul Ivano: Paul Ivano, interview by Anthony Slide, May 12, 1976.

359 negligées: Michael Morris, Madam Valentino: The Many Lives of Natacha Rambova (New York: Abbeville, 1991), p. 187.

360 "a Goya woman . . .": Photoplay, November 1922, pp. 61, 92.

360 love of luxury: Norman Zierold, Sex Goddesses of the Silent Screen (Chicago: Regnery, 1973), p. 98; Jeanine Basinger, Silent Stars (New York: Knopf, 1999), p. 243.

360 black onyx: Negri, Memoirs, p. 272.

361 Chaplin was half crazy: Ibid., pp. 205ff.

361 "carefree schoolboy . . .": Ibid., p. 279.

361 *"a lie"*: Alfred Allen Lewis, personal communication, June 15, 2001; George Schönbrunn, personal communication, September 7, 1999.

361 *"man so locked . . ."*: Negri, *Memoirs*, p. 264.

361 *doubts about his manhood:* Ibid., p. 269.

361 *"morbidly frightened . . ."*: Ibid., p. 267.

362 *"He was crazy about Natacha"*: Agnes Ayres, quoted in *Boston Post*, July 10, 1938, n.p.

362 *"I'm engaged to no one . . ."*: RV, in Bernice Scharlach, "The City's First Night Club," *California Living, San Francisco Examiner*, September 22, 1974, p. 43.

362 *"In the home, I love quiet"*: RV, in St. John, *Love, Laughter*, p. 176.

362 *"To my imperative . . ."*: Inscribed RV photo in Negri, *Memoirs*, facing p. 192.

362 *Other male lovers:* Robert Florey, *Pola Negri* (Paris: Publications Jean-Pascal, 1926), p. 53.

363 *his own little horse:* JV, interview by Kevin Brownlow, June 3, 1977.

363 *home movies:* Jack Grant, "Long Missing Valentino Film Found," *Movie Classic*, undated Valentino clip, Wisconsin.

363 *"When they took the floor . . ."*: *Photoplay*, May 1926, p. 88.

363 *Murray-Mdivani marriage:* New York *Daily News*, June 28, 1926, n.p.

363–64 *"From day to day"; "When they are on-again . . ."*: *Photoplay*, July 1926, pp. 78, 139.

364 *"Darling, you must learn . . ."*: Norma Talmadge, in Negri, *Memoirs*, p. 273.

364 *Lake Arrowhead: Variety*, May 8, 1926, p. 17.

364 *"The only dirt . . ."*: Valeria Belletti, letter to Irma, February 2, 1926, Special Collections, AMPAS.

364 *the Tiffin Room:* Scharlach, "The City's First Night Club," p. 43.

364 *he crashed: Variety*, March 3, 1926, p. 26.

364 *"His dangerous career . . ."*: *Los Angeles Examiner*, March 19, 1926, n.p., Valentino clip, AMPAS.

365 *A poll of fans: Los Angeles Times*, December 22, 1925, section 2, p. 9.

365 *"Heaven knows I'm no . . ."*: RV, in John K. Winkler, "I'm Tired of Being a Sheik," *Collier's*, January 16, 1926, p. 28.

365 *in the future:* Ullman, *Valentino*, p. 170.

365 *"The feminine portion . . ."*: RV, quoted in *Motion Picture Magazine* interview, undated clip, Valentino scrapbook, NYPL.

365 *"one appears to be . . ."*: RV, "Confidences et Souvenirs," *Ciné-Miroir*, February 24, 1928, p. 131.

365 *he would retire:* RV, quoted in *Motion Picture Magazine*, October 1925, p. 34.

366 *"He made no complaint . . ."*: Frances Marion, *Off with Their Heads: A Serio-Comic Tale of Hollywood* (New York: Macmillan, 1972), p. 141.

366 *second attempt:* Cari Beauchamp, *Without Lying Down: Frances Marion and the Powerful Women of Early Hollywood* (New York: Scribner, 1997), p. 191.

366 *careful preparatory work:* Richard Koszarski, *Hollywood Directors, 1914–1940* (New York: Oxford University Press, 1976), p. 33.

366 *When he lifted her:* Irving Sindler, taped recollections, courtesy Sylvia Valentino Huber.

366 *"He loved character work . . .":* George Fitzmaurice, quoted in *Los Angeles Times*, August 24, 1926, p. 3.

367 *"I didn't enjoy . . .":* RV, "Confidences et Souvenirs."

367 *"I don't want to be . . .":* RV, in Norma Talmadge, "Rudy as I Knew Him," New York *Daily News*, August 26, 1926, p. 2.

367 *"I am grabbed . . .":* Banky, quoted in *New York Journal*, June 30, 1926, n.p.

368 *"WE WILL GIVE YOU . . .":* RV, telegram to W. K. Kellogg, in Mary Jane Parkinson, *The Kellogg Arabian Ranch: The First Fifty Years* (Arabian Horse Association of Southern California, 1977), p. 67.

369 *Kellogg's son suspected:* Ibid., p. 88.

369 *Jadaan's film career:* Ibid., p. 113.

369 *"I guess that's art":* RV, quoted by Irving Sindler, taped recollections.

369 *"physically worn out . . .":* Frances Marion, *Off with Their Heads*, p. 142.

369 *for his next projected picture:* New York *Telegraph*, May 15, 1926, n.p.

370 *new contract: Variety*, August 25, 1926, p. 1.

370 *he would coproduce:* AV, quoted in *Motion Picture Magazine*, September 1924, p. 82.

370 *weekly returns: Variety*, July 21, 1926, p. 6.

370 *"Then he staggered . . .":* *Photoplay*, October 1926, p. 104.

370 *to the Cocoanut Grove:* Ardmore, *The Self-Enchanted*, p. 185.

19: DEATH OF A GOD

371 *"[Valentino] wore a silver ring . . .":* San Francisco *Chronicle*, July 16, 1926, n.p.

371 *"Rudy donned a Chinese . . .":* S. George Ullman, *Valentino as I Knew Him* (New York: Macy-Masius, 1926), p. 181.

371 *"Pink Powder Puffs":* Chicago *Tribune*, editorial, July 18, 1926, n.p.

372 *"Rudy repeated the words":* Ibid., pp. 189–90.

373 *"It is a printed utterance":* RV, quoted in *Theatre*, October 1926, p. 68.

373 *The Italian code of chivalry:* Luigi Barzini, *The Italians* (New York: Atheneum, 1986), p. 183.

373 *letter . . . in the Chicago* Herald Examiner: Ullman, *Valentino*, pp. 187–90.

374 *later identified as:* Gene Siskel, *Chicago Tribune*, June 28, 1977, p. 15.

374 *they eventually heard that he was suffering:* AV, interview by Kevin Brownlow, June 3, 1977.

375 *"tacit retraction":* Ullman, *Valentino*, p. 201.

375 *"He was jaunty, friendly . . .":* John Chapman, New York *Daily News*, August 26, 1956, n.p.

375 *"Valentino felt that . . .":* Jack Dempsey, with Barbara P. Dempsey, *Dempsey* (New York: Harper & Row, 1977), pp. 196–97.

375 *"That boy has a punch . . .":* Ullman, *Valentino*, p. 193.

375 *"POWDER PUFF? WHAM!":* Unsourced clip, n.p., Valentino scrapbook, NYPL.

375 *he repeated his offer: Chicago Post*, July 29, 1926.

375 *"READY FOR ALL COMERS! . . .":* Unsourced clip, NYPL.

375 *Atlantic City:* Ullman, *Valentino*, pp. 207–8.

376 *Lorenzo Tucker:* Richard Grupenhoff, *The Black Valentino: The Stage and Screen Career of Lorenzo Tucker* (Metuchen, N.J.: Scarecrow Press, 1988), p. 27.

376 *Chicago, New York returns: Variety*, August 4, 1926, p. 7; August 11, 1926, p. 5.

376 *Fans tore off:* Ullman, *Valentino*, p. 196.

376 *"the beginning of a new era . . .":* Will Hays, in David A. Cook, *A History of Narrative Film* (New York: Norton, 1990), p. 258.

376 *At the Colony:* Adolph Zukor with Dale Kramer, *The Public Is Never Wrong* (New York: Putnam's, 1953), p. 218.

377 *"in the blaze of midday . . .": Theatre*, October 1926, p. 39.

377 *photographed there with his arm around:* Schuyler Livingston Parsons, *Untold Friendships* (Boston: Houghton Mifflin, 1955), photo facing p. 132. I owe this reference to David Stenn.

377 *Rahman Bey: Variety*, July 28, 1926, p. 4; Ullman, *Valentino*, pp. 198–99.

378 *"a sequence of artistic achievements":* RV, quoted in *Theatre*, October 1926, p. 39.

378 *"I have never had . . .":* RV, in Helen Louise Walker, "Last Interview," *Motion Picture Magazine*, September 1933, pp. 30, 73.

378 *"I have everything . . .":* RV, in Adela Rogers St. John, "Valentino: The Life Story of the Sheik," part 4, *Liberty*, October 12, 1929, pp. 73–74.

378 *"curiously naive and boyish . . .":* H. L. Mencken, *Baltimore Sun*, August 30, 1926, n.p.

379 *"nervous indigestion":* Adela Rogers St. Johns, *The Honeycomb* (Garden City, N.Y.: Doubleday, 1969), p. 170.

379 *"Yes, from forty to fifty . . .":* Harry T. Brundidge, *Twinkle, Twinkle, Movie Star* (New York: Garland, 1977), p. 77.

379 *"seized with terrible pains":* Parsons, *Untold Friendships*, p. 125.

379 *a living-room conversation:* Dorothy Wigman Raphaelson, personal communication, December 13, 1999.

379 *"I have never been treated . . .":* Marion Benda, quoted in New York *Graphic*, August 18, 1926, n.p.

379 *Barclay Warburton, Jr.:* Various clippings, private collection.

380 *"full of soft lights . . .":* New York *Daily News*, August 17, 1926, n.p.

380 *noisy gatherings: The New York Times*, November 15, 1927, p. 16.

380 *George White's* Scandals: Gerald Bordman, *American Musical Theatre* (New York: Oxford University Press, 1986), p. 413.

380 *"We had some drinks . . .":* Harry Richman, quoted in *Los Angeles Times*, August 28, 1926, n.p.

380 *Ullman's secretary:* Grace Case, personal communication, May 12, 1999.

380 *"profound shock . . .":* Dr. Harold Meeker, quoted in *The New York Times*, September 4, 1926, p. 3.

381 *it took several hours:* AV, interview by Kevin Brownlow, June 3, 1977.

381 *"The doctor told me . . .":* Dr. Arthur S. Bogart, personal communication, June 30, 1999. I owe this contact to Stuart Oderman.

381 *Neapolitan curse:* Phyllis H. Williams, *Southern Italian Folkways in Europe and America* (New Haven: Yale University Press, 1998), pp. 171–72.

381 *"Did I behave like . . .":* RV, in Ullman, *Valentino,* p. 210.

381 *"HAVE JUST HEARD . . .":* NR, cablegram, in New York *Graphic,* August 18, 1926, n.p.

381 *that their past differences:* NR, *Rudolph Valentino (Recollections) Intimate and Interesting Reminiscences of the Life of the Late World-Famous Star* (New York: Jacobsen-Hodgkinson, 1927), p. 123.

381 *A special room:* Michael Morris, *Madam Valentino: The Many Lives of Natacha Rambova* (New York: Abbeville, 1991), p. 183.

381 *He asked Ullman:* Ullman, *Valentino,* p. 82.

382 *"I am stunned . . .":* Pola Negri, quoted in *Cincinnati Commercial Tribune,* August 16, 1926, n.p.

382 *Stiller:* Pola Negri, *Memoirs of a Star* (Garden City, N.Y.: Doubleday, 1970), p. 292.

382 *medical bulletins: The New York Times,* August 17, 1926, p. 1; ibid., August 21, 1926, p. 3.

382 *"By no means . . .":* RV, in Ullman, *Valentino,* p. 212.

383 *"I just want to see . . .":* Ibid., p. 213.

383 *phone messages:* Unsourced clip, August 18, 1926, NYPL.

383 *"How much longer . . .":* RV, quoted in *The New York Times,* August 19, 1926, p. 1.

383 *"RUDY BRAVE . . .":* New York *Graphic,* August 17, 1926.

384 *had passed the crisis point: The New York Times,* August 20, 1926, p. 1.

384 *Jean Acker arrived: Los Angeles Times,* August 22, 1926, p. 1.

385 *"Why should I go . . .":* RV, quoted in unsourced Valentino clip, Wisconsin.

385 *Last Rites: Moving Picture World,* September 4, 1926, p. 2.

385 *"Hello, Chief":* RV, quoted in *The New York Times,* August 23, 1926, p. 1.

385 *"Thank you, Frank . . .";* *"Wasn't it an awful . . .":* RV, in Ullman, *Valentino,* p. 217.

385 *"Don't pull down . . .":* Ibid., p. 218.

385 *"Doctor, do you know . . .":* RV, quoted in *The New York Times,* August 24, 1926, p. 1.

385 *"California was his kingdom . . .": Moving Picture World,* September 4, 1926, p. 17.

386 *"His breathing was . . .":* New York *Daily News,* August 25, 1926, p. 4.

386 *"VALENTINO PASSES . . .": The New York Times,* August 24, 1926, p. 1.

386 *"I am unable to state . . .":* Death certificate 22164, New York City Department of Health, August 23, 1926.

386 *"there was a hole . . .":* Dr. Harold Meeker, quoted in New York *Daily News,* September 4, 1926, p. 3.

387 *"and that is something . . .":* Quoted in *Variety,* August 25, 1926, p. 5.

387 *Agatha Hearn:* M. M. Marberry, "The Overloved One," *American Heritage*, August 1965, p. 85.

387 *Peggy Scott:* Noel Botham and Peter Donnelly, *Valentino: The Love God* (London: Everest Books, 1976), p. 216.

388 *"one of the finest . . .":* George Fitzmaurice, quoted in *Los Angeles Times*, August 24, 1926, p. 3.

388 *"We are grieved . . .":* Joseph Schenck, quoted in *The New York Times*, August 24, 1926, p. 3.

388 *grosses of $1 million:* Tino Balio, *United Artists: The Company Built by the Stars* (Madison: University of Wisconsin Press, 1976), p. 56.

388 *life insurance:* Unsourced Valentino clip, September 8, 1926, AMPAS.

388 *"one of the greatest . . .":* Charles Chaplin, quoted in *Los Angeles Times*, August 24, 1926, p. 3.

388 *"May the thoughts . . .":* Gloria Swanson, quoted in *The New York Times*, August 24, 1926, p. 3.

389 *"My heart is too full . . .":* June Mathis, quoted in *Los Angeles Times*, August 24, 1926, p. 3.

389 *"the type-man . . .":* New York *Daily News*, August 24, 1926, p. 17.

389 *"He passed through the depths . . .";* *"When I was . . .":* Los Angeles *Times*, August 24, 1926, pp. 1, 3.

389 *"placing itself prone . . .":* *Variety*, August 25, 1926, p. 44.

389–90 *"What a power . . .":* *Moving Picture World*, September 4, 1926, p. 17.

390 *"The sidewalk was strewn . . .":* Eddie Doherty, quoted in *New York Mirror*, in Frank Mallen, *Sauce for the Gander* (White Plains, N.Y.: Baldwin Books, 1954), p. 79.

390 *"One person a second . . .":* New York *Daily News*, August 25, 1926, n.p.

391 *A police captain said:* *The New York Times*, August 25, 1926, n.p.

391 *wax effigy:* Lawrence T. Quirk, *Quirk's Reviews*, August 1978, n.p.

391 *"It was not so much . . .":* Heywood Broun, quoted in *Literary Digest*, September 11, 1926, n.p.

391 *George Ullman would testify:* New York *Daily News*, August 26, 1956, n.p.

392 *Black Shirts:* *The New York Times*, August 26, 1926, n.p.; Mallen, *Sauce for Gander*, pp. 3, 84.

392 *"This has gone far enough":* Ullman, quoted in *The New York Times*, August 26, 1926, p. 5.

393 *"I have lost . . .":* Pola Negri, quoted in *Los Angeles Times*, August 24, 1926, p. 3.

393 *"She is on the verge . . .":* Ullman, quoted in New York *Daily News*, August 30, 1926, p. 2.

393 *a note from Dr. Meeker:* Ibid., August 31, 1926, p. 3.

393 *"a premiere for Pola Negri":* Ben Lyon, "Swanson and Valentino," an episode in the series *Hollywood: The Pioneers*, written, produced, and directed by Kevin Brownlow and David Gill, Thames Television, 1980.

393–94 *"I cannot help that I have not . . .":* Negri, in C. Wyche Beinhorn, "Pola Negri: Temptestuous Temptress," *Take One,* September 1978, p. 38.

394 *a doctor who:* New York *Daily News,* September 6, 1926, p. 3.

394 *Honorary pallbearers; twelve-car cortege:* Ibid., August 31, 1926, p. 3; *The New York Times,* August 31, 1926, p. 1.

394 *High Requiem Mass:* The New York Times, August 31, 1926, p. 5.

395 *Louise Brooks "cried unashamed":* New York *Morning Telegraph,* August 31, 1926, n.p. Thanks to Thomas Gladysz for providing this clipping.

395 *telegram to Alberto:* Unsourced Valentino clip, August [25?], 1926, AMPAS.

396 *Natacha's plea:* New York Telegraph, August 27, 1926, n.p.

396 *"Mio fratello . . .":* New York *Daily News,* September 2, 1926, p. 2.

20: AFTERMATH

397 *came with guitars:* AV, in Kevin Brownlow, *Hollywood: The Pioneers* (New York: Knopf, 1979), p. 185.

397–98 *"We were all one . . ."; "Rudy never . . ."; "He never . . .":* New York *Daily News,* September 3, 1926, p. 3; ibid., September 4, 1926, p. 4; ibid., September 6, 1926, p. 2.

398 *At Chicago's La Salle:* Ibid., September 4, 1926, p. 4.

398 *a six-foot-high floral:* Los Angeles Times, September 4, 1926, p. 3.

398–99 *In Yuma; "Miss Negri sobbed . . .":* Ibid., September 7, 1926, p. 2.

399 *"They didn't even buy him a grave":* Paul Ivano, in "Swanson and Valentino," episode in *Hollywood: The Pioneers,* written, produced, and directed by Kevin Brownlow and David Gill, Thames Video, 1980.

399 *"beloved June":* RV to Adela Rogers St. John, *Los Angeles Examiner,* November 11, 1950, n.p.

399–400 *Los Angeles Breakfast Club:* Los Angeles Times, August 28, 1926, n.p.

400 *"The ceremony moved . . .":* Ibid., September 8, 1926, p. 9.

400 *pallbearers; mourners:* Los Angeles Times, September 8, 1926, p. 1; unsourced clip, MoMA.

400 *Goldwyn had been summoned:* Unsourced Valentino clip, September 7, 1926, AMPAS.

400 *Rex Ingram turned down:* Alice Terry, interview by Anthony Slide, May 10, 1978.

401 *"stretched their fingers . . .":* Lisa Mitchell, "A 50-Year Swoon Song for Rudolph Valentino," *Los Angeles Times Calendar,* August 22, 1976, p. 1.

401 *"He leaned toward":* Los Angeles Times, September 8, 1926, section 2, p. 1.

402 *cash advances:* Unsourced Valentino clip, November 7, 1930, AMPAS.

402 *"grief stricken":* Ibid., September 6, 1926.

402 *might try to contest; coexecutor:* Ibid., October 6, 11, 1926.

403 *"Everybody talks about . . .":* Ullman, quoted by William Self, personal communication, December 5, 2000.

403 *debts:* Unsourced Valentino clip, May 20, 1930, AMPAS; unsourced clip, MoMA.

403 *"I resorted to some tricks"*: Ullman, quoted in unsourced Valentino clip, May 20, 1930, AMPAS.

404 *"Although I dislike . . ."*: Ullman, foreword, *Catalogue, Estate of Rudolph Valentino*, (Los Angeles: Eureka Press, 1926), p. 4.

406–7 *"Women stood . . ."; Carrara marble sculpture:* A. L. Woodbridge, "When Rudy's Belongings Were Sold," *Picture Play,* April 1927, p. 16; Robert Florey, *La lanterne magique* (Lausanne: La Cinémathèque Suisse, 1966),p. 159.

407 *netted a disappointing: The New York Times,* May 4, 1927, p. 28.

408 *"I try to get the Grecian . . ."*: AV, quoted in "The Tragedy of Valentino's Brother's Nose," *Literary Digest,* September 21, 1929, n.p.

408 *Jean died: Los Angeles Times,* September 26, 1996, n.p.

408 *forced to resign:* Unsourced Valentino clip, August 18, 1932, AMPAS.

408 *final settlement:* Unsourced Valentino clip, April 11, 1934, and December 11, 1934, AMPAS.

408 *Romero moved in: Los Angeles Times,* February 6, 1935.

408 *Doris Duke:* Ibid., April 10, 1995, A, p. 1.

408 *Falcon Lair for sale: Hollywood Reporter,* November 1, 1998, n.p.

409 *a fatal heart attack:* Unsourced clip, Locke Collection, NYPL.

409 *"a torch lighting . . ."*: Burnham, quoted in unsourced Valentino clip, Wisconsin.

410 *"He seemed more reconciled . . ."*: NR, *Rudy: An Intimate Portrait of Rudolph Valentino, by His Wife* (London: Hutchinson, 1926), p. 145.

410 *"being suffocated . . ."*: Ibid., p. 193.

410 *"He spoke only of . . ."*: NR, quoted in unsourced Valentino clip, November 25, 1926, AMPAS.

410 *reference to Pola:* NR, *Rudy,* p. 207.

410 *All That Glitters:* Michael Morris, *Madam Valentino: The Many Lives of Natacha Rambova* (New York: Abbeville, 1991), p. 192.

410 *"I'm in business . . ."*: NR, quoted in unsourced Valentino clip, March 29, 1928, AMPAS.

411 *Mallorca: Los Angeles Examiner,* August 16, 1934, n.p.

411 *She fled:* Morris, *Madam Valentino,* p. 220.

411 *heart attack:* Ibid., p. 223.

411 *haircut; Gurdjieff:* Ibid., p. 224.

411 *Natacha published:* Ibid., pp. 228ff.

412 *Natacha's death:* Ibid. p. 258.

412 *willed:* Last Will and Testament of Natacha Rambova, Surrogate's Court of New York, March 13, 1967.

412 *Pola Negri claims:* Pola Negri, *Memoirs of a Star* (Garden City, N.Y.: Doubleday, 1970), p. 195.

412 *double portrait:* Unsourced Valentino clip, 1930, MoMA.

412 *Negri's later career:* Eve Golden, *Golden Images* (Jefferson, N.C.: McFarland, 2001), pp. 121–22.

413 *"He was the only man . . ."*: Pola Negri, in A. J. Liebling, "Paysage de Crépuscule," *The New Yorker*, January 11, 1964, n.p.

413 *she choked up:* Alfred Allen Lewis, personal communication, June 15, 2001.

413 *"We Will Meet . . ."*: Published by Shapiro and Bernstein, 1926.

413 *"There's a New Star . . ."*: Written by J. Keirn Brennan, Irving Mills, and Jimmy McHugh, Jack Mills, Inc., 1926.

413 *she sued William Delehanty:* Unsourced Jean Acker clip, July 14, 1930, AMPAS.

413 *Holy Cross Cemetery:* I owe this information to Allan Ellenberger of the Valentino e-group.

414 *"Lady in Black":* San Francisco Chronicle, August 24, 1977, n.p.; Al Ridenour, "The Grave of the Unknown Mourner," *Los Angeles New Times,* September 7, 2000, n.p.

414 *Wilson insisted:* Irving Shulman, *Valentino* (New York: Simon & Schuster, 1967), p. 478.

414 *Russell Birdwell: New York Sun,* August 24, 1938, n.p.

414 *"For this stunt . . ."*: Paramount Press Book for *The Sheik,* 1938, Paramount Collection, AMPAS.

415 *"she had seen Rudy 432 times . . ."*: Memo to Mr. Quirk from H. Kennedy, September 15, 1930, Photoplay Collection, MoMA.

415 *"part Day of the Locust . . ."*: Mitchell, "A 50-Year," p. 1.

416 *Leslie Flint: Psychic News,* May 12, 1973, n.p.; Alexander Walker, "Leslie Flint," *London Independent*, May 10, 1994, n.p.

416 *"Now that Valentino is dead . . ."*: Stark Young, *New Republic*, October 13, 1926, p. 217.

417 *"because of popular demand":* James Hay, *Popular Film Culture in Fascist Italy* (Bloomington: Indiana University Press, 1987), p. 86.

417 *"a little impotent":* Mastroianni, in Israel Shenker, "The Man Who Made Apathy Irresistible," *The New York Times Magazine*, December 12, 1965, p. 58.

418 *a distant cousin:* Sylvia Valentino Huber, personal communication.

418 *"I'm not imitating him . . ."*: Moreno, quoted in *The People*, January 23, 1927. I owe this reference to Kevin Brownlow.

418 *"had left vacant . . . The war brought into being . . ."*: Moving Picture World, September 11, 1926, p. 93.

418 *1930s successors:* Boris Nicholai, "Would Valentino Be a Star Today?," *Motion Picture Magazine*, September 1934, pp. 40, 82.

419 *Anthony Dexter:* Dexter's original name was Walter Reinhold Alfred Fleischmann. He later took the name Walter Craig.

419 *Alice Terry ended up suing:* Kalton C. Lahue, *Ladies in Distress* (South Brunswick, N.J., and New York: A. S. Barnes, 1971), p. 298.

419 *Jean Valentino sued: Variety,* December 12, 1979, n.p.

419 The Legend of Valentino: Directed by Graeme Ferguson, first shown in New York on KPIX-TV, May 24, 1961. Thanks to Ned Comstock for providing this information.

420 *off-camera comments:* Alexander Bland, *The Nureyev Valentino, Portrait of a Film* (New York: Dell, 1977), p. 27; Diane Solway, *Nureyev: His Life* (New York: Morrow, 1988), p. 410; *France-Soir*, September 15, 1977, n.p.

421 *"to make good in he-man . . .":* John Dos Passos, "Adagio Dancer," in *The Big Money* (New York: New American Library, 1969), p. 207.

423 *"One night she pretended . . .":* "The Holy Door," *Stories of Frank O'Connor* (New York: Knopf, 1952), p. 326.

SOURCES

AUTHOR INTERVIEWS

Michael and Virginia Beck, Kevin Brownlow, Dana Serra Cary (Baby Peggy Montgomery), Claudia Balboni Chiurazzi, Nan Hudnut Clarkson, Agostino De Bellis, Louise Di Modica, Allan Ellenberger, Leatrice Gilbert Fountain, Howard Gutner, Charles Higham, Sylvia Valentino Huber, Gavin Lambert, Richard Lamparski, Betty Lasky, Alfred Allan Lewis, Diane Mathis Madsen, Michael Morris, Patricia Neal, Stuart Oderman, Dominico Orlando, Barry Paris, Dorothy Raphaelson, George Schönbrunn, William Self, Anthony Slide, André Soares, David Stenn, Tracy Terhune, Amanda Vaill, Connie Van Wyck, Alexander Walker, Marc Wanamaker

UNPUBLISHED INTERVIEWS CONDUCTED BY OTHERS

Anthony Slide for Astoria Oral History, American Museum of the Moving Image: Jetta Goudal, Lois Wilson

Kevin Brownlow: Alberto Valentino, Jean Valentino

Columbia University Oral History Research Office Collection: Mae Murray, Nita Naldi

Agostino De Bellis: Nicola Napoletane, private communication

Anthony Slide: Virginia Brown Faire, Robert Florey (written answers to written questions), DeWitt Bodeen (letter), Paul Ivano, Doris Kenyon, Ivy Crane Wilson, Lois Wilson

Jean Valentino: Alberto Valentino (tape provided by Sylvia Valentino Huber)

BOOKS

This list is limited to books not cited in the notes.

Ben-Allah (Newman). *Rudolph Valentino: His Romantic Life and Death*. Hollywood: Ben-Allah Co., 1926.

Blum, Daniel. *A Pictorial History of the Silent Screen*. New York: Grosset & Dunlap, 1953.

Bodeen, DeWitt. *From Hollywood: The Careers of Fifteen Great American Stars*. South Brunswick, N.J.: A. S. Barnes, 1976.

——. *More from Hollywood*. South Brunswick, N.J.: A. S. Barnes, 1977.

Caffin, Caroline and Charles, *Dancing and Dances of Today*. New York: Dodd, Mead, 1912. Reprint Da Capo, 1978.

Castro, Donald S. *The Argentine Tango as Social History, 1880–1955: The Soul of the People*. Lewiston, N.Y.: Edwin Mellen Press, 1991.

Chierchetti, David. *Hollywood Costume Design*. New York: Harmony Books, 1976.

d'Amico, Silvio, ed. *Enciclopedia dello Spettacolo*, vol. 9. Rome: Casa Editrice Le Maschere, 1962.

Everson, William K. *American Silent Film*. New York: Oxford University Press, 1978.

Gifford, Edward S., Jr. *The Evil Eye: Studies in the Folklore of Vision*. New York: Macmillan, 1958.

Gissing, George. *By the Ionian Sea*. London: Chapman & Hill, 1921.

Hanson, Patricia, and Alan Gevinson, eds. *The American Film Institute Catalog of Motion Pictures Produced in the United States: Feature Films, 1911–1926*. Berkeley and Los Angeles: University of California Press, 1988.

Hollander, Anne. *Sex and Suits*. New York and Tokyo: Kodansha, 1995.

Katz, Ephraim. *The Film Encyclopedia*. 3rd ed. New York: HarperCollins, 1998.

Kimmel, Michael. *Manhood in America: A Cultural History*. New York: Free Press, 1996.

Klepper, Robert K. *Silent Films, 1877–1996: A Critical Guide to 646 Movies*. Jefferson, N.C.: McFarland, 1999.

Lockwood, Charles. *Dream Palaces: Hollywood at Home*. New York: Viking Press, 1981.

Lyttelton, Adrian. "Politics and Society, 1870–1915," in *The Oxford History of Italy*, ed. George Holmes. New York: Oxford University Press, 1997.

Magill, Frank. *Magill's Survey of Cinema: Silent Film*. 3 vols. Englewood Cliffs, N.J.: Salem Press, 1982.

Maltby, Richard, and Ian Craven. *Hollywood Cinema: An Introduction*. Oxford: Blackwell, 1995.

McConathy, Dale, with Diana Vreeland. *Hollywood Costume*. New York: Abrams: 1976.

Morton, H. V. *A Traveller in Southern Italy*. New York: Dodd, Mead, 1969.

Munden, Kenneth W., ed. *The American Film Institute Catalog of Motion Pictures Produced in the United States: Feature Films, 1921–1930*. New York: Bowker, 1971.

Nochlin, Linda. "The Imaginary Orient," in *The Politics of Vision*. New York: Harper & Row, 1989.

Oberfirst, Robert. *Rudolph Valentino: The Man Behind the Myth*. New York: Citadel Press, 1962.

Peiss, Kathy. *Hope in a Jar: The Making of America's Beauty Culture*. New York: Henry Holt, 1998.

Russo, Vito. *The Celluloid Closet: Homosexuality in the Movies*. New York: Harper & Row, 1985.

Schickel, Richard. "Rudolph Valentino," in *The Movie Star,* ed. Elisabeth Weis. New York: Viking, 1981.

Schulberg, Budd. *Moving Pictures.* New York: Stein & Day, 1981.

Shorris, Sylvia, and Marion Abbott Bundy. *Talking Pictures.* New York: New Press, 1994.

Sklar, Robert. *Movie-Made America: A Cultural History of American Movies.* New York: Vintage Books, 1976.

Slide, Anthony. *The Big V: A History of the Vitagraph Company.* Metuchen, N.J.: Scarecrow Press, 1976.

————. *The New Historical Dictionary of the American Film Industry.* Lanham, Md.: Scarecrow Press, 1998.

————. *The Silent Feminists: America's First Women Directors.* Lanham, Md.: Scarecrow Press, 1996.

Spears, Jack. "Nazimova," in *The Civil War on the Screen and Other Essays.* South Brunswick, N.J.: A. S. Barnes, 1977.

Studlar, Gaylyn. *This Mad Masquerade: Stardom and Masculinity in the Jazz Age.* New York: Columbia University Press, 1996.

————. "The Perils of Pleasure? Fan Magazine Discourse as Women's Commodified Culture in the 1920s," in *Silent Films,* ed. Richard Abel. New Brunswick, N.J.: Rutgers University Press, 1996.

ARTICLES IN PERIODICALS

This list is limited to articles not cited in the notes.

Blok, Anton. "Rams and Billy-Goats: A Key to the Mediterranean Honor Code." *Man* 16 (1981): 427–40.

Bodeen, DeWitt. "Rudolph Valentino." *Screen Facts* 3, no. 5 (1968): 1–27.

Douglass, William A. "The South Italian Family: A Critique." *Journal of Family History* 5 (Winter 1980): 338–59.

Ingram, Rex. "How I Discover Them." *Photoplay,* June, 1923, pp. 37, 116–17.

Jennings, Dean. "The Actor Who Wouldn't Stay Dead." *Collier's,* July 2, 1949, pp. 26, 60–62.

Lambert, Gavin. "Fairbanks and Valentino." *Sequence,* no. 8 (Summer, 1949): 77–80.

————. "*The Sheik*'s Leading Man at Falcon Lair." *Architectural Digest,* April 1994, pp. 122ff.

Lampinen, Patricia M., ed. *The Rudolph Valentino Newsletter,* 1995, 1996.

Marmin, Olivier. "Trois Faunes." *Saisons de la danse,* no. 260 (September, 1994): 48–49.

Mathis, June. "Pursuing a Motion Picture Plot." *Photoplay,* October 1917, pp. 24–25.

Prédal, René, with Robert Florey. "Rudolph Valentino." *Anthologie du Cinéma,* no. 45 (Mai 1969): 217–80.

Smith, Frederick James. "The Tragedy of Fame." *Liberty,* October 9, 1926, n.p.

Strother, Celia, ed. *Rudolph Valentino Newsletter,* 2001.

Taves, Brian. "Paul Ivano." *Classic Images*, September 1984, pp. 30–31.

Tully, Jim. "Rudolph Valentino." *Vanity Fair*, October 1926, p. 87.

Valentino, Rudolph. "Is the American Girl Playing a Losing Game?" *Metropolitan*, January 1923, pp. 40–41.

Wanamaker, Marc. "Historic Hollywood Movie Studios." *American Cinematographer*, March–April–May 1976, np.

Wennersten, Robert. "The Second Mrs. Valentino." *Performing Arts*, February, 1978, pp. 16–18, 22, 42.

Williams, Craig A. "Paul Powell: Outspoken Innovator of Silent Film." *Classic Images*, December 1997, pp. 32–C3.

WEB SITES

Rudolph Valentino (maintained by Agostino De Bellis): http://www.deor.com/valentino

Rudolph Valentino (maintained by Donna Hill): www.geocites.com/_rudyfan/rudy.htm

Rudolph Valentino e-group (maintained by Tracy Terhune): groups.com/group/Rudolph_Valentino

The Silents Majority (maintained by Diane MacIntyre and Spike Lewis): www.silentsmajority.com

The Valentino Nook (maintained by Lisette Rice): cyberflapr.tripod.com/vnook.htm

DOCUMENTARIES

The Legend of Rudolph Valentino. Directed for television by Graeme Ferguson. Producers Saul Turell and Paul Killiam, 1961. Wolper-Sterling Productions. DVD, Image Entertainment, 2000.

Rodolfo Valentino: Viaggio nel mito / Voyage through a myth. ASH MultiMedia (Corte del Molini 7, 36100 Vicenza), 1998. Interactive CD.

Rudolph Valentino: The Great Lover. Produced by Greystone Communications, Inc. for A&E Network. Martin Gillam, Producer. VHS, A&E Home Video, 1995.

Swanson and Valentino. Written, produced, and directed by Kevin Brownlow and David Gill as part of the series *Hollywood: The Pioneers*. Thames Video, 1980.

ARCHIVAL MATERIALS

At the Margaret Herrick Library of the Academy of Motion Picture Arts and Sciences (AMPAS), Beverly Hills, California, I relied on the books, periodicals, and Valentino clippings (as well as clippings on individual films and on others who knew or worked with Valentino) in the Core Collection. I also drew from the following in Special Collections: Valeria Belletti letters; Gladys Hall Collection; Joseph and Jeanne Henabery Collection; Robert Z. Leonard Collection Scrapbook; Metro Ledger Book; Paramount Collection (Scripts, Press Books); Adolph Zukor Collection (letters). The Vertical File Collection has a copy of the *Catalogue for the Estate of Rudolph Valentino to Be Sold at Public Auction Commencing December 10, 1926*.

In New York City, at the Billy Rose Theater Collection of the Performing Arts Library, New York Public Library (NYPL), I relied on several Valentino scrapbooks, which are now all transferred to microfilm. When I started my research, some scrapbooks were still in their original form; in some cases, the clippings I found were so fragile that they may not have been microfilmed. The NYPL Theater Collection also has clipping files on other individuals and on specific movie titles. In Special Collections, I used the scrapbooks in the Robinson Locke collection for material on Valentino's pre-Hollywood career as an exhibition dancer with partners Bonnie Glass and Joan Sawyer.

Also in New York City at the Film Study Center of the Museum of Modern Art (MoMA), I consulted letters and other documents in the Photoplay Collection, clippings and documents on Valentino, and files on specific films.

In Austin, Texas, I consulted scrapbooks in the Gloria Swanson Collection at the Harry Ransom Humanities Research Center (HRC).

In Washington, D.C., at the Motion Picture Division of the Library of Congress (L of C), I consulted film-related periodicals.

In Madison, Wisconsin, I drew upon the extensive Valentino clipping file at the Wisconsin Center for Film and Theater Research (Wisconsin).

In London I read one Valentino letter and consulted books, clippings, and periodicals at the British Film Institute (BFI).

In Castellaneta, Italy, I visited the Museo Valentino and several sites connected to Valentino's childhood.

In Paris, France, I read periodicals at the Bibliothèque du Film (BiFi) and scrapbooks at the Biblithèque de l'Arsenal (Arsenal), Département des arts du Spectacle. At the latter I also consulted letters in the Jacques Hébertot Collection.

In San Francisco, California, I consulted clippings from the collections of the California Historical Society and the San Francisco Public Library. I consulted dance-related periodicals and clippings at the San Francisco Performing Arts Library and Museum (SFPALM). I read microfilmed periodicals at the J. Paul Leonard Library, San Francisco State University. I also drew upon books and clippings in my own collection.

VALENTINO FILMS

At the Motion Picture Division of the Library of Congress I screened *Virtuous Sinners, Camille, Moran of the Lady Letty, The Sheik, The Eagle, The Son of the Sheik*, and a trailer for *The Young Rajah*.

At the Film Study Division of the Museum of Modern Art I saw *The Four Horsemen of the Apocalypse*, a section of *Patria*, a trailer for *All Night*, one reel of *The Wonderful Chance, Blood and Sand, Monsieur Beaucaire*, and *Cobra*.

At the Film and Television Archive of the University of California, Los Angeles, I saw *An Adventuress*, *The Wonderful Chance* (on video), *The Conquering Power* (on video), and some news footage for Hearst News.

I saw a restored print of *The Eagle* at Photoplay Productions, London. The Nederland Filmmuseum, Amsterdam, allowed me to see a copy of *The Delicious Little Devil*.

Michael Yakaitis of the Library of Moving Images, Hollywood, allowed me to see surviving footage of *The Young Rajah*.

I saw *The Married Virgin* at the Academy of Motion Picture Arts and Sciences.

I saw excellent prints of *The Four Horsemen of the Apocalypse*, *Camille*, *The Conquering Power*, and *The Eagle* on Turner Classic Movies, cable television.

INDEX